GW0866680

LOST YOUTH

Volume 1

Christian S Simpson

authorHOUSE®

AuthorHouse™ UK Ltd.
500 Avebury Boulevard
Central Milton Keynes, MK9 2BE
www.authorhouse.co.uk
Phone: 08001974150

First published by AuthorHouse   01/28/2011

ISBN: 978-1-4567-7435-6

This book is printed on acid-free paper.

Thank You

To my beautiful Mother (RIP) who I love with all my heart and who I miss ever so much. To my Father (RIP) I am sorry that life didn't turn out quite how you wished but I do always have many memories of the good times and when smiles were shared. I miss you both so much, from your loving son.

To my beautiful sister, who I love dearly and will always be here for you to look after you and protect. I will never leave your side and that I promise with all my heart as I love you dearly, from your brother.

To my beautiful daughter Angel-Grace, you are my everything and I love you so much. I am so proud of you always and forever from your Daddy.

To my blood family in New Zealand especially Frank and Beth. Sorry for all the trouble I once caused in my early life in New Zealand. I hope one day you both can see I have turned out to be a decent person in the end rather than a troublesome young man that you both remember me as.

To my Nana Davis (RIP) and all my other blood family in New Zealand. You all are in my thoughts and I hope that one day we can enjoy a drink together in memory of Nana Davis who sadly passed away after I left New Zealand.

To my blood family in Scotland, my grandparents Grace and George and my uncle and auntie and cousins. You all know how much I love you all dearly. Thank you for always being there for me and never casting judgement over me and my ways.

To Wim Bosman and the Bosman family in New Zealand. You may not be blood family, but to me you are and always will be family. Thanks all and also to Rob and Frank for looking after the girls and making such good husbands and being there for them both since that dreadful day back in 1992.

To Irene Manuel thanks for being there for my father and giving up so much in the name of love and friendship as you were so special in my father's life.

To my step brothers and sisters the Manuals. We are from different backgrounds but we always saw eye to eye and I am sorry that my father took your mum away but he only ever meant well. Respect to you all.

To the Mitchell family in New Zealand, Kath and John, Chris and Damon. Again you are like an extension of my family. Thanks for all that you have done for my family. I will never forget and I love you all.

To my 3 close pals in New Zealand, Chris, Campbell, Sackza and everyone else who were there watching me grown up, going through hell and back and sometimes being a loose cannon. None of you ever left my side. Respect always given.

Michael Mercer of Hadlow School, thanks for always believing in me and also those staff at Wellington Activity Centre who tried their best to help me further in my education when no school in all of New Zealand would give me a second chance.

To the SS MC club house, past and present members, you were more than a MC 1% club to me from such an early age. You were family to me and in my heart I will always be SS MC even though I don't wear the colours on my back.

Craig and your brother (Rebels car club) thanks for what you guys done for me, always remembered and never forgotten.

To all the other clubs and gangs that I was involved with, all I can say is that although at times in all honesty you really don't offer the youth of today much apart from a life of crime, but by writing this book you all in some way have been a part of this success story so I salute you all for that.

To the Wellington (New Zealand) police force maybe it was a good thing you caught me when I was young and at least the judge never threw away the key. Although I battled with many of you when I was growing up I guess you all were just trying to do ya job. Now many years on I understand the shit I used to get from you all as I guess you didn't wish to see me spend many years behind bars as that for sure was where I was heading up to my last arrest when I was young and placed in jail.

New Zealand's such a beautiful country and I am so proud to be kiwi and wear the silver fern with pride and of my Maori roots. I do miss New Zealand but I guess it just wasn't the place for me. One day I will come home and one day I hope to have a decent drink with you all.

Lastly a thanks to Ronnie, Reggie and Charlie Kray for what wasn't expected at all with the hand of friendship, RIP you three.

Mel thanks for being a great mother to my daughter, you truly do an amazing job and though we don't see eye to eye I respect you always as the mother of my daughter.

To my sweetheart Stacey, thanks for always being there for me through thick and thin when others in the past have had to walk away. I ain't the easiest of people to live with at the best of times. Thank you for the love you have given me and allowed to grow into something very beautiful, even when others attempted to push us apart and try their best to ruin our happiness. What we have no one can ever take away as true love is here to stay forever more. Love you Stacey with all my heart and forever will.

To Freddie Foreman and the Foreman family who have been there for the last 15 years of my life. In many ways like another family to me who have seen me go through so much but at the same time grow in strength and seen me learn from my past mistakes. You never gave up on me when at times many others did. Fred since I lost my father, you have been there for me and I can't thank you enough, I love you so much.

To Tricky as well, thank you for believing in me and seeing more depth than others never bothered seeing. You're a true friend and you mean the world to me.

Steve Wraith again encouraging me to write a book and Stephen Richards for all your wisdom in helping me on this journey when I first put pen to paper you're a good man.

Dave Courtney who many judge and say bad things. Again you never done me any wrong and in the early years you were always there for me and so thank you, I will never forget your kindness.

To the endless MC 1% club member from various clubs up and done the country and very much in London I know none of you wish to be mentioned in my book, but this is a big respect going out to you all, you know who you are.

All the British gangland families I have met and which have never done me wrong but been good to me over the years. Respect as well to you all and to those who sadly passed away such as Joe Pyle (RIP always) and Tony Lambrianou (RIP).

Bron and Neal Porter who gave me so much encouragement to write a book when I never believed I had it in me to write a book, so many thank you's to you both.

To all those in New Zealand who failed me, doubted me and turned their back on me well look at me now standing as tall as a mountain and in the end actually doing pretty damn good with this life of mine. To all those who done me wrong in New Zealand, maybe I have forgiven but only because I know karma deals with those when you're least expecting so don't stop watching over your back.

My last message is to the youth of New Zealand and to other countries who find themselves lost in youth and looking at gangs for that excitement and purpose. Please look ahead as gangs in no way are glamour and you're better off joining your local boxing club, or ruby club. Please take it from someone who knows too well, as trust me the life you'll lead will be short or if long then a long life standing behind bars of a prison. Trust me on my words and make good of yourself even if everyone around you has given up on you. This should be more of a reason to prove them all wrong exactly like I did now so many years on.

And to add my very last message to the youth of today, please say no to drugs as they will only destroy you and many. Many times costing you not only your family and loved ones but also your life. Drugs do absolute nothing for your life and those close to you. Drugs only take away things so please hear me out when I say that from the heart. I have been there and it may have seemed very rock n roll at the time but what a lonely dark place in life it actually was. When things came crashing down there wasn't no one there apart from a few who really cared. I was one of the lucky ones, you might not be one yourself.

God Bless and Be Lucky Always from Christian

Volume 2 will have thank you's from the UK and other parts of the world.

Chapter one

SWINGING 60S AND SWINGING FISTS

My very first memories of growing up date back to how frightened I was of living inside my childhood house. From a very young age my house seemed haunted in so many ways. It brought such terror to me from within my own bedroom and surrounding rooms. Throughout the earlier years I would hear the most chilling sounds which would carry through the entire house. Certain going-on's within the house would cause such nightmares to me and if those weren't enough to scare me there were nights where outside my bedroom window a certain person would also bring me to sheer terror as a young child.

I lived in this house in a nice suburb called Miramar in Wellington, the capital of New Zealand, with my mum and my father and my older sister, all whom I loved very much. Our family was like no other that I knew. In those earlier years I thought that every family was like ours. How wrong was I? As I grew up become to know and learn how other families bonded and behaved.

Our house was three bedrooms with a hair salon that attached to the side of the house. My mum was a talented hairdresser and this was always her dream to have her own hair salon. My Father being the generous man that he was made my mum's dreams come true. He had not only brought a new house for his family, but also one with a shop front that was turned into a hair salon for his wife to fulfil her dreams.

My Mum didn't have to leave far for work but simply just go next door. She was the happiest woman alive but not long after very dark clouds would come over that house and stay for many years to come, as long as we lived as a family together in that house.

My Father left his birth country, Scotland at an early age of 16. First getting work on the docks in the East End of London. Back then it was tough down on the docks, but you can imagine how tough it would have been for a young kid of that age.

His days would be filled with working the docks, and the evenings drinking with the older chaps who run the docks. In those days, these were the busiest docklands in the whole world, where men were real men among them all.

At the pubs in the East End where my father could get served a beer, being underage, what would have been just a couple pints on his first night soon became more.

Once working on the docks gaining a weekly wage, not to mention the many other ways he made a few extra quid down on the docks, through stolen gear to all sorts of trades. My Father, as did most, got himself involved and only to make a few extra quid than normal. As his takings got higher the wiser he got. He was a hard worker then and with more quid in his pocket, those earlier few couple of pints soon became twelve.

That's all he wanted to do after a hard day of work was to go to the pubs, unwind and have a drink with the other fellas. He would spend most of his time in the pubs of the East End and on weekends the big dance halls where he would come across gangs.

This is where he came across The Kray Twins. They would be drinking in a few of their pubs back in the East End. My Father was never part of The Firm nor was he a gangster but he was becoming a hard man even at a young age.

I am sure that was due to the guys he was working alongside of on the docks as every man back in those days who were dockers was as hard as nails and equally the men whom he went onto travel the seven oceans with as he started to gain work on board ships, getting to see the world though always returning to the East End which had become his home away from home.

I have been lucky to meet a lot of old time dockers at a certain dockers clubs in south London and though they now old men, you can still sense how very staunch they are. You can imagine how hard they were back in their prime. All of them I have met through Freddie Foreman and his brother George Foreman.

The dockers are all gentleman and I always have such a great day among them all listening to their stories of back in the day. My Father while working on the East End Docks and aboard many ships became involved in union work back in those days and also in his years after in New Zealand.

He took all this knowledge with him from his early days on the East End docks and aboard the many ships he worked on, leading on to helping out so much in a huge way with dockers Union and Sea workers Union in New Zealand.

I would later myself get involved in unions. As a young man, while I was over in America doing security for a British film company, I managed to have meetings with the biggest Union in the world that are a huge powerful force in America, The Teamsters.

It was through these meetings that would go on to play a part in my input into forming a security union in the UK. My learning and knowledge of unions had been handed down to me by my father plus Freddie Foreman who was a great positive influence on me when it came to making the correct decisions to do with the rights of the workers.

The Union was formed by not only me but also Joe Pyle Snr and mainly his son Joe Pyle Jrn with other members of The Firm coming on board to benefit the security industry.

This passion of mine to form a union for the right of workers was due to my Fathers early days in the East End. My Father himself was involved in unions, to what scale I am unsure, but it was a huge part of not only his early days on the docks and aboard ships but also throughout his time in New Zealand.

While he was out at sea he was a voice among many. Whenever he felt that the crew were not being treated correctly he would always speak up. My father would also rally together the other younger men who would be looking for work on the docks or on ships but had been taken advantage of by their employers. Some of those ending up with poor wages or not many workers rights, my father would always fight the corner for the underdog.

My Father was so hard working that whenever he was not aboard a ship and was based in the East End he soon began bar work at some of the clubs in the west end that the Kray Twins had control over or had money involved in.

My Father had a passion for cooking so my father went on and started to work in a plush restaurant to help out in the kitchen.

The Kray Twins weren't all about beating people, murder and protection. They also helped their own and looked after many folk.

My Father didn't know the violent side of them. He wasn't a witness to any of their crimes or what was going on in their personal lives.

It makes me laugh when you hear folks speak and they tell you, "yeah my father worked for the Krays, he was their driver or he was part of their Firm." These types of pricks you just want to chin them for their bullshit. Why can't they just be honest and say that maybe at one time their Father's life they were simply drinking in the same pub as the Krays rather than spin some yarn.

When I used to visit Reggie Kray in Maidstone prison and Wayland prison, while he was serving his 30 year jail sentence (Reg ended up doing 34 years behind bars locked up in jail) we would always laugh about and joke of how many drivers he had lost count of having as everyone on the outside seemed to think they had driven him or his brother Ron at one stage of their lives.

They would also talk of how they were on The Firm, when in all truth The Krays didn't have a bigger Firm than that of any major crime Families at the time. There were so many people that claimed they were on the Firm that realistically there could never have been that many if what everyone claimed was true.

It brought so much laughter to Reggie Kray in his later years and he didn't mind as long as they were only spinning yarns and not using his name to better themselves or to gain money for themselves.

When visiting Reggie Kray I would sometimes pop into the pub across the road by the gates of Maidstone Prison with either Charlie Kray who was the Kray twins older brother or Roberta (Reggie's wife to be at the time) or senior gang members of The Firm.

There were always different men drinking in there who would hear that I was waiting to visit Reg and they would tell such bullshit stories about them knowing the Kray Twins until Charlie Kray would turn up and then they'd shut their mouths.

I still get it often to this day. If conversations of the Kray Twins ever come up or of the Foreman Family also, people claim to know Freddie Foreman. When I ask Freddie in person, he hasn't a clue who the person is and has in most cases never even met the person.

After working so hard in this kitchen at the plush restaurant my father had impressed the head chef so much that he was offered a full time position.

He never again worked for the Krays again in their bars or clubs in the West End.

He was given a full time chef job in the kitchen of this plush restaurant so he gave up his days of working the seas for now and went on to cook amazing dinners for the rich and famous, royalties and even now and then for the Twins whenever they came in to dine.

He never collected debts for the Krays, he never killed for them, and he certainly never drove for them. He was now simply a chef in a restaurant and he loved it. He would hardly see the Kray Twins anymore as this job soon became his life and this is where he met my Mum.

My Mum was a young stunning lady who had taken a hairdressing course in New Zealand as this was where she was from. She was a kiwi, her blood line was from England and also she had Maori blood in her as Te Rauparaha who was a great fighting Maori Chief (A legend in New Zealand's history) was my Mums Great, Great Grandfather.

After my Mum taking the course in New Zealand she travelled over to London like so many other young New Zealanders did, to be part of the swinging 1960s of fashionable London. She wasn't so much on holiday as she was looking for work. She somehow managed to get work on film sets as a hairdresser.

At one stage she even became friends with the wife of a famous British film director whom she had cut her hair for while they were over from America.

One evening my Mum was invited out for dinner with them. Dinner was served at the world famous restaurant, Simpsons on the Strand, which was the restaurant that my father was now working in the kitchen as a chef. This very night, after dinner, my Father had finished his shift or was simply taking a break and enjoying a quiet drink.

My Mum noticed him on his own and excused herself from her table and went over to him. Thinking that he was a diner of the restaurant she asked why he was drinking by himself and where his friends or guests were. My Father asked her if she had enjoyed her meal, she replied it was the best dinner she had ever tasted and with that he asked her if she would like to have that every night of her life.

My Mum looked puzzled and asked him what he meant by that. He told her he wasn't a guest at the restaurant but he was one of the chefs and asked her out on a date.

My Mum thought this was quite romantic and said she would let him know at the end of the night and went back to join her table for drinks. On leaving the restaurant she found my father outside enjoying a ciggie while waving down a London Black Cab.

As he opened the door of the taxi, he looked over at my Mum whom he had noticed to be outside, he asked her if she enjoyed dancing more than good cooking. With that she replied yes, so he said jump in and that she did, getting into the taxi with him.

My Father took my Mum to a private members club up West End, and they danced the night away. This was the very start of their romance and as the night ended my mum stayed the night and woke with a breakfast fit for a Queen.

That following night he took her out to Mayfair for dinner, chatting away to each other all the time my father taking her hand in his. Over the next few nights of the weekend he showed her his London Town.

By the end of the weekend, as promised, he cooked a romantic dinner that melted in her mouth. After dinner they were out again among all the lovers of the night. He took her to all the best clubs in town, even the ones owned by Freddie Foreman and also by The Krays. Between Freddie Foreman and the Kray Twins, they had the best clubs of London in the swinging 60s.

All the famous stars, music stars including The Beatles, Eric Clapton, The Who, Rolling Stones to name a few would drink or perform in their clubs. They also had all the showbiz stars from America, who would come over and visit these clubs such as Frankie blue eyes, Judy Garland and George Draft, to name only three from so many.

Within this short space of time, the Kray Twins were keeping a low profile as the police were now building a massive case against the Kray Twins.

At this point even some of the members of The Firm were speaking to the police and not long after all of them were in the Old Bailey Court Room Number One for what was the most expensive and longest running court case in British legal history which resulted to many of them doing long jail terms such as Reggie Kray and Ronnie Kray.

Many of The Firm was put behind bars for a very long time and also their brother Charlie Kray and Freddie Foreman, who only got out the year I was born in 1975. Freddie Foreman had been released with the Kray Twins older brother Charlie, who in years to come on my arrival to London in 1995 would have a lot of contact with me.

In 1995 Reggie Kray had telephoned me from Maidstone Jail to tell me his brother Ron Kray had died and it was time for me to come over to show my respect. It was Charlie Kray who many times would take me down to see Reggie Kray in prison once I arrived in the U.K as a 20 year old back then in 1995.

I would work with Charlie on many charity events. One point we fell out but that was due to a third party and once that matter was laid to rest after we found out the truth behind the troubles, we become good friends.

Sadly he lost his son Gary Kray and also Charlie lost his own freedom for a second time when he had nothing to do with what he was being charged with. Such was the case of the murder of Jack the Hat, which Charlie had been sent to prison with others though Charlie had no input in any way to the murder of Jack the Hat or the disappearance of his body. The body of Jack the Hat to this day has never been found.

Many years on and very late in his age when he was an old man in his 70s he was being falsely accused of being part of a £70 million pound cocaine deal. Charlie Kray was set up by undercover police officers, which did have an ill effect on his health but also on Reggie Kray getting freed after 30years of life behind bars. Sadly Charlie Kray died while locked up for something he had nothing to do with.

In the five years I got to know Charlie Kray, he was anti drugs, he looked down at anyone who took drugs of any form and he would leave a party or event if he knew that someone was taking drugs as he was so against drugs.

He was not involved in anything that was suggested at his court case, a court case that I would watch from the court public gallery in support of Charlie Kray as he was a good man who didn't deserve his freedom to be taken away from him. Even with the great skills of his lawyer Michael Mansfield, who is in my eyes was one of the best lawyers in the country?

A truly gifted man of law, even Michael Mansfield couldn't save Charlie Kray as when they threw the book at him, the Government and the police wasn't going to let a free man walk. Now they were wishing for his brother Reggie Kray, who by this time had served his recommended 30 years in prison should have himself been freed.

But the police and the Government had a plan and they were sticking by it even if it meant that they take Charlie Krays freedom away from him and also deny Reggie Kray of his own freedom.

I always wonder if my Dad hadn't got out of the East End, which had become his home away from home since the age of 16years old would he had like many others got involved with the firm back in the 1960s and ended up serving a long prison sentence which then would have meant my Mother and my Father would never have ever met.

I wonder where my Father's life would have leaded, if he, as so many others in the East End had done, followed the Kray Twins into a life of crime and then into many years of a life behind Prison bars.

Reggie Kray remembered my Father, as we spoke about my Father on many visits. Reggie Kray did say he didn't think my Father was the type who would have lived that life, though my Father wasn't straight as in a do gooder, he was not a career criminal in any sense of the word and yes he may have been part of a few little things down on the docks as every man working there in those times, am sure would have had their hands in a few pies.

As for anything more serious my Father would never get himself involved and more than likely would have turned his back if offered anything serious.

My Father would have been too young back then to have been on The Firm.

When my Father found out years later that I was visiting Reggie Kray, he didn't approve one single bit. One evening it even led to a punch up between my Father and me.

Although he didn't have a bad word to say against Reggie Kray, he just didn't want me getting mixed up in the underworld of London. By that time it was far too late. From the fight that we had, he made it pretty clear that back then he didn't have interest of ever being a part of it all.

Straight work took him into working at Simpsons on the Strand and then from there into a romance with my Mum on meeting her. He was in a way saved from a life of crime and of one of possible jail and that's all due to a beautiful lady coming into his life, that being my Mum.

What my Father didn't know was that sadly a month earlier to meeting my Mum and her leaving New Zealand, she had met and fell in love with a young man by the name of Wim Bosman. A Dutchman who had came to New Zealand in search of work, as like my Father had gone from Scotland in search of work in London, and as my Mum had from New Zealand to London in search of work.

My Mum, while she was enjoying the times in London with my Father, the dates my Father would take her out on and the way he swept her off her feet and the connections my Father had, that meant she was going to the best places in town during these times.

My Mum was falling in love with my Father though while being in love with another. Is this possible? Is someone able to love two people equally? I doubt it is. I for one can see someone feeling love for two people but to equally love two people, then I can't see anyone being able to share their heart as such.

During these times I am sure while my Father courted my Mum, that her thoughts were not miles away back in New Zealand thinking about Wim.

Soon it came time for my Mum to return to New Zealand. My Dad pleaded with my Mum to stay and start a life with him in London as all was going so good between them and happiness for both of them was something that speaks of true love between two people.

She missed her flight, to stay in London with my Father as London was now her new home. As the months went by my Mum started to miss her Family and home more and more. She wanted to go back to New Zealand and show off what she had been taught in hairdressing in her time in London. Even at that young age it was her dream to have her very own hair salon.

You've got to remember that back then New Zealand's standard of living was still very much unknown to many people in the UK. There were lots of boats that were going out to Australia and cheap they were. If you wanted to move your whole family out to either Australia or New Zealand it was only £10 for English and also Irish families to board these ships in promise of a better life.

Many were packing up their lives, their homes and making that move over seven oceans away. After a period of time my Mum explaining to my Dad what a beautiful country that New Zealand was and such a great way to live and how friendly the people in New Zealand were and also how much work out there that there was and about her own family.

My Dad decided to make my Mum even happier so with a few contacts he still had through the docks of the East End, they boarded a ship and in comfort they sailed to New Zealand. So as my Father had said goodbye to Bonnie Scotland years earlier, now he was saying goodbye to old London town. He was leaving everything behind him, including his own family in Scotland and crossings seven oceans for the love of a woman.

They settled in Wellington, though this was not my Mums home town. She was born in New Plymouth, the middle of the North Island, under a great mountain. In all the surrounding towns her Family had saw mills and also dairy farms. Her own Father was a very well respected member of the Local Council and also a senior member of the Freemasons in New Zealand during his own life.

My Mum had a big family. She had four brothers though her twin sister that died at birth. My Nana had also lost another daughter, so my Mum was always looked after by her Dad and her Brothers. It was a very loving family. My Nana was so lovely and such a strong woman.

I don't remember my Grandfather, I am unsure if he died before I was even born.

My Dad found work straight away in restaurants in Wellington, but they were nothing compared to the restaurants he had worked in London. I don't think it matched his drive so he went back to working on the docks this time in the port of Wellington.

There he found many British workers, whom he could relate to and as he knew about this trade then he fitted in fine and soon become part of the union.

He loved the sea so on taking even more wages he started work on the inter-island ferry service between the North Island and the South Island of New Zealand. Wellington is at the tip of the North Island and this is where the ferries would leave and return from.

They were happy times for both my parents. 1970 came and they had my beautiful sister. My Father wanted to provide even more for his wife as now he had a daughter so he gave up the ferries and started to get even bigger wages by working on huge ships that would travel for weeks on end, sometimes months.

My father worked on Oil liners, luxury cruise ships and container ships. The sea was in my Fathers blood and he travelled the whole world so many times, going to every major port all over the world, bringing home so much money through all his hard work and days at sea. He used to tell me such stories of how he travelled the world's oceans and seen so much of the world.

Soon he could afford an even bigger house for his family. This was great for them both, as when left to go away again he promised my Mum that upon his return he would buy her, her very own hairdressing saloon. After making love he left for the sea and on his return to be told that my Mum was pregnant again.

He was on top of the world and he kept to his promise and brought a bigger house for my Mum as the family was now growing. Not only had he brought but he managed to find a property that had a shop built on the side of it. He transformed the shop into a hair dressing saloon for my mum.

While my father was out to sea again my Mum brought all the things for the salon that it needed, everything brand new. She had the entire shop front done so it was ready for when she was ready, as at this time she was still carrying her next child, that being me.

Then it was the year 1975, and I was born. My sister had just started school and across seven oceans Freddie Foreman and Charlie Kray were getting out of jail. On the day they were both freed, the police then tried to charge Freddie Foreman for the murder of Ginger Marks and attempted murder of Jimmy Evans. Ginger Marks was a thief.

As for Jimmy Evans, he was gangster, a safe blower as well. Jimmy Evans was a close friend of the Kray Twins. Jimmy Evans wife had fallen in love with George Foreman, one of Freddie Foreman's brothers, which lead to her having affair behind Jimmy Evans back.

On Jimmy finding out, one night he took Ginger Marks with him and went to George Foreman's house. As they went to his door, they had unscrewed the light bulb on the outside landing and knocked on the door.

As George Foreman was much respected and didn't have any enemies, he went to the front door and opened it, only to be blasted at close range by Jimmy while Ginger stood there and watched this happen.

Most men would die from being shot at close range by a firearm, but not George Foreman, as he was from the old school and had played a part with his brothers in winning the war against Nazi Germany.

So with some rest in hospital, he was soon good again and as neither Jimmy nor Ginger had masks on that night, they came for George. Well what a huge mistake that was that they both made as it would soon cost one of them their lives.

Freddie Foreman, as any brother would, went and took care of business. Most brothers in the same situation would sort it out but Freddie Foreman done it his way. No one and I mean no one fucked with the Foreman Family. Soon after the shooting of George, both Jimmy and Ginger were called onto a job they thought was taking place in the heart of the East End.

On arriving to the East End, Jimmy and Ginger came under bullet fire on a busy street just near the famous St Matthews Church (The Church The Kray Family services were all held in), only a few streets from the Krays Family house. When the bullets went flying and Jimmy saw it was Freddie

Foreman holding the gun, he knew there and then that the bullets had his name on them.

Jimmy pulled his friend Ginger so to shield himself. Ginger took the fatal bullets to his body and head, dropping dead instantly on the pavement as one thing Freddie was, was a very good shot. Jimmy drops his friend and runs for his life, hiding under a lorry that was parked on a nearby street.

Freddie Foreman looked everywhere for Jimmy. With Ginger laying there cold dead for his body to be discovered, Fred had to return to the body and throw it into the boot of his motor before any on lookers saw the body of Ginger Marks.

As for Jimmy Evans, he escaped down the road and went running to the Krays. Ronnie Kray turned him away as neither of the Kray Twins wanted trouble with Freddie Foreman, whom they respected a lot more than they did Jimmy Evans. Jimmy had nowhere to turn. So Jimmy became a dirty grass, naming Freddie Foreman as the killer of his friend Ginger Marks, the same friend whom Jimmy had shield behind to save his own life.

So upon Freddie getting out of jail he was rearrested to face the murder charge of Ginger. The key witness of the case was Jimmy Evans, who in court pointed the finger at Freddie standing there alone in the dock of the court. What a shock Jimmy got after grassing up Freddie, who by now was known more than just Brown bread Fred but as The Godfather of British Crime.

When the charges were dropped against Freddie, you can imagine from that point onwards Jimmy Evans went into hiding and is still in hiding to this day. No body of Ginger Marks has ever been found.

See what I mean no one fucks with the Foreman Family. You now understand why Freddie Foreman is known in gangland circles as Brown Bread Fred as brown bread in cockney slang means dead.

To this day, Gingers body has never been found. Only due to Freddie admitting the murder on a TV show and in his first book titled "Respect" in the late 1990s. It was only then that the truth came out as to where Ginger Marks disappeared to, and that was out to the shipping lanes of the coast of Newhaven, cut up and feed to the fishes (Mafia style).

Chapter 2

THE HAUNTED HOUSE

1975, a young healthy baby boy was born, that being me.

I was born into a loving home and a new home that my Father had brought for my Mum and a brand new hair salon that was next to our house. It meant she didn't even have to travel far for work, only through a door in our lounge into her own hairdressing saloon.

Once my sister was old enough to go to school this made my mum happy as she could then open her new business but I think what she wanted instead of such a hard working husband, who she hardly ever saw as my Father would always be out at sea. She wanted a husband at home with her and more so a husband to help take care of her new born baby.

She couldn't even think of opening her salon as there was no one to look after me so for the first two years, the business didn't open and she become just a mother. One with dreams and one with a business next door that she could only walk inside and design, not during those first few years open the front door for customers.

Now this may have caused her to be depressed I am unsure, but at this stage while my Father was away so much, it caused her to have thoughts again back to her first love of her life that being Wim and for what reason that trail of thought passed through her mind.

I am unsure when the affair happened but I did know it was before I was born in 1975. When I was older, my Mother and even sometimes Wim as well, would taut my Father saying that Wim was actually my Father. Even telling me this when I was older, when my Father had left New Zealand to go back to the U.K.

This was the cause for so much of my own self discovery, not knowing who I really was after hearing this being discussed.

My Father was spending so many weeks away from home, he would then drink heavy as most ship crews would. Most of the crew on the ships he worked on were either Scottish, or English or Welsh and the Irish.

All being far from their own homes so all would bond together as one and that was made so through them all drinking on the ships. Many of my Fathers good friendships were formed among these men, whom he had met during his days of work on the many ships he took work on, to support his Family that were back at home now in Wellington.

These men were hard as nails and they all stuck together through thick and thin.

My mum wanted my father around but at the same time she couldn't give up Wim, I think when I came along, life was more settled as my sister was five years old, so as mentioned already off to school.

Now that dream of my Mums to run her own saloon was very much put on hold as now my mum had me to look after all by herself.

Three years passed, my Mum found out about a place called Saint **Barnabas** which used to be a place for orphans and children that parents couldn't cope with though by the time I had been placed there it was mainly for children whom parents were in full time work, who needed their kids to be looked after in the day. My Mum placed me in there during the day as then she could finally open her business.

So during the day I would spend my time being looked after by a bunch of women who seemed very so strict. Even though I was only three years old, I do have memories of that place.

It seemed to me a place that was very over bearing and I never understood why I was there. I am sure this brought on my early bad behaviour as all of my life up to this point I had been at home surrounded by the love of my parents.

My mum looking after me while my father was away but for some reason now, I wasn't allowed that during the day so I would play up to the people who ran this place in attempt to get back to where I felt the most safe and that was at home, and not at this new place where these women with their loud strict voices and many with big crosses that they wore around their necks.

The place had a huge symbol of Jesus on the cross outside, and I was told that if I was bad, that's where I would end up, something that stayed with me all of the time I was there, as to a three year old that something a bit extreme to say to a little kid.

If I was ever naughty then some of these women would hit me, this is something that I never had experience from either of my parents so I become even angrier

14

which lead to more mischief. I can tell you from the moment I got home; I would cause a riot, be it in the house or running a mock through my mum's hairdressing saloon as I resented her sending me to this place.

It came to the point that my Mum couldn't look after me while she run the hair salon, with no one at home to look after me when my Father wasn't home so I was then kept even longer at the place that I hated to early evenings. By that time my Mum had finished her days work at the saloon, she could look after me in the evenings. Looking back now even a worse decision to put me at a place I hated most days being at, as my behaviour you can imagine just got worse.

The following year I was off to kindergarten, something I hated even more to start with. This was only for half days, so my Nana would come down to collect me, while my Father was away on the ships as the only other person who could watch over me was my sister though she was only by then 9 years old.

I can remember the first day I was dropped off to kindergarten; I was picked out of all the kids to go to the front gates and meet the postman for the mail and to bring it back to the teacher who was looking after us all.

It was maybe a lesson in trust and a lesson in responsibility, well I can tell you now, I had different things on my mind and a lesson to teach them, which was how to escape. I jumped over the gate, by passing the postman with his smile and his post outstretched in one hand and I was off like a jet.

Remembering my house was only on the straight and narrow down the street at the fourth corner. A teacher in hot pursuit after me, though with a skip through the traffic, I left her for dust as I reached my Mums hair salon. I run through the saloon into my lounge and to my bedroom.

Yes I would have embarrassed my Mum in front of her clients, more so as the teacher came through the door in search of me. My Nana came in and placed me in her arms asking what was wrong, she was worried about me, taking me into the lounge and calling out for my Mum.

But in came the teacher who without even any respect towards my Nana, grabbed me from my Nanas arm and attempted to drag me by the arm out of the lounge and back into the saloon, well I wasn't going to take that so I went nuts trying to pull away, but the teachers grip was even tighter on my arm to the point of making marks, so I reached over closer to her own arm with my head and I bite her so hard.

I let go when she had, after to the point drawing blood from her arm with my teeth, which caused her to yell.

That was enough for her, she let me go, so I run back to my bedroom and in came my Nana again followed my mum. My Nana was having a go at my Mum so I ended up staying there for the rest of the day with my Nana spoiling me as Grandparents do to their own Grandchildren.

I stayed at home for the rest of that week before having to return the following week only because my Mum telling me my Father was soon coming home from being away at sea, and he wouldn't be happy to hear what I had done. Never again on returning to the kindergarten, I was given the chance to collect the mail from the gates.

A year later, I had started school. I was ok with school, although not on my first day but school soon grew on me, plus I had my sister attending the same school so she would look after me but at home the house that I knew and grow up in to this point, started to become what all I can describe as a haunted house.

By this age I could feel a distance starting to form between my parents as I wasn't seeing them spend as much time together as they used to in my earlier years. Not feeling the happiness around the house that I once felt as a very young child. I was far too young to understand, it was due to my Mum having an affair.

My Mum not knowing during her time in London that she would find herself falling in love, returning to New Zealand living her dream of owning her own hair studio. Those first few years, I guess was so very happy for them both, but what my father didn't know was during the times he was working away, doing his best to provide for his wife and his family, that my mum having everything she could ever ask for, was relighting her first love that of the Dutchman, she had left in New Zealand to come to London.

This first love was the love of her life even though she had my father give up everything in London to make a new life for her and him and to provide for his family as best as he could. All this didn't seem to be able to turn my mum away from her first love and during the time that I was born soon the affair began.

An affair of dangerous passion and one that would come to terror for us all as from my very early memories I must have been only three years old when I first heard the shouting inside the house, the house that I always knew from this point on as the haunted house at night time.

The quietness of the night would be broken by screams, terrify screams coming from behind my parent's bedroom door. What was taking place I never did know at that young age, but it was terrifying to hear, I could make out it was my beautiful Mothers voice, that would be shouting out for help but at this age I was helpless to help.

What I would find out in much later years, the cause of this terrifying noise one night, was that my Father returning one evening from being out to sea for many months went to put a new family photograph of all of us into my mum's purse as she had only a photo of myself when I had been born and also a picture of my sister so my father wanted my mum to be carrying around a family photo.

One thing that meant a lot to my father was family, it was the most important thing in his life it's what he lived for and what he breathed for as he loved us so much and so did my mum but what he was too find would break his heart in two as beneath the photograph of myself in my mum's purse was a picture of her with another man. A photo taken in a picture booth of her and what my Father would find out would be the love of her life.

Her very first love was to a Dutchman by the name of Wim Bosman. My father's blood boiled and tears I am sure dropped from his eyes as there was a picture of his beautiful wife, my father's love of his life and the mother of his children but in that picture he now had in his hands wasn't of her with him. Nothing my mother could say would stop such pain and hurt rush throughout my father's body as there weren't any excuses for a photo of another man to be in his wife's purse.

My father would be told that the photo was an old photo taken of an old flame from a past relationship and she hadn't realize that the photo was still in her purse and she assured my father that she no longer was in contact with this man , but she was. My father believed her to make my mum happier he even done up the house, gave her a grander bedroom, and a new kitchen. He did feel bad being away at sea for so long but this it showed through good wages meant my mum had anything she wished for.

Before my father went away again, she was very happy with what he had done to the house but he would go away with that photo playing on his mind and as he spend so long at sea he would go back to a past time of his drinking that started in his early days in the East End after working on the docks.

He would join all the older set into the drinking pubs of the East End and the dance halls getting a taste for drink and sinking many pints and shots taken with each pint he would drink as a chaser from the age of 16 years and onwards. Now in his later 20s, he was really throwing them back; drink would play a heavy part on his life, it actually in years to come be the death of him.

My mother did love my father but she couldn't put the love for Wim out of her heart and within a month of my father being away again she would start up the affair and carry on seeing Wim, a man behind my father's back.

While my father was the most loyal of men, very old school, never once did he cheat on his wife even when visiting every major port around the world, where his work friends would be off the boat and into the first whorehouse. My father would be just happy to enjoy a drink or few and never once get into bed with another girl.

He wouldn't wish to break his wife's heart nor lose his family through cheating and when he said his marriage vows he meant them and so did my mum but she just couldn't stop carrying on this affair and sooner than later she would be caught out and this would bring terror within our house, frightening for us all.

I am unsure but somehow my father found out that my mum was actually having an affair. He came home from a pub one evening having drunken twice the amount that he would normally drink and he confronted my mum about this, and again she lied to him. My Mum saying there was no truth in what he had found out but he had proof somehow and again asked my mum.

Soon a fight broke out very late at night, waking me in my bed I could hear their voices, louder and louder they got and not laughing as I had heard for many years but this was shouting. Something I had heard previous but now I heard things being thrown and soon something smashing. Here I was in the pitch black and not knowing what was going on but feeling so scared, wishing one of my parents to come in to let me know all was ok.

No one came and then that's when I heard more than shouting as I heard my Mothers screams, screams that I will never forget even 30 years later if I close my eyes I still can hear them from that night and many nights that would follow.

Things would get worse, soon I wouldn't be just hearing such screams but I would be seeing what the cause of them was and this is what made the house feel even more haunted as if it had an evil entity inside that house. Due to my father not being at home as much as most husbands were, I am sure that he felt it was the cause of his wife having an affair. He went on to give up his work on the big ships, that he loved so much, to spend more time with his wife and his family.

My father took up work on the interisland ferries that take passengers and also livestock between the two islands of NZ as then he would no longer be away from home as he had been for long periods as on the ferries he could do 8 days on and four days off.

This it seemed to work as my parents got on better and it meant I would now see more of my father and spend more time with him I hoped, which did happen when he come off the ferry from working. Though his first day off, he would spend it sleeping after working and living on the ferry for 8 days then the next he would spend time with me but the next two days he would be at the pub with his friends.

He wouldn't get home till so late at night that by that time I would already be in bed fast asleep and by the morning he would be recovering and hung over. He wouldn't get out of bed and then he would be off to work again for another 8 days.

My mum would be working so hard herself each day in the saloon till late so only in the evening she would see my Father when he wasn't working but that was only after he had come home so drunk from the pubs.

One evening I remember my father yelling at my Mum that his dinner that had been cooked for him was cold by now, driving him into rage he would fly and so would his cooked dinner, fly all over the floor and the kitchen walls as he would throw his dinner plate in disgust as the food was no longer hot as he wished it to be.

All of this I would hear from my bedroom and wish the fighting would stop but it didn't and it would only get worse. My father was changing due to all the booze he was drinking as now he would be drinking in the day as well as late into the nights. Perhaps this was it due to the broken heart he was carrying around with him as I know from conversations I had with him in his later years that on seeing that photo and then finding out my mum was having an affair truly caused a broken heart that never was mended so was all this drinking to drown the pain that he was feeling.

What was to come was no excuse for what he went onto doing as the howling terror of the haunted house would come alive even more, and it was frightening for a young boy who had maybe just turned four years old and already had a year of shouting and smashing going on in the middle of the night and those screams behind my mother's bedroom door.

One morning after a another night full of terror I noticed at the breakfast table my mum wearing a pair of sunglasses and asking her why, she just tried to change the subject then I watched her break down in tears as she reached up into a cupboard to get a drinking glass for my milk and as she reached up it seemed she felt a terrible pain in her ribs and with that it caused her to cry.

I had never seen my mum cry in front of me, it really hurt to see her like this as she just didn't seem like herself as if she had become beaten in spirit and then I noticed when she went to wipe her tears away removing her sunglasses that's when I saw her black eye. Her eye was nearly closed and it was a mess like she had been hit by a train , she told me she had fallen in the night, I was too young to know that she was telling me lies covering up for something so much worse.

What had gone on behind her bedroom door was that my father had come home and woke her up with more accusations of her affair. My mum being asleep rolled over on her side putting her back to my father and telling him, for the very first time, to fuck off as she had work the next morning. With that my father, the father who had been so loving and caring for her all those years, attacked my mum as she laid there in their bed.

She couldn't protect herself from the many blows that he struck her with, breaking two of her ribs as he laid into her and then doing damage to her beautiful blue green eyes with a close fist punch to her face.

She had nowhere to go and no one to call out to as he undressed himself and got into bed and forced himself on to her, which is rape in my eyes and nothing less. There was a woman, his beautiful wife whom he had just beaten, and now he was forcing her to make love to him. This wasn't love nor was this sex as this even within a marriage was rape as I know for a fact that my mother didn't want to be anywhere near my father after what he has just done to her.

With his rage like a devil that soaked into the walls of that haunted house. Everything that house took in and everything it witnessed, I am sure just made the house even more chilling and filled with terror. I was only over the hallway in my own bedroom, and could hear my mum being beaten that night but I didn't realise it was her who was being thrown around. I thought it was just my father smashing a flower vase but never would I ever think he would lay his hands on my mum.

My mum never would tell me that, the following morning what had happened as she kept with her lies that she had fallen over in her bedroom. As for my father who was fast asleep, when awaking and never remembering what he had done nor did even get to see my mum's black eye as my mum had gone into the hair salon having to try and run her business as best as possible in so much pain and still wearing a pair of sunglasses telling clients that she had fallen down the stairs leading up to the front porch of our house.

My father going off to the pub as usual and coming back that night when seeing my mum's eye as he was again really drunk, calling her a liar as he hadn't remembered what he had done the previous night due to the amount of drink he had consumed before reaching home and beating his wife up so badly. He truly would have black outs and not remember anything, he was such a different man when he was very drunk than when he was sober.

He was sober when he had nights to work on the ferries , he wouldn't turn up to the boat drunk ,but it wouldn't take him long getting drunk on the boat and that's what he would do. He now was always pissed whenever I saw him.

While he was on nights, there was only one person my Mum would run to and that was to Wim her lover and this could mean that my mum would get a babysitter in. My sister and I at night would be in the house with a baby sitter while my Father was away working and my mum was away with her boyfriend, not her husband, such a dangerous game of love she was playing but a game she still carried on playing.

At least the nights when my father wasn't in the house, I would get a better night's sleep but still suffering from great night terrors. I always felt there was something haunting about the house. It wasn't a nice vibe and things were very uneasy.

This wasn't my only worry, as someone else would come along to contribute to making my early years very unsettling. I would know him as simply The Monster, a man that would bring more terror to me as a very young boy but not within the house but from outside the house. Escalating my troubles so much so that with these horrors combined it would only draw me away from ever wanting to spend time there.

I recall the first appearance of The Monster when I was only 4 years of age. He was a weirdo who lived in the neighbourhood. He was around 50 years old, very creepy, and I can recall he had thick black eye brows that were overgrown and would stick out. As I look back now, I am 99% sure he was a child molester as he was just so creepy and what he would do was of no normal behaviour.

His wife would always get her hair cut in my mum's hairdressing saloon. That's when I first saw him, or let's say when he first noticed me as while my mum used to cut peoples hair, I would always run in and run out of the hair salon causing trouble whenever I was bored. I noticed him sitting there waiting for his wife to get her hair done and the way he would look at me was so unsettling and gave me the utter creeps.

Some afternoons while I would be in my lounge which was the room next to the hair salon, clients would walk on past me while I watched cartoons as they were allowed to use our family bathroom if they wish to and this Included him, though he would stay there and try and talk to me ask me what I was doing and just the way he would speak to me, it's as if his eyes were undressing me while he spoke.

I hated whenever I saw him in the saloon waiting for his wife, as once he saw me his eyes would light up. This made me want to leave my lounge immediately and go from enjoying my cartoons to climbing up and away from him into my walnut tree in my front yard and stay there until I could see him and his wife walk off down the road.

Only then once I could see they were gone I would get back down from the walnut tree. He just had this horrible effect on me, and I wouldn't be wrong about how I sensed he wasn't a good man. That even became more evident one afternoon when I had come home from kindergarten.

In that year before I was attending school I came home on a specific day that I remember so clearly. I went into my bedroom to get my football that I would kick around my yard in my Liverpool football kit that my Grandparents had send me over from the UK. I had just finished getting changed and my bedroom door swung open. I was thinking it was my mum but there stood the man staring at me.

I don't know how long had he been standing behind my bedroom door for, but he gave me such a fright. I tried to get past him as he was standing in the doorway. I felt trapped, just wanting to get out he asked me, "is this your bedroom, Chris?" I hated anyone from that moment onwards calling me Chris. He then followed with, "is this where you sleep at night?" I remember the hairs on the back of my neck standing on ends as he rolled his eyes around at me.

He was such a big fat sob of a man, greasy black hair that was turning grey, slicked back, and those huge bushy eyebrows that would stick out so crazy. He smelt of a musty smell and booze, not like the smell of my father after he drunk, but more of a whiskey type smell. A smell, I can think of even now to this day and only have I ever smelled from him and no one else I have met.

I managed to push past him and out the kitchen door I run, not even kicking my football around, instead climbing straight away up into my walnut tree. From there I watched him pop his head out of the kitchen door looking for me.

As I sat there in the tree, quiet as a mouse, watching him come down off the porch and looking around the side of the house where my bedroom window was, then back into the house he went. I didn't get down even after I saw him an hour or so later leave with his wife. I was so shaken up by him looking for me and by coming into my bedroom.

I told my mum at dinner time that he had come into my room, and she said maybe he was just lost looking for the bathroom but of course he fucking wasn't as he had used the bathroom many a times. He wasn't lost at all; that I knew for sure. I wasn't making a scene, but my mum told me not to worry.

I didn't even bother trying to tell her that he had also followed me out to the yard, as she didn't believe me so I gave up trying to convince her that he was a wronging as she believed that he hadn't done anything. What else could I say to make her believe me that he was dirty old pervert.

I would find out that my claims were 100% correct as that night the winds were up. Wellington is known as one of the windiest city in the world so winds were nothing unusual. At night the braches on the bushes by my bedroom window would make noises against the window panels, like a screeching scratching sound, but this evening I woke up with more of a solid tapping noise.

Thinking it was one of our cats maybe trying to get in as some nights they would stay out rather than coming in, so I jumped up out of bed opened the curtain to let one of the cats in, but there looking straight back at me wasn't one of our family ginger cats, but it was The Monster's face looking back at me.

I didn't see him to start with as it was dark black. Then he moved his face closer to the window and with the light of the moon, I saw his big evil eyes then he wiped his lips with his tongue.

I screamed and run into my mum's bedroom telling her what I had seen so she came into my room and looked out the window, but couldn't see anything and so my Mum shut the curtain and took me back to bed. My mum telling me I must have been sleep walking and having a bad dream.

Telling me he wasn't there as she put me back to bed. What I saw that night was The Monster. It wasn't a bad dream and it wasn't a nightmare, it was for real. I had seen him with my own eyes.

This wasn't the last time he would tap on my window at night either. Our house was on a corner so he could come into the property from two different directions. He would return many a nights, no one ever believing me and no one ever questioning him.

I just spend more time up in the walnut tree so I would never have to see him when he was waiting for his wife to get her hair done. That didn't stop him at night coming back, as some evenings, not always, but some evenings hearing that tapping noise again outside my window.

It would wake me up and I would just be frozen in my bed, too scared to yell out to my mum or my dad. It wouldn't matter because by the time I had, they would check out the window always telling me, I had again been having nightmares.

How I wished they had believed me as it just made the house so much more frightening for me. I didn't for many nights slept well. Most nights, I would sleep with the light on, as now the dark was even scary to me as if it wasn't for this bastard being outside my bedroom window which would wake me up, then it would be due to the serious fighting that now was taking place inside the house between my parents.

Their fights only got worse, but I don't think my father for the time being, struck my mum again. His drinking hadn't slowed down so night time would always be very unsettling whenever he returned drunk.

My mum's ongoing affair wasn't found out again until leading up to my 5th birthday in 1980. I had only been at school for four months and something made my father suspect that my mum had made contact with her lover again. One thing he didn't want to happen is lose his wife to another man and he certainly didn't want to lose his family.

He had tried to do so much for us although finally it became quite clear to him that his drinking was causing a lot of problems and that his moods towards my mum were getting out of order and their fighting was becoming more regular.

He thought that to save his marriage, the love of his life that he would return his wife and himself to where they first had met and to bring back the romance that they had.

That was back in the late 1960s and it was now 1980 with so much that had gone on as with the beatings my mum had taken, with the mistrust my father had in his wife and with the serious drinking problem my father had but for now for the sake of the family unit then my mum was happy to give it another go.

She very much had such fond memories of London; neither had she met my father's family from Scotland. Maybe it was time to move on from our house in Miramar something even as a 5 year old child, I very much wanted.

We were soon off on a plane heading for the UK with a holiday on the journey there. My father treating us all to and if once we got to the UK and liked the place so much, be it London or Scotland then the plan was to sell the house back in NZ and my mum's business and set up a new life in the UK. That could change everything for the best and also in my father's eyes then his wife will be far away from her lover back in NZ.

Chapter 3

LONDON CALLING

The year was 1980 I was 5 years old and my sister was 10 years old when we landed at Heathrow. We had stopped over first at Singapore, I can remember how I played up, becoming a naughty child. I think before this, I was just mischief but now I was ever so naughty and escaping was one of my trades.

One evening when my sister and I had a babysitter looking after us in our grand hotel, I decided to follow the music that was being played, some floors down from our suite as there was a ball going on. I spotted my mum and dad dancing together, holding one another and smiling; it was so beautiful to see them again like this after the recent fights at home that I started to hear so often go on behind closed doors.

As I watched them dance, until the babysitter grabbed me forcefully. This hadn't happened for many a years, last time it was the kindergarten teacher so I knew what to do as I had learned from my parents fighting to scream and shout as when I could hear my Mum fighting with my Father, it sometimes stopped my Dad shouting at my Mum behind their closed bedroom door when they heard me scream.

I would be awoken in the pitch black of the night hearing my Father raise his voice at my Mum, when my Dad would see me standing at their bedroom door then he would let go of my Mum, when my Dad would see me standing at their bedroom door then he would let go of my Mum so I yelled at the babysitter but it didn't work as she just threw me back in the direction on the landing of my parents suite, where my sister was who was up in bed watching the telly.

I was having none of it and more the babysitter felt like dragging me, more I put up a fight to the point that when she was hurting me by grabbing me, it was making my blood boil.

What the babysitter didn't know was she had just driven me nuts by laying her hands on me so I jumped on her foot as hard thinking she would let me go but she just held me tighter so in the end I kicked her in the sheen as hard as I could.

I didn't like having to kick her but she had her nails right in my skin and she was being so rough with me and all I wanted was for her to let go off me which she did though my quick kick to her sheen left her screaming which brought a sudden stop to the music below and with all the hotel grownups guests, whom were at the ball looking up at me as I had my made my way back down so I could just see my parents being happy together up till this point that is.

There I was with my blue sooky blanket and a teddy in my hand in my pjs, my parents noticing me was the end of my parents loving moment, I had wreaked it. Back in the suite due to me escaping from the suite, kicking the babysitter, brought on a row between my parents so all was lost and we were back to how things were in the haunted house.

The thing is my parents would never hit me or grab me so whenever someone did, be it at school, a kid hit me, and I would just go into a mad rage and seek to hurt them for causing me pain. I was never one, ever just to strike out at anyone, I was behaved in that sense, though was naughty in other ways.

A few days later we were off to Hong Kong, where at the gates a official man, customs or a police officer with a huge gun strapped around him took my teddy bear and torn at it which brought me to tears. Later on, in years I found out this was due to my father having so many stamps in his passport, they for some stupid reason thought he could have been a drug smuggler.

One thing my Dad was anti drugs all his life. I think maybe my mum in her time in London tried a few things what were going around in the swinging 60s back then as in purple pills though in NZ, she never took drugs of any sort.

We were off to London. We arrived there in the morning; I can recall the black cab driving us to our hotel, which was the famous Dorchester Hotel on Park Lane in Mayfair. My Dad really wanted to lay it on for my Mum, was he doing all this in way of saying sorry for how he treated her at times, or was this honeymoon for them, for my mum to get Wim out of her head. I am sure all of the above.

We checked into the hotel, we were so tired but my Dad wanted a drink. He left for the bar and returned hours late with another fella. Only before my Dad died, I found out this other person was the English comedian Peter Sellers, who my Dad had known during his years in London in the 1960s.

I remember them being around the same size in height while my Dad was introducing Peter to my Mum and us kids. My Mum was happy to have met Peter.

Soon afterwards we were sleeping, what I didn't know at the time was that Peter Sellers, that late afternoon or early evening had a fatal heart attack in his own suite at the hotel and died, which was sad to my Father as he loved his work on the radio and also on the big screen.

It was lovely for my Father that on touching down again in London, hours later he had bumped into someone he had known from his past.

Soon we were shown all over London by my Father. My Father knew London like the back of his hand, he showed us all over London and we went down to the East End, ate pie and mash, one evening we went for a curry down Brick Lane.

I remember all the different cultures and the smells and tastes of the food that swept down the street and nearby lanes.

Even as a 5 year old, I loved this place and how then at that early age, old London town was drawing me near.

Who would think that 15 years on, I would be again through the streets of the East End, though next time knowing and befriending many of the shop keepers, the pub landlords and the florists and the suit makers and the diamond sellers and back street shops workers, but more than this who would have dreamed or thought that in 15 years I would visiting the gangland boss Reggie Kray for the last 5 years of his life and including the last 5 years of his 30 year prison sentence.

Also being in the company of Freddie Foreman (The British Godfather), who single handily would play such a huge part in my life, ensuring that I stay on the straight and narrow, and that I don't get myself involved in crime as I had when I was a kid then teenager and a young man growing up in New Zealand involved in gangland.

Though of course I am not saying all the time I was a saint during my latter years in London as I was far from it but at least with the kindness of Freddie Foreman and his family, including his Janice.

They all gave me so much support and love to only better myself as a person, which forever more I will always hold them all deeply in my heart and in my memories ever so fondly.

No one could dream that I myself would become part of the Kray Empire as it stood with the passing of Ronnie Kray.

I being part of The Firm and working directly at times for Reggie Kray while he was still serving his recommend 30 year jail sentence that was handed down to his twin brother Ron and himself in the late 1960s.

I would also become a good friend of Charlie Kray , the twins oldest brother and get to know all the gentlemen who were known as The Chaps such as Roy Shaw , Big Albert Chapman, Johnny Nash, Joe Pyle, Charlie Richardson and Tony Lambrianou just to name a few.

I sadly during my time in London would take part in Charlie Krays funeral which was sad as Charlie was a gentleman through and through, a very special man in so many ways.

Then onto Reggie Kray own funeral, after being part of his life, the final five years in London to when he sadly lost his fight of cancer after first making contact with him when I was only a teenager living on the other side of the world, seven oceans away so knowing Reggie personally for over 8 years of my life.

No one would ever think that Ronnie Krays death; this was the reason why I had been called back all those years later to this London town, the tough streets of the East End.

Soon after all our sightseeing and places we had been were over, my father took us all out to a plush restaurant, Simpsons on the Strand. Where back in the late 1960s, my Father had met my mum, and where they had started their romance. I can remember wearing my best suit that my dad had me made from a tailor from the back of Mayfair.

I looked smart in my blue suit and tie, maybe this was the beginning of a villain in the marking. All I needed then was a pinkie ring and I would have looked like a mini gangster but the suit of course wasn't to make me at the age of five look anything like a villain.

To dine at such a plush British restaurant, one had to not wear causal but be ever well dressed, and that day we all very much did. Soon we were leaving London and heading up the country to stop off at Manchester as just outside Manchester, we had family through my father and then we went on to York where I was stung by a bee while eating a strawberry jam sandwich.

After a night in another lovely hotel, we headed to Scotland to visit my Grandparents and also my Auntie June and my Uncle Raymond and my two cousins whom my Father hadn't ever met before, as they were born while he was in New Zealand.

My father hadn't seen his sister since he run away when he was young and to be with his Mum and his Stepfather whom he always knew as his Father, it was a joyful time for my Father and for all of us as one Family together and my Scottish blood family are so lovely and ever so dear to me.

I even named my daughter after my Scottish Grandmother. My memories of Scotland are set within my mind, some of the best childhood memories I could ever in my whole life ask for. I loved the people and the country and more so the country side, the Highlands.

We got to see the highland games and also the tattoo games and what have to be a highlight was the stories being told late into the night of the loch ness monsters, as we sat in a village pub not too far from Loch Ness. Listening to these stories of the sightings of Nessie, my mum the following day hired a car so we could travel right around the lock for me to try and see Nessie.

Even with a great imagination at that age of 5 year years old, I never got to see Nessie and her young, out there somewhere on the lock. For years I would any chance I got on my return to the UK would always go up and revisit the Loch Ness, it's beautiful but more so it brings memories of a time where my parents not once did fight and for me to have that small window of happiness through my childhood memories is something ever so dear for me forever more, to hang onto.

We spent a lot of time in Scotland, living there to see if this was the home that was to be our new home but sooner than later my father would drink and my mum to be honest had second thoughts about saying goodbye to her home NZ. Her business as well, that she had built up also she missed her family dearly.

I think with the blast of the winter that soon was to come and my father drinking heavily, more than he would back home, my mum made the right decision for us all to come home. My father wasn't happy and asked my Mum what was wrong with bonnie Scotland. The thing was to my Mum there wasn't anything wrong; she loved it and also the warmth from my grandparents and the friendship with my father's sister.

My Mum was thinking of us kids, what was best for us, and that was NZ, what we knew as home. Soon we were back on a plane to New Zealand; I am sure Wim somewhere was again on my Mothers mind. Though the last few months, my Mum and Dad were getting along so much better since their time away from New Zealand.

School I was dreading ,I had just been away for so long, I had to play catch up in school, something that I didn't enjoy as I had missed so much and all the other kids seemed to be more advance, I wasn't slow nor a slow learner. No one knew that I was dyslexic. I found school at times a lot to take on, but I never complained nor did I ever take days off.

School to me was an early escape, from the nightmares that I would suffer from hearing my parents fight on our return to New Zealand, within months of getting back. I am sure parents who fight, never realise what effect they are having on their kids but believe me, I did suffer. I am sure that goes to all the kids who have been brought up in a violent home having to hear their parents shout at each other all through the night.

Lennie Mclean, the very famous bare knuckle fighter, after I had met him for a second time, in his pub The Governor in the East End , we had a conversation about witnessing, hearing or being part of violence as a child. The first time I met Lennie through the London Gangster Dave Courtney but Lennie I felt, was standing over me and very much giving me a cold shoulder in his pub, the first time I met him.

But after I had Reggie Kray call him vouching for me, letting him know that I was one of the good guys, the next time I was in his pub having a drink and on Lennie walking in, he was a proper gentleman and we had a good chat, he was friendly as a pie and that late afternoon, the conversation was interesting and he opened up a little to me.

This giant of a man told me how his childhood was effected by violence from within his own family house. I know that many children are affected by violence within their home that they grow up in. Even some people reading this book, you may well also be affected by what you witnessed or still do witness in your family home.

I hope my book is of some help to you, and I do wish that you seek help to have this violence stopped as in this day and age you have many outreach groups you or whomever it is being effected by domestic violence to go to for help, before it gets out of control.

In my Mums day and age, she had no one to go to as back in those days there were no groups that were set up for such women to go to for help. In her darkest hours and there was many of them, as I am sure for the people reading this book, who can relate to this, have also themselves many dark hours so I do wish you all the best, I very much do.

I felt glad that my Father wasn't at home all the time, only due to the violence though I loved my father dearly. I am sure my Mum, even more so, though of course I did miss having a father, as the other kids Dads would be there for them on school outings and to watch them in the track and field days or while playing football.

I didn't have this, not that my Father didn't care as he did very much so, it was just his work would take him away for weeks on end even months.

I can remember during the Falkland War, my father set off and joined a ship that was used for supplies to the battle ships and the troops. He would send us letters home that my Mum at night would read to us. While in other houses, kids would be getting read bedtime stories, but we were being read exciting real life stories of my Father during those times.

He was never part of neither the Royal Navy nor the Royal Army, he was still very proud to serve his country in some way during the war. He came back from there with even more stories, stories that I could share at school among all the other kids in my class as not many, if any of them had even be out of New Zealand, some had travelled as far Australia with their parents and families, but never further than there.

They were always interested in the stories that were handed down to me from my father on his returns from the seas and the countries, he had visited. I would never swap my parents for their parents.

I would have swapped their peace and quiet behind closed doors for the whole wide world, if I had the world in the palms of my hand, as soon things got worse and worse when I was soon turning the age past 7 years old.

Chapter 4

BLACK AND BLUE

As my sister got older, she would travel out of the neighbour to be with her friends after school. My dad being away at work, my mum would be having that affair with Wim so she would race off, when she had the chance to see him, guessing maybe my sister would be there to look after me.

My sister who now was 12 years old, I had turned 7 years old. I would many times find myself early evening in the house alone, my mum would only get a baby sitter if she was away for the whole night, but if she was away just for the evening, being it while my dad still living in the house, many times they wouldn't be speaking due to my dad beating my mum, which meant he would be at the pub till late, not knowing I would be at home by myself in the evenings.

I would once it became night, turn on all the lights in every part of the house so to get rid of the darkness. I would never go into my bedroom as my bedroom was frightening to me due to that monster tapping at my window. After a while I would be scared to even be in the house alone.

I was very grown up for my age. I knew how to cook myself dinner.

I would go on to, after my father left the family house for good, cook my sister and my Mum dinner many times as I had after my dad left, become head of the family at such a young age. I thought at the time I was the boss.

As for the house, it didn't get much better for me, so at night I would lock the front door, climb up in the giant walnut tree. Up there I would feel most safe. I would watch the busses stop outside my house and wonder where would they go to and what else was out there past this suburb of Miramar. I wanted to find out, that was for sure but a little at a time.

I would day dream, thinking what all the other kids would be doing right now. Would they be listening to their parents fight as that's what I thought went on in every household, as it did in my own house. I had been at this age, invited to other kid's house but I never noticed my sister going to her friend's house too often as they would knock about at malls and shopping centres.

Something I asked why she did and why she wasn't fond of other people's houses, she told me that it felt weird as she would watch fathers come home and kiss their wives and dinner would be served on a table for all to be around the dinner table, all to enjoy the food together. That wasn't a normal family, as what we had at home, we both believed was to be a normal family, wasn't it.

As we got older, experiencing other friend's households, we realise what was happening inside our house, what we both would hear and witness during the nights, before we had to go to school was not normal at all. Something we didn't share with others at school.

My mum worked so hard for us, everyday she would be running the salon after a night of being beaten with a black eye, she would wear sunglasses and try to hide her many bruisers with makeup. She started to have a weight problem.

I think during this time she found out Wim had been cheating on her so with one man who would beat her and the other one whom she would run off to and give up everything for him as she was taking beatings due to being unfaith to her husband, to only find out that the man of her dreams, the love of her life was cheating on her, must have made her feel so less of herself.

Food like anything can become a friend, my mum didn't drink too much, she would when socializing and she smoked a fair bit but back in those days everyone smoked. She didn't take drugs though later in life, she could have been taking sleeping tablets and also tablets for her weight up until soon after my father left the family house.

My mum went and got a operation that dropped a lot of weight of her, she never was overweight after that but her health did suffer a bit during these early years and with me who had severe asthma to the point on many nights, I had to be rushed to hospital and kept in hospital for long periods of time.

This was with me for my early years, I can remember at night waking not being able to breath and passing out at times, trying to shout for help then waking up with our family doctor their injecting me with drugs to open my airwaves and putting me on a machine. There was the times in hospital, whenever the call in the night for the doctor wasn't going to stable my condition.

This scared my mum so much, that many a nights, she would sit in my room with me not leaving my side and would get her own mum down so to look after me. My nana moved to Wellington, so she could always be near. I am unsure how much my mum ever told her brothers and her father and her mum about my dad beating her. I know my uncles would have gone for my dad, if they knew. I doubt they did, as they all seemed friends, getting on with my dad.

My granddad, I am unsure as he died before I was born but I do know he was a good man and so were my uncles and aunties. We would as a family travel and visit them all up in the country. They all lived in the North Island, around the base of the middle mountain as that's where the family businesses were, be it dairy farms and saw mills.

My mum's youngest brother would take on the family businesses, the saw mills that my Grandfather owed. Uncle Frank would branch out to become in his years the leading forest pine saw exporter of all the country, he is now worth over 20millions pounds+, and is one of the richest men in New Zealand, my Grandfather would be so proud of him.

Going back to my days of the aged 8, I would as by this time get into sport in a huge way. It was a way I would fill up my days after school, be it swimming classes or track and field, I would put my name down for any sport activity. I found playing soccer on the weekend my passion, not many kids would play the sport but I took to it like a duck on water and my social circle soon branched out.

I was at the same school as my sister, Worser Bay School, that's when I first seen bullying. I didn't really understand it, but I was not going to allow myself to be bullied. I remember one of my first sports was judo; my mum got me involved in that. It brought me great confidence, which lead me onto stepping up to my dad, whenever he would come around the house to fight with my mum in later years.

I just wanted to protect my dear Mum as good as I could. I would find myself leaning against the door that my father would be trying to kick in, as my mum wouldn't ever leave the house to get away when he did get in. She was too embarrassed for the neighbours to see her beaten up, but I would take my mum's hand and get her and my sister out of the house across the roads to a neighbour's house for my mum to be safe.

Someone would always call the police from a neighbouring house when seeing my father chase us down the street in the middle of the nights. Sometimes the police would be too late, and my father would get hold of my mum and drags her back into the house.

Other times my dad, it seemed had left the house after we had got away so we would go back to the house, one door still hanging off its hinges and to bed we would go, only to find out my dad hiding in the house.

My mum would be trapped to take what was a horrible beating. The amount of booze my dad would drink would make him switch so nasty. We kids would just be told to stay in our rooms; we would listen to what was going on. As I got older I would go into my mum's room, try to fight my dad, to no luck apart from when he saw me crying he would then feel ashamed of his actions.

When the police would arrive, they really didn't under domestic violence so they never really acted on it. It was my father's house and as much as my mum's. The Police couldn't make my father leave, if my Mum didn't wish to press charges which she never did.

Sometimes the end result would be ok and my father would just fall asleep after the police had left but other times, only minutes after the police leaving then all hell would break loose. There were times, the police would turn up and my mum would be stronger enough to ask the police to take him away though never pressing charges against him as she too was old school in many ways, and even though my father had just beaten my mum up so badly, he would shout at her while the police attempted to take him away.

My father would fight his ground; knocking over any copper who put their hands on him as he would yell out, it was his fucking house, his wife and none of their fucking business. More cop cars would arrive and my dad would be wrestled to the floor. I hated seeing him handcuffed, my mum always feared for the next morning as more than often the police would just released him when he sobered up.

My mum would have us kids to get off to school, while running a business that was connected to the house. My mum would have to go into work and making out nothing was wrong. One of her best friend was Kath Mitchell, she used to run the shop across the road, her husband John worked on a radio show anyway their kids were to become my best friends and they were like family to us,

I think it was Kath who my mum would speak to about my father, a few times as we would run over to her place sometimes above the shop to hide from my father, if my father had called to say he was on his way over.

But during good times, it was lovely and it felt like a real family, and soon my father said to my mum that maybe the cause of it all was due to my father being out to sea and then coming home and drinking so heavy. I think the very heavy drinking was the main cause of it, full stop.

My mum used to plead with my dad for him to stop drinking as now he would wake up have a drink and drink all day, though still be capable of doing normal things and holding down a job as it would take a lot to get my Father pissed.

At this stage my mum did find me even more difficult to control. I had for many nights been left in that house by myself, I would still climb up the tree as an 8 years old and think of where everyone else would be and also where those buses did lead.

Through my sport, I had become friends with other kids but they all had to be home by 6pm and in bed by 8pm. This wasn't a rule for me so to hang out with them after school which finished at 3pm then do our sport activities that would go till 530pm, it meant I could pop to their houses.

Sometimes if I was lucky I would stay for tea but then I would be walking on home by myself and with nothing more to do, not wanting to go back to my house so I would wander the streets of the neighbour and come across kids much older than me. These kids were 14 years old and 15years old, but to hang out with them, I would have to prove myself as such a young kid; it was not cool for them to have an 8 years old hanging about.

Now these were not kids that were smart or well educated, I found these kids many of them were like me, no fathers at home to discipline them so here I had found kids who I could relate to. They all had BMX bikes, which meant they could travel deep into the neighbourhood.

I wanted to be part of them, not knowing at the time what I was being part of, which was actually a youth gang. I would find youth groups among my sport friends who all lived as normal kids but these older kids whom I met wandering the neighbour, were out to cause trouble.

I was soon put to the test, keeping an eye out for them while they shop lifted to quite a big scale for these kids. That was just a start of many things as they were into destruction of properly, rugby clubhouses, people's houses and schools, also they were would break into people's houses but that wasn't my cuppa of tea, I wasn't ever a thief though mischief like, I wasn't a scumbag of a kid who would rob someone's personal house.

I would look down on them whenever they would talk of doing so. They would even end up breaking into my own school and smashing that to pieces.

I didn't enjoyed all of their crime related activities but my evenings, otherwise would have just been sitting up in my tree, so at least with the local youth gang, I was seeing some of my neighbour and going on adventures and yes some things were fun even though wrong, but being out late at night with these kids was so much fun.

By the time I would get home at night my mum would yell at me, my sister would wind her up and tell her to ground me. My sister and I used to fight like cats and dogs, I would be jealous of the freedom she would have, as now she was 13 years old, she was allowed to go to parties, stay over at her friend's house for the whole weekends. I couldn't do this; I felt I was older enough to.

In the end, I gave up on my family and stayed out with the gang making trouble through the suburb for many a year's then smoking pot for the first time. I hated ciggs, I tried them once, hated them plus with my asthma and my sport my lungs were too tight when it came to inhaling a ciggs. I never knew why all the kids at school would sneak off to smoke a ciggs.

My school performance around this time started to drop and what I was learning in the evening with the gang, was all crime related. Soon we started to get bigger in size of our gang; we named ourselves the Miramar warriors. The word warriors taken from a movie, I had watched on video. My mum was one of the first in the neighbourhood to get a video recorder. I would get movies out at the local video store, take my mum's video player and would watch these movies at one of the kid's house, when his own mum wasn't home.

He was the only boy of the gang who I knew where he lived as with the other kids they would never let any of us know where they lived. I think many were ashamed as they lived on run down estates, and as for some of the others, they were taking beatings by either their father or mother so they never wanted us to meet their parents.

Any movie, the first movie I watched on tape was "Rambo", then "Thriller" the Michael Jackson music video and then "America werewolf in London", not the best selection of movies for a 8 year old but I was past cartoons and I was hanging around with older boys so I would always pick out horror movies or violent movies, as the boys loved to watch those types of movies.

Because I had been to London, all the kids loved hearing of me being in London as some were so poor that their families would never be able to even afford to travel out of Wellington, so when I would speak of the sounds and smells of Brick Lane or the guards outside St James Palace.

The kids would dream of one day them all being able to go to such places, sadly for many it would only ever stay as dreams as many in their older life's, ended up spending a lot of time in prisons, some lost their lives through gang related violence so dreams for many of them , simply stayed dreams.

One night, one of the older boys said he would get me a BMX bike, if I swapped the video recorder for it. A BMX bike was any kids dream. I said yes and later that evening he came back with a bike for me.

I rode it home like I was the new kid in town, a few streets from my house; I had the police stop me. This was the first of many dealings I would have with the police. I was taken in the back of the police car, driven home and my mum being told I had stolen a bike from a nearby street. I hadn't I protest, later finding out that the kid had nicked the bike to do the swap with the video recorder.

After the police left, my mum hit me around the legs, accusing me of being a thief and that I wasn't though I had taken our video recorder but I hadn't stolen a bike. Here I found myself among many thieves as that's how they would pay for their dope and anything else they wished for.

The only thing that I wished for at the time was for my mum to believe me, but more I told her I hadn't stolen the bike, more it seemed she accused me of nicking it, so after that I just thought fuck it, I will go out and do whatever I fucking want and her, my mother nor the police can do anything about it.

At school I didn't keep up with the programme, just day dreaming of what I would be doing that night with the gang. As for the bullies at school, well I started to form my own gang within school, which didn't go down well with the teachers. I saw it as in numbers the bullies couldn't do anything so we ended up having the bullies on our side.

As they couldn't take on a small size school gang so I would soon have them operate for the school gang. I would introduce the more rebel kids among them, to the older boys from the Miramar Warriors after school.

In the evenings, they would sneak out at night and meet the Miramar warriors this now brought our numbers over to 30 kids in total, which was a proper little gang forming to the point that we were being noted by the local police as we would just walk the neighbour 30 handed, causing trouble.

Any break in or anything that had been smashed, the police knew it would be down to us, some nights we would all be rounded up by the police.

My mother having parents turn up to our house, telling my mum to look after her child better and stop having me be a bad influence on their own children. My mum would take no shit, telling them all to fuck off and get off her land.

Soon it became known that I was some sort of tear away, and that my father hardly was at home.

At the school gates, I would hear other parents say my mum was a bad mum, but you know what, my mum was the best mum in the whole world. All this used to upset my mum so I never asked her to drop me off to school, instead I would ask her for bus fare, though school was only up the winding hill, I could have walked it but instead I would bus it to school, it was my first time on the bus.

Teachers would say to my mum that I was too young to be travelling on a bus by myself. My sister was now in her intermediate school so now I was on my own at Worse Bay School. I had been on my own in many ways for a few years already so catching a bus was fine, so I didn't understand what all the fuss was about.

Thoughts of travelling even further on buses soon caught my attention even more. One night I went out with the gang, we were heading over to south Miramar as the older kids had found a girls home there, where girls were locked up due to all sorts of crime or due to running away constantly from home so they were placed in care and this was where they would be held for the meantime.

We would go over there, chat to the girls by the pavement, and show off to them by doing what was the craze from American at the time break dancing. There would be us with our lino and our break pants, doing all these dance moves with a loud stereo playing, looking like, I can imagine right fools, apart from the guys who could really dance well, I wasn't one of them that's for sure.

The older boys would be smoking their dope, some of the older boys who couldn't afford to put cash into the weed, would bring stolen booze from shop lifting. We all would go back late at night, get some of the girls out and all head to a local park, where kids would be having sex for the very first time, lots of dope be smoking and drinking happening.

One of the girls who hang around us from the girls home, kissed me which was my very first kiss, then from that kiss we would play about with one another, though she and the other girls thought I was like 12 years old or 13 years old. The older boys would laugh, putting the girls off me. It become a regular thing, the girls coming out with us late at night home, it kept us away from causing trouble on the streets as girls were all that as on our minds.

At this time my school, had been having meetings with my mum. My dad had found out as my Mum blamed my father that I had become uncontrollable as his lack of being a father which then caused even more trouble at home whenever they both were home, which just made me runaway even more at night and stay out with the gang , constantly being brought home by the police.

Even though some nights I wasn't getting into trouble, the police would still send me home but the rush I was getting from being in a gang was too much, so again I would be out and my mum just couldn't cope with me.

What did my parents expect, as after many years of being in a house that was filled of violence, or nights that I found myself alone in the house then I truly wished I was anywhere else than home. The gang gave me the escape into evenings of adventures, even if it meant my schooling was slipping, I wasn't going to give up the gang as they had become like another family to me.

Finally my mum had enough not of me, but of my father and his rages and her being beaten to the point, that my mum ended leaving the house and for a short time stayed at my nanas house and then getting a flat nearby but never telling my father where it was. My dad would be at home looking after us, then later the pub would come first so he would be out late and no one again to look after me or look over me but I couldn't leave as if my dad came home and I wasn't there then I would be in the shit, so back to my tree I would climb.

One evening while I was up in the tree, below me appearing around the comer of my house, I could see someone walk around the side of the house, I didn't see who it was as I kept still in the tree and didn't say a word, then I heard that tap, tap noise, it was The Monster. He was back, I watched him stand outside my bedroom window, that's when I heard him call out "Chris". I watched him unzip his trousers, he started to wank against the side of the house, this was the noises tap, tap that he had been making all these nights, it was his body weight against the side of the house that cause this noise.

I frozen as scared as I saw what he was doing, then when he finished he walked away out of the front gate. I didn't get down of that tree until I saw a taxi pull up, it must have been around 1130pm as my dad got out of the taxi so drunk. I jumped back down and unlocked the door and went into my bedroom, even more scared than any time before. That night I slept with my light on and done so for years to come as a young child in that house.

The Friday of that week, after school I was speaking to my dad, he had managed to get the address where my mum was staying so he asked if I wanted to go and see my mum as she had someone else looking after the saloon while he was in the house. Her friend Helen Scully was running the saloon for my Mum, and when my father was away on the ferries, that's only when my mum would come back to work again in her saloon and stay over at the house in the evening to look after me and my sister.

That Friday I mentioned, my father and I went over to see my Mum in a taxi, my father never drove as when my mum was carrying me in her womb, my father crashed the car and nearly killed all of us though I was in my mum's womb, the doctors thought for sure my mum had lost her baby due to the crash so ever since then, my mum was the only one who ever drove the family car.

We got to my mum's flat; my dad knocked on the door with me, his son behind him. On my mum opening the door, she got such a fright, she tried to shut the door but my dad forced his way in. There in the kitchen was Wim, my mum's first love. For the very first time these two men had met each other, this man was the cause of the entire break up and all the years of misery in my father's eyes, not the booze.

In some way yes my father was right, but was it also true love that was the cause of years of unhappiness. Was it the volume of booze being drunken by my father night after night that was actually the main cause? I can remember to this day as if that day was only yesterday what went on moments after my dad laid his eye on Wim as a fight between two men that went on, past a normal fight right there in front of my eyes.

My father attacked Wim with all he had. Now my father was short in height, Wim was 6 foot five in height and as strong as an ox. It in a way, remained me of watching back Roy Shaw and Lennie Mclean on old footage of their bare-knuckle fights as it was so violent, my father fighting with Wim as if they were true bare knuckle fighters.

Roy Shaw and Lennie Mclean were at their peak of their time, the finest bare-knuckle fighters in the world. My father was far from that but hell did he give a good fight that day against Wim, in what was soon the wreak of my mum's kitchen. The only thing that broke it was lots and I mean lots of coppers came rushing in and breaking them up.

Both covered in blood, also my mum she tried to step in and was hit mistaken this time but with such nasty punch that cause her not to be able to even speak. Its violence like this which that truly was a lot to take in being only 8 years old, as it was a fight that was bloody to the point of one of them nearly dying.

My father was lead away first in handcuffs; this was yet another brush with the law my father had got himself into and every time it was due to do with violence.

He would always let his hands do the talking even though it was destroying him as again he would be lead to a police cell. I had told my mum that this weekend I was going on soccer tournament and that one of the parents was to pick me that evening from the house.

I just wanted to get away from all the violence and I didn't like seeing my father fighting like that and I knew deep down neither did my father as he was a good man, he was just fighting for the love of his life and his family.

I knew Wim was there to look after my Mum and so even though I wasn't on a soccer tournament that weekend, it was only being held locally and not as I told my mum out of Wellington, I just wanted for the first time to be on my own, I was so upset by what I had seen.

My mum gave me some extra spending money, she felt so bad to what I had witnessed that she actually gave a lot of spending money, and I told her I would catch the bus back home as she was in no state to drive. She told me not to tell my sister if I saw her nor my nana. I told her I wouldn't, as I said goodbye to them both, leaving out the front door, to wait at the bus stop.

I counted my money it was about $40, I normally would only get $5 a week. Thoughts came into my mind of what I could spend this money on. I caught the bus back to mine and got change quickly, seeing my sister who was with her best friends Angie and Joana. I actually fancied most of my sisters' friends but when you're at that age, you're telling them they look ugly instead of how nice they really looked.

I showed them the money I had, which my sister was convinced I had stolen it out of the till in mums shop. I hated people falsely accusing me of things I never did, so I ended up having a fight with my sister, shortly finding myself being attacked by all three. I let them win that fight as I never ever hit a girl after seeing for all these years what my father done to my mum.

Off I went, out the night meeting up with the gang .We went to the girls home, I put out some of my money so we were stocked up on booze, not beer this time but vodka something I hadn't tried before. The Maori boys in the gang all had their dope, some of the girls on this night were happy just to run away from the home, something that never was spoken about.

I did notice one of the regular girls weren't with us, I asked where she was. Tuesday of that week I was told, she had hung herself in the home. We don't know why but it made it us all very sad, this was the girl who months earlier had been my first kiss and now she was dead.

Something I didn't understand and taking a look back at the horrible looking building that is was, with bars on some of its windows, it was if she was standing in one of the top windows looking at us leaving her behind. I stopped the group and said hey there she is.

I was sure of what I had seen; pointing up to what window I thought I had seen her in waving back at us. I not knowing what that part of the home was, until one of the girls said that room was actually the girl's bedroom that was the room she hung herself in.

This was the start of my belief in ghosts, not knowing at that time how I had with my own eyes seen the ghost of my first kiss. We all went to the fish shop which was across the road from my house, the boys played on the games machine and we all had fish and chips.

As soon as it got late, the shop closed, everyone as normally they could by this time would all go their separate ways. I looked over at my house, the haunted house, I thought of The Monster and I just didn't want to be their alone even though hours earlier I did wish to be alone.

I, for the first time asked everyone back to my house. As the girls who had escaped from the girls home, had nowhere to go we all crossed the road to my house.

I first checked the house to see if anyone was home, it was pitch black. No one was there so I pointed over for everyone to come over, and they loved it. We got on the vodka, drinking it straight, what a shock to the system that was and we partied.

My mum's Elvis records came out and we all got complexly shit faced on Elvis, The Beatles, pot and vodka then running out of vodka I pointed to my parents well stocked liqueur cabinet where there was over a dozen bottles of booze.

Neither I nor the older kids had any clue what all the different bottles of booze were but it didn't stop any of us drinking as much as we could.

We drank one bottle after another, being more wasted that I had even got. They all said that I for sure was now part of the Miramar warriors that was after months of running with them in the evenings getting up to trouble whenever possible.

My house looked a bit of work place as my father had been doing the pace up for a second time, thinking maybe this was the way to get my mum return to the house in previous weeks. I know that the rest of the house was being done up so I was sure that would include my bedroom.

On hearing I now had become part of the gang, I went out on the front porch and got a can of spray paint of one of the Maori boys who was so wasted from dope, he had turned the colour green, and it's known as a whitey.

I took the black can of spray of him; he was our tagger who style would spray paint all of Miramar with the words warriors everywhere. This is what I decided to do on my bedroom wall. I had everyone join in and write whatever they wished to add, it was fucking wicked at the time and a lot of fun was had that night.

We partied on until we all got sick; the girls had sex with a few of the boys. Morning came; I woke up on my mum's bed with one of the girls across me and one at my feet. I still had my clothes on but a lot of love bits on my neck so something did happen that night, I was just too drunk to have remembered.

That morning as I could cook and cook well, something I learned from my dad, so I done everyone a breakfast and it which was fit a king so we all eat, looking and laughing at the mess of my bedroom wall and the state of the lounge where we all had been drinking throughout the night before.

We decided what we were to do for the day, I told them that I had soccer on so I couldn't miss it and would they all come down watch me as my parents sadly never did watch me perform on the pitch, as often as I wished they had.

Now and then my parents did but not as often as all the other kids parents did. I told the gang that afterwards on Saturdays, I would normally go fishing with my dad, if he was off work so I suggested that we all do the same after I finished playing football in this local tournament.

The beaches weren't too far away from Miramar, only over a hill and there below the other side were miles upon miles of sandy beaches. I felt so happy all of them watching me that day on the football pitch.

I can remember the expressions of all the other kids, what they thought and more so their parents when I rocked up with 9 boys who looked ruff as hell and 4 girls who were looking like they for sure weren't your normal girls next door.

Anyway after the matches we headed back to my place, my mum had accounts at the local's shops across the road that I could use whenever I wanted food or anything such a lunch for school.

I went across with a shopping list and brought tons and tons of food and drink for our beach party, that we decided to throw after we had been fishing as the girls thought the idea of fishing was boring so we promised to hold a bbq down on the beach among us all and invite over other members of the Miramar warriors.

I probably spend over $200 worth of food and drink that day. We loaded up all the bottle of booze that we had not drunken from my parent's liquid cabinet and found some of my mum's packs of smokes; we now were in good supply of food, smokes and drinks.

Soon more joined our gang on the walk over the hill to the nearby beaches and it was what was the start of a proper party with fishing rods being shared around so all the boys could have a go at fishing, some never had fished before. The rods my dad had brought me to fish over the weekends, he was home and when he was sober, it was one of the things that he did love doing with me and I enjoyed it as well.

It was mid evening we had been out all day, now partying; older kids started to join us for more fun into the evening. I noticed a few motorcycles; the guys riding the bikes all had the patches of the Satan's Slaves Motorcycle Club on their leather jackets. They had been riding around the bays most of the afternoon, soon parking up their bikes near us.

Satan's Slaves Motorcycle Club, a motorcycle club that had the title of the most feared 1% bike club in all of New Zealand.

How then I never knew that these guys would play a huge part of my life in only a few years to come. Once these bikers had noticed we were only young kids they left us to enjoy our gathering of a party, though some of the girls got chatting to the bikers.

One actually got on the back of one of the bikes and ride of with them, which meant we now had only three girls left to party with.

What did turn up next was the Maori kid who had been sick the night before on my front porch, he had more than just dope this time around as he had a bread bag but no bread, as it was filled to the top of mushrooms, not just normal mushrooms but magical mushrooms.

Such a drug was something new, to me and new to some of the other kids but we were the warriors and we were partying, so anything would do to keep the good times flowing and hell did they do that.

I can't start to explain the energy and the buzz, what came over my body, what was flowing through me, every inch of my body, my mind being taking to another planet it seemed, and my soul just coming alive.

How peoples face started to change and how the rush and the joy of this drug, just took me somewhere that I felt like I belonged to this place where ever I was being taken in my mind and my soul.

It's as if we all were no longer a gang but more a tribe as we danced around our beach bond fire, chapping our hands like great Maori chefs and watching the moon appear even closer to us.

Just belonging in the sky, the moon soon had become ours and we all would be touching the moon, holding it tight in our arms.

Lying on the beach looking up at the stars hearing the water hide the tide, we were all enjoying what had so far been one of the best moments of my life. One of the girls that were left out of the three remaining girls was resting her head upon my chest.

I held her hand knowing the marks on my neck from the drunken night before was cause by her, but this night I felt passion. I felt like a wild animal, I wanted to roll the whole moment up into a ball.

I wanted more and more so I took more and more and more and more I got out of it. Out of my body razing from the floor, it seemed, I felt I no longer were there.

It was magical and it lasted all night long, I was wishing it was going to last forever more. We all awoke on the beach where we had laid hours earlier and there was the sun rising in the sky to meet us all on this Sunday morning of ours. Soon we were all heading back to mine, leaving everything behind.

I couldn't find my fishing rods, they had disappeared, and all had gone. I wasn't for now worried as I was still slightly feeling the buzz of the evening before. A few of the boys rolled up some joints that soon were lit, as we walked back up over the hill with the beach now behind us.

This weekend had seemed the best that there was, how I didn't want it to end. I beg for everyone to stay on for more but they all left me there still in a dream like state as the girls they said had to find somewhere to sleep.

There was talk of them going up to the city as they knew of people, street kids they called, which would sleep on the streets. This was the last conversation that took place before they all left me near my house, that day. I unlocked my front door and went into my house.

I found my bedroom to be so beautiful with all their writings up on the wall, I fell asleep so peacefully, soon though to be awoken, awoken sharply as shit was about to hit the fan.

Chapter 5

STREET KIDS

My mum appeared over me asking what the fuck was going on, and then I saw Wim standing next to her. She was telling me we had been robbed, I lay on to my side and asked her what was she on about.

She said her jewels have all fucking gone and other things from her bedroom! She didn't even ask me about the giraffe all over my wall but she did tell me the police were on their way. (She didn't know that I was home as she called them the minute that she noticed her jewellery all gone - thinking I was at the soccer tournament).

The second day of soccer I had missed due to, yes the drug taking from the night before.

As the police arrive, they had asked my mum who had keys as there seemed to be no sign of a break in and she told them I had been away since Friday early evening and so that it must have been a break in. They did their bits and pieces - whatever that is the useless pricks call police work.

My mum wrote down what was taken as in the jewels but what she hadn't noticed in all this time was the video recorder that was swapped many months earlier for the bike that the wanker coppers had said I had nicked weeks earlier.

I didn't know wish to see yet again police in my house as by now I had got a lot of hate for them even at this early age I hated them so while the police were looking around my house I pretended to be asleep until the police had gone.

I explained to my mum that I had a few friends over, "what school friends" and I told her no other friends which she straight away knew I meant by my youth gang friends.

I just couldn't believe that one of them had stolen from my house and more so my mum's jewellery it made me so mad with rage and I felt so disrespected by them for robbing from my house.

Respect was one thing I had been brought up with and it meant a lot to me.

I told my mum the video recorder was my fault and that all the booze that had been drunken was to be blamed on me as I wasn't going to grass anyone up even though someone, one of them had robbed from my house. She couldn't believe I was hanging around with such kids after they had already got me in to trouble. I told her I had taken the booze and that I would find out who had taken the jewels.

I also pointed out the wall in my bedroom was also down to me but that right now was the last of her worries.

Feeling so terrible for my Mum, and feeling so angry towards whoever stole from my house, I made it my goal to track down who had been at my house and to get back my mum's jewels.

I was dead set on, all I needed to do now is search for those whom at been in my house, this was something that wasn't going to be easy in the slightest.

The following morning, my Mum wasn't speaking to me and soon I knew my Father was going to be home as I heard my Mum take a call from the female police officer who had been to the house.

I pleaded with my mum not to tell my Dad. I was shitting a brick so I made sure I wasn't in the house when he returned.

I went out and walked the neighbourhood, but I didn't know where any of the gang lived in their own family houses as I only ever met up with them in the evenings when I found them wandering the neighbour or when they were playing the game machines over at the fish and chip shops.

I decide to pop over to south Miramar to the girls' home, but near the gates I was told to move on by some bloke with a large set of keys.

I waited down the road and as it went early evening I went back and managed to whisper one of the girls over to me. I asked her about the girls that I had been hanging out with and also about the robbery of my Mums jewels.

I was told that since those girls run away a few nights ago, none of them had returned out of the four girls so I was back to square one, no closer on finding out whom out of everyone had nicked from my house.

I walked back to home; I was too scared to go into the house and ashamed as to having things taken from my beautiful Mum so I went up the walnut tree, my safe place over the years.

I sat up there and looked over to the people coming and going out of the fish and chip shop knowing that I would finally see one of the boys out of the gang go in there.

As I was doing this, again I noticed the buses come and go, which reminded me as to some of the boys taken the girls up to the city.

The city I had never been to by myself as my travels had only been as far as the neighbouring streets or the beach over the hill, the city to me at that age seemed like another country away.

Soon I spotted one of the boys placing his push bike outside the fish and chip shop so I climbed down the tree and darted over there. He was one of the Maori boys, I asked him if he had taken from my place, he said no and asked what was nicked so I told him some of my Mums jewellery.

He said actually one of the girls he was sure had taken some things as he noticed her in my Mums bedroom while I was sleeping near my Mums dressing table so it must have been her, we both agreed.

I had already remembered and he commented on, that she was one of the girls that had gone to the city, as the only girl who had not come back the second night was the girl who had hopped on one of the motorbikes at the beach when the Satan's Slaves motorcycle club members had been down at the beach.

Thank fuck for that as I wasn't going to be knocking on their place asking questions, plus at that age I wouldn't even know where to start to ask where they lived as I had only ever seen them ride on their Harley Davidson motorbikes that time at the beach.

It's the first time I had ever seen bikers in my whole life, though as you will read they will be a huge part in my years to come, unknown to me or them at this time in my life.

I left the fish and ship and went back across the road to my house; my Mum letting me in via the kitchen, my dinner was ready. There was no sign of my Dad, so I asked had he returned earlier or was he still at the pub.

My Mum sat me down and explained due to my Fathers behaviour and due to them now not being able to live together though she said they still loved each other that my Father wouldn't be staying at the house for a while.

He wasn't allowed to due to some court ruling when he appeared in court that Monday morning.

The police had kept him locked up all over the weekend, my Mum had been given a court ruling against him so it meant he wasn't allowed 100 meters from the house and that he had returned that afternoon though with the female police officer who had turned up to my Mums flat when he had fought Wim.

My Father was escorted into the house by a male police while the female police officer had spoken to my Mum explaining the details of the court ruling, it was only for a short period but it seemed to make my Mum more calmer and not full of nerves.

Though where was my Dad out there somewhere, I hoped he was ok and I wished I had been at the house when he had turned up.

I didn't know that this day was one of the worst of his life as he was being forced out of his own house, away from his kids.

He loved his kids so much and his family was his life, was everything to him so now all this it seemed had been taken away from him.

The behaviour of my father triggered by large amounts of drinking and also my Mums affair, meant my father having to leave his family home for good.

I went to bed that night thinking of my Dad and was hoping that he could return back to the house though not with his fists or the noises of my parents fighting as I did miss him that night as I fell asleep with both my cats in my bedroom and my dog as comfy for me.

The following morning I was awoken as school day I had to go to, the day earlier due to my father being released from the police cells and not knowing what was going to happen as in case we had to leave due to more violence.

My Mum had let me take the day off but today was like a normal day. My Mum gave me my bus fare and said I to get my lunch from the shops across the road to put it on her account as she was settling the bill at the end of the week.

I left the house, I didn't get myself any lunch as due to all the money I had placed on her accounts for the food and drinks I had put on credit the week earlier for the beach party.

I knew that I would be in the shit when my Mum also found this out which again didn't sit too comfortable with me, I hated upsetting my Mum when she was looking happy

I didn't catch the bus either that day; I walked up the hill to school and kept my money in my pocket.

I just wanted to take a walk so to get my head around that now my Father wasn't going to be living in the house, it was a lot to take in and I dare not tell the other kids at school as they all had perfect families.

I didn't want any of them looking at me in a different light.

School went fine, I got bored at lunchtime as no food to eat and also during play times I always felt the kids were so young when they played their stupid games, as I was so much older than my years and to watch them at playtime running away from girls who wanted to kiss them and chasing other girls to kiss.

I really thought these kids so haven't lived as only the weekend earlier I had done more than just kiss, it was clear to see on my neck by the love bites I had.

I can remember the teachers thinking I had some form of rush, not knowing actually I had love bites or even worse that I had done magic mushrooms for the first time, but who could I tell no one as didn't relate to any of them.

I did have my own mini school gang but that was very soft, we would just walk around trying to look hard and beat up bullies and try and get more kids to join us but most kids were normal kids and they would go to school simply to learn and play.

Learn I would, I did find some things hard due to dyslexia but I was doing ok in many subjects and would give it my best, but my mind would always wander as into what I would be getting up to that night or what I had done the nights before.

I got home again by not catching the bus as I went and walked after school the friendly family up the road dog and then I went to soccer practise and for the first time I stayed on later at the park.

I had found a soccer ball in a nearby bush so I played with it for hours, kicking at goal, thinking I was a Liverpool player against Everton in the F.A Cup and winning the game in the final minute with the goal of goals.

As I was playing about, I noticed a real football team turn up to the park; it was Miramar Rangers, the biggest professional football team in Wellington.

The park I would discover was their training ground and as I had never been in the park this late of night I didn't know that previously but here they were so I sat on the side and watched them.

Their coaches trained them so hard and do training that I had never seen before; I was such a happy kid that night even chasing the ball for them when it went out of play.

I walked home with my new football the happiest kid in all of New Zealand.

I got in and told my Mum about the Miramar Rangers and told her I wanted to go to the park every evening they were practising which was late in my Mums eye as they would practise from 8pm till 1030pm and by the time on this night I had come home at 1045pm so she was worried about me as I had been out all night and not told her.

She knew I could look after myself but she always wanted me home for dinner when she was home and not to be out late but many times what would happen there, as I have mentioned many evenings when she herself wasn't even at home and I was too scared to be in the house by myself as my sister wouldn't hang about.

She would be off as soon as my Mum left and as for the time my father was at shore well he would be in the pub till when ever long so even though my Mum as she was on this night trying to lay down ground rules.

Well sorry but it was far too late for that as I was too old in the head to be given times of to be home and as my father no longer was in the house at all then I very much was the man of the house more so now than ever before.

There were actually nights when my Mum would be in the hairdressing salon and nor being out to pop out to cook us kids dinner, it would be me who would cook dinner for my Mum and also my sister as well.

Next morning again I didn't get any food from the shops for my school lunch and as I got out of the house to head to the bus stop that would take me up the hill to school.

I stopped at the bus stop nearer the shops and ask a women where does the bus go to and she told me to Wellington city so I took a note of what she had told me. That day I worked out that the bus stop directly outside my Mums saloon must be the return bus from the city.

I didn't want to be late for school but I decided to keep my bus fare as I had a plan to do with the goal that I wanted to achieve which was to find the girls in the city.

I now knew how to get there and I knew I would be able to get back home safe but school was first so I walked up the hill into the school gates with a step in my foot as I was nearer to finding out where these buses went which I had in the evenings in the walnut tree always wondered where they would lead to.

Soon I was going to find out as I would be boarding one of them.

That afternoon, with no football practise for myself, I had track and field so I done that as fast as I could as I wanted to plan my trip into town, it had been on my mind all day at school and track and field very much wasn't.

I went to both bus stops that I had been to that morning before school and with my school bag I took out pen and paper and copied all the information down, the time tables and distances and places of departure and returns.

With all of this, I spend my time in my bedroom while it was light outside and worked out how far in to bus journey I would have to take that would put me in the city and also what the latest return bus to get me back home.

I took my school bag into the kitchen and made some sandwiches and placed them in my bag with a pint of orange juice and a apple and back in the bedroom extra jumper for warmth then went into my mum's hair salon and told her I was going again to watch the Miramar rangers football team practise at the park so she said that was fine.

I stood at the bus stop buzzing with excitement as this was it, a day I had dreamed about for years and it was even more special as I was on a mission.

My Mum would be so proud of me when I would walk back in the house with her jewels, that is how I saw it but how very wrong was I to be as I didn't get any where further than the bus driver as even with my fare I had kept, it wasn't enough to travel so far.

It was only enough to take me on a short journey and with only having the money from Tuesday and Wednesday then even if I had put the two fares together, I wouldn't be able to get back.

I was guttered as I step off the bus at the same bus stop I had just stepped on.

I went to cross the road back to my place but some of the gang was at the fish shop, calling me over asking where I had been the night before? I told them about the football team practicing and that this evening I wanted to get in to the city to track down the girls.

Among the gang were two of the boys who had taken the girls up town so they said they could help and said "don't pay to get on the busses, just jump into the push chair and wheel chair lockers that were at the side of the Wellington buses or the open one at the back of the buses."

All the buses had an area at the back of the bus, like a cuppy hole what I am unsure was the use of these would be for, and on one side of each bus there were lockers.

The kids said that you could fit inside one of them for the journey as long as you didn't mind being in the pitch black and not seeing where you were heading. Jumping out if a driver came to open it or at the end of the bus route.

The back of the buses were always the best as you could see out where you were heading and ya could fit two kids in easy or three at push though you would have to hold on so not to fall out.

I begged with the boys if they would take me up to the city and get me on a bus. No one wanted to as they said week nights were boring up town and the police who would walk the streets would just grab ya.

You would find yourself in the back of a police car heading home, so even though I was still willing to risk it, I took their advice.

They told me Friday night is cool up town, loads of people and loads of mischief.

Even though I was still very young and by many years, to even be in the gang, they liked me a lot and said they would help me out so we all were to meet on the Friday outside the fish shop.

I went to pull out my sandwiches to share among them all, and they laughed at me and told me to grow up.

I must have looked young doing that and having a packed sandwich and the orange juice to go to the city so I went back home feeling as young as my age as I run across the road.

The next day seemed to go on forever and that evening again soccer practise for me then spend the evening watching the senior team play and got their ball for them as I had the previous Tuesday night with a few quiet thanks from the team.

Friday came, this was the night I had been waiting for and when it came, I made sure I didn't pack any sandwiches and there as promised were some of the boys at the fish and shops.

We waited for a bus to pull up as people who were also waiting for the bus boarded the bus. A few of the boys sneaked in the lockers, I was with one of the boys on the back.

Fucking hell it was cool though slightly dangerous as the bus picked up speed and more so when there was traffic behind.

If any of us had fallen off then for sure the car behind wouldn't have the time to brake, you would be run over at speed so hanging on as tight as it meant the difference between life and death.

I can recall as we got out of Miramar and there in the background it was going further away, soon I was in areas unknown to me travelling for ages and ages now stopping at bus stops on the way.

A good 45mins later even an hour I was told we had just made town, we all needed to jump out soon.

All the boys knew exactly which bus stop to all get out, so the kid with me tapped hard on the lockers as we were the first to jump off as the bus stopped to pick up more passers so the rest of the boys got off.

There all around us was bright lights and so many people walking on by, up and down the streets.

This was like another world to me, the streets of the suburb so was many miles away and nothing compared me to this.

There were pubs and drunks were the first thing I saw which made me think of my Dad. I wondered if that busy pub was one of the pubs that my Dad would be drinking in but for now I just followed the other kids and kept close to them.

Getting lost I was worried about as I had no idea where I was apart from somewhere in the city of Wellington.

We were heading to where the boys would buy their dope from; I was told it was a real gang's headquarters by the name of Black Power.

Black Power in New Zealand isn't like the black power movement you know of as in America.

BP in New Zealand is the second largest gang behind the Mongrel Mob. BP members though are 99% Maoris and very proud to be Maoris, they do have some white members so are not all anti white though many are and that's fact.

They do respect their elders as in Maoris and the history and conflict that the Maoris in New Zealand have suffered but as gang is a gang and though BP do a lot for communities, they are very much deeply involved in crime and a lot of their members are in NZ jails and the prison system from all sorts of crime from drug dealing to murder.

The gang was formed in the early 1970s in Wellington and now have a gang house in every single town across New Zealand.

There is not one town where they don't have a gang house and if they don't cause trouble in that town then Mongrel Mob do, another gang that was formed in the late 1960s.

Ross Kemp (who is well known on British television screens as an actor and TV personality) covered the Mongrel Mob in his well received TV show titled "Gangs."

If you missed that Television show then Google or YouTube mongrel mob and you will see how ruthless they are compared to their main enemy that is Black Power.

So there we were walked finally coming to a huge fence, what looked like a factory or warehouse behind it.

We were let in as the massive gates opened and we greeted by a giant of a man with a gang patch and a tattooed face, fuck he looked scary at the time. He let us in to the noise of dogs barking, not friendly dogs but guard dogs a few pit-bull looking dogs.

We were taken inside this place BP signs and gang signs everywhere and the smell of weed so very strong, the young kid who was with us started to talk Maori to this gang member then he was lead away.

We stood there for ages; I wasn't shitting myself though some of the older boys seemed to be frightened as more gang members came out all looking very tuff and making our gang the Miramar Warriors look like a Girl Guide group as these guys were the real McCoy.

Then out came someone who I had seen around Miramar in a big V8 car not knowing who he was, but always knowing it was his car I could hear in my neighbourhood before it appearing as it was American Chevy which made more noise than any other car I had heard.

This guy was the president of the BP, the national BP meaning he was the boss of all the BP across New Zealand.

His name was Rai Harris and when he walked in the room you could feel his presence as everyone moved out his way, not just us kids but the heavy tattooed BP members.

He asked how we all were and it seemed some of the kids knew him quite well as he spoke to them at length then came over to me asking who I was.

I told him I was the kid who lived across the road to the row of shops mention my street as he had lots of time driven down my street so he must have lived nearby I guessed.

Finding out that he actually lived in the next suburb just past Miramar North, he asked me did my parents know I was here and I told him no. He asked had I run away from home and I told him no.

He then asked what brought me to the BP headquarters so I explained about the girls from the home that had nicked from my Mum.

He said that those girls had been here and they were now living over on K St.

K St didn't mean anything to me but I said thanks for letting me know, one of the other kids knew what he was meaning by K St and said once they had scored their dope we would go over there.

Rai left, I was now in a hurry to where ever K St was. I asked one of the boys to hurry up the Maori kid who had gone inside the building to get the dope.

I was told he wasn't allowed in there and neither was I as only gang members or trusted gang people could go in there.

The kid out of our gang, I found out his uncle was one of the BP members that why firstly the gate had even been opened to us and secondly why he was able to score dope from this place. We just had to wait near the barking dogs and the heavy smell of dope.

Finally he appeared red eyed; he was as stoned as a fish that became his nick name of that night.

I was lead out with the rest of the boys with the loud bang of the gate closing behind us and we walked on down Manners Street, noticing punk rockers and skinheads coming out of a music venue down the road.

The Maori kids in our gang shouting out abuse to the skinheads as flying empty bottles came hurling our way as we were chased down the road but none of the skinheads caught up with us in their dock martin cherry boots and white shoe laces.

I asked the Maori kids why cause trouble with people twice their age? I was told that skinheads were scum they were our enemies and they hated the black power and they would always cause trouble and they were racist but the thing was I fucking wasn't Black Power; I was Miramar Warriors so I really couldn't give a fuck about what ever BP thought were bad news.

I would myself unknown to me or my friends at that age would become a skinhead myself for many a years in four years time and some of these friendships that I now had in my own gang would soon be broken.

Finding ourselves in the future years on the other side of the fences but here for now the boys I were hanging around with were my brothers in arms.

That night anyone with a skinhead or looked like that to these guys was scum so they kept on causing trouble past the night clubs and the pubs.

It was exciting being chased, having bottles thrown at us, it become more fun throwing bottles back whenever we came across a group of skinheads.

There were many around this part of town, and as for punks too many too count. How weird that these people were hanging out only a few streets away from where the BP headquarters were as for sure both would clash whenever they passed one another on the streets.

We soon reached another building, though no warehouse as I expected to see when we reached the street. It wasn't K on the street sign; the building was just a massive 4 storey house, very run down.

We went to the front door, we didn't even have to knock as one of the boys opened the door and in we went.

Downstairs no lights were on, it was a mess as we walked up a flight of stairs again all lights were off but we could hear voices up the stairs.

I asked where we were, "shouldn't we be going to K Street?" I asked one of the boys. It was explained there this was K Street, K Street standing for Kids Street.

This house was owned by the BP, they didn't use it due to many police raids for the years as it once was a holding house for the supply of drugs but now to show the government they were doing something positive as a gang then they allowed the many street kids of Wellington to live there.

Let me tell there were many street kids in New Zealand, in Wellington so many from broken homes or kids who were abused by their parents or sexual assault so they would all run away.

Many would end up on the streets well here at least they had a roof over their head to keep out of the cold and wet, and in numbers I am sure they would safer at night.

I hadn't met one of these street kids until we went to another floor and there in a few rooms were at least a dozen kids.

They looked like trouble to me, very scruffy and mean looking. Most were Maoris, none my age, more the age of the other boys out of my gang.

I was introduced to some of them, they didn't really give me the time of day, and it seemed they just wanted to know if any of us were carrying pot. We all had a smoke and once they got stoned, they seemed friendly as we sat in one of the rooms, mattress and blankets all over the floor.

I needed to use the bathroom but wasn't going to wonder around this place by myself as in a room next door could hear more voices, actually at that moment I wished I was at home as didn't like my first time in this place.

It seemed I had nothing in common with these types of kids and I kind of felt quite posh next to these rat bags but I was never a judgement of anyone, I never have been in life.

One of the boys asked about the girls, and we were told this is where they had been staying but they weren't in any of the rooms.

The boys looked around; we couldn't stay as we had the last bus to catch back to Miramar so I was disappointed on the walk back to the bus stop.

My mood only changed when I was promised that we all would go back up again tomorrow night. On the back of the bus we went and travelled home exactly the same way we got there, holding on tight to the back of the bus as we travelled back this out of the city into the suburbs.

Soon came my street but no one got off the bus at the stop who were passengers so we went further until finally the bus stopped at a bus stop and we walked off back to the direction of my house.

The time must have been near 1am, I never thought about how late I had been out to until getting home. Reaching home I noticed many lights on in my house; I came in through the back door and was confronted by Mum who was crying.

I guessed maybe my Father had been to the house but no, she was crying over me, saying that she thought my Dad had come and got me.

She had called the police as she was terrified that he had taken me, I said why would Dad do that and not to be silly, hoping I could go straight to bed I was tired but then she asked where I had been and that I had to tell her.

I didn't so I said I had been to friends place and she knew it wasn't one of my school friends house as their parents of course would have rung her to tell her that I was staying over at their place.

She went from tears to yelling at me knowing I had been out with the older kids that I had been recently hanging around with and the same kids she knew were something to do with her jewellery going missing.

She said to me I was never allowed out at night. I had broken her trust and I was now grounded.

Grounded, what the fuck was that?

I had been out all night to get her jewels back, it's not like I did want to be out this late.

In all honest I loved being out at night, I felt so grown up and also it meant time away from my house the haunted house, anyway I was send to bed.

Great as I was exhausted so I was happy with that and TV back in those days finished at 12am so it's not like anything was interesting on the two channels, that all the TV had back in these days two TV channels, how weird remembering that.

Saturday meant football, and I wasn't grounded from that so I went off to my match, and scored 4 goals.......no I didn't, I didn't even score one goal but I did tell the kids in my team I had been up to the city without my parents, none believed me as that was unheard of. I had and I was on for going back up again that evening but being grounded how would meet the kids to get out so I could go back up to the city.

I had to use my head and work this out on returning home after the game, I was well behaviour, helping out with lunch then my Mum pooped out. I am sure to go and see Wim but she was back by evening time, so I didn't have the chance to sneak out.

I went to bed and laying there still thinking about meeting the boys, I waited till my Mum went to bed. I went to the salon and looked out the shop window, across the street were the kids at the fish and shop hanging out so trying to wave over to them in the saloon but they couldn't see me.

I went and got a torch out of the kitchen and back into the shop I went, flashing the torch until getting one of the boy's attention, and he came over.

I slipped a note through under the door asking him when would they be catching the bus and he with the use of his fingers said 923pm bus they were going to catch so I said I meet them across the road at 915pm.

I went back to the kitchen put the torch back and as my Mum had taken my set of keys off me from the previous night. Her thinking that would mean I wouldn't leave the house at night as I wouldn't be able to get back into the house. She did think that through well, I guessed.

I needed to get out and I very needed to get back in, I didn't want to climb out my window as I was scared that the monster might be on the other side of the window if I opened the curtains as I had that time to see the bastard steering back at me.

I didn't wish to use the bathroom window as it was on the same side of the house as my bedroom window so the imagine of the monster put me off so I grabbed a tea towel and quietly opened the kitchen door, jamming the door with the tea towel.

I then went to my bedroom and got warmer clothes on and out I went through the kitchen door again jamming it with a tea towel so it didn't make a noise when I closed it but more so, so I could get back in when I returned later that night.

I was out of the house, just hoping my Mum wouldn't wake in the night. I joined the other boys; we waited for people to arrive at the bus stop as the bus would only stop if someone wished to board it or if a passenger wanted to get off at that bus stop.

We had to wait and the 923pm bus came and went as no one was at the bus stop but time wasn't on our side. We had to reach town and then get to K Street, then back to get the last bus so we were all back home by the end of the night, more so by the time my mum woke up.

Finally someone boarded the bus, a bloke and his girlfriend, we got in the back again and this time around I enjoyed the journey even more. I didn't hold on as tight and felt more comfortable, though yes still was a buzz travelling like this.

We reached town and the route to K St was the same route we walked the night before.

I got to know the few streets and the different pubs and clubs that we passed even though this was only my second night up town but the night before everything had seen as in landmarks really soaked in to my head so I remember certain things from the previous night.

We got to the house and again we let ourselves in. No one was down stairs, I thought to myself that none of the girls again would be here out of the girls from the girl's home but as we reached the second floor I heard a toilet flush.

Out of the bathroom came one of the girls. At the time I was really happy to see her then I remember why I was here so I asked her where my mum's jewels were?

By the look on her face I fucking knew she was the one who had stolen from my mum's place so again I pushed with the question and thankfully the boys wouldn't let her past me on the stairs as she looked like she was going to do a runner.

She told me it wasn't her idea and that one of the boys had put her up to it.

I didn't believe her, demanding my mum's jewels back.

The boy, who she had just accused of putting her up to stealing from my house, grabbed her and yells right in her face, his mood went nuts as he shouted at her calling her lying whore then lots of street kids came running down the stairs asking what was going on?

I told them before they reached the girl as one appeared with a long knife so I was worried they were going to stab someone even me.

They jumped in between everyone; the street kid with the knife in his hand said what's wrong?

I thought they were speaking to someone else but looked at me what's wrong"

I said she was the thief of my mum jewellery and with that they demanded louder for her to tell them the truth and where the stuff was.

She now was shaking, she said she had sold them but unbelieving she said it, and not only I sensed that. The main street kid who seemed like he was in control until he slapped her so hard across the face, she fell to the floor and what I saw next was horrible as he kicked her in the stomach, it was horrible to see and reminded me of my parents fighting.

I wanted to reach down and shield this girl, yes she had nicked out of my house but she didn't deserve this and also the street kid still had this long knife in his hand and couldn't watch her being stabbed if that was what was maybe on his mind as he was gripping it really hard.

I could see his knuckles red through the blood rushing to that hand that held the knife.

I went down to maybe I guess protect her, she then moved her hand in her bra and out came my mum's rings and her other hand went in her jean pockets and out came a necklace and other jewels.

She begged the street kid not to hit her anymore, and all the jewels she handed me I thought that was all she had taken but as she sat up on her knees holding her stomach with one hand she confessed that there was more but she had indeed sold those pieces for dope to black power when she first reached up town on the Sunday and she was very sorry.

I accepted her sorry but the street kids weren't and told her to fuck off before she got even more of a beating.

I couldn't understand why they were standing up for me, then I thought now they had seen the jewels I would be robbed myself by them. They pushed her in the back telling her to leave the house straight away. She ran down the rest of the flight of stairs.

I was taken back up the third floor the room where I had been before and still the street kid was holding this long knife which was very off putting to me as he spoke to me.

One of the boys put their hands on my shoulder reassuring me that everything was ok, anyway the street kid said that there was a strong bond among all the street kids and they wouldn't allow a thief to live among them as they wouldn't trust that person so that girl had to go who they thought would nick from one of them.

I sat with them asking them lots of questions and found out that though some of them go out to steal that is only from the shops to get clothing as the black power would only provide them with some food to the house and sometime blankets etc but as for other things they needed then they would go out and steal, be it from shopping malls or drunken people they would find asleep outside the night clubs in the streets nearby after falling out of the nightclubs drunk, the street kids would then search them while the searched for wallets.

Now and then they would snatch handbags, so even though they were a band of thieves themselves, they wouldn't steal of one another and their stealing was only to cloth themselves or keep them warm and never for dope they told me, that I didn't believe as they all seemed to have one thing on their mind and that was to smoke dope.

He was making them out to be more angels. I was too learn that if they kept out of trouble while living in this house and proved to the black power that they could support themselves, never asking the black power for anything then they would be picked out by the black power and the male street kids as they got to a certain age were then taken in under the wing of the black power as in prospect for the BP gang which is the start of a journey to become a member of the gang.

Once they had prospected for the BP gang then they would go onto bigger things, what I mean by bigger things, I don't mean a house in the country or a job I mean crime for the gang more than likely selling pot and worse crimes anyway here and now I was grateful for them for what they did and asked if there was anything I could do for them and they said never to forget them and more so never become one of them, something I very much wouldn't wish to be and I will always never forget them that was for sure.

Outside the building when we left, the boys and I found the girl outside the house crying. Saying now she had nowhere to go, she was on the streets and many of the other street girls she had met in her week up in the city all would be either raped or forced into being a hooker on the street corners, this I didn't want to happen to her so again my heart went out to her even though she had nicked from my house.

She was around 16 years old and she looked so frightened, the boys told me to leave her and not to give her the time of day as we walked off and looking back at her not knowing where she would spend the night and hoping she would be safe.

We got the last bus home just in time and this time the bus stopped outside mum's saloon. We jumped off the back and out of the lockers the other boys appeared. I thanked them all for being there for me and helping me as they all went in their different directions. I crept back into my house, so happy that my mum was still a sleep and that she didn't know I had got out of the house.

Now I had her jewels back, I just wanted to wake her up and tell her as I was so happy but I knew not to as too many questions for now would have been asked so I went in to my bedroom and placed out all the rings and necklace and the other bits and pieces into a glass I poured some water in the glass as some of the jewels looked dirty and smelled of dope as maybe in the girls bra that's where she kept her dope.

I fell asleep and woke before my mum, making her breakfast and on the tray I took into her room with the jewels and explained to her that some of my friends had found the girl who had taken the jewels.

My mum was so happy with breakfast in bed not realizing that on the tray were her jewels until she sat up in bed. I placed the tray on her lap, she went through it all and lucky only maybe two pieces were missing and what had come back to her was the most important jewels out of it all as some had been passed down from her mum and also some of it had been brought my Dad back in there early days in London in the swinging 60s.

Among all what was taken, now back was her wedding ring that my father had brought her. She had not been wearing it lately but she did explain it brought back lovely memories as she told me about her beautiful wedding day that my father had given her.

That morning we sat on the bed she went through all the stories relating to each piece of jewels and speaking loads about her wedding day and so many things including talking about Wim as well.

We spoke for ages, I listening to her as she was smiling so much while holding up her jewels as you could just see in amazing eyes that lovely memories were flooding back to her mind of years that had passed during good times of her life, and that even included good times she had had with my Father.

I let her be so her cooked breakfast didn't go cold and as I went to shut her door to say "I Love you". I heard her say the words back as the door closed "I Love you too".

That is something I would hold onto for many years to come as within less than 8 years I would never again hear those words spoken from my Mum, nor hear her voice ever again. I closed her bedroom door for her to enjoy her cook breakfast I had cooked for her.

The peacefulness of that Sunday morning wasn't going to last long as there was a knock on the door, a loud thumping knock and one we had heard many times before.

It was soon about to smash the peace and quietness that my Mum had just shared with her son.

Chapter 6

ANOTHER BRICK IN THE WALL

AGE 7 to AGE 10

That knock on the door could only be one person. It was a very hard knock as if soon the door would give way, and indeed on my Mum opening the door with me standing behind her, looking past her I could see my Dad standing there not looking happy at all until he saw me which changed his whole expression on his face from anger to joy.

My Mum was in the middle of speech reminding him about the court judgement against him not allowing him to come near our house or to be in contact with my Mum but there and then I just knew he hadn't turned up to row with my Mum but he had come to see his kids and that is all he wished for, was to see me and my sister.

I had the feeling that my Mum was going to close the door on him but I am glad she never did as for sure the devil within him would have come out and it would have been World War 3 right there on our doorstep and no one wished for that on this Sunday morning.

My Mum still questioned what he was doing at our place and she said that quite firmly, the very first time that I could recall that she ever had such a strong voice when speaking to my Father. She wasn't shaking when speaking to him and stood her ground as she had every right to ask him. At the same time you must see it from my father's point of view as this was his house as well and this was his family. He may have lost his wife but he still had his beautiful daughter, my sister, and his fast growing son, that being me.

My Mum stayed within the open door side of the house but I rushed past her and got a hug from my Dad and asked how he was. He asked my Mum if could he come in as he noticed my sister walks up the hall way but still my Mum wouldn't let him in even after my sister also ran over to hug him. Both my sister and I asked my Mum, please let Dad in as it was us he had come to see and though he knew by turning up that he could be arrested for this, the love of his kids was much stronger than worrying about getting arrested.

Finally after my Mum trusted his motives, she allowed him into the house but she didn't feel comfortable from the moment he walked in the door. Once he was in the house she didn't have the same strong voice that she had towards him only minutes earlier. She went into her salon even though it wasn't open but I think it was only to get away from him.

My Dad and we spent all day in the lounge. We watched the television show, Some Mothers Do Have Them, the British comedy and it was a right laugh. We laughed so much that afternoon together with our father. Then my Mum came out of the salon, and back into the house. She must have spent at least 5 hours in her saloon just sitting in there so to not be near her husband.

When finally my Mum did come out she only spoke to say that she felt it was time for my Father to go. He asked for another hour more and he even used the word please. Both my sister and I asked her please can Dad stay, so she said she would go out and that when she came back he was to have gone by then. He looked happy and we kids were happy as well.

I am sure this didn't make my Mum too happy that we wished for my Father to stay. Once my Mum left my Dad decided to cook us all a lovely lunch so he popped over to the shop and brought some food to cook. He would always cook such lavish food, fit for a king and food that was good enough to be placed on any modern restaurant menu.

We ate so well and I had eaten far too much. After lunch, my Father noticed that there was no booze in the drink cabinet. He asked if my Mum had held some type of party and I said no but was making sure I wasn't grassing myself up as in telling my Dad about my pals and those girls from the girl's home being at the house. I am sure that's when my Father's mind went wandering as he then asked had Wim been to the house and was it him who had drunk my Fathers booze but I said no.

My father started to get very restless. This is because as a heavy drinker, he needed a drink and drinking for my Father sometimes came first before his own family. During us doing the dishes my father said he was just popping out for a while, I knew that meant to a pub. I wasn't bothered as I was just a happy kid that day to have spent some time with my Father and more so that my Father and my Mum hadn't had a fight.

After I finished doing the dishes, I felt tired so I went to bed and my sister went and visited friends. I had great dreams and a very peaceful sleep and awoke to that same banging on the door. I knew it was my Father so I opened the door and in came my Dad, it had fallen evening and it was dark outside. I noticed my mum's car in the drive though I didn't know she had returned as I had been sleeping.

The first thing my Father asked was where my Mum was. I told him I wasn't sure as I had been sleeping. I could tell he was very drunk as he walked past me shouting out my Mother's name, Lorraine. He pushed open my Mum's bedroom as he marched through the house. She wasn't anywhere to be found. I wasn't sure if she was in her bedroom until I heard my Father's voice raise behind the closed door of their bedroom. I put my ear up to the door trying to listen but I didn't have to listen hard to hear their voices as my Fathers voice was raised and I could hear him accuse her of allowing Wim drink his booze and that as one man leaves another comes in the door.

She wasn't happy that he was applying she was a slut and she told him to fuck off! The row got even bigger and the door flung open as she was running from him. I grabbed onto his leg to stop him chasing her and told him it was me and my friends who had drunk the booze making sure that he heard correctly and that it wasn't Wim. He stopped dead in his tracks as he understood what I had told him but instead of getting angry at me for drinking his booze and for underage drinking, he just used this to have another dig at my Mum who had stopped short of reaching the kitchen after escaping him from the bedroom. He was saying now she wasn't a fit mother and she couldn't even look after her kids properly.

This comment was a comment too far for my Mum as one thing she was, was a good Mother though yes she had faults as she would leave us at home at times to look after ourselves but that was maybe because we seemed so grown up for our younger years. We could look after ourselves much better than most kids our age.

This meant my Mum had trust in us not to need a baby sitter at most times but perhaps only for me if my sister was staying over at a friend's house and if my mum would be away over night or if my Dad had been away at sea.

My Mum marched back up to my Dad and pushed him so hard that he went flying back, ending up on his back. She reached down and tried to what looked like drag him towards the back door but as she had forced him half the way up the hall way he got hold of her leg and pulled her down. She fought not to go down but she too ended up on the floor trying her hardest to get out of his grip, but she couldn't as he moved himself now on top of her.

It was horrible as he grabbed her face bashing her head into the floor. She tried her hardest to get him off her but again he bashed the back of her head on the floor. She had her hands in his face then managed to grab his shirt and rip it from the buttons but his rage just got worse. I tried to get hold of his wrist so he let go off my Mums hair but he was too strong so I jumped on him and grabbed him about the eyes so he couldn't see and that for a moment meant he let go off my mum which gave her enough time to slid away and get up.

She got hold of me once she got to her feet and we went running out the kitchen door around the other side of the house and across the road to some neighbour's house.

My Mum was shaking like a leaf with marks on her face from where my Father had grabbed her. Her hair was messed up so she tried to straighten it as she was knocking on the neighbour's door, composing herself when the neighbour came to the door. Letting us in straight away when realising it was my Mum, the neighbour knew what was going on and yelled at her own husband to call the police.

Even though I am sure my Dad knew that soon the police would be on their way, he never tried to flee but stayed in the house. Afterwards we would find out he was in the kitchen sitting at the table after feeding our two cats as if nothing had taken place. This time when he was cuffed we found out he didn't put up any fight, he was lead to the police car without fighting the police.

I know for a fact my father hated himself for fighting with my Mum, though many times he was so drunk that he wouldn't recall what had gone on during their fights.

A female police came to the neighbours house, asking if my mum wanted a ambulance as by this time my mum had a tea towel with ice on the back of her head, there was a massive lump from what my father had done but my Mum didn't wish for any medical help nor did she want to charge my father for assault. She was just happy that we could return to the house knowing he again would be spending a night behind bars that is until the police would let him out again in the morning.

With this in mind and with the fact that my father had turned up and then turned nasty my mum slept the night in fear for what else he would do and guessed he would be back again to cause more trouble. It was at the back of her mind all Monday but while she was in her salon for some reason she felt safe as there were many people around as in her staff and her customers.

After school every Monday I had judo after school and this session I asked the sensei if he could teach me more advance usage of the sport. I always saw it as a sport and nothing more but soon with these private teachings I felt I was learning more and much quicker than the others kids who were my same grade. I think my Mum first put me forward to judo in a way she could see in years to come as I got better that I could forever more there after protect her from these attacks from my Dad.

As for me I was happy to stay on in judo class rather than having to go home as with what happened that Sunday evening made me feel even more put off with the house as it was so upsetting at a young age seeing that go on between my parents. I was only days away from turning 10 years old and all that house brought me was upset. I had witnessed far too much and by now it was making me not enjoy my home life, even though my Father no longer lived there, it just showed that it didn't mean the violence wouldn't stop as Sunday evening proved that very much.

When returning from judo that evening I found Wim in the house and again he was there in the morning and again on Tuesday. I guessed he had moved in but no it was just for my mum's peace of mind if my dad was to return. I felt this was wrong though because if my dad had returned, knowing this would have made things so much worse as that's what was the cause of a lot of this anger, that plus whatever volume of booze my dad drunk on the Sunday was the cause of my mum and my dad fighting.

I just didn't like another man in the house and no one was ever going to replace my dad even though he had been awful towards my mum, he was still my dad and I would only ever have one mum and at the same time only ever have one dad.

By mid week I had Wim telling me when my bed time was while I was in the lounge and I thought who the fuck does he think he is? I anit being told what to do by him and I never had a bed time to go to bed so if I wanted to watch TV until late then I would as I wasn't going to have my mum's boyfriend tell me what to do so I told him so, but he encourage my mum to put me to bed and she did which made me into a angry young man that night and smashed my toys against my bedroom door. My mum came in with a wooden spoon and hit the back of my legs.

I couldn't believe it as she had never hit me ever. I wasn't going to stand for this plus I wasn't going to have Wim in my house as when my dad was never there, I was the man of the house and since he had gone I was very much the man of the house.

Once I had got myself together as fuck it hurt that wooden spoon against the skin of the back of my legs, I marched into the lounge as I still could hear the TV on.

There on the settee was my mum having sex with Wim, a sight I really didn't need seeing but I couldn't let them see me standing there. I couldn't cause trouble as I went in there to go bananas to let Wim know I very much was a handful and to let my mum know that never again she could hit me with a wooden spoon as all hell would break loose.

I had grown up all my life hearing my mum being hit or beaten by my father and what I tried to do on the previous Sunday to protect my mum after my dad had attacked her well she wasn't going to ever hit me as well. I wouldn't stand for it even if she had when my dad did what he done to her for years, well sorry but I wasn't standing for it for one minute. Was I told to go to bed that night just for them to fuck each other in the lounge well fuck that I thought as I went back to my bedroom?

I was in such a bad mood the next morning. I could see my mum was sorry for hitting me the night before but I just blanked her, only speaking to her to get my bus fare. She had found out about the credit bill across the road at the shop so she had put some code word on the account which stopped me from ticking food or adding anything to her account so now instead she started to give me cash for school lunches but that morning like many others I started to walk to school keeping the money, not spending the lunch money either.

After school I would just come from whatever sport activity I had and cook myself the size of two meals that would fill me. I started to get in the habit of eating breakfast with lots of fresh fruit and skipping lunch but eating at least two meals at night and walking to and from school. By the end of that week in all the lunch money and bus money I had saved a fair bit of cash, a fair bit for a 10 year old.

It was soon a few weeks and Wim was in the house many evenings though he lived in a huge lovely house of his own. I didn't like having rules in the house. I was no longer allowed to spend time with the gang in the evenings and really my life revolved around school and sport.

I loved sport but I missed hanging out with the gang and that sense of freedom. I would only see them some evenings when I was sent over the road to get fish and chips on a Friday evening. I wasn't allowed to stay with them which I hated as they were spending now more of the weekends in town rather than around the neighbourhood.

You got to remember these kids were much older than me and soon even some of them now had real motorbikes rather than just BMX so their adventures sounded so much better than mine had become though I had sport nearly every night of the week which I guess kept me out of trouble. I had judo two nights a week which was encouraged by Wim who was very good at Judo himself. It was something from an early age we bonded for the first time and from then onwards I didn't mind as much when he stayed in the house though it did take a lot of getting used to.

I had soccer two nights a week plus a match on Saturdays and then I had track and field once a night, and swimming sometimes and gym. Not weights of course but mat work. I was crap at that and it was a bit too girl like for me but my mum would support me in all my sports and encourage me to go to each class, was this because she was proud of me?

Yes I am sure she was but as I got home each night to find Wim there, I then started to think that it was due to my mum wanting to spend more time alone with Wim. She also at times had the girl, who had started work in my mum's saloon from day one Helen Scully, cover the saloon meaning Helen could run the business single handed while my mum wasn't there. Helen was now a hairdresser with all her courses she had passed with flying colours and also what she had learned from my mum.

Helen was a family friend and though she had a mum and dad who were both lovely and great brothers she was like a second daughter to my mum. They really had a great relationship working and as friends so when Helen became more confident in the saloon then my mum would take it easy some evenings and spend more time with Wim at our place which by this time I hadn't been happy with that idea.

Every time I was sent to bed I would sit in bed and my thoughts would go back to the street kids I had met and how they had no one telling them what to do and what time they had to go to bed, so with all the money I was saving now I would be going to town but not as I once travelled on the buses hanging on the back but I would be able to pay the correct bus fare and also get home by bus. I would have a little money while in town so one evening I planned it. I thought I would hook up with the gang across the road at the fish and chip shop and tell them all that I would again be going up town with them.

I sneaked out of the house one night, I had my house keys again by now from my mum, so it was easy getting out of the house and back again when I wished.

I am sure my mum was still awake in her bedroom with Wim when I left the house. I hurried across the road to the gang, telling them I was up for going up town with them but they said they were taking their bikes up town and there was no place for me as the other older boys without motorbikes would be riding passengers on their motorbikes.

It was the very first time I felt the gang not wanting me around them. Had the age gap just got bigger or was I just now too young to hang around with them? I was pissed off after all I had done for them. I had climbed through windows for them which I hated doing as it didn't feel nice. I didn't mind getting into fights with them or causing trouble with them during the last few years but that night when they made a point of not involving me, it really hurt as I felt they were brushing me aside, well I didn't like it one single bit.

So firstly I unplugged the space invaders machines they were playing on as it meant they lost all their money they had put into the game. Childish I know but hey I was only 10 years old. Wait till what came next, as when I went to leave the fish and chip shop after unplugging the power source of the game machines I was hit in the temple by a crackling punch.

I stood still with my hand to my ear that was ringing and the pain was intense as I wobbled outside, turning around not hearing what they were saying and not knowing which one of out the 12 kids who had done it. I was about to do something that would I hope effect them all. It would affect our friendship thereafter and I knew that as I stepped down from the pavement and with one big kick I hit the first of the motorcycles lined up and watch as the first bike landed at speed onto the second and then second dropped on the third right up to the sixth bike all ending up in a row piled up on one another.

I ran for my life as I knew if they had got hold of me they would forget all the years that I had spent with them. They still would have given me more than just another punch to the temple.

I reached my front door grabbing for my key. I couldn't get the key in the lock as they had nearly reached me but just then the door opened. Falling into my kitchen in the nick of time, and into Wim I fell with about 9 of the boys chasing me to the kitchen door. The first one with no fear in his face come flying through the door. Wim just moved me gently out the way and with such a punch the kid just went flying and when I mean kid he was 18 years old. The rest of them just stood still and out came Wim 6foot 4, a bloke ya just wouldn't fuck with.

Wim told them all to get off the property and not ever to come back. They all nodded shit scared and picked up their mate who had come around by then from the punch and walked him back and themselves over to the fish and chip. That was the last time I would ever hang around with them again; I hated thinking about that as I lay in bed after my mum seeing what the trouble was all about.

I told her I had a row with them and was hit so I pushed over their bikes, she thought there was more to it after Wim told her about how many had been chasing me and they were it seemed after my blood for what I had done to their motorbikes.

It was the first time I was grateful that Wim was in the house as he had saved me from a serious kicking. From this moment on Wim and I became very close and I could see the good he was doing for my Mum and more so the love he had for my mum. It was Wim who brought my mum happiness which to me meant the world so from this stage onwards Wim and I also got along and he never became a replacement Father. No man could ever replace my Father, though Wim did become a good friend and I always respected him as long as he never tried to lay down the law to me. I would only ever listen to my mum and my father as no one else had the right to tell me what to do, something that I would stand firm ground on if ever anyone apart from my parents told me what to do.

While I was in bed, my mum did say they were no good and she was glad that I wouldn't be hanging out with them anymore and that I could just stick to my straight friends at school rather than the local gang. She had a point as I am sure I would have only gone onto get into more trouble with them and they had tricked me in getting my video recorder off me for a nicked BMX and real friends don't do that. I was thinking off all the negative things about them as there on my wall was still the spray paint with Miramar Warriors and all their names up on my wall, it reminded me that if it wasn't for their help I never would have got my mum's jewels back, which again made me think back to those street kids I had met back in K Street.

My Father in all this time had been out to sea, I think he took the job to try and get away from the pain from losing his family. The police may have warned him if he kept on breaking the injunction that the court had placed on him that he could find himself in jail and that would be worse effect onto his kids and if anything the love of his kids were the most important thing to him. I was sent a birthday present and a card that meant so much to me from my Father as I thought he had forgotten my 10th birthday but he hadn't which meant the world to me.

I think my mum was finally happy in life, she had the man of her life, her first love and she had her kids now living a normal life and her son was no longer involved in gangs. She had seen it as maybe a passing faze but unknown to her, for me it wasn't. It would soon reappear in my life as once Wim stopped staying at the house less and less then I was feeling I was in control of the house again and that was to do what I liked as I didn't have anyone telling me to go to bed at a certain age.

My mum still tried to enforce these new rules that had been laid down. I wouldn't stand for any of them so my mum had a fighting battle on her hands and when she couldn't win she would then hit me with the wooden spoon. I just couldn't believe it and it started to turn me to dislike my mum as I couldn't believe that she was trying to bring in punishment.

My mum never enjoyed hitting me with the wooden spoon, it was her only way to try and control me as I was out of control whenever I got myself into a rage and my behaviour would drive her to her breaking point as I was a little fucker, so full of mischief, such handful to say the least.

I was sure it had been Wim telling her too as he may have seen me as too much to handle. I didn't have any displine of any sort in my life which yes I didn't but the way my mum would get to the end of her rag after trying to tell me to go to bed or whatever and I wouldn't do it then we found ourselves clashing.

So much to the point that even though the house was calmer without my dad living there, I would when in one of my moods cause stress for my mum.

I didn't want to be there anymore and I couldn't hang out with the local gang anymore so I caught the bus by myself into the city one night. I had remembered the walk to the street kids so even on school nights after heading up there a few times late at night I would find myself hanging out with street kids.

Some would sleep ruff as I found out it wasn't all good back at the house that the black power gang had given to them to sleep in. I would get to meet many of them and share the money I used to save so they could get McDonalds as a treat. I would also bring them in some of my clothes and shoes when I saw them barefoot and in tattered clothes.

I would just tell my mum that a kid at school had bullied me for my shoes as a few kids would do that to other boys so she didn't have a clue that I was giving so much away to the street kids. I just even at that age really felt for them and yes many couldn't relate to me as there I was a middle class kid running away from a house when I never had the problems that many of them had.

I mean with the Miramar Warrior boys well some of them were from broken homes as in their own parents would fight like mine did or they were from broken homes as I was but all of those boys each night could go back home at the end of their nights after they had wandered the streets causing trouble and mischief.

But with the street kids they couldn't go back to their homes as they had more than broken homes, some had one or both parents in jail and they had run away from care. Then there would be the others who would open up telling me dreadful stories of things that had happened to them. They would all tell me more while they were high from sniffing glue and cans of fly spray or paints as that's how they would get high if they couldn't afford pot.

It was so low of a depth for them to go just to get high but when I would sit with them and hear them speak it was no wonder they wanted to escape life and being straight. Some of them not only the girls but even some of the boys had been raped by their own fathers or other family members and other such awful things that would seriously make me wish to help them and that were even if I could get them to laugh or a pair of shoes.

I was so happy that at least they had K Street a place to live for some of them who chose to live there but as I said it turned out to be not always safe for them there. I had been told though never witnessed it myself as I would only travel up at night two or three times a week to see them.

On arriving sometimes there was talk of horrible acts going on when certain black power members would turn up and rape the girls not knowing that these street kid girls were at K Street not only in finding a roof over their head and a warm blanket but most of all they were looking for a safe place where they could sleep.

Just knowing that their uncle or their father weren't coming in the middle of the night to rape them, so just think what a nightmare it would be when they were raped by gang members. None of them ever went to the police and they now were living on the streets and never to return to K Street.

Some ending up as working girls on street corners then getting hooked on heroin and like anywhere in the world be it UK or America or Australia, no one walking past these girls would ever stop and try to help them. No one would see them as someone's daughter or someone's sister or even in some cases someone's mum but only as a drug user or a working girl.

These girls had no chance of help and many would die such a lonely life either by dirty drugs or dirty men or in jail or killing themselves. Hell if I was a rich man back then I would have helped them so much just to give them a chance of a better life but I was only a 10 year old kid.

It used to trouble me so much hearing their stories and that they had all given up on life. All they could see was a future for the boys and not any future for them.

Many of the boys were to join the black power gang so when other gang members would turn up the boys wouldn't say no when told to do certain crimes and serious crimes not petty ones. I mean bank robberies and even taking the rap for patch members who had committed a crime.

The older boys in the street kids would walk to the police station and give themselves up for the gang as after a few years in jail they would come out as a man with a better chance of getting a patch and with a patch then they had made something of their lives and they were someone in their eyes and in the eyes of the gang.

So in a way yes black power were doing something good as in providing shelter for these kids but it was just a form of recruiting them in later years. Firstly into a life of crime then into the black power, this for most would be just a life of crime.

As for the girls if no one saved them then they wouldn't save their own lives. A few managed to get away by getting jobs in shops that would normally end in them robbing the shop themselves or nicking a set of keys that at night the boys would go back to rob.

Some nights after spending a good six months with the street kids they actually treated me as one of their own and here I was again in some sort of a gang.

I was growing up quick and having my eyes open to so much in the way of crime and surviving becoming very street wise which is an education in its self.

My new friends lived not even day by day but hour by hour as they had no direction, no hope and no life. Some new kids would come and live there, they would try to bully me but as the ones who had been there the longest they would stand up for me. It felt at the time that I was spending more time with the street kids than I was at home and as for my parents well even six months later my mum never caught me sneaking out so she knew none the better.

My Father had been living in a building which was in central Wellington where ex-seamen or seamen who was in-between boat journeys would stay before their ships sailed off. It was like a hotel for seamen so he had no idea about my new friends and the time I was spending with them, he just guessed my mum was looking after me.

I did miss him and due to him not being allowed to come to the house then I wasn't allowed to see him. He could only call the house phone on certain nights or some weekends to speak to his kids for the time being while certain court orders were being put in place.

Sometimes though if he rang up drunk and started shit down the phone to my mum then she would hang up and unplug the phone so we didn't even know he had called as my mum wouldn't tell us, which made me think as weeks went by within the last six months that he had forgotten about us.

I didn't know about their divorcé battle or custody battle that was going on as my father very much was fighting for us plus also demanding the house to be sold so he would at least get something back out of everything that he had built, but my mum was not going to let him have a penny that easy.

It seemed, though at a young age of course I didn't know any of this, she didn't want him to have a penny for all those beatings she had taken from him over the years. She just wanted him out of her life completely but me and my sister still needed a dad and he was our dad.

Finally we were able to see our Dad as the courts had allowed it. It seemed forever since we had seen him. We were to meet him with my mum in a restaurant in town. We arrived at the restaurant, I can remember how excited I was and also my sister was so happy to be seeing our Father.

My Dad wasn't there as she sat down and waited, it wasn't long but I can remember mum wanting to go as he wasn't anywhere to be seen but we told my mum he will be here. Back then no one had mobiles so we couldn't call him. My mum decided to wait and so glad at the time she did but as soon as he arrived we noticed he was drunk which my mum didn't like.

I wasn't bothered as I was used to my dad being drunk. We all ate, it was lovely food and my dad kept on drinking. He was being good and really trying his hardest with my mum, but I felt my mum was being quite rude and just kept saying to him that he wasn't there for her but the kids so to stop talking to her.

I think he was just trying to be that gentleman that many a times he was as whenever my mum got up from the table my Dad would stand. Something even to this day I do whenever sat at a restaurant table when a woman or women are present. Anyway I thought my dad was being lovely to my mum,

I just wished they hadn't broken up and that my dad had never hit my mum in the past as they were my parents and I loved them both so much but I was much closer to my mum.

Soon my mum wanted lunch to finish and my dad reminded her that he had not seen his kids for six months and she gets to see them each day so he pleaded her for us to stay but she said she had things on that afternoon so we were to go as she wasn't going to be late. My dad mentioned Wim saying "That bastard can wait!"

I wasn't sure if it was Wim who my mum was speaking about but you know something I am sure my father probably wasn't far from being wrong.

This single comment caused my mum to say that's it, we're leaving and that the lawyer will be in touch for the next visit and with that it caused the row to get even tenser. My father hated that for him to see his own kids he would have to wait to hear from my mum's lawyer so he said stop the crap lets sort it all out between us here and now, no fucking lawyers.

My mum called him a joker and we soon followed her out while my father stayed back to pay the bill. The lunch must have cost loads as it was a fancy restaurant and we all ate like kings having anything we wanted.

As we got to my mum's car I sat in the back and my sister was in the front with my mum. All of sudden my dad appeared at my mum's car driving side and opened the door calling her a rude bitch that he hadn't even said good bye to his kids.

She said he had the chance to do that at the table. This just flamed my dad up and my mum should by now known not to wind him up especially when he was drunk as he went nuts.

He went for the keys of the car to stop my mum driving off but she slammed the door a few times on him till he got out the way. She finally shut her door locking it straight away telling my sister and me to do the same.

He did look like a mad man that day. Even as I went to close the door I think that was the only time that my dad frightened me as if he was going to turn on me. He was so angry so I went to do what my mum told me to do as in locking my car door but as I went for the lock all of sudden my door flew open. My father reached inside and grabbed me, and told my sister to open her door but she wouldn't.

My mum was crying saying his name "Please Steve leave Christian alone, give him back please", but he said "No!"

"If you're going to treat me so bad then he is coming with me!" he said as he slammed the door, walking me down the road with him.

We got lost in the crowd, he explained to me he wasn't going to hurt me and that's when I thought of course he's not as he's my Dad and he never has hurt me in the past so I was happier now to follow him as we went from one street on to the next. We reached where he had been staying since losing his home, the home he had built for his family.

This building he now lived in as I explained earlier was a large building with many floors and an entrance like a hotel. My Father took me up a few sets of stairs and we reached what was his room, a one bedroom number with a sink in it, a single bed and a wardrobe and really that was it.

He said he needed to show me what was now in the mean time what he had to call home. It was in my Fathers eyes such heartbreak as after all he had done in his life, where he had started his own journey, how many countries he had visited, the women he had fallen in love with, the reason why he had come to the shores of Beautiful New Zealand, the house he had brought and the saloon he had made possible for my mum, he had now lost the love of his life and also the family house and all he had left was the love of his kids.

That room he would place his head at night to sleep, how lonely and bitter that must have been for him as I felt his pain and I think he could see that in his own son eyes as he could see it was upsetting for me.

We then went down a flight of stairs and there was pool table and in another room a TV room. Also a bar area so he went got me a cola and a bag of crisps while he had a beer. I met some of the others who lived there. We sat down with some of the British seamen and my Dad and I watched the Two Ronnie's on TV, a proper humour and something since I was a young kid would watch with my dad on TV back at home.

This was great all having a good laugh together but it was short lived as soon many police officers came running in throwing my dad to the floor and grabbing me taking me down the stairs while I looked back at my father who I had just been sharing laughs with pinned to the floor with police all over him. I hated that, I fucking hated it.

I was driven to a police station and sat in some meeting room being asked over and over was I alright? Had anything happened to me? Like if I had just been taken by King Kong. Nothing was wrong, apart from the image I had of my father being pinned down on the floor by the police officers. That was my only concern and nothing more.

I didn't like the police asking me questions so I asked to leave but they said my mum was on her way. I wished it was my dad so I knew he was ok as he hadn't done anything wrong.

He's my fucking father, that's not a crime.

My mum arrived to the police station to collect me and she explained she had been at Wims house and not at home. That's why the police couldn't reach her on the phone straight away. That's when the penny dropped and it was due to Wim that the lunch with my dad was cut short as it was Wim after all who my mum was seeing after lunch.

I wasn't happy. I demanded to be back at my dad's new place but the police had informed my mum at the police station when she collected me that he would be spending time in the police cell until court the next morning. They were going to charge him for possible kidnapping and that's why they were asking me loads of questions. Even a fucking head doctor turned up treating me like I was five year old kid. I told the doctor to fuck right off! I just wanted to go.

It was my Father and he had never done me any wrong so what was all the fuss about. Then to be told that my father might indeed be charged with something and that I had the next day off school as we had to turn up to court.

I didn't sleep all night I was so worried about my Dad. This divorcé had gotten so bad and I didn't like it as yes my mum was hurt in the marriage and my father was a bastard at times towards my Mum when he was in drunken rages, no doubt about it but now my mum had got her own way.

My Dad was no longer at the house so why did things have to get worse before they got better. It was badly affecting me and I started to blame myself as all this wouldn't have happened the day before if it wasn't for me. If I hadn't been to that lunch and then in the car well then my Dad would not be in a police cell, so a lot of guilt was going through me. I know now it wasn't my fault but try to see all this through the eyes of a 10 year kid.

My plan was to run away, my mum had brought me a tent earlier that year for my 10th birthday. I had a girlfriend called Melanie who was my first girlfriend. She was a younger sister of my sister's best friend Angie Berg. Melanie had stayed over at mine when Angie Berg stayed over to see her best friend my sister that evening.

It had been my tenth birthday weeks earlier. Melanie and I slept in the tent in the front yard that night, of course nothing happened though I tried my best but was kicked in the balls so I didn't try my luck after that.

Anyway this evening we both done the same again, sleeping in the tent pretending that we weren't in my front yard but that we were in the middle of the forest somewhere or at the beach with no worries in the world.

My plan was once the court cases were over with as with my mum and my dad then I was going to ask Melanie whose own parents had broken up, to run away with me and live in the tent. I was 100% planning it from the time morning came and my mum took me to one of the family court meetings.

I was placed in a separate room and I never got to see my dad while at the family courts. I sat with my mum's lawyer and another head doctor they just wanted to know the facts of what went on so I told them my entire father wanted was longer time at the restaurant with us and so did I.

He had been away when I had turned 10 years old so he very much wanted to make up for that and spend the whole day with both his children. I also added that he never grabbed me out of the car but it was me who opened the door and it was I who got out of the car and asked my father could I see where he was living.

My mum's lawyer kept on saying don't lie but I kept to my story and then my mum come in and they chatted and she asked me to tell the truth. I told her to tell the truth, she was thrown back by what I was saying so asked us for to be alone.

She asked me why I was lying so I told her what I had seen. My father's tiny room and how sad he looked and that he was so upset. I said he just wanted to spend time with me he didn't want to fight with you.

My Mum was taking all this in and then asked for her lawyer to come in and said she wished to take back her statement of events from the day before.

This seemed to piss off her lawyer as a lot of people now were rushing about and when my father finally appeared in court that morning. I didn't get to see the case go in front of a judge as I was still in this room at the courthouse but the outcome was the case was dropped.

The case that could have brought a kidnapping charge of my father, something he never did. I am just so glad my mum listened to me as how terrible it would have been if she hadn't.

Not just for my Dad but also for me and my sister as a family unit. Even though the family home was broken and the family bond was rock bottom, it was such a mess and it went on to affect me and to run away was now on top of my list.

Thinking as the 10 year that I was, that running away was going to solve the problem but it wasn't, it was just going to get me into a lot of trouble and fast.

Chapter 7

RUNAWAY

My parents divorce was very hard to take, so many rules sent down from the courts. My father had to buck the line to be sure to see us but I think for everyone involved meaning my mum and dad they knew now that it all was effecting, us the children badly. How many people out there have made this mistake by not thinking about the kids involved but only themselves which can have such an awful effect on the kids.

I think a lot of damage was already done through my mum trying to make sure she hurt my father as much as she could for all he had done to her in the past as still many nights my dad would call and sometimes my mum would let us know and other times she wouldn't. Not to be hurtful against us but very much against him. If he dared say a wrong word on the phone to my mum or if he rang up drunk and drunk most of the time he was.

What my mum didn't see is what I saw that day he grabbed me and that was insight into how one day in the life of anyone you could have everything, then the very next day you could have nothing. It could all be taken away from you.

This was affecting my father's health and also increased his drinking. One good thing was he had found himself a new house and one near the beach front in Seaturn which was only over the hill from us. He also started to date a Maori lady whose first husband had died, I am unsure how as it never was discussed.

Irene had to raise 7 kids by herself after the death of their father and in a very poor part of New Zealand called Porirua.

A city, as it was classed, just outside Wellington. Though it may be a poor part of New Zealand, it shines proud when it comes to Family belongingness and also a strong community spirit as everyone who lives in that part of New Zealand always sticks together through thick and thin.

They don't care about some bullshit class system, they care only about Family and what's most important. Well the Manuel's were no different, if not actually stronger than many families as they were a staunch family looking after one another was most important to them. Plus they all respected their

Mother through and through as many Maori families do, equal respect for the Mum as well as the father.

While my father was working on the interisland ferry between the North Island and the South Island, he had met Irene she had been travelling with a Maori performing group as Irene had very strong ties with the Maori population and very much its culture. She also had blood of a very well known Maori tribe and they were fighting tribe back in the early days when English first settled in New Zealand.

It was the type of relationship you wouldn't guess would form but out of a friendship that grew a strong bond and as both had lost their partners, her husband in death and my father's wife cheating on him and leaving him then their heartbreak maybe brought them closer together. They also both enjoyed drinking. Irene drank booze but no near as much as dad but she was still a big drinker.

My father's lawyer had told him he had to get out of the place he was living. Obviously my father wished to do that as it was not a nice place to live. His relationship with Irene got stronger and my father was no longer in shock to what happened in his life as in losing his family. With a solid new home and now only ever working on the ferries as he had given up all the vast ships he had worked on in his life, he now just stuck to the ferries. This would all go in his flavour to being able to have all more contact with his kids.

I never knew at the time my father's life was changing for the best, I still felt to run away would solve the problems.

So one night I packed up my tent and out I went. I didn't catch the bus but I walked and walked over the hill and down heading towards the bays that stretch right around Wellington and as I got near the navy base on Shelly bay I put up my tent. Due to all the walking I feel asleep and woke in the morning, hidden in the bush where I had set up camp.

I didn't have much money on me so I went and brought a hot dog and ice cream at a take away van and then went back into the bush. I had nothing to keep the boredom away as the second day went from afternoon to evening and I wanted to explore the navy base.

I saw the many lights on and all the activity that had been going on so at the drop of darkness I went over through the windows and could see some people watching telly. In another out building I could smell food, hot food so I went over there and the kitchen was massive.

I noticed the kitchen staff taking in trays of hot food into the mess so as the kitchen was clear I run in and grabbed a pot which was full of steaming food. With a towel I held it so I didn't burn myself and on the way out I even had time to put a kitchen spoon in it and off I went back to my tent.

It was too dark to see what I was doing but I worked out it was mutton stew. It tasted so delicious and with that my belly was full. I got under my only blanket which was the only thing I could fit into the bag that carried my tent and wrapped up for another night away from home.

Thinking to myself that my parents had one less thing to worry about but what I didn't know was my mum had been calling the police after speaking to all my friends' parents and not knowing where else to look.

My Mum thought my father had grabbed me again so the police were waiting at my father's house when he came home from the pub. There was his new girlfriend explaining to them that I wasn't there and I had yet to stay there as she hadn't even met me yet. I wasn't there though they had to look in the house and then report back to my mum saying I wasn't there.

Now I had my loved ones worried but I hadn't thought this through. Nor had I left a note. The sun came up and I went to the take away van that was parked up near the beach but I didn't even have enough change left to get me a buttered bread roll and they wouldn't give me any food. The only place was the navy base but it was daytime so I went back to the camp and seeing the empty cooking pot only made me hungrier.

I really hadn't thought this running away thing through correctly. I leaped out of the tent and went down back to the kitchen where the door had been opened the night before, probably to let out the heat of the kitchen, but as I went around the side of the building and darted up to the window it was too busy in the working kitchen to get away with any food without getting caught so I thought I would go to K Street and see the street kids as they would help me out.

I still didn't have the correct money even to catch a bus so I got on the back of one of the buses and then had to change the bus. Not knowing I had caught the wrong bus I soon after a bit of travelling looked out and noticed the streets all looking like many that lead back to my house. The next minute I was at my bus stop outside my mum's saloon, many miles away from K Street.

Thinking of all that distance I would again have to travel and the thought of being so hungry was never far from my mind so I jumped off the bus and with my keys managed to get into my kitchen and to the fridge but as I slowly opened it, I could hear my mum crying.

She was crying worse than ever I had heard her cry before and also even worse than she ever had when even my father would hit her. I had to go in a find out what was wrong with my beautiful mum so I stepped in the lounge and when she saw me, I just knew the tears were for me.

She got up and instead of being happy to see me she seemed angry trying to speak while she was crying. I couldn't understand the words that were coming out of her mouth.

There she was alone and in a state so I cuddled her and said everything was ok. It wasn't until she had finally calmed down she made a call to the police. They were to the house in a flash and not being very nice to me at all.

They were cold towards me and it seemed my mum didn't like one of them yelling at me saying I had caused so much trouble and questioning where had I been. I wasn't there to answer questions. I was hungry so I went to the kitchen to make a sandwich and pour myself a cup of juice but the fridge was slammed shut and there in my face again was this copper threading behaviour towards me. I told him to get the fuck out of my house, telling my mum to tell the police officers to leave.

She didn't know what to say. Yes she was angry as I had gone missing and walking back in the door without a worry in my head and after giving her a cuddle then the only thing on my mind was food.

This didn't impress the police officer and maybe the prick who had yelled at me out of the two of them was only trying to play the tough cop.

Later on I would realize why he was so angry as they had been out looking for me when I was told his own son had years earlier gone out with some friends eel fishing and had fallen in a river and for days. He searched for days only to be told his son's body had been found and his son was dead.

It was hard for him to then be looking for another missing boy around the same age and as I wasn't given them any respect then that made him mad. As far as I was concerned I didn't like the police as I had known them over all those years fighting with my father and the very last time pinning him down on the floor but this cop didn't know all those issues I had with the boys in blue and for him shouting at me, it just made things worse.

I didn't have issues with all police officers as some did seem caring and understanding. Whenever they were called to the family house and so I didn't have a hate for every police officer as many of them were only doing their job. In some you could tell they did care but I disliked them whenever they put their hands on my father and anytime they did the same to me in years to come.

How glad I was when they left. Looking back now I should have been more understanding towards the two police officers as they were only trying to do their job. They had been out searching for me, while my Mum was thinking the worst, but I was only a young kid at the time and was not to know better.

I tried to have my food in peace but now my mum was shouting at me. I was sick of this fucking house and all the raised voices, although I didn't like seeing my mum crying as she did earlier, I really didn't need to be shouted at again just after I had been shouted at by some police officer so I slammed my bedroom door and asked to be left alone in my room.

My mum wouldn't give up asking where I had been so I told her where I had been near the navy base and that my tent was there and if she didn't stop shouting at me then I would in the middle of the night go back there and not come back as I was sick of the shouting.

That night my mum came in checked on me when I was sleeping and for many nights she would always check on me while I slept. I myself never knew as I would be sleeping.

At the end of the week I was taken out of school by my mum and had to see some councillor, I didn't enjoy that as what was all this about?

I was a normal kid and it wasn't me with the problems, it was my parents and yes they were causing a negative on me due to their fighting. I did blame myself for some of their fighting and rows, that's why I run away but it didn't deserve me having to see a councillor.

I rebelled against my mum even more. When I got home after seeing the councillor all I could think of is the morning when I went to the takeaway van and not having enough of my own money. If I did I would have lasted longer out there in the bush and not have come home. Though I was frighten by the pitch darkness of the bush with all the animal noises around me and being alone, but you know what being in my house I felt more frightened as a child there and that was in my own house where most kids should feel the most safest.

That following Saturday I went out by myself after soccer was over and asked around in Miramar central at the shops for weekend work as from now on I wanted to have my own money.

After everyone saying no due to my age, I then went into the video store and I asked the owner who I knew. He would get his hair cut in my mum's saloon and his wife and their younger kids. He knew who I was and said yes I could help out on Saturdays. I was given $25 each Saturday to help out from around noon or whenever I had finished playing football on Saturday morning and I would work up until 9pm.

I was as chuffed as I had gone and done it myself and I was earning my own money so no longer did I feel trapped. It meant even more freedom plus my mum was proud and also my dad.

For some reason each Friday my mum would still take me to this councillor and I didn't like where it was heading. To me it was all shit and nothing good was coming out of it. Why not my sister who was by then 14 years old going on 15 years but my mum believed more so now because I had my own job, that less and less I was listening to her. She kept on following through with stupid house rules causing us to clash.

I felt as though I was behaving older, it seemed to me I was being treated more like a child and I didn't enjoy it.

Not only in my head at the time was I the man of the house but now I was very grown up as I had a job that I was being paid for.

Within a month I had $100 dollars that was pretty cool for a 10 year old kid. Life was going good apart from these counselling sessions.

Finally through court agreements I was able to spend time over at my dad's new house. It was a great pad so every second weekend I was allowed to stay over after I finished at work. On the Sundays I would be able to go fishing again with my Dad and even better for whenever he was working on the ferry because when it ported in Wellington I would go on the ferry with Irene and do the crossing to the South Island. Then in the morning the return crossing to the North Island and that would get me into Wellington in time for school. Normally my mum would pick me up and get me to school in time.

At school I was too grown up compared to the other kids, ok not in the class room but in life. Many of the other kids were boring and so young for their age. They would play at lunch time such shit games in the playground and I had cash, I had a job and I had what I thought was an exciting life.

I couldn't relate to most of the kids. Although I had some great friends but what I started to feel more and more is that I couldn't relate to the teachers. I felt they were looking at me in a different way due to me going to a councillor each week. I am sure they all were talking and thinking either I was fucked up or that my family was. I don't recall any other kids at school parents being broken up and I didn't know how much of what the teachers knew about my parents break up. I was becoming a young man, living life not in school as all the other kids were doing.

I was living my life out of school and I was getting bored of school, not the lessons as I loved learning but bored of the social aspect of school. I even started questioning teachers if they told me what to do.

By now, after having the run ins with the police a few times already in my life and having no discipline in the home, then these people who were teaching English, maths, and art etc, I wasn't letting them then tell me what to do. I would leave school during my lunch break and with my wages I would have fish and chips for lunch at home and then return for school but the school said no this which I didn't enjoy as sitting with kids with their robotic lunch as in an apple, a sandwich, or a carrot talking about maths class.

Fuck that I wasn't going to eat boring jam sandwiches with peanut butter. If I felt like a coffee with my lunch I would walk down the hill and make myself a coffee from my mum's hair salon that she had installed a machine for her customers, but even this didn't go down well with the school, so I had my mum run coffee up to me or fish and chips at lunch time as then the school would be happy as I hadn't left school grounds.

Whenever I was at my Fathers place there was never any mention of what time I had to go to bed. I could stay up all night as my dad would too due to drinking. He gave me more freedom than he ever done when he lived in his new house and while he was working on the ferry I could run riot.

I was allowed to watch the English football that would be screened late at night, plus play darts. I learned how to play pool on a rocking pool table due to the rough seas. I also started to learn how to play pool very well and in general I was enjoying spending all this time with my dad. I think he made sure I enjoyed myself so he knew he wouldn't ever lose me or that I didn't wish to be in his company, while maybe at the same time my mum thought she was losing me and that my dad was playing a game by giving me more freedom than she ever did, as back in the house when both my parents lived there then it was my father who used to be more strict and my mum who gave more freedom.

Soon I got my ear pierced without my mum's permission. At school when they told me to take it out I wouldn't and had my mum fight in my corner but the school didn't like this. After when I told my dad about the councillor he went nuts and told my mum that it had to stop so eventually it did as the last few times she made me go I just sat there and said nothing so it was a waste of time.

I had learned for many a year's never to tell a soul of what I had witnessed as a child with what I saw going on in the house with my parents fighting so I wasn't going to start now with some head doctor who was speaking to me like I was 5 year old kid. It didn't go down with me and every car ride back home with my mum she would get an ear full from me for making me go there.

Soon I quit track and field which meant my mum had me in the house extra afternoons which wreaked her time with Wim when he came over to the house. He would always try and involve himself, which he wasn't doing any harm but there was no place in my life for another father. It actually didn't help me in anyway though Wim would get me involved in tennis on Sunday with him and my mum which I very much enjoyed or time spend with his two own daughters Roberta and Heidi, whom I enjoyed both their company very much so and in many ways it was like having three sisters as over time they become just that, like sisters to me.

My Mum and Wims lifestyle was much healthier than my Fathers, but my Dad was fun. I learned how to win money in darts and pool and soon when playing his drunken mates, aka the crew on the ferries who all would have a drink and once they were drunk I would place money down on the pool table. I was only a kid they would be happy to play me and I would lose the first few games and then clean up if I could on the next.

Soon sport was becoming second best to going out as I would take my mates from school on weekend trips with me on the boats we would fish in the ports of the side of the boat and meet girls who were travelling with their parents as passengers up on board and we would have little romance going so some journeys as young kids do when the go on holiday.

I think my mum didn't like the stories I would come back with after spending time on board the boats as I soon would be drinking booze, not in front of my dad but once they all were asleep me and my pals would drink their beers in the mess room and get drunk but make out we were just sea sick when we couldn't walk straight or when we were sick from all the beer.

Such stories were getting back to my teachers at school as other parents were telling the teachers that they didn't want me hanging around their kids at school due to finding what they had got up to with me when I was on the boats with my dad.

We had a big important cake day at school, win prizes and all of that but seriously making fancy cakes in my eyes was a boys thing to do so I protested and said I anit making no fucking cake so my Mum ended up having to make it for me and also my best friend Chris Mitchell got his Mum to make him a beauty of a cake.

We so would won first and second prize, that is if we had managed to make it to school with both cakes as on our walk to school we ended up just eating our way through not just one of the cakes but both, arriving late for school telling the teachers that we left the cakes by mistake on someone's fence while I was doing up my shoe laces.

If it wasn't for our faces being covered in chocolate cake then I reckon we could have got away with that but we didn't, and even our Mums were phoned about this from the headmaster, how stupid was that over two lost cakes, how anal was he about the whole matter.

Monday came and I was dropped a class half way through the year and always had my desk at the front of the class so the teacher could keep an eye on me all do with a fucking missing cake, ok two cakes.

It made me feel neither dumb being dropped down a grade when I was far from dumb, I was one of the brightest kids in the school, ok maybe not at maths etc but I wasn't slow nor ever a slow learner.

The headmaster being dropping me down a grade just made me feel like such an Outcast and me never was stupid but this made me feel like a fool so from then onwards I would make the teachers life hell by getting my old school gang up and running again.

I had driven out most of the bullies as I was anti bullying of other kids but when it came to the teachers then I would make their days not as peaceful as they once were. It didn't take long before they called my mum to the school and I was given some warning for misbehaviour and encouraging other kids to follow suit.

I was told I had behaviour problems, but I didn't I just would take on authority, be it at home or at school and I wasn't going to change but now it seemed due to all my outburst and some of the kids not being as strong willed, I then was losing my school gang and this to me meant a lot of friendships at school suffered as they wanted to believe they were rocking the boat let's say but when it came to being put in line by the teachers then they would do so.

Deep down I knew they wished to be as much of a young rebel as I had become uncontrolled and if I didn't have many friends left now at school, not because they didn't want to be my friend but because they didn't want to get themselves in trouble as these were the kids that fathers may not ever have beaten their mums but wouldn't think twice about using a belt on their sons or beating their sons if they had misbehaved at school.

When I mean misbehaved, nothing serious I just wouldn't take orders from teachers as they were only ever just that teachers, they were simply there to teach and not throw their weight around as many would do, sorry but I was having none of it, I never had and wouldn't then when I was 10 years old.

That year of my life, I feel so much changed for me and I guess also my Mum.

For the very first time my Mother standing up to my father and being honest to him by showing him she didn't love him anymore even to the extent if it meant the break up completely of the family that both of them knew for all the last 14 years since my sister was born.

My time with the street kids what I heard from their stories about such horrors like some of them telling me they had been raped in their own homes and how bad things were for many of them in their family houses, worst than I ever witnessed by my parents fighting as these kids were beaten and worse.

That age for me had been such a eye opener than any year before and I was growing up ever so quick as that year is where I put all those first years of my life in to the past and it's there where things took a turn and things got worse for me even though there were many times of happiness as in spending time again with my father, having my own job and seeing my Mum happy thanks to Wim.

Maybe school and my time at my house weren't going well but I think myself and my sister were coping better than most but even I didn't know and nor could you while you read this book ever think how these next ten years would start with death and end with death with death also in between.

It's going to be hard writing the next few chapters but I promised myself I would write a honest book and I did warn you that this was going to be a journey with so much heartbreak as well as good times so what comes next is more of my journey.

One that I wish for you to keep on turning those pages and stay on board with me as I write because trust me reader, I am digging hard to put words on paper as I am going where I have for many years blocked off to the back of memory never wishing to seek those memories out as to remember many things back in my life will bring back such pain but this is my life and this is my journey, a journey I promised to take you all on from the very first page you read and then turned to read the next page.

Chapter 8

YOURE SO FAR AWAY NOW

Things started to seem better for everyone, my Father was happy as he was able to see his kids often and it meant my Mum had every second weekend just to be with Wim, which I know she enjoyed the peace and quiet.

School had told my Mum that the only way I would be allowed to gain my place back in my own age class was if my behaviour had come down a peg, if I was willing to stop challenging the teachers, but this wasn't just it.

I also wouldn't be allowed to socialise with some of the other kids, as their parents wouldn't allow it as they said I was too much of a powering influence over their children as they the parents were from good back grounds and were parents whom would raise money for the school then they had a very must say in the running of the school even though they were only parents but all were on the school board.

It pisses me off that I was moved down a class which effects my learning and my education due to what outsiders had to say with the running of the school, this in turn made my education suffer but they had more of a say than one single pupil did, so my mum had to agree to terms that I was given.

Soon I was off to some boot camp style set up over the course of a month, my father wasn't too pleased but if he dared say anything against my mum's choices it meant that she would stop the visits which would bring back the angry within him as my mum played many silly games with my father still.

It was as if I was a porn in a chest game as that's how I felt many times when I would be used to hurt my father by my mum, and in not telling him I had been send away to this camp made him very angry which I don't blame him for and I wish he had been near to get me out of the place.

It was a tough place to be in and most of the kids were rebels themselves but all were bullies, where I wasn't as they had kids at their schools following them through fear but at my school kids followed me through not fear but due to excitement and fun.

Hell we all were only kids and we weren't getting up to much mischief all I was showing them was freedom, no restrictions as they had in their own homes by their own parents and they had while they were in school by the teachers.

I was like a breath of fresh air to the kids in my school but here at the boot camp I wasn't a breath of fresh air to anyone. These kids were serious when it came to causing trouble and harming others including me.

At night there would be beatings carried out by the strongest and hardest of the boys, I managed to avoid that on the first few nights but listened to the other kids getting hit with hockey sticks and fists.

Each morning the tough nuts as I called them the bullies had more and more boys now in tail of them as more and more beatings they gave out then more and more would join them out of fear.

The only thing those first few days I joined was the church group. I had been to Sunday school when I was much younger but after that church never played a part in my life until this week.

Each day I would spend time in the day between behaviour classes. I would be learning church classes and I must say it had a good effect on me as it was a positive experience as for the early evenings I was taking in negative experiences, learning about all the trades from the jack the lads, from credit card fraud, to cheque fraud and robberies of chemists and other crimes that the tough nuts were teaching some of us.

See maybe I was here at this boot camp for the wrong reasons as I wasn't rebelling against school where these kids were.

They would hardly even turn up to school where as I would love going to school to learn. I just felt it difficult at times but back then no one picked up on the fact that I was suffering from dyslexia so that was causing me some frustration.

As for challenging the teachers, well due to not ever having any form of discipline at home then I hardly saw my own parents as authority figures so of course I wasn't excepting the teachers as authority figures, I only saw them as one thing and that was teachers to teach me skills and learning but not there to tell me what to do as when they did that's when I would stand my ground.

As for the kids whose parents thought I was getting them into lots of trouble at school and outside school well they were wrong as all I was doing was letting these kids live a bit as in their own homes with such strict parents they weren't living their youth not having fun, and what 10 year old kid doesn't get into a little bit of trouble now and then.

As the tough nuts couldn't work me out and noticing I had formed a few of the kids around me that they had yet broken by midnight beatings with hockey sticks, well I soon was on top of their list.

I wasn't aware as I thought I had actually befriended some of them quite well as one day at the church service after taking a call from my mum informing me one of our cats had been run over.

The loss of my first pet as a kid was my dog that had been nicked and I was guessing by the monster man but to hear when many miles away that a pet had died and one that I had grown up with over the ten years was sad for me. I was upset when I left the telephone call so I went back in to chapel and I said for the very first time a pray to God. Something I hadn't done before but something that did help me feel better as I felt I was sharing my pain with God or Jesus then I left the chapel back to my dorm and fell asleep.

I was awoken with my pillow over my head and great blows into my body; something that was hard was hitting me. It was pitch black, I couldn't see nor breathe due to the pillow being held over my head.

I tried to fight whatever was happening to me but I was being held down and I couldn't fight back even all the judo that I had been taught couldn't save me as I lay there taking these blows to my body. The lack of air I felt myself drifting that's when my mind when back to earlier while kneeing in the chapel saying my prayer surrounded by calmness and quietness which soon came to me while I was being beaten.

No longer could I feel the pain nor could I hear the blows to my body as I drifted more towards the time spend in the chapel; something spiritual happen as I truly stopped feeling any pain all together and felt very at peace even though I was being smashed by what seemed to be fists and a piece of metal.

The beating was all finished, the cowards, the tough nuts had all run away back to their beds and I was the only kid who ever took a beating not to cry or to get one of the staff members.

I just laid there wondering what had happened to all the pain. Where had it all gone and through pray did something more happen, I said another pray as I fell asleep a few hours later as my ribs and chest and my legs were giving me a lot of discomfort where the blows from what I guessed was hockey sticks had been brought down on me in the beating I had taken.

Waking up my body looked like it had been through ten rounds with Henry Copper the British boxer as I had bruises all over my chest and my rib cage and also my legs, my face had been protected by the pillow thank God and I could walk but I was in pain and discomfort to say the least.

I was asked by staff how I had got the marks I simply told them that I had fallen from my bunk bed and I felt too much pain to enter class so they allowed the morning off as I very much had somewhere to go and that was back to the chapel.

I found one of the members of the boot camp in there she told me how Jesus had entered her life and how she gave her whole life up for the church, and how she as a person changed and changed for the best so taking this all on board I explained that I felt some type of connection the night before when I fell off my bunk bed and hit the floor.

I wasn't going to grass up the tough nuts and I didn't even see who had attacked me as they were cleverer than that.

Anyway she went ahead and said I should except Jesus into my heart and so I did, that's when I become a Christian, I wasn't forced by my family or by the church itself but I found it through being beaten which sounds weird but then God works in funny ways.

On leaving that chapel I did feel so much better within myself though as all the staff had heard about me excepting god into my life many of them didn't leave me alone and kept on preaching to me which was a turn off as I didn't need to be brain washed as I had my own experience and I was just happy with that and also the earlier talk I had had with the one member of staff back in the chapel.

As for the other kids, many took the piss out of me but that didn't bother me as it showed to me how stupid they were as what they couldn't expect or simply understand then they would use that as a excuse to be nasty but I was above that and after taking such a beating the night before then sticks and stones so didn't hurt me and even if I were to get another beating I was sure that even that wouldn't hurt me as I had found myself among all these brain dead drop out losers and I would on leaving this boot camp so leave them all behind in the dirt.

I never knew or found out who had attacked me out of the kids were it the tough nuts or were it some of the sheep in among the kids who had to give out the beating to save their own skin or to follow suit, whoever it was were cowards as never did I get challenged one or one as I know in my heart who would have won that fight.

I did make friends with some of the Wellington based kids and though some were part of the tough nuts gang, they were to me no different than kids from Miramar warriors, again older not much direction in their lives, they hated school any form of it and they were very much on the ladder to becoming criminals, I think I learned a lot from these guys and I would see them again in my not too far future.

I left the boot camp, yes a better person but that wasn't due to anything that this place provided as all it provided was terror for kids who couldn't stand up for themselves, fear for kids who had been used to being bullied, power to kids who were used to being the bullies in their own schools, and knowledge of crime to all kids who went to this boot camp, that's fact as nothing else happened there apart from beatings or dishing out beatings.

What happened to me wasn't there for me waiting but it was personal and could have happened anyway though it's something that I did take out of there and on returning back home instead of having a go at my mother for sending me.

I was happy she did though when she seen the bruises on my body she wasn't happy at all but again on myself noticing them as they were very bad even to a week later, but they in turn made me never wish to be in that situation again as in being beaten like that so I upped my game and my effort with my judo and I started to take now three nights a week and also some Sundays.

Thought I wouldn't take Sundays to go to church as to me a pray at the end of each night was good enough for me and as long as I learned to be nicer towards the teachers at school then I felt better as a kid, this I did try more and also at home and towards my Mum and also Wim as well as he now was very much a part of the family and my sister I stopped fighting with her as often as I once used to so we got on so much better as well.

My upbeat in judo came success as soon I wasn't no longer just part of the Miramar judo team but now I was part of the Wellington judo club and I was fighting in tournaments, I was so proud but again I never had my parents there to see me, like how all the other kids whatever age they were had their families watching them, still always got me down a lot but I still tried my very best for myself if anyone.

As my judo went on leaps and bounds so did my soccer as soon I wasn't now playing just for my school but I was playing for Miramar rangers under 12 even though I was only 10 years old, I was playing two grades up and doing well with that so sport had again been the front runner in my life, rather than gangs and what a great feel good factor I had through this but again the balance in my life would swap over and balance became unbalance.

My success in sport and also that at school I was trying so much better meant that Wim could see that I wasn't such a little bastard after all so he would give up more of his own time and no longer try to dictate to me as he knew that would be a losing game so instead we would play tennis together and also on going to his house for the very first time.

It was such a grand house in one of the nicest area of Wellington looking down across wellington from a tall hill, he had many houses that he had brought over the years and had done very well with them that he rented most of them out he had successful motor business with garages throughout Wellington.

Wim would work hard for his money six days ahead and over the years it meant with millions in the band he could enjoy the good things in life and things he liked which included nice cars though he would drive himself day to day in a ford escort but in his garage he had some lovely motors and also his house had antique furniture which were worth a fortune.

Wim loved his work and also playing sport and he loved using the gun club as a sport as well.

I was 10 years old when I first was handed a gun, and it felt good even more so when I fired it, this is something with Wim that I looked forward doing was going to the gun club with him and my mum.

I started to use the gun club with Wim as many times as I could but as I was so keen and as Wim was busy doing others things so not always could he take me to the gun club so instead I managed to talk my mum into buying me a gun, something she very much was against but Wim talked her around to it.

It was only a 22 rifle, now u had to be 16 years old to have such a gun like this in New Zealand so the gun stayed locked up at home and only when I was going to the gun club could I have the gun but that beat the purpose as I wanted to use it say for target practise in the real outdoors , soon over time my mum allowed me to use it with trust outside the gun club as Wim would find suitable places I could hit targets such as tin cans etc but other than that it stayed mostly of course under lock and key.

I went away with a girl I was dating named Sarah Black, she was around 13 years old or 14 year old I think I told her I was 12 as she wouldn't have dated me if she knew how young I really was.

Anyway I went on holiday with her and her parents and my mum let me take it with me then as we were going up the east coast of the country to sand and surf but also her dad and I would go shooting, he would be after rabbits etc.

It's weird as he himself had never held a gun before and here I was a 10 year old teaching a grown up firstly safely rules of handling a gun but also how to load the gun and fire it. I am sure if he knew I was 10 years old and not 12 years old going on 13years old then he would not have been as carefree taking lessons from me.

I know myself I wouldn't even let a 13 year old take a gun for any type of holiday but in New Zealand its different as many of the farmers kids all had guns to go out shooting on their farm lands from that age, the only difference was I was a city kid and not a country raised kid.

I was sensible for my age and more so whenever I handled the gun as I knew it wasn't a toy and I would only ever use it for target practise and in a safe area so I wasn't some wild child walking the streets with a gun, to me target practise was just another form of sport and I wasn't doing anyone any harm.

One person who didn't like hearing about this and made a point of it one night down the phone was my father and it drew him to come over to the house and confront my Mum about it.

My dad was anti me having a gun at my age and he hit the roof when he got to my house, he demanded mum open the door and she wouldn't. I asked her not to call the police and I went outside to calm my dad down.

I think from all the confidence I had been getting lately in judo I truly thought I could take my dad on, of course I couldn't but at least I felt within me that I could protect my mum as here I was doing just that but as I was outside talking to my dad reminding him that he still could be arrested for turning up to the house.

He was so drunk as well that I knew any sign of police would just mean the worst outcome, but what I wasn't expecting was that while I was speaking to him, my mum was on the phone not to the police but to Wim.

Wim was on his way around, when he arrived he went through the saloon door and appeared at the kitchen window, worse though telling my dad to get out of the yard.

Well that was it as this was my father's place and Wim wasn't the one ever to tell my dad to get off his own land so with that as Wim shut the kitchen door after yelling out that order to my father, my father didn't knock on the kitchen door but flung the whole door of its hinges and down came the door ended up on the kitchen floor as again for the second time in their lives another bare knuckle fight took place.

It was scary for my mum, she called the police, for me unlike the first fight between them which shook me, I actually now older watched this fight to see the two different styles of fighting to see the punches being laid and the others missing, it was as if I was watching a boxing match but one more suited for the Roy Shaw rather than my own father.

Soon the police were here and my address 88 Rotherham Tce Miramar must have been a red dot for the police as whenever they came they came in force and through what was where the door stood they flung themselves in, my Father cuffed and send in police car.

My father well he again was placed in the police cell for the night to sober up and hear what his actions had done and that was he wasn't allowed to see his kids for a while, this was unfair as he was only being a good father as in he was concerned about his 10 year old having a gun but my mum started to learn that if she got me whatever I wanted then I would behaviour more at school and more so at home as if I didn't get what I wanted then I would be a handful.

I would go as I learned the saying "going walkabout" which meant I wouldn't sulk in my room if I didn't get my own way or what I wanted as that is what other kids would do, well I would simply get a bus and fuck off up to the city where my mum would be worried sick as she didn't know where I was and who I was with as normally I would go and see the street kids at K Street and wander through town, get entry via a fire escape door into a movie theatre so we could watch movies for free.

I would hang out with the tough nuts who I would see at the video game parlours in the city where we're would burst open machines to get money and we would be at the bottle stores having students go in to buy us vodka and Jack Daniels and at that age we would be drinking everything neat from the bottle so all would end up so drunk and sick everywhere that the buses drives wouldn't ever let me on.

I would either have to jump a bus as we called in back then or if I was even too drunk to hang on to the back of a bus in the trolley basket at the back of the buses then I would work out the route home walking always taking the bus route by foot even though maybe it was the long way home but at that age I didn't know any better.

Many nights being picked up by the police and driven home, my mum being woke in the middle of the night by the police to drop me home. If she ever said anything negative then the following night I would be back out again and more I hanged around town more I hanged around the tough nuts they were soon forming a steady youth gang and they would be even worse than Wellingtons own street kids.

They would bring in the interest from some of the street gangs such as the Samoan gang called the peacemakers, maybe a silly name but these guys carried long knives and I mean not kitchen knives but knifes they would use out on farm lands in their own country but over here when they fought against the Maori gangs and the fights were on the streets in Wellington they would pull out the knives and chop at whoever was the other gang, in public.

These frighten fights would happen mainly on a Friday night in Manners Mall whatever gang would hang around to fight one another, the Satan's Slaves Motorcycle Club who commanded the most respect out of the gangs (they are a 1% motorcycle club not gang) would pull over and watch these gang fights go on and it would give them a idea who were becoming stronger on the streets out of the gangs and if any were ever a threat towards their own strong hold of gangs over Wellington.

I would steer at these guys on their Harley Davidson's and British bikes and go up and talk to them they would encourage me to get among it all and fight as well which I would though not against the peacemakers as these guys who just chop you in two so here I was now weekends day time would be sport but nights would be fighting and touring around the city drinking and partying as once we kids would hear of a party we would turn up 50 handed.

So if u had answered the door to 4 kids and told those 4 kids to go away well just around the corner was another 46 kids and we would rush in and in we would go to fuck the party up though if we were allowed to party, and that didn't happen often as u can imagine then we would behaviour ourselves but that didn't happen much.

We all were little tearaways and in all we would be following the older kids while many following me out of the new comers and soon I would bring the street kids and the tough nuts together so in total at one time during that year we must have excesses 100 kids in total, now that's like a little army and it caused a lot of problem for the police but for the gangs they loved it as it was picking pot for them as in which gang as you got older would you end up in.

The street kids mainly went black power and the pacific islanders who go with the peacemakers and other gangs that were born out of their own countries and other gangs would also be having a look in from the outside.

If the ban hadn't been on my father as in access being stopped on him seeing his kids then my connections again with the street kids and the youth gangs up town would not have been as great as I would have been spending usually my second weekends with him but as he wasn't allowed to see me then those weekends so after sport I was running amuck.

As for the other weekends well in the evenings my mum kept on wanting to spend time with Wim and normally at his house and me being there well I was only in the way so I preferred staying at home by myself which lead me to going up town and causing a muck.

My mum was too scared of losing Wim so she gave him as much of her time as possible as he was known to have had affairs that broke my mum's heart into at the time though I was too young to know about these affairs back then but looking back now is that karma as my mum had a affair with Wim and that's how my father's heart was broken and so when Wim had a string of affair over the years behind my mum's back was that jus karma biting her in the behind.

I didn't know the great fear my mum had in losing Wim but I do now realise that's why she would spend so much time with him rather than with us the kids as she knew she was never going to lose me or my sister but she feared she would lose the man of her dreams.

During this time everyone had forgotten about my father and again when he was barred from seeing us he took this very badly, it would cause him stress and also rows with his new girlfriend Irene.

Irene had family problems of her own as out of her own 7 kids she too had troubles with her youngest who was 15 years old and he found it hard to except his own father dying when he was a young age and I guess none of her kids did and they for sure wasn't going to except my father as replacement father, like I wasn't going to except Wim as my father.

So there were many issues going on there and Andrew, Irene youngest boy kept on finding himself in a lot of trouble back in Porirua so my father deicide to move from Seaturn the lovely place he had by the beach and get a bigger house so at least then he could have Irene kids stay over when they wished, he hadn't yet met all of them for some reason.

Irene didn't wish my farther to meet them until maybe she knew she had my father as in the way of a future for herself.

They were all grown up and many had young families of their own so the move to a bigger house meant that whenever they wanted to visit they could and they could stay over which made Irene happy so to start with my father met Irene three daughters and during that time it made my father miss his own daughter.

When Andrew would stay then my father would miss his own son so more drinking was taking place so to cover the pain of not having his children around and after the distress of the house move and hearing about me being brought home by the police drunk etc then with that on top and not knowing when he was going to see his kids away, and even more drinking.

My father collapsed in his house and was driven to hospital; he had had a brain h which is when a blood vessel in the brain breaks and bleeds something very serious and life threading.

He was close to death, we were at his bedside with Irene and also my Mum, as maybe my mum didn't love this man who was laying there near to death but she still remember that within him he did have a good heart and that's when on the way home from the hospital she would tell us stories about when they first met and at the Simpsons on the strand restaurant and about the Kray twins clubs though at that age the name The Krays didn't mean anything to me.

Over weeks my father seemed better a little anyway but then he had another one while he was in the hospital he had collapsed in the bathroom as he didn't like the nurses having to wash him etc.

He was too old fashion and far too stubborn for this and he didn't like others ever making a fuss over him so he thought he better wash himself one morning but the strain and the stress of getting out of bed and walking that distance to the shower room while still very poorly meant a second brain h he had while in the shower room.

The doctors said it was too close to call if he would live.

My father had to be in hospital longer than anyone thought and soon as he got some of his strength back, he demanded drink to be brought in thought the doctors back then in the mid 1980s told him he was never to drink again as high blood pressure caused by stress and drink was going to kill him, that's if his liver didn't pack up on him in a few years time and kill him.

He was told he wouldn't see 60 years old maybe not even 55 years old if he kept on drinking like he did as he was killing himself by drinking the way he did.

You never think by drinking heavily that really it will all one day catch up on you and you will end up in an early grave. You only have to look at the kids of today who drinking excess like many of us did in our early 20s but for those of us who kept on going and didn't stop past the Saturday nights of drinking and found themselves like my father did.

Drinking every night and then all of a sudden that drinking was just not all of the nights in a week but also all of the days in a week, well sooner or later it's going to catch up on you and when it does its by then for sure far too late as none of us in this life that we have been given can change back that clock though many of us stupidly believe we can.

How scary it is when we finally realize that we can't and we all are only given this one life to live, let's hope for some that there is something called reincarnation as for sure I do know of some souls that do need a second chance in life.

On a visit to my dad we went and saw Irene pouring my father a neat whiskey and my mum asked her what the hell was she thinking, and grabbed the drink from my dad before he could slip it, the women were at each other and this wasn't a fight I wished to see as that's my mum and she is too much of a lady to be fighting but she had every right to take the drink away from my dad and it showed she still cared.

Irene loved my dad, and it was my father who made Irene brings booze into the hospital for him to have a small drink.

My Mum she did still I am sure love my father in some ways though yes 100% she did of course care about him and the father of her two kids so to see him being handed booze well that's was just madness and my mum then looked at my father in disgusted and said "Stephen go head and kill yourself and as for you Irene you anit a good example to my children by having them watch u sneak booze into the hospital for their father when its bloody well booze that put him in her in the first place." and with that she left us to see out our visit with our dad.

Irene wasn't the only one who sneaked in booze for my father to drink; many of his friends who he worked with would as well.

As soon as my Mum had gone, he had a drink in his hand telling us not to worry everything would be ok and a wee little drink is nothing to worry about, we didn't know any better, we were just glad that our dad was sitting up in bed talking to us rather than laying there looking like he was on deaths door as he had looked the weeks previously.

Soon he was out and at his new place resting and Irene looked after him so well, getting him back to good health, she did love my father a lot and it made me happy to see my father happy again and in love though he wasn't one to ever show his emotions in public but we all knew he loved Irene.

My sister and I were able to visit him again and that where the very first time I got to meet Andrew Irene youngest son and his best mate George who had one eye, now if I thought that all the kids in my life I had meet earlier were mischief like well nothing compared to Andrew and his mate George.

These two 16 year old kids wouldn't just be drinking at their age but they would be getting up to some serious mischief and that to me brought on a close friendship with Andrew and his best mate George as these two were proper little villains at the time and that suited me fine as it meant days out with them two were always going to be fun.

We would be on the piss, vodka or whiskey anything we could get our hands on while we were out and drink, we would in the evenings when we weren't near Andrews Mum or my Father.

These guys were a head of their time when it came to mischief as in they would walk in places and out they would come with more money than I had ever seen before.

You got to remember there were no cameras on street corners back then and no mobiles so the only think the shop keeper had was a shop phone and more time than most George would come running out the shop with the phone in his hand and the shop keeper would be either knocked out by a single punch to the head from Andrew or if the shop keeper didn't come out of the shop then George more than once would have tied up the shop keeper with the cord from the phone.

All this time me and Andrew are standing out the shop thinking George had just gone in for a packet of smokes, neither of us knowing we were actually being part of a robbery without even knowing and a armed robbery as maybe

George didn't have a gun but George always carrier around a hammer and to the staff of shops he looked fucking scary.

George was a legend in his own right and with the strength of Andrew behind him then no one was going to fuck with George, even though he only had one eye he still got throw a punch that would knock the best of them out.

These two were proper Porirua boys, Andrew was a giant for his age and though both could turn to violence at the drop of a hat, Andrew had a big heart and he was a dam good friend of mine who would end up becoming a step brother to me.

They were always hooded up in those days as George with one eye was a bit of a giveaway when the police arrived on the scene and asked shop keepers who they should be looking for anyway what I wasn't aware of the first few times that I was the lookout man after George would do over bottle stores as soon as he appeared from any store he would just shout run so I always thought that he had just been caught shopping lifting and that's why we had to be on our toes.

We would be back either at my dad's place hiding the booze and the money or we would go in to the bush and hide and drink away till we all were drunk them we would go and get a feed and transport would always be taxis, till one evening between them they would hot wire a car.

Cars back in those days in New Zealand some were from the 1960s so they were easy to hot wire and off we would go all over the whole of Wellington, it was good times but if I had ever been caught in their company in a nick motor then hell shit would have hit the fan with either of my parents.

The mischief with them was low key compared to what the street kids now were getting up to as soon after nearly getting caught George stopped what we found to be his hold ups as in the end we all would have ended up being grabbed for that so that came to a end after a few times George getting away with it.

As for the street kids who I had known for a number of years, they all were getting older now and at the start of their times in gangs so any evening with the street kids now stared to get even more reckless.

Some nights if they had run out of booze themselves or if they had been told by gang members to get booze for their gang clubhouses say if there was a party being held and all the booze had been drunken as New Zealand wasn't a 24hr place unlike New York or London.

When they wanted more booze and this is years before the British did to gain goods mainly jewels and entry into banks etc well these street kids were only ever after booze and ciggs so they would ram raid the front window of a shop while it was closed in their stolen cars and in we would dart to get the booze.

I couldn't just stand there and watch these street kids do on their own as again I had to be accepted and if this was to follow what the older boys were doing then I did so, as I was young and stupid. The thrill of it all was so great and this is what adventures were like, for me but to the street kids well this was nothing new to them and it was very soft compared to what they were getting up to for their chosen gangs while I was around.

Sadly more than many lead this life as it was the only life they knew, they had no chances to better themselves, and if there were chances put in front of them, those chances all came from gangs who's only gain would see these street kids commit more crimes on their behalf's leading to jail sentence and sometimes death, be it suicide or gang related deaths or drug overdoses.

The street kids I knew back in those days, I bet not many of them are alive today as all they had going for them was the life of gangs after living a life on the streets and not many make it through though some probably did reach the status of becoming a fully patched gang member in one of New Zealand's many, many gangs.

I hope some got through it all and found an escape or are actual positive change to their lives, to better themselves as though they were street kids and a lot done many crimes.

Not all of them were bad kids and some were staunchly good to me and I was a working class kid more so white, and a kid who could have anything I wanted or asked for from my Mum.

These kids never judge me as any better than themselves and neither did so I was accepted into their tight circle as at the end of the day, it seemed any form of a gang always draw me near though not any old gang- it gave me a strong feeling of belonging.

My dad didn't know any of this was going on he would have had a heart attack if he had known, Irene didn't either but she knew her own son well enough so knew we were getting up to some form of mischief as to play tennis and soccer wasn't Andrews thing nor was it Georges.

I wondered what Irene's older boys were like as Andrew spoke of them with sometimes with a glow in his eyes as if he was taking of giants and sometimes Irene would speak about them with a huge smile and a smile would appear across Andrews face as not if they were saints but in a way only a brother can speak about another and he always went on about how staunch they were and ruthless, they couldn't be any more staunch than the black power members I had met that very first night I had been taken to K Street, oh how very wrong was I.

Chapter 9

THE MOB, A WEDDING AND THREE FUNERALS

I soon would find out the true meaning of staunch and that was through Irene's oldest sons who as would Andrew and their sisters become my step brothers and step sisters as what I didn't know was that the reason why Irene and my father were having a celebration drink those months back while he was in the hospital as because they had just gone in engaged to marry Irene but none of us kids on either side yet were told until the day I met her oldest sons.

As each one pulled up in roaring v8 Australia made fords and Holden cars I knew they weren't going to be bank managers nor real estate officers as far from it as the first one marched up the steep stairs to my father's house that he now had in a suburb a fair distance away from Miramar unlike the last place he had which was near to our family home anyway as I saw my father go out to greet Irene's oldest three boys, boys they were not as these were grown men.

I went to the front door and could hear deep voices a few hellos and then a voice asking where is Ma, and that's when the door swung open and there standing in front of me was a huge Maori Billy I got to say the scariest looking Maori I had ever seen and I had seen a few in my life but this guy was fucking naughty looking to say the least and that was just from the look on his face.

I could see he was wearing some patch, a gang patch then next another one came in, Patrick he looked no different than the first though twice the size and then came a third Lenny also gang patch and looking fucking mean, and when I mean fucking mean I mean that times one hundred as these three guys were the reason why there is a word in the English directory Staunch.

All three were senior members in the Mighty Mongrel Mob of New Zealand and one was one of the founding members.

These guys weren't just gang members they had gone on to form the biggest gang that has ever set foot in New Zealand, these guys are what since Ross Kemp has made a TV show on called Gangs and a book as well but that was all done in the mid 2000s, I was here in my dad's house a ten year old kid in 1985 and these guys were soon to become my step brothers and not people you read about in a book or is flash over the news on telly.

To anyone else in all of New Zealand you wouldn't wish ever to come cross Mongrel Mob in let alone your street and for sure not your house as in those days in the 1980s this gang brought fear to every household that wasn't connected to the life of the mob and though the press played on this a lot and made every gang member out to be scum, which wasn't the case.

There were some good folk among the mob and many were family men such as my now to become step brothers as at least all three of them knew what Family meant and though the Mob was their Family, their blood family came a equal first and so did now their extended family well me to start with as they still had issues with my father marrying their Mother but that was understandable.

Even with such differences they respected my father and that's all he wished from his wife to be kids and in no way was he going to try and be any type of father figure to them as he was far too old school for all that as he was there to look after their Mother to give her a good life and to make her happy, he wasn't going to be interfering in any of their lives or their way of lives.

Now I knew why Irene had never told my father up to this point that her sons were senior members in the mob as he wasn't one for gangs and as for the Mongrel Mob well they had such a bad name through every village, township and city in New Zealand.

No one liked the mob but the mob didn't give a fuck and as for the Maoris' who would embrace the black power gang as the black power gang were proud of their Maori roots and background well the mob were different as many couldn't give a fuck about their Maori back ground as their back ground for many of the mob is just that the mob and nothing more and nothing less.

The Mob let you know by how they carried themselves that they can be your worst living nightmare, which lead onto most of New Zealand hating them, the black power were there main enemy.

The Black Power are huge in numbers and in some towns liked by locals through what they give back to the young Maori communities but one thing that Black Power hardly do even in numbers is ever attack the Mob as no one really fucks with the Mob in New Zealand.

Black power they may be many though not many would clash with the mongrel mob of Porirua and more so as the Mob grew in greater numbers themselves from a small gang out of Petona and Porirua both near Wellington, to what they are today and that is to have become the biggest gang in all of

New Zealand and even to this very day they still very much are that and still growing in every township there is.

Over in the UK there is just nothing to compare them with as they are a gang that could only ever be found in the land of the long white cloud, it's scary to think that the beauty that is New Zealand has some very nasty naughty people lurking in the darkness.

To me though you know, I thought fucking hell as after coming across all the tough nuts I had already met in my life and the Miramar warriors, the peace makers, the youth gangs and other Wellington based gangs all look like pussy cats as I studied these three men as they sat in my father's lounge.

looking over me maybe they were thinking fucking white honky, as I just wouldn't keep my eyes off them and if my interest about gangs were soon disappearing well with the arrival of these three, then gangs again were about to become a even bigger part of my life and for the wrong reasons.

There is no right reason for my involvement in gangs but at that age it's hard to see that at the time though when you only that young and with all the previous involvement I already had, had in my life when it came to gangs.

Its only now at this age I can look back over my life and I am one person who can say it, that gang involvement on any level anit staunch for any youngest though at the time it may seem like so through the eyes of a youngest who is easy impressed but if you found yourself young and easily impressed by a gang then that means you going to end up easy mislead and that's like the most easiest way to throw away your life as you know it full stop.

If u anit born into a gang then you should just turn your back whenever you find yourself on the outside of a gang looking in as maybe it might seem full of some glamour and at times it very much is but once you are inside of that gang then it anit too great looking out as there is no way out for many.

If you were born into a gang then you can find yourself having no choice and you know no other life so that gang becomes much more than simply a gang but it becomes your family and at times your one and only family so you learn to embrace that gang for the right reasons and there are no hidden motives awaiting for you.

As for Billy, Patrick and Lennie my soon to be step brothers well the mob even though they all had a family of their own, the mob come first and foremost and that's what made these guys very well known leaders among the Mongrel

Mob up and down the country as everyone knew the Manuel brothers and no one fucked with them.

They had between them done enough jail time to also be feared in every prison up and down the country and I bet Andrew being their youngest brother felt the most protected kid in the land and that also then meant their mum who they worshipped was the most protected mum in the world.

If my father ever hit her, I wouldn't want to think what would have happened to him as I looked at him drink his pint while sitting with them, but my father also was staunch and he didn't need no gang patch to back that up, he was known as angry Steve as u get on the wrong side of my father and he would fight u bare fist to the death.

He may not have been too tall but he could throw a punch and take one as well but most of all he didn't fear a soul and even though these three in his lounge were over whelming to me they very much weren't to him, he had been on many a working ship in his day and had worked on the docks of the east end and also lived in the streets of the east end and had come from a land of giants and hard men , that being Scotland so nothing and no man did he ever feel fear of.

He offered them all a beer and they got catching up on who was who and this was a time for them to get to know each other, break the ice let's say and also the shook for my father as he didn't expect three mongrel mob members to walk on in the door but he had to except them as they were his wife to be sons and he as a father knew how much family meant as what he had gone through with the breakup of his own.

Though over time from this first meeting even however hard he tried the thing was they were never going to truly excepted my father into their mothers life and there would be many rows that would go on at times when they came to the house whatever time of the night and day.

I don't think some of them meant to cause rows, I think with some of them they were just testing the water as at the end of the day Irene was their Mother and their only parent after losing their father so she meant even more to them than any other time in their lives and she was their Grandmother to their kids so they needed her very much as a leading mother figure as much as my father wished to have her as his wife to be.

My father put up with it for the time being as he had to look after his failing health and also he had a wedding to arrange and pay for , and with my father he never did things half he would always go full out and do everyone proud.

My friendship with Andrew grew and now I knew how and where he and George had learned all the tricks of the trade from but in hanging around with these two it meant the positive steps I had made previous were now fading as when I wasn't in their company I still would be getting up to mischief with other groups within Wellington as mischief seemed to give me a buzz, in a way playing sport did.

Though mixing in with other groups, be it youth gangs I still found myself always the youngest by many a years and so I was time after time always tested to how far I would go as into proving myself, constantly being challenged.

Also every time I went out to Porirua with Irene to visit her sons and family I was even getting more of a taste for a life in gangs as here I was in their manor a city that was at the time more controlled on the streets and in the neighbourhoods by the mob than the local police force.

When the wedding date had been fixed and it had been come more real to her older boys that their mum was too remarry then they wouldn't visit as often at my father place as they didn't wish to accept it.

At that age as a young kid I guessed they felt he was taking their mum away from them though they were older but due to them losing their father now in some way they thought they were losing their mum as well so my contact with them would be in their own manor on their patch of tuff and out there Irene was so respected by everyone.

She had for many a year's worked in the justice system trying to help the young kids out who kept on reappearing in the youth courts so among all the Maoris she was very much loved and respected but as for her sons who run Porirua single handed with the mob.

They weren't as liked but more so feared as you could see the fear that run through the town whenever you were out with them on the streets as no one dared even look at them in the eye so they had the place very well sewn up to how that gang would run towns and cities and that's from a street level with fear and then respect among their own.

My father knew when he wasn't welcomed so hardly ever went out to Porirua, as if they didn't like him then he had tried his best and couldn't give a fuck as all he was doing was trying to give their mum a better life.

They didn't see it like that though Irene's daughters still would come and stay some weekends but as the brothers had their voices always heard then Irene would spend more time out in Porirua with them all.

The bigger house that my dad had been rented now seemed more empty weekends as I didn't see much of Andrew or George hanging around either.

I felt for my dad during this time as here he was being so kind with a open door and always looking after everyone cooking them great feeds whenever anyone was hungry and always sharing his beers as he had himself had accepted all of Irene kids, be some gang members he didn't care as over time he had got to know them not as mobsters but as who they were as people and knew they all were good people.

All he wanted to do was look after Irene as she meant the world to him.

He soon moved house and got a smaller place one though which was in the middle of town on a hill that's street sloped down to downtown right near Courtney Place.

This was exciting to me as the city that I had once many years back always dreamed of and that at night I used to jump on the back of the buses to get to and explore now were just there outside my father's front door.

Good times they were but still very naughty times as I could wonder into town meet up with the gangs and cause ciaos then just walk back home which was mins away if ever the heat got too much and we found ourselves being chased by the police.

Only streets away from my dad's place were lots of hotels that I found out the street kids would go in packs of four and break into rooms and take everything.

And I mean everything from the mattress of beds to blankets and coffee mugs everything from the room and they would sell it to the black power as they would put everything into their clubhouse or they would do up k Street for the other street kids so they had new sheets and blankets and mugs and boiling kettles.

Well me, I wouldn't break into any of the hotel rooms as such but I would nick the booze trolley from the maid serve when they used to load up the mini bars in the rooms.

We would just come along and take it and out a fire exit across the car park of the hotel we would go with the trolley and all the booze and sell the mine bottles of booze down at the game parlours to all the kids. Soon we would have everyone in the place drunk and we wouldn't tell anyone where we were getting all this gear. After we had hit a hotel so many times, we would just go to another.

This was better for me as no one was being hurt and I weren't robbery someone's personal belongings, that type of crime I didn't like ever but to a rich hotel well, it didn't seem as personal and it was so easy as again in those days security wasn't like it is now where there are security guards and cctv on each floor and the keys are plastic cards.

There was nothing state of the art about these hotels and everything was fair game soon we would be stealing of the back of the Lorries that would turn up with the goods such as cuts of meat that we could easy get rid of.

When we had some of the stronger boys with us then they would even take the TVs out of the hotel rooms and carry them as long as they could because we would only have to walk in to gang related pub and that TV or side of lamb would be sold within seconds and we would be in the money.

As I told Andrew and George about this one weekend they came to stay at my dad's new place then they too would join us but when seeing that the gear was going mainly to the black power gang then both put me right about the rivalry between these two gangs as I didn't know at the time that the two gangs hated one another nor that black power were the enemy of the mongrel mob.

Andrew though not part of the mob himself like his brothers were, his loyalty was to the mob so from that point onwards I stopped having any contact with the street kids and didn't ever go back to K Street which was run by the black power gang. It meant being at home with my father at his place rather than hanging around with the street kids.

Though I did miss them, I guess in away Andrews warning to me, kept me out of trouble so now my weekends at my fathers were spend in pubs while he drunk with his mates from the boats or the docks. Boring as it was hours on end drinking coke a cola and eating bags of crisps listening to grown men talk about life, football and women oh and World War 2 and those Germans would always pop up in conversations as they all were British.

Now and then I would hear the surnames Nashes, Krays, Richardson's and Foreman's come up in conversations but again I was too young to know they were speaking about the strongest Gangland names in British History. I was missing out on all the stuff the kids were getting up to with the hotels and other things that they all had going on so no longer was I earning a bit of quid on the side and causing no mischief at all.

Soon my father's wedding day was to come, in the mean time I had been come friendly with all Irene's family and they liked me though the mobsters couldn't believe I was selling stolen gear from hotels to the black power and asked me to put a strong word in with the kids who were doing it.

I did by which they were told not to ever sell anything to the black power, I am unsure if they listened as these kids were after only one thing and that was the dollar so any loyalty on their behalf would come a second behind making themselves some instant cash.

I didn't fancy as a kid getting caught up in serious gang warfare as these gangs on sight of one another would murder each other and without a flick of a eye lid they would and they still do to this day so with me bringing in the mob to the youth gangs then that dived it all as some stayed true to the black power as the streets kids did, and some of tough nuts went to the direction of the mob in Wellington.

As for the Miramar warriors they were now of an age they were only keen on motorcycles so they headed towards the older boys who had links with the Satan's Slaves Motorcycle Club who ruled Wellington with an iron fist.

There I was soon to have step brothers in the mongrel mob, knowing the black power from an early age due to the Miramar warriors scoring dope from them and also my connection to K Street and the street kids and in time I would myself have a involvement with the Satan's Slaves Motorcycle Club as around this time my sister's boyfriend Stephen Rowe started to prospect for the Satan's Slaves Motorcycle Club.

The Miramar warriors out grow me and moving on to motorcycles plus I wasn't never again the favour of the month with them after tipping over their bikes outside the fish shop so here I was a young kid who had always been involved in gangs.

Not purposely but had found myself involved with one or two but here I was involved, connected to so many and to stay enjoying a free life as in mischief and being excepted by the older boys and the gangs, where was my life going to take me further down the paths with the gangs and if so with which one.

My father's wedding would make that decision for me due to the carryon of so certain people but first I had to be there for my mum as news had reached us that her brother peter was dying.

Peter was so young only in his 40years, his son Peter Jrn had just made the Hawke's Bay rugby team to play against the British lions who were touring, and word was that Peter Davis Jrn was about to become a All Black, after he done so well against the Lions they ended up beating the Lions. My cousin Peter Davis played such a great game, he done the whole family on my Mums side so proud, and everyone in Hawke's Bay.

Sadly my wonderful uncle died and Peter Jrn now he being the head of his family had to look after his mum who had lost her whole world in her husband, the whole family took it so badly and it was the first time I had been around death.

I had not know death before, only from losing a cat but this was personal in a family member and though my cat was like a member of the family, this was my dear uncle Peter who I had so many great memories of and so much love and he was a great uncle and a great dad to his kids, a great brother to my mum and his other brothers and a great son to his mum my nana.

I had never seen a church used for a funeral, as I had only been in a church for Sunday school for that time I was at that boot camp and I had gone in to the chapel for pray but her now as a 10 year old child I was discovering sorrow, grief, a and heartbreak in so many faces all family related and due to one of my family dying to that horrible thing called C, I don't even like spelling the word.

It took him so young and when he was doing so well in life and had a amazing family, it's such a shame and I can remember asking so many questions as a child does as to where has my uncle now gone and why etc, staying at his place in Dannvillvie was never ever the same again and he was very much missed for ever more.

I thought that type of sadness would only happened once during my younger years but it seemed ever since I first learned about death through my uncles funeral then I noticed it all around me as on visiting one of my mum's friends she was half Maori and half pacific islander.

She had about 3 sisters all were close to my mum and all were funny ladies, well one day while we sat at table chatting to this lady friend of my mums, all of a sudden she leaned forwarded and while looking into my eyes, I could see in hers I am sure also a coffin being carried.

I know it sounds unreal and a bit dark but it's something I remember clearing seeing and I wasn't high or anything we were all having a cup of coffee and I liked this lady a lot and she was always very kind hearted to me but that day when I saw this imagine in her eyes I moved back a little as she landed forward then next min she laid her head on the coffee table and was cuffing a lot.

My mum called for a ambulance, on leaving hospital the rest of the ladies life was spend in her bedroom in bed as she now was on her death bed, she too had C and like my uncle didn't know until it was far too late, but with her she really didn't have long to live.

When the doctors told her months, how very wrong they were as each day we would go back and visit her. She seemed to even become more and more ill, she was fighting hard and she was suffering a lot in pain. She didn't wish to return to hospital so it was there in her bedroom that she died and she died while we were in the room, my mum was holding her hand as she slipped away.

I will never forget the moment she died and how I am sure I felt her still in the room with us all but this time not in the pain that she had earlier been in, I had experienced death now first hand and for a second time I was to attend a funeral, this time knowing due to my uncles funeral what a funeral was but this time something that I had seen in her eyes only a month earlier when she had fallen ill at the coffee table.

As there at the end of the church as we walked in to the packed church was the coffin, the very same coffin that I had seen in the ladies eyes.

As the church service went on, I faded into my thoughts back to that day as what I had seen in this ladies eye as I remembered back to the details and then looked over again at the coffin sitting there studding it even more to make sure that it was what I had seen in her eyes.

Even to this very day, I can say it very much was that. Whatever I saw, was it the face of death and why had I seen this imagine that soon weeks later would appear at her own funeral.

I was too young to understand and even now I don't understand but it was something that I thought was common between people to show a sign that they soon would be dying or for them as if this lady herself knew that she soon would be in a coffin as her own life was too come to an end.

It was something I didn't think much of as I was only discovering death for the first time in my life with these two funerals but there was even going to be more but the third brought such sadness to our house. It broke my sisters heart as the third was her best friend and unlike my uncle, who my sister loved very much so as we all did.

Well unlike an uncle, a best friend you see every day (be it at that age of only 15) each and every day and during school then after school as well.

Angie Berg was her name and she was more than my sister's best friend, she was like a sister to my sister. They would do everything together. Angie's parents had broken up, her mum was lovely and her father was cool, his name was Ian and he was like a cool cat mirrors imagine of Bob Dylan in his style of clothes and his lifestyle.

Ian was a hippy and as free as a bird, he had a cool British motorcycle and a sunken beach house that was two stories high and had a jungle at the back and the front with an outhouse as well; he lived for his two daughters Angie and Mel.

Angie was my sister's age they had gone to school together and still was at school together, Mel was my age same birthday and same year, and she was so pretty that when we were young she was my girl.

Me and Stacey would go up the coast to Angie's house where her dad lived as he would play the guitar and my sister and Angie would get high, while me and Mel would roam the beaches for beach shells and play with her friends and also the friends from neighbouring houses it all was so laid back and just so cool, no hassle as in with the city and everyone was just a chilled out souls. Then on Sunday nights we would all get the train back to Wellington and Chrissie, Angie and Mel's mum would pick us up as she lived near our street back in Miramar.

My sister and Angie loved David Bowie and boys and going to parties, both had boyfriends and both would be smoking pot behind my mum's back and their social group was a fair few girls, from Joana to Emma and so many more from in and around Wellington.

They had such a cool social life that I would always be envy of as they seemed so grown up and my mum would let them do what they wished, it was only me my mum tried to keep on the straight and narrow, probably because my sister wasn't really getting up to much trouble she and Angie and the rest of the girls were just being young teenage girls, living their lives like no different to other girls their age.

They were as I said so much like sisters in so many ways and though I could be a brat of a younger brother towards many of my sister's friends at that age I was, but with Angie I never was as she was special and she was so full of life and always smiling whenever I saw her.

I can't remember the last time I saw her but I do remember the very day my sister came home from school and my mum's saloon and our family friend Helen Scully had something to tell my sister, she told my mum first who couldn't take the news in and was too upset to tell my sister so Helen came in to the lounge and while I was there with my sister she told her that Angie's body had been found.

The night before on a stormy night, Angie had had a terrible row with her mum and run out of the house to make the long journey to her father's which was on the Kapati coast hrs by car out of Wellington much further than even Porirua though heading up that same direction on West Coast of New Zealand.

Angie got the bus to the main Wellington railway station she phoned her dad Ian to let him know that she was on her way then she bored what was the last train but for some reason this train stopped short of arriving her stop where her dad was waiting to collect her from the railway station.

She had rung the house to let her dad know that she had got off three stops earlier as that where for whatever reason on this night that the train stopped but that call was unanswered as her dad had already left the house to go and collect her the station the train was meant to have finished the journey on.

As her dad didn't answer the phone and it was a very stormy night, very cold and rainy with howling winds then Angie didn't wait at the phone box to recall her dad, she decided to take the walk to the direction of where her father lived which was miles away.

Such a long walk but she still did in the winds and the rain, maybe she just wanted to get home after such blazing row with her mum, maybe she was feeling the cold so the only ways to warm up would be to march on home.

The journey the last leg home she took, she decided to follow the motor way so from being at the railway and walking the streets she decided to get up on the motorway and found the traffic signs towards her father's town but she never made it.

While her father waited and waited for the train to come in and it never did, he then checked with his ex wife if Angie had returned back home but she hadn't returned back to her mums.

He then called the train company and they informed him that the train for whatever reason had stopped short then he drove to the last stop where the train had been and asked around the very few people who were there but time had since pasted when that train had came in and Angie had got off the train to do her walk home.

He then checked up and down roads but still no sigh of his daughter so in thinking maybe she had got a taxi home he knew she had her own key so he drove home calling out his daughters name as he entered the dark house turning on the light seeing that nothing had changed.

He went down to her bedroom hoping she was already in bed fast asleep but the room was still the very same since she had last slept in her bedroom.

He then called Chrissie one more time and both then called around all the friend's house that night including ours as I remember the phone ringing in the middle of the night as both parents were checking to see if maybe Angie had simply gone to a friend's house but still there was no joy.

Then of course even more panic settled in and such great worry as soon they had to make the decisions to call the police as Angie was now a missing person.

My sister went to school as normal the next day but with something missing, and that was her very best friend, her best friend that they would grow old together be at each other own child birth and each other's weddings and there for each other through thick and thin but this wasn't to be as that day my sister came home, it was Helen who had to break the such sad news that Angie, my sisters best friend had been found death by the side of the road of the West Coast motorway.

It was too much for my sister to take; she destroyed the lounge breaking what was above the fire place where the heater sat. She broken down in tears as did everyone that day in our lounge and in many lounges throughout Wellington as Angie was so very much loved and my sister best friend was taken from her on a cruel windy stormy night.

No one to this day knows what happened to Angie no one knows why she didn't stay at that phone box as she would have finally been found by her father or on his return back to his place she would have called again and he would have been back to answer that call.

No one knows who killed Angie, though they did say she wasn't sexual assaulted and the cause of death was a hit and run, but whoever was driving that car that night when on hitting Angie never stopped to check on her and this was what haunted every one since as how could someone hit a person on a car and then leave them to die, how could they not think that they themselves still could save this person and be the hero rather than the villain.

For whatever reasons and there are no reasons even if you are over the limit drunk behind the wheel of the car and you hit someone on the road it's got to be in you as a human being to stop the car and make sure you can save that person's life as when it comes to court then you would have been seen to do that one single act but on that night who ever and how ever they hit or run Angie over.

They didn't stopped and kept on driving and that was what made this experience of death so much worse than the others as to watch all the grief that Angie best friend my sister go through and to see Ian and Chrissie both for wrong reason feeling guilty due to all the what ifs.

Mel lose her sister that she loved and looked up to so much, and then to see the turn out to the third funeral that I had been a part of with three different people all different ages, all differently connected to me.

I had now come to learn that life is short and with life comes death for us all whatever the age and this would be something that would repeat its self many times, the face of death throughout my life after these three funerals.

A wedding soon was taking place, many months later and there we all were dressed smartly at the head of the table, I was there with my sister who had been dating a guy who would become a member of the Satan's Slaves motorcycle Club, and at the table was the bride and groom, Irene and my Dad in this lavishly spend wedding.

It looked like something out of Goodfellas movie though with lots of Irish men and Scots and English and people from Wales, no that's not the start of some joke as there were Maoris' and pacific islanders, a mixture bag of all sorts among us all to attend my father's second marriage.

My Father had claimed down a lot and though prior he would raise his voice at Irene only once or twice, he wouldn't go for her, they had arguments like everyone else did in relationships. He wasn't the same violent man that he had been towards my mum plus his health due to stress and booze wasn't the best but he was still as fit a fiddle and he loved his wedding, all Irene family were there as well to celebrate.

I was sitting next to Andrew and my sister and her boyfriend Stephen Rowe and there was so much free booze going around and Maori performing groups and also Scottish highlands band. They had the best of both worlds and there was even some underworld faces among the men that had flown in to attend it. It was held in Wellington's biggest hall at the time.

You can imagine how many guests in total there were, but there were three men missing on Irene side out of family and they were her oldest boys as they had not excepted this wedding and they wish to take no part so no one was excepting them though it was breaking their mums heart that they weren't there from the start and it also was disrespectful to my father as even though they were leading gang members of the most ruthless gang in all of New Zealand.

He still excepted them as his step sons and as part of the family as he wasn't embarrassed by them, as they had done me no wrong apart from show a lack of respect and he wanted this day to be the happiest of his new wife's life and for all of them to see how happy their mum was and how happy everyone could be, that wasn't much to ask but what took place next was uncaused for.

As in came not just one of the sons and not just the three of them, as that was what everyone was waiting for from Irene's side but in came following them a whole chapter of the mongrel mob, Porirua chapter and at least 60 gang members walked on in to my dad's wedding.

All the Scots and all the Irish and all the English and all the welsh stood up as if it was going to go off as these men would back my father through and through as maybe the mob had turned up mob handed but they had turned up to the wrong wedding to cause trouble as my father's friend older and wiser in age, some had lived through the troubles of Northern Ireland so nothing scared them and some had fought alongside the Krays so nothing frighten them.

Some had fought in world war two so nothing frighten them and I think out of the mongrel mob who had turned up to cause trouble then they knew if they started it they very much would have to end it and there would be murders there on that dance floor.

As my father went and approached them asking what the fuck were they all doing here and that only of the sons could stay and a few of their close mates and other senior members but as for the others he stood his ground and told them to all fuck off and when Irene said her piece.

A few of the Maori guests then the rest of the mob did leave to be confronted outside by the Wellington police who had never seen a whole chapter move from out of their clubhouse and come to this part of Wellington.

The police in Porirua had thought they were actually on their way to over throw the black power gang in Wellington as it looked like for sure a gang warfare was soon going to take place rather than them actually only going to a wedding of one of their leaders mothers.

Not sure what would have happened if all had stayed as I am sure it would have gone Pete tong anyway the ones who did stay all got really drunk and the ones who left only stayed out the front of the hall so the gang members inside were sending out drinking to the many outside.

In the end it mean all the booze soon run dry but this time we had all been in there since the day time and these late arrivals didn't show up till around 2am so the wedding by then was all over and my dad and his new wife had had enough.

Thinking I was going home with my sister and her boyfriend my dad left but before he did he said to his new son in laws "I am not her to replace your father, I am her to give your mum a better life and I will make sure I do that, with u or without u all, so be supportive or destructive as it will only mean one thing and then u will lose your mum." with that he left.

I know for a fact that Irene's oldest sons hadn't turned up to cause trouble and they were respected when they all had a talk with my father. As for turning up with the chapter well that to them were their family as in brothers in arms and many of those mob members not knowing my father well the loose cannons out them didn't really give a fuck, they were the ones who were waiting outside, they just saw it as a excuse to get out on a Saturday night and do what they do best and that is be mobsters.

And there I was surrounded by 60 mongrel mob members and Andrew their youngest brother soon Andrew told me that they all were heading back to my father's house so I thought my father was there to let them all in but he had checked into the honey moon suite as the most expensive hotel in Wellington.

I didn't know that soon turning the corner of my dad's road and walking up the hill I wasn't happy to see what was going on and I thought to myself there is no way my father would be letting this happen at his house so I thought maybe he had been hurt or attacked by gang members as I run up the hill with Andrew but as I entered the house my father wasn't there.

Nor were Irene or my three older brothers who I hoped were but they had left to back out to Porirua with the chapter that were meant to follow them out though many of the loose cannons mobsters never did take to their cars to follow my step brothers instead with all the booze they had from my Dads wedding they decided to have a party in my dad's house.

All partying and many smashing my father's house, being animals but they knew no better and at the time many were so drunk and high that they were too fucked to know or maybe care.

I know if my older step brothers had been there then none of this would have carried on.

The younger ones just trying to show off to the older members though their behaviour was to them was sound as all they were worried is that none of the gang member take the booze taken from my dad wedding to their clubhouse as they wanted it all here at my father's house.

They had a party to get rocking and if my dad had returned well then they were going to show him how it would be from now on and who would be boss and how if they ever wanted to rock up to my father's house firm handed as they had done then that's how thing were going to be.

I sat there and looked around and saw many mobsters who were being disrespectful in my fathers and Irene's house but then thankfully I saw my step brothers who had returned after realising that many of the other mobsters hadn't followed them back out of town. They came back to get everyone and when they saw some of the younger ones being disrespectful to not only my father's house but also to their mums house well they went mad.

A few beatings were dished out by them to one or two of the scumbags, who were causing trouble and to a few among them who had tried to bully me.

Andrew had done his best to try and protect me from some of the wankers who were trying to bully me but once my older step brothers rocked up again they were saying "Don't touch him he's our brother!"

I looked up to Billy and Lennie and Patrick in that moment and thought they were speaking about Andrew their blood brother but they were speaking about me, their step brother and in that moment I saw that they had good hearts.

They were still just horrible hurt over the loss of their father and what they knew now would be the loss of their mum as there had been talk of my father taking Irene to live in Scotland for them to start a new life together, but unlike their father was lost to death, their mum would only be lost to my father but still for these grown men that was maybe too much to take in.

For the very first time I had now felt totally excepted by my step brothers, though different in so many ways, they on that very night stood up for me and in doing so let me know that for the rest of my life they always would be there for as brothers and in that moment it meant a hell of a lot to me.

I stood outside my father's house and noticed loads of police cars were parked across the road but the police far too scared to go near my father's house while it was full of 60 mongrel mob but slowly many of them started to leave on the orders not of the police but of my step brothers.

Soon the house was empty of all gang members and left behind were some family friends of Irene's who with Andrew and I cleaned up the mess that had been made and all was back to normal by the time the sun rose the following morning.

This entire unknown at the time to my father and his new wife but when he finally did come home and heard what had happen. Massive changes were soon to take part and because of what had happened that night, it now meant yes they would be making Scotland their new home but at the same time because of what had happen I would lose my father through the actions of some loose cannon mobsters.

That change was too much for me to take on board at such a young age as I really needed a father in my life as all young kids do.

Be if the family unit is broken or not, as what son doesn't need his father.

Chapter 10

HOME AND AWAY

The house on arriving back for my father and his new wife could have looked like it had been turned upside down and then shaken all about if I with the help of Andrew and Irene's family friends hadn't cleaned all the mess up.

I know how upset Irene would have been and also how angry my father would have been if the house hadn't been cleaned up after the mess that was left from the partying in their home from the night before as before we started the clean it did look like it had been somewhat thrashed.

Thank God they all had gone as even though my father couldn't have taken on the gang, he for sure would have taken some of them down and they would fallen by his angry as what he could have come back to.

Heads I am sure would have rolled and fists at some stage would have been exchanged.

What he did notice on returning back with his new wife was many of his personal belongings had been taken. I am sure if my step brothers had known this at the time then they would have very much acted on my father's behalf.

They wouldn't have put up with that and it was disrespect of the highest level that some shitbags who had been in my father's house had actually stolen stuff but at this stage the following day who could you blame as everyone who had been inside the house from the night before had all gone off course.

Only 48hours after they had just got married my father was just full of utter angry. It really wasn't a good start to any new life and a better life that he had promised his new wife but this was not his fault and he was going to stand his ground as one thing that he didn't like was disrespect like any man who was from the old school as respect is key to everything, how a man should conduct themselves.

My Father went on to the ferry as he had a 8 day shift to do, I think it gave him time to clear his head and also he had just paid out a serious amount of money for a great wedding that did take place but until it was wreaked by unwelcomed guests and also what went on in the aftermath back at his house.

I went and joined my father that following weekend and by then he was in higher spirits as some of his work mates who couldn't make the wedding were making dam sure that they were throwing a party on board of the ship for my dad so he was drunk and happy drunk and all the British songs were being sung among all the merry men.

That night he spoke to me for the first time as an adult and said that he felt the only way to make his new wife happiness come true was to maybe think about taking her to Scotland for truly a new life and one without stress and worry.

As many years earlier he just wanted the best for his first wife my mum and make her ever so happy and give her everything she wanted which he did but her affair and love for another man wreak all of that so here was my father in a position to do it all over again but this time to get it right.

As we sailed back into Wellington harbour and what a beautiful harbour it is indeed then I thought about my father's health and all the sorrow and heart ark that he had been in over the last many years, was it my place to stop him as I guess he was asking me in some way of my approval and how I would feel if he made the move back to Scotland.

A place he hadn't been for many years and a place that was home sweet home, where his own mum was and his step dad and also his sister and her family was, but the love for his own two kids was what truly was stopping him from making this decision.

I told my mum about the conversation I had with my dad and I think the first thing she thought was I going to decide to go as well. Even though she didn't say anything I really felt that was what she was thinking, by the way she was asking me questions.

My primary school days were soon up as from the next year I would be going to intermediate school but where that still wasn't decided. At school I finally had been doing really well back in my own class.

Some subjects I was getting good grades on, it seemed a lot of the other kids had given up at the last hurled but I was taking my exams very seriously and also my sport had managed to pick up more.

My lifestyle outside of school was very still unbalanced and I was still hanging around with the wrong crowds and getting up to mischief and into trouble with the police.

Something I was always picked up on the street either due to getting into brawls or just general no good, that was put on due to peer pressure at that age where other kids would bait me on. The hotel scams had been caught on, it was the only way we could afford to get loads of booze for the weekends of partying.

It had been two weeks since I last saw my father as I headed over to his house. I could hear his voice down the street where my mum dropped me off as she stopped dropping me of near my father's house due to the problems she had with my dad in the past.

I went to the house and he was screaming at Irene and she was giving it back as well then he turned around and I saw a black eye on his left eye and I asked what had happened but he wouldn't say as he told me to leave my overnight bag and that we were on the way out as he slammed the door behind him.

We went to one of his regular pubs, he had many pubs that he would drink at and that it was as if he owned the pubs that he drunk in. He never had to put money behind the bar only when he was buying other drinks and he would do that often as he was very generous but as for himself he wouldn't need to buy himself ever a drink as every pub would pour and serve him as much beer as he wanted so hell did he always get drunk and that night like no other was the same.

All the years as a youngest I spend waiting in pubs, if I could save the time then in that time I now could have walked to the moon and back as not one day when I was with my father would I not be in a pub.

Even when we would go fishing we would either start at a pub or end up at a pub and when I would visit him at his places after he had moved out of the family house, then again we would be in a pub each day and night when he wasn't working and even then on the ships he would be sinking the beers back.

Boredom never really got to me but I know it did for my sister as with me I had pool tables or dart boards to play and stories of the English football teams to hear about be it West Ham Utd or Liverpool F.C or Chelsea etc so I was always taken in by the talk of football by all these mates of my father. Some had had been to Wembley themselves over the years and watched firsthand the F.A Cup being lifted by their teams.

They would talk about the great snooker players and the dart players of that era who would take their shots at board with a beer in the other hand. On this Saturday my father's speech was again about moving back to the U.K and he was telling his mates what they thought about his possible move back to the U.K.

He later on that night let me know that the black eye was from one of Irene's son who had turned up to the house and so wanted somewhere to crash the night so came to his mums place and when my father opened the door he stood his ground and told one of my step brothers that he wouldn't be staying under his roof so to fuck off and find shelter under a fucking nearby tree in a park.

Well with those words that's when fists when flying and though my father I was told stood toe to toe with him, the younger man soon win due to strength and youth, quickness and madness I guess ended up winning that fight so the end result meant my father ended up with a black eye and a broken few ribs and Irene had her son blankets and pillows for her son to sleep on the settee.

Well that was the final nail in the coffin as if his own wife wasn't going to stand by his side as in the decisions he made then he knew he had a losing battle and more so even a bigger battle on his hands as if one of the sons was happy to strike my father and if his own wife wasn't going to back him though my father was out of hand by what he said to his son in law but in saying that punches shouldn't have been thrown either way.

My Father was to give his new wife a huge decision that she would have to give an answer to by the end of the year which was very soon as he wasn't going to be spending the next Christmas in New Zealand where sadly fists could have flown again in the heat of any further more drunken rows as he didn't wish for anyone's Christmas to be wreaked. He though how lovely it would to finally again spend a Xmas with his family in Scotland whom he knew would welcome Irene with open arms as the Scots very much do to all new comers.

November was upon us and my sister's birthday. She had thrown a party back at our place but I found my sister crying in her room. She went to speak to me but before even spoke a word I just knew what the tears falling from her face were due to and that was because Angie her best friend wasn't there to celebrate that very special birthday with her.

My sister would never give up the ghost of Angie and her death would always stay with her forever more, it was so sad to see and I was hoping that the birthday my father had planned would cheer her up a little which was the following evening.

We went to my father's house and then off to a restaurant a very plush restaurant in a high raise building right in the city of Wellington. My father this evening was even drunker than normal something my sister didn't like seeing at all and he only got worse, soon falling of his chair and also saying to the restaurant manager that the food wasn't cooked correctly and demanded in front of everyone to see the chef.

He would do this many times it was embarrassing to say the least but what topped the night off was that he took underneath the bottom stairway by reception brand new carpet rolls, that was looking like it was headed for this new restaurant as maybe the carpet hadn't been fitted in time for their grand opening.

Well all that carpet that was rolled up still in plastic sheet wasn't ever going to end up on the restaurant floor as my father ordered a people carrier taxi and roll after roll went in the motor back with us to his house. Why I wasn't sure but my father was chuffed though it kind of wreaked my sister's 15th birthday celebrations.

His level of drunkenness was not due in any way of trying to wreak my sister's birthday but it was due to him making the decision and also Irene as well that for a better life and for her happiness that they would move to Scotland and I think this brought on great sadness to him that he was leaving us behind also for Irene with her great big family, it truly wasn't a easy decision for her either.

Irene would be leaving behind her family but most had families of their own and all had houses. What Irene was going to miss the most, was her grandchildren but she knew one day she would return and she had a new family that she hadn't met that would take her in and also a great life was waiting for.

My father that night just couldn't bring himself in telling us as he knew as we were young that we would miss him so much and as for me to have my father not even in my family house but not to have even my father nearby it was a cruel blow to take but I had grown into a young man by then so another emotional knock I could take. Yes I know I was still only ten years old but I was unlike any ten year old anyway at least I still had my mum near and so I wasn't going to be all alone was I.

For my father to move to Scotland then the family house had to be sold as thankfully my mum was kind in divorce and didn't take my father for every penny he had like most women do in a relationship break up.

I would know that for myself when I was older ....hello to a certain person.

So with the house on the market, my mum's live as well was to move on, had she now given up the heartbeat that she had in her saloon? She had it for now 10 years, was there anything more she could do with it, as she had built it to such a success and I know the ladies would miss her and what she had brought to Miramar.

Xmas was soon and at least my father had a early xmas with us the kids and that meant we could enjoy two Christmas and also my mum threw a xmas party at her saloon which brought a person whom I wished to not ever see as there with his wife was the monster.

The man who had been for so many years causing me terror by tapping at my window at night and creeping me out when ever his wife was getting her cut. Always looking at me in a pevery way. That night I didn't hang about and so wanted to tell my mum again about him but as in the past I guessed I would never have been believed that is till after xmas past and a few days after my following birthday.

Though before even my birthday came two things were going to happen and one was that my father was true to his word to his new wife as they stepped on the plane and waved goodbye to New Zealand.

It was a very sad moment for all concerned and all I now had to fall asleep with is dreams repeating dreams that I would be one day seeing my father again and that would be in Scotland. It's the only thing that some nights would stop me crying those following nights after he had got on that plane. Though my father could be the devil, he still was my father and a very loving caring father who was so missed by my sister and me.

I missed my Father dearly the moment I watched that plane fly into the sky and I to this day wish he had never left but in doing so he did keep that promise to his new wife as happiness is what he very much provided for her and also she did for him as they very much did love one another, everyone could see that including us kids on both sides of the families.

The sale of the house soon came through and the salon as well and school was finished but where I was heading after looking at some local schools where all my school friends had gone onto but due to my good school reports and the promise that seemed to shine in them and the praises I was given by those same teachers, who for years I would fight and challenge and now were saying to my mum on her very last teacher and parent night, that she should look to better higher education for me.

Now that is what I was told but was it all the truth as I was being driven out of Wellington over a mountain range and to the Wairarapa to a town called Masterton which was hours and I mean hours away from Wellington with a massive fucking mountain range between the two.

The car, my mum's pulled into these school grounds and in the car park near the tennis court was the type of cars that you would only see in a movie as they were flash sports cars, European cars and then there was the teachers straight out of a royal house, it seemed by their speech as they weren't taking kiwi English but the Queens English.

In each class room we visited was the children all dressed like that their school uniform had just come of the shop that very day and they all stood up as we went into each of the class rooms then there was what looked a dorm where kids would call home, it reminded me of that boot camp I had been to earlier in the year.

There was playing fields not like at my last school which was two small fields but here was large rugby grounds not just the one but three and cricket pitch with its own pavilion and batting nets and also there was a football pitch as well. What the fuck was this place with a massive pool; I actually hadn't ever seen anything like this before. It was a private school for the rich and elite, it was Hadlow Prep School, and what the hell was I doing here?

I was just some city kid but one who had a past with gangs and street kids and an upbringing watching my mum being beaten, I didn't fit in with these kids one single bit so my mum was mad to even think of this place for her son.

But on that car ride back she had already made up her mind and with the sale of the house that was to buy her a trendy one bedroom apartment with a folder out couch that when I would be coming home which was only once a month for 48 hrs. If you were in a top grade sport team then you wouldn't even have 48hrs once a month a home, you would get 36hrs.

I was never good at my sums but I tried my very best to work that out and it meant in short my life over the next two years were to be spend at school 24/7 and then once in a blue moon I would be back in the big smoke, I didn't like the idea of this at all.

The money from the salon and the business would solely be used on my education as this place wasn't cheap; it was in the top 5 most expensive schools in the country. It just wasn't for me, I wasn't posh and I wasn't from a posh background which would play on my mind very much so all the way back home.

But as school soon was finished then my mum had to make a decision and though I didn't want to go there, I just wanted to go to a normal school with my mates but my mum wanted me to get a good education or was it that now my father was gone and that meant he wouldn't be having me every second weekend so that meant more time with her son rather than her man Wim.

Was my mum really caring about the type of education I was to get as why then wasn't my sister send to a private school and also there were private schools nearer to Wellington than this one. I just have a feeling it was maybe a bit if both and as I was getting older, mixing more with the wrong crowd and not being controllable by my mum. Now my father had gone then she would have more on her hands so was it all of this as well which meant the difference between home and away.

Another year was up and soon I wasn't going to be in Wellington long so I made the last few weeks very messy and made sure that the street kids would never forget me or my pals from the gangs.

I dared not tell any of them where I was heading as I didn't wish myself to look any better than them as we all had been equal over the last two years and a half years and through good times and bad times most had been there for me.

I know many mislead me and maybe crime suited them more than me well at least a life of crime as they hadn't anything else to fall back on. They never were given this chance that I was being given, from here onwards I could truly become anything I wished.

Was I going to end up an airplane pilot when I had made it through to the other side? I had to first some entry exams and didn't think I would pass but I did which just made my mum full of so much joy and happiness.

Was what was handed to me a golden education or was it a way my mum could live the life she wanted which was for Wim at his beck and call rather than having a soon to turn teenage boy to look after?

I still felt angry that out of all the schools I was it seemed being send the furthest away, I didn't like it and I made sure that xmas day wasn't one that I would let my mum enjoy as all the presents in the world that she had brought me I only saw as tool for her to try and win me over.

I wasn't happy so in between Christmas and New Year's Eve I think I spend two of them over at k Street. These street kids didn't get presents, all they got was black power gang send them over some food for xmas day so I gave away lots of my presents that I had received to the kids who had no mum or dad being there for them or handing them what they wished for which in all honesty was some real love, something none seemed to ever had received in their own homes in their own upbringings.

I felt connected with them though I came from a very loving background as in the love both my parents had for my sister and I.

I didn't feel I would be able to connect much with the kids where I soon was heading and unknowing to me I wouldn't see many of these street kids again. These last two days were my farewell to them all, yes some were high on glue and others were stoned as, but I never judged them when I first met them that very first night and on that night most were high on glue and dope so they were no different to me than they were on these last few days.

When I got back home my mum had though I had run away though by now she knew never to call the police as I had enough of them hassling me for doing sweet fuck all so another home visit by the police wouldn't have done my relationship with my mum any good.

Due to Angies death then that's why my mum said she was concerned so I understood that but then I wasn't allowed out of her sight and even on New Year's Eve I was taken to a family friends place where the adults all got dressed up and out they went to some party and left us the kids in this house with a babysitter.

The babysitter was only around 18 years old. She really couldn't say much and in the end she paid us money to keep hush as she really wanted to be with her boyfriend so she went outside and hide a key underneath the mat of the front door for him to arrive and let himself in quietly in case any of the parents had come in, he was to met her in one of the spare rooms.

As for us kids we were all downstairs in the cellar which had been formed into a play area with lots of mattress down on the floor for us kids to crash out on and we had a TV with a game machine that we could play computer games through the TV soon we all got bored and after lots of playing fighting where the TV its self had been knocked down and wouldn't work again so the lights went out as we all fell asleep.

I woke for some reason I am not sure why but I looked over at the doorway and I could make out a person standing there with a ciggie in his hand and then to his mouth he would drag on it as that's when I could make out it was a male.

I guessed it was maybe one of the other parents who had just come back to check on his son or daughter who was sleeping nearby me but he never called out a name, he just stood there looking over us all.

Something I sensed then wasn't right so I dare not allow him to see that I was awake then he turned around and left.

I just knew he was a bad man. I am not sure why I got those vibes then I heard a door shut, it sounded like the glass front door.

I tried to wake one of the other kids up but I couldn't so I thought I would see who had come back hoping to see my mum as I went up the stairs turning on each light as I felt out for light switches on the wall.

Each step I took I can tell you that I felt scared as the darkness that appeared in front of me just felt unkind and then as I moved from the top stair I could tell no one at all was in the house.

None of the parents had returned but what about the man I had seen who had come in and left again?

I wasn't sure and didn't have the answers to these questions as reached the top of the stairs.

The fear hadn't passed until when light after light was turned on in the entire house.

The babysitter was nowhere to be found, on calling out to her so I returned the stairs.

Thankfully some of the kids too had pretended to be a sleep when they noticed the man with a ciggy in his hand over looking us.

Most of us stayed awake until we heard the front door being opened, thinking it was our parents returning but it wasn't as it was the babysitter returning back.

We asked her if her boyfriend had come down earlier where we slept but she said he hadn't.

I told her we weren't fucking lying and some man came down stairs smoking a ciggy.

That's when she informed her boyfriend didn't actually smoke and for us not to say a word about her leaving us alone.

Once the adults including my Mum returned later on, I told my mum about this man but no one could report a crime as crime hadn't taken place.

The spare key was found to be missing from underneath the doormat so at least that proved to the adults, that we were telling the truth about some random man had entered the house.

All I know was a lock smith came to that house after we had gone and change the locks. The next few nights before my journey to my new school, every night I had nightmares about the man and I felt like such a child my first night at boarding school as I was awoken by the matron as my nightmares could be heard throughout the dorm.

Some of the kids thought I was home sick or missing my parents, which as with other kids was the case but not in my case to the extent of bringing on nightmares. This was all due to that New Years Eve and the man with the ciggie in his hand.

So there I was now at boarding school and it seemed I wasn't fitting in as I was having these unrestful nights but it wasn't due to being away from home.

I was never home sick and as I had already spend evening away from home plus my house to me was always seemed haunted so anywhere else from my own bedroom I was happy with.

It did take me ages adapting and I did feel like a complete outsider as many of the boarders at this school had been the previous year to the school.

The school was a boarding school for ages 8year old to 12year old boys only and day school 5 years old to 12years old. I soon was 11 years old so there were only kids older than me by one year and a bit. Many were local even the borders and everyone was rich or well off and that was seen each and every day by what kind of running shoes they had to their pens and anything that was brought in by their parents.

It as if they all shopped at Harrods Knightsbridge and me only shopped at Oxford Street. Massive difference even the kids from a farm background all had the best of the best which just made me feel like a second class citizen among them all.

I was a rough diamond to say the least.

The school I can't really fault as it provided everything you could wish for but hell did you have to buck the line "Yes sir no sir".

It was full on and always we had prefects. well in my eyes many were just snakes, grasses who would grass ya up for anything just to get brownie points from the teachers and these kids could also get u detention if they saw you break a school rule. Not only had you had to watch ya back from the teachers you had to from some of the students as well.

Many were brown noised pricks that I couldn't stand as for bullying not much went on which I was surprised as I thought like that boot camp I had been to there would be attacks but there were not many at all.

Though for the first time I could see how other kids really could be so cruel towards the weak, if they were a slow learner or overweight or wore glasses then that form of bullying was in full swing and it would break kids to the point that they would leave the school within the first few weeks or month to have time off due to such wickedness from other pupils.

I found this to be utter disgusting as these kids were miles away from home and as they lived on school grounds then there was no escape. Name calling and behaviour towards them just less of beatings, I am sure some of the kids would more have preferred being beaten rather than the torture they were going through with verbal abuse.

As I get older I think back to how cruel kids can be to one another in schools, be it state schools or private education. It runs in all class systems, be it if you from a poor background or a wealthy one.

For whatever reason kids do bully and schools have to deal with the victims among their pupils but so many don't have voices as they are too frighten to and how I strongly believe that this issue should be more highlighted to help the kids being bullied first and foremost.

Equally to try to reach out to those kids who are bullies themselves. There is always a under rooted issue or problems maybe at home that causes them to turn so nasty towards other kids.

As I get older I think back to how cruel kids can be to one another in schools, be it state schools or private education as it runs in all class striations be it if u from a poor background or a wealthy one, for whatever reason kids do bully and schools have to deal with the victims among their pupils.

Many sadly don't have voices as they are too frightened too. I strongly believe that this issue should be more highlighted to help the kids being bullied first and foremost but equally to try to reach out to those kids who are bullies themselves as there is always a under rooted issue or problems maybe at home that cause them to turn so nasty towards other kids.

The first month at school was new to me of course as it was a new school, new surroundings but the fact that when the bell went at 330pm, that meant at a normal school u were off home apart from if you were part of a sport team but here at this school you had nowhere to go.

This school was lessons, teachers, sport and church equalling a timetable that was as strict as anything that I could ever imagine and that was just anti how I was used to living my life back in Wellington.

To start with bed time in the week was 730pm and lights out at 8pm then up at 630am each morning to go on a 7.5km run.

What was all that about and as for classes there was even classes after dinner which was to do your prep work, homework. If u didn't pull ya weight then it wouldn't be doing some lines on the chalk board but you would be canned and I mean canned. Again what the fuck was all that about?

If you misbehaviour in class, that could mean if you didn't call a teacher sir or if you didn't stand up for when a teacher walked in the class then you would be asked or pulled by the ear to the front of the class and in front of all the kids you were with ya hand out then wacked across the hand with a belt.

Again what the fuck was all that about? None of this I was used to and soon made that aware to my father who wasn't going to have any of it. I started to hate my mum for putting me in this place and if I ever wrote about it in a letter home well all our mail was checked so the letter would have to be re written and phone calls were listened in on.

I am sorry but prisoners get treated better than this and I was only a young kid but I couldn't rock the boat as much as I tried my hardest as if I were to rock the boat that seriously then at the end of the month when I were able to go home for 48hrs they had in their power once your parent or parents signed that dotted line then you were in the hands of this school.

They would take anything away from you if you were trouble and that meant visits home and all I wanted was to get maybe not back home but just anywhere out of that school as here I was for the very first time facing displine and authority that I couldn't tell to fuck off or run from.

It was all around me including these senior kids, senior kids by one year, who acted like I did when I was 7 year old. They were twats but even I had to stand in line for them so you can imagine what kind of raging little bull I was when I reached home on a bus that travelled over the mountain range and back through into Upper Hutt and then Lower Hutt from where I could see the night lights of Wellington.

I was glad to see my mum I had missed her and also my sister. My bedroom didn't look the same all the writings on the wall had been covered up and most of our house was looking like it was ready to leave as in our belongings were mainly all packed up.

The saloon had been sold and work was being done on that so my mum and Helen Scully now were working together in a neighbouring suburb called kilburnine. The following morning my mum had to go to work so here I was at my house after being away for so many weeks and I was alone.

It didn't feel nice so I called my father for a chat and told him about the strict rules and everything else, maybe I made the school to be out to worse it was as he demanded to speak to my mum and when I told him I was by myself he wasn't pleased his blood level I could tell had shot through the roof and he asked if I wished to come out to Scotland.

Oh how cool was that going to be. I could quid this school and get on a plane and all would be good as I knew my father would look after me and my grandparents would spoil me. But on telling my mum she made a point that, which was never going to happen. She wasn't going to let me thrown away my education.

When I went back to school the following night on the bus there were girls who were borders at the sister school of Hadlow as Hadlow was part of a trinity of schools.

St Matthews had borders, only girls who aged from 8 years old to 18 years old so that journey back among the older girls finding out their school was only three streets away meant to me as I fancied a few of the girls then maybe night times could become of interest to me.

Also on the bus were older boys from 13 year old to 18 years old and they were from the brother school of Hadlow , Rathkeale. That's where most of the boys from Hadlow would attend their senior years. This school was located further out of Masterton on 100 acres of land deep in to the bush and farm land but my mum dare not send me there as I had two years still to go at Hadlow.

So for sure by the time I was 13 years old my mum would let me back to Wellington or in the meantime I would be out in the U.K where I had great memories still from the last time I was out there.

From now I wouldn't stay put and I couldn't challenge these teachers or the German matron so I put my head into my school books as did all the other kids.

I didn't let go off my free spirit or the rebel in me and I wasn't going to become one of the other kid's robotic like, to the state they all seemed like sheep just following one another. Yes I did step in to line and found in doing so then I would get more chances to get out and if I had done well on the sports field then it would mean travelling to other schools and not local ones up every other prep top private schools around the whole country.

As long as I were on the top two sports team, be it cricket or one of the top 8 tennis players in the school during the summer months or in either of the two best rugby teams or the top flight football team of the school in the winter months. Either way through good behaviour or great sporting skills then there was a chance that I would be getting chances to get on out.

As for now the only time I was ever allowed out was the morning runs where I would fall into trouble with the local Maori gang as mentioned by the name of the nomads.

Where from being hit with a studded belt I got my revenge back by fucking up their clubhouse and then for whatever reason finding out while I was recuperating with my leg that had been opened on their barbwire, that their clubhouse had been burnt in some other bigger attack guessing from the mongrel mob as they too weren't far and were the nomads' greatest enemy in these neck of the woods.

After my leg got better and I had been home a few times once a month for 48hrs but even by now though I had been at the school for 4months, I was still feeling like an outsider due to the other kid's wealth.

I had kept my head out of most trouble and all was going good plus soon was going to be my 11th birthday and I was able to spend longer time at home over this period as my mum didn't want me to miss Anzac Day as my Grandfather had fought in the war so every year we would raise early to be there at dawn to remember all the New Zealand and Australia solders who had lost their lives during that war.

My Mum had requested special permission for me to be off school even past my birthday and the school had granted that.

But what was to come on that day was something I will remember forever and finely my mother now knew what I meant by that man who I knew as the monster, who used to tap at night on my bedroom window. My mum would come face to face with him and she would then onwards know why I always called that man the monster whenever I spoke about the pevery creepy man that he was.

Chapter 11

THE MONSTER

My 11th birthday April 20th 1986 was a Sunday and I could celebrate as I didn't have to return to boarding school till the following Sunday as I was also home for Anzac day that was the following Saturday so the evening of my birthday my mum held a party for me with all my old school friends from my previous school and the neighbourhood.

I managed to get some booze past my mum so my bedroom was where everyone would dart to, so to get themselves a drink from underneath my pillows as I had a few bottles of Jack Daniels. As the night went on my mum clocked that half of the kids were shitfaced as many were sick and others were dancing like prats to cheesy music. Maybe hey, they were just crap at dancing like me but I could hold my drink a little bit than the others and I wasn't going to look a fool by trying to dance in my front lounge.

By the end of the evening it was a great success as I got so wasted from the Jack though by the morning I had what would become often in my life a massive hang over so I started the week feeling rough.

It felt weird being back at home for so long as I had only been used to the 48hrs journey back home that I had been given from boarding school once a month. All my mates from Miramar all were there like my best friend Chris Mitchell and his brother Damien and my good friend Campbell.

Monday though they all during the day had to be back at their own schools so boredom crept in and all I wish to do was go to the gun club with my mum's boyfriend as I really enjoyed target practice and a friend of his owned hand guns that we could sue at the gun club, which to me at that age was exciting though I hadn't got used to the kick back the gun would give once fired.

If I were at home when my sister was there with her friends then I would just annoy them all for a bit of fun. They would hang out with my sister such as Jane, Rachael, Leigh and Joanna and many others back at the house but at that age not many had the time of day for me as I was simply just Stacey younger brother and they all were more interested in smoking weed in my sisters room, without my mum catching them rolling up joints.

My sister's boyfriend Steve would bring puff over, he used to always have so much of it and I worked out he and his circle of friends were selling it as he always had plenty of dough on him and he had just brought himself a new bike, a Triumph 750 Bonneville which would be his first bike of many in those early years of his life before he joined the Satan's Slaves Motorcycle Club.

It was a wicked bike and I would start to look up at him. He wasn't any James Dean but very much an outlaw of a person and a rebel within that I could relate to as I know in his younger days he and the others had all been tearaways.

His best pal who was known as Zombie and he too was another one who wasn't far from trouble and he would follow Stephen in to the Satan's Slaves MC at one point in years to come he would become President of the Satan's Slaves MC in the late 1990s though leaving the club for reasons I am unsure of.

Zombie was dating one of my sister's friends and there was talk of all of them getting a flat together after the sale of my mum's place so my sister would be moving out of her family house before she was even 16 years old.

Young it may have seemed but we both had grown up so quick and we knew how to look after ourselves from such a young age so to go into the big world and have her own flat at the age of 15 wasn't nothing major as it would be a flat with a friend of hers and their boyfriends so it wasn't like she was going to be living by herself.

Her boyfriend would look after her, through the sale of dope that she wasn't aware of the extent but between him and Zombie at their own younger ages of 20 years old they were becoming very well known for obtaining great puff in Wellington.

They were never ever short of the stuff and soon that would become more than just dope as it would become acid then soon coke as well, once they had trust of certain Mr. Big and a lot of cash flow behind them.

As an 11 year old I would study them and learn from them, all the maths that had to go into selling gear but with the maths correct then just pure profit and to me all they were selling was a plant, a bit of weed. Where the harm was in that, no one was being harmed and everyone seemed happy.

The people who would come to my sister's house and score the weed and Steve and Zombie who would be selling the shit, I am sure if my sister clocked onto what kind of set up they had she would have moved out.

She only guessed they were selling a little bit just among friends in their social circle but slowly and surely these boys were getting in to the big league and moving on to high grounds in the years to come, I would be caught up in all and it would cost me so badly.

A great loss but I only have myself to blame for being so overwhelmed by the colour of money and thinking wow to these two and others lifestyles of outlawing and free spirits.

I should have seen them for who they were at the time which was dope dealers but when you that age anything impress ya and at the end of the day they were good fellas, they never done me harm in these early days of mine.

Zombie out of that early social circle is still a very dear friend to me to this day.

If there was ever a self made man done good and a business man who done well through both bent businesses leading to straight businesses then he is a success story in his own right, no one would ever thing it all started from selling a few bags of weed in the 1980s.

He now has gone straight and has a family and doesn't involve himself in any such business as what is mentioned when he was in his 20s.

I wish him the very best in life and his family as well.

Now going back to the week I had off school. That's the very first week, I saw something more than just smoking weed as weed for me I had gone off since becoming a part of the private boarding prep school that my mum had send me.

Sport was taking over my life and success in sport at a young age and that was really the only thing on my mind and being away from Wellington, boarding at this plush school then I was away from weed so it went out of my mind as well as my system so even this long week now back in Wellington I never ever even smoked a joint when one was around.

I wasn't a smoker of ciggs, I saw them as the cause of my uncle peters death so like many other kids who would smoke ciggs, I never did all of my early years nor even through my teens but as for puff I didn't see that as a health risk and in a way harmless.

So this week ended by without being stoned, I didn't even get up to the city as I hoped to do but I think I felt too ashamed to knock around with the youth gangs who I had been knocking around with and getting into a lot of trouble with before being send off to boarding school as by now they had heard I was attending some posh school. I am sure they would have believed I too had turned posh.

I hadn't as I never forgot my background anyway I didn't want the grief from them and more so to come across I was any better than them. I would have just wanted them to except me as they always had in the past but I was sure they wouldn't have due to them still being exactly where they were in life the year before to now.

Unlike me they were never handed this great chance in life to make good. I felt for many of them as if only they had been given a chance in life then they would have become good spirited people rather than a life of crime involved in gangs.

How though back then I wished I kept on repeating that to myself in my mind as I would at times take it for granted and also not ever think what would happen if it all got taken away from me, something that I should have consider when I made some stupid decisions over the years that were near.

We all make mistakes from the making of a decision which turns out to be the mighty wrong decision and most times we are unable to go back to redo the mistake and make things better.

I guess it just called growing up and life but there are those out there who learn from their mistakes and then there are others who simply don't and continue to make those wrong mistakes so they become repetitive in their own lives.

I think we all know someone who does this within their own lives, be it a family member or a partner or a close friend but what can we do as our lives are to be lived by us and not told by others how to live our own lives and we mustn't ever tell anyone else how to live their lives.

Friday night came and I had to be in bed early as on the following morning, my Mum and I had to be up at 430am so we could make the 6am Anzac day morning service. My Mum decide to eat out as a treat for me to a new Indian restaurant down the roads that had opened up in the time I had been away at boarding school.

I don't think I had tried India food since when I was 5 years old down Brick Lane in the East End of London with my parents so I was looking forward to eating some hot spicy food.

On arriving back home after the restaurant neither did me or my mum were feeling too well and the toilet was getting it from both of us as while I was in my bedroom feeling more sick with tummy cramps and I could hear my mum being ill in the bathroom every few mins.

After I had finished with the loo the bathroom stunk to the point that she had to open the bathroom window, "Don't blame me." I yelled out to her "blame the dodgy curry I had down the road." as had been coming out my behind as well as my mouth.

I was like the bird out of the exorcist and I anit kidding ya though my head wasn't spinning around but my guts was and it was flying out like I was a human water hose, sorry but I was that poorly.

I managed to close my eyes and sleep finally come over me, then maybe two hours later I heard my mum shout. A shout I hadn't heard since those days when my father used to live in the house. I didn't like hearing my Mum yell like that.

It was so loud that it woke me up, I thought fuck it's my dad but then remembered he no longer lived here any more and more so he didn't even live in the country anymore.

I rushed to my mum's bedroom but she wasn't there in the bed I started to panic like I was in some horrible nightmare so I yelled out to her then heard her shout again.

Her voice was coming from the direction of the bathroom so I ran in and what I saw was terrifying as there was my mum in her nigtie and above her, half his way in through the bathroom window which my mum had left open hours earlier after I had been using the loo was the monster trying to climb through the window.

He had just spotted me standing there in my pjs; my mum was trying to push him back out the window. Hitting him but it wasn't doing much as more of his weight was coming through the window.

This was the creepy man, who used to sit in my mum's hair salon whenever his wife would get her hair done by my mum, and he would sit there and whenever I was in the saloon waiting for my mum to finish work he would look over at me so creepy with a disgusting look on his face.

I knew as a young kid he wasn't a good man and he was evil. I could sense it the moment I first seen him and I was proved to be right, though for years no one would believe me but after this night they so sure would.

Anyway next door to the bathroom was the kitchen as I looked around the bathroom to see what I could use to hit him but there wasn't anything worthy to grab so I run into the kitchen and hanging up above the stove as my father had a great kitchen put in for our house was the pots and pans hanging up so I grabbed the first one that was near.

I run in and on one movement jumping up on the toilet bowl with the same movement came my swinging arm and whack I got him straight above the ridge of his noise he then let go off his grip on the bathroom shelve, which he was using to pull himself in but he didn't let go fully.

He just slipped back at bit, hanging out the window so I just raised both my arms and held on to the pan and came smashing down this time on the top of his head and with a yell he let go and fell out the window.

What the fuck was he trying to do? Murder us? What was he going to try and grab me? The fact that he was after my mum as well made me so fucking angry as here I was being what I had been for so many years the man of the house and protecting my mum.

Suddenly my rifle came to mine and as I had been out shooting that day with my sister's boyfriend Stephen. I had never given the gun back to my mum to lock away when I reached home; it was still in my bedroom.

I run into my bedroom, it was leaning up against my set of draws so I loaded and grabbed my beautiful mum, she was too scared to reach over and grab the flinging window which now was wide open up hanging out the frame.

We couldn't get the lock and she didn't want to reach out and I knew not to put the tip of my gun out in case he grabbed the end of it so we sat on the floor and I just kept it pointed, we were waiting for him to reappear.

My mum was in such shook and she was even to scared to go in to the hall way to reach our only phone in the house to call the police. The rest of the house was pitch black, the bathroom light was the only light on then suddenly his hand appeared and his arm so I fired a shot but before I even aimed.

It gave me such a fright when his hand appeared again trying to pull himself back into our bathroom before I fired that shot so after he had disappeared with the gun going off, I then went flying out the bathroom I thought fuck him I going to kill the bastard.

Holding the gun that night let me tell you made me feel very much this time in control over that bastard causing any upset to my Mum and more so ever again towards me.

Firing that shot I can say hand on heart was for the right reason as he was coming for us to harm us.

I wasn't not only going to protect myself but first and more so my beautiful mum as if anything ever happed to ya mum then you going to protect her, right.

So I went into the kitchen for some reason raising my voice louder and louder as I got to the kitchen door and as I open it I just thought he would now be there so I fired another shot which missed my mum's car.

Loading the gun again I swung myself off the porch and to the wall tree maybe I had seen some cop and robber TV show or a old western movie as I pulled myself up hard against the walnut tree in my front yard but trust me I wasn't trying to act out no telly show.

My heart was racing so fast and though I was shaking, I was just thinking to put a hole in the creepy bastard and with that thought I threw myself into the open of my front yard, away from the walnut tree and pointed down the side of my house where the bathroom window was and also my bedroom window and I fired.

I thought I heard a slight moan, and then rustled in the bushes was a figure leave fast heading out the other end of our property as we lived on a corner house so he could make his escape without passing me.

I didn't give up chase instead I quickly run back in to the house and slammed the door shut. My mum had heard the shots asking me in a panic had I shot him? I replied that I didn't think I had. She could tell in my eyes that I truly wish I had.

Now things had got just crazy as there we were in the bathroom me holding a gun after firing off the gun in the middle of the night after what had happened. My Mum asked me would I close the window, I knew by reaching up there was no way this time the monster wasn't going to appear as he was way gone.

Who knows by the sound of the moan I had heard then at least in some shape or form he truly was injured. From a bullet I doubted so.

We didn't panic though we both looked panicked and all I could say is "I can't go to jail as I got school on Monday." That's all I could think not being late for school. I don't know why but it showed how much I started to respect that private posh school for the very first time since I had been attending as a boarder.

Were we going to call the police? No fucking way, tell them what, I had just attempted to kill a man with a gun, that wasn't locked up in the gun cabinet and that should have been under lock and key. It wasn't self defensive as I had purposely left the house and went outside to shoot him. Maybe if I had woken up in the house and he was in the house and attacked me or my mum then I could maybe have the right to fire one into his skull but here and now I was sure I was now in the shit big time.

At least my mum wasn't telling me off as I had got the gun for the only reason to protect my mum.

Now she as the adult had to think how to clean up the mess and sort the situation out so first thing she did is ask me what my father would do in this situation. Firstly no way would he call the police if he had shot a man or even if he had fired a gun.

He would make sure he would disappear, well at least the fucking gun he would get rid of so that was our plan. We could see mums parked car out from the kitchen door.

My mum was too scared to run to the car and drive us off as she had a feeling the man was somewhere if not dead then even more angry as he looked like a craze man when he had tried to get in earlier through the bathroom widow. My mum sure didn't wish to bump into him again especially outside where he could grab her or me.

I wanted to be that knight in shining armour for my mum so it was down to me to get control again of the situation as I had done earlier.

First thing first we had to leave the house and get rid of the gun. I told my mum to get her car keys and also a towel from the bathroom, she wouldn't go in there without me even though the window was now locked so we both went in and I placed the gun in a towel then I went to the tool box that was at the bottom of the cupboard in the kitchen and all the markings on the gun and sanded down so no trace back to us of this gun after it was to be dumped.

I then after wrapping it in the towel, with a saw I cut off the barrel and also then with a hammer smashed it constantly what was left of the gun in the towel, so to stop anymore loud noise.

Our neighbours were used to noise coming from our house over the years with all the raised voices whenever my parents used to fight or loud music being played from either my sisters bedroom or mine so while I smashed away my mum had put some music on the ghetto blaster so to cover the noise even more so that I was making with the hammer.

Once the gun was broken into smaller pieces, we got some of my fishing gear and in a bag threw the gun parts and also the towel as if for any reason we were to be stopped driving in the middle of the night then my mum was going to tell the copper that she was taking her son night fishing which isn't unusual in New Zealand.

We left out of the kitchen I had a fishing knife in my hand just in case he was still about, if he was that silly enough to still be hanging around.

My Mum started up her car and we were off. We took the route around the bays as I told my mum I wanted to throw the gun out to sea but not anywhere near a swimming beach so we drove right around the bays.

We ended up having a row while we were in the car as how many times over the years that he would be outside my window tapping on my window and I would tell her but her never believed me.

I reminded her about the night a few years ago when I had seen him outside my window while I had been in the walnut tree and also that it was his face previous to that when I had open the bedroom curtains and he had been steering in.

Finally now after what happened my mother believed me as she thought I had just been suffering from night terrors that I had most of my life but those night terrors are something completely different as with these night terrors I awake but with a loud buzzing noise in my ears and then a feeling of being held down not being able to move as if someone was sitting on my chest and my whole body becoming unmoveable.

When trying to shout or yell out not even being able to do that plus sometimes when these night terror succour I get a feeling of leaving my body. It's so hard to explain but every time I have also sensed something or someone is in the room when this occurs so for all my years of telling my mum and also my dad about this creepy man who I would name simply know as the monster as that's what I would call him, they always thought I was just having night terrors.

One thing for sure I am just too glad that my mum now got to see for her own eyes that this monster was for real and no fucking part of my night terrors. He had made my life in my own home like a living nightmare due to the creepy bastard outside my bedroom window some nights.

Scared me from the young age of 6 when it first started I can recall and not having my own parents believe me for all those years made it even worse.

We were as planned to go still to the Anzac day service as if nothing had happened as we wasn't going to let this make us miss showing our respect at the morning service as that meant a lot to both of us.

We drove to a place called Red Rocks which was around the bays on the coast of Wellington where the seals would come during matting times. It was there that I threw the parts of the gun out there to sea as this was a place of the sea where no one would ever go swimming due to the seals.

We didn't go back to our house instead we went straight to my Nanas flat as we were to collect her as she was coming to the dawn morning service. We arrived a little early but she didn't seem to notice and she made us a coffee each and some toast as my belly hadn't anything in it due to being sick from the night before.

She asked my Mum was she ok as she sensed something was up but my Mum after drinking her coffee, said she was fine and that morning we all went and paid our respects to the returned service men and the men who fought for Queen and Country but sadly never made it back to their loved ones and their families.

I had to get back on the bus that evening for school so after we dropped my nana back to her flat, my mum and me went back to the house. It was day light so we looked around for signs of blood spilled or a trail of blood but nothing was found. We sat in the house my mum really spooked out still and I didn't want to leave her.

She told me she was going to stay at Wims and also the house was already half packed up, if not all and that in only a week she would be moving out so she wasn't planning to stay in that house one more night as I think even to her she saw that house as a haunted house in many ways as her memories of that place, like mine wasn't nice and even only recently I found pictures of the house on the internet and it just brought back terrible memories.

The Walnut tree still stands and the house looks a little difference but to me it still in those recent pictures looks like the haunted house that I knew and grew up in.

Not only was I happy to leave there but very much my Mum. We never saw the monster again and to this day I don't know whatever happened to him. All I hoped is that he didn't go onto be a monster for any other kid and with what happened that night when I fired those shots at him , that to him it scared him enough and that whatever new family that moved into that house 88 Rotherham Tce , Miramar, Wellington never was woken at night by tapping noises on the bedroom middle window as I wouldn't wish another child to have to relive the nightmare that I had to live through for many years of my younger life due to that bastard who simply was known as the monster.

I am unsure if I would ever wish to visit that house again even now I am a grown man I am sure it would make the hair on the back of my neck stand up if I ever were to stand in front of that house again though it would be great to pull off the wall paper in my old bedroom and see all the writings on the wall as that for sure would bring back many memories and I reckon if all the wall paper was pulled off it would be like looking at a piece of art and hell that would bring me back many, many years as those writings up on the wall were of a Lost Youth, my Lost Youth.

Chapter 12

TEACHER AMONG TEACHERS

1986 aged 11 / 1987 aged 12

Arriving soon back at school, settling in with everything that was going on with the school such as sport activities and learning new subjects.

I wish now I had pushed myself further with sport as I felt if I had set my mind to my given sports I would have done even better that what I was showing at a early stage of my sporting life but unlike many of the other kids, my mind was elsewhere at times.

Though one sport I was very good at and did have huge passion for and that was the game of cricket.

There is only one man in the world I can thank for this and it isn't my own father as he enjoyed football more which as you would have read in other chapters of my book then I too did love football, Liverpool Football to be correct but I did like cricket and it's a sport I am so glad I was taught by a man called Carl Gill.

Carls Gills wife was one of my mum's dearest friends Leonie who was such a lovely lady in so many ways and she was always there for not only my mum but also me as a young kid.

Leonie had time for everyone and she was such a warm hearted lady and so giving of her time and whenever my mum had a problem or something on her mind, she would always call Leonie or go over to Leonie's and Carls place for a cup of tea and bring me along.

That's where the game of cricket becomes such a good thing in my life as it was at Hadlow I first began playing the game.

As a young boy I used to go to the Wellington cricket ground and watch great players like Sir Richard Hadlee play against the Aussies and other international teams and though I loved watching the game, I was always doubted in myself that I would be any good as a player well if there was one man who could turn that around for me, it was Carl Gill and he sure did.

He even made his way all the way up to Hadlow one weekend and practised with me in the nets and taught all the other kids how to play and wow what a difference it made as we went on to win the following weekend and win we kept on doing.

Every time I would go on to the playing field, it was what Carl had taught me how to be such a great player for my age that would just make me do wonders in each game, I don't recall ever having a bad game even when I was on the losing side as playing the game of cricket just gave such a great buzz and really made some very happy moments for me.

I really wished my own Father had got behind me more as a young kid when it came to sport as what a difference it made when Carl gave me hope and encouragement.

Both Leonie and Carl were such a great influence in my life and always I will be grateful for what they done for me and their friendship they had with my mum as though my mum had many friends, Leonie and her family, including her daughter Jackie were so special to my mum and us as they themselves seemed more like family than just friends.

I hope they all are fine and well in life as there are true stars in their own right and such lovely people.

My Mum was very lucky to have such good friends in Leonie and Carl.

And as mentioned in further chapter of the book, Carl and Leonie arranged such a treat for me when a visiting international cricket team came to play against New Zealand's international cricket team in New Zealand on a tour of the country.

It was a boys dream come true and something that I will remember for ever as it was magical then for me and still is when I look back over it.

As for study at Hadlow, what was holding me back was my dyslexia which wasn't picked up at any of my years of schooling as I seemed to have a method of covering up for the mistakes, be in grammar or general learning but it so held me back though I must say it just meant for me that I would have to study twice as hard to keep up with school lessons.

How I wished that first year a teacher, any of them would just give me more of their time but I never was given that, though to be honest I never asked for it as I felt I would have been looked upon as a stupid kid or a slow kid, neither of them I was.

I did love learning and learn I did, also by now I was streetwise through my early years of living in the big smoke Wellington. I got to say probably more grown up in many ways that may of the other pupils but they were miles ahead when it came to the classroom.

Some so much better on the playing field than I hoped ever to be though don't get me wrong, in some sports I wasn't far behind to the best of them and if I had just been as focused as some of the best among the kids when it came to sports I would have easily matched a few of them at any given sport that was played out there on the playing fields at Hadlow Prep School.

I was always thinking of the fun and the mischief I could get up to when back at home on the weekends in the big smoke rather than thinking more on what I was being taught in the classrooms.

My sister had moved in her own flat and how more exciting that was for me, as her friends would be there all grown up and all looking so fit, wow I would think as I sat around them watching them all get ready to go out to the pubs or clubs.

How even at that age I wanted to join them as the following day I would pop back around to my sisters place and hear of the drunken fun times that they all would have got the night before and seeing my sisters boyfriends Harley Davidson motorcycle parked outside and also her flatmates boyfriend bike, I started at that young age looking up to them as some type of role models.

I hadn't any role models in my life but things would be a changing in times to come as one day someone would walk into my life; people like these are hard to find in life.

We all may only get the chance to meet one such person. What I am talking about is someone who can make a huge difference on your life, walk into your life and touch your life with teachings that can forever more shine at times throughout your own life.

Equally the person can give u a sense of belief in your own self and a belief in knowing that in every negative there is a positive, believe me there were many negatives to come through out my life, many dark clouds and times of despair which would have me thinking back to this person and what he had taught me at such a younger life.

There aren't many people they we learn from how to become better people in our own lives at a young age when we find ourselves heading down the wrong path in life. There aren't many people who are happy to give so much of their time to troubled kids, if there were then so many kids at a young age would be saved from continuing down the wrong path and heading for even more trouble times ahead.

It's too easy these days for teachers just to walk into their schools solely just to teacher English, maths etc but not to really make any more commitment apart from to take classes.

You can't blame them as their wages don't match their skills and all the time they already give by just teaching and at the end of the day they have their own lives to go back to and deal with and also all that homework they must check and then to put together the work for the following day of class.

They really don't have the time to give much more and when a kid is trouble then most of the time that pupil really doesn't want any help and would have been a nightmare throughout class so why would a teacher want them to spend any more of his or her time with the pupil.

If only so many more teachers would just reach out, well this would have such a lasting impression on many of today troubled youth and it would steer them away from a life of crime and instead give them a life that they themselves could be happy with in obtaining life goals and making dreams come true.

In this day and age the youth if not helped at school on any one to one level are then not going to gain life skills if they don't find them at home, where maybe their parents have given up on them a long time ago or their parents may not even be there at home to keep them on the straight and narrow and in some cases maybe their parents sadly are abusing them.

So Where else are they going to pick up life skills, if even none of their teachers are able or not to care in some cases that much to a least give these kids some of their own time and more to give the kids of today who can come across in school as trouble a second chance to make good of themselves.

Well this man not only gave his time to me but to so many others and his life to that school Hadlow Prep School.

His name was Michael Mercer, you will learn about this incredible man through turning the next few pages and I am sure after you have finished reading then if you are a student at university you may as well have such a man or woman among your teachers or if you are no longer at school like myself that you too can think back and say yeah I had a teacher like that but then maybe you were someone who was never blessed in meeting such a person, having such a teacher among teachers which is a shame.

Maybe I was just one of the lucky one, as I know of some great teachers who are friends of my mine. One being Geoff Thompson who is a kiwi and teaches in the East End of London now that anit going to be easy but when we have sat down and spoken, it's how he gives his time to the kids in every way through their bad times and the good times and as the kids listen to him then he also listens to them and this is one of the differences between a teacher and a good teacher.

You are there not just to teach the kids abut also to listen to them and speak to them more than just about what is on the blackboard, to guide them when you can see they have no guidance's at home or in their own lives

And though as a teacher you stay a teacher but it's never wrong being a friend, a friend for them to listen to their future dreams and their life goals as many don't even have life goals and this where as a teacher, I am guessing you can make that little bit of difference as happened to me with set goals I was given to achieve at my time at Hadlow when Michael Mercer arrived to teach at the school.

Ok maybe I never become a airline pilot as I wanted to be from a young age watching the planes fly by my house as I sat up in the walnut tree escaping the sounds of my mother being beaten by my Father and dreamed of escaping with my mother to protect her for ever more from any more horrible beatings that were taking place in a house I only knew as home.

But for me to have achieved the things that I have in my life truly couldn't have been done without the input that Michael Mercer had in my early years. I had no goals up till he taught me how to place goals in one's own life and to achieve them at the same time to believe in dreams as with hard work and putting everything plus that little bit more in to the class room or the sports field.

That little bit extra of hard work will pay off in the long run and you will find yourself living out your dreams.

The hours spend with these kids some may be difficult in class for so many different reasons could be just the turnaround in not only their behaviour but also their learning within class.

If any teachers are reading my book then you as a teacher maybe not know at the time to you but maybe you are the only friend they have in that whole school, if they being bullied or in some cases they just don't fit in.

I was never bullied but many times didn't feel like I fitted in as some of these kids I went to school with came from the best backgrounds surrounded by wealth and well I was just from a working class background and I was just a lost city kid who for all my earlier years watched in horror as my father would beat my mum like a raging mad bull, so I didn't have a upbringing in a normal family home like these other kids had so I couldn't relate to them in many ways and I dare not open up to any of them as in doing so then it would have even showed more how indifferent I was to them.

But with Michael Mercer over time I could talk to him and these many talks made a major difference on my time at Hadlow as you will get to read as the pages turn to do with this part of my life as I had been given such a great start in life after the horrors and unsettling start to my life that I had.

Being enrolled at Hadlow as it was and still is one of the best schools in all of New Zealand ....and that's fact even better now I am sure after hearing that Mr. Mercer is now the head of that school.

So you see what I mean by one man not just giving his time to the school but his whole life as we talking over 20 years on and that man is still there and I am very sure changing kids outlook on life in such a better way and also their teachings and more so never giving up on the kids like myself who was never going to reach the top of the class or whom had problems from his past as when other teachers would have put us to one side or never give the pupil a second chance or just saw as trouble rather troubled, then we all need a Michael Mercer in our school life.

Also for our own kids trust me, you all like myself would wish a Michael Mercer in your own child or children's schooling years as if one person can make a different then such teachers, men or women who have it in their heart and in their assembly speeches to their daily teachings in the class room and their moments with pupils to chat with them, to listen and to advise.

Well you just can't get better than such a teacher as Michael Mercer, especially for me as I didn't have a father in my life at the time.

My father had left back for the UK to start his new life with his new wife and through many court cases my mum fought hard not for me to be joining him even for a holiday she would fight his court requests to have me even out there on holiday.

She was too sacred that I wouldn't return that maybe he would talk me around to staying over there. For her at this time in my life the most important thing for her was my education.

I wish I had respected that so much more now looking over back at these years but sexy girls and motorcycles that's I would see come and go at my sister's house well that is what I looked forward to more and more and that's when sadly drugs creped in to my life.

Not at this stage of my life as in taking them, yes I had smoked pot before but the hard drugs I hadn't taken but I would witness many a weekend to my sisters friend taking them be it coke or speed and in my eyes it just made them more funny or as if it gave them more of a wow factor and soon I would see her boyfriend as a role model as he had everything in life- no rules and like a outlaw a law within himself.

What a rebel he came across in my eyes with a huge American v8 and a Harley Davison motorcycle and always lots of cash that I would find out later over time that he was earning by selling drugs.

While I was at school learning about economic studies, he was at my sisters place doing the maths as in selling drugs, with him and my sister flatmates boyfriend well the two of them were doing really well when it came to moving drugs throughout Wellington, something they would keep hidden from my sister.

I doubt she would have wanted to be dating a drug dealer but they weren't shy of showing me what they were up to, maybe they were showing off and as they knew I was no grass meaning I wouldn't tell my sister what was going on plus my Father always taught me at a young age loose lips sinks ships and as for my Mum, hell no would I tell my mum as I didn't want to never be not allowed to spend time at my sister place.

My sisters friends among the girls would make a fuss over me, some would pretend to flirt towards me and the older boys would though at times give me beatings when I would get in the way but most of the times I felt like I was being treated like one of their own or as a young brother I guess would be treated by a older brothers.

How wrong was I and how this was the beginning of the end to a education that could have made me become a airline pilot which was one of my dreams that Mr Mercer had taught me to believe in was my dreams.

I was allowed at home freedom, unlike at Hadlow I had none and this strict control was the very first that had ever been placed upon me in my life so even as hard as I would try to be the little rebel that I was, it was a losing game to win with the teachers at the school as they always had the upper hand plus punishment back in those days meant getting the cane or a belt across the hand.

How if schools in this and age over in England practice that, then I can tell you the kids of today would be more in hand rather than little tear a ways at school that I read about constantly in the British press papers.

One thing which did very much work was displine and trust me it was handed out when one of the kids were out of line, never excess but always fairly, not in an incorrect manner though at the time when I would be caned I would think it was unfair.

Maybe the school was given the displine that I needed in my life as the rebel in me if given a chance would be trying his hardest to get a little following and have the other kids follow my word and my way of life rather than that of the teachers.

The only person I had a big moan about was the matron, sorry but she could be a right bitch and she was at most times unlovable. She was just struck in her ways and what she said was the end of it, there was never any debating with over anything.

With this woman there was no debating, her word was final even when she was in the wrong. She would have a go at me for something I had no part in as in when the boys would fight in the dorm and I would come in as peacekeeper to break the fight up but at the same time she would arrive and I would find yourself outside the principal's office for fighting.

I would end up being punished for something I hadn't even committed; times were hard when she was on the war path.

School so far was gliding along and I was fitting in better that was expected though a few touchy moments as the morning on that run when I was attacked by the scum that they were the nomads the local gang down the road but as mentioned in a previous chapter I sneaked out one night from school and I got them back by doing what I done on their club house so I was happy with that.

The only have times I would ever leave the school was to sneak out and visit the girls over at St Matthews School whom I had met and got to know quite well on the school buses to and from home.

Once a month together we all would bus it home as buses were provided for the kids who boarded and lived a distance from the school such as the Hutt Valley or Wellington. The buses would be filled with the girl boarders from

St Matthews's and also the senior boys from Rathkeale School as these two schools make the trinity of the three schools including Hadlow.

Now the girls were always fun to have on the bus but the older boys would just be acting as bullies, some soon found that as their down fall bulling us younger boys from Hadlow. I would have them sorted out and all the bully soon stopped and the girls from St Matthews loved seeing these sleazy acting bullying older boys put in their place one Sunday early evening.

As on a Sunday when I was getting ready to go back to Hadlow to take the bus ride there I was at my sister place saying goodbye to my sister, and I spoke about being bullied on the bus by these kids well her boyfriend overheard and so did a few of his pals so as my mum arrived, my mum wasn't too pleased when the guys asked if they could get a lift with my mum in saying good bye to me on the bus.

She thought it was quite odd and also she really didn't want the other parents seeing the biker looking blokes get out her car as she would have felt embarrassed so she said no but if they really wanted to say goodbye to me then they could follow us in their car.

Some took the big v8 American motor that belonged to my sister's boyfriend while three of them got on their bikes. It was like I had outriders to the journey to the school bus as we drove through the streets of Wellington. I thought hell this grand but knew my Mum didn't think it was great as she drove with her head down so no one knew they were with us.

As we arrived to the school bus my mum helped with my bags and gave me one of those hugs u only get from your mum and a wave goodbye she would always have tears in her eyes when she was saying goodbye to me.

She loved me so much and I think sometimes felt bad that she had sent me to a school so far away that she couldn't visit me as often as the other kid's parents could nor watch her son play cricket or football or rugby when the other kid's parents were there to support their kids.

What a different to me that would have made if I too had two parents like the other boys watching me from the sideline as I would have played every game as if it was my last and I would have score ever try or winning kick to goal or bag those 6 wickets.

That never happened my Mum watching me play sport at Hadlow though actually once against a rival private school from the North Island of New Zealand on a sports trip to their school to play them in cricket I actually did bag six wickets but sadly I recall only score 17 runs though managed a great catch at slip (Carl Gill you taught me well).

Anyway going back to the farewell of my mum, so as she was waving goodbye I soon was joined by my sister's boyfriend and also his friends as they too stepped onto the bus.

They went up to the Rathkeale boys who for many a time bullied us the Hadlow boys but when my sister's boyfriend and his mates stepping on the bus that late afternoon, well what a shock the bullying kids got when they were shaken up a little and warmed never ever to bully me or any of the boys from Hadlow on the bus and to stop sleazing on to the St Matthew girl who would always sat at the back of the bus.

With these few spoken words they all shook my hand and said "safe trip Christian".

Oh and what a safe trip it was not just for me but everyone on board and even the bus driver didn't even have to tell kids to behave themselves as not even the Rathkeale boys made a sound on the whole journey back as their mouths still wide open from shock of being put in their places earlier on even to the extent I am sure some of them had poo in their pants from the earlier fright they all had got.

None could believe what had just happened to them before the bus had left from Wellington.

This for me was great as from then onwards I would always be invited to sit at the back of the bus with the girls from St Matthews who some among themselves were rebels like myself so a few would dare me to meet them one night in the week.

I would get up in the middle of the night make my bed as if there was someone still sleeping in just in case the matron would do a little night walks through with her torch on after lights out.

If the light from the torch had swung onto my bed it would have looked like I was there in my bed when actually I was many streets away having many a kiss with one or two of the girls from St Matthews.

So my sister's boyfriend now had become more of role model but in a sense a hero and this was going to be my downfall from doing ever so good in my mum's own dream of her son getting the best education in all of New Zealand as my sister's boyfriend started to and his friends have more contact in my life those years just before I had become a teenage.

One weekend they actually drover up and took me out on a day trip which was allowed. Every boarder was allowed a day outing with family once a month, if your parents or family wanted to visit you. They could take you out for just the day so my sister made a request that was granted so one weekend on a Sunday she arrived with her flatmate her and their boyfriends.

I was taken out for the day, we drove around Masterton and went to a pub in the country for lunch where the boys brought me a bottle or six of beer and though it would be funny getting me drunk for the day and drunk I got then having to return to school making sure that I complaint of a sore tummy so I could go straight to bed to avoid any contact with the teachers who would be taking shifts on days and evenings to look after the borders. I avoided the matron to make sure matron didn't smell beer on my breath.

Slept like a baby that night I sure did but awoke with a banging head due to the beer I had drunken the previous afternoon but matron wouldn't believe I was still feeling poorly from a sore tummy so at 645am in the morning 7.5k run I had to do the other pupils. That run was one of the longest runs of my life as I was throwing up within two miles of it not due to being unfit but because my belly was still full of beer from the day before.

A hangover from hell followed me around school that day and never leaving me for the whole day. My hangover didn't leave me at school that day but what did arrive at school that very day was someone who would change my life there at my school Hadlow.

A real role model and someone in that time in my life that I was needing and a figure in my life that I was lacking which was a positive role model rather than the negative role which was my sister's boyfriend.

Into the school came a new deputy headmaster and into my life came with that a teacher, a friend, but most of all a impact on my life that would carry on throughout my life, a remembrance of one man from all of my years of schooling that was by far a positive role model and this young man name was Michael Mercer though to us kids we knew him as Sir.

As with on a sunny late evening in old London town speaking to the teacher over here in old London town whom I mentioned Geoff Thompson and hearing the way he spoke so proudly of his given job, that being a teacher.

Seeing his passion he had when he spoke of his job and the well being for the kids he teaches and also making their lives that more interesting when they are in his class, when many probably wished they weren't at school until they met a teacher like Geoff.

He lightens their days and makes learning so much better and he speaks to them one on one on their level which I guess some even wouldn't get this from their own parents.

Well on hearing Geoff speak that night, it reminded me of the impact that Mr Mercer had on my years at one of New Zealand's leading private schools and for any school to have a Geoff Thompson or a Mr Mercer then that can only in rich the school and the lives of the pupils they teach.

Chapter 13

A FAREWELL AND A SUDDEN DEPARTURE

So here was a newcomer Mr Mercer at Hadlow, who went onto change so many things and have such an input into my life at school. He was one of the good guys I would meet in my life and what a difference he made on my learning in the class as any subject with him I started to reach such high grades even if he wasn't the teacher taking the class, he was still very much encouraging me to do that little bit better than normal plus as a P.E teacher he was pushing me even further on the playing fields.

He would every morning join us the pupils for the morning runs so my health as in fitness was just going from leaps to bounds and that meant I was making one of the top teams in any given sport I had taken.

leaving many in my wake as I would make a difference on the playing field than I ever had in my life when it came to sport as I was becoming a leader in teams I was in and not in a rebel manner or as a captain as I never captain any of the sport teams I was in but in a positive fashion, picking the team spirit up if ever we were losing or behind in a game.

Always heading for one result and that was to be on the winning side though if found myself on the losing team, I could take this as well in good spirit.

My past outbursts on the sports field had come to a halt as I used to bring in my teachings of judo when playing certain sports such as rugby and that used to cause many fights that I had been the cause of.

That was due to if I came up against dirty players that would play dirty to try and put weaker players off whom were in my side. Whenever I came up against this method of playing, I wouldn't play dirty back nor would I run or try to avoid them as I would seek them out on the opposite playing team and I would take them down in close quarter by using a judo move and that would normally put most at bay but then there were the others who would just want a all out fight.

I would always step up to the mark and fight I would, which never looked good in the front of the coach as I was playing for one of the best schools in the country.

Fighting in public or any fighting just wasn't ever something that they would stand for so I was shut down quick during my first year at Hadlow and as for fighting in school I only fought if I was ever challenged and that would happen from time to time, which would only cause me to hammer whoever stood in my way that had brought on such challenges with my fists.

I had learned from my time with the youth gangs, the type of violence I showed was too over bearing for any of the pupils whoever attempted to attack me as it was the last thing they ever did, but due to the damage I would inflict on them by defending myself, I would also find myself being punished unfairly.

I was noted by all the teachers from the matron saying I had a violent temper, which I feel I didn't. It's just I wasn't weak and I could stand up for myself but the school saw it differently but with the arrival of Mr. Mercer he saw it as not a problem.

Something that seemed negative that being my tempter and he thought of ways to channel my tempter and that was through what the head teacher at the time disagreed on but as I had spoken about how calming that judo was for me then Mr. Mercer would bring in a Zen Do Kai Master from Palmerstone North Wolves Club who would with some of his higher graded own students teach me the art of Zen do kai which is a free style marital art actually one from Australia from a gentleman called Bob Jones.

I would lean how to control my tempter through self discipline, this done me the world of good and soon many of the other kids were following me as in taking up class to start with once a week then to twice a week.

This was doing me so good but at the same time it was, I guess giving me to much confidence. When it came to spending holidays in Wellington and those weeks away as now I was given even more freedom from my mum so I was allowed to go out into the city and hang out without having to sneak out of the house.

For me and my friends from the city then this would be where we would go up town on a Friday night as girls were on our mind and up town is where we could meet many on our school holidays.

At that time of my life girls very much were no.1, whenever I went up to the city but also me and the boys would find ourselves fighting as well due to us meeting up with other kids whom also were up town hanging around the malls and fight we would.

Never losing many that I recall but of course not winning all but with my two combined martial arts I was for my age turning into what was a very good forced fighter for my age group and impressing a lot of the older boys but that was never a good thing as soon I would find myself being baited on by them, or evening having to fight them as they wanted to put me in my place to teach me a lesson.

It was testing me in what I was capable of in my fighting skills. At times bringing me straight back down to earth if I was thinking I was too clever for my own boots but in general I was still getting up to a lot of mischief and being away from school I didn't have those good influences in my life, which were such a blessing while I was at boarding school doing so well.

Everything was going well when I was, that is at the school living far away from Wellington because as soon as I would reach Wellington for those weekends at home, I would be back among it all through my sister's boyfriend and his friends.

More I hanged around them, equally what they were teaching would be soaked in by my young brain as with the schooling I was learning and progress from Mr Mercer at school so in a way it was like having an angel on one shoulder and the devil on the other.

Only time would tell which would win in making my life a better future for me at such a young age as I had everything to live for and being a student at one of New Zealand leading schools was something that I could just capture and turn it into even better results in all aspects of my life.

But with girls I soon I had a girlfriend by the name of Penny Smith who was many years older than me. She was around 14 years old and she thinking I was maybe only a year younger and what we got up to was just short of full sex but things were leading that way very quickly whenever I saw her while on home leave from School.

I had dated many girls even by this young age though trust me I still had a lot to learn about girls.

I can recall one girl who I dated and then called her sister on a date, without either of them knowing I had dated each other well when they found out they thought they would get me back, good and proper.

They did by both asking to go on a double date with me and getting me really drunk on a bottle of vodka.

Their own bottle of vodka they had poured out and filled with water so as we sat in the mall after seeing a movie and I was thinking I was the man, well oh no as these clever girls had something planned for me, and that meant I wasn't even going to get past first base.

Soon as they got me drunk and I mean very drunk I was taken to a car park the suggestion was to be naughty where no one could spot us so on arriving in one of the more empty floors of the car park my jeans were soon removed and then was my shirt as I was laid down and told to close my eyes. I couldn't close my eyes as every time I did, I was spinning due to the booze these girls had thrown down my throat.

As I tried to sit up I thought to myself hey where the fuck are the girls as I thought I was in for some treat then as I stood up that's when I saw one of them with my clothes and trainers rolled up saying "this for dating one another behind our backs, you asshole".

"What u two sisters? Never! You gotti be kidding." I tried to use as my get out of jail card but that wasn't going to cut the biscuit as the younger out of the two threw my clothes over the side of the car park.

We must have been like 8 floors up, I looked over the side and they had landed on a roof of a building that was being built, I had to pull myself in before I fell over the side as well due to how very drunk I was.

But still it hadn't hit me that these girls were getting one over me to the extent of them leaving me standing there in my underwear as they took to the fire exit stairs and run they did.

I couldn't catch up as I got to the top stair as I was far too drunk and I didn't even make it down one set of the stairs.

What the hell as I too had no money as my money was in my jean pocket and in those days no mobile phone and stuck in the middle of a car park probably the most drunk I have ever been up to that stage of my life.

I couldn't sleep as I was spinning every time I tried to close my eyes, I couldn't get to my clothes and hey the girls really had gone and left me. This was no joke and there would be no naughty play for me but a mission ahead on trying to get home and on a busy night through the capital of New Zeeland just in my underwear.

I tried getting a ride with a bus but the driver just laughed in my face and so did everyone on the entire bus and at the bus stop as I had to wait for another bus in my underwear in the middle of the city.

As they say when ya want a bus there are never any and when you don't need a bus then two come along at the same time.

As I was in the middle of town I couldn't just jump on the back of a bus as I had done years ago as too many people would have seen me.

I had to run and run I wasn't doing good at all as every foot step I seemed to take I would fall myself due to the booze but thankfully I made it just to the outer limits of the city and found a quiet area where there was a set of lights and a bus stop.

All I had to do is hope someone caught the bus from this bus stop or that the bus would be stopped at the lights but neither happened for a while but thankfully someone got off the bus so on the back I went and home sweet home I was.

But I wasn't as my mum wasn't home and she always had great locks on her door ever since my father used to break down the door so easy at our last place so in her new flat even though my Dad now was living overseas she still had great solid locks put on the doors so no way was I able to get in so I had to get to my sisters place and by this time I was sick and exhausted and just wanted to get inside.

On reaching my sisters and knocking on her front door and no one inside at her place either, well I couldn't wait outside as it started to rain so I punch my fist through her glass panel door and in I went straight to her bedroom, putting on some of her boyfriends clothes a motorhead t-shirt and a pair of black jeans then crashed out on the bed.

That is till I got up in the middle of the night and open one of my sisters boyfriends draws and thinking it was the toilet I pissed in it filling it up with all the vodka that was inside of me and then back on the bed rolling over as the ceiling was spinning around and around so throwing up all over the bed then falling asleep only to be woken up near 5am from my sister and her boyfriend who had been out to a house party.

Well the two sisters had got me good and proper and I learnt never to date one girl well dating another and more so if they were sisters, and always to make sure never get the wool pulled over my eyes again like that.

It was only till the next day I could laugh about it and hell I did but my sister's boyfriend wasn't too pleased when he open his draw and all through his hidden supply of dope which I hadn't noticed while half asleep pissing on it, he still went ahead and sold it telling people who would come to the house to buy the weed, while my sister was out of the house, it was just sticky buds that's all and they didn't smell of piss.

You know what they kind of did as I could smell the bag of weed every time he would pull it out and it stank of piss, he wasn't happy with my performance at all so I stayed clear for the rest of the year from him and also ever drinking vodka to excess.

Girls I kept chasing and school was becoming more settled by the year was out, I had achieved so much in that first year and now I had my second and last year to do at the school now though as a senior pupil.

What I didn't know was that through my good work and myself no longer having this rage that seemed within me in the first year and for seeing some leadership skills in me then Mr Mercer had put me up as a school deputy prefect of one of the schools houses.

That was such an honour at any given school that had a system of prefects especially a private school and a leading one as there were only four school houses so there was only four prefects of each house and four deputies of those same school houses.

The only most senior pupils above the perfects were the head boy and deputy head boy so I was very much in a league that held great respect among the school, be it the teachers really for the first time and other pupils many thinking how did I end up with this title.

Maybe I was a leader as I showed so much strength and I wasn't weak plus I thought more as a older kid I guessed as in making decisions as I never replied on others and I would take the lead when many of the other kids were just like sheep they would only ever follow rather that lead.

My sport came alive as now I was reaching each top or 2nd team so I was travelling away with the teams playing against the best in the country and would stay with other pupils and their parents when playing against them at their school grounds in sports.

When we had visiting teams to us then my uncle Frank and his wife who were both supportive to me during this time of my life as they lived in a town that was only two townships away from Masterton, in Greytown as my uncle had brought out single handily the best saw mill in that part of New Zealand which was located at the bottom of the mountain range in the township of Featherstone.

As my Mum lived over and beyond the mountain range so whenever I had to host then I would do so at my uncles house which help me not feeling distant from the other kids who could host fellow school team players.

In turn it meant a better bonding among both teams until that is both teams reached the playing field when we would met them again to thrash it out on the playing field to gain more wins and become the leading sports team of the country in our age group within the private schooling system.

The best of the best and I was one of them as by midyear my grades in class had shot through the roof and midterm I was reaching in the top 5 and also coming first and second on more than two subjects which meant placement on the honours board if I were to pull this off by the end of the year and nothing was stopping me from doing so.

I was now 12 years old though going on 16 year in many ways, I had school sorted.

My relationship with my mum was good, so much better than ever before and thankfully I had my uncle Frank and my auntie Beth near, who truly were there for me and gave me so much love and support as if at times they were my second parents as they were the ones that would come and watch me play sport and also just be there for me.

It meant so much to me and truly made me a better person while at school having my uncle Frank and my auntie Beth in my life during those years.

I say I had school sorted; it still was tough going at times so I mean I had school sorted as in my own happiness and success that I was achieving be it on the sports field or in the class rooms but still there even more tough laid times ahead.

I was in regular contact with my father whom at the end of the schooling year wanted me out to the UK for the end of school holidays something I was hoping to happen as I hadn't seen my father for a few years.

What I had spoke about to do with Carl Gill and Leonie Gill came true as I had members of the West Indies cricket team whom at the time were the best in the world personally come and visit me at their house as a few of the players were childhood friends with Carl Gill who as mentioned was a great role model when it came to sport.

That man taught me how to play cricket and his wife Leonie Gill was a dear friend of my Mum, she was such a lovely friend to my mum and also to me and my sister.

I was loved very much by the other pupils for this who all were cricket mad but it also brought some resentment and jealous as I returned to school with a signed cricket bat and also photos with the great legends of modern day cricket as the West Indies cricket team at the time were like in another league above all the other international teams at the time.

I could feel at times a lot of petty backstabbing towards me by some of the wealthy boys who thought it was their right in status that they should have been given the prefect position rather than me.

Fighting started to occur in the dorm again though I wouldn't get bailed or fooled into fighting as it was going to mean that my position be taken and I wasn't going g to give it up as I had earned it and it was given to me in such a risk or gamble that Mr. Mercer took in making me a prefect above the others, who may in others eyes be more suitable than me.

But soon I was tested and would it be falling in line as to how the other prefects would jump to doing the deed without a second thought or would I do what I had been taught by Father and that was not to ever grass?

I took what I had know was right and not grass up on what I seen two pupils do and that was one had sneaked in some pot of one of the day pupils and like in every school across the land the kids would have a smoke of ciggs in the changing rooms but these two kids had taken to smoking dope getting stoned.

Now I had smoked pot a few odd times in Wellington but never would I think of smoking it while at school or having anything to do with it at this stage. I walked in to the changing room with two other kids; both were wealthy kids who had always been jealous of me, the kid from the city. We entered and that's when I could smell it was weed but the other kids who were with me would never ever in their whole lives ever had smelled dope before.

I simply asked the two smoking the weed to put it out remaining them that they could be expelled for this but that was as far as I was going in my duty of being a prefect.

Now here was the chance of some of the stuck up kids to score brownie points for being grasses. They were like teachers pets but of the worst kind, they wouldn't stop sucking up to any of the teachers, just to get brownie points. These kids were in my eyes simply rats.

They told me if I were not to tell on these boys then they would rat on me for not letting it known to any teachers and as being a prefect it did mean you were the eyes and ears for the teachers when teachers weren't about plus you had other duties all that were fair and brought around something good for your given school house mine being Rutherford House.

I loved doing all the duties that was placed upon me but one thing I wasn't was a grass and I wouldn't grass these kids up and so I made a deal with the two wealthy kids, that if I gave up my title then they were not to rat on anyone.

I for sure wasn't going to grass up the two pupils who I had found smoking a joint as no way was I going to end their own chance of a great education as that is just pure bad karma to do that upon anyone.

So before the two trouble making wealthy kids could rat me in, I made a decision that had never been made in all of the many years of the history of Hadlow and that was I gave up my position as deputy prefect of my house. This was such a shock to the whole Friday assembly when I done this in my speech.

The only person I felt sorry for was Mr. Mercer but I felt I done the correct thing and I looked around at some of the teachers who seemed please I had given up my title and many of the boys did as well, and there were the two rats among them all who had got exact what they wanted.

One of them rather than be happy just with that he would rock the boat and become such trouble for me over the next few months.

I would be given so much abuse by the boarders for what I had done as they said I had brought shame to my school house and that this was not correct so in a way I had black sheep myself.

You know what I didn't give a fuck what they all thought, the brown nose prats as what I done was right and not abuse my position ever of power and when I was placed on the cross roads I didn't take the sewer hole of the rats as I didn't grass up anyone as if I had then due to my actions I would have there and then got two boys expelled and that would have wreaked their lives as in a education and that would have brought such shame on to their families.

Even more so if it had become known among others as then the school its self would have been in more shame than it seemed to be by me resigning as a prefect.

Due to the lack of respect I now held among the kids, it drove me more now in the hands of my sister's boyfriend and his mates, who now had become prospects for the dangerous motorcycle club in all of New Zealand, who were the Satan's Slaves Motorcycle Club.

On my weekends home I wouldn't just find myself at my sister's house but now down at the headquarters of this clubhouse. It was a place that was filled with staunch men some among them were the hardest men in all of New Zealand.

Some were killers and most were criminals of the highest order, none accepted fear but all were fearful to others, be it at the time the police, the general public and rival gangs as no one dared fuck with these guys that were serious and here I was a young kid of 12.

I had been down their clubhouse in the past but never been up at the bar drinking among them and due to leaning how to play pool and also darts all those years earlier on the Cook Strait ferry across the two Islands of N.Z with my dad, well I could win money from playing some of the bikers mainly after they had drunken enough beer and I could clean up on a few games of pool and take a few dollars from some of the visitors.

My face was maybe young but my way of thought wasn't and though was treated as a kid I wasn't treated as a child of my age but one much older.

I liked this and it gave me bigger balls so whenever I went back to school and was given any abuse from the little rats at school well I would just wake them in the middle of the night with a mask and hockey stick across their knees for all the abuse that I had to take that I never reported to the teachers.

I no longer was going to take any shit and I fought my way sadly out of grace and into a bad light. My mum was for the first time called to the school which I wasn't happy with as I thought it was a bit too much as I wasn't falling out of line in school but I was just standing up for myself. I had the awful matron jump on the band wagon and she would make life a hell backing up on the side of the kids who were giving me shit.

She was truly being an utter bitch. I don't know why after so many years the old hag was still the matron, they should have brought in a younger women that the kids could get on with and relate to rather than this old hag as she wasn't the kindest of a women and she too would get into the act of punishment by whacking us over the back of the legs with her slippers.

Fuck that used to hurt and the way she would cut my toe nails, she would nearly rip the toe nails out of the skin at the end of my toes. I still can feel the pain from just writing about this. I was having enough of her backing up not the decent kids as she saw them as the shit stirring bastards that they were so it had to come to an end.

No longer could I dish them out beatings as they all would point the finger to me even though I would get them in the middle of the night, even though there were never any witnesses but the matron would take their word over mine.

One night while we were allowed to watch a movie called Stand by me, it's about a few kids who run away and their adventure following the train tracks.

Not too far from my school were also railway tracks that run through Masterton and would go all the way for many miles to Wellington as there was a major tunnel cut through into the mountain range. I thought that's the plan, to get away from the witch of a matron and the grassing kids, I would follow what I had just seen in this movie and have my own adventure.

I packed away a hidden bag, over days I would add things to it such as dried food and also a small blanket, a few books to read plus a torch then I would hide the bag away in a bush near the playing fields at the back of the school.

I would also on my morning runs work out the direction of the train tracks and the quickest way to reach them from leaving the school by foot when I was to make my escape.

This planning all went on for a week. One afternoon I went to put some apples into my bag but I was seen doing so by the deputy head boy of the school. Catching me putting a bag together he soon clicked something was up as he was a smart boy and I thought he for sure would grass me up as it was his duty to do so but what surprised me, nearly you could say into a shock as he asked me could he come along.

I thought it was a trick but he said he had never done anything such as this before and on watching that movie it just seemed so cool. He was sick of his strict parents and he too was sick of the matron and what I didn't realise was in many away he was like the first hippy kid I ever met apart from Mel Berg.

He said he loved listening to Bob Dylan while all the other kids would listen to cheesy pop music and here was a kid who enjoyed folk music and also he enjoyed The Doors.

This was my first time I listened to Light My Fire, L.A Women, all the sounds from Jim Morrison's voice, the lead singer of The Doors. I fucking loved it as it played on his tape cassette back in the dorm.

I hadn't taken my bag in; I left it still hidden in the bush. We sat in the dorm and spoke for the very first about running away and he said he had always thought I was a cool kid and he wanted to be my friend.

I asked him really he wasn't going to tell on me if I was to run away and he promised me he wouldn't. When asked if he could come along I said to him that's not my decision to make and neither would I ask him. He simply said would I at least tell him the day or evening that I was planning to escape and he would make up his own mind if he would too escape. I really didn't believe him that much, I just thought he was in away letting me know that for sure he wasn't going to grass me up.

I thought of giving him a different day all together that I was going to run away and a different time so if he was grassing me up or tricking me then he would have been given false information but in the end I just told him the truth. I was never one to lie so I let him know that the very next Saturday, be it rain or shine that I would be making the adventure come true once dinner had finished. Early evening before night showers we were allowed playtime within the school grounds so that was my time to escape before night roll call back in the dorm for bed.

It gave me an hour and half or two hours to be hopefully clear of the school on my route that I had mapped out to Wellington.

I had set myself a route to get back to the bright lights of Wellington, home sweet home by following the train tracks up to the beginning of the mountain range; I would then cross the mountains by foot.

By going over the mountain range I knew where the nearest huts were in the mountains as at school we would do so many treks up into the mountains and stay overnight so as a pupil I had covered most of the mountain range.

In theory it sounded easy and safe but in reality it would have been a nightmare and maybe cost me my life as this wasn't a hill but a mountain range.

Firstly though I had to escape and make it to the mountain range which by foot was at least 6 hours maybe away as it was three townships away with a lot of miles between each township.

I guessed to run that distance then maybe take three hours but to walk then yes at least 6hours so if I left at 6pm I would reach there by 12am.

Start my climb into the mountain range using one of the public paths for trekkers and raise up in to the mountain as after a hour of trekking then would come across the first hut for travellers, which I could enjoy one of the many meals I had and wrap up with my blanket and fall asleep out of the cold away from the wild animals, and sleep till morning break then take the next trekking part of the adventure and make the summit by the following night fall.

Again to sleep in one of the many shelters then following morning down the back of the mountain and overnight half way down it again to get rest and eat and sleep then following morning I would arrive at the nearest town on the other side then across the tracks of the train again I would follow for at least one or two days of marching along, I would finally reach Wellington.

Home to rest and tell my mum that I never wished to return due to the nasty matron and her side kick of prats who were the brown noise boys of the school, rats.

What a mission I had ahead as I quietly said a farewell to the school that had done me so well for the last year and a half. I collected my rug sack bag and started my sudden departure.

Just then hearing my name being called I thought for sure I had been found out, grassed up or spotted. I turned my head around slowly, there he was the deputy head boy with his own make shift carrier bag. He was for real when he said he wished to make this journey with me. We both set off on foot towards the railway lines to begin our adventure that was ever so exciting for the both of us.

No one had ever as a border even run away from the school in the school's history so again I had made the Hadlow history books though again for the wrong reasons. I had, had enough and thought out the way the school was a better place without me and it wasn't anything wrong with the school that drove me out.

The blame was down to the matron and some of the very brown nosed little bastards who I just couldn't stand. I couldn't knock their lights out fairly one on one as I for sure would have been expelled for any more such acts then I had nowhere else to turn part from exit.

Here at least I had a friend to join me so it was going to be even more of an adventure than I had hoped. I had enough food for two so all was good, we weren't going to starve and that's what was most important as we walked along like two mini backpackers through the town that we had known as home for over a year and half.

looking back now and then, seeing the school disappear even further into the background of this sleepy little town, where the train tracks soon would be in front of us as we could in the reaching distance hear firstly and then see with our own eyes the trains go moving past through the town and out of town which was exactly what we both wanted to do, and that was get out of town.

Out of town quick is what we did before it went dark and the torch needed to come out as we crossed the railway bridge. Fairly similar to the kids had in the movie when it came to crossing a huge railway bridge though for us we made it across the very first train bridge without a train coming running passed.

Everything seemed going in our favour in the very first few hours but it was getting dark quick and also ever so cold but you will have to read the next chapter to find out where our adventure lead us to and if I had made home sweet home with my pal in tow.

Chapter 14

STAND BY ME

The rain came down on us as we run along the train tracks. The darkness of the night came in all around us with flying trains, at times forcing the both of us to jump into farmland fields below the banks of the train tracks so neither of us was hit by the moving train.

Having to climb the bank to get back up to the tracks, only to come flying down them every time another train came by. In the end we decided to follow the train tracks from within the safely of the farming fields so we walked through one field to another and another then coming to a dairy farm full of live stock.

We jumped over the first fence passing all the cows, wondering if it's true when a cow sleeps standing up that if pushed, the cow simply falls over sideways only waking when on the floor with four feet up in the air thinking to its self how the hell did I end up in this position.

We tried to see if there was truth in that but these were New Zealand cows the size of range rover 4x4 motor vehicles. There anit no way two 12 year old kids going to have the strength to push a cow over. We headed for the next fence and then we both got buzzed. Giving both of us such a fright as we had walked straight into an electric wire fence that was in the middle of the field to place it into halves.

Now we were trapped behind a live wire electric fence and 50 sleeping cows so we headed to the bottom of the field towards the main road trying to avoid bumping into standing sleeping cows. By now we had had enough of walking through cow shit and being electric by the fence wires that we couldn't see in the pitch black of the night.

I didn't want to use my torch as it was only for once we had reached the mountain range, also wanted to keep the torch out of the wet as it was only a house use torch rather than a travelling torch. I couldn't risk our only source of light to be out by the time we had reached the mountains.

We jumped over the gate and walked along the main highway road. The nearest town was miles away and there was a lot of traffic on the road. We were guessing by now that we had been noticed by not being in the dorm for our roll call to bed so we guessed by now that there would be a party now out looking for us. All the cars that came past we jumped down to the ground and kept out of oncoming lights of the cars so not to be spotted, in case it was a police car or even worse our headmaster out driving looking for us.

We were in small running fresh water streams which are a common sight along country roads in New Zealand, which meant for us as the rain was falling we were not just covered now in soaking rain along this route we now were up to water in our boots. Still having to duck down when ever cars came past so we both decided to enter one of the nearby farms due to just not making much distance through the streams and along side of the main road.

As for the railway tracks they had pulled away right out into the countryside as we no longer could even see any trains out to the left, where we had come from much earlier back. The only way now for us was by following the road as we knew we were heading in the right direction towards the mountain range.

We must have been away now 5 hours as it was nearing midnight. I had timed it would only take us 6 hours on foot to reach the mountains but still they were miles away ahead. Now and then we could work out the ridge way when the light of the moon shined down upon the mountain ridges. Remembering actually how massive these mountains were. It was going to be a mission to climb them but that I still felt confident in.

We went back to the farms and over the fences, long as we weren't with live stock and found ourselves in open fields then we were fine. We now tried to pick up the pace which we did as we had moved through one township but out the other side of the township we had more farm land and by this time the ground was just soaked through. Water blogged which meant mud every step we took, many times losing our boots and ended falling many times on our faces.

We were now covered in mud and cow shit and our backpacks becoming even heavier after the worst of the rain fall had finished hitting us. We decided to reach a barn in one of the farms and take a rest to get our boots in order and work out a better plan as we now only had two townships to go and then the mountain range to hit.

We got some food out of my backpack and just as I went to put my teeth through an apple, the door swing open and standing there was a farmer with a fuck off shotgun.

We were frozen; he looked around but his head never looking down in the corner where we were sitting. If he had, had a farm dog with him we would have been found for sure.

If he had got a fright and his first reaction was to just fire a shot as farmers on their own land in New Zealand were known to fire away before asking questions due to them having so much live stock stolen and gangs stealing their farm machinery.

Kiwi farmers are not to be messed with as their farms are like their castles as it's their livery hood, more than usual past down from generation to generation as with my own families farms that my uncles had in New Zealand. Which are more than likely to be in the hands of some of my hard working cousins to run until they pass the farmlands on to their own kids in years to come.

We sat as silent as a mouse after seeing the shotgun, which of course was surely loaded. Scared the kid who had run away with me that's for sure as maybe he had never seen a real gun in his life before. He did seem to have lived a shelter life compared to the life I had lived anyway we couldn't let that fright end our journey and there was no turning back now.

As for an adventure it sucked, wasn't nothing like on the film and we hated it. We open the barn door as quietly as possible, we looked up to the skies and the heavens had truly opened even worse that before.

We couldn't hide out in the farm barn due to the farmer's house only being meters away. His kitchen light was on; we could notice a TV flashing inside as well so we knew he was still up or even maybe out there in the pitch black looking around his farm on some kind of security patrol as what else made him come to his barn.

Maybe he had heard the barn door open as we entered moments earlier before he himself checked on the very same barn that we were hiding in.

We didn't want to hang around to end up both being shot so we cleared out across the main entrance and back to the highway. We again were on the same route ducking and diving every time a motor came past; we had only made it up the highway for maybe only 2miles.

I was tucked on my jumper; looking back I could just see my friend had fallen into a creek. He had done damage to his waist as he seemed to have twisted his body when fell onto the side of the bank above the creek. Rocks had been pushed into his side as he was holding onto his right side of his hip which was giving him pain.

The rocks underneath the water that we couldn't see, we only felt them when we would try and take careful steps. Sooner or later one of us was going to take a fall. At the same time we were holding on to lose rocks in the side of the bank trying to balance ourselves up right keeping both our heads down and out of sight.

I took a look at my watch time now was 1230am, probably the latest this kid had ever been up. He had he couldn't or didn't wish to go on any further and just wanted to get back to school but there was no way after making it this far that I was willing to throw in the towel.

Ok maybe I wasn't ever going to make it in these weather conditions up the mountain but there was no way I was wishing for the long walk back to the school in defeat.

I said let's find somewhere again with a bit of shelter so to get out of the rain and to sleep then we can see how things are for tomorrow so he agreed with that. I had to though carry him as he had lost the will to go on. His legs and he was shaking due to the cold and wet so I carried him as good as I could to the next township.

Right on the outskirts of this town was an old fashion homestead pub so we walked around to the back of that where still we noticed inside through the window a few gents and a dog having bottles of beer pasted over to them in the salon bar. We could peer through in the bay window and at the back of the building were many cars and pickup trucks even at this time of night in the car park.

There was a lorry with an opening at the back so we slipped both up on the back of the lorry and with the cover from the rain, we were as happy as Larry but neither could sleep with the noise of the rain hitting the canvas of the roof and sides of the lorry.

I took my blanket out of backpack but it wasn't the warm blanket that I was hoping it to be as every where the rain had got in. I needed to put something around my pal as he was shaking and not looking the best. The entire colour from his face had been drawn out of his face so I went to see if there was somehow I could get into the homestead to at least find something to keep him warm.

I climbed up the side of the building using the fire stairs and through a window I manager to get in. I dared not walk further in to the place as I heard music bearing from another room and also a lot of voices all laughing, drunk they sounded so with one pull I just torn down the curtains and took that with me.

The curtains were heavy so I knew they would do for now and back to the lorry I went, covered my pal up so he had a bit of warmth. He was still in soaking wet clothes so not doing him the best of help as what was causing his skin to be cold were his own wet clothes.

He said he had seen a TV program that to keep warm sometimes to piss ya self helps in outdoor situations but as he suggested that then I thought I can't have the kid pissing himself to keep warm then having to smell piss in this confined space so I said lets go knocking on the pub, at least we then very much out of the rain. He hadn't been too a pub before let alone a homestead out on the country, where all the locals would come after their days out working in the farms.

He was scared for some reason, and I told him he had nothing to worry about as I jumped off the back of the lorry he still covered in the curtains. I said no leave them as we can't walk in with their curtains that I had just broken in to the homestead and nicked as then of course we would be in for a kicking from the owner or the locals. The curtains were thrown underneath the wheels of the lorry, as we went knocking on the front door to be greeted by a well built man with hands as strong as a boxer someone like Freddie Foreman.

He asked what were we doing hanging around his front door at this time of night, thinking we were brothers looking for our father among the locals who were still drinking in the bar. No we replied, we are cold and hungry and we have run away from Hadlow.

Everyone in this part of the county knew Hadlow even the rednecks or the township people as it was the posh school, very famous indeed.

He let us in after he had a good laugh when heard we had run away. He called for his wife an overweight woman with facial hair, who had the most softest of voices and was so caring towards us and gentle. We asked them please don't call the police and not the school, not for now anyway as we didn't wish to face anyone from the school at this point.

They agreed after hearing our stories, we added a few to make out the place was so bad as more we spoke more sorry they felt for us. Soon two baths were run for us and warm clothes, children's cloths close to our size were handed to us so we both in separate rooms up the stairs had a bath each and then afterwards we were clothed and warm again.

Back downstairs into the bar area they had cracked open the fire for us.

We asked why they still open at this time of the night, they replied that it was their eldest daughter's wedding that had taken place earlier that day, so her herself and her husband and wedding guests were all upstairs partying away in celebration, after such a lovely day.

Their eldest daughter wedding that had taken place earlier that day, so that's the noise I heard earlier when I had ripped the curtains down from one of the bedrooms upstairs.

How bad was I feeling now as they were so nice to us both and even better to come they came out with big slabs of lamb as they had a lamb on the spit earlier in the day so we were given so much food that had been left over from the wedding reception.

After that, we were taken again upstairs to the party that was in full swing and we joined in as well as we could. It was a bit over whelming for the fellow pupil but while he was tapping his foot to the beat of the music I was away with bride dancing with her and the other ladies.

She did turn to me after she also heard about my escape from school earlier that night and she commented what a great adventure it sounded I had been on to get this far. I thought yeah it finally did feel like a adventure, rather than a struggle as it had been for the last 5 and a half hours.

Things finally felt better for my fellow escapee after the falls and knocks he had taken to get this far after being electric on the wife fence, maybe nearly being shot by a right wing farmer and then having to walk through creeks, falling over and ending up in cow shit in farmland fields. Well how the night was ending for us all had truly made up for all the last six hours.

But as they say all good things have to come to a end and what we wasn't aware of, was the owners wife had called through to the school letting them know that we were here and we only found out as the dutchie was being passed to the left hand side by a few of the wedding guests who were getting high. It was me who had the joint in my hand though I wasn't smoking it I was just passing it to the left hand side when out the window we could see blues and twos pull into the car park below.

We thought we had been grassed on but then the lovely women said she had to as if we were her sons and then she would be worried sick so she hadn't done it to wreak our night. We kind of understood but for sure our night was totally wreaked as two country coppers came in making out as if we had escaped from a high security prison. Fucking hell it was only a boarding school and why the coppers, why not the school headmaster picks us up?

We found out in the car ride back that it was a scare tactic. Hey we were both stoned as fuck and asking them to put on their sirens just for the banter, but with no reply. We asked for them to put on the radio or did they have any Doors or the Rolling Stones that we could listen to for the car journey back?

Also cheekily asked them if they could stop in to any late night petrol shop if one happen to be open as we now had the munchies but none of our requests for a bag of crisps or great music went down to well. All we got a dirty look in the rear view mirror from the copper behind the wheel.

Soon puff the magic dragon was going to disappear in a puff as smoke as what we had done came crashing down on us. We reached the school and were pulled out of the cop car like two criminals.

The headmaster was there, fuming! Explaining how a major search party had been out looking for us including we were told the police from Masterton and surrounding towns and that our families were worried sick and even was the matron we had been told was worried sick about us, that bit about the matron I couldn't believe.

The head master said in the whole history of the school that no one had ever run away! Be it a day pupil or a bordered and it had brought great shame to the entire history of the school.

We were looking at getting expelled, this hadn't crossed my mind and that now became something very real which would have broken my mum's heart and also all the progress that I had so far achieved. How far I had come to this point in my life from the early years of hanging around with street kids and youth gangs getting into trouble and a early life of crime so on seeing Mr Mercer I asked if I could have quiet word with him, before any life changing decision was to be made.

I made sure to outline that it wasn't the other pupil idea and I also added so to save his skin that it was all my idea and that actually the other boy didn't wish to take part but I had kept on at him, which in the end making the kid come along so the whole thing was my fault.

I was the only one to blame as I wasn't going to put the other pupil in the shit. I wished to take all of the blame on our behalf as I felt he had more to lose, but looking back now really in all truth it was me who had more to lose if I

Christian S Simpson

were to be expelled as that would have been the end to any chance ever again in my life to better myself in such a school.

I noticed Mr Mercer have a long talk with the headmaster which seemed to go on for a lifetime as we stood standing out his the headmaster's office, waiting to hear what was going to happen to us.

First the deputy head boy was stripped off his title, as the headmasters done that then I knew we weren't being expelled well at least he wasn't anyway. The headmaster wouldn't have made a big issue about taking his title from the boy as we would have just been expelled there and then though the time was 3am in the morning.

There wasn't a smile to be found in the headmaster office. What was there waiting for us, was his cane and fuck he caned both of us not 6 times which was I am sure the rule but 12 times each, it hurt like hell.

Though in some pain each time I was canned, all I did to block out the pain is think back to where we started off the night across railway lines and bridges to falling in cow shit and being buzzed by live wire fences to ending up at a wedding reception. Eating great portions of fine New Zealand lamb and dancing badly with some wedding guests. It did bring a smile upon my face even while thinking of the car ride back in the back of a police car to now being canned at 3am in the morning.

It was just a funny moment that was had and it had turned into such an adventure even if we never made it to the top of the mountains.

Shorty after being canned on our backsides we were send to our beds in the dorm. Once the matron had gone, well the dorm erupted as if we were greeted like return war heroes from the war. What we had done just, become a cult status for the rest of our days at Hadlow.

Though the kid who run away with me had his role as deputy head taken from him, what he had been given as a replacement from everyone of the students was something that he just loved having the title for and that was a rebel without a cause- a true outlaw in the eyes of the other kids, who none of them would ever have had the balls to do what he or I had just done, it was truly priceless.

Through all the three schools from Rathkeale to St Matthews, we were known among every single student. My bus journeys home and back, now some of the girls were even keener on me and as for the boys of the Rathkeale College whom had at the start for the year tried to bully me were now befriending me. Our story was spread around through the grapevine.

The way I made it up to Mr Mercier for making sure he had changed the headmasters mind around from expelling me for running away, was to gain the very best results that I ever could get in my class.

I scored 1st in class on two subjects, the lowest position on some subjects was 4th place also with all my great grades on final exams I had done what no one would even foreseen me as doing and that is gain a place in my final year on the honours board. As for sports I now had be given a regular playing position of the 1st 15 rugby squad so my talent on the playing field which had been worked on for those two years, all that hard work at training sessions had all paid off in the long run.

My mum was so pleased and so was even the head master as from escaping from the school to coming back and doing the best I had ever done on my two years since leaving home which was commented something that even the school was proud they had turned this troubled young kid from the big smoke around and made him that year one for their finest improved students.

I was so happy in all I had achieved, some of the those goals that were set out for me by Mr Mercer and how I had even done so much better than was expected of me but most of all I had made my mum the most proudest Mum in the whole world and she was so happy and that alone meant the world to me.

I soon was told that in the post was a letter from Rathkeale offering me a place at Rathkeale Prep College due to my rugby skills I had shown on the playing field plus also due to the success story that I had become.

For me to be offer this was a once in life time opportunity for a working-class boy , though it would meant being at another boarding school and this was if not the leading private school in the country at the time with Christ College in Christchurch in the South Island coming a close second.

12 years/13 years old I would be going into the school and coming out of there with the world as my oyster at the age of 18 years old after spending 5 years at the school as a boarder. 5 more years of such an education then I could be anything I wished and reaching for the stars would be so easy. Any job that I wished to have taken up once I finished the next five years at Rathkeale would come so easy as long as I kept up with all the hard work from the previous two years and carried on setting goals and achieving them.

I didn't want to do go on to a another boarding school though as I was hoping these last two years at Hadlow would finish with me returning back home to Wellington. My mum enrolling me into local college, but my mum was just too proud and she believed so much that I could go onto better things. My uncle Frank and his wife Beth also were backing the decision that I stayed on. Mr. Mercer said this is your chance in life to even become more of a success story; it would be like a rag to riches story in many ways.

My Father was sad as it may mean for that coming Christmas holiday I wouldn't be travelling to the UK to visit him. He and my Grandparents were so happy though when I send them the results through of how well I had done in final year exams at Hadlow.

I agreed with my mum so to make her happy, that I would go to Rathkeale. The forms were filled out and I set a exam separate at Hadlow that was submitted to the Rathkeale and also my final rugby game seemed to have brought great interest as well by a few more people from Rathkeale who came to watch some of the best players including myself play, out of the students who were heading for Rathkeale the following year. I found out as well that I would be placed into rugby house when arriving in the New Year at the college.

Now all I had to say was farewell to a school that I didn't to start wish to be at but over time had grown on me and had changed this young troubled kid into someone that I could be proud of and also very much my Mum and my family. How it actually done me the best of good being so far away from Wellington and out of reach of the gangs and all the trouble that I would be getting up to if I still had lived in Wellington. As long as I was away from Wellington then I would be out of reach of the many gangs and their pitfalls and everything negative that surrounded them.

I had to thank Mr Mercer for all he had done, as in giving me a chance and believing in me. He was such a great influence on my schooling and on making me reach for the stars, also for how he backed me when for sure I was nearly to be expelled for escaping that evening earlier in the year. I truly had so much to thank this incredible teacher for as without him showing up at that school then I am not sure I would have gone on to better things and changed my life around for the best.

I then got onto the final bus journey back to Wellington and was welcomed by the senior boys from Rathkeale, who were going to move up a year at Rathkeale to become last year's pupils at the school. They would be attending the school when I was to become a junior student the following year.

I could see in their eyes mischief thoughts, which soon I would find out many had never forgotten me for showing them up in front of the girls and the other kids on the bus when my sister boyfriend and his mates came on board to put them in their place after all the bullying that had gone on in previous years.

Also as they knew I had in my past smoked a little pot, then that meant I was going to become part of a certain group within the school where drugs for cash came first and foremost for many of them above even class. They were seen by many as the in crowd with money to spend and access to drugs for the pupils who were of the age experimenting with the use and abuse of drug taking.

They had I would soon found out at the school, dope plants grown in the bush surrounding Rathkeale. The dope plants had been handed down from senior students to them, which had been growing over many a year's. They were growing out in the grounds of the school as the school was over 100 acres very deeply set in the country side.

It was no interest of mine to get involved in any of that as I was going to that school to only better myself and try my hardest not to put a foot wrong and for now I didn't care about any in crowd at the new school. My thoughts were on a magical Christmas that was a few weeks away as I now had weeks of school holidays to be filled with joy and happiness.

But what I didn't know at the time, that these older boys on the bus would be the destruction of my success story. Singlehandedly, they would be a destructive force which would take everything away from me that I had earned and worked so hard towards.

The start of the end was actually near and also the very end of the golden education that I had studied so hard for. Where I had put my head down for the last two years into my school books and all the learning, training, blood, sweat and tears on the playing fields, all the time and effort I had put into sport and turning my school results around that had got me a place at Rathkeale, this all was going to be taken away from me.

All of it to go up in a cloud of puff due to puff, the end was near, or as Jim Morrison would famously sing "this is the end my only friend, the end" in one of his songs. Here for me the happiest time in my whole life, I would find it all come to an end.

Chapter 15

YOURE GOING DOWN AND GOING DOWN FAST

Back home to Wellington to a welcome home with open arms from my Mum and all my friends. Everyone was so happy to see me after the good news that had been spread about my acceptance into Rathkeale, one of New Zealand's leading private schools in the entire country.

After how well I had done in my end of year school exams at Hadlow, I was one very much looking forward to this Christmas. Wow, my life was perfect in every way and I no longer felt like an outsider and I was looking forward to attending college and doing my very best.

I said to my Mum that I was popping out to see my sister over at her place as she had now moved into her second flat since she had moved out of home two years ago.

This flat was bigger, it was a house and so there were more flatmates and that always meant more visitors due to also her boyfriend still selling drugs and her flatmates boyfriend as well. I don't think my sister still at this stage knew what was going on as to the level of drugs they were moving nor to the extent of how many different drugs they were now selling.

When I reached the flat my sister had gone already out on a girlie night with her girlfriends so the house had only her boyfriend and also a few of his mates there and my sister's flatmates boyfriend. I was let in and a bear hug followed that nearly crushed my ribs, I walked into the lounge and there on the coffee table was so much coke, nothing I had ever seen before apart from on well known American gangster type flicks.

I knew it was coke; I had snorted a line of coke in my past once when I was 11 years old, only small line by these same people but never had I been offered it to this extent, with a promise of joining them to a party if I would carry the drugs for them.

I know what a fool I would be if I were to say yes but I would only have to leave and go and spend the evening at my mum's apartment with my mum, and that to me on my first night of my xmas holidays seemed ever so boring compared to joining the excitement of a party.

It sounded too good so I lend down and snorted a line of coke and placed bags down my underpants and jumped in one of the motors as we headed out to Stokes Valley about a hour's drive out of Wellington and party we all did.

Though I had positive roles models such as my uncle Frank and also Wim and at my last school Mr Mercer but none of those people were around and these older guys to me were also role models though negative ones but in my eyes they were doing me no harm at the time and again it was a thing of being accepted such as what I always seem to need when I was younger by the youth gangs etc.

Maybe it was due to not having a father in my life. I am unsure but also these guys in my eyes were cool and true outlaw type guys, rebels. That had always been a tag I was given since an early age so in many ways it seemed I had a connection with them and could relate to these types of people so much better than your normal Mr Jones, if you know what I mean.

The girls are the party were loose to say the least, taking their tops off after a few too many drinks. Partying to the sounds of ac/dc, motorhead, deep purple, and The Doors, a band I really enjoyed. Actually all the music some new to me and some I heard down at the Satan's Slaves MC being played in the past so I was enjoying it all and very much so the party and half naked girls running around as I had seen nothing like this before, it was fucking great.

With the sounds of The Doors, I went into the bathroom and enjoyed more of the coke which was making me feel like I was on top of the world.

Soon I had many people coming over to me asking if I were Christian. I thought fucking hell I am popular tonight, soon realizing though they all were after the drugs I was holding. Mainly the coke and not so much the weed so I set up in the kitchen where I was close to the guys who had driven me to the party so no one would rob me as there were some heavy looking guys there.

Many I could see had knives foddered into their belts, each time they went into the fridge to get themselves a beer I could see a lot of weapons as they reached over to take a cold beer out of the fridge, even one having what looked like a handgun.

This wasn't the type of party where anyone would want their 12 year old kid being at, but for me I loved it. I felt a wave of trust over me from my sister flatmates boyfriend plus I was buzzing just counting all this money each time someone else scored lsd or coke from me.

By the end of the night I had no coke left and all the lsd tabs had gone and only a little bit of weed left. My pockets just full of pure cash, so much cash that I didn't have enough room in my jeans to put my hands.

We drove back to Wellington, which was a fast drive back and a reckless drive but I was used to their driving after hanging around with them now over time.

We reached my sisters place, I was asked to hand over all the money that was shortly counted in the car. There was over $6,000 in cash, now to you that may not seem a lot of money but to me it was so much quid.

Once the money was counted I was handed $100. Five £20 notes, that was fuck all compared to all the money that went into their hands and for the very first time they realized that maybe my birth date meant I was 12 years of age but 12 was only a number.

I was unlike many other 12 years old so I wasn't going to be mugged off so I told them I want 10%. All my years of schooling meant that I could work out the maths and yes 20% would have been better but if I could get 10% out of them then that meant $600, which to any kid in New Zealand was a hell a lot of money.

They moaned and then I had them rowing between themselves until they agreed to handing me $500 which was short of 10% I had tried to get from them. They handed me $500 in cash as long as next time I would come out with them again and do the same. With the colour of money now in my hands, I didn't give it a second thought and so said yes but from then onwards I could command 10% and nothing less, agreed and agreed it was.

After the money had been hidden somewhere in the house, our night wasn't over as we drove away and went to the Satan's Slaves Motorcycle Club House.

There was a steaming party going on there in full swing even though it was near 4am in the morning by this time, but they had a round 30 guests into the clubhouse from different 1% Motorcycle Clubs from the South Island whom were on a Club Bike Ride.

Satan's Slaves MC was the first MC Club when coming of the interisland ferry from the South Island to the North Island. As long as they were friends of the Satan's Slaves MC then they were allowed to of course ride into the clubhouse and party hard.

I was able to buy my own beers and I had a great night. Some prospects would be giving me a bit of shit, but with hell to them as they looked like pricks by picking on a 12 year old kid, as with the senior members they just let me be and I got on with playing pool and getting drunk.

I had learned to hold my drink so much better ever since those two sisters got one over on me so I never lost the plot where drinking at this such young age. As I had been snorting coke back at the party in the end about a grams worth then later on that night when I asked for more I was charged $300 for a gram out of my money.

I wasn't allowed to snort it in the clubhouse as the Satan's Slaves were anti any drug use inside their clubhouse and anti the sale of any type of drugs so I was told not to let on to any of the members I had coke on me while there. All of this made me feel very grown that night among all this lot.

I didn't leave till maybe midday the following morning. I was so wasted walking along in the sunshine. By now I was hungry so I ended up at the petrol station on the corner of Luxford St and got myself a sandwich then waved down a yellow taxi.

By the time I had paid the fee of the taxi and worked out all the money spend on all the drinks I had brought from the night before and also the coke I had brought from my sisters flatmate before I reached the clubhouse, I had only around £50 dollars left from the $500.

I wasn't too bothered as I didn't see it as my own money and I would do it again so to get more money, whenever the next party was on.

I fell asleep a happy young man and woke up that evening with a knock on the door a friend of mine Sasaka Campbell had come over to see how I was as he hadn't seen me for ages.

His mum was a friend of my mum's for many years and he and I got on well. His sister was the same age as my sister so our family would mix a lot together, he also had a younger brother who was around my own age group. Sasaka came in piece of tinfoil that had around $20 worth of weed, known in New Zealand as a bullet.

I rang my mum to finds out where she was and if she was coming over. She told me she was at her boyfriend Wims place and so I told her to stay there the night as Sasaka was staying over as he would take the settee to sleep on and it meant I could crash in my mum's bed.

But more than that it meant we could get stoned in my mum's apartment and not has to worry about smoking it outside and getting caught by any of the neighbours.

My mum told me there was lots of fresh food in the fridge but after the first joint was smoked I was too stoned to cook. I told Sasaka I had $50 dollars on me so we would order in some pizzas and that we did. The pizza was dropped off by a kid who mustn't have been any older than 15 years old.

I asked him how he got a job as a pizza delivery man at his age. He went onto let us know that it was his father business and he worked in the pizza shop for his Dad but whenever his father was away then he would take one of the pizza bikes out as a excuse to be able to ride a motorcycle and get out of the shop.

His name was Carl and he seemed like a cool kid, as I went to give him the money for the pizza, he asked was it pot he could smell? Asking why he would ask such a question, he said as his dealer wasn't answering his phone so he was wondering if he could get a joint from us.

Now this is where it all started from as I went in and told Sasaka to hand me over some of the bullet. Sasaka said no he can't buy any of it as it's all he had, I said to Sasaka not to worry as I could get more so he handed me over most what was left apart from a joint and with that Carl then gave me $20 even though it was short of two joints.

One we just had before we ordered the pizzas and the one we kept for later. Carl was happy and grateful and said any time in the future when I want to order pizza he would give me discount. A friendship was made but also as I said the very start of things to come, none being positive though I wouldn't realise this to the following the year.

We sat back and ate the pizza while listening to a great blues record of B.B King the blues legend, while getting stoned more. Finishing the last joint, we had run out and Sasaka started at me asking why I had given our pot away. I told him not worry as we could go to my sister place as her flatmates boyfriend sold dope. Sasaka eyes lit up, soon we were on our feet walking the pavement heading to her place.

On arriving we scored some weed and finally I could see my sister who wasn't too pleased that I was being sold dope but Sasaka told her not to worry, it was for him rather than me. She didn't then have a go at me in front of her flatmates and her friends as I hated when she ever done that.

That weekend I and Sasaka got so stoned. When he went to leave he asked if he get more weed for him to take back home? I took him again around to my sisters place, but as we were heading there he said he didn't have enough money to cover the whole amount.

I went through what I had left which was a bit of money after paying for the pizzas. I handed him that and in the end with what he had and what I gave him, he could buy himself $40 quid worth of dope and still have his bus fares home. He was a happy guy as I walked him then onto the bus and I headed home with no cash though I had 48hrs earlier had $500.

The holidays were going well, my mum was happy to have me home when I was home but I was always over my sisters hoping that her boyfriend again would be taking me with his pals to another party. The next time I went out with was when they headed out one afternoon to meet the guy who they were themselves scoring off.

I was to stay in the car though I knew why they were heading to this place due to the conversations they were having in the car. When they came back to the car I was handed a huge wrapped bag, too big to put into any jean pocket so the whole package went down my jeans and off we went. This time not straight back to my sister's place but to one of their close friends called Stonney.

Stonney was huge in height and weight, he was known to be kind hearted and also he was known at the same time to have a tempter, which I would see over the years.

His temper at times remind me off my own father as Stonney had a raging tempter towards anyone who upset him but these early day he was ok around me. He still would be fine towards me as I got older though at one stage like many others, he would take the piss at times.

You got to remember these guys were over 25 years old and had been in such circles where guns, drugs and violence were common so they had become hard as nails as they got older and in ways ruthless which made them an interest of the Satan's Slaves Motorcycle Club.

That evening after I watch them separate all the drugs and bag everything up, out came one of Stonney flatmates who was a stripper at a local strip club. We headed off in his motor and went to her strip club; I was holding the gear during the car ride there.

We got greeted by the owner who hushed into the dressing rooms and there in front of me were so many naked girls. I thought I was in heaven as it was just unbelievable, I wasn't complaining that's for sure. Out came the drugs I was holding and all the girls every single one of the girls took drugs from me mainly this time speed and then some threw the correct amount of money for the coke.

They hadn't seen what I had seen earlier back at Stonney place, watching certain people present who were cutting the gear up with other things added so they were able to make what they had brought even last longer and that to them, meant more cash.

I didn't take on board what I was getting involved as I truly didn't feel I was getting involved in anything. After we left the strip club with a couple of grand and the owner had given us a round of us drinks them we went with one of the girls onto a stag party where she met another girl there.

Both the girls stripped off and they had some fun with the guy getting married. I waited next to Stonney who was making sure the girls were treated correctly and if any of the house guests wanted to buy any drugs, which a few did so that mean another grand in cash for him.

We ended the night in a pub, an old pub actually that my father years ago used to drink in though he never ever had anything to do such people as Stonney as my father was anti drugs.

The Governor of the pub knew I was Stevie's son so allowed me to have a beer as long as I sat in the restaurant part of the bar and not in sight as I was only 12 years old.

The night finished I was dropped home with $300 in my pocket. This was great as within the two weeks of being at home on school Christmas holidays I had earned myself $900 just short of a grand and really I didn't have to do much.

What if I had been caught? Though too young to go to jail but the youth courts surely would somehow handed out something for, if not found selling drugs then at least for having them on my body as in carrying them. All that was far from my mind as this was the most money I had ever seen go through my hands.

During this time I was still seeing a girl by the name of Penny Smith though we called her Penny Lane from the Beatles song. She was around 16 years old now and sooner than later I ended up having sex with her and then couldn't stop after that first time though I had played around with girls in the past from an early age, it was here when I was no longer a virgin.

For the rest of the holiday I was just pure fucking. I couldn't get enough of it and I fallen deeply in love as ya do when u 12 years old, the only different is back in those day most of the 12 years old were only holding hands going to the movies with their girlfriends but here I was taking her back to mine and not stopping with her till morning come.

My mum knew what I was up to and at one point left condoms for me which made me feel so embarrassed anyway all was good and my involvement with Penny after xmas had taken me away from hanging around with my sister's boyfriend so it was a good thing, it seemed sex had saved me from getting into anymore trouble.

As for knocking around with Chris, I was going to college parties with him rather than parties that guys would be carrying guns or knives and I carrying drugs as was the score when I hung out with my sister's boyfriend and his social circle of friends.

These colleges' parties were all through the local surf club that Chris was a member of and though I couldn't surf, they didn't mine me rolling on with them. The parties were great but sooner than later my life would repeat its self from the first weekend I had been home on these holidays.

One day Sasaka called me one day at my mum's house, due to not having mobiles and neither having a answer machine I would lose so many calls from my other friends such as Campbell Palmerton who was a good decent kid, he lived on my old street back in Miramar and he had always kept in contact with me since our first school that we went together to, Worse Bay School.

Anyway I didn't get to catch up with him this time during these holidays as I was busy with so much going on in my life. Sasaka was calling as he wanted me to score him more dope but as he couldn't smoke it at his place, he asked could he come over to mine so I said that was fine.

I got him $100 worth of dope and he gave me the cash when he arrived as I had used some of my modelling money to cover his costs. We called for pizza again and Carl true to his word gave us discount and again asked if he could score of us.

We sold him some weed when he dropped off the king size pizzas as Sasaka and I had the hell munch on through being so stoned of the weed so we ordered like three family sized pizzas. Carl asked for my number as he said he had shown and smoked that last bit of weed he got from me with some of his friends, who all now wanted to score from me.

But the thing was I wasn't a drug dealer. Never wished to be one and only due to events unfolding that were linked to each other then I was finding myself selling the shit. Not for myself but for others as if people asked me if I could sort something out for them then I would.

Not for the money but just due to my nature of being a old fashion gentlemen and in a way I didn't see harm in sorting Carl some weed as who was that hurting and also it meant my sister's boyfriend and his pals thought more of me so I was being looked upon now many years above my age and that I felt good about.

I went and scored a lot of weed from them and remembered seeing how they would break the weed up to smaller bags and how to make profile from what I had paid out for it. On calling Carl once I had scored the weed he wanted he arrived this time a few house later on his bmx with his best friend Trevor who said he was collecting some weed for his father who owned a taxi company in Wellington.

Within one week my phone at my mum's place wouldn't stop calling as Trevor's father friends and other taxi drivers wanted to score weed and I had Sasaka buying a few bags but I had to bring him in on it so he could bag up the dope while I was on the phone keeping an eye in case my mum would turn up. Carl would come past with pizzas and take bags of dope to his shop and be selling it now himself.

I would meet Trevor who asked if his dad could meet me and turn up to collect dope from now on but I didn't wish anyone else to meet me. I was moving many ounces of weed a week and counting my cash and spending it on whatever I wanted, all the best things in life.

It also meant I could spend more time down at the Satan's Slaves Motorcycle Club as I had money in my pockets which made me feel like a grown up though I was still just a young teenager but I didn't feel like one at all.

I never told any of the members of the Satan's Slaves Motorcycle Club that I was selling weed as I am sure they would have given me a ear bashing and they very much wouldn't have been happy to find out. I enjoyed spending time down at their clubhouse, I felt so at home as in safe and welcomed and I could drink all dam night if I wanted as there wasn't many bars in town I could get into due to my age.

I wasn't looking my age, people would think I was 16years old but still too young to be in bars and drinking. I started doing a lot of it at the surf parties and the college parties I was going to and selling a weed as well but now instead of taking weed to these parties, I was being encouraged to take coke to try and sell that.

The profiles were higher but among the college kids and the surfers they had no money for coke, all of them just wanted to get high from puff. I was always left with a few grams of coke which stupidly I would make my way around to see Penny.

Penny's mum smoked weed which meant she loved me coming over as I would always give her a small bag of weed, let's say on the house. I and penny would once her mum had gone to bed stoned, we would get out the coke and get Charlied up. Something that meant the following morning I would owe $600 for snorting two grams of coke so all my profile from my dope would have to cover that but the worse thing of this whole thing was , now had I been hooked on coke (purposely or not)?

I started to get the flavour of it and that early buzz from first use of coke and that for anyone isn't a good thing. Let me tell you coke isn't nothing great and more so can destroy a life and so much more harm to not only your health but very much to your life and who you are as a person.

I must have truly in those six weeks had over $20,000 go through my hands. I was holding it for someone so the $6,000s and $5,000s all added up and though only a small % of it was mine, it just opened my eyes to a hell of a lot of money. Wise I thought at the time I had become though silly at times as in snorting my own profile. The use of coke was something that would dance in my brain and all who I shared it with.

Everyone knew through me they could get so high so I was making friends left right and centre all though for the wrong reasons. I guess as 50% were my friends as they liked me and 50% were hanging around for the drugs that now and then being so high myself I would share a lot of the drugs and not expect money back as I just loved everyone being so high.

It seemed good times and a school holiday that I would always remember back fondly but how now I wished that maybe I had flown over to the UK to have spend those holidays with my Father in the UK. I know my life would have taken a different course on my returning to New Zealand, instead of within six weeks ending up what you could call as a drug dealer at the age of 12 years old.

Never looking at me in the mirror as one, but in the eyes of the law and many readers of this book then you would be judging this period of my life as being just that, a drug dealer even at the very young age of only 12 years old.

Just think only 8 weeks earlier I was away over on the other side of the mountain range in school, safe away from everyone who was a negative in my life. I was doing so well in lessons and scoring tries out on the sports fields, nothing could have been going better for me and now here I was now finding myself smoking a hell of a lot of dope which was yes getting me stoned but forgetful and I was putting on weight due to all the pizzas I was ordering because of the munchies.

I had mood swings going on from the coke I was snorting and it being mixed with speed so my sleeping patterns were now all back to front and as a 12 year old I was drinking amounts of booze as if I was a 25 year old so not only was my head suffering but also my body was taking a few too many hits.

Soon the school holidays were up and I was heading off to my new college. My mum and one of Wims daughters Roberta drove me up to my first day, all the boys loved Roberta when the spotted her walking in the dorm of Rugby house as she was very good looking so that was a nice touch as I had new pupils asking me about who she was when my Mum and her had left.

Both Wims daughter Heidi and Roberta were very good looking. Their mother was an attractive lady as well and her good looks combined with Wims features made both their daughters stunning in looks.

I settled in very well at my new school and was so touched that my mum drove me up as this place now would be my home for the next 5 years. A long road ahead but I was happy to be here as Wellington had got a bit too much in the last few weekend though I missed Penny a lot so I would start writing to her often.

I am glad I had the two years of Hadlow behind me as it meant I could find my feet at the new school much easier and also there were many faces from Hadlow who also had become students here, moving straight from Hadlow as I had done so it meant I already had a few friends.

The next few evening after a week had passed I would be visited by some of the older boys who knew me from the school buses, the same boys who would be smoking puff before they got on the bus. Here in Rugby House there were also bullies who didn't give a fuck about who I knew back in Wellington though the boys from the bus did try to warn many not to miss about with me, not that I could win every fight myself.

I didn't lose many over my years at boarding school and that's to gaining brown belt and one black tip in Zen do kai during my time at Hadlow leaning the marital art. I only wished it was able to follow me through to the next college as I would have gone onto becoming a black belt and even higher that I know for sure. I loved the marital art and it was such a great benefit to my well being at that age and even now I still have the teachings of the marital art very much in me.

At Rathkeale I could do serious harm if pushed. None of the kids could really fight, well not as a true fighter so I had things like round house kicks and elbows and other things that I could lash out with though within a month I was canned after picking up a pool stick and not play pool with it.

A older kid had cheated me out of a winning game of pool which had money riding on it and I was fuming but as he was a large lump, he had come from a farming back ground and was strong in size with a massive head and bigger fists so on weighting him up I thought my balance of knocking him out was slim.

I picked up my pool stick and struck straight to the throat then the bullying bastard went on his knees so I struck him again over his back as I was sure he was going to get up like the incredible hulk and come at me but after striking him a second time he wasn't getting up fast as the second strike to him broke the pool stick.

Other pupils run and told the house master who came in and grabbed me by the ear, he was a wanker and he was the type of teacher who enjoyed canning boys. It's like he got some rush from it as he caned me so fucking hard that I just wanted to smash him in the jaw, I was that close from hitting him and he knew it.

I was so angry that I was being canned when this senior boy had cause the trouble anyway after I was hit I went out into the grounds and running away soon came again to my mind but I couldn't for the sake of my mum I was only at the school for a month at this stage.

Anyway as I kept on walking I could smell weed. I found some of the boys smoking it who caught the buses with me. I was asking them did they bring dope to school as that would be so risky. They took me for even a longer walk and in among the bush were dope plants, some that had been grown from previous students who no longer were at the school.

They didn't know much to do with plants, I knew a little. I knew when to pull the buds and more what part of the plant actually to smoke as these kids didn't even know what to smoke as some had even been trying to smoke the leafs of the plant. With my minimum knowledge I helped them by pointing out what part of the plant to smoke but that's as far as my help went. I didn't want to be any part of their dope plant growing on school grounds.

They rolled up a few decent joints and smoked away, offering me a joint to share in smoking with them but I said no as to me smoking dope at school was if anything stupid and I didn't want to get caught smoking dope at school as for sure I would be expelled on the dot and that's something I didn't wish ever to happen.

They asked could I get hold of good dope back in Wellington, I said yes. Why the fuck did I say yes, because I was really fucking stupid? After falling out with the bully and being canned it made me so angry that I now wanted to be part of these guys at collage as they were the in crowd.

I knew with their backing in school I wouldn't again find myself getting any of shit from other pupils as I was sure these guys would help me sort out any future trouble while at school as they were the senior boys of the college.

I would late find out they all were doing lsd and having séances which was leading to them doing weird shit that was going on the weekend that we were at school. It was only once a month we could go home like at Hadlow. Soon the weeks went by quicker than I thought and it was the end of that month and we were to go home.

On this bus journeys I got to see some of St Matthew girls; it was nice seeing them again. Some friendships grew and grew even on a simple bus journey back home from school, a lot could go on the between the pupils of the three schools on the back of those buses.

My first weekend back, I spend it with Penny. I didn't even get to see any of my friends nor even my sister I was told she and her boyfriend had broken up. I wasn't sure what he had done but she had kicked him out and now I was told he was living at the Satan's Slaves MC headquarters but she still had the same flatmates.

My mum didn't really either get to me see which was upsetting for her as he had planned to take me on a lovely dinner to celebrate my time so far settling in at the college.

When I got to the bus stop on the Sunday evening after the weekend break was over the older kids were as normal smoking weed. They asked if I wanted some but as I had a straight weekend of no drugs so again I said no to them.

While on the bus I had my Mum waving goodbye and also Penny as well which was nice. The ride back was talk from the senior boys on the bus was of what I could get in the way of drugs. I said I could get them weed but that's all as I didn't want to let them know anything more than that. I actually felt uncomfortable even telling them I could sort them out some weed but in doing so, I knew this would mean even more backing from them while I was at school.

If I came into any trouble from other students then I knew they would sort it out for me there and then and that would lead onto calm life at Rathkeale. That's all I wished for rather than on going fighting with bullies or assholes who would be happy to cause me problems.

I told the senior boys that if they wanted, as long as they had the cash they could meet me over the next weekend break in Wellington in four weeks time. I also said I wouldn't be willing to risk bringing anything to school as it wasn't worth it as I had nearly been expelled from Hadlow and I so didn't want to be expelled from Rathkeale.

I couldn't risk this but they pushed on and on but still I said no. I told them if they wanted something then on the next weekend in four weeks time that we were all back in Wellington, that's when one of them could sort and arrange the money between them and then he could come and meet me somewhere to get the weed.

The next four weekends went by quick at school. I done quite well in the track and field day which I was happy with and I had made loads of good friends in my own age group in my classes and my boarding house who weren't into drug use and were just good guys who studied hard and played hard when it came to the sport fields, such as myself.

It meant I wasn't in much contact with the older students and not once did I even go out and check on the dope plants that were growing on the school grounds when asked by the senior boys to come for a sneaky smoke as I wasn't interested in getting high while at school, it just wasn't my thing.

The month passed and as I didn't swap phone numbers with any of the boys on the bus then I was never called to meet up for them to collect any weed so on the return bus journey back, they were fairly upset that I hadn't in their eyes used my own brain and brought along some drugs for them to buy.

I felt they tried to stand over me for a moment. They clocked from a conversation I was having with one of the ex pupils from Hadlow now was also attending Rathkeale, who previously had been bullied badly by the senior boys, that my sister was no longer going out the guy that had threaten them the year before.

They then thought I no longer had any back up if they tried to bully me but by this time I was soon turning 13 years old, I really didn't need any back up especially from kids who were only 5 years older. I warned them not to fuck about with me.

Slap! I was slapped in the face by one of them and that was it even before the bus had left from across the road of Wellington railway station. I went off my nut, attacking the student like a wild man. It took at least 9 of the kids all to hold me down but it was too late as I had broken his nose as I punched him within moments after he slapped me.

I was so going to be expelled for this until the bus driver pulled the bulling bastard of the bus and called over to his parents telling them that they were to take his bags of the bus and that he wasn't allowed to be on the bus.

The kid had slapped me, I didn't know right in front of the bus driver so the bus driver who for years had actually had enough of these rude bastards giving me shit over the years, was happy for the senior boy to get his just rewards by a broken nose. Finally someone had hit back rather than allowing being assaulted and taking it, which was something all of my life I never allowed anyone to lay their hands on me.

The others warned me that his friends at school might get me back for this and they did as I was laying in bed one morning before the dorm wake up call. Some kids came running in and held me down and bashed me with a pillow case filled with snooker balls. The blows to my body were so painful but I was in my blankets, I couldn't do anything to defend myself.

I knew their faces, one of the boys was the boy who first shown me the dope plants that were grown on the school grounds so I thought I would get these bastards back. Not all the in crowd were bastards or part of this attack on me.

I didn't care as due to their behaviour towards me and also for no one warning me about this planned attack which I know many would have know was going to be taking place, well fuck them all as I would get them all back where it hurt.

After the cowards had done their attack, I got up though feeling badly injured, I managed it out of the dorm in my slippers and my dressing grown and went to the wood work class which I just kicked in the door and off came the hinges through the force of the kick.

This made my chest swore from the earlier attack but I was steaming mad and I was after a knife not to stab any of the students who had attacked me but I was on a mission. Out I went with a knife into the school grounds out to the bush and straight to the where their dope plants were hidden.

I hacked away at them, tossing them all into the stream and I felt fucking good by doing so then I threw the knife away in to thicker bush and went back to bed. Missing out on breakfast as I stayed in bed that Saturday morning and also I didn't take part in sport, telling the House Master I was feeling very unwell.

The next two weeks I really didn't have much to say to anyone and just wanted to be home as I didn't know who my friends were among them, and who had it out for me.

The bus journey back home, I had the kid who slapped me say he was sorry for what he had done. The boys were saying "Go on shake his hand, he means it."

He said sorry so with that, I thought not to hold a grunge as I did have 8 more months of the year left and 5 years still at this school so I didn't want any more fighting or such negative things.

I didn't like my name being highlighter as a fighter and I wanted on my return to school after this weekend home just to get my head down again like I had at Hadlow and do well for the coming midyear exams and get ready for the rugby session that soon was upon us.

I had so much to look forward to when I got back to school again. I would prove myself as a success story as that's what got me here in the first place to this school so I wasn't going to be held back as I felt I had for the last few months, not showing my true abilities.

On the bus pulling into Wellington across the road from the Wellington railway station I was asked my home number by the kid who had slapped me. I though yeah its cool that he had my number as though all the plants at school had been destroyed, none of the kids were any wiser that It was me as they all had thought one of the teachers had come across the plants and destroyed them.

I knew none of the kids had any access to weed so if they wanted some then fair enough I would get them some if they asked. At least then, they all very much would have to fall into line and if any more shit from them then I would cut their supply of as I had by cutting down their plants as they truly knew no one else who could get them weed to smoke.

These guys were big smokers so it's like they needed weed like they needed their left hand, if you know what I mean. To show them there was no hard feelings between us all and if they all were stoned then at least they wouldn't be casing me anymore trouble.

Friday night, I was told that my sister ex boyfriend was out on his first weekend leave from jail. He had been in jail up on the hill, Mt Crawford Prison. Mt Crawford was a very old and naughty jail that sat on a hill though classed as a mountain which looked over Wellington City and the beautiful harbour below. It was filled with 85% gang members and was one of the most violent jails in all of New Zealand, housing many murder inmates.

The jail was run by the Satan's Slaves Motorcycle Club who had many members and supporters in the jail. Those inside kept things tight and even the screws knew who were really running the jail. My sisters ex boyfriend had been in for gang trouble and for assault. There was a drink up for him at the Satan's Slaves MC Clubhouse so to raise a few quid him on his release.

The Satan's Slaves Motorcycle Club always raised money for members or club prospects that were locked up in jail. I went along to the fund raiser and met up with my sister flatmates and her boyfriend Zombie who now had become a patched member of the Satan's Slaves Motorcycle Club.

My sister never went down to their clubhouse once she had stopped dating Stephen and even during the time she had dated him she hardly would go there down there. It wasn't really her scene. I had a great night and the money I earned from winning a few matches of pool I put all of it into the money jar that was for Grot aka Stephen.

When I got home in the early hours I rang Penny to ask her to pop around. She had the hump that I didn't ring her the night before when I had arrived back into Wellington on my school weekend leave.

Being drunk, I just thought I can't be asked with a row so I hanged up the phone. That Saturday was the 22nd of April, I had turned 13 years old on the 20th of April which had been the Thursday but being at school I didn't really celebrate so tonight was my official birthday party.

Party I did. I had a great party held it over at my friend's house as my mum's flat was too small to hold everyone. We partied though with his parents there, we weren't able to get too drunk so I brought everyone back to my sister place and there we all got seriously smashed on booze and partied it up. I didn't invite any school friends, only friends from my past in Miramar.

On the Sunday I was hung over when my mum woke me up. She said she had forgotten to give me a phone message from the day before. She told me some kid was trying to get hold of me since early Saturday morning as he had twice asking after me.

I called the number; it was the older kid from school who I had beaten up on the bus after he had attacked me. He asked could he meet me before the bus ride back to school. I said couldn't he just meet me at the bus but he said he wanted to smoke some weed by himself before meeting up with the other boys so I said fine and to meet me in town at the games parlour.

I got dressed and went over to my sister place and woke up her flatmate. I got some weed of him without my sister knowing. The money I had on me to pay for the weed was birthday money I used to cover the dope for the older boy and the other boys until I would get it off them later to cover the costs.

I then went into town and waited nearly two hours which I was pissed off with. The dope wasn't for me but there I was wasting my whole day firstly collecting it for others and then having to wait for one of them to meet me.

That Sunday I really wanted to spend it with Penny. We hadn't seen each other all weekend and more so after she had a go at me over the phone early hours of Saturday morning so I really wanted to see her and I am sure she wanted also to see me before I had to get the bus ride that evening, back to school.

Finally he arrived I asked for the money and he said I would have to wait till I got to the bus as the other boys would be sorting me their share of the money as he made out he was only there to pick it up from me and that he didn't have any money on him.

I wasn't too happy but I couldn't give the dope back to my sisters flatmates so I handed it over to the him, telling him the money better be there for me later before I even board the bus as I had used my own birthday money to cover their dope which I wasn't too pleased with.

I went and met Penny, having lots of sex through the afternoon then got home just in time for dinner that my mum had specially made for me. After such a lovely home cooked Sunday British roast lunch, the type which is always the best when they are cooked by ya mum. You know the types with all the trimmings.

I was then driven to the bus and on the bus I stepped wanting my money but the boy who I had given the dope to, wasn't on the bus.

I was fuming as where was he? The other senior boys weren't too happy either as it was their dope anyway none of them would hand me over money until the kid turned up with the dope. We guessed that he had been driven to school instead, as some times parents would make the effort to do the long drive than always the kids catching the return bus back to school.

We arrived at school around three and a half hours later, I was so sleepy after shagging all day and felt still a bit hang over so I went straight to my bed. I was about to throw my bag into my cupboard when suddenly the bearded knob head of a prick House Master appeared and told me to take out my bag and place it on the bed.

I asked what was going on and he asked me to open it in front of him and had I brought anything back that I shouldn't have? I said no of course not, and what was his suggestion, as I didn't have a clue what he was on about.

Then he said he was searching for drugs. Next minute my bed was turned upside down and a proper search going on. Fuck me dead, a copper walks in with a sniffer dog, what the Hell was all this about? I was lead into his office no one telling me what was going on. Then like a wanker his only words were "You're going down and going down fast!"

Who the fuck did he think he was? Some fucking cop from the American hit police television show C.H.I.P.S or even worse the American police television show Cops, you know what I mean.

I had no idea what all this was about and his stupid comment only got my back up but what was to come wasn't what anyone was excepting, very much not what I was ever expecting too happen. It shock my world as I knew it, big time and a feeling of utter numbness came all over my body and throughout my state of mind.

I truly was numb; it's the only words I can explain to how I was feeling at this point in time with what happened next to me.

Chapter 16

HELLS BELLS

YEAR 1989 AGE 13years old / 14 years old

I was sat down in shock by what was going on; by the way I was being treated like a criminal.

Thinking to what the fuck was going on. Why was I being searched for drugs? I would never ever bring drugs to the school.

Hell I may have smoked dope back in Wellington now and then but I wasn't a big dope smoker or the like. I had never brought any to school and never smoked dope at school. Not even one puff on all the joints that I had been offered while at school by the senior boys throughout the last few months in the school grounds.

I wasn't like many of kids at school, all getting fucking high on lsd and them tripping out thinking they were all speaking to the dead or nor was I like any of them by getting stoned every night of the week that they could, while boarding at school so what the fuck was going on here.

Soon the copper who had the sniffer dog from earlier had returned from his police car after locking the dog up.

He and the house master tried to play bad cop, good cop, what the hell, like I had never had run in's with the old bill before.

I had been held in police cells many a times before I had reached this age of 13. It was only recently that I had kept myself out of trouble with the law ever since I was send half way up the country to boarding school rather than hanging around the big smoke that being Wellington, so their silly scare tactics weren't doing fuck all to frighten me.

They must have thought I had never seen a police officer in my life before but oh how wrong were they as I still had the memoires fresh in my head of all the times the police would rush into my house I was growing up in as a young child and fight with my father wrestling him to the ground and handcuffing him in the house or out in our front yard.

Then to all the times I had while growing up fall outs with the police whenever I was being hassled over petty crime that the street kids were pulling off, for hanging around in youth gangs in the malls of Wellington, for fighting with other kids on Friday nights up in the city so I was so very aware of this bad cop good cop shit that they thought they were being clever doing.

I didn't hate the police in general. Many who had dealings with me when I was a youngest were actually friendly and at the end of the day most were just doing their job and if that meant keeping me off the streets and out of trouble or giving me a earful whenever they got hold of me then this was no harm in that so in no way did I think all coppers were wankers but there were a few in my time who had mistreated me and that stayed with me while I was a young kid and then a teenager.

I just wanted to know what all it was about as they had failed in finding any drugs on me as I was never going to be bringing any drugs ever to school so I truly still at this point didn't know what the hell they were on about.

Then just to shame me the copper told me to undress. What was he a gay friend of the House Master who I was sure though married as was well gay.

Undressed I got, all my clothes now being searched then I was able to get dressed again and I asked what was going on as still they hadn't said much, only asking me to hand over the drugs.

"What fucking drugs?" I was getting wound up by now I was angry as I had just got off a long bus ride, I was tired and I just wanted to get to bed to sleep. The copper went out of the office with the house master and they spoke for a while then he left, nothing more from him was said to me as I heard his patrol car speed away out of the drive way.

The shitbag wanker of a House Master hadn't finished with me yet, he still wanted to play bad cop even though he had no one there playing good cop, the prick.

He told me as I wasn't being honest and that due to me hiding the truth from him that in the morning I would have to report to the headmaster and that he would be writing the headmaster a report. "A report for what and what was I hiding?"

I question the House Master but he wouldn't give me an answer, he just sends me to the dorm to bed. The other kids were full of excitement as a police officer had been called to the school so it was something fairly big for them but I wasn't impressed. I lay awake thinking what was all that about? Had someone who didn't like me tell the school that was I bringing drugs to the school?

I thought back to all the fights I had been in, and the only one in my head to make sense as to someone trying to get me back was the kid who I had done with a snooker stick as I didn't think of the kid on the bus who I fought, making trouble for me as he was the kid who wanted drugs from me in the first place so he wouldn't get me in trouble as we had made up on the recent bus journey home, would he?

Next morning came and everyone went to breakfast as normal. All the kids, the entire school were now talking about it and everyone was coming up to me like I was some celebrity even kids whom I didn't even know were coming up to me.

All which the teachers didn't like this and especially the wanker House Master of mine, who stopped me short of eating my breakfast and took me by the arm into the direction of the headmaster's office.

I hadn't had much previous contact with the headmaster of Rathkeale though he did come to Hadlow the year earlier and watched me and some of the other kids in a game of rugby and to speak to the pupils including me who had reached the honours board so I had met him previously and of course had seen him around the school grounds, though really ever spoke to him as I was no brown nose kid, unlike many of the other kids.

I told him that no one had told me what all this was about and that I wanted to know. "It is your right to know." he replied back and then his words were

"You are being expelled from Rathkeale Prep School for selling drugs to a fellow pupil, this is not acceptable in the rules of the school and I as headmaster have no other choice apart from expelling you."

"What I never sold any drugs to any pupil and last night none were found on me so what proof do you have?" I asked him.

He followed on by telling me that the pupil who I handed dope to back in Wellington, that is. On him taking them from me, he went home and rolled himself a joint in his parent's garage and that his father came in and found him smoking a joint.

His father being a police officer then question his own son and found out it was me who had given his son the dope after his son had grassed me up, the low life grass!!

Then his father a police officer in the Wellington police phoned the headmaster who had become a friend of his over the years his son had been an outstanding pupil of Rathkeale.

You got to remember the boy was much older than me so had been a pupil at the school for many years and also both his father and the headmaster were free masons so they talked on a different level than most pupils parents.

Anyway the father had told, informed the headmaster of this and said that he didn't wish his outstanding son to return to the school until I the drug dealing pupil had left. I was to be expelled straight away for what I had done.

Even though it wasn't on school grounds and even though his son had brought the weed and called me in the first place to score some dope but that wasn't an expelling crime when fuck off, course it was!

If I was to be expelled then that grassing fucker should be as well!!

But it never happened. The headmaster called my Mum and told her the news. My mum's heart just sunk.

By the end of that morning I was on a bus back to Wellington.

You know I never said a word against that other pupil the grassing fuck. I never told the headmaster anything, not giving up any of the boys nor told about all the drugs that were throughout that school as I was old school through and through, and was taught never to rat on anyone even if they did wrong against you.

One of the boarding houses at Rathkeale you could buy tabs of lsd for your weekends at school but I didn't tell them about that nor did I never tell them about the dope plants that were growing on the school grounds as one thing I wasn't, was a fucking grass!

Here I was losing everything I had achieved so far in life.

Gaining a place to one of the best schools in the whole country and doing so well at my last private school that I had made it onto the honours board and been excepted into Rathkeale Private College.

All the thousands of dollars of money my Mum had put into my education, all gone down the drain.

All the hard work I done all now lost due to a grass.

Why couldn't he have just told his dad he had got it from a street kid up town rather than pin point me.

You know why as he had never forgiven me for when my sister boyfriend had stepped on the school bus the year before and shook him up by the scuff of his collar for bullying younger kids.

He had felt so shamed for being put in his place in front of a whole bus full of kids and more so in front of the girls on the bus from St Matthews that he hadn't near let it lay low.

Also when he had slapped me the month earlier and I had smashed his nose and done him good and proper, well the handshake he offered me when he said sorry was not a real handshake but a fake one that belonged to a grass!

This kid didn't realise that by grassing me up he would not only have me expelled from my school but he had destroyed what was my future and everything I had done in the past to get this far. He was putting my life in his hands from the moment when he mentioned my name and grassed me up.

It was the end of what could have been something so grand.

I was in shock on that bus ride home and so very much feeling for my Mum to what she was feeling as this not only turned my world upside down but also my Mums and what shame it would bring on her that her only son who had been doing so well against all the odds was now expelled for selling drugs.

If only when the older kids had asked me on the bus if I could get them drugs, I should have just said NO as then I wouldn't have been there on this bus riding home by myself with the mountain range soon behind me and with my education of the highest level left behind me as well.

I arrived home and my mum was in tears, my sister told my mum to ground me so I had a go at my sister then she left.

I said sorry to my mum but not to worry I told her as we would fight the schools ruling, and I will get back to that school but all we tried, the school said NO.

It was heartbreaking for my Mum and also for me even though I know what I had done was wrong but it wasn't done at school, it was done hundreds of miles away and in my own time. I could do whatever I wished in my own time as the school were not my parents nor allowed to set rules when I was at home as that was just bollocks.

I was driven now to get that grassing bastard back for upsetting my mum and wreaking my education as I would have gone and done so well at Rathkeale as I was so focused, and then this happened to me.

It was unbelievable but there was one person to blame in my eyes and that was the grass so I now wouldn't let it lay as in making sure I teach him a lesson.

At the time if I still had my rifle, I would have probably shot him the bastard if I had the chance as that's how mad I was at the time and that's how much I blamed him for this mess that now I had found myself in.

I had just turned 13 years old only the week earlier and I now after all those celebrations, I now had been expelled from such a high profile successful private school.

My first year, my first four months into college but now I was sitting at home going through names of schools that my Mum wished for me to carry on my education but with the words expulsion on my last school report then not many wished to even interview me. One did though a private college St Patricks out near Upper Hutt on the outskirts of Wellington.

St Patrick's was a great school and one of the leading private schools in all of New Zealand so when they took a interest in me due to more so because of my Hadlow end of year school report so with that I was taken to this school and shown around.

All went well but they wouldn't have a position for me till the following year so though it was a negative but there was a positive to the outcome of that as at least I would be accepted by this private school.

I think mainly what they could see in me was me bringing to the school my rugby skills but all this I would have to wait a year and my mum wasn't going to have me sitting around her apartment for 8 months.

She kept on looking at getting me into a new top school but again many wouldn't take me so she looked closer to home rather than boarding schools and Wellington College for Boys were happy to take me on.

Though a state school, but the finest of colleges for boys in Wellington and run like a private school. It was quite a posh school on the outside looking in.

I was kind of happy as it meant I didn't have to board at a school but my mum only had a one bedroom apartment. It was ok for when I came home from boarding school once a month as the settee was a fold out bed so that was fine but to be living there full time, sharing the place with my mum well the apartment was too small so one of us had to go.

And it was my Mum first as she would stay at Wims house most evenings but that only meant for this 13 year old, trouble and I would end up bringing it on my own door step.

In the months from the moment I was expelled to when finally a school was willing to take me on, my mum made me get a job across the road at the panel beaters and car spray paint garage after my failed attempted at being a teenager model.

I met up with my best friend from my childhood, Christopher Mitchell who had become a surfer but also he had managed to pick up some modelling work. He said the money was sweet; it was mainly TV work for adverts and also for magazines selling surf wear etc so I went to see his agent but I had to change my looks I was told and look more like a surfer.

So my mum put me in the salon she was working at and I had my hair dye so I had blonde coloured strikes and then had some photos done and I was on the books and managed to get into some magazines. Chris thought the money was great but over the next two weeks I only made $250 and many times was send home from photos shots as truly I wasn't no model like many of the other kids so I kind of jacked it in though Chris went on and did quite well from it, he had the height and the looks when I just looked like a duck out of water.

So a real job was soon thrown on me and that was at the panel beaters and car spray workshop across the road from my mum's apartment. All this was alien to me so manly my duties were sanding down lorries and petrol tankers which would take so fucking long and it was just pure boring work but I had to do it so I could pay board at my mum's place as I had the run of the place to myself so my mum thought if I wanted to act grown up then I would have to cover the house bills through my wages.

I was running a house at the age of 13. I could cook as I had learned how to cook as early as 7 years old so looking after myself was no problem and now Penny loved it as she could come over and we would party it up.

My work which was only across the road would be knocking on the bedroom window at 7am waking me up. The boss's oldest boy would be shouting out my name so soon he and I would come to blows and worse.

He was a fuckwit from the start. He thought he was going to end up member of Black Power though he was only a run around for them. They used to sell his is old man stolen car parts so he thought the gang wanted him to join.

I had my three step brothers, all Staunch Patch Members of the most Powerful Chapter of all the Mob Chapters in the entire country, Porirua.

Patrick, Lenny and Billy Manuel, whose names you would have read in previous pages, these three me were the fucking real McCoy when it comes to Gang Members and they were leading New Zealand Mobsters.

No one and I mean no fucked with the Manuel Family as these three brothers would take care of business ,their way privately or by the way of the Mob. Either way you would be fucked if you crossed them or you had done wrong.

You would be even more fucked if let's say you were a black power member who's car broke down in Porirua but then again the Black Power were far too scared to ever be anywhere near the city of Porirua, due to one family, one gang and three brothers that being Patrick, Lenny and Billy Manuel and the gang being The Mongrel Mob.

You could say they were as powerful in their own manor of Porirua, as was to the Kray Brothers in all of London; though of course different in many ways but similar in some and all were family men through and through.

I couldn't wait till me and my work boss son fell out with me as I was going to love smashing the daylight out of him. He was much stronger and he was much older than me but I would at least get in one good punch when ever that time came.

If I were able to get in a decent second punch well that would be for my step brothers as I know all three would have loved to have taught some dirty prick like him a lesson as he was as much black power as my nana was a hells angels, do you know what I mean!!

He needed a wake up lesson.

Black Power when they used to come into the car wreakers, I knew they were always up to no good and the sons of the car wreakers took the BP as their protection. I am sure that suited the BP very well as it meant in all honesty they the gang had major control over their fathers business even if their Father didn't wish for that but it was too late as one of his sons, let's say was in bed with BP so the father couldn't say sweet fuck all.

Having my Mums apartment was fine as in living arrangements though I didn't like the job but it was bringing in cash. I was getting $300 a week, not much only $50 a day but it was something and now I had my own money so I was going out every weekend with my friends none of course had jobs. They all were at school so I would cover most of the costs when it came to drinking.

We would get people to walk into bottle stores for us then we all would just get so drunk going from party to party. Most never being invited to any of them but through all the different schools my mates went to then they would each Friday find out who was holding a party and that was that.

I was making a name for myself as yes someone who caused mischief but who also wouldn't back down to anyone so I started to get a reputation as a fighter , more so during the times of heading to these house parties across Wellington .

I didn't get to see Penny for around three weekends in a row as I was always out with my mates. They knew I always had cash so they would get to me first before Penny could arrange us doing something. Even some mates would wait on my doorstep across the road from work waiting for me before even I had finished work as they knew Fridays was my pay day.

My circle of friends became bigger and also I started to have girls after me which meant Penny ended our relationship though I never cheated on her. What was a 13 year old doing in a relationship anyway?

All my friends were having the time of their lives, a girl at each party and nearer enough a girl in each part of town we would travel to so I jumped on their band wagon and times were good. I had fun with lots of beautiful looking girls and had the time of my life as a young teenager should.

Rathkeale was now not even a thought in my mind, though very much what was a thought constantly in my mind was the grass as I hadn't finished with him.

Many friends who were backing me to get him back so one Sunday after a weekend of boozing it, I got a few of the guys together and I waited at Wellingtons main railway station for him to get on the school bus that would travel from Wellington to Masterton .

Right there on cue he turned up. It appeared his mum was dropping him off.

I waited for her to drive away and clocked where on the bus he was sitting and also noticed it was the normal bus driver. He was a good guy so I went up to him and shook his hand asking how he was and was it ok if I said hello to a few old school friends on the bus before he started on his journey? He said "Yes of course that's fine."

Right then I just felt a rush go through my body as if I was as strong as ten men and it was reinforced when I climbed on the bus and spotted the grass sitting there with a pack of cards in his hands.

He turned and saw me walking up the middle of the bus. My eyes fixed solely on him and if my ears had shut out every other noise as I walked past all the other kids. I couldn't hear them though they all were speaking among themselves or to me but everything was silent, a cold silent until the grass got up of his seat and extended his hand as if again to offer me a handshake.

It was as if time had stopped and then everything went into slow motion. I pulled back my right shoulder and let go while twisting my body of all my weight that now was behind my fist as it landed straight on his jaw. Blood went flying across the bus, landing on me as he fell back and then due to the arm rest of seat he came forward.

I couldn't see his eyes in his head. I could only see the whites of his eyes as if his eyes had rolled back into the back of his head. Just then his head came down as his body was slumping I put with all my lower strength, my knee into his face and watched his head as if it had been whipped lashed in a car crash then his head bobbled as he hit the ground.

He had broken teeth from the first punch. His lip cut open from when I hit him as he didn't close his jaw quicker enough when I hit him the first time. He didn't have time to move his speaking tongue out of the way quicker enough which caused him to bite down hard on his tongue.

He had bitten it nearly in half as the blood was pissing out of his mouth and as for his nose well if he thought it was broken badly last time I hit him, this time his nose had been crushed by the power of my knee when it had landed right on the tip of his nose.

The grass was out by the first punch and the knee to the head just meant he weren't getting up in any hurry. I looked at everyone on the bus and told them if any one and I mean anyone was to grass me up about this then there would be serious trouble as I would be back and I pointed them down at the pile of shit at my feet and said "This is what happened to grasses, so not always is the grass grasser on the other side."

With that I left the bus and waited for the blues and twos to turn up to my house. I was for sure that one of the kids were to grass me up, I didn't expect anything less but Sunday soon become Monday and Monday become Tuesday and no knock on the door so I thought I was in the clear then on the Wednesday, while I was at work over the road from my mum's apartment I noticed a police car turn up.

The passengers' door opened. I noted a cop getting out banging heavily on the door of my Mums apartment and leaving what looked like a note in the letter box as the car drove off.

I run across the road once the patrol car had gone and checked what it was. It turned out to be a note from the police officer who happened to be the grass's father threading me to keep away from his son or else.

With a few threading comments I thought fuck him as well so now I had the beef with the father. Who the fuck did he think he was to be threading a 13 year old kid? Bad luck if his son had been knocked out, he should have taught his son how to fight rather than teaching his son how to be a grass. That night I went with a good pal of mine and I took some paint from the workshop and we went to the wankers house splashed his car and also his drive way and took the paint can with us and left, then the next morning I showed my mum the note and she rang him.

He started screaming down the phone at my mum about his family car being fucked and accusing me but my mum told him I was indoors with her all the night before and I hadn't gone out once.

Even though she hadn't even be home the night before, let alone watching TV with me but she was backing her son and she wasn't going to take no shit of a prick so she said if he wanted to cause trouble then this note would be handed to her lawyer who would take it up to have him charged with threading a minor.

She said she would go on to get a order against him that made it against the law for him to come near our house, similar what she had done with my father and how all this wouldn't look good for him. She ended by saying "keep your druggie son away from my son and I will keep my son away from your son."

That was that, she stood up for me though she knew what I done wasn't right but these two had fucked up my education so she had backed me all the way.

I was so chuffed by her support and felt so good for smashing the son and getting one up on the father even though he was a senior policeman but he went out his way getting me expelled due to making a huge issue over it.

So let's call what happened to his flash little motor was Karma.

My days of working at the panel shop were becoming such a bore and the owners sons who worked for their old man, one of them was getting right on my nerves about a lot of things. He just thought he was like the boss of the place when ever his father wasn't there.

The thing is whenever his father wasn't there, I would pop over to my place and chill out and the son would come over banging on the doors yelling at me to get back to work or else!

I opened it one afternoon after hearing him banging away on the door saying if I didn't come out he would get some of his black power mates to get me out so told him to fuck off!

Then letting him know I would be back over in my own time, with that he grabbed me by my working overalls and pulled me out onto the landing trying to push me down the stairs. What was the prick doing? He was stronger than me and I couldn't push past him while he was on a higher stair, but as we got to the bottom I without thinking just chinned him and down he went, my hand was so sore after that puka punch.

Now I had trouble right on my door step and it was not like I could go back to work and I knew not to go back up the stairs so I fucked off to my sister's house.

She was throwing a drink up, kind of house party so I called my best friend Chris Mitchell and we both got so pissed up. People had run out of ciggs so we said we would go and get some.

Chris ended up just putting a brick through a shop front and in he went and took some ciggs, so random. He wasn't a tear away like me so it was very unusual behaviour from him anyway we came back to the party and everyone loved us as we brought them packets of ciggs.

Nothing else in the shop was taken, just 6 packets of ciggs. I am sure the shopkeeper was shock to find that all is stock minus only six packs of ciggs were missing after what would have looked like a break in.

We got so drunk of Jack Daniels back at my sisters place that I was sick for ages in the loo. Chris went to walk me home as I could barely stand up and was just too drunk as I would have downed near to a litre of Jack from my first drink to my last between a short period of time of drinking heavy.

As we got near my mum's address, Chris thought he saw a shadow across the road outside the panel shop and he wasn't wrong as the two brothers from the panel shop stepped out of the dark and confronted us as we tried to cross the road.

I was drunkenly saying didn't he get the message earlier? With that I was punched straight on the nose and heard it break. Blood coming out of my nose like it was a waterfall. I was struck about two more times.

Chris was doing his best to defend me and in the end the row ended with him taking them both on and though flying some good shots soon they were hitting him with rounds of punches that he couldn't defend but that didn't stop him and he fought on to the end.

We were both still on our feet and Chris had landed some great punches on them. They fled though not really in defeat but neither was Chris as we both stood our ground though Chris had done most of the fighting protecting his best friend me, as true friends do for one another.

Chris got me up the stairs and knocked on the door seeing the lounge light still on. My mum was at home, she opened the door asking what had happen to me. I didn't tell her who had attacked me so she gave up on asking either of us and started to clean me up as my face was covered in blood. Chris and I were left with a bag of peas to place on my face as I started to look like the elephant man.

The following Monday I didn't even bother going to work and no one came knocking. My mum didn't know I had caused trouble at work, she thought I was still working there.

It was uncomfortable coming out of the flat as every time the two brothers would be there and the father as well, who thought now I was a little shit for attacking his son but his son was a dickhead anyway and as for his older boy, he was ok.

He had never given me trouble and I guess the night I took some punches from him, he was only doing what one brother would do for another and that was sticking up for his brother so I had no problems with him.

I did want to get the other one back but again it was right on my door step so I didn't feel comfortable doing anything, well not straight away.

I would keep on going out up town but now with no wages I was struggling. I stared to mix with some kids who were from out of Wellington, they were shop lifting teams. In and out they would go through all the big shops, nicking shit and selling it all on for a small profit. On weekends they would go one further as they would use quiet weekends mainly Sundays to break into warehouses, sometimes getting great results other times hitting a miss and go.

They would take me out on pieces of work. Many times nearly getting caught but many of them didn't care as they knew nothing else. The thing was I was a bright kid and had so much going for me. I wasn't like these dead head kids but I liked their company. I would turn a blind eye to what they all were up to but to get money of my own then I would have to follow suit and in I went with them over a few times into warehouses that they had target and struck.

As for shoplifting, that wasn't my thing. I saw it as such a petty thing to do, nicking shit out of a shop. I actually would look down on them for shoplifting as what's the point of it? Sweet fuck all to be honest and how embarrassing it would be to stand in front of a judge for shoplifting so it wasn't something for me.

I then ended up around this time of my life out at a bike club (MC 1%). They weren't allowed to wear a back patch as the Satan's Slaves Motorcycle Club had already busted up one of their clubhouses in Newlands as they were going around saying they were a 1% MC Club.

Well no one was allowed to do that in Wellington nor on the outskirts as the Satan's Slaves MC was the only bike club that were ever to wear bike colours in Wellington. This bike club MC 1% was now in Johnsonville, not far from Newlands where their first clubhouse was shut down by the Satan's Slaves MC.

Since moving they had quieted down a little but still run as a motorcycle club. One of their members started to date my sister. I was unknown to many of these bikers as I was just a kid who hanged around their clubhouse with a couple of the other younger kids who would be selling their stolen gear to them. One of the members who were a friend of one of my sister flatmates boyfriend told them that I was a good kid so that meant I started to get treated well.

Likewise when I was at the Satan's Slaves MC headquarters and more so when the Satan's Slaves MC came out to check up on this MC club and saw me there drinking. The Satan's Slaves MC asked me to keep on going out there, just to make sure the 1% MC Club always spoke of the Satan's Slaves MC in good terms and that there was no speech of the 1% MC Club getting back patches of their own.

As if they had or even spoken about it then it would have cause a biker war to go on as the Satan's Slaves MC would have seen that as a direct insult and also a threat. The Satan's Slaves MC for sure would have come out on top of that one if these two MC Clubs ever clashed.

I had decided to go up one night when I heard they were holding a party. About 15 of us kids, oldest probably only being 17 years old, I being the youngest all got drunk first at the nearby train station.

It was cheaper for us to drink straight out of the bottle from the bottle store rather than buy booze from their clubhouse. We all got slightly too drunk at the rail station and started to cause a bit of trouble to the point many people telling us they would call the police so we told them all to fuck off.

How embarrassing looking back now my behaviour towards normal straight people who were doing us no harm but I guess we were being loud and 15 odd kids, it's going to look bad even though we were only having fun ,mucking about. Doing what normal teenage boys do while they are being teenagers.

Play fighting as we left the platform, heading out towards the car park we spotted a bunch of locals kids coming off one of the trains, all steering at us, like we were scum so that was it. We stopped play fighting among ourselves and charged them all fighting, many fleeing.

We were on top of cars jumping around, about 25 boys. Ten of them and us lot all fighting each other then the blues and twos showed up so we all run as fast as we could but stupidly most of us ran towards the motorcycle clubhouse.

We were let in by the huge gates at the entrance. The bikers thinking that the local mongrel mob in the area was chasing us. We all ended up in the club house then next minute not one or two police cars came zooming down the path route but up to four police cars.

The bikers weren't happy at all as they had of course inside the clubhouse some of them holding drugs and others a few guns as well inside due to earlier problems they had been having with the local Mongrel Mob so a lot of the bikers were tooled up.

More than likely some were wanted by the police so one of their senor members by the name of Sticks kicked us out down to the fence and through the gate spoke to the police.

Sticks telling them that we hadn't anything to do with it and the only reason why us kids run here who none of the bikers knew any of the kids, including myself was due to us being chased by the mongrel mob.

Now if a copper wants to make a good arrest in New Zealand then many would love just to arrest mob members as the police see them as their number 1 enemy. Off they went down the road to rustle up some of the mob members who hadn't anything to do with the earlier fighting in the car park of Johnsonville railway station.

I didn't think it was wise of Sticks putting the mob up as they had a house in Johnsonville very close by and I knew in Sticks doing that then he was bringing even more future trouble to his own clubhouse. The mob member who lived there had Mongrel Mob tattooed over his forehead, he had never done me any wrong anytime I had walked past his house though he wasn't happy when these bikers moved into town as Johnsonville is only a small suburb, and it's not even a town.

Unknown to Sticks the mob found out that the bike club was to blame for the mob house being visited by the old bill so they were going to attempt to teach the bikers a lesson, that lesson soon followed.

The following weekend we turned back up to the bikers club house now more like 20 of us as some of the locals boys we had fought the weekend earlier now had come on board with us. We now very much were a strong little youth gang with members not only from Wellington city and the suburbs but also out as far Johnsonville so I named us "New Order".

What with us growing so big, all the boys agreed I got t shirts printed up with our youth gang logo of a skeleton firing a sawn off shot gun and with the words New Order above and New Zealand below.

As we stood outside the gates buzzing the gate, none of the bikers would let in as we had caused trouble the Friday earlier. Just then from behind us came a white Ute, we thought it was just more bikers turning up in a motor but then out of the passenger door came the barrel of a real shot gun.

Shots were fired in our direction so we all got down as they let the gun do the talking spraying the gate and fence around the club house. It was the mongrel mob coming to let the bikers know they weren't fucking happy.

We kids were shiting ourselves though none of us were shot.

The fucking bikers didn't even come out. We were hoping they would be running out of the club house with their own guns as they at least always had one firearm in the clubhouse.

The Ute truck backed up and sped off. We were finally let inside, which was meant to be for our own safely but again we were give more of a blasting for bringing even worse trouble down to their club house.

What the fuck were they on? As if their member Sticks hadn't bullshitted to the police that it was the local mob that had caused the previous week trouble in the car park of the railway station then the mob wouldn't have come down this following Friday to let off some shots.

For many weeks there was a very uneasy stand down off between the local mongrel mob and Johnsonville motorcycle club.

I had a feeling I was going to get shot anytime I turned up to Johnsonville. A lot of us, the kids thought that as we all had hair shaven off and looked like skinheads. A skinhead youth gang which our appearances just lead us to standing out more for the mob, and some of them would wait in the car park at the station for when we come of the train.

We had to walk through the car park to get to the biker club house and there were always a few members of the mongrel mob with chains and bats ready to smash our brains in so we kids were fucked.

I expected more from the bikers out there but none would ever come to the railway station and stand up against the mob. I realise why the Satan's Slaves would never let these bikers call themselves a 1% club as they might have been staunch among themselves behind their giant security gates, but many of them were fuck all when it came to squaring up to the local mob. Though I know a few would have taken the mob on as they did have some heavy men among themselves including Sticks, Wayne, Alan and Andy and Baldric and a few others.

One who was very tuff and all terms of the word was Jason White, fuck could that guy have a row and back it up time after time as no not many people who wish to get themselves into a row with this guy, he was all about fighting and the thing is, he very much knew how to fight and fight very well indeed.

Wayne as mentioned above also could take on a small army and come away still standing tall as he was a no holds fighter, more than just a street fighter but a very good boxer in his own right.

It was me who went forward and spoke to one of the mobsters explaining we are only kids and we enjoy drinking at the clubhouse, so be it their problem with them and not ours as long as the clubhouse was never fire bombed while my mates were drinking inside with me then I was happy.

I said to this mobster while he had a few others around him who I could see they didn't give a fuck we were kids, they would have been more than happy to smash the shit out of us. Whoever this mobster was with mongrel mob tattooed over his forehead, he at least gave me and my pal's right of way and never again did we ever have a run in with them personally though the mob finally after many a year drove the motorcycle club out of town. They never ever again formed a bike club anywhere in that part of outer Wellington.

Sadly Sticks lost his life riding his bike and he was very much sadly missed by many, many people across New Zealand as he was a good guy and a true biker through and through.

Only recently I have heard also that Baldric more recently lost his life while riding his motorcycle and that his crash was something like from a horror flick – it's sad to hear he died as he was a great guy and a friend among many.

Alan also died in the time that I have been in London, though he was a bully in many ways but still any death to hear from folk back home isn't nice to hear but unlike Baldric, Alan died from drug use, an overdose was what I heard.

As for my youth gang, they went on to make me their leader. I was now running my own gang. We would spend weekends drinking and causing trouble against other street youth gangs and I would get the markings of the gang tattooed on me and still have to this day as a reminder of those early years in gangland New Zealand.

Gangs for me as a teenager growing up in New Zealand took over my life as it does for so many kids across all of New Zealand. There are more gangs per head of population in New Zealand than in any other country in the world. The youth gangs of New Zealand are fearless and the older Gangs such as the Mob are one of the most dangerous Gangs in the entire world though as least with the Mob, many of them have a sense of duty not just to their brothers in arms but also to their blood family. With this correct balance then they always bring their own kids up very well and try to steer them away from ever joining a gang themselves, or at least leaving it to the choice of their children when those children get to a certain age.

For those you have no idea about gangs well in many young kids eyes, a gang is a family. Gangs very much are that, an extension of one's own family or a new family where one doesn't have a family themselves.

Of course gangs are negative, but not all gang members are and some good does come out of gangs, even if it's a little but at times that little bit can last a life time and that belonging to a gang can also last a lifetime and it can be all good.

Never judge a book by its cover, they say. Well never judge a gang member by his colours as I have meet some very decent mongrel mob members in my time in New Zealand and though by far the most dangerous gang of them all, they never done me no wrong. As for my step brothers, all of them I hold the up most respect to and forever will as they are family and family, be it blood family, step family or gang family well in my eyes family always comes first.

My mum was fuming as her son had become a little terror and now involved in gangs on a bigger scale. I had school soon again to attend and that meant my first day at a muti cultured school. I turned up looking like I was a member of the right wing, it really didn't go down well at my new school and the past would repeat itself, which no one saw coming apart from me.

Chapter 17

BEEN HERE BEFORE

AGE 14 / 15 YEAR 1989 /1990

The year just been 1989, had me turn up to a new college, a new beginning and a new start. I had been excepted in the very late part of the year so didn't really get involved in most aspects of the school and felt I was placed in a class that was out of my league as the kids were all so bright.

I couldn't match them in the class room also the class size was so much bigger than I had been used to. I never had that one to one teaching like I had at my private schools. This school just seemed too busy for its students so I felt a drift a little but still giving it my all though.

After school activities were not suitable for me as I was drifting away further through now with all this time I had on my hands which brought on a lot of boredom that lead onto more contact with gangs in Wellington. Unlike when I was at boarding school stuck on the school grounds, here I was walking out of the new college in the heart of the Wellington city with not much to do in the evenings. I was left to do whatever I wished so anytime my phone went and it was friends or others asking me out then I would do so.

So my evenings were spend out till very late, sometime 3am in the morning then I would have school the following morning. One thing I did do was my homework every afternoon after I come home from school. That's the first thing I would always do but after that I would be out, either in the gang I had formed which was the New Order or I would be down at the Satan's Slaves Motorcycle Club house drinking beer, playing pool.

If not down there then I would be out with Stonney while he looked after the girls at the strip club as in to what kind of drugs they wanted for their night at work. I would be carrying for Stonney which brought me in an income each time I went out with him.

On my 15th birthday in 1990, having one of the girls come and visit me at my house. It was a treat by Stony and the others so I was given a session. Let's say that made me turn up to school the following morning with a huge smile on my face

What then lead onto this was I would have the girl every night she finished work come back to what now had become my apartment as my own mum who owed the place felt that I had taken her home over and that she wasn't allowed to turn up when she wanted. She felt very pushed out of my life as I was changing quick instead of being just a rude teenage I was in many ways becoming a young man but a very moody young man due to all the drugs I was taking. A lot of coke was being now snorted up my nose so my mum in my eyes seemed to be always in the way, at times still treating me as a kid. She just loved me so much so always wanted to make a fuss over me but I didn't want my mum around as I didn't like being treated like a kid. I had become very in depend and I felt I was my own man.

My mum came over one night after she had a row with her boyfriend Wim and in she walked into the bedroom, and there I was having sex with a stripper who had brought one of the other girls over as well for some fun.

My mum didn't know what to say, nor did I. I closed the door and there was a silence then the girls all cracked up laughing, my mum fell asleep on the settee and left for work in the morning before any of us got up. I had to be up next dressed in my school uniform and get Angie the stripper, who I was seeing, for her friend to drive me off to school so I wasn't late for my first class.

As we were heading for school, Angie was in the front of car giving me head and next minute I was in the school grounds being dropped off by two blonde strippers. Teachers looked in shock as I got out of an old banger of a motor and had two birds blow me kisses.

Sometimes after school I would have my peers collect me on their Harley Davidson's and I would be driven to the Satan's Slaves Motorcycle Club house to help around the club if they were expecting visitors or I would help out with doing general duties of the clubhouse.

I would be seen to giving a helping hand when ever asked. Something I would enjoy doing as they had become a huge part of my life in every sense of the word as like a extended family.

I could cook and cook well so then even when other 1% Motorcycle Clubs were down to stay, bikers down from up north or from over the South Island then I would help the prospects of the club who were on kitchen duty with the cooking to feed all the hungry mouths. In the evenings when the clubhouse was full I would be asked to go up to Wellington's red light district to the strip clubs taking the visiting bilkers to see all the girls.

Soon Angie put me in some business as her and many of the girls worked in hotels in the day time as maids so they would steal credit cards and they would be up to all sorts selling their personal service to businessmen and ripping them off. Many times they would be blackmailing some of the men for lots of money.

With the credit cards that I was handed from Angie then after school I would go with Stonney girlfriends younger brother who was around 20 years of age, we would drive around buy lots of booze and beer kegs with the credit cards. We would go through the back door of many of the night clubs and pubs in Wellington and very much the strip club we would sell them the booze for a knocked down price and make shit loads of cash.

We also would have many cards transaction slips backdated so it looked like the card holder had been drinking in the strip club or clubs over the previous week. The owners would put the slips in with all the other card slips and off to the bank he would go. This scam went on for a good year which meant I was rolling high in more money than any kid at my school.

Soon I wanted to branch out more than just Wellington as I had done many years earlier when I wished to branch out of just Miramar. The only way was to learn how to drive but the only car I had access to be my mum's new car she had just brought.

When she slept at night over at her flat, Chris Mitchell my best friend who could drive at his age, would sneak the car keys out and drive we would around Wellington at night. He gave me driving lessons and we found having a car was just so much better, though of course if we had been caught by the law I would have been in the shit.

My mum one night waking up to go to use the bathroom saw that I wasn't there as I always would be asleep on the fold out bed settee in the lounge ever she ever stayed over anyway this night she realised her car keys was missing and though she guessed straight away that it was me who had taken her motor, she didn't call the police but waited for me to return.

I was given an ear full and warned that she would next time call the police if I kept this up nicking her car. Though in my own eyes I only saw it as borrowing her car. My Mum said she would call the police if it happened one more time, I doubt she would so I kept on doing it to the point that she would park her car around the corner from the house in another street and sleep with her keys.

She caught on that I could only drive an automatic, so she swapped her new car and changed to a manual. I never had learned how to drive a manual though my peers seeing me drive around my mum's previous car all thought that I could drive. Some nights when I would be leaving a party with them and they all were pissed up; they would get me to drive their own motors and nearly killing everyone on the way back from whichever party we had just been to.

These cars they owned were massive Australian v8 cars or American cars and I could barely see over the steering wheel, ok not that bad but still very bad poor driving each time I got behind the wheel of any of their cars.

For my recent 15 birthday I asked for a car for my birthday present from my mum. You could back then get a learners licence when 15 years old but of course I wasn't given a car but what I was given was a new gun. I was chuffed as it was a shotgun and I would go clay pigeon shooting with it and also up into the bush on farm land for night hunting with kids who I knew whose parents owned farmland, we would just go general shooting out on the farm or into surrounding bush areas.

It actually kept me out of trouble and away from the bright lights off Wellington and out of trouble that I was generally getting into.

My mum knew if it wasn't for a gun all those years back when we had the monster try to climb into the haunted house back in Miramar then something could have terrify happened to us both.

It wasn't like I was gun crazy; many of the kids at my last boarding school all had rifles though they all did live on farms so they needed them or had an excuse for them. I was just a city kid but I was always safe using it and never stupidly.

It did in power me though for some reason knowing I had a gun though I kept it quiet as I wasn't allowed at that age to have one so in the eyes of the law I was breaking the law but for me to go out shooting at gun clubs with Wim was harmless and also to good hunting in the bush on my friends parents farms was also harmless, I wasn't doing anyone any harm nor was I getting up to any trouble.

A lot of New Zealander's went hunting and in New Zealand per head of population there are more guns in New Zealand than anywhere in the world so it was a rare thing to have among many Kiwi Folk.

My weekends going into the bush or into the mountains would soon come to an end as what I found in the bush one day was a dope growing business.

There were shit loads of plants huge plants, something I had never seen before in my whole life. Yeah ok I seen a few plants growing at Rathkeale but nothing compared to what the hell I had mistakenly stumbled across one day while I was in the deep part of the bush on the outskirts of Upper Hutt.

I only found it by mistake as I went off the beaten track. The first thing I did was tell Stonney about my find. We went back up the following weekend, pulling as many plants as possible then taking some back to his place. He being greedy sold most of the dope while I wasn't around so I didn't get a huge share of the profits even though it was me who had come across all these dope plants in the first place.

I was told not to go back as it would have been home grown by a local gang and if I was ever caught then I would have been shot there and then if found stealing the plants.

Dope in NZ is a huge business and all controlled by the Maori gangs who wouldn't cut your arm off, if they caught you stealing their dope as they would kill simply cut your head off instead if they caught you and that's fact as they would kill you, no doubt about it.

Soon some of my peers now had gone from having me carry their drugs for money to now they were handing me drugs to hide at my mum's place. They would come around so many times and noticing actually that my mum wasn't living there, and that I would be there by myself so it was a perfect place to hide drugs as a safe house as it wasn't a known address to Wellington CIB.

I started to hold a lot of their drugs there and this meant again cash coming in for doing just that plus I would be ticked a lot of drugs for my own use, which I would have to pay back the following week with no excuses if I didn't have them the money. They would turn on me nastily if I didn't have their money even though we were all in the same boat together let's say as in we all were very close in this circle of people but again I was so many years younger by miles.

At this age I now was drinking more often up at bars and clubs in town. The police would pull me out of clubs and bars and constantly drive me home for underage drinking. If I was even fully searched they would have found drugs, but I kept all the drugs in my underwear so lucky never was caught with drugs on me.

My Mum hated me being driven home by the police and was now trying to set down home rules but it was too late for that now. As long as I was still doing ok in school then she was happy as her main concern was for me to get a good education. Education I would be getting, but more so in selling drugs and being streetwise rather than an education in the class room.

At school there were problems starting to appear. Not so much from lack of trying in the classrooms as I always put my head down and done my work and never did I fail to turn up to school. Many a times though I would be hung over or coming down from coke use from the previous evening while out partying or I would be up all night having sex with Angie so I was struggling a little to get through a whole day of school.

Some of the other students I wasn't at all getting alone with and that would bring on trouble sooner than expected which again would seem to turn my world upside down, all for the wrong reasons.

My mum found drugs hidden at her place one evening when was clearing away a few things. She threw the drugs straight out and only leaving a note for me when I came home early hours of that morning with Angie.

My mum's note read that if she ever, ever again found anything like this in her flat then 110% she this time would call the police. Her threats of calling the police on me as if I was for taking her car and now for drugs were soft threats in my eyes well that's how I took them anyway. She wasn't happy with the older crowd I was handing around with and most I had met through my sisters' social group so she would have a go at my sister.

My sister hadn't anything to do with drugs and it wasn't her fault that I was hanging about with certain people. My sister had her own life to live and she didn't need to be brought into whatever I was getting up to as she had no knowledge what I was up to. To her I am sure she just saw me as a troubled teenager like many teenagers are and she hadn't a clue what I got up to wasn't none of her concern though she worried about me like my Mum did as both loved me dearly even though I could be a little shit at times.

My sister moved into my mum's flat while she was in-between flats. Her boyfriend Tony tried to act as my big brother but him and I did clash a lot. I had a go at my mum about them two living there as now my own space had been taken and I was then sleeping again in the lounge which I didn't like so I made their life hell, always annoying them as much as possible and always inviting around as many of my friends as possible.

I told Tony as well during this time about the gun I had. He asked my mum if he could go shooing with me, my mum trusted him that he would act correct so we went out and sooner than later the gun now was store at my mum's flat rather that at Wims place. Tony got work at Wims garage, he knew about cars and being out of work at the time he now had a full time job working for Wim also side Frank who had worked for Wim for years and was a decent chap who I always got along well with.

As for Tony, I didn't like having an older brother figure. He would fight with me and due to him having a second Dan in Zen do kai, he would hit me and over power me in fights to the point one day I lost it and went for my gun and pointing the gun at him, pulling the trigger. The gun wasn't loaded but he didn't know that while he was pleading for his life but once the gun didn't fire, he gave I such a kicking and he hide the gun.

I complained to my mum but she backed up Tony, which lead onto he become like the gun keeper of the gun. The prick then had it cut down and I know he used it in some hold ups of some sort as he soon had a fair bit of cash.

My sister and Tony finally moved out, my gun going with him. Tony telling my Mum the gun had been sold as he thought that was best thing for it but later on I would find it hidden at my sister's house among Tony's belongings so I took it back one afternoon while he was out. By now my gun was useless to go hunting with as it was a sworn off shot gun, what a naughty tool that is.

Once I had managed to get my sister out and her boyfriend Tony then I had the place for myself again but now I had a drug debt handing over me due to my mum throwing away the drugs she found. This meant I owed some heavy people money so with that I was a given one choice and one choice only by them and that was too take on more drugs (what now looking back was a sly way of making me sell their gear) with no money going to me as my little profile would be going to them.

I would have to take on more drugs to cover the remaining debt; this went on for many months until I was out of that debt.

Not only was I in debt with my peers over drugs but they had hooked me on drugs. I not sure if on purpose but I now became a steady drug user and what a shame now looking back over to this part of my life as I had so much going for me only a few years earlier.

Due to them, their contact with me in this stage of my young life and their drugs, they messed up my head as I wasn't no longer focused as I had once been and drugs now were a huge part of my life, be either selling the shit for them or taking drugs myself for my own personal use.

I now was in their hands, in debt to them and hooked on drugs. How glad all these years later I have finally given up any contact with drugs and drug use. To any young kid or drug user reading this piece of my book, I just hope that your life sooner than later becomes much more clearer to the abusive self destructive use of hard drugs and that you give them up as all drugs do, is destroy lives and dreams and it's just pure evil.

Trust me I have been there. As they say brought the t-shirt and worn it. It destroyed all my dreams and a huge part of my life, how young I was back then not realising it and how very weak of a person I was to take that path of drug use and selling the shit as well. Please take this on board and look at your own life as mine was wasted from being just that......wasted.

Well having so much drugs around me meant I would be taking the drugs myself and that would be more debt as I was taking loads of drugs and for the first time LSD.

I loved LSD, I can remember my first acid tab with my sister flatmate boyfriend and his girlfriend and my sister and her friends up at a pub called the Lord Nelson Tavern in Wellington.

I recall the pub carpet mobbing up and down like waves in an ocean and the wall paint dripping down of the walls. I was getting such a great feeling of being on acid for the very first time, so trippy then getting hold of one of my sisters' friend Leigh. Leigh was one of many of my sisters friends I would end up sleeping with as I had come of age in their eyes by this time of my life as I looked at least 18 by now though I still only 15. I had been enjoying girls company for many years so when it came to the bedroom, I knew very much what to do in pleasing a girl.

I now was running the youth gang very well; all were skinheads in appearance which lead me to meet the leading skinhead firm in NZ, based in Wellington and also to new drugs. These guys were called Drudges' (miss spelt). They had a very British skinhead sense of style as in fashion and they would appear like the skinheads from the cult film A Clockwork Orange.

They had a house in front of the Satan's Slaves Motorcycle Club, but after the SSMC found them shooting up heroin in their clubhouse which the Satan's Slaves MC was so anti (most 1% bike clubs are) so the SSMC burnt down their house and they were out on their own to fend for themselves.

I started to sell the skinheads acid and other drugs. There was a skinhead outlet, a house that many lived in not too far from my mum's apartment. They were into robbing chemists, I went on a bit of work with them one night they broken into a chemist and in we went taken a lot of the drugs back at their place but I didn't know these new drugs so I wasn't as daring or more so as stupid and scum like as in taking the drugs the method they would be taking them.

Their drug use was in form of shooting up the drugs in their arms and feet by needle use as they all were into needles. I wouldn't ever take the drugs like that so down my throat lots of time I would drop different colour pills to see what was the buzz I would get, not knowing what it was I had taken but no way would I ever put a needle in my arm.

They were the guys that got me in to Ska music and also Sex Pistols, The Clash, The Sound of Oi, and other punk and skinhead style music. Music I hadn't ever heard before but started to really enjoy more so ska beats, and bands like The Specials and Madness etc.

Even though the SS MC didn't like me hanging round with the skinheads, the New Order guys loved it as that's what most of them were into as in was right wing movements, white power stuff.

White Power this extreme wasn't my thing. I always had many friends from all different cultures and back grounds but soon that was to change.

As at school I had a pacific islander be racist towards me one morning going into a classroom and I wouldn't take. I step him out and had him in a judo hold until he said sorry to me for what he had barked out at me but just as a teacher walked by and pulled me as saying I was being agro and that I was the one being racist.

I wasn't. It was this kid who had said some things about the colour of my skin and not I about the colour of his skin. I never saw people for the colour of their skin, I saw everyone as an equal and all I wanted him to do was say sorry to me.

Soon all this started to cause friction between me and the pacific islanders at school, all for the wrong reason as many of them I played rugby with and also were friends with. All they saw me as was someone who had a skinhead and that they knew I was in a gang called the New Order. They soon were turning against me, some trying to do stand over tactics on me which I couldn't understand as many had been good friends in the same rugby team so I couldn't understand the threats I was getting and how now they were classing me as a racist, I did not like that at all.

The skinheads soon found out and said they would sort the problem out but that was the worst thing to happen. The following Friday, they turned up waving Nazi flags and as the pacific islanders left the school grounds after school was finished for the day, there was a huge fight.

Many people injured and all hell broke out, I was in the middle of the fighting. I was being attacked by some of the trouble makers on the Pacific Islander's side and all I was trying to do was break up the fights. After being hit too many times I then fought back and more trying to get at the kid who had caused all this trouble in the previous week at school. The same kid who had been racist towards me in the first place. All this was caused by him and now it had seriously got out of hand as had the fighting which was totally out of control.

By the Monday morning I went to college as normal though carrying a black eye. One thing for sure are pacific islanders are great fighters, they never ever stand down to a fight and if they ever get knocked down they soon back up on their feet. They great natural boxers and that I had learned from the previous Friday as the fight seemed to have last forever though it only went on for around five minutes but it wasn't a pretty sight. Even bystanders run for their lives as it was like a true street battle going on in front of everyone to witness.

I was called into the head master office and spoken to about fighting. Fair enough being told off for being in a fight but where were all the other boys, why only me?

I then was told that the school had been send another report or taken a phone call from Rathkeale in the time I had been a student at Wellington college stating that it come to their attention that I had been growing plants at Rathkeale.

Those plants that the senior kids had shown me, after which I had destroy thrown them in the stream, I didn't know that just through the thick bushes there was a few more plants that I had missed. Well I was soon told these plants were found and that the kids including the grass had said they were mine, the dirty fucking pricks. Now as least I knew why when ever my mum tried to have Rathkeale change their mind about my expelling, she was given even a firmer no to her pleads.

I was then told by the headmaster of this, my second college that due to the racist up stir and the planned gang attack of some of his pupils, my fellow pupils on the Friday previous then he had no choice but do what Rathkeale had done and that was to expel me.

Expel me! What! No, no not again! I couldn't believe what I was hearing as here I was only 12 months later being expelled again. I had been expelled twice in less than my first two years of college.

My poor mum when was given the call by the headmaster. She drove straight up to the school and she wasn't going to take it neither was I. Firstly I wasn't racist and secondly I wasn't the cause of the fight on the previous Friday. It wasn't unusual for these same kids to fix up fights between rival schools and beat the living day light of the other kids plus most were bullies within this same school but the school would turn a blind eye due to how many trophies on the playing field these kids were winning for the school, and that meant a lot to the school.

They were teacher favourites' some of these kids as winning things on the rugby field meant a hell of a lot to this school. Why was I the only boy to be taking all of this as it wasn't fair but the school didn't give a shit as my track record wasn't really the best as I had been expelled from my previous college that being one of NZ`s leading private school and now I was being expelled from the capital city of NZ top state college. All the debating my mum tried then it was a lost cause.

She even took it up with the NZ education board but my mum was send a letter saying that even they went with the schools final decision.

I was out on my own and again broken my mum's heart. My dreams for doing any good with my education were just now dismissed. I had kept up my high level of learning and exam results were improving and also on the rugby field as I was being looked at for a school rugby tour of South America, now all that was shattered.

There I was such shame among my family. My mum was just so in shock she truly couldn't believe it as though maybe home life wasn't the best but at least I wasn't failing her in school or myself.

What school would take me now? Expelled for selling drugs and so called growing drugs on school grounds and then being expelled for arranging a gang fight at school, a brawl that no school had ever seen the size of and for being expelled for racistism.

I may have become a bit of hero among the skinheads and also the New Order gang that I had formed that now were thinking I was the business but what at the cost of my education and trust me I didn't feel like a fucking hero!

No school was taking me on. None in all of the entire country had any interest in me at all, not even one single school would take me on. I was blacklisted from every college in the whole country.

The only people who were now taking a deeper interest in me though at this time very much were the Satan's Slaves Motorcycle Club as here they could see a future member once I had come of age in years to come. In their eyes they were seeing a youth gang leader, running his gang intact and being able to hold myself well when ever in their clubhouse and for having real passion about their Motorcycle Club and everything it stood for.

Crime I was learning quick about, fighting I would and would with anyone. I was being lead down such the wrong path by now my own youth gang that very much was coming of age and I needed saving.

My mum couldn't control me and I had it seemed given up on myself, by now robbing chemists at night with the skinhead outfits and then getting so wasted. Being involved in brawls up to town in Manners Mall with my gang and other youth gangs and just being surrounded by everything that is negative in such gangs.

My mum would come home find me crawling round the floor after taking lots of V`s and acid, tripping off my nut listening to The Doors with pals and girls having a house party in her lovely little one bedroom flat. She telling everyone to fuck off then in the morning telling me to get up and get out! She had, had enough!

I didn't want to see the sunlight let along me my Mum standing over so telling her to leave me alone. Horribly telling her to fuck off due to my head being filled of drugs and nasty mood swings the following morning.

Just one horrible side effect of taking drugs such horrible mood swings. Well that was it, she couldn't take any more. Next minute I know I'm being woken up again but this time not by my beautiful Mum but by police officers who I fought as they dragged me out of bed without saying a word to me. I didn't know the fuck was going on and soon I was in the back of a police car handcuffed and soon down to the police station.

I was told I was being handed into care as my mum couldn't control me anymore. In a boys home I was send that late afternoon. Arriving there, being placed in a lounge type room surrounded by gang members, black power gang young members mainly.

I was the only white kid. I wasn't like any of them, I was highly education and bright. I didn't belong in this place I had come from a good background and a good home so fuck this as a joke! I was off, I escaped.

Escaping, one thing I had become good at times is as a young kid so I managed to get out.

I went and stayed at Stonney place and other friends and also some nights down at the Satan's Slaves headquarters on the run from the police and also the boys home and also my own mum until my mum had the court ruling lifted off me though when finally did hand myself back in, I was send back to the boys home for one week until all the paperwork was arranged for me to again be in the care of my mum. I wasn't too pleased about this, I was fuming.

A week full of fighting with rival now gang members who were out to teach the New Order a lesson but ya see I could fight so I did, just to save my own life. My Mum finally agreed for me to be out of care completely but saying I couldn't live at her flat and that stood as a court order when I was to be released so a suitable place had to be found to home me as I was still only a minor at the age of 15 years old.

It was agreed in family court that I moved into Sasaka house to live with his Mum and him and his younger brother. His Mum was one of my Mums long lasting friends so the courts were happy for me to find shelter there at hers with her supervision.

That was ok as she had granny flat underneath her grand house. It was in such a rich area of Wellington and she was cool but I did miss my Mum. My Mum would come and visit me and I wanted just to live back at her apartment but she was trying to be strong so she said no as if staying where I was, was teaching me some sort of lesson then she hoped that I would come out of this stage in my life as I had turned into a right little rebel and she couldn't control me.

My Mum knew I was a good kid as I was. I was just in the wrong crowd and hanging around with the wrong type of people for my age plus I was involved in the dangerous world, the evil world of drugs.

Anyway as for Sasaka Mum, she found trying to keep me in order wasn't easy as I would be out all night and bringing girls back and being my own man though in the days I would get bored so I got a job at fruit and a market place which I enjoyed but only being paid $200 a week for a whole week's worth of hard work.

Well I had learned I could earn so much more than that from selling drugs as that's what I had been taught even since the age of 12 years old. A world of drugs but due to all the years of drugs playing a part on my life I now was hooked on coke at $300 a gram, very expensive and then acid at $40 a trip.

I would take at least 5 to 10 acid trips a weekend taking two or three at a time, my whole weekend I would just be on one long acid trip. Soon came getting random tattoos done on acid and having the tattoos all on acid, it was madness and craziness and then came crime to pay for the drugs. Fraud was my main thing and then of course selling drugs, I was playing into the hands of my peers without even knowing it at the time.

So it meant even getting placed more into crime, such as the credit card frauds and also taking drugs to a club owner in town so he could sort out all the clubbers with drugs. I was doing this all to pay off my drug debt to my peers. My life was by now just seemed lost and all heading for a life of crime.

It seemed I didn't have a choice in the matter due to the pressure from my peers over the drug debts that I still owed them from when my mum flushed down the loo all their drugs that she had found in her flat. My own personal drug debts to them were also only getting higher and higher as I got higher from taking the shit.

I know my mum was only trying to do good, maybe shake me up and at least she didn't call the old bill when she found the drugs that time in her flat but she had no idea the amount of trouble and danger her actions put me in and how it all would come to scar me for life, not emotional but physically.

I would with stolen credit cards that I mentioned earlier have hand to me by certain maids who worked at the some of the hotels in Wellington. By day time they were maids in the hotels who would steal credit cards and other things then get them out to certain people who would pass them to me in the day after finishing work. I would get myself busy to many of the clubs and bars, one being the Diner and another being the strip club where there I with certain members of staff would zip zap the cards on those very old credit card machines.

Each slip we would back date it so it looked like whoever the card holder was had come in for a period of a week and we would mark each transaction for around the sums of $130 to anything up to $600 depending on the place of business then out of the money I would get my cut.

The girl would get her cut and the club or bar would get their cut and the certain person who would match me up with the girls would get his cut. We never were greedy and the cards would be returned back to the hotel room in the safe or the bedside draw also when whomever it was came back to the hotel nothing was a miss and at the end of the week each club would take the transaction slips into the banks with all their many other non fraud transaction slips and they all would be cashed there and then.

Nothing would be traced for the meantime and when times anything came up well in those days there was never any CCTV cameras so the police were fucked and we would make shit loads of money. The girls at night would go to their evening jobs that being strippers in the red light district and working later, some of them in the saunas so many would themselves end back at hotel rooms and more than likely the client was married so when he slept or was so drunk that's when the girls would also robbed them.

More than many times the client wouldn't get the police involved as it wouldn't be worth the breakup of his marriage. I would then be called and I would go the strip clubs and do their credit card as they had previously been there the night before so again we would back date the card on transactions and then off to the bank that morning before the card was reported lost.

The club owner would get the cash and even when the card was reported lost by the time we reached the banks, the bank of course would still pay out on back dated transactions as before the date of the card being reported lost, more times than the cards be reported lost than stolen.

This time of my life was turning wild as I would end up shagging some of the girls and when other bike clubs came to Wellington such as the Outcasts MC or the Outlaws or the many bike clubs from the South Island, who were friends with the Satan's Slaves MC then I would take them to the strip clubs for nights on the piss.

The bikers all would pay to shag the girls over in the parlours which meant lots of earnings for the girls so I would be given treats and extras and was very much liked by the club owners in the red light district of Wellington.

Soon through the heavy people I was doing all this for, I was placed with another guy and with the credit cards we would travel across all the massive booze wholesale stores (unlike what you see in England but more like the size of the hype supermarkets in France at the ferry ports, where the size of a supermarket just sells untold amounts of booze) to buy booze in bulk.

With the booze we brought we would sell it all at knock down price to the 1% bike clubs. All the bike clubs had private bars in their own club houses so any 1% MC that got on well with the Satan's Slaves MC, I and this fella for miles around we could travel by Ute or pickup truck and drop off booze to the 1% MC clubhouses.

We would do the credit cards to the max over a short period of time, load up the booze and sell the booze cheap then to the clubs and bars after the motorcycles clubs had got their booze first from us.

There was many back hand dealers going on in the red-light district and most of these club owners were not straight acting in business. The booze would flow in and out we would go onto the next place. Only once we had trouble after dropping off lots of booze, a club manager told us he wouldn't pay us telling us to fuck before he called the cops on us.

The cheek of him trying to do a stand over tactic on us so we just super glued that certain nightclub locks with heavy glue knowing as utu glue (it's what the street kids would be using to get high by sniffing it) then with some timber, nailed the timber against the entrance of the door and the back door and poured petrol underneath the door so they for sure could smell the petrol.

We weren't that nutty to light the petrol but what we did do next is get a car battery and with the leads place it on the mental door handle of the door. We yelled out "You all are going to fucking burn!"

Well they of course run for the doors, only to get a fucking shock of their lives, soon a empty wine box full of our money was thrown out of a upstairs window so in the end the wanker paid up without getting burnt.

We undo the door and went in to discuss the shit he had been trying to play but this we went with two baseball bats from the back of the Ute and smashed up all the booze they had just got off us, telling them they would never be looked after again.

Around this time I started to date the girl who I was seeing more often, one of the girls who worked in the parlour. She was an Australian girl called Angie who I mentioned earlier on.

She was a lovely girl and no not a whore or a slut even though she worked in a parlour. I met her through a friend of mine and who also was a close friend of the Satan's Slaves Motorcycle Club called Stonney (who in his later years would become a Satan's Slaves member himself). He was a nice bloke, a bit money hungry when it came to greed but a good guy and when I had fall out of with my mum I lived at this place after I ran away from the care home.

His girlfriend was a hooker and Angie was their flatmate. Stonney used to drive them around to stag dos and make sure they weren't mistreated and then at night he would drop them off to the parlour and sell drugs to get a few more quid in.

It was his girlfriend's younger brother than he would lend the Ute for us to drive around to do the booze.

It was Angie who worked in the hotels with her other friends who would get us the cards so at the age of not even 15 that year, when my mum couldn't cope with me I would stay out with Stonney and friends.

His best friend was dating my sister at this time but my sister had no time to these girls and didn't like me have contact with this seedy side to Wellington.

None of the girls were forced to doing what they were doing unlike what I have seen with my own eyes in the street of Soho where the girls mainly from Eastern Europe are forced into that.

My time living with them they all would be ranking in so much money that they all would love going to work and ripping off sad business men who most couldn't even get it up I was told and many were cheating on their partners and their kids.

Some of the girls enjoyed what they were doing plus they all had sugar daddies so some would come back with paid holidays and diamonds, even at that age I thought fair play to them as long as they not are being forced into this line of work.

I know there is a much bigger picture over all, but all I am saying is the girls I knew who were doing this, all were happy and weren't in any way sex slaves.

What I did notice of course all of them had massive issues from their childhoods and all were addicted to mainly the bigger drugs such as coke and speed and these cost a lot.

Most of the girls to cover their drug costs had to work most evenings as drugs came sadly first and foremost for many of them above anything else.

There I was living in this world while my mum was at Wims happy, as now I had come to age where she felt she didn't need to be looking after me though she was always worried about me and no way did she ever know the world I had now got myself involved in and she didn't have a clue what I was up and also the drugs that I were now surrounded by, not a weekly basis but a daily basis when among this circle of people.

Fuck I had been looking after myself for many a years.

I wasn't getting any lesson in life that at that age I should have been getting from my parents as I was at that age learning about coke and lsd, fraud and crime ,vices and also living a life past my means as I was getting a addiction I am sure to coke, back at the young age.

Whenever I was not making quid on the stolen credit cards as not all weekends would be good and during starting to take coke to much as well, $300 a gram is a lot of money after you do 3 grams of coke in one evening so I would have to do more than just fraud just to cover the costs of what coke was going up my nose, so this where selling drugs such as coke and speed came into play.

Soon I was even having Angie over my place. My mum met her many times, and really liked her. My mum never questioned the age gap.

Angie was older than my sister, so around 9 years older than me.

I know this seems weird to think but Angie like many, thought I was so much older than my age. To start with I wasn't ever in a school uniform and I would always be dressed and acting as if I was older.

Unlike many of my peers I knew how to treat girls well and I never cheated on them and when my mum was ever staying at Wims place then I had a pretty cool apartment I could take Angie or whichever girl I was seeing at the time to, and with the supply of drugs I could just get then Angie and I would just get sooo high all through the night and fuck for the whole night until the sun came up the following morning.

Soon personal debts started to increase all due to drug use and partying 24/7 though my mum said that I wouldn't be able to borrow more money off her as I had gone to her asking to bail me out but not telling her why the reason I needed money.

The sums of money that in truth no teenage kid should be asking from their parent or parents anyway soon after school classes in the afternoons I had to find work and that I did first with a removal company but I resented my mum for not just giving me the money as I saw it as she wasn't helping the problem as my debts brought on a lot of stress as to where to find the payments that were being asked from me from the peers who I owed money to from my drug use.

I was a bastard to my mum during that time. At the end of the day, it wasn't her fault as she didn't have a clue why I needed the money as I would hide so much from my mum, I am sure if I was just honest with her then she would have paid off my debt but more so I know she would have got me help for my addiction to the use of coke and drugs but instead of being clean with her as in explaining the situation I was in.

I just more a less slammed the door shut on her and one evening while she was at Wims calling me on the phone to try to talk to me about the troubles in my life, I never took the calls instead I packed my belongings and I went and lived at my sisters.

What a cool hang out it was at my sisters place. Any of the flats my sister ever had in Wellington were fucking cool to be at as always filled with in my eyes great people and most of all always partying plus my sister did have some very hot friends so I loved when time I spend at my sisters place and what I liked most as well was my sister always treated me as a equal.

My sister would take me to the pubs with her and her friends and they would get me into the nightclubs and also I would go to many parties with them all. Even at a young age that I was but now my age wasn't a question to anyone as I never acted my given age in any sense of the word.

It reminds me of the ausssie and kiwi's house in Brixton London, where Chesse and Sarah and the others called home away from home as in just proper party house.

Back in then those years back at my sisters' place, none of her friends minded me handing out.

My appearance was now different as well compared with the year earlier when I was of the age of 13 as back then I had blonde hair but now I had a skinhead and I looked the part as well.

A year earlier I was handing around down at the surfs clubhouse many weekends and I started to dress and look like a surfer though trust me I couldn't surf to save my life but I loved the hang out down on the beaches near the surf club houses and also the girls, wow they were hot the beach babes. Everyone always was up to mischief at these proper beach parties that would take place near the surf club in Island Bay.

I and Chris Mitchell were doing modelling at the time so we had to look the part and that meant look like pretty boys, we had dyed our hair blonde. The modelling was just for magazines and also the odd TV ad that we tried to go for. Chris got more work than me but I didn't mind as any bit of work that either if us got, meant we would be paid and we always shared our money among us both and saved it to party hard on the weekends at the beach parties with the surfers.

Soon actually Chris took to the water and picked up the art of surfing and to be honest he was very good at so sooner than later he went and brought himself a board and he would surf most weekends but he always still would party hard when it came the evenings on the weekends.

I was useless at surfing so I used to just pretend.

I had been out on the waves but failed and instead of trying again and again and finally getting the hang of it, I merely just gave up and would lay on the beach catching the sun while sitting next to someone else's surf board so looking the part though not ever doing the magic on the waves as the Wellington surfers would and would very well including Chris.

My friends could surf, some surf well.

Chris Mitchell used to be able to pull in all the surf girls so we all would with some fit beach girls end up shagging them on the beach watching the sun go down.

It was good time until two things happened to me which made me stop even more hanging around with my own age group.

One incident was when I was pissed on at a bus stop.

One evening when I was really drunk leaving the surf club, I fell asleep at a bus stop, and a car with a few guys drove past, they seen me a sleep there so they done a u turn and came back parking their car outside the bus stop where I was laying asleep due to too much drinking earlier down at the beach.

A few of them got out of the car and decided to piss on me, waking me up. I looked up and clocked one of them, who was a dickhead who lived in the local area by the name of Sash Jackson.

I would make sure I got him back for what he done. He was around 8 years older than me, and he thought he was the big man doing this to me in front of his fuckwit mates.

He doesn't know how very close the following night he came to having his parents home set alight as trust me I was fuming by what the wanker done but at the time by the time I came around and had clocked what the wanker was doing.

I was far too drunk to get to my feet quicker enough and also even if I had got to my feet after he had pissed on me, I wouldn't have been in no fit state to even be able to throw at least one punch as I was that drunk.

The only thing that stopped me setting his house a blaze was his parents were at home at the time the following evening I turned up to his doorstep to get the bastard back for what he done to me.

The coward himself wouldn't come out of the house when I turned the following evening with three of my pals, but instead his father came out on his behalf.

What a gutless bastard to hide behind his father's trousers, anyway I would seek him out in Wellington and get him good and proper as I wasn't going to let that lay low, no fucking way.

I am just glad for the time being I didn't do anything stupid as in set his house a blasé. I was just so angry at what he done so revenge at the time was No.1 on my mind when it came to that little prick.

Chris love was the next guy who attempted to a few years later to fuck with me.

Jackson I would in my life go and fuck up very badly and enjoyed getting him back for what he had done to me.

At that age of 13 years old no kid had ever taken the pie savoury out of me.

I never had been beaten up by this age, not even lost a fight.

So you can imagine my sense of angry at having some wanker piss over me while I was asleep and couldn't do anything about it. It may have been a right joke to him and his mates at the time but it was in my eyes a cowardly act.

I was all ready very well trained in Judo and had taken Zen Do Kai for a few solid years so I knew how to look after myself.

I just wished I wasn't in such a drunken state that evening as I know one on one even with the age difference I would be able to put that prick on his back and any one of his fuckwit mates who had stepped out of that car that night.

Around this age, looking like a pretty boy as I did made me feel like a weaker person as I could sense others would treat me as if I was soft and yeah maybe as I dressed like a surfer and I looked like a pretty boy then many older boys would think I was a easy target to take the piss out of so I knew my appearance had to change as I didn't like anyone taking the piss out of me.

Also I wasn't no surfer, I only dressed as one and looked liked one so I had more of a chance picking up the hot beach babes but what I wanted more was respect and to be treated no longer as a young kid so soon at one of the parties away from the beach, all my hair came off in one go and there I was awoke the next morning with a number haircut.

I didn't look like a pretty boy but instead I looked ready for the army with my skinhead new haircut, it was a massive change of an appearance to say the least from one extreme to another.

My best friend Chris Mitchell didn't follow suit but he did have the blonde in his hair grow out and soon went back to his normal appearance and though I left the surfing social circle, Chris by now had fallen in love with not only the beach babes but also the art of surfing so his weekends were for one thing only, and that was to catch waves and spend his weekends out in the surf of the beaches of the Wellington coast.

Though I should have learned from being so drunk that evening where I had fallen asleep at the bus stop and with the way I would drink far too much but instead of me calming it down and not drinking as heavy, well actually in all truth I would even drink more and get myself into even worse states.

So worst that where my mum would get me to hospital to have my tummy pumped after arriving home from a drinking session which out done any kid of my age or even senior kids. Drink so much that I wouldn't remember anything including at times my walk home.

Sometimes leaving house parties and I wouldn't reach my front door till at least 24 hrs as I never could make it home in the drunken states I was getting myself into.

I would sleep anywhere but home only due to not being able to even walk in a straight line so I would just fall asleep in someone's front yard or garage or a set of bushes.

Such was the state I was in that very night when I was asleep in the bus shelter on the night of the bus stop incident which as clear as day now I still can remember as with other memories from over my life and time growing up in New Zealand.

Sasha Jackson firstly kicked me that is what woke me before he started to piss on me and as I tried to get up, I recall he placing one of his feet on my chest holding me down holding me down s he continued to piss on me like a scum bag that he was and when he finished with his mates laughing on, he then as I struggled more to get to my own feet and by the time I had the strength to push his foot off me, he with the same foot started to kick out at me around the face and head as he made for his escape in the waiting car of his mates.

Not happy memories at all but a few years later, less than two years later I would get him back though at a cost due to the coward not being able to fight his own battles.

Second time running, is what exactly he did and that was run for his life though after hiding behind others who took it in their own hands to do damage to me and damage to the extent that I was in a inch of losing my life, less alone simply losing a fight.

One evening Sasha had entered a club which was called the Naked Angel.

It was the very first of such a club in Wellington in the early 1990s, a very Andy Warhol style type nightclub.

What was known as a true acid club at the time.

The reason why I was there was because the owner knew I could get good acid. The owner would ask me to come in on the weekends and sort him some acid tabs plus whatever other drugs I could bring him as his club was based on people being off their faces as it wasn't a disco but a true drug cultured type of nightclub, so each weekend he would buy loads each weekend from me.

He would have the doorman sell the drugs for him.

The club was up two flights of stairs, the doormen always being at the bottom of the stairs and what I noticed was that whenever there was a fight upstairs by the time the doormen had found out about the fight, there would have already been blood spilled on the dance floor which in turn meant the police being called due to trouble at the club.

The owner was always off his face on acid it meant that he was very near to being closed down due to the police noting drug use inside his club as everyone in the club were high and didn't take a police officer to notice that as it was plain to see by anyone who visited that club.

I didn't feel comfortable dropping drugs off to him after a while as the place was always having visits by the police so I said to him that he needed more security inside the club but he said he just couldn't afford the extra wage of one more doorman.

So now and then when I was in the club if there were trouble upstairs I would throw the people causing the trouble downstairs to the doormen as most people in there were just buzzing from acid, so they wouldn't put up much of a fight.

It wasn't a staunch club in any way at all so any trouble or fights always wreak the club and more visits by the police was putting me off from dropping off more drugs as I didn't wish ever to get caught with what I was carrying on me as I didn't see myself as a drug dealer as I was far from one in my eyes.

I was just sorting the owner out as it meant I could have free drinks and party in a night club in Wellington when I was under age so it suited me fine to do this for him once a week with what benefits I thought I was gaining in return though in all fairness now looking back. I was simply being used but at that age wisdom is far to find and I thought I was something special though of course looking back now I wasn't as all I was(was a mug) a proper fool for someone's else benefits, rather than my own and soon I would find this out the hard way.

Sooner than later though the owner started to pay me a wage as less trouble at the club meant firstly more people drinking there and enjoying themselves and that meant more people buying drugs from his doormen which brought in pure profit to him and also most of all it meant for him less visits by the police.

Wellington police I guessed thought maybe the owner had cleaned up the nightclub so they never visited much from then onwards.

What it did cause was the regular doormen not liking me at all. This teenager me, who was at this time was still taking school classes at the Correspondence School in the day then coming to their club in the evening to bounce the club. They never knew it was me who was supplying the owner who in turn made them hold the drugs in the club.

There was a lot of tension there whenever I arrived.

Things were going good as I had my school correspondence in the days going well and in the evenings I had my foot in the door of a club and I had Angie visited me when she left the parlour so my mum spend more time at Wims.

My Mum had by now it seemed given up on me.

She had no idea I was involved in drugs of this scale and she thought my evening job was working in a clock room at the club as she didn't know I was using my martial arts that I had been taught since I was young to stop fights.

Fights that I was only comfortable with stopping as I wasn't a great fighter so it was only if I felt I could have the upper hand when trouble started that I could steer to the doormen.

Over a period of being in the club every weekend, I did have a lot of back up by the regulars of the club.

I had access to what they wanted, which was drugs but I was calm and not ever giving it the large. I wasn't stood in a position as a doorman but I would float around the club partying it up and if there was trouble I would do my best to lead it out.

All was good in my world, then that prick Sasha Jackson walked in one night with a few friends. He didn't notice me as he headed to the bar area passing me where I was standing and nor when I went up to him and asked what the fuck was his game the year or so earlier when he pissed on me in the bus stop.

He just pushed me out the way and I thought bullocks though I was the one never really to cause a fight I just smashed him from one end of the club to the other.

He was a good fighter I had been told and though he was many years older which meant he would have more strength but I gave it to the prick as his mates watched on then as quick as the fight finished I went into the bathroom to clean his blood of me that had landed in my face from his nose and lip after watching me run cowardly to the set of stairs to the lead down to the entrance of the club, so thinking that was the end of him.

I didn't think to hang about or to make sure he had actually left as he wasn't in any state to put up any more of a fight as what he had already given seemed to be his best and he not once shook me.

I had proudly won that battle and made him look like a girl in front of his mates; none had bothered to even back him up during the period of them watching Sasha get the living daylights knocked out of him.

I truly don't think ever since then I have done so well as in landing such great punches, one after another in a fight as I might not be a boxer but that night

I felt like a proper heavy weight and a skilled boxer at that, which I am not but everything seemed to fit in place with the flying fists when they connected on his chin and nose.

After I washed all the blood away from my clothes as good as I could and also from my face as he did get himself in some good punches, so I noted I too had a bleeding nose though he landed a few punches, they were piss poor in strength. He punched like a girl.

I then went for a piss while I was in the bathroom, that's when I heard the bathroom door behind me open, though I didn't get sight of who it was in the mirror, but I could tell more than one person had entered the bathroom at the club.

Suddenly I was slammed forward into the trout and I was hit many times to the side of the head.

My front of my face was already now itself bleeding from being slammed into the wall.

I tried to get my body around so I could see who was attacking me. I managed to get facing them; there were three Pacific Islanders all punching me and one throwing kicks as well towards my body.

I was trapped and couldn't even get in one punch as it was like something I hadn't ever experienced like this and there wasn't anything I could do to defend myself so I had to just cover up my face as to block these heavy head punches that were coming my direction. One punch after another, so quick they were and so powerful.

The many punches to my head and a few getting through to my face were all painful as I moved my body back to try and cover up more and move away from reaching distance, then as I thought I could make a run to the door that's when what I thought was a punch to my right eye, blood appearing pouring down my face from the strike.

I managed to get free as far as the door and stumped out of the bathroom then with a heavy push again I was hit from behind which spun me around facing the guys again who had attacked me.

But as I was now out of the bathroom between the bathroom door to the stairs nearby leading down the main entrance stairs, I was grabbed and flung in this direction. Grabbing one of them but my grip didn't last as I was nearly picked up off my feet and thrown backwards down the stairs of the club landing right at the bottom where the two doormen stood after hitting many stairs on the way down near the bottom of the stair case.

No one had seen the attack on me take place in the bathroom though people had seen me get thrown from the top of the stairs but it was done so quick that even if anyone wanted to try and help or at least stop the attack upon me then no one would have had the chance to do so as these guys weren't fucking about nor slowing down

As for my earlier fight upstairs with Jackson then it seemed the doormen as normal missed that due to both of them standing at the bottom of the club at the entrance outside.

I landed by their feet, I couldn't even pick myself up nor even my left arm nor would it take any weight either.

Were these guys trying to kill me as I had been beaten so badly?

The doorman didn't even help me up on my feet; I had to do that myself.

I got to my feet telling them to shut the fucking door.

I was sure these three nutcases, who had just given me a serious beating, were going to any minute come racing down the stairs to finish me off.

Doors never were shut, and suddenly the three guys appeared at the bottom of the stairs.

Thank Fuck they had finished with me as they run down the hill, soon followed by the owner who said firstly he couldn't call a ambulance as the police would be called and I was under age to even be drinking in his club, let alone working so he told me to leave the outside of the club.

What a prick he was, as all he cared about which was clear now to see was his drugs in his office that meant more to him than me bleeding and covered in blood on the entrance of his club after all I had done and risked for him weekend after weekend.

Anyone could see that I seriously needed medical attention.

My face had been sliced and stabbed open as a few of the punches I had taken in the attack actually some were with the use of a knife, what I thought was a punch to my face earlier in the attack in the bathroom had actually been a stab wound just below my right eye.

I hadn't seen my face in a mirror in the bathroom during the attack but all I could see was so much blood dripping down onto me and tasting blood in my mouth, I was covered in blood, my own blood and the pain I was in that I started to feel as for now I think I was still in a state of shock from the attack.

I thought most of the blood was from my nose, but it wasn't till another 20 mins later I would be taken in a ambulance to the nearest hospital with a stab wound to my face just right eye, missing my right eye by less than a inch.

After all I had done for the bastard was all that was going through my mind as I walked away from the club, very unsteady on my feet then noticing blood from my mid drift as I started pulling up my shirt there was a gash across my stomach as well so then I knew a knife of some sort had been used in the attack.

I knew also something very wrong was with my left arm as I couldn't even move it or raise it and it was causing me great pain so were both my hands.

I couldn't move it and it felt so much pain and every time I wiped my face there was just tons of blood in my hands I knew my nose for the second time in my life had been broken and I was guessing my eye lid was cut by the punch I last seemed to have taken.

I got a bit further down the street until the doorman at the live music venue called The Car Park, who knew me through the Satan's Slaves Motorcycle Club, came to my rescue.

They called for an ambulance straight away and also were the first people to apply some first aid. They even commented what a state I was in and how bad things looked face wise upon me.

By now my right eye had filled up with blood and also had nearly closed from all the punches that side of my head and face I had taken.

Ambulance soon arrived came and got me. A police officer who saw me dripping blood outside the door of The Car Park Nightclub thought it had happened there, so they questioned me in the back of the ambulance well the medical team were working on my face.

I was then being told I had been stabbed in the face.

All the police got to hear from me was that I had been mugged in the street, that's all I would tell them.

All the way to ambulance I was stirring out of my left eye looking at the ceiling of the ambulance, thinking to how badly attacked I had just been through and how well these guys could really fight

It really showed up my age, and to even attempted to bounce at a club that age, I soon was going to end up getting unstuck but I never expected to be attacked like that, and more so for now I didn't even know why they had done this to me, as I had no rows ever with these guys in my past.

It's just ashamed that the coward Sasha Jackson could not take his earlier kicking from me, one on one as a man as I suspected he had something to do with it as he must have had as the attack only came moments after I smashed him to bits.

One thing it taught me, I was no boxer as I didn't even get one punch in against these guys and a good boxer or even a half decent boxer I am sure would have at least got one of the bastards.

I was taken to Wellington hospital; the doctors had to do surgery on my face as I had been opened up very badly on my face down to the bone of my right cheek bone.

What fucking animals to have to attack me as a pack and for nothing I had done wrong against them and even if I had, no one deserved to be set upon like this.

How I wished I knew who they were or where they lived as I know the Satan's Slaves M.C would have tracked them down and done them good and proper.

My x rays showed a broken left arm, a broken left collar bone and a stab wound to my stomach just below my left rib cage, a stab wound to right side of the face, a broken nose, and a broken right hand.

To my face, a skin graft as well from another part of my body.

My face looked so bad when I arrived to my mum's house with her opening the door the following morning seeing her only son, in such a mess.

I couldn't speak due to my face injuries but one thing I didn't do was to come across weak and I didn't want my Mum in tears as she was when she opened the door to me so I was as tough as I could be and strong though by this stage I was even in more pain than I had been the night before when the attack took place.

As for trying to have a laugh in such a mess all I could think of that made me have a laugh to myself was for sure that was the end of my brief modelling days over with, though of course I didn't have a career in modelling as I didn't have the most featured of faces to start with but now one thing I did have was a big scar on my left cheek so I now was never looking like a pretty boy that's for sure as it over the next few days.

Kind of in a way suited me and it made me look like a kid who could have a proper row but rows weren't on my mind for the time being, I think I had , had enough of them for the time being so for now it was about getting some rest and getting better, something that my mum made sure I was getting as she looked after me as any mum would for her son.

The beating did I think looking back make me more of angry kid though and not in a way that I ever went out looking for trouble as I hadn't in the past, and I sure hadn't to receive this beating but towards people I was more angry in general as I truly felt I had been let down badly by the club owner as on that night I did feel I was inches from losing my life and all he could do was wash his hands off me.

I for sure now was going to mark his card and try to get to the bottom of why I was attacked.

I was then weary of everyone who seemed to be doing me favours or offering me benefits as I guessed in the end they all would turn out to be how the club owner had treated me so I closed in to only being in the social circle of my peers as I saw them as people who wouldn't take me for a ride and who were out for my best interests.

Many of them were but looking back now many of them weren't but again I was still ever so young and had so much to learn about people and their behaviour and patterns in certain friendships, if that makes sense.

I did get to see more of Angie as she would come over to my mum's flat while I was there still recovering from my injuries so that was nice having her around for company and some naughty sex in the days.

As I didn't leave my mum's flat for a while as I was still in the dark who had attacked me and why so in the back of my head I was expecting maybe the three fellas to kick in my mum's door and finish me off.

I am sure some of these thoughts were due to the weed I was smoking at the time as I was doing that most days, just getting stoned as I had time off from doing my correspondence school so my days were just staying indoors at my mum's place and getting stoned was what was taking over my days and more stoned I got then I guess more paranoid I got thinking these guys were still after me and trying to track me.

Smoking dope to that extent doesn't do anything good apart from mess ya thoughts up and bring on horrible sense of paranoid but it did at times help the pain relief as I was in pain all over my body from the broken bones and also the force of the attack I had taken.

Angie soon moved in to Stonney's place. Stonney's girlfriend Mel was a stripper, who worked with Angie so that meant I would have more of a reason to go and see Stonney sociably and get myself out of the flat.

Most weekends from this point on while I was still getting over the attack, I would be spending time over at Stonney house having Angie in the sack if she was home which done me the best of good as I wasn't just spending 24/7 in my mum's flat but soon I stopped seeing her as much as I had other things so much more important to take care of which was at the core of my family due to such sadness and trauma hit my family.

Life at the age of 15 within my family came all crashing down as what happen to my sister next.

Grey clouds it seemed kept on hanging over me or my dear mum or my lovely sister. We just weren't meant to taste happiness as something awful it seemed was always waiting for us. It was so much to take in and it was a very dark, many dark hours and weeks for my mum and me and more so for my beloved sister Stacey to come, more than what I had just gone through with by a mile.

Chapter 18

GREY CLOUDS

My Mum had phoned to say that my sister hadn't made it back from the funeral that her and her boyfriend Tony at the time had attended.

Tony had ridden my sisters' motorcycle to the funeral, a Triumph 350cc tiger motorcycle.

I don't know to this day why my sister had brought herself a motorcycle back when she was 16 years old. My sister had been dating since the age of 15 years old a guy called Stephen Rowe, a very staunch guy who would ended up joining the Satan's Slaves Motorcycle Club.

He was a local boy from Miramar. Many young men of his age group who had interest in bikes well most would at one stage have contact with the Satan's Slaves MC as they were the only bike club in Wellington. Many would stay on and in their 20s many would prospect for the club, many would fail though some would do well in the eyes of the motorcycle club.

Stephen was one as he did go onto becoming a full patched member of the club become a fully patched member but as his life lead into the world of the Satan's Slaves MC, my sister lost interest in him.

They would row a lot and the relationship came apart. This was my sisters' first very long term relationship though in her younger years while she still lived at home she did date a guy by the name of Shane Dally, he was sound as a pie. Shane was a local kid, a bit of a tearaway but a decent guy to my sister.

She had been in a bike crash with Stephen just months before they were to break up and had surgeon done on her knee and was lucky not to be injured even worse.

She had come of the back of the bike when they crashed just outside Wellington after a bike run with a few of their friends who also were travelling on bikes, who were all living together in the same flat that my sister and Stephen had, which was just around the corner from my Mums place.

Most of the girls who lived there were dating guys who were connected to the Satan's Slaves. Their boyfriends either trying to get into the club and many becoming members in their time. One actually went on become in later years the president of the club, his name was Andrew Masters.

Andrews's younger sister was a friend of my sisters and like my sister Andrews sister didn't take much interest in the club either, though at this time I very much did.

I used to spend a lot of time down at the Satan's Slaves MC Clubhouse with Andrew who was known as Zombie and also my sister's boyfriend Stephen Rowe who was known as Grot.

The Satan's Slaves clubhouse was a old warehouse and also next door to it was a old repair shop for cars and bikes. My Mums boyfriend Wim had actually sold both the warehouse and the repair shop to the Satan's Slaves many years earlier which they connected both buildings and made it in to one of the biggest clubhouses out of all the motorcycle clubs in New Zealand.

It truly was something else, with a massive bar and a stage also living quarters for up to at least 20 members of the club and also state of the art security so they could never ever be under attack by any other gangs and also they had all there American and British bikes well locked up under guard plus with a work shop so the members could work on their bikes and huge American V8 cars.

They had high fences and also gates and solid steel doors that even when the police tried to raid them, the police simply couldn't get in so had to go to extreme lengths over the years by trying to break in via using bulldozers to gain entry into the clubhouse. Their headquarters still stand there to this present day on Luxford St in Wellington.

My mum never knew that from the earlier age of 11, I had been knocking about with them down at the Satan's Slaves headquarters.

Anyway back to the day of my Mums phone call to me telling me that my Sister and Tony hadn't arrived back from their friend's funeral that had taken place.

One of my sister's friends had been killed in a motorcycle crash.

Tony decided to ride my sister bike to the funeral with my sister on the back, though it was my sisters bike, he just didn't want to look like a girl by being ridden by my sister and having to be a pillow passager to a girl on a bike as that's something not seen as cool.

After the church service there was a wake, where everyone got drunk in celebration of the friends life that had died so young in life from a motorcycle crash, and drunk they all did get including Tony.

Who after the Funeral though my sister didn't want him nor her to be riding the bike back as they were so out of Wellington and to leave such a nice British motorcycle on the side of the road as any local gang would have seen that and nicked it though Tony convinced my sister that the best thing to do was just ride back to theirs so after a row, they got on my sisters` bike again with Tony riding the bike at the front.

They never made it back home that late afternoon.

Tony tried to over take a bus on the inside of the bus but the bus started to pull in so as Tony thought he would undertake the bus from the inside while the bus started to pull into his lane which was the bus lane but Tony instead of slowly down or allowing the bus to pull in, in front of the bike. He decided to pick up the speed of the bike to try and pass the bus on the inside.

Tony crashed at speed right into the side of the bus as it pulled in and my sister was flung into the front doors of the bike then her body was thrown under the bus and she was run over by the bus.

All the weight of the bus going over her right leg, her body being dragged a few meters before the bus could come to a final stop.

My sister went into an instant coma and was in a very bad state. I can't even start to explain how serious the injuries to my sister were.

My mum had been given a sos phone call from Wellington hospital which after receiving that dreadful call, my Mum called me that afternoon telling me what had gone on.

We hadn't been speaking much lately me and my Mum but as she told me my heart went out to yes very much my sister but also to my Mum as she didn't stop crying down the end of the phone, I never ever liked hearing my mum so upset.

When my Mum arrived to pick me up she was in no state to drive as she was shaking like a leaf.

My Mums car was an automatic which I could drive so I then drove her and I to the hospital. I know I was only the age of 14/15 years old but truly my Mum was just shaking with panic as the hospital had told her on the phone how very life threatening state my sister was in.

As we arrived to the hospital, we knew there and then how bad of a state my sister was in as a priest was giving the last rights over my sisters' body.

My sister had slipped out of her coma and died.

The doctors were all over her as we watched from behind a glass screen and then we saw the machine with the heart beat come back on, they had brought her back but she was still very much in a very bad way and also a very deep coma.

The doctors didn't think my sister would make it through the night and a few times it seemed they had lost her again as she was that near to death.

My sister was in a coma for over a month in that hospital and it broke both my mums and my heart to visit her seeing her just laying there, no movement what so ever and her eyes closed as if she was in a constant sleep.

It's such a painful thing to go through for anyone and how do u get strength everyday not knowing if your loved one would ever wake up and if so what state will they be in when they wake up, very much so when it's a terrible crash like this as due to what extent are the head injuries.

You don't have much of a chance when you are on a bike and involved in such a crash like what my sister was involved in.

One morning many weeks into my sisters coma in hospital when my Mum arrived to see my sister and held my sisters hand as she did everyday that my sister was in the hospital, this one morning though as my mum was speaking to my sister while my sister laid there, my sister opened her eyes ever so slowly and the doctors run in after my Mum had informed the nurse in the nursing bay that my sister had opened her eyes.

Soon she was speaking and over the next few day there was no lasting damage on her brain but as for her leg it was very much nearly cut off but they managed to save the right leg with hours and hours of surgeon and implants as her upper thigh had all but been removed and as for the bones then they had to be mended with pins and metal rods.

My sister had so much plastic surgeon done as well and when she left the hospital she left in a wheel chair as for her being able to walk again, the doctors were unsure as her left leg had been so badly damaged in the crash and by the weight of the bus running over that part of her body.

It was such an awful time to see my dear sister in that hospital and also my Mum nearly losing her only daughter.

All our family rallied around but me and my mum wasn't still talking as I never had forgiven my mum for when she had called the police on me whom had had me put in to care.

I couldn't live with rules. I never have and I never will as I am my own person and one with such a free spirit.

I had to report weekly to the local police station even though I hadn't committed any crime, well not to their knowledge.

At this time in my life the police kept a close eye on me as my name had been taken down so many times when I was in the company of known gang members and they wanted to see what my involvement on long term or short term was with gangs.

I can recall being arrested in Wellington on many nights and getting a beating by certain police officers though not every time, and not by every police officer whoever arrested me but a few sure did get laid into me over my younger years in Wellington.

I think the police thought this was a way of me gaining respected to the police though trust me it didn't and maybe they thought it would make me turn my back on gangs and come away from being such a mischief teenager but by this time of my life, gangs were in my blood.

Gangs had been such a major bearing on my life ever since I was 8 years old. I knew no different and as for gangs to me they were and had been like a second family to me from the very first gang that I hang out in my neighbourhood to the Satan's Slaves Motorcycle Club, who were known to be the most feared gang/motorcycle club back in those days.

I felt safe in gangs, more than I did even in my own house.

When my Mum or my Dad wasn't about in my early years then Gangs were. Gangs were there for me during dark hours though looking back now at the age of 33 years old, I do know that Gangs were my downfall.

They were the reason why I started to take drugs, why I started to sell drugs, why I was expelled from both of the schools, the reason why I lost out on such a good education and the breakup of relationships.

The trouble that I was getting myself into was all due to gangs and also the crime that was in my life was all down to gangs.

The arrests while I was under the age of 16 years old meant I was only appearing in youth court as I was too young to go to jail. There were times when I was of a young age in my teenage years when I was locked up in police cells and some police officers would come into my cell and beat me.

One time I had a fire hose put on me after being stripped searched and thrown into a police holding cell completely naked. I don't know if that was for them to get their personal kicks from but I was only a child, though in their eyes I was a criminal or worse a gang member.

The time the police came and got me from my Mums place to put me in care, they had to drag me out kicking and before they could get the cuffs on me I managed to kick out but as soon as they got me into the car and I was cuffed, I was sat on in the back seat and hit so many times that at least one of my ribs I am sure was broken.

Arriving to the police station I wasn't allowed out of the cell till I had calmed down I was told, even after taking such a kicking from them so I calmed down and asked what the fuck was going on?

Why had I just been dragged out of my Mums flat straight from bed with no questions being asked?

Next minute I was taken to a care home for boys in North Miramar. All the other kids were gang members from either black power or the mongrel mob and they were dangerous kids. What the fuck was I doing here among all these lot, I thought to myself as I very much didn't belong in this hell hole that's for sure.

I wasn't going to hang here for long, that's for sure so after working out the size of the security of the building and the staff on the first evening I was there (which was a Friday) I made my escape plans for the next evening.

Escape is what I did as I managed to get out through breaking a lock off a window and that was me free as a bird.

I headed straight for the Satan's Slaves Clubhouse and was let in by Zombie who asked the then president of the club Billy Cluston if I could stay for just the weekend which was granted to me so I slept over in the clubhouse for the remaining part of the weekend. On the Monday I headed over to Stonneys house and that become my new home for the time being.

I contacted my mum though not telling her where I was but telling her that no way was I going to be living in a boys home nor was I happy about being placed in care.

My Mum explained I was now in care so it wasn't here decision where I was placed so I told her if she wanted to see me again then she needs to do all she can to get me out of being in care of the state.

I wasn't to tell her my whereabouts, which I know frighten her as she only wished for the best for me and she was worried with not knowing where I was.

My mum calling the police was a cry for help as she no longer could take care of me, not due to being a bad mother as she wasn't that as she was a great mum but it was down to the fact that I wasn't an easy kid to look after.

I had grown up too fast and I didn't act like no teenage of my age would act, plus due to the partying and lifestyle I was leading then I wasn't controllable.

Putting me in to care though wasn't going to solve any issues and if anything I would have only become more of a lost youth so over the next few weeks she spoke to the government agencies that were involved and also to the police as they were now looking for me as I had escaped so there was a warrant issued for my arrest.

The police never did find me even after they went down to the Satan's Slaves Clubhouse to look for me, they had no idea where I was and that suited me fine.

Finally my mum said if I were to hand myself in then she would through the courts have me back though I wouldn't be able to live at her flat as she truly couldn't cope with my behaviour as at the best of times, I was a little shit to say the least.

I agreed to hand myself in though I wanted to know what had been discussed and where would I end up before I handed myself in. These questions had to be answered before I gave myself up.

A dear family friend of my mum Glenis Campbell said she would take in me and that I could live with her and her sons who both were good friends of mine. Once that was in written paper and agreed by all parties involved, I finally handed myself into the police and was picked up from the police station by Glenis soon afterwards after spending a few hours in a police holding cell.

My new home was her lovely house in a nice suburb of Wellington.

Everything was so much better in my life including my personal relationship with my mum, who would come and visit me on the weekends. I still was slightly angry with my mum by having to call the police on me weeks earlier that lead I to being placed in care but at least now I had my freedom back.

There was still certain agreements I had to stick by and If I were to get into any trouble or arrested for anything I would be placed back into in care but this time I would be sent to a even worst care home that I had been in and possibly one that was out of Wellington, which would mean being completely out of reach from anyone and many miles away from Wellington if I wished to escape for a second time.

You know what I still would have escaped even if the care home was in the South Island of New Zealand as however a mission for a young kid of my age to have made it back over to the North Island, I know for fact that somehow I would have done it.

For the time being I was happy too not get myself into any trouble and actually I went and got myself a job at a fruit and veg shop, packing the stock in the morning and then serving to customers in the afternoon.

It gave me a wage and something to fill my days up with so for the time being I was happy though most of my money went on buying dope with Sasaka Campbell, the oldest boy of the two Campbell brothers.

Sasaka loved to smoke weed and as I wasn't ever going out as I once was used to doing then smoking weed with him became my weekend enjoyment and at least being stoned indoors wasn't getting me into any more bother with anyone, more so with the law.

It was while I was staying at the Campbell's that I had got the call from my mum to say that my sister was in hospital so during these times I was allowed to stay at my mum's flat again as that was nearer to the hospital than where the Campbell's house was.

Mum and I were finally able to bring my sister home back to her flat that in the time she had been in hospital had holding bars fitted at the front stairs of the front door for my sister to be able to pull herself up out of the wheel chair and into her flat with the aid of crutches.

Also a toilet had been fitted that my sister could move across from her wheel chair and use and also a shower bath had been fitted so she could wash by herself.

She was still a long time away from full use of crutches.

Her boyfriend Tony had all only a broken ankle in the bike crash, so he had been let out of hospital months earlier and was living at my sisters flat with her flatmates.

One of my sisters flatmates was one of the girls who seven years earlier had run away from the girls home in South Miramar whom I had the girls back at my place when my mum's jewels was stolen though this girl wasn't the girl who had nicked it whom I found living with the street kids in K Street.

This girl was the girl who jumped on the back of one of the Satan's Slaves motorcycles when they had stopped near us at the beach party that we were having anyway as my mum went and opened the bedroom door leading into my sisters bedroom there laying in the bed was tony my sisters` boyfriend and that girl both in bed together.

My mum went nuts and so did my sister. It broke her heart as how cruel a blow was that, if I had known where my shotgun was that he taken months earlier (saying he had sold it) was actually in my sister's house hidden, I swear hand on heart I would have shot him with no worries in the world.

With what my sister had just been through due to him crashing the motorcycle, my sister didn't deserve this or to be treated like this, actually no one did and it proved how heartless he was and scum.

He was send packing after some bullshit that they had just fallen asleep together after takings some acid. It didn't take long for most of Wellington to find out what he had done among some of that circle including the Satan's Slaves Motorcycle Club.

Tony was hurt badly in an attack in his new flat; he was beaten so badly I was told.....well that's called karma isn't it.

My sister was only 19years old having to learn to walk again and with the rest of her life in front of her still but now having to face it with such injuries a nightmare.

She had amazing friends around her Joanna Smith, Mike Quinine, Jane, Tammy, Kate (Tim's Sister), Leigh and Abby and Rachael, so many others too many to mention but all of them were there for my sister.

I was so grateful for them all being there as good friends to my sister during times like this as it made a huge difference on my sisters outlook on life and she coped as a person during these dark hours.

Events and sadness that you just couldn't read about in a book as whatever it was be it bad luck or just utter grief, we were soon as a family too be on the end of so much more.

It would spin our lives out of control, mine publicly and my sisters privately and my Mums own life would be effected forever.

Chapter 19

THE CULT OF VIOLENCE

YEAR 1990 AGE 15

With what happened to my sister, seeing the strain and heartbreak that caused my mum, I didn't wish to give her any more problems so we sat down at the Campbell's and we spoke about getting my life sorted. Back to some form of schooling education was first and also to be living again at home.

We tried many other schools but not one single private or state school in all of NZ would take me as a pupil due to having been expelled twice. My education was still very important to both my mum and also to myself.

We fought for a place through the New Zealand Education Board and social welfare services. It was against the law not to be attending school at such an age so in the end both came on board to help me get back in to the education system though even with both these government bodies behind us, helping out even they couldn't convince a school to enrol me for the time being though one school did take me on for sports.

St Patricks College in Wellington which was not too far from my mum's flat and it was this school that at least for the time being took a interest in my rugby skills so they as a school let me train and play for one of their rugby teams as they had heard that I was a very good rugby player for my age.

This gave me something to look forward to each week as I would train with them twice a week and also play on Saturdays. One of my first weekends was a round robin tournament, where we managed to make the semi finals after beating many of the other national teams.

I was spotted by a rugby coach who took me on board to play in a sevens tournament which in New Zealand at that stage had become fair interest due to the famous Hong Kong Rugby Sevens.

I wasn't no near as good to even think I could make such national teams when I got older, but for now I was as good as many on the school playing fiends each and every Saturday plus it seemed I had bigger balls than most as in I would go, in for those tackles and not be scared to take a hit as I for sure would take down a few players when I was steaming along with the ball under my arm.

All in all, it's something I needed at that time in my life as it got me away from partying it up every Friday night as I took my rugby serious on the Saturday mornings and felt proud that this school took me on.

Also I found myself no longer smoking weed or getting high as I once used to so my overall health and well being was so much better and I felt better within myself and such people as my mum could see a huge change in me, which was lovely during those times after all I had been through in my life up to this age.

Even though I wasn't allowed to be a pupil at Saint Patricks School, it was nice to be a part of such a great school in the way of sports and to do my very best for them on the rugby pitch.

Still though I had so much time on my hands in the week that I decided to get another job which was near my sisters now new flat that she took after leaving the flat where her ex tony had bedded one of her flatmates. My sister didn't wish to be living there anymore after what had been going on there while she was in hospital.

My sister just wanted a flat of her own and also for her to get decent rest and more so for her injuries from the bike crash to mend.

She got a flat up on the mountain in Wellington, Mt Crawford. On one side of the mountain it would look down on all the bays and the beautiful harbour then on the other side of the mountain it looked down on Miramar the suburb where both her and I had grown up in. On the very top of the mountain was a jail, the only jail in Wellington called Mt Crawford.

The jail would be filled with gang members and it would be known to be run by the Satan's slaves as the jail was on their manor and it had many of their members locked up in there for many a crimes.

It was always known as their nick. The Satan's Slaves being in there in numbers always controlled/stopped a lot of the gang violence due to the numbers of Satan's slaves being in there at any given time which suited the prison staff as it meant less of their own prison officers had to deal with much trouble from the other rival gang members that were locked up in there.

There were always only ever a handful of black power and mongrel mob and other gangs which meant all these other gangs that were at war with one another on the outside couldn't come together in numbers inside the prison to take on the Satan's Slaves in there.

No one ever pushed the Satan's Slaves off the no.1 position in that jail plus the Satan's Slaves had a few screws in their pockets that would make life easier for them to operate while inside the jail.

The job I got while living at my sisters place was working for a trucking company in Miramar. I couldn't drive a truck nor did I have a licence to drive any of their trucks or vans so I would be there to move around the stock that was on the floor at the depot placing it all on the back of trucks then going out in one of trucks and unloading the gear of with the help of the truck driver.

It was mainly office equipment such as photo copy machines and bulking old computer systems, anything that you would think of that would be in a working business office also we had to take old machinery away as well from office spaces that companies had gone bust or help other companies relocate to new office spaces.

It was heavy labour but it was ok though I was the youngest by at least 12 years or more which would lead on to having to do all the shit jobs around the warehouse when I had come back to the depot after my regular work had been finished before time.

One thing I was and that was a hard worker so I dint mind put more effort into my job than many of the others.

I was proud of my job, but within a few weeks it meant I had to give up the rugby as I wouldn't make it to rugby practices twice a week as I would be working. Unlike the other kids in the team who of course would be at school and not be working after school so for me it meant by taking a decent wage each week and holding onto my job, I would lose out on my sports.

I was very disappointed with as I was becoming a very exciting young player.

My final game that was played at home, again for the second time I had interest in my rugby skills, this time from a local rugby manager from Ponki (miss spelt) rugby club.

He told me that when I got to a certain age if I was still playing rugby then to give him a call and try out for one of his teams, this made me so proud.

It was sad when I played in my last school boy team as I could have gone places as I was starting to pick up my game so much better than most on the pitch.

Work meant wages and wages meant money. I would put some of my wages aside as in savings rather than be as I was in the past with wages, just blowing them up against a wall on booze and partying.

I would sleep some nights at my sisters flat as it was near work and then some nights at my mum's flat while she stayed at Wims house so I had the flat to myself and some evening still I would stay at the Campbell's.

The Campbell's address was what was on my court order and actually it's where I was meant to be staying each night and nowhere else. No one from social services would ever rock up there in the evenings so I always chanced it by not staying there every single night of the week.

Social Services would always inform us when they were coming around for one of their meetings with me to see how things in all aspects of my life were going on during the time after being placed out of the care of the state and into the joint care of Glenis Campbell and my mum.

My mum and I stopped clashing and she was happy seeing how well I was doing with the job but still education was on the back of her mind, and even though she was still asking schools to take me on, none still would.

My sister started to be able to walk much better as time went by. She went in for even more operations to have her leg skin graphed and also to have silicon bags placed in to her upper thigh as that's where the bus had run over her.

A lot of damaged was done but with each new operation and plastic surgery done on her leg, she was feeling much better and was getting around so much more plus she now had a new boyfriend who we both knew as his family were good friends with my mum.

His name was Nick, he wasn't a biker, he was in staunch car club though, the biggest in all of New Zealand by the name of The Rebels(not to be mixed up with the Australian 1% bike club by the same name).

The president of the Rebels Car Club and his brother both had through my time up in town drinking at the bars and clubs had become good friends of mine. They were two Maori guys, the staunchest of Maoris you could ever meet.

They would fight 20 men if they needed to and I am telling you now I would put a bet on either of them two in smashing the shit out of 20 blokes as these two were something else.

Don't get me wrong they weren't violent men as they were true gentlemen first and foremost but if you fucked with them then they would come looking for and hunt you out where ever you may be.

They wouldn't give a shit if you were firm handed or if you had a gang to back you up as they would fight any men standing in your corner and they would always come off best.

Craig only being short in height but fuck could he fight and Mike his brother being a giant could lift a man up with one arm and throw them a few meters up through the air and that would only be for fun before he actually done you any harm.

They weren't crazy nor trouble makers, they were just very much from the old school and they had manners and principals where many folk had forgotten either which made both Craig and Mike shine so much more than many people in certain circles in New Zealand.

I didn't know of any man who didn't like either Craig or Mike and you could see how well respected they were through how many friends they had from all different walks of life as these two treated everyone with equal respect and that's all they expected in return.

They had some lovely motors, all American and also their clubhouse was a good place to have an early drink before hitting the nightclubs.

All their members were friendly and easy going though some were staunch but none were bullies and all treated me very well even though I would be the youngest to be found drinking in their clubhouse, but I always had a great night in there and was always felt welcomed by Craig and his brother Mike and their members.

I will always have good memories of both Craig and Mike and also the Rebel Car Club as they were good times when I spend evenings with them all.

Craig and Mike are the type of guys who you truly could call friends for life and though it's been nearly 14 years since I have seen or spoken to either of them, they are always very much in my thoughts whenever I think back to my time in New Zealand.

One day I very much would love to be able to have a cold beer with both of them – I do wish them all the best where ever they may be in New Zealand and whatever they may be getting up to as they always were successful in any business they were involved in.

Two very special guys and friends like that are hard to find on any journey through life.

Now that I had given up playing rugby, it meant if I didn't work over time on a Friday evening I would go up town with my sister after getting paid and I would get pissed up and then party it all through the weekend as I had no rugby to play on the Saturdays.

Many times after going out on a Friday with my sister and her friends I would end up sleeping with a few of my sister friends who now we're all going on 20 years old and so fit and some were just sexy as hell well actually all of them were but not all would wish to have me in the sack with them but I still would try my luck with a few and a few I ended up in bed with.

Saturday nights were always partying and then in the week nights I would be over at the Satan's Slaves clubhouse on the drink or be helping out with things they needed doing in the clubhouse.

I wasn't doing drugs though I was still drinking which was it seemed at the time my only vice from previous years.

By this time my relationship with the Satan's Slaves had become even stronger. My sisters ex, ex boyfriend Stephen and also his mate Zombie (who still is a very close friend of mine) had both been in the club a few years so they always let me go out and about with them and party it up.

The older members such as Scotty, Bacon, Scuff, Red, DD, Lou, Stan, Rob, Spoof and Greg to only name a few out of many good men that the club had at the time I would have upmost respect for them and also for Shane a old member who went to Australia to set up another bike club over there though by a different name to the Satan's Slaves.

The MC 1% Club that Shane set up was a success(and still is going strong today in Australia) so after knowing it was in good hands, he returned to New Zealand and rejoined the Satan's Slaves MC. Shane had a brother who was very solid with the club and also was a top man, always fair to me whenever I met him back in my younger days hanging around at the clubhouse.

I recall Billy Cluston as well. Billy once was the President of the Satan's Slaves MC; he was like a wild man, proper staunch. Billy was very wild through his actions actually just fearless might be the right word to use when speaking about him as that's one thing he didn't have and that was fear of anything and anyone.

Billy was always good to me and so was someone else who was known as a right nut case by the name of Hitler who again was a former president of the Satan's Slaves. Hitler as he was known was one of the most dangerous men I had ever met. He too was fine as with me and actually I got on well with both him and Billy Cluston.

These guys had a lot of time for me as long as I wasn't cheeky and not make a fool out of myself especially in front of travelling other 1% bike clubs that were stopping by and as long I didn't let the club down in anyway and that I could hold my drink as good as any other, which among these lot I got to tell you was fucking hard as they would drink till the cows came out and more.

Bacon was another member who had been with the club for many years, he had lost an arm in terrible bike crash but he was still loose as hell, and he was the member who would make sure the clubhouse was always in running order; I had a lot of time for him as well.

They all were hard as fuck, but many could turn on you suddenly if u said or done the wrong thing and they were all dangerous and probably the most dangerous bike club in all of New Zealand at the time.

There are loads of bike clubs up and down the country in New Zealand but the Satan's Slaves were far the most feared and they had built that reputation up from being lethal when they needed to. Their men could fight and if they got bored of using fists many would just ya stab ya to dead or if they were in the mood then just shot ya head off with one single blast.

The Satan's Slaves were blamed on most of the cities shootings and gang related murders that went on in and around the capital of New Zealand though many a times getting away with murder.

This was a time before anyone had heard of the Australian underbelly crime related shootings and murder that recently have come to light in Australia and around the world through books and also a television show both by the same titled Underbelly.

No one messed around with the Satan's Slaves, and I can say I took many a beating from them at times as did prospects that didn't stay in line.

I do recall from these times is I myself getting into many fights with the prospects that used to attempt to bully me. The Satan's Slaves members never bullied me, yeah I would get a back hander if I had been out of order but the prospects never stopped trying it on me, always trying to pick a fight with me due to how young I was.

I can remember my first ever fight in their clubhouse was between me and a probate someone who wanted to join the club so wasn't yet a prospect but was on what 1% clubs call probate - a time period where they work out to see if you worthy of just prospecting for the club and even after prospecting you anit guarantee of course for many years your colours / back patch to the club.

Even after 3 years of prospecting, they could still make you do another two years and then tell you after 5 years that you weren't worthy to wear their colours.

So probates were at the bottom but they still could be dangerous as they all had the most to prove to the club and its members.

This night in front of the then president Scuff, a probate tried to bully me and when he throw a punch in my direction I wasn't going to go down in front of the club and though there was a mighty age gap between the probate and me, there was no way I was going to lose this fight.

I was thinking if I were to win this fight then Scuff or some of the members would attack me for beating up a probate and if I were to lose then I would then as well be attacked after taking a beating so I felt I was in a no win situation.

I decided then to do my best and fight to what could have been to the death of either of us. The only thing the probate didn't know was that I could fight and fight good for my age as all he saw was a 15 year old kid.

I was strong then from all my heavy lifting at work and labour and I was fit due to all my years playing rugby and I could fight due to my years of learning the great martial art Zen Do Kai and also from my years of judo.

I had taken a few beatings in my life which meant I could take a punch and still fight on so I did and this fight went on from in front of the bar then into the toilet which was to the right of the bar if you were standing facing the bar.

I smashed his head timeless times against the pisser until I saw the lights go out in his eyes, and he had been knocked out.

I then thought I was on for a massive beating as I walked out of the bathroom covered head to toe in my blood and the probates blood for Red and Scuff both to say to me "Where the other fella?"

I told them I had knocked him out, and with that another member went into the toilet and drag the guy out slapping him a few times to get him around.

When he came to, a senior member got hold of him even more and just slung him out of the headquarters door and told him to fuck off and then a member got the guys Harley-Davidson and pushed it up outside the gates and just let it crash to the floor next to where the guy had been thrown to the floor by the other senior member.

Bang!!!! The huge reinforced gate closed and a beer was placed in my hand and a tap on my back as if this guy couldn't beat a 15 year old in a fight then he anit worth shit to the club.

After that I didn't have too many problems with any probates.

Though it wasn't the last of my fights in the clubhouse, and for now all the prospects kept from hassling me until one night Glenn, a friend of Stonneys who started to prospect did end up having a fight with me.

Glenn was a decent guy, and we both got on well but for some reason he felt like he needed to prove himself in front of some of the members so he started on me, out of the blue and for no reason at all.

I just took this as a sign of bullying as he was much older than me and it wasn't right he picked a fight with me as there were others in the clubhouse that night who were his age group, who he easy could have picked a row with but no, no he wanted to cause me problems.

I knocked him down at least three times but he still got up again and again and came at me. In the end I had to pull out a knife and warn him that I would stab him no doubt about it so for him to fuck off and stop showing off in front of the members.

By that time we both were knacked from the fight so in the end it was called a truce though in all truth Glenn wouldn't have dared to come forward while I had the knife in my hand as he for one knew that I wouldn't have thought twice about putting it in him so I not to lose the fight or face in front of the club.

He had a lucky escape as I was still fuming that he actually had started on me as we had always got on so well and I thought he was a mate anyway over time we made up but I always watched my back there onwards whenever a prospect got too drunk or started to act loose in front of the senior members or any visiting 1% motorcycle club.

I wasn't there to be fair game for any of them and I hated bullies in any form so I would always fight my corner even if it meant that I would lose as I wouldn't ever let any one walk over me and I had a fighting spirit in me that would come alive whenever I felt threatened.

I don't know why he started at me that night as we had been friends for a few years as I knew him from stonney but at my age many people always started at me at parties and I would just lose the plot and go for them, with more than they would ever have.

I think it's one good quality that the club saw in me at that young age as one thing I had, and that was balls....big balls for my age and I wasn't ever like some kid but very much many years my senior so I was always taken serious and I would act so which meant I was treated more like a adult than a 15 year old kid.

I had been going down to the clubhouse ever since I was 8 years old, so to me the clubhouse felt like more my home than these probates, who would come in and try and join the club and fail or the prospects who would come and go as only the best ever did make it to gaining their full colours.

Trust me I saw many fail, maybe that's why a lot of prospects would try and start on me as they didn't like the fact at times I would be treated even better than them by the senior members.

The thing was the club had seen me grow from a kid of 8 years old and now seven years later I was still hanging around the club house and if anything I was putting the club first and foremost in my life, maybe even more than a few of the prospects were.

For me the Satan's Slaves MC was very much my life, like another family that always were there for me through the dreadful times I had been through in my life up to this stage and also they were like brothers to me.

As I said earlier yeah a few times I got a beating when I deserved it from a senior member but you know what, the very next day I would be back knocking on the clubhouse door, black and blue but still showing where my heart was and that was with the Satan's Slaves MC.

My loyalty very much so was my honour and that's more I can say about many others as I lasted the distance and showed my true colours time after time, more than others did and at the end of the day I was only up to this stage in my life 15 years old, now that is saying something.

All the members very much knew where my loyalty lay and how very important the club was to me and how I respected the club through the bad times and good times and how one thing that grew as each year that I grew and that was my support for the club.

AC/DC the massive heavy metal rock band from Australia was playing in Wellington one night so I went along to go to their concert. From a young age I always wanted to see them perform live and this was my only chance as they were only playing one night in Wellington so I was so over the moon to be going to the gig.

While I was in the rugby grounds where the gig was being held, within only ten minutes of arriving and jumping the fence to get in, I was attacked and punched a few times by members of a staunch gang. I never knew this gang had a club in Wellington.

I knew the gang had clubs all the throughout the Valleys in the Hutt, just outside Wellington but I hadn't never seen a bottom rocker (lower patch of a gang member stating where they from below their gang patch) with Wellington written on a patch apart from of course the Satan's Slaves or the Black Power.

I thought "fuck yous, you dirty fucking bastards!!!!" as I hadn't caused any problems with these guys and I hadn't ever seen them before in my life but they thought they were tough smashing the shit out of me.

To them I would have looked like easy prey and they probably thought I was some right wing skinhead as by my appearance but I didn't give a fuck about the reason or reasons why they were smashing the shit out of me as all I wanted to do was to see AC/DC play but these bastards were wreaking my evening by stamping on my head.

I wasn't there to cause any trouble and I didn't even give these guys any shit so they were just picking me out to give a beating to as I was alone.

Well as the blows stopped to my head until I was nearly knocked out. I managed after the attack to my feet slowly once I knew for sure they had gone and I wandered back out of one of the gates.

I knew one of the security guards Mike who for the time being when he saw me with blood across my face came to my aid but when I told him who the gang was that attacked me earlier and had done this to me then he didn't want to know, nice one how charming is that.

"I could have been stabbed if they had got their hands on me rather than just put the boot into me or even worse!" I told Mike but he said he couldn't do much about it as he said there were many, many of those gang members all through different parts of the crowd so he was powerless to act.

I wasn't going to report it to the police as I wasn't any grass but fuck them I wasn't going to let this lay low that's for sure.

I said to Mike fair enough I wasn't asking him to do anything about, as I was just letting him I would be coming back.

Mike thought I was heading down to the Satan's slaves to tell them about it but they had New Zealand Outlaws MC from Napier, Sein Fein MC from Upper Hutt, New Zealand Outcasts MC from Hamilton, 45 Club MC from Auckland, Southern Vikings MC from the bottom of the South Island and Road Knights MC from also the South Island and also a 1% MC Club from Christchurch all drinking in their clubhouse.

The concert grounds was only a few street from the clubhouse so the Satan's Slaves MC themselves thought that a visiting gang in numbers might be silly enough to try it on with them that night at the clubhouse, not realising that inside they all were tooled up to the max and with some of the most violent men from among many of the toughest New Zealand 1% MC clubs from all over New Zealand all inside their club house.

Any gang that night who would be foolish enough to even think of attacking the clubhouse would for sure have left in body bags and that's hand on heard as that day I saw some of the fire power that they had and it was enough to fight even a small army.

No gang that night fucked with the Satan's slaves even though they didn't know the Satan's slaves had all this back up but as for me I was going to be running to them for help over me being attacked as I didn't want to look small in front of the bike clubs and I had my own tool, that was in mind.

I got a taxi home and picked up a massive carving knife from underneath my bed and I called a pal from Newlands who was in the New Order gang with me.

He collected me, parking many streets away from the concert grounds and I tucked away the carving knife and went into the concert through Mike who was on the gates still. He knew I was going back to either look for trouble or to take another beating so he wouldn't let me back in to the concert.

He didn't know I had a massive carving knife tucked under my jacket but he just wouldn't let me back in he was saying he was doing it for my own good.

I went back to my pal's car and we waited till we heard the music finish as you hear the band playing for miles around.

I didn't think I would get to see the pricks that had attacked me for no reason at all but as I was getting out of the car, I spotted one of them and then the rest heading up the other side of the road. I couldn't believe my luck and more so when one stopped to take a piss and then three more joined him, just like sitting ducks they were.

I run into the middle of the road and straight for them stabbing two of them from behind.

One I knew I got with a decent blow.

I knew also that there was a lot of police around at the time near the concert grounds more so after the concert had finished plus there was many people starting to wander up from the bottom of the street so the last thing I wanted was anyone calling the police before I had made my get away.

I just wanted to scare the living daylights out of them, and let them know how very close I had got to killing them.

But one of them who I got in the back of his legs as his legs just went to jelly as he fell quickly to the floor and the nearest one to him also hit the ground, well actually all of them dived for cover but these two dropped like bags of potatoes.

If I had been struck again, I would have done serious damaged but I needed to make my get away.

It still meant two of them took more than they had earlier dished out to me rather than my night ending by getting a beating earlier that I didn't deserve.

I was off back across the street running up to my mate's motor that was slightly over the hill on the road so no one saw what motor I got into as we sped away.

I knew by the time I had made it to the car then I was as safe as can be and more so as we got out of there. As if I was chased by the ones I didn't managed to get then who knows as one of them could have had firearm on them and they would have made sure that they would do me close range and to a early coffin.

In New Zealand there are more firearms per head of population than anywhere else in the world, like there are gangs.

It was so easy to get a gun growing up in New Zealand and more so by having strong gang connections as every third man in a gang had a gun so I wouldn't put it passed them for such people to be carrying a firearm.

One thing this gang was known for throughout New Zealand during these years was murdering people. It's what they did in their spare time so I knew getting home as soon as possible, well away from that area was putting it lightly in my best interest.

My pal took the knife I had used and was being destroyed just in case what happened came back on me.

I waited in my mum's flat that night thinking I shouldn't have given the knife away as just what about if we had been followed and they were on their way to my mum's place to burst in and putting one in my head. I really didn't feel too safe and though it was best to get over to Satan's Slaves clubhouse so I did after hiding away at my mum's flat for a few good hours.

When I arrived at the clubhouse in the early hours of the following morning on telling them what I had done, they went nuts telling me to fuck off and not turn up to their clubhouse after I had just stabbed someone and more so gang members as the police if they were called would be straight around to the clubhouse asking questions.

I told them no one saw it but I was given a slap and had the guard dog bite me when a member placed a punch on my chin for showing up after what I done and due to them all maybe having firearms that night already down at the clubhouse they didn't need to be raided due to my stupid actions.

They had to get some of the own guns out, and out quick! All the hand guns had to leave, the hunting rifles stayed like the 303s etc though as some of them had licences for them though such guns weren't permitted to be held at the clubhouse.

I was told to fuck off and so I did, not turning up to the clubhouse for weeks as I felt that they all now hated me or looked at me as a stupid kid when all I was doing was standing up for myself though a normal kid wouldn't have gone to that length but sorry I always reacted to the extreme if someone done a wrong against me or if I was ever mistreated.

Fair enough when I was in the wrong I could take that and when I used to get a slap at the clubhouse I could take that but to be beaten up at a rock concert for no reason at all then I anit fucking taken that and I sure didn't.

I have no regrets over stabbing the gang members who had beaten me up as how else could I have got the bulling bastards back. I couldn't have a had a tear up with them as there were too many of them to fight and so I would have been on the losing side of that and these guys do kill for a hobby and that's fact. Most who are in the jail system are all in for murder so I knew if even I tried to fight them they would have done serious harm to me.

As I wasn't going down to the Satan's slaves to drink in the week nights, I tried to drink with the guys at work but the warehouse floor manager who run things wasn't having any of it.

I tried to be in the mess room where there was a pool table and a fridge of beers that after work the guys wouldn't go home straight away but they would hang out there and bring in their own beers in the morning to be drunk after work.

They all mostly just sat around and talked shit and had a few games of pool so this night I tried to do the same and they kind of cold shouldered me apart from the Maori bloke who I would always go out on the truck with as he was sound as pie.

He would bring some pot to smoke so after a massive hard day of work had been finished we would park the truck up somewhere and he would get stoned and enjoy the puff before we had to head back to the depot. He only smoked weed in front of me as I was the only one he trusted as he knew I wasn't a grass and was sure some of the others would have grassed him up if they had seen him smoke weed while working.

Anyway this one night, about two weeks after the ac/dc concert stabbing which had by now been reported in newspapers.

And the following night after I had it seemed I had been cold shouldered by the guys who I worked with, I was playing the warehouse floor manager in a game of pool and I won so I asked who was in line in next for the pool table. The next person I beat in the following game as well so I was on a roll and feeling good about my pool playing skills.

All of a sudden the pool cue was taken of me and I was told to give up the table but I said "No, that's not how it works!" and then I added "Until I get beaten I will stop playing!"

I went to get my pool cue back but it was raised above my head, in that the manager wanted me to try and jump up to reach it up he was much taller than me. I wasn't going to be jumping for any one.

I told him stop being a prick, and with that next minute I was pushed in the back by the supervisor who was a dickhead at the best of times, he had no life apart from driving trucks but now he had been working from the depot, never going out much on the trucks anyway so he was just a moody asshole.

I thought to start with he had made a mistake by bumping into me but then he again pushed me in the back making me unsteady on my feet so I turned around and asked what was his problem?

He then removed the beer I had been drinking, one of the cans I had brought and poured it down the sink which was located in the mess room where we would make our lunches or cups of coffee at lunchtime.

I asked what the fuck was he playing at, and he took me I was too young to be drinking and as he was the supervisor then he would be constraining the rest of my beers in the fridge.

I told him like fuck he would, and that's when he stepped up to me.

You know what by this time I had already lost the plot from being baited by the other wanker who had taken my pool cue so I didn't know which one I would attack first, then it became obvious which one of the two I would go for first as the supervisor lean down to take my beers out for the bottom of the fridge so he was the most easier target so I line him up, and crack got me the sweetest of blows right on the side of his chin.

Down he went, not out though so I laid into him with punch after punch making sure he wouldn't be brave after that as he put up his hands to stop the blows to his head.

Then it was on to the wanker who had taken the pool cue from me. He was just in shock as to what he had seen and before I could even leap on him to start kicking the shit of him for making me look a fool, he yap out "You're fired, you're fired!! "which made me stop in my tracks and then I had some of the guys grab me and also the Maori guy who was my friend telling me it wasn't worth it.

The look on some of their faces were of great joy as firstly I think they loved watching the fight and secondly they all I am sure wished they had in their time given the supervisor a kicking as I had done.

I left telling them as it seemed I was under age to drink then they could finished of my beers in the fridge as I was just so full of rage but I understood they were being friends to me by making me think straight as in not to carry on fighting any longer.

I went to my sister house telling her what had happen but for now not to tell mum as though I was told I was fired, I in my own eyes didn't think so the following morning I woke to go in to work as normal and that's just exactly what I done.

I rocked up to work as nothing had happened and clocked in and went and to sort out the documents that were to be ready for that morning so the Maori chap and I knew what we were doing for the day but when I was spotted in the depot by the md, he called me over to his office and asked what was I doing at work as he had found out what had happened and that he had to back up his floor manger with what decision he made.

But I said I was being taken the piss out off and also I was pushed twice in my back.

The md went onto say after I explained my side of the story that due to the violence that I had inflicted on his supervisor that he now was off work for a week even maybe longer.

What a pussy as I hadn't broken his jaw, I had just made him look like that twat that he was in front of everyone at work but the md wasn't moving on the decision. He went onto explain that it's lucky it is not a police matter and that I wasn't being charge for assault.

Fuck him!! I wasn't in the wrong and I wasn't going to be losing my job over this so I called my mum who was at one of Wims garages doing his account books and told her what had happened and that I anit leaving this place.

Wim and my mum arrive around 30 mins later as I wouldn't leave the depot.

Wim had a word with the md, heated words were exchange from inside the office between all parties as I was waiting outside the md office that's when the floor manger came up to me and told me that he himself was going to do me good and proper and the best thing to do was to leave there and then. He didn't know that the man and woman in the md office was with me, he didn't know that the big man yelling at the md was my mum's boyfriends so I just told him to go fuck himself.

And I went into the md office to hear the md say to me ok you can have your job back but you know what I thought fuck him as well.

I didn't want to be working for the gutless bastard I was so angry that it took Wim and my mum to have to come down to get my job back when after I had explained to him earlier what had gone on.

I wasn't in the wrong but still he hadn't believed me and then only minutes earlier while waiting outside his office was being threaten by his floor manager so I said no thanks to the job and told him to look out his window as I marched up to his floor manger and just punched so hard right in the face at the bridge of his nose.

It felt like my hardest punch in the world, flooring him though breaking part of my hand and crushing one on my knuckles on my right hand that still is missing to this day as I hit him so hard that even before then and since then I truly haven't in all my life hit someone as hard.

He was out to it before even his head hit the ground, and with that I walked to the car park and waited by Wims car. I saw the Maori guy put his hands up in the air and so I waved to him and then got an earful from my mum as she was fluming with what had just happed after she had left work to come all the way down for me to argue about me being fired and to get my job back for me.

As for Wim he said "That's my boy!!"

I didn't like Wim saying that I wasn't his son and I wasn't no boy, though I know he didn't mean anything by it, he was just proud to see me a 15 old kid standing up for myself.

It gave me great confidence and I went back to the Satan's slaves clubhouse that night for a drink actually taking Wim with me as he hadn't never been down to the Satan's slaves clubhouse since he first sold the land to them and the outer buildings to make into a clubhouse there so we all had a good piss up.

The Satan's slaves' laughed when they heard Wim tell them the story of me telling the md to look out his window as I floored his floor manger.

I sat there enjoying my beer, not worrying about my damaged hand as it was badly swoony, giving me lots of pain though after a few shots of vodka I was feeling fine and at least the following morning I could sleep in as I didn't have work.

Not only had I been expelled from two schools, my first two colleges but I had also now been fired from my first real job as the fruit and veg market store job wasn't in my eyes a real job nor was the video store when I was a kid, and as for the spray paint and wreakers yard well to me that wasn't a proper job as I was skilled for it and it didn't last too long.

Not to me not knowing the trade it wasn't though everyone who worked there were highly skilled in what they were doing but not me so the job I had just been fired from was in many ways my first real job as I was paying tax on it and it wasn't wages under the table plus I had a work position as in role at the job so I knew what I was doing each and every day but it wasn't highly skilled.

What did ya expect I was only a 15 year old kid who hadn't even done exams yet and had been out of the schooling system now for a long time though that wasn't my choice or nor the choice of my mum.

The main school exams were in the last year of each kids schooling when they reached the age of 16, the exams are known as School Cert.

As a pupil you can stay at school till you actually 18 years old, it's known as higher education. I think it was known as that in those days but with me here I was in no man's land as no school would take me on and my last job I had just been fired from for attacking a senior member of staff and then when given my job back knocking out a member of the management.

Such was life but I wasn't feeling cocky as all I wanted to now try and do is make my mum proud as I had tried my hardest to improve my life and I had given up all drug taking.

I had calmed down a lot and been working so hard in my job and also in bettering myself but with losing my job and how I lost it then I did feel I was letting my mum down. She just wanted everything to come good for me and not always be called on the telephone about my antics or trouble that seemed to be following me.

That's all that mattered in life as I had let her down so many times in the past few years and I just wanted her to be proud of her one and only son, that being me.

As to see my mum finally happy after all the pain and sorrow and heart arc that she had lived and been through I wanted to be the person in her life who could provide her with happiness.

I had become the man of the house ever since my dad had left and I felt it my duty in life to protect my mum and my sister, not to bring my mum troubles or worries as I seemed to have been bringing her over the recent years that had just passed.

All the troubles I had brought upon my mum over all those years I wished to change that so she wouldn't have worries anymore in her life when it came to her son.

I just simply wanted her to be happy not part of the time but all of the time and to start to enjoy her own life more as she did seem very happy with Wim which was nice to see.

A smile to be placed upon my mum's face was long overdue after all she had done for me, stuck by me through thick and thin, never given up on me and even when I was up to mischief and trouble she did give me chance after chance until it came to much and the police took me away but that was now forgiven as I could understand her reasons for that as I was at the time was I have admitted out of control always high on drugs.

Even that I now knew was probably for the best and I really was out of control as a teenage so at least I myself had started to grow up more and think of my mum more so rather than just live a life of no rules and no walls as I had seen through the lives of the Satan's slaves.

My mum didn't want her son growing up to become one of them, all she wanted was her son to become good and make something of his life while I still had time to do at such an early age.

All I needed to do is work out how to control my tempter as what was starting to become a regular thing was my own violence and that wasn't going to get me any where fast in life.

I needed to try and work out how to channel my violent tempter though I was very peaceful and calm 99% of the time but when I was pushed or someone tried to bully me that's when the short fuse would go off and maybe it was due to what I had witnessed as a child though I wouldn't ever be violent towards women but any man who tried to bully or put me down then it was open game.

What I saw my mum go through growing up in that house I knew as the haunted house, I would stand in any ladies corner to fight their cause whenever I saw a women being mistreated. It would make my blood boil if I ever saw a lady being mistreated I would go to their rescue straight away even though it was none of my business.

I was ever so protective over my sister as well and so much over my mum as these two girls were the most important people in my whole life. My mum and my sister, I wouldn't ever let any harm come their way.

It was as if since I was a little kid getting them out of the house into neighbour's houses after my father had or was trying to attack my mum, that I would be their protector and protect them as much as I could. I would as I got a little older living in the haunted house try to fight my father off whenever he went for my mum while he still lived in the house or when he used to return to cause a fight.

It had become part of my make up as who I was, and that as to protect my mum as best as I could and also my sister as best as I could though my father never ever went for my sister or I. He never once laid his hands on us.

My tempter whenever I was in a situation feeling myself threaten or was threaten then I would just see a red mist and I would go for that person not realising what my actions could lead onto while I was in that rage as in the case when I stabbed the gang members at the rock concert.

When looking back now I should have just left the concert after taken the beating and just gone home to bed rather than seeking revenge to the point that I did as I could have easier wound up facing a murder charge.

I know as a 15 year old I was far much older in mind set. I had lost a lot of my childhood and youthfulness during my years of growing up (that's why I titled this book of mine Lost Youth).

I was living a life like a man in his mid 20s, and nowhere like how other 15 year kids were living their lives, which is a shame as it's as if my childhood was taken away from me and that I never got to be a kid or enjoy life as a teenager.

I was (it seems) robbed of my younger years due to the cult of violence.

Chapter 20

NEW ZEALAND INK

YEAR 1991 AGE 16

In 1990 in London, the premiere of a movie called The Krays a true story based on the Kray twins, London's leading gangsters in the 1960s and the biggest crime family in British history.

The two main roles of Reggie Kray and Ronnie Kray were played by Martin Kemp and Gary Kemp though neither at the time were main stream actors as they were actually pop stars, in a famous British band called Spandau Ballet which were one of the biggest bands in the world during the 1980s.

The lead singer was Tony Hadley who in my time in London I got to know through his tour manager a close friend of mine by the name of Dave Williams also Tony Hadley was a close friend of Greg foreman, Freddie's oldest son so many a nights when Tony was out on tour he would pop into the foreman's pub to have a drink with Fred and Greg after he had just done a gig in London.

Tony is a proper old school gent so are the other members of the band that I have met like John Keeble who was also in the band and he still tours with Tony plus has his own band now as well, they all good fellas and so is Dave Williams.

Both brothers though played their parts in the movie so well and have since gone to become very good TV and film actors since their roles as Reg and Ron Kray.

I have met Martin a few times in the late 1990s, first time was at the national TV awards in London and also he starred alongside Freddie foreman's son Jamie in a TV series which had a gangland feel to it called The Family, so met him again through Freddie Foreman and Jamie.

Jamie Foreman is one of the best and well known British actors who has been in massive film productions and is still one of the British leading male actors.

The film didn't reach NZ till at least a year later this is where my knowledge of the twins came from to start with as my father never spoke about them until many years later after I had reached the U.K as an adult and we rowed, actually fought one another when my father discovered my personal friendship I had with the Kray Twins, more so Reggie Kray in his later years and also his older brother Charlie Kray.

My own father didn't speak much about his time in London to me when I was younger all the conversations I had with him was in later years, more so after he knew I was visiting Reggie Kray in prison .

The end of 1990, things finally came good I had been accepted into a education centre, though it didn't sound to promising as it was a centre that kids who were to be classed as the worst kids in the normal school system of all of New Zealand were send to.

Be it they were violent or they like me weren't accepted into any normal school throughout the entire country.

some were school drop outs, some were just too dangerous even at a young age to be in a normal school and many were on the verge of being in gangs, most hated school and all of them were above the term naughty.

At this centre there were no teachers but people who would help you learn and there were no class rooms either.

All the work was send in by correspondence school work, that would only be send to kids who lived right out in the middle of the sticks on farms where there was no local school or kids who lived on say on houseboats or yachts so this was the way they still would do their school work to get themselves a education.

Each subject was posted to you and you nearly had to self teach yourself how to take your own lesson, though it was written out clearly how to follow each page etc, and there were the helpers at the education centre who would help.

I do believe I was the only pupil who went there and was excited to get my school work and do as much as I could each day.

I loved learning, be it history or other subjects also this was a way I could get my school cert so I had something I could show for myself after so many years of my education being stalled due to expulsions.

The only thing was it wasn't easy learning among this environment as some of these kids were disbursed to say the least. We all would be searched, patted down each day arriving to school.

They were looking for weapons and drugs as a weapon in some of these kids hands meant trouble as the fights that broke out when there wasn't weapons used were very hard core.

Many kids had to be restrained until police would turn up and take them away but they would be back as this place had a no expulsion rule that is apart from if someone done something to the extreme.

Fighting among the kids was a common thing, they would punch the shit out of each other, but with me I just wanted to get on with my school work and do as good as I could.

This was my very last chance of any form of education and I wasn't going to fuck things up even though at times it was hard contracting with all that was going on around me.

Now that I was back at school (if you could call it a school) at least the year was ending on a high. Christmas time and New Years Eve time I very much also ended the year getting high myself as a treat. Soon into the New Year, most weekends I was either stoned or I was when mixing with my peers more often than in the past year.

I now had all afternoons free and evenings so I found myself taking and getting such a liking to lsd more and more plus everything magical like mushrooms.

Maybe I was taking a step backwards but with all the free time on my hands, I think it was just boredom creeping back in and due to as they say being in the wrong crowd.

I was always in the wrong crowd as I didn't really have many straight friends as all my friends or social circles were up to one thing or another.

As I was doing good in my schooling and the fact that I was finally again getting a education and one that I was taken seriously (I always took my schooling serious at whatever age I had been while in education) I then thought as I was doing so well with school then I could party it up a bit on the weekends.

I didn't see the two world's co riding with one another but looking back now it wasn't such yen yang situation as I tried at the time to convince myself it was.

As for my gang New Order we were still going strong and being at this new school it was easy to recruit new members as they all were bad as hell and it meant among all the nutter's at the centre I could at least have a little back up when trouble ever headed my way.

I was now looking like a skinhead and acting the part soon there was talk of getting the gang name and symbol tattooed on a few of us so I went to see the Satan's slaves member Stan who was a tattooist and the clubs tattooist asking him if he would do the ink for me.

There was talk among the Satan's Slaves if they would allow me to get a gang tattoo but I argued the case saying it was my gang and it was a youth gang so there should not be a problem as it wasn't anything connected to the Satan's Slaves Motorcycle Club.

They said yes as long as I don't get the bottom rocker to say Wellington on the tattoo because as far as they were concerned no one gang or bike club would be having Wellington as their bottom rocker.

Soon afterwards one drunken afternoon while handing out with members of the New Order we got our money together and went to see Stan again and out came the guns, the tattoo guns.

I was first and it took a few hours to do and by the end of it Stan didn't want to tattoo anyone else so they made an appointment to get theirs done the following weekend.

There was only 6 of us that I agreed for them to get the gang logo done out of all the gang but you know what that following weekend out of the six who were meant to get it done, not one did so I ended being the only one ever to have it tattooed.

I felt embarrassed that they had made Stan wait for them that following weekend as that meant he lost out on money aka other tattoo bookings he could have taken so I went around to his place and he done more ink on my other shoulder. I didn't wish Stan to lose out on a day's wage, It was loyalty to the club and I had a lot of time for Stan.

So now age 15 there I was my mum not even knowing that both my shoulder were now covered in ink and one being a gang related tattoo and I won't be telling you what the other shoulder had done on me.

Soon though I got the taste for ink and so wanted more and more done but it cost money and me being at school wasn't earning me any quid.

I started to sell pot on the side as it was the only source of income I could make though I had to hide my pot so my mum never found it or any other drugs again in her flat.

That would have just broken her heart and she would felt so let down by me, something I had promised myself never to do to my mum again, that is let her down.

The New Year was moving by fast but what was missing out of my life was sport. I think with any New Zealander especially as a kid, we kiwis soak up any sport activity it's such a huge part of being a kiwi.

I rang the rugby manager from Ponki rugby club and though I was only 15 years old, his squads age group was min under 21s which meant ya had to be 21 years old to play but he remembered me.

He said for now at least I could go to the training grounds and train with them which I did and learned so much about the sport and even in practise I took many hits but would just get back up again and do my best against grown men who were so talent rugby players.

Mid 1991, I got my acc payment from when I had been stabbed in the face in the naked angel night club that I had been given a job as (while bringing in the managers drug supply for his regulars) a onlooker doing security for inside the club and that I had been beaten up so badly that my face you couldn't even recognise it was me.

I had my arm broken and ribs when I was thrown down the set of stairs after being attacked viciously in the toilet while going for a piss by the Samoans due to the in-house security who has gone against me and didn't like me working there.

I was given a cheque for £7,500 it was such a lot of money for any kid my age. I had been awarded it due to the lawyer who represented me telling them and showing the old modelling pictures that I done back when I was 13 saying that now with a massive scar on my face I no longer could ever get modelling work again.

Trust me I would never have got much modelling work as I got older as I was far from being a model but it worked as I got a good pay out for facial scaring and the loss of earnings.

In a way being stabbed in the face didn't do me any wrong at all as I had pure cash in my bank account but living the life I was leading was maybe a not a good thing.

First thing I did was go out and buy a V8 Valiant Charger car that belonged to Bacon, one of the Satan's slaves members who sold me his car which was his pride and joy.

I wasn't even yet 16 years old and I didn't even have a driving licence but that didn't stop me from buying a car and driving it, even driving it to school some mornings though I was told that I wasn't allowed it on school grounds as they the staff knew I didn't have a driving licence to drive.

I had never been given proper driving lessons apart from all those years earlier from my best friend Chris Mitchell when we used to take my mum's car when she was sleeping so I was probably the worst driver on the roads.

At that age you don't think and it gave me such a status that was until I crashed it one night leaving a night club into a parked car as I was so high on lsd that the parked cars along the road were last of my worries as I was tripping out thinking I was actually a airline pilot and that what I was flying was actually a plane.

I thought I was flying above the parked cars and the other traffic so when I went to fly over a park car to turn left as the traffic lights were red ahead and I wanted to turn left before them as I thought I could as I was in a plane.... then crash I hit the parked car and hit it at speed as I thought I was taking off.

I still couldn't work it out how I hit the car until I was pulled from the car by the friends I was driving asking me what the fuck kind of driving was that and how the hell had I not seen the park car.

My conversation to them as we left the scene wasn't making any sense to them when I was telling them that we hadn't been in car that I actually had been flying them in my own plane.

What a trip that was but it meant my car was left there as I couldn't go back and reclaim it so it ended being recovered and then placed in the police pound.

Something I couldn't go to in saying to them the next day yeah sorry that's my car, I thought it was a plane and oh yeah I don't have a licensed to drive it but here's the paper work to say I am the owner.

As that would have just got me in more shit and I didn't need that, another brush with the law.

So now every night I was going out it wasn't by transport of my own car but maybe that was a good thing though $2000 down the drain but I still had another $5,500 left.

I went out one night again tripping off my nut, a good trip as in those days all my acid trips were great.

I and my sister and her boyfriend and some friends had gone to watch a band play that a friend Andy was in, they were a covers band he played base and at every gig he played there was always trouble.

I got in to a fight the moment I went to get served my first drink by some knob head and as the doorman were telling me to calm the fuck down or I would be out.

They knew I was close to the Satan's slaves so they never in this club done me no wrong and they weren't part of the security company from the naked angel club so I knew that I wouldn't be expecting to be set up and stabbed again.

While they were having a go at me for the fight I got myself into, I noticed a blonde girl from behind one of their shoulders who was a skin head style girl. She looked about 23 years old really hot with cool dress sense, very British and she was talking to some bloke, or more so he was talking in her ear.

Now I anit one at chatting girls up, I am very shy though at the same time very forward but I wouldn't be one of these guys to go and be sleazy towards a girl or to use cheesy chat up lines.

As the doormen had finished given me there last warning, I looked over again and saw this girl looking back giggling away at the way I was being read my rights and I could tell she was disinterested in whatever the guy who was speaking in her ear.

I was high as a dove, I was and with ecstasy in my pocket that I had brought at the club I went over to her grabbed her by the hand and said "Hey babe you coming with Me." with a naughty smile upon my cheeky face.

Leaving the guy in some sort of shock as we left the nightclub which was named The Car Park, walking on past a fight that was happening at the front of the long queue and hearing the bass from Andy Evans guitar play out to a Rolling Stones number Jumping Jack Flash, I walked on by with the girl holding her hand neither of us had even spoken a word.

Stopping outside a shop front window I placed my hand in my pocket and unwrapped a few loose acid trips placing one in my mouth, seeing what I had taken she opened her mouth and in went a acid trip, my kind of girl I thought to myself.

I then noticed two policemen drive slowly down the street, stopping to give me a funny look. By now I must have looked very high as I had already taken two acid trips before that one being my third.

As they went by I told the girl I had got some Es and that placed a smile upon her face so out came a few Es and we went up the road to the very next bar so we could drop our Es with a few drinks.

I was asked id at the front door which made me just laugh and say to the two doormen "Are you beings serious boys ?" "You guys wouldn't show me up in front of my girl, would ya?" and with that the doormen moved the rope and in we went straight to the bar to down some Jack Daniels on ice while we took the Es and drank more Jack.

It was only then that I asked the girl her name. She told me her name was Kiren and mine I said back was Christian with a laugh that she found funny.

Within 30mins we both could feel the acid and the Es mixing together, the buzz was too much so we walked down the road heading down Courtney Place in Wellington, looking at all the bright lights and all the drunken fun loving people walking the streets.

Too many on the footpaths so we took to the road more a less walking through the steady going traffic, neither of us knew where we were heading but just then in front of us we came to the massive movie theatre house.

The signs said The Doors, and for some reason we decided it would be a laugh to go to the showing of a movie.

What a fucking great choice as we sat there buzzing off our nuts watching such a amazing film come alive right there in front of us on the screen, The Doors and Jim Morrison though only a movie but to us the movie was for real thanks to the drugs powering through our minds and bodies.

We ended making out in the isle afterwards once we got back to a row of seats that weren't the ones we had been earlier sitting in viewing the film, I stood back up and just pissed everywhere as I didn't want to be missing out on any of the movie.

I was getting shouts not to stop pissing but just to sit on down again which meant most others that night in the movie house all were as well off their faces on one drug or another.

I got to say that night, that trip was my best ever though your first is always the best as its undiscovered territory but this one this evening just rocked my boat, everything about it was beautiful.

Hours later I was in bed with her and still in bed with her till the Monday when she had to get up and go to work.

I had there and then fallen for her, I told her I was 17 years old going on 18 years she believed me though in all truth I was only 15, my 16th birthday was only a less than a month away but I didn't tell Kiren that nor the fact that I had school to go to that morning as we both left her flat with smiles upon our faces, naughty smiles I may add, proper happy ones.............you know that!!!!

I asked my mum that week for her not to come around to her flat as I had met a girl and I wanted my new girl over a lot so my mum said that was fine so I invited over Kiren to my mum's flat later part of that week and cooked her dinner.

I asked Kiren over dinner who the guy was whom was in her ear back at the nightclub on the previous Saturday where I first laid my eyes on her.

Kiren told me he was someone she had been dating and that was her third date with him and how she felt bad by now not even returning his calls as he had done no wrong. She said he was just boring, unlike me who seemed full of surprises and mischief like. Oh I fucking loved hearing that!

We spend like every night tonight I either at her place or she at my mum's flat, though the nights I went over to hers I would leave my school work at school as still couldn't tell her how old I was.

Having her at my place was ok, though my mum would be interested in the girl who had made her son ever so happy but now it dawned on me that I was living at my mums and to me that didn't feel cool now I was dating a girl so many years my senior.

I had at least $4,000 left as I blown $2000 on the car I crash, and $1500 on partying it up, that's not much money when you going through a lot of drugs and drink and the odd movie.

So I asked kerin if she would move in with me. , We had only been dating like 2 months but I felt it was time for me to move out. She dais yes a few weeks later so we got a really cool cottage only like 20min walk from the city from all the clubs and bars. It was up on a hill and it was number 5c Wright St, Wellington.

The cottage must have been at least 90 years old as it was old as, but it was such a cool pad and it was my first home so just like my sister had done 5 years earlier I now at the age of 16 was living in my own pad.

My mum used to come around making sure I was ok but I didn't like this as it made me out to be young but looking back now fuck I was only just turned 16 years old, every other 16 year kid that I knew was stilling living at home.

I told kiren that I had a job on the dust bin trucks as each morning I would be the first to leave as I would be off to school and then Kiren would be off to work.

The way I sorted rent was out of my acc money I paid rent for the first six months in advance and Kiren paid the bond so she thought I had used wages to do that but at least we now were rent free for six months but I knew somehow she would find out that I was going on 18.

She did when it was my 16th birthday and my mum invited her and around to Wims place for my birthday dinner though we had already just moved into the cottage by this time.

As we walked up the stairs to his house was a huge giant banner that said happy 16th birthday.

I told Kiren that it was a silly joke but as we got inside, everyone wishing me a happy 16th including both of Wims daughter who had Happy 16th birthday cards then Kiren pulled me aside and asked me was it true so I said "Yeah but don't let it fuck things up and as for ya friends just don't tell them."

I think she felt very uneasy when she first found out as she was 23 years old going on 24 years old, 7 years older than me but I still kept hush about school as that just wasn't cool and I think she would then have thought to herself "What I am dating a school kid."

But as I have said many times I was far older than my age and all I needed to make sure was to treat her good.

I cooked the best dinners in the world and I was always house proud and I did treat her very well and was a gentleman plus looked after her and spoiled her as much as I could.

I was just always worried about money so on speaking to my peers telling them my situation, they all knowing that I now was living out of my mum's place then they went back to me holding drugs for them. That was there way of helping me out; in their eyes they were doing me a favour.

Each week I would hide stuff in my cottage for them and they would give me a payment for doing so.

It used to be weekly they would sort me something but they worked out longer the drugs were in my place then more it cost them so after a while they would give me just a single payment.

I know I was stupid in many ways and maybe yes they were just using me but it meant I could keep up with appearances and also drugs now had been in my life for over 5 years so at the time I didn't see any wrong in it and I was gaining the trust of some very heavy people.

But like anything this soon leads onto more things to come but for now I was just happy making some money each week by doing this favour for them and being paid for it.

A neighbour two doors down soon moved out and in came a Maori fella and his wife and two kids.

I knew from the moment that he was a gang member but I didn't know which gang. I would say hello to him every time I past him on the path and always noticed he had a joint in his hands each time he would stop to say hello.

Also what was new was now that I was 16 years old I had gone on from just practising with the rugby club to be put on their bench for matches, I was only 16 years old playing in a under 21 years old team and that meant so much to me.

To be honest I was probably the weakness member of the rugby team but when anytime I was given a run in a game I tried my best.

I was always a forward in my own age group but I wasn't bigger enough or stronger enough to be part of this highly skilled forward pack so I was always covering the wing position and that's due to having good speed, I don't mean speed as in the drug but on my feet, I could always make the distance and scored a try or two so my rugby was coming along good and so was my school work.

I was nearing my end of year exams and only two things happened that year at school that was a highlight in some way though neither educational but interesting and one was when a car rolled up to school, a car I had remembered seeing when I was young back in Miramar and the driver whom I had meet 8 years ago when I was only 8 years old and that was Rai Harris the National President of the Black Power Gang.

I didn't know if he would remember me and I was right he didn't as I tried to speak to him but I guess in his eyes I looked like a right wing skin head so he didn't give me the time of day and the guy who was with him, made a mental note of this.

He turned out to be his son John Harris; he had just come out of borstal for an attempted armed robbery I think that took place somewhere up in Auckland.

He was locked up as a youth after the failed attempted on a hold up when he was 14 years old. He now was 17 years old so he done 3 years of what sentenced he was given and in those years he behind bars he had lost out on an education. His old man had found out about this educational centre so was making his son now become a part of our school, in a way doing something good for his son as any decent father would.

John from day one was offish with me and didn't like me at all. I never had many dislike me and I always don't like the feeling when someone is not willing to get to know me and does not like me for whatever personal reasons.

I thought I would make it something of mine to get to know him as all the other kids were shit scared of him apart from me as he wasn't too scary though a tough guy but how many of them had I already met in my life, and I was becoming one myself.

He was in good company as there was a Maori kid called Jacob who was black power through his own father and uncles and there was a girl called Bianca whose father was black power so every day these three hanged out together.

Soon John was wearing a black power t shirt to school and Jacob was as well so I came to school the next day in my New Order colours that were on a t-shirt but was told by the head master that I wasn't allowed to. The head master told me due to me being expelled from my last school for so called gang violence then he didn't wish me to be stirring shit up here.

I said if he asked John that he himself wouldn't wear his colours then that would be fine but the headmaster or director whatever title he had wasn't going to rock the boat with Rai Harris so said no.

The director had been a person who I could speak to and one that helped me out a lot with my studies whenever I needed help but here when it came to something that was social to do with school he wasn't taking my side.

I felt this wasn't fair as not only was I the most behaved but at lunch time the kids were encouraged to take turns cooking school lunch for everyone even if was just mince meat and veggie's in a pot or some pasta.

The other kids though would just find somewhere to all go and get stoned and not do sweet fuck all in the kitchen apart from me who would feed them all with whatever there was to feed them with.

In the end I thought I anit being praised enough for everything fucking good I was doing at this place and I felt I was being over looked through all that I was doing good in a positive way while at school so I thought fuck it........... It's time to turn things upside down.

One morning while on the way to school I went and picked some magic mushrooms that would grow all over different parts of New Zealand, including in Wellington so there I was picking the mushroom before arriving to school.

Placing them in a bag and then in the fridge they went while I sat down and got on with my morning school work.

Lunch time came so while I started to cook a massive stir fry for everyone, I added in all the magic mushrooms and of course served the staff first including the director(I did have manners....you know what I mean).

John Harris came in to get a feed, I told him not today mate as I didn't want him going on a trip but he demanded he was served some food so I told him "John go out and take one look at the staff and then tell me if you want some of this special brew?"

A term used when drugs such a mushrooms or dope is added to a food dish or added to a boozy drink.

John came back in the kitchen wetting himself nearly due to his own laughter.

I just had to take a look or myself what had made me full of giggles so out I went into the main room to take a look. There in front of my own eyes was the director crawling around on the floor in his office at the far end of the main room.

He seemed to be hiding under his desk with the only other member of staff who had not brought their own lunch this day so also had eaten what I had made.

She was Lucy in the Sky with Diamond, proper off her nut.

The other staff hadn't a clue and it was only me and John who knew what had taken place. I headed back into the kitchen to dump what was left in the wok but John wanted to fuck up some of the kids so he took in turn to serving them up what was left and sat there like a kid just waiting to see what happened.

Let's say that day will always stay with me as the Magical Mushroom Wednesday.

The staff never thought it was there food that had been touched they thought someone had put something in their cups of tea while they weren't looking.

As for the director he stayed in his office all afternoon after finally recovering and not knowing what had come over him. He was still there even when we left; a member of staff had called for his wife as they didn't know what was wrong with him.

Nothing too serious to worry them or for them to call the police as many just had belly laughs but at least for that day I for sure turned everything upside down though of course I couldn't take the credit for it.

I walked from school that afternoon with both John and Jacob; we all ended up getting pissed up in town in the black power pub in Newtown. I was the only white person in there and with a skinhead haircut well I wasn't getting many handshakes but just frosty looks though that didn't put me off standing my ground and sinking many beers, one after another even drinking some of the old boys under the table.

Both John and Jacob asked me to their clubhouse the Black Power gang clubhouse but I said no as I was on the other side of the fence.

At school from that day onwards we all finally had become friends but out of school they were black power and I was as they saw me as a skin head but it did built unlikely bridges.

Soon all the kids wanted to be using the kitchen at lunch time as many including John I would teach them how to make dope cakes for us all so we would be so stoned come afternoon once cakes and tea break had finished.

Christian S Simpson

One afternoon I was too stoned to get a bus or train home I ended up having to call myself a taxi with a tummy too full with cakes and a head to fill with stoniness.

While john and Jacob still wore their colours black power to school, I did one day just to take the piss turn up in a white power stated t shirt, the director went nuts and then said to me that my short number hair cut was offensive and that I would have to grow my hair as he didn't approval of it.

John when he saw the white power t shirt knew that it was a personal dig to him and Jacob but not in a piss take of a way, it's just he was allowed to be wearing black power and I wasn't even allowed to wear my own gang colours New Order so I went one step further by wearing that t shirt that day.

His only comment was that I had big balls for a white kid and it was lucky his old man wasn't visiting the school that day but at least it meant he and I never came to blows and all was good.

We would have a laugh and a photo of that time would have been so black and white as we were representing the opposite things in life because of our involvement from early ages of being in gangs.

One thing for sure was that I wasn't going to be getting my hair cut, and at the end of that week on the Friday I went and had a drink with the Wellington skinhead firm.

The Satan's Slaves MC didn't like hearing about this and more so when they saw me down at the Satan's slaves MC clubhouse the following evening, with the side of my head tattooed (My loyalty Is My Honour) though not having the ink work done by Stan but instead by the skinhead firm whom the Satan's slaves didn't get on with at all during those years.

Why those words on my skin in ink, well all through my life I had been taught one thing from a young age and it started from my dad and that is how important loyalty is - be it to your family first and foremost then to your loved ones and to your friends.

I had this always inside my heart and everyone who knew me knew one thing about me and that was how strong my loyalty was so I wanted to have it imprinted on me.

Why the head you ask? I think because when I asked by the director of the school that I had to grow my hair, I knew by getting the tattoo done there it meant I would have to cut it even shorter.

I mean to the point where this was no hair there at all and to turn up to school the following day and no more wearing gang symbols on t shirts or jackets but now he couldn't say go and wipe that off and when it came to suggestion that I to wear a hat during school hours, I told him to go fuck himself as he couldn't make me cover up what at the time and still to this day is a important part of me and that is my loyalty.

Though I never regretted having it done, and my girlfriend thought it was kind of sexy at the time.

It was stupid getting the tattoo done right on the side of my head especially as when I get older I will end up going bald so for all to see all of the time, which was something I really didn't back then as a young kid put much thought into.

Some people's reaction to it was shock horror but I am still proud of it and as many kiwis have tattoos and it's very much are a part and parcel of being a New Zealander.

The history of tattoos on New Zealand go back hundreds of years and as for Maoris they have their tribe tattoos for everyone to see including many having front facial tattoos.

Maori tattooing has become worldwide fashion art work even the singer Robbie Williams has a whole shoulder done in the Maori art form and many high profile actors and sports men do as well.

My mum wasn't too happy, and that's putting it lightly as she was ashamed by her son now having a head tattoo. I have lost count of how hats my mum ended up buying for me during the first few months as she just couldn't believe what I had gone and done.

As for tattoos I started to want more and one night went too far in wanting more as I had been partying with a guy who was known as Cool Ken and a few of his friends from Lower Hutt and Upper Hutt.

Cool Ken was cool most of the times that is when he was on medication as other times he was a nuttier. He had been in and out of mental hospitals due to being schizoid but you know what he was a nice guy and mental illness is just that a illness and as long as he was taking his tablets then he was fine and was a dear friend of mine and more so my sister during the years to come.

Anyway him and me and few other pals had come across a plant that was known in south America and also in Mexico, that many native tribes including the American Red Indians used to take the juice from the flowers and boil it and drink it as this would take them to the other side as in the outer world (spirit world) where they would see their ancients' and go on journeys (to you and me tripping).

Well us lot weren't from no South American tribe and none of us were American Red Indians either but we all wanted to try the juice so we boiled it one night ready to see where the hell it would take us all.

Kiren came over to see what we all were up to, sooner than later we all were drinking the stuff and fuck trip did we what.

One guy thought he was John Wayne I think that was due to all the earlier talk about American Indians as he kept on seeing many, even naming them.

I didn't see any American Indians but I was having a dam good talk to Winsor Churchill, Bobby Kennedy, Rudolf Hess and Elvis, who I thought looked similar to John Lennon when he placed on purple shade of glasses.

I was speaking to these three about the murder of John F Kennedy and that what part did Hoover have in it all.

I really thought they all were there though I couldn't understand what Hess was speaking about as he was talking in German but all the others when Elvis had stopped singing I could understand.

No one else apart from me could see them.

Cool Ken thought he was a pirate hiding treasure in the back yard; yep he was even digging up our friend's back yard putting pints of full milk and cereal boxes such as weetbix in the holes he had dug.

It was really loose what was happening to us all as we would go in and out of our trips.

One of the guys with us was actually a talent artist as in he wasn't famous but he could draw so well.

We all convinced him that he was tattooist and then we busted open the stereo for Cool Ken to make a tattoo gun and someone had some correct ink as one of the flatmates who wasn't home was a tattooist which was lucky as after a while the make shift tattoo gun failed half way through one of the guys getting a tattoo done. It didn't turn out to be what he had asked for but he was so tripping off his face he didn't realise till a few days later.

Then it was my turn, it's so lucky I didn't end up with a tattoo of Bobby Kennedy with Elvis as the guy who was doing the tabooing was himself tripping and I should have know from the fuck up of the first tattoo he done on the other friend that I shouldn't have been as eager as I was to go second for the ink.

I asked him to tattoo the devil on me. Satan don't ask me why as maybe it was something I thought of to do with the Satan's slaves I am unsure as I was off my nut but one thing I knew that Satan himself hadn't arrived among John Lennon and all the other people who I thought was present in the room.

During that tattooed that was being done, I can remember looking over at Kieran.

She had only drunk a little of the juice with one of the other girlfriends who were there so she wasn't as bad as we all were as in off her face but I remembered her smiling and I thought she looked so beautiful so I told him while he was still working on my first tattooed that I wanted to get another one done as well of my girlfriend.

So he finished doing the first one that was on my right leg on the calve and then went on to do my next one which he placed on my left calf.

I am sorry but I don't know what trip he was on! You know what I should have asked him before he even put ink to my skin even on the way home I hadn't even bothered looking at what he had tattooed as I was too busy on the motorway into Wellington from Lower Hutt telling Cool Ken to pull over as there were loads of hitch hikers on the motorway.

There wasn't but to me there was so from earlier meeting Elvis and the gang I now was talking to people from Sweden and Wales and Cuba and New York City everywhere else who we had picked up to give a lift to into town.

A few days later Cool Ken told me I had him stop over 20 times to pick up different hitch hikers who weren't even there but only in my trip. He said he stopped so many times that had there been hitch hitchers well even if he was driving a bus there still wouldn't have been enough room for them all on a bloody bus.

I was told I even opened his car boot to put their back packs in and that all on the way back to Wellington I told them the best clubs and bars to go to and the brief history of Wellington City.

Kiren by this time had left me at the party as her and the girls found us too much while we were tripping out. I don't remember even making it home, I only remember the part of being in the lounge talking to famous dead people and what the other were up to as in the pints of milk being buried in the back yard and also the tattooing that was being done on everyone but from that point on I don't remember much.

Kieran said I didn't get home till midday the next day.

Cool Ken tells me that he broke into a boat as we reached a boat yard near Wellington after coming off the motorway and that about four of us ended up trying to sail around the harbour.

Well he did think he was a fucking pirate after all.

As for the ink work, art work it so wasn't and two tattoos that for the rest of my life I shall wish I never had. They're only good at telling this story as to how they got there and why.

As the devil tattoo isn't off no bloody scary looking devil but of a devil, one will blonde hair, firm tits and fuck me boots.

I am only guessing my pal though that he was tattooing my girl who had blonde hair and really firm tits but she wasn't wearing fuck me boots and she didn't look like the devil.

But to him she must have and as he was tattooing the devil it must have been when I asked him to tattoo Kiren on me half way through him tattooing the devil then that's what made him try to put the two together.

As for when he was meant to then tattoo Kiren, all I can say is I have a tattoo of a women with red hair who had snakes in her hair like the Greek myth but hey this one is laying on a pillow with a phone cord that is attached to the pillow and with a phone in her hand.

WTF comes to mind if you ever get to see it and as for those who have well the laughter is heard over mountain ranges as everyone who has seen it just can't stop laughing out loud, including me.

Let me carry on telling you as it only gets worse but to you whom is reading this it will even more funnier as her hands are black gloved and one hand has six fingers and as for the rest of her well she's in a black bra and has pull up stockings, oh with high heels! Now how the fuck is that meant to be my blonde hair girl and when has anyone ever known a phone to be plugged into a pillow.

The guy not only fucked up my tattoo requests which weren't that hard to follow, but he also went and fucked up both my legs as I used to never worry about wearing shorts etc.

These days it's very hard to find me in a pair of shorts as these two tattoos if I don't get the chance to explain them to people then all I get when I been away on holiday is balls of laughter and hey I don't blame people from having a proper laugh as I still do when I take off my pants and see them there along both of my legs.

As I said they could have been worse couldn't they..................nope!!!!

Chapter 21

HOPE AND GLORY

AGE 16 YEAR 1991 / 1992

Hope, I had lots of that going into my exams. My school exams had to be taken place in a real school with real teachers and under real exam settings so I was off for the different exams over a week to a girl's college as they were the only school willing to have me sit my exams.

All the boys colleges in the Wellington region wouldn't let me sit my exams with their pupils, they saw me as trouble and too much a threat to their pupils and also too much of a talking point among their own pupils if I had been in their exam halls.

What the hell were they on as I wasn't cannibal lecture, do you know what I mean!!!!

All I wanted to do is my exams, even up to this point my girl still didn't know I had been going to school for the past year. I must have been the nicest smelling dustman in all of town anyway when I arrived at the girls' college; I was very happy to be among them all as I entered the school hall and sat my first exam.

Following day I was back with a smile on my face, due to lots of the girls being so dam pretty as most New Zealand girls are.

I sat there among the girls thinking to myself all these girls were my own age group and these are the girls that I should be courting but even though many were stunning, I couldn't see myself wanting to go to the movies with any of them.

I guessed that's all they probably did when going out on dates rather than getting up to mischief which was by now kind of my second name.

As for movies actually I had taken Kiren back to that same theatre house where we had seen The Doors. We could it seemed only go to the movies whenever we were high and not to normal movies as we got so bored watching love stories or comedies or horrors as everyone else would go and see.

For us the memoires of that very first night when we had watched the movie The Doors, it had become such meaningful thing between us both and movies after that just never seemed the same apart from that is, if we had taken acid first.

So we would go to see art house style films that neither of us could understand but being high as a kite it always made the film more interesting and then there were French movies we would go and see, thinking we were cultured.

I kind of enjoyed the French movies and then there was always the music late films such as Jim Hendrix playing a gig on the isle of Wright which just rocked or a film about Woodstock that made me even more get into those bands of that period as I was never into pop but more rock from the 1960s and also the 70s.

I can remember the week I was taking my exams I decided one night after having a row with Kiren that I would drop some acid.

I was in the cottage by myself and bored, she wasn't going to be back as she was staying over at her friend's house so I took the acid and had a few people come by and buy some weed so as it was a nice night for me enjoying my acid and having a few dollars in my pocket.

While we all smoked a few joints outside the cottage, I was shouted over by the Maori neighbour who had moved in to the flat recently a few doors down.

He asked if I knew of anyone who could sort him some weed so I told him I could and I went on in to get him some then my trip started to come on even stronger while I was getting a bag of weed together for him.

I went to his fence to hand it to him but he wasn't to be seen so I walked up beside his house and as I went to knock on the door, the door swag gently open.

From outside the house I couldn't hear any shouting earlier but as I stood there looking now inside the house, he was over his wife yelling at her in Maori as she cowering down behind him.

I saw him take his belt off around his jeans and then suddenly he struck the floor next to her.

I was sure I was just tripping so I wiped my eyes but on removing my hands from my eyes, he was there right in my face.

I flew back as only moments earlier he had a belt in his hand and serious shit was going down between himself and his wife but as he told me in English to come in and close the door behind me. I couldn't see her or even hear her though she had just been right there.

He slammed the door behind me and told me to take a seat at his table. I took a good look around and everywhere I looked there was something in Maori, this guy was as Maori as you could be. He even while looking at the bag of weed was talking to himself in Maori.

The first thing he said when he glazed in to my eyes (as if he was taking my soul away). He looking straight through me with the coldest eyes I had ever seen.

All of a sudden flash backs from the haunted house came back to me for the very first time. Scenes from my father came to me as what I had just witnessed was domestic violence.

It wasn't my place to say anything and the presence of this guy shooked me up so I was just in a hurry to get my money and leave.

I didn't wish to be around him after what I had just seen go on. I had only seen the guy ever when I used to pass his fence to get down the ramp from my cottage and then this time when I saw him go nuts at his wife and smash his belt against the wooden floors of his lounge.

I didn't know the guy at all.

But as I stood to leave he said "No you smoke with me." He yelled out something in Maori then his wife appeared with some money in her hand and handed it to me, she didn't say a word, she just left and disappeared into a room closing the door quietly behind her.

I was already too stoned to smoke more but I didn't wish to offend him so I sat there and watched him skin up a joint and light it soon afterwards with a huge grey cloud of smoke being blown into the room.

He then asked me was I a Satan`s Slaves, and I said no though one day very possible.

I guessed he had asked due to how many times he had seen members of Satan`s Slaves turn up to my house from time to time.

He went onto tell me he had spend time in Mt Crawford jail with them and though he was a Nomad gang member (the vice president of the gang) he found the Satan`s Slaves he was banged up with in jail all ok guys.

What the fuck had he just said I said Nomads, and not just a gang member but the fucking vice president!!

That's the gang who I fucked up their clubhouse when I was 11 years old attending Hadlow in Masterton, and now here I was on the other side of a table with their second main man.

The stoniness had just taken over the acid and I was thinking fuck me dead as all sorts of things were going through my mind.

I got proper paranoid as I started thinking he knew somehow of what I had done against his gang all those years back, but he couldn't know could he?

My mind wasn't taking the dope too well but then the acid wouldn't let me move my legs for some reason so even when I was telling myself to "Stand up Christian." my fucking legs weren't taking no notice of my brain.

Being on acid is one thing but being that stoned of some of New Zealand's finest dope on top of acid is mind fucking at the best of times but in this situation the stoniness was like times 100.

I couldn't look at him in the eyes, and for some reason I had to stop myself from blurting out "I done ya fucking clubhouse it was me!"

When there was silence I thought to myself had I just said out loud what I was thinking?

Fuck I had never been fucked up before on acid and though the trip hadn't turned bad, I just for the first time wasn't in control of the acid and that soon became apparent when next minute (after he said something which was only to the extent of pass the ashtray) I cracked up with laughter.

Uncontrollable laughter like a fruit cake even to the extent I was trying to tell myself to calm down, act normal and laugh at whatever he says that is funny.

Pass me the ashtray wasn't funny but it didn't stop me from laughing my head off.

Then he started to laugh saying "Che bro, the weeds fucking good ah bro." and that just send me off again into balls of laughter, so much that I had tears in my eyes.

He himself started to laugh out loud to the point that he farted and sneezed at the same time with a big bogie that flew out of his nose and landed right on my cheek.

A big dirty black green bogie was sitting on my face. It only made him laugh more like a nuttier as I wiped it from my face and tried my hardest not to breathe in whatever crawled out of his arse.

The grey clouds from the joint were now a blue colour due to him either shitting himself due to so much laughter.

The smell was unbearable to the point that I couldn't hold my breath anymore and ended up throwing up my dinner all over his table at the same time he had outstretched his hand to pass me the joint.

His arm and hand was covered in chicken strew, so much so that even his tattoos on his arm were covered up by my sick.

I looked up and caught his eyes and for the first time I saw some kindness in his dark eyes and we both just crackled up laughing together like two kids.

We had connected through such a weird 15mins of smoking a joint, him covered in sick and I am sure pants full of shit.

I had wiped the bogie from my face, my lungs full of dope and that awful smell but we both had smiles on our faces as I finally was able to stand up and use my legs to walk out the door.

As I walked out the door, we both agreed that the pot was fucking great and that though we weren't from the same background and on any normal day of the week in any given pub or on the street we would be seen as enemies.

We did say to one another while shaking hands goodbye that after those few minutes in each other's company we had become friends and from there onwards he would always buy weed of me.

Shit loads of it to the point I noticed he was selling the stuff out of his house as he had loads of visitors come on by to his home.

Something I wasn't too keen on my own place for many reasons.

Anyway I got to know him really well for time and I found out that the only langue he spoke in his house was Maori 99% of the time as he saw English as a forced langue on his people, the Maoris.

Every time he spoke to his two kids and his wife was only in Maori and also they would only speak Maori even to me though my Maori was never the best but it was something I thought was great to hear a family speaking in their own tongue.

Hearing them all in speak in their own tongue and being a very proud Maori family, he wasn't going to let his kids ever forget their background or never ever forget their roots as their people once were warriors.

That night I left his house and went back to my mates over at the cottage all who asked if I was ok?

I had been away for 30minutes so they were had been worried.

I tried to explain what went on but I just couldn't as it sounded all Pete Tong, I guess you just had to be there.

I didn't sleep that night as due to the acid. I was a fool that I had taken acid; I had my final exam that following week well at least it wasn't the following morning so I had a few days to recover before this next important exam.

I should have left celebrations till all the exams were done and finished with but due to the row with Kiren and my mates showing up, one thing lead to another as they do when ya got a few mates around and drugs nearby.

I never mixed drugs with education as in I didn't light up a joint before setting a exam and never taking drugs while at school when many others did. I did take my education seriously.

I used to do my home work and prep work on exams staying back after school to do it when others wouldn't but then again I couldn't bring home work home for Kiren to see as that would have been the rabbit out of the bag.

I felt I had been living a lie, as if I was hiding an affair from Kiren though I wasn't as all.

I hadn't ever told her was that I was still attending school but it did play on my mind lots and the recent argument was over her thinking I was hiding something.

She thought I was cheating on her as I was so secret about my job and also early evenings I would come back not telling her where I had been.

Where I had been? Well I had only been staying behind at the centre to do my prep work for the exams and not with some other girl as she suspected.

One thing I wasn't was a cheater.

The last two months I had studied so hard. I hoped I would (due to this heard work) do better than I first thought so I didn't need to be being accused as a cheater.

I was so loyalty and hated whenever she accused me of being unfaithful as trust me there were many times that I could have cheated but I never did and even on the final day of exams I was invited by some of the school girls whom I had got to know to join them to a party they were holding at one of their houses in the posh area of Sliverstream.

A lovely suburb Sliverstream, located out in Upper Hutt. My uncle Frank used to have a massive house there with swimming pool and games room; it was so lovely the house and very much the surrounding area.

As It had been a few weeks of exams and also of months of studying I thought yeah I deserved to celebrate and as I couldn't share it with Kiren but only the ones who had taken the exams with me then I thought why not join them, take them up on their invite and with no thought of getting up to any mischief with any of them.

It was nice of them to invite me so out I went on the train, thinking that they would invited some other boys but I was the only guy there and there was like 30 girls.

How I wished I was single as it's a boys dream come true as girls , girls and more girls...........what else could u ask for as a 16 year old kid surrounded by all these lovely girls(My Loyalty to my girlfriend stayed true).

Guilt did I come over me even though I wasn't cheating or getting up to any mischief.

I thought "Wow this is the fucking business!!" Maybe it was a good thing being expelled as no way if I was still at boarding school would I be surrounded by half naked girls as many were stripping off as the house also had a pool and the parents were away all weekend so girls were dipping in and out of the pool.

I had to pinch myself a few times thinking maybe I was simply dreaming but alas I wasn't.

It was like having a lovely cake right in front of me and not allowing myself to taste the cake, not even a little piece to bite.

It's just I was too loyal to even take a bite of the cake but I can tell you that many of the girls were teasing me to take a bite well making me feel as horny as hell in all honesty.

I just wasn't going to go against what I had in my heart and tattooed on the side of my head and with what I had been brought up to believe in.

I needed others to see where as I knew no one would believe me that I was actually being surrounded by 30 girls and all having a proper right time and more so when even soon more girls arrived.

No one would ever believe me. I did a head count and there were 47 girls and just me as this was a girls only party it seemed from last year students of that school but as I had set all my exams with them and got to know them, even sorting many of them out with weed then they saw me as ok to come along and party and that suited me fine.

I just knew no one would believe me when I arrived back to Wellington later that evening and it's not like I could go home and tell Kiren while pillow talking to her after making love "Oh by the way babe I just been partying with hot girls." as she for sure would have stabbed me there and then.

So I called the Satan's Slaves clubhouse and spoke to Zombie and that was that he and Diz and a prospect at the time known as Carl Cumstain (I know but really his first name was Carl) all about a hour later rocked up in one of their cars and even though over the phone Zombie thought I was telling a porkpie.......that's until the front door of the house was opened by a girl and as they walked in, there were just girls everywhere.

You should have seen their smiles as I never seen three guys smile like how they did that night when they first walked into the house party that was going full swing.

I had forgotten to tell the girl whose parents owed the house that the Satan's Slaves were on their way so she got such a fright to start with when she opened the door to see 3 bikers standing there and naughty looking ones at that all standing there with hard on's.

Once I let the girl know that they were with me, most of the girls were ok though a few stuck up girls left the party as bikers were no go to them.

With the guys arriving, some coke thanks to Carl came out and so now the party was in full swing and the pool was full with no longer all half naked girls but also naked girls and one naked biker as Carl cum stain jumped in completely naked..........I guessed he needed a good wash.

Not to go for a swim but just to firstly wash himself as he would for weeks never wash himself as this man didn't even work out what soap was for and he hadn't ever worked out what a shower was.

He was called Carl Cumstain because his black jeans were covered in his own cum and his black Motorhead t shirt that was also always covered in cum stain.

Carl, after he would have sex with a girl he would just wipe his cock on his clothes and never ever clean his jeans or that fav t shirt of his.

Carl came out of the pool like a different man. Zombie though it was time Carls clothes needed a clean so in the pool they went which meant a dark colour came in that side of the pool in a instance when his clothes hit the water so that was the end of the pool party for the time being.

Now the bikers were chasing girls in and out of the house and let's just say after about 20 mins if that and after all the foreplay then if you had a camera and a film crew there then you would have got a least 3 porn movies made as some of the girls weren't shy and sex was very much on their mind even if it meant they were letting Carl cum stain share a bed with them.

I still stayed true to my word and didn't join in whatever was going on in the bedrooms as I stayed in the kitchen and just drank the place dry.

Once the bikers had got their rocks off and Carl had shared out all his coke then back on the big V8 Ford they went. I joined them as by this time all the booze had run out and it was getting really late.

You know just a quick note , one great thing back in these days was no one had mobiles so if you were out late into the night , ya never had your girlfriend hassling you where you were or whom with...........It was bliss back then.

I had to get back home as the following night was my sisters 21st birthday that my mum and my sisters friends had put together for my sister after all my sister had been through so they were all making sure that this was going to be my sisters night.

I very much wanted to make it home not too late on that Friday so there wouldn't be no moodiness at my sisters 21st birthday from Kiren towards me for being out all night.

There were many times Kiren would at times get moody when I walked in the door drunk or off my face with a smile after having a wild night of partying without her.

Zombie dropped me off my place once we reached back to Wellington but Kiren wasn't there.

I could tell she had been home and gone out again, I was guessing she was in a mood as maybe she had waited for me to come home and as the time now was 1am she must have got fed up and gone back to one of her friends house anyway I was coked up so I knew again I wouldn't be sleeping that night and I didn't feel tired so I decided to come back with zombie to the Satan's Slaves clubhouse to get on the piss so back in his motor I went heading down towards Luxford Street to get on the drink with the other Satan's Slaves.

Loose Lips Sinks Ships is what my father always taught me well this night Carl cum stain I wished he had known that saying as Carl when we arrived to the club house told senior members where he had been.

Next minute Carl was wearing what was known as the sheriff badge.

The sheriff badge only came out when a member or prospect had got hold of a few party girls and not let anyone know so to have all the fun for themselves (that's if the girls let the person have group fun).

Carl Cumstain returning to club house, given it the large that he had been at some party, not bringing any of the girls back to the clubhouse for a party but instead party it up himself with the girls well you can tell how annoying and pissed off that the other members felt hearing this.

They pinned that sheriff badge to him and without going into too many details he was given a bad night by everyone around him.

He wasn't allowed to leave the clubhouse, at one stage he wasn't even able to walk far as he had a ball and chain around one of his legs so it's not like he could get away.

What was done to him was very naughty but he was a sheriff as we all kept our mouths closed and said nothing at all.

If Carl only knew to have said nil then he wouldn't have taken what was being put out to him.

The only good thing was that Carl wasn't a grass as none of the Satan's Slaves are, so he never put me or Diz or Zombie in the shit as fuck that as what was happening to him wasn't my cup of tea so Zombie and me made out we had just been over to mine and as for Diz he had said Zombie to collect him to bring him down to the clubhouse.

As it was Friday night, it meant Friday Club at the clubhouse which meant this evening that close friends of members and prospects were allowed to invited guests down for the Friday Night Club so by the time I got there, it was in full swing, a few strippers and lots of partying going on as well.

No member's wife or girlfriends were allowed at the clubhouse on Friday nights so you can imagine what kind of night most Friday nights was.

All good until that is the noise control turned up on this evening.

By now everyone knew which neighbour kept on calling the noise control agency anyway the Satan's Slaves who opened the front security gate were told if noise control were to return they would take the stereo system.

The thing is the club had about 7 working stereos so time after time they would just through the huge gates pass through one of the stereos this went on for about two hours then the police turned up outside the main gates with the noise control in hand.

The police couldn't ever force entry that is without a jcb (bull dozer) as the gates were steel gates. Security was very strong on the property and the entrance into the clubhouse itself. No one could gain entry by force apart from if they were driving a bull dozer at high speed to crash into the clubhouse.

The police weren't going to cal out for a jcb at now 4am in the morning but what they did do was call the Wellington Electric Board Company.

We first noticed a man with a extended ladder climb up the electric post and that meant they were trying to shut down all the power to the club house.

There's only one thing that's going to stop that so Diz and myself went with two water hoses and hosed down the guy before he even reached the top as if he had been at the top, he wouldn't be a wise man if we had the water on him so down he came as quick as a rat down a water pipe.

Next minute the police were on a louder speaker with all sorts of threats!

Diz being Diz wasn't happy that out of all the many neighbours one had spoilt the party and he thought fuck them and that included his opinion of the police as well.

Within the clubhouse where the bikes were all parked, Diz got into his Kingswood motor and asked me to open the second set of gates once he started the engine running.

I opened the second set of gates and with that, Diz speed past me as I watched about four coppers jump out the way of his Diz car then suddenly Diz turned the corner slightly (he wasn't braking) as he went flying into the house where the neighbour lived who complained about the music being too loud previously that night.

His car went up in a cloud of black smoke as he crashed his car on purpose into the wooden house the whole front of the car went straight on through and stayed stuck in what looked like a lounge room.

Diz was mad as hell most of the times but such a diamond of a bloke and so loyal to the club over many, many year.

I just hoped he had put his seatbelt on as he hit the house with some power.

Next minute all the coppers were all over him dragging him out and I saw one copper run in my direction he had jumped over the main wall so I quickly locked up the side gate and then the big inner garage doors.

The Copper wasn't going to get far as I then opened a smaller door and set out two of the clubs guard dogs in-between the garage door and the outer gate where they bite the copper ten times if more as he had nowhere to run.

One of the dogs, a white English bull terrier ripped the policeman's pants off him when the policemen was trying his best to climb back over the front wall again to get back to where the other policemen were.

The other policemen all were still jumping over Diz as Diz was still putting up a great fight with them even though he had just crashed his car into a house and now had more than eight police officers over him trying to get him in to a back of one of the police vans.

I thought it was funny at the time and my night so far had been an interesting one to say the least though as I walked back into the club house it still was going quite bad for Carl Cumstain but again I shall not say what was going on with him.

Soon we were being told on a speaker that they were calling backup, and back up came as the first we heard was someone in the back yard of the clubhouse so me and a member went down to look through the strengthen bullet proof windows to see what the police were up to from behind the clubhouse.

The member and I looked out to see what we could see, next minute I noticed one red dot on his forehead and then letting him knew he looked towards me telling me not to move and there on my chest was two dots and more appeared on him as well.

The fuckers had brought in the firearms unit, and though we both were behind bullet proof glass neither of us moved as we watched these police officers with their guns aimed at us take position in the back yard.

They didn't move and neither did us.

We could barely see them as it was dark out there but they so could see us standing in the back room as the light was on and then next minute the lights went out with that we both ducked down but there was no shots fired.

We creped along the ground working out the way back to the main clubhouse where the bar was..............that wasn't due to us being thirsty(that's for sure).

A few members had torches and there were at least 60 people in there, we kept bumping into every one telling them what had happened and they said look out the fucking front.

It was like they had called in the army as most coppers out the front now were carrying firemen.

We noticed the guy up the ladder had managed to do his job and that Diz was nowhere in sight but still his car was and the grassing neighbour was out in a dressing ground looking at the Ute that was now part of his lounge.

The music was out and so were the lights but one thing the Satan's Slaves are not and that is party poopers as Greg one of the senior members appeared under candle light with two generators he was dragging along with the help of Grot.

All they did is light a few more candles then get a light that you use to look under cars when you working on a car.

They hung the light up high which was blazing light like a Christmas tree from the power of the generator.

The whole bar area was now lit up. Next the music was back on and as long as they had the generator going then they were happy as that party went on all morning till past noon.

The police not all but two cars stayed outside in the street most of the night but there really was fuck.

All they could do was sitting in their motors as they weren't joining the party that's for sure.

Even the noise control came knocking again for whatever reason but this time no one even bother opening the gate to them and all the many guard dogs were let out into the back yard and also the front of the second gate so no one wished to be bitten by nasty guard dogs that just loved to bite.

Hadn't it been made clear that the party and music would only stop when the Satan's Slaves had decided it would and not when some Muppet had returned with another fine to stick to the front door.

How it ended was the club was fined well over a thousand dollars, a expensive party.

Diz never of course got his car back and he was arrested and charged with dangerous driving, damage to property.

Diz was also charged with carrying a dangerous weapon as he hadn't dropped his knife that he carried with him before he got into the car so that was found on him when he was pulled out of the car by the policemen.

All in all he got a year jail sentenced that he spend six months of the sentenced up in Mt Crawford.

As for Carl Cumstain he never sheriff girls again and he started actually every Friday night going up town with some of the other prospects getting girls to come back to the clubhouse for the Friday Club antics that went on well members wives and girlfriends were not about.

Many as you can image said no but a few nights, a few girls would come down and realise what a good party night was actually down at the club house.

All the previous horror stories that they had heard about the clubhouse with what went on behind closed doors wasn't all that bad as lots of straight people who weren't in any way trying to join the club would have a great time at the clubhouse with their girlfriends and nothing ever bad happened to them.

As long as they were respectful and never out of line then all was good and it was all about having a puka night on the Friday nights and that was for sure to always happen as it was Friday club night.

For those who came down and took the piss well then it would turn into a blood bath as I saw many people come within inches of their lives whenever they were bang out of line.

What did they expect as no one took the piss out of the staunch 1% motorcycle club in all of NZ and think they could get away with it.

Not always was it smelling of roses and smiles to be found as there was some horrors that went on but it's not my place to say what I witnessed as they say Loose Lips Sinks Ships.

That afternoon I managed to get back to my place, so rotten drunk that I couldn't even speak to my now friendly neighbour who was in his front yard with one of his kids. I gave him what I thought was a wave but may have looked like a half hearted attempt.

I didn't like one side of him, and that's the side that reminded me of my own father though my father was never as nasty as this man at times were at times to his own two kids as in beatings he would dish out which is something my own father never ever did.

I knew when my neighbour over time would go for his wife or even slap his kids far too many times if they hadn't done what he asked.

My own father not once hit us. My Father had rows with my mum when he was completely drunk , going into a mad rage but my neighbour would just flip over the smallest thing and he wouldn't care if I was sitting there witnessing it all.

Some of the guys who would turn up to his place used to try and steer me out or make me feel intimidated but bullocks' to them as I had grown up with heavy people and no one ever could use stand over tactics on me,

Those who did all I can only guess have small cocks as they need to try and give it the big when all they are basically are just cowards.

Though they all looked dangerous fuckers and I didn't ever like when he would tell them that the dope was coming through me as I wouldn't put it pass them for them to break into my house at gun point even if their second in charge had told them to leave me. One thing with Nomads they are even in my eyes one of the most dangerous of all known gangs in New Zealand even more than the mongrel mob and that's saying something.

The mongrel mob love to be known as the scum of the earth when it comes to gangs. The mongrel mob on a international level are notorious but as for the nomads (who once were members of the black power gang) were in the end even too dirty for the black power so they were kicked out by the black power senior leaders and that's how they came about to be known as the nomads throughout New Zealand.

They once raped a doctor and his elder mother after they had broke in to his house to rob him of whatever drugs that was stored at his practice in Otaki, a small town in the North Island of New Zealand.

They followed him one early evening after he left his practice and when he arrived at a house they suspected it was his house so the burst in after him and raped not just him (a man on man rape) but also his elderly mother who was disabled.

I am sure they killed both of them though I can't remember as the crime was just so shocking at the time.

It made not only me but every New Zealander sick and made them the nomads very much the worst gang in all of New Zealand.

There only two doors down from my front door was my neighbour who wasn't part of what had happened in Otaki as that were another chapter and the nomads who committed that unspeakable crime.

The members involved acted alone as they were junkies in need of a fix but why they went and did what they no one will ever knew as its past belief.

My neighbour two doors down were still second in charge of this gang and he was a dangerous man in many ways.

I was always of course weary of him and a few times he actually knocked on my door (probably just wanting to see if I had more weed for him) but I never answered my door and told Kiren never ever to open the door to him or anyone when she was alone in the house.

This made Kiren frighten especially when I was out of the house and all she knew about this neighbour of ours was when she could hear from our bedroom window his wife cry for help as she was being given a beating by him. Kiren didn't like him one single bit and would never ever speak to him.

She actually hated being in our cottage by herself from the moment he moved in down the road and more so when he started to sell dope from his house. The scum bags that would sometime be on the path way leading to our house would be there when Kiren would come home from work so I told her not to worry that I would have a word to Wim.

I asked my mum if I could get another gun. She didn't like the idea so told me just to go to the shooting range whenever Wim would but I wanted one for peace of mind to have inside the house for personal protection, not just to take to a shooting range.

I knew that if I showed Kerin how to use a gun, how to fire one safely and how not to see it as something to use against me in a row then I knew Kieran would feel safer if I were out one night say over at the Satan's Slaves having a drink.

Wim took Kiren with us shooting one day to the shooting range, my mum would come along though she only fired a gun there only once as she wasn't too happy with guns nor at Wim having a few at his house.

My mum wasn't keen on me having another gun especially after what happened many years ago. I couldn't talk Wim or my mum around so I ended up getting a shotgun through Jacob via is black power connections; it was already sown down so was easier to hide for me in my cottage.

I ended up never letting kiren know about the gun to start so the gun just stayed hidden in our bed base, Sooner than later I did let Kiren know about the gun as I was spending more time out in the evenings though not once did it ever need to come out.

The gun did make Kiren feel so much more comfortable in the cottage when she was by herself which in turn made me feel more ok about leaving her there when I had things to do and sort out.

Going back to the Saturday of my sister's birthday I arrived home and just crashed out. I was dead to the world by the time Kerin woke me up which was only mid afternoon so I had only had two hours sleep.

Kerin thinking I had been asleep all day and from the evening before but I hadn't so I told her to join me. We feel asleep till around 6pm when Kiren was shuffling me to get up and have a shower as we had to be at my sister 21st birthday by 8pm.

I was so tired after two days and nights of being up all due to drug taking, and though I had gone to bed in a good manner I had woken up in a foul mood that's what drug taking does to you.

Maybe yeah everything is fine and cool when you're as a high as a kite but when you come down, you come down crashing. Your mood changes so fast, you become such a bastard so snappy towards anyone around you.

I went and had my shower in a foul mood and then as kiren was taking hers, I went back to bed telling her that I didn't want to go too early and that for her to go and I would get another hour sleep but she wasn't having any of it.

The only way she was going to get me out of this bad noise was to jump into bed and have sex with me; she knew how to please her man

So after all that went on, we were off heading to the party that was in the rugby club house that I was a member of (Ponki).

There were hundreds of people who turned up at least two hundred showed up; my sister had so many friends and God so many sexy friends. A few as I have highlighted I had in my past slept with though not loads but about 7 or 8 of them I had ended up in bed with after one or two drunken nights partying it up.

I and Kiren sat at the head table with my mum and Wim, my sister and some of her close friends. It was such a good party and everyone was enjoying themselves and partying with smiles galore including my sister which was so lovely to see.

As the night went on, now and then each one of my sister's friend came over to say hi so I would of course stand up.

I had been taught to do is i.e. Stand up whenever a lady stands up herself from the table or returns to sit down or comes over to say hello.

It's just manners that my father and my mum had taught me such manners from a very early age.

Even before I had gone to the UK many years earlier I knew my manners so here of course I stood up and greeted my sister's friends who had come over to say hello.

A few times while sinking many beers, my mum (who had seen how much of a drinker I had become) commented that I should be slowing down on the intake of booze.

I told her not to shame me, I wasn't a kid though I was only 16 years old 6 months but I was actually drinking better than a few who were at the party and ever so smashed off their faces.

Soon afterwards throwing back a few more beers, along came a girl who had been friend of my sister for ages.

I stood up to also say hi when suddenly Kerin grabbed my leg and told me to stop greeting my sisters friends as she was getting fucked off by it.

I told her not to be so silly, knowing she was jealous I thought I would play on it just a little only to be a twat but not a bastard. Most of the night Kiren had kept a tab on me as to who I had pervious slept with out of my sisters friends.

Well on the head table alone I had slept with 3 of the girls out of the 10 who were sitting with us and this alone got Kiren back up.....big time.

Kiren wasn't too happy anyway as another one of my sister friends came along I stood up to say to this friend of my sisters who hadn't seen since I was like 9 years old.

She comments how much I had grown up since the last time she had seen so I went to give her a friendly kiss on the check but she said out loud "Oh no! You're older enough now for a proper kiss!"

At which point she started to put her tongue down my throat in front of my mum, Wim and my sister, but also in front of my own girlfriend, who then stood up next to me while this girl was still kissing me.

Kiren then picking up my glass of beer, smashing it over my head.

She fucking glassed me at my own sister 21st birthday...can u fucking believe that!!

I can laugh at it now looking back, but back then I couldn't as I was dripping in blood from a cut the glass had made on the back of my head.

It hadn't hurt when she crashed it against my head and I am just glad it was only a pint glass rather than the tall bottle of beer that I had been pouring the beer out of into my pint glass right next to where my glass of Jack Daniels was at the time.

I am sure when she flipped and she made up her mind she was going to glass me that she decided which one or what to use to do it before actually going through with doing the damage.

Even the dj stopped and everyone on the dance floor as there I was standing there blood pissing out of my head all over my white shirt.

This girl the friend of my sisters who had kissed me thinking what the fuck as Kerin leant over to what looked like she was going to knock this girl out.

Kerin was a lady but a lady who knew how to throw a punch.

Wim jumped in between the girl and Kerin so Kiren didn't get a chance to do anymore damage.

Then my mum said to me "How could you Christian?" "Wind Kiren up like that and wreak my 21st Birthday."

"Hold up one minute!" I replied.

"My girl had just glassed me and I was being pointed out as the bad guy.... what the fuck was that all about!" as I looked around and saw Kiren now in tears s if I had done something wrong to her.

My mum took her to the bathroom and then came and got me and took me in to the men's toilet to try and stop the bleeding.

I was fuming as how dear my own mum take the side of my girl as she had been the one to wreak my sister 21st birthday not me.

I went back out in the hall to say sorry to my sister but fucking hell everyone was up on the dance floor, dancing away like nothing had even happened.

I was glad I hadn't reeked the evening so I told my sister to go up on the dance floor and join her friends.

My sister's boyfriend Nick at the time was the only good guy who came over to me and said a ambulance had been called, but I didn't think I needed a ambulance.

I told the caretaker (who I knew) to cancel the ambulance. Nick said to me the bleeding wasn't stopping; explaining to me I had a gash in the back of my head that truly needed some medical attention to it.

Nick went onto say he himself would take me there to the hospital to get stitched up.

A few of the Satan's Slaves who had come along, all said "I can't believe you been done by a girl and you anit doing anything about it!"

What did they expect, me to give her a hiding?

I wasn't into beating girls up so I didn't even bother replying to their comments.

I knew I wouldn't be living this one down for a long time.

My mum came outside looking for me making sure I was ok as I was walking to Nicks' car. ,

My mum was telling me she wanted to take me to the hospital and for Nick to stay but I said "No way Mum this is as much Stacey's night as it is yours so stay!" "All will be ok." "I love you mum."

I then got into Nicks car and headed to towards the hospital.

At the hospital I went in and got stitched up, telling the nurse what had caused me being bottled by my girlfriend.

She didn't believe me as she thought I must have done more too deserve that but I hadn't even done anything, maybe it was karma biting me back for being at the school girls party the night before even though I didn't do anything there either but I shouldn't have been there and for sure Kiren would have done worse than just bottle me if she knew I had been to such a party.

I headed home once my wound had been stitched up.

I felt too embarrassed to return to my sisters 21st birthday party after what had gone on so I asked Nick to drop me home.

We pulled up to the cottage and in we went but who was standing there with no smile on her face was Kerin.

Kiren still going off at me demanding I tell her who the girl was that I had kissed.

The thing is I hadn't seen that girl for at least over 8 years so I couldn't even remember her name but Kerin wasn't having any of it.

She was in a devil of a mood to say the least.

I thought for the first time about was it wise to have a gun that Kiren knew about its whereabouts in the house as I said good bye to Nick.

Ne had to get back to the party so I went to bed and that night I slept with one eye open and one eye closed thinking of hope and glory.

Chapter 22

SHEEP SHAGGERS

YEAR End of 1991 / 1992

AGE 16 YEARS OLD / 17 YEARS OLD

I waited for my exam results after what was a pleasurable xmas time though I was still a little moody towards my Mum for taking Kerin side the month earlier at my sisters birthday so I hadn't spend xmas with my Mum this year that was the very first time I actually hadn't spend a xmas with my mum.

My mum went to her brother's house over in Greytown but I stayed put in my little cottage and then had New Years Eve down at the Satan's Slaves' clubhouse.

I was invited on my first trip away with the club, which was to head to the South Island on a bike run so I was excited to start this New Year.

I didn't work out that some of my peers again were just using me to carry their drugs for them from one island to another island.

It was only when we went to board the ferry that what I saw down at the docks there many police who wasn't going to let over 50 bikers take the passenger ferry and neither was the crew of the boat either.

They saw trouble when over 50 bikers from many different 1% MC clubs roaring up to get on board.

I didn't feel used at the time by carrying some of my peers drugs who were travelling among the bikers as I felt honoured that I was being taken on my first bike run as I was 4 months short of my 17th birthday so still young in mind.

All I wished was to keep in with the club as by now they were the biggest influence in my whole life.

For many years of being maybe yes I had been mislead but until I got my school cert results I didn't see my much earlier dreams of becoming a airline pilot ever coming true.

I hadn't given up that dream as long as I didn't get myself into any more trouble or caught for a few things that I had taken part in then I still had so much belief in myself.

The police were talking to the main presidents among all the bike clubs that had joined the Satan's Slaves for this club run.

I noticed the police doing searchers on each and every bike and most of the bikers but there were too many bikers and not enough police to have every one searched.

I spotted a few of my father's old work mates walk towards the live stock ferry that was also in port so I said to some of the crew who I knew through my father, if they reckon we all could get a board that.

They said yes they wouldn't say no as that ferry was just full of truckers so a few bikers wouldn't make any difference so I run over to the Satan's Slaves president Scuff and told him yeah I got us all a lift, after explaining to him what the score was.

Scuff let everyone know then all the tickets got changed and bike after bike boarded inside the transport ferry and as the back of the ferry shut closed the Wellington police couldn't do much as the bikers had been given the green light.

Once on board, everyone locking up their bikes against all the truck that were filled with livestock .All the animals were heading to the slaughter houses on the South Island.

Everyone all headed for the bar on board and cracked open bottles of beer as we waited for the ferry to leave port.

I was asked time after time to keep on checking on the bikes, but after doing this twice before we even left port, I didn't see there was no need to so as I knew the ferry well as my father used to work on this ship, I went down to the crew mess.

I found a few of his old friends who I thanked and had a beer with them. They all asked after my father who was known as Angry Steve as many times he was just that, but they never knew the reason behind this though you all now by reading this book understand why he might have gone to work so many times being angry as his wife he knew was having an affair.

Maybe it was after he had to leave his own house that he become even angrier in life.

He wasn't angry when he got remarried and nor when he had his own place and never since he returned back to Scotland as he was very much loving being back in Scotland and around his very much loved family.

After a few beers with them, I went to check on the bikes again and found a few of the members down there and also Carl Cumstain.

I had a lot of time for Carl. I knew Carl years before the Satan's Slaves ever did and so had spend some of my earlier years with him when he shared a skin head house that was known as a party house in Wellington.

It was Carl who actually first shaved my head and had thrown me my first British made Doc Martin boots.

Carl was a naughty skinhead, he wasn't one of the drug skin heads out of Wellington and that's how he was more accepted by the Satan's Slaves as they got to know him and trust him among their own tight circle of people.

Carl was white power through and through, unlike me who had Maori friends, Carl didn't like anyone whose skin colour was anything other than white and he would get himself into so many fights being very far right winged. One on one he was a nice guy, and I always let his speech about white power go through one ear and out the other.

I asked what they were doing again down among all the trucks, the smell was awful due to all the livestock.

What was even more awful was seeing how many sheep that the truckers had shoved into their trucks as none of the sheep could even move and they all were pushing out between the gaps in the trailers.

A few of the bikers looked over at me seeing these helpless sheep saying to me "We see you have spotted Carls girlfriend." as they undone the back of one of the trucks and pulled out one of the sheep.

These were the Satan's Slaves, so I knew whatever they had planned has got to be sick.

I had seen them do many things that were sick over the years. Sometimes thinking they run a circus at times when it came to animals as many times I seen them with their German Sheppard who was 15 years old, a giant of a dog, vicious as, who was at times the main star.

If ya got on with the dog then you never got bitten. I got bitten many times but over time tried my best to befriend the dog.

A dog I seen with my own eyes have sex with the most sluttish of girls and trust me there were many slut like girls who loved to be gang banged down at the clubhouse and also to allow buff the German Sheppard to fuck them.

Hand on heart as they used to rub honey on their pussies and let Buff lick that then they would go doggie style and let the dog with a little help fuck them ....no condom.

Seriously even if there was a condom at hand, it still was wrong though Buff the dog fucking loved it.

Loose lips sink ships I say no more but I got to finish off with this story of being on the ferry.

So I knew that something was going to be happening to the sheep, what it was, I couldn't even imagine.

As we pulled out in to the harbour, this ferry always left first from the Wellington port as it was the slowest out of the two Cook Strait Ferries.

It had to due to what was aboard as in weight so it stared of first and then the passengers ferry would come out next into the harbour, full of families with their kids and loads of Japanese tourist and Americans as well.

So there we are now on the top decks looking out over the beauty of Wellington and its harbour and with about now 15 bikers and a sheep.

One of the bikers girlfriends came out on deck and was asked to hand over her handbag by her boyfriend whom opened the bag and after looking through it pulled his hand out with lip stick and also some VO5 shampoo and some make up powder.

He told a few of the bikers to hold the sheep tight. He place bright red lip stick on the sheep's mouth as good as he could and then also some pink make up powder over the sheep's face.

Now at this point the sheep looked funny as if this is all they were going to do then that was not too bad.

I loved animals and never liked any animal to be mistreated. I hated hearing about those cruel bastards that you read in the papers who put kittens in microwave ovens or put fireworks up a dogs ass and as for all the animal cruelty in the world I hate it and all the animals that these big companies so experimenting on as it doesn't sit well with me and I am very pro animal welfare.

But what I was too witness next and again realising I was with the Satan's Slave , some very sick minded men among them as next minute Carl Cumstain was grabbed and told "There's ya bitch, now fuck her!".

With that and no delay he poured some of the VO5 into the palm of his hand, he seemed to already know what part that the shampoo was to be played into all of this, as he rubbed it around the arse of the sheep.

He then dropped his trousers and no I anit one to look at a man's cock but when he dropped his trousers, the sick bastard already had a hard on.

This is the same bloke who came to the school girl's party and had about three of them in the sack all at the same time.

I just hope they made him wear a condom as I wouldn't put it pass him having every STD that there was and probably some new ones, unheard of diseases that he carried.

What was about to happen in front of me showed that he would fuck anything if it had a pulse, it didn't even have to human as he put his cock into the sheep and started to fuck it.

It was too much and the sheep for sure wasn't happy as it started to kick back and needed others to hold it tight while Carl Cumstain didn't stop fucking it.

No wonder why the kiwis are called fucking sheep shaggiers as Carl Cumstain was doing exactly that fucking this sheep like it was his girlfriend.

I couldn't look as it was too much and to hear the sheep make noises in between all the laughter that was going on.

I looked up and there was the passengers ferry gliding on by past, with the parents of kids putting their hands over their kids eyes, but as for the Japanese tourists they were all out on the deck of their ferry with their cameras in hand all recording it.

What kind of message is that giving to them about New Zealand? You know what none of them seemed disgusted but then again they are a nation who still to this day kills whales for no reason at all.

I know many Japanese people who all are very respectful towards me when I speak to them about their nation still needing to kill whales, when there is no need to kill whales.

They all just go in to a massive debate which in the end doesn't make any sense, especially when they speak in Japanese.... You know what I mean.

Anyway back to the sheep, the poor old sheep!!

I said come on Carl stop it now, and he turned to me and while still fucking the sheep said not till I cum or you will be next.

With that a massive cheer went up and he fucked even longer and then what was the sickest part of it was that he came inside the sheep...one sick man.

As he pulled out and wiped his cock this time not over his t shirt because he was wearing a Satan's Slaves MC club t-shirt and if he dared wiped cum on that he would have been thrown overboard so he wiped his cock on the wool of the sheep.

Up went his jeans as all of a suddenly as we could hear voices coming on deck that didn't sound like any of the other bikers.

The guys including Carl Cumstain who now had a sweat on, picked up the sheep and they threw it kicking over board as it hit the water below making mini waves as it bobbled up and down.

Now that was cruel but I was remained it was off to get killed anyway so I was then told what was the difference how the sheep was to die but it just looked so sad bobbling up and down to drown after being raped by a biker, and one whose name was Carl Cumstain.

The prick as that's what I thought of him after he wiped his stinking hands over my face as we all went into have a drink.

I thought fuck him as I managed to sneak his glass of beer and took it in to the nearest toilet so to wash my face of the smell of sheep's shit and then I popped out my cock and pissed in his beer, cooling down the side of the pint with the still running cold water so to make the glass no longer warm from my steaming piss.

I went back into the bar area and said to the Satan's Slaves I think Carl deserves a drink for what he just done and a yell went up as I handed Carl Cumstain his beer knowing he would give it the large by drinking the beer in one go.

Down his throat went a glass full of kiwi piss.

I done it for the sheep, God bless the sheep.

When we landed on the South Island, there were some police cars waiting there who tried to give what you could only describe as a police escort out of Picton (the first small town you get to at the top of the South Island).

The Police couldn't keep up with the bikers as the bikes all roader off which was too a week of madness, fun, dangerous encounters, far too much drug taking and some loose times and that was just me.

All I will say as we visited other bike clubs and it's not my place to comment on anything to do with those clubs or what goes on in their clubhouses as again loose lips sinks ships but I can say they all were great hosts and fucking know how to party.

Kiren wasn't too happy that I had gone away with the club, she actually told me not to go but sorry no woman tells me what to do and as long as I behaved myself then she had nothing to worry about.

The thing is she knew what the Satan's Slaves were like so she wasn't happy at all when I came back and gave her a kiss.

The first thing she did was check my cock, for what I am unsure as it was the same looking cock that had left the house only a week earlier.

Anyway at this point she didn't like me spending so much time down at the Satan's Slaves clubhouse.

I wasn't no longer at school but she still thought I had this rubbish bin job so it meant each morning I would leave the house pretending to go off to work though where I was just going was down to the clubhouse to spend my days down there, playing pool or helping around the clubhouse.

I was waiting for the exams which were due any time now and soon they came.

I done so fucking well I was so proud of myself, but the dream of being a pilot was now very much behind me and I really didn't know what I wanted to do.

The only two things it seemed I was good at well the three things I seemed I was good at one was cooking, one was protecting people and the third was crime.

I never saw myself as a criminal, though the police very much saw me as one through all the times I had been arrested over the years and all the violence they knew I had been connected with and them knowing how close to the Satan's Slaves so the police saw me as a up and coming criminal.

I had done a few things already up to that age but there was still this inner part of me who didn't wish to go down that path and as long as I had hope and goals to achieve then I would do the best I could with my life.

I went around a few restaurants and got a kitchen job in old homestead that actually my father worked in when he first came to New Zealand, it was one of the first jobs he had and in my sister years she too had worked there.

It was an old fashion hotel with three big bars and a massive restaurant it was called Fallangans.

The job I was given wasn't the best but I had no format training in a kitchen, I had only learned as a very young kid how to cook from watching my Father when he lived in the haunted house with me.

So unlike my father who was a level of a chief, I was only the kitchen dish washer so I didn't even get to be near any of the food (not to eat it but just to help out).

I guessed you got to start at the bottom and work your way up.

At least it was a job and I never was late and always done my best and over time offered to help the kitchen staff to even do a little prep but I wasn't given the chance and told just to clean this or clean that.

I didn't like how some of them were talking to me, treating me like a kid as didn't they see the danger sign meaning my head tattoo as that should have showed them that I wasn't some normal 16 year old kid and if be, I would step any of them out and thrash the shit out of them.

Lucky it never came to blows and to keep hold of my job it meant that I would have to bite my tongue and keep my head down which I did but it just wasn't what I was looking for as in work as I knew I could cook.

If I was only given a break then they, the chefs would see I had some talent and also that I was very much eager to learn from them all.

After a month of working there, I was still washing pots and pans so I thought I would give it one more month and if by then they didn't even let me near the food prep or involve me then fuck it as I wasn't going to be turning 17 year old as a fucking dish washer.

I can remember going to the Satan's Slaves clubhouse at night complaining and all they could say is "Ere cook us up a feed and stop fucking moaning about your job!" I guess I had that coming to me.

Around this time Wim would come down to the clubhouse more and more, he even had brought a brand new Fat Boy Harley Davison in the new year,

I think he saw through my relationship with the Satan's Slaves and their free spirit lifestyle, his own lost youth as in that he came to New Zealand when he was so young after living in Holland when it had been taken over by Nazi Germany so of course his own childhood had been somewhat robbed.

His own parents hiding Jews on their farm as they though weren't Jewish themselves but they had heard what had been going on as in the death camps so on finding some Dutch Jews hiding on their farm land they never handed them over to the Germans but kept them hidden until the war was over.

The Dutch always look after each other they always have and always will, it's in their blood to do so.

Wim had worked all his life on the farm and on coming to NZ he hadn't stopped working every day he would work.

His hard work meant he had a few million in the bank as he had used his money wisely in property as well buying a few houses and land and also motor garages throughout Wellington.

Wim was very well off but he was not flash in anyway and he wouldn't show off his wealth, he kept it under lock and key but due to working so hard he didn't get to live out his own youth and he always liked motorcycles while growing up. He himself having a few in his younger years so he went out and brought the Fat Boy Harley Davidson and then he even brought a second brand new Harley, a Soft Tail Custom.

There weren't many people in NZ with two brand new Harleys. Why did he have two? Wim said if I were to get my bike licence then the Soft Tail Custom would be mine as my 18th birthday present in just over a year's time.

My 17th birthday was near but it would take a year to pass my driving test but look what was at the end of it for me.

Was he trying to win me over or was he seeing me as a son he never had as he always had a lot of time for me.

As long as he wasn't trying to replace my own father then I would be happy and as long as he never tried to lay down the law to me I was happy.

I now was very anit establishment as in I wouldn't take commands from anyone be it the law or a parent that being my mum as I now had become a man for my age though I was only nearly 17 years old.

As for work I went looking for another job while I was still working at Fallangans as I wanted to stay in the kitchen arena but one where I was doing something with food so I headed down to the ferry where I had been only months earlier aka the sheep.

I spoke again to some of my father's old work mates who said I was far too young to work on the ship in the kitchen but they would give me the contact name of the company that worked on shore and did a lot of the food that was pre served on board the ship.

With that I thought all was good and it turned out to be as I got a job with the outside catering contracts that were based on the docks.

In a way I was following in my father's footsteps as in working on the docks, but he had done real work on his times on the docks, I was only making hundreds of lunches and dinners.

I rang my father in Scotland who was so proud of me.

Also a very good thing was once I got into work and work I did then drug use came to near a end as I was working 6 days a week from early mornings onwards where I had to be at work so to help get the first food orders etc onto the morning ferries.

I couldn't afford to get off my face in the evenings or on the weekends and then expect to get to work and make food orders up.

Finally I was doing some cooking and though it was only light prep but I was at least given a chance into working in a real kitchen and this kitchen was at least 20 times the size of a normal working kitchen.

I was learning so fast and so much, also not only was my father proud of me but also my mum.

She seemed the happiest ever in all her life.

She was 42 years old and she looked so beautiful and there was talk of her and Wim finally getting married.

Wim had just paid for a trip to Holland to take my mum.

The holiday to Holland, they were going to be taken late May so to get Europe's first half of the summer, my mum was so excited.

The only thing she didn't like talk of was me doing my motorcycle licence and getting the bike as she never wished me ever to be on a bike after my sister's terrible accident a few years earlier.

My Mum begged me to always stay off bikes but apart from that being the only worry on her mind and in her life about her son as she finally had seen that I had come good.

She knew for many years I had been taken drugs but here on my now 17th birthday she knew that my taking drugs was a thing of the past and that I was taking my job so seriously.

My Mum finally could see a bright future for me and also I could as well.

No longer did I wish to become an airline pilot as all I wanted now to become was a chief.

Cooking was in my blood it seemed and it was something I truly loved doing.

My 17th birthday it seemed like a 21st as I had a massive pub and club crawl throughout Wellington and though there was no coke snorting or acid taking I did party it up in the end but it was my birthday and I didn't have work to go to the next day.

The next day I did get woken up in the afternoon by a few of my peers who had brought around the pot that I used to sell and drugs to store in my cottage for them.

I said I was finished with all of that as I now had a job so no longer did I need to rely on selling pot to make up a wage nor did I need the payment to be holding their drugs as I was now earning my own money through the steady job I now had.

They thought I was joking and asked if I was taking the piss as I told them again no but they sat me down and went onto how they had for many years looked after me and if it wasn't for them I wouldn't have gained the respect I had for my young age and that I wouldn't be handing around in the circles that I was in.

They went on to say that all because I had a job that didn't mean I had to stop from holding the drugs and also selling a bit of pot.

They talked me around to it, to seeing things their way.

In all truth I was really being told I didn't have much choice and they went to tell me that my name had been mentioned in a recent meeting that I to be included into a few more things in the following month which was May.

Nothing more was said as they left my cottage and I hide what was handed to me.

What could I do? These guys were and had been my peers for many years; I couldn't just turn my back on them. More than that I wouldn't be allowed to even if it meant that in my heart I felt I finally had come good after so much crime and drugs, not getting anywhere in my life.

Now here I was with a good job and just wanted to be like everyone else earn money through hard work but they my peers weren't going to be letting go off me, they very much had their craws deeply inside of me so business as normal would go on.

Though, as for the pot I cut my profits a lot as I just went down to the Nomad vice president and handed him all the dope on tick (he didn't have to hand me any money till he had sold it all),

I told him he could take the dope at a cheaper rate than normal. He was a happy man with that, more money for his kids and for beer (his wife nor did he work).

They were on the welfare and the kids were missing out what all the other kids at their local school would have so at least I letting him take a bit more of my cut of the profits, then it meant his kids wouldn't be suffering as much as they were used to.

I now think with him selling dope around the clock and with all that money coming in then his wife wasn't beaten up as much as it meant he could treat her and he was too busy selling dope to be beating up his wife.

He knew if he did beat her and the police were called then he couldn't risk them being called to his house due to the amount of dope that now was hidden in his house rather than previously in my cottage.

I am sure my peers wouldn't like to know that their dope was in the hands of one of their main rivals as in the Nomads but as long as it was getting sold and they were getting their money then I know they were happy as all they cared about was not me, but just there cash.

Cash is what made these people happy, nothing more and nothing less.

Chapter 23

ANOTHER ONE BITES THE DUST

YEAR 1992

I was now 17 years old, feeling I had lived such a life already, an interesting one in many ways, a life that had aged me in so many ways but a life that had made me strong and also tough.

Anything the world was to throw at me, I very much was able to cope with ....that's what I believed as I had been through a lot in life and I had managed to come on through to the other side, quite well I felt.

The month was late April and soon was May.

May was the month my Mum was going to be travelling to Europe with Wim, for Wim to see his family in Holland. It was there in Holland, that everyone knew he was going to ask my mum to marry him.

It was like seeing two kids in love as I saw them on my birthday briefly.

By now I felt too grown up to have family birthday dinners as I once used to have with my Mum and with Wim.

All I wanted to do is just go out into town and get very drunk indeed which I ended up doing on the massive pub and bar crawl that I mentioned.

I didn't have time to do a evening dinner with my Mum and Wim though I popped in to see them briefly the afternoon of my birthday.

My mum was a bit hurt that she wasn't going to be spending quaintly time with her only son over his birthday which was important to her but no longer was I her little boy, I now was a man and spending time with my mum just wasn't cool.

I didn't see my Mum for over a week and a half after my 17th birthday nor had I spoken to her as I was busy with work and my own home life plus also I was being brought into some meetings to do with something that I was being put into by my peers.

Though at this time I still very much was left in the dark as to what that was, for the time being.

SATURDAY 2nd OF MAY, 1992

Saturday 2nd of May, my Mum came knocking on my door. Kiren yelled out to me that my Mum was downstairs so I got out of bed as I had been on the drink the night before as now instead of working 6 days a week, I was able just to do a five day week which suited me better.

I was so hung over and I didn't know why my Mum had turned up out of the blue to my cottage so I went down stairs to see what was up.

She had come around just to see me as she hadn't seen me since the 20th of April (my birthday) and she wanted to make sure I was ok.

She had brought lots of seafood around with her. My Mum knew how to win me over as New Zealand seafood has to be the best in the world.

As I ate into the seafood, my Mum asked me about my job so I told her that I now had a future planned that I would stay with this catering company till I learned many more skills and that when I was 20 I would then love to get a job in a plush restaurant and get a trade as a chef and then in my mid 20s to travel the world.

I went on to tell my Mum that my over all dream would be to open a restaurant with my father in Scotland or even London as I would love to give something back to my father.

That's when she first talked about my father's early years in London. It's the first time she talked in-depth about how they met and the restaurant that he was working at and how that she had met one of the Krays (I unsure which twin it was at one of the clubs that my father had taken her to).

I then told her I heard of that name the Krays as at the time some of the movies house was showing the Krays movie (still not knowing anything about them apart from my mum explaining to me that they were gangsters).

I asked her had my Father been a gangster? She replied no but he so could have gone down that path if he had stayed put in the East End of London during those times and if he hadn't come to NZ when he did.

My Mum explained my father was a god man but he just had a vicious temper and that yes he had an at times a shady past but he wasn't no villain, unlike The Krays.

I sat and listen to her telling me about her times in London and also for the first time about the breakdown of the marriage and some of the violence that took place when I was young.

It was if she needed to put the record straight and to open up to be at peace with herself.

She never told me about the photo of Wim she used to carry around with her.

That photo is what triggered of my father being violent to towards her and what was the giveaway when she was found out to be having affair (this I wouldn't find out about for many more years from my father).

My Mum did explain that she didn't hate my father and that she did very much love him but that she was just in love with Wim at the time she met my father.

She went on to say she at the time didn't think she never would see Wim again so she allowed herself to fall in love with my father.

With the birth of my sister, the right thing to do was of course get married as back in those days it wasn't looked fondly on if you had a child out of wedlock.

Then a few years after my sister was born, she and Wims paths crossed again.

This wasn't on purpose, it just happened. At the time Wim was married but not happy as his heart he told my mum belonged to my mum, and so the affair then began as my father she explained was always away at sea.

My Mum never meant to have hurt my father or to be unfaithful but she explained the love she had for her first love Wim was just too much.

Passion came between them both that they just couldn't let go off, though it destroyed not only her own marriage but also Wims first marriage.

Since then neither My Mum nor Wim ever remarried.

They after my father left my family house then started their relationship in the open, this time without having to meet in private or behind closed doors.

My Mum understood (she tried to explain) she knew how pain that my father had felt as Wim had also in their time together cheated behind my mum's back but what my mum felt was nowhere near the pain that my father had felt.

My Father had lost everything, his wife who had given up his own life for and then he lost his kids and his house so what my mum was saying, she really didn't feel the amount of pain that my father had felt and been through.

This afternoon was very strange as there was my Mum in a way saying sorry to me for everything as a child that I had to go through and all the unsettled nights and the witness of such extreme violence but my mum hadn't need say sorry to me.

I had turned out all right and she had been through so much herself remembering the many evenings she had been beaten up and look what I did in my early teenage years, how I had failed her by being expelled from two schools.

The times I would nick her car, all the times I wouldn't listen to her and I had taken the piss, the time she found drugs in her house and the times she would come home to her flat to find me in her own bed with girls when I was only young and I should have been thinking of school lessons the following day rather than getting my leg over.

Then the times I was in hospital after being stabbed or in many fights. The times I would come home with blood dripping from my nose and she would have to clean me up or the times she found me so drunk with sick all over me that again she would have to clean me up.

All the nights I would out without her ever knowing where her son was and the time her house was robbed by a low life girl from the girls home and even before that when the police would drive me home finding me out wandering the streets at such a young age.

It wasn't my mum who had to say sorry to me, it was me the son who should be saying sorry to my Mum.

She then told me how very proud she was as with my job and the goals that I set myself and that my father would be so proud of me as well.

She told me she would very much like a nice evening all together, my sister and herself and Wim and also Kiren before my Mum and Wim flew out to Europe on Tuesday 12th which was in ten day time.

Kieran reminded me that it was Mother's day the following Sunday so I said to my mum "Hey we will 100% do something then ok." "Next Sunday night I promise we will go out for a proper plush dinner."

My mum loved the idea of that so I went onto say "I will sort it out and that we will have a great night" "My treat in saying thank you for being the best Mum in the whole wide world!" with that it brought a tear down by Mums cheek so I wiped it with my hand and told her not to cry, everything's going to be a o k.

I then made a joke that when she would be returning from Europe she will have a huge rock on her finger and that Kerin and Stacey could arrange the wedding for her. Kerin and my mum got on so well and they laughter as my mum said her good bye and left.

That afternoon I sat there thinking about all my mum had said.

I didn't understand why on that day she shared all this with me.

I day dreamed trying to picture my parents back in the 1960s and how it must have been so exciting for my mum after what she had told me about all these top night clubs also the name Krays stuck in my mind.

That evening over a few drinks I told Kiren I was going to call my father. I had always written him letters to Scotland and also to my grandparents in Scotland but I hadn't written to him for a while though I had called him the month earlier to tell him about my job down on the docks.

For some reason I just wanted to speak to him again to let me know I loved him.

My Father felt so far away from his kids being seven oceans away and he felt he had already missed out so much on not just my life but also my sisters' life.

I wouldn't be able to make the call though till the following morning due to the time difference of the two countries.

SUNDAY 3RD OF MAY, 1992

The following morning when I woke up I dialled but Irene telling me my Dad was of course at the pub but she would call the pub and get him home as one thing that would bring him home to have his dinner would be to get to speak to his son.

I called back in half an hour and he answered the phone, it was like all his Xmas had come all at once.

He loved hearing my voice on the other end of the phone and when I told him I had been on one of his old ferries.

Not telling him I had gone aboard with the Satan's Slaves motorcycle club or 50 bikers and for sure didn't tell him about the poor old sheep but did let him know about that I saw a few of his old work friends and that I had a beer with them in the mess room as I had forgotten to tell him all this when I spoke to him last.

My Father said he can't wait till the day he has a pint with his son, a proper drinking session that will be he went on and said and then he laughter.

I then made his day by telling him about my present job still going ever so well (supplying the outside catering for the Interisland ferries) and told him where I was located which was right on the dock side.

He was as my mum just so ever proud of me.

I then told him of my dreams and my goals and about the restaurant idea in London, he said how about Scotland?

A proper Scottish family restaurant that sounded even better to my ears.

My Father told me he was head chef at a Italian restaurant in Scotland and that whenever he would leave work in the evenings to pop into his local pub for a lock in, he always wished that it was his own restaurant that he was leaving each night so I told him don't worry we will have that sorted.

He asked how my mum was. You could hear in his voice how much he still loved my mum.

I told him my mum had been along to my cottage only yesterday and how she spoke about their times in London, and she went on to tell me about the famous night clubs he had taken her to and the restaurant he was working at.

That's when he told me the name of the restaurant Simpsons on the Strand.

I then asked him who the Krays were. His voice changed, when he said "You don't need to know about them." "They gave me a lucky break but they were very dangerous men."

He wouldn't say anything more, even when I asked more he wouldn't say anything, changing the subject asking about my Sister.

I told him that I would be calling her today as I am arranging a special mother's day next week for my Mum.

I didn't tell my Dad about my Mum going to Europe nor didn't I mention Wim either.

The phone call made me so happy and also my father.

I put done the phone after saying good bye and I just felt so happy in my whole life, everything was perfect and nothing could take this happiness away.

I just wanted to get on with organizing my mum's mother's day and as for whatever I had to do next Friday with my peers I really didn't want to as now I had a future all mapped out, it didn't include anything that was criminal related nor drug related.

Whatever it was though I had to go through with it and I decided that after this last time of taking some pot from them then I would 100% make it the very last time and tell them straight.

If they had a problem with it then I would take whatever they were going to serve out to me as hell by now I could take a beating.

If they went over the top then I always had my shotgun to protect myself or if need be I would speak to the Satan's Slaves telling them to get my peers of my back as I had done too much of their dirty work by now.

I didn't want to have the risk over me anymore getting caught with so much dope as then my goals I had set would never be fulfilled and that I would never make it to Scotland to open up a restaurant of my own and more than likely I guessed I would end up banged up on the Mountain in the notorious Mt Crawford jail.

My last thought was it can't be anything to bad whatever they had lined up for me to do next Friday after work (8th of May) as I am sure it was probably just a few more bags of dope than normal, and so really I didn't have anything to worry.

I was in a good mood after getting off the telephone to my Father, the sunshine was hitting my face through the cottage lounge windows, so I picked up the phone to speak to my sister next to tell her about arranging something for next week when it was Mother's Day.

There was no answer on her phone so I left a voice message. That day Kiren and I after making love and without having one of our silly rows, (no row came as I or her hadn't been high on drugs from the night before) we both were feeling the sunshine and day as it was....that was, a very good day for us.

We went out and brought my mum a few mother's day presents.

Kerin was going to make up a gift basket for my mum. (Kiren was very creative and arty).

It looked great when she done her magic touches on the gift basket when we arrived back home after being out shopping for the afternoon.

Our neighbour came over knocking on the front door so I went outside to see what he wanted.

He told me he had nearly run out of weed. I had to tell him nothing till the following Friday.

When I got back inside the cottage, Kiren had a go at me as she thought that I wasn't going to be selling any more dope so she had a moan at me.

I told her just one more time and then that would be that and for her not to reek what already was a lovely day between us.

I told her about my bright future of how I wanted to run my own restaurant and how my father had suggested it be in Scotland.

"How cool was that!" I said to her as we lay on the couch and listened to some Neil Young and then Bob Dylan on the record player.

It was a sunny lazy afternoon so nothing too heavy but just a afternoon chilling out, finally falling asleep to the sound of Eric Clapton playing one of his classics.

I woke up and it was dark so I woke up Kerin, asking her for the phone so again I could call my sister. At the very moment when she passed me the phone, the phone rang.

It was my Mum, she was crying down the phone.

To ever here my Mum upset, upset me.

It remained me of my childhood.

After only yesterday seeing how happy my Mum was. What had happened in the mean time to make her so upset?

I asked her what was wrong. She told me that my sister's friend Tim was on a life support system in Wellington hospital.

Tim was out of every guy my sister ever dated, was my sisters' soul mate.

If my sister could have wished to spend her life back then with one man, it would have been Tim out of her boyfriends she had dated.

Tim by far was the one who made her the happiest during her previous years.

Though he himself had many problems and one was a drug abuse but he was a gentle soul, a hippy and one who lived that life style, free as a bird.

Tim was a kid from Miramar, who my sister knew most of her life.

Tim was like the male best friend of my sister. Angie was my sister best friend until she sadly was killed and Tim were not a like Angie in any way but they both were the dearest people my sister had in her life.

My mum told me my sister was at the hospital with Tim's family, his sister Kate was a friend of my sisters so at least at the hospital they had each other.

What put Tim on a life support system was he was out at a party in Peotone just outside of Wellington the night before.

Tim and his friends, all high on whatever drugs they were on, decided to ride-surf the roof of a combo van.

Tim was on top of the van roof (car surfing it was known as).

What no one was expecting was the driver for whatever reason put on the brakes all of a sudden.

I am unsure if someone or something had run out in front of the van on the road or if he was playing a silly game as in getting them off his roof.

One thing for sure he didn't know what was about to happen next, due to his breaking all of a sudden was that Tim went flying head first over the van.

Tim hit the road ahead at speed with nothing to protect him as he fell and was flung straight down on to the road head first.

Smashing his head open there and then instantly becoming brain dead.

His lifeless body lay on the road and in those days no one had mobile phones, there was no nearby house to call for help so some of his friends tried their best to save his life while other run for help.

But by the time the ambulance came, there was nothing anybody, not even a specialist doctor could do to save Tim even after operations to his head.

Tim was brain dead; the only thing keeping him alive at the hospital in the special unit was a life support system.

That night, in the middle of the night his family decided to turn the life support system off as there was nothing the doctors or anyone could do to help him.

Tim had been living only one street from my cottage so Kerin and I that night went around to his house and laid flowers outside his house and spoke to his flatmates.

Carl Cumstain was there at the time, as Tim had a huge arrange of friends from hippies, to hard men to bikers to many pretty girls.

Tim was loved by so many and dearly missed by hundreds, my sister being at the top of that tree as Tim loved my sister so much from the first time he ever met her to the very last time he ever saw her.

The following day the body of Tim was placed in an open coffin and brought around to his house. The coffin was placed in his front lounge with him in it as the Irish celebrate do at a wake such as this.

I was at work that day but after work I went around to say good bye to him.

There he was in the open coffin in the middle of the lounge.

It wasn't at all weird but very moving as people were drawing peace signs and Greenpeace signs on his coffin.

People were smoking dope and playing the music that he loved the most, so many different bands were being played on the record player from Patti Smith to Pink Floyd.

Everyone in that lounge was drinking and smoking, talking to Tim.

Tim would have loved all of this while looking down from heaven.

He would have been so proud and I know for a fact his body wasn't just in that room but very much also was his soul as he was among all his friends, partying with them in spirit form as one thing Tim did is party like no other and though he had a drug problem, he was always a good guy.

My sister was there she looked so upset I could tell, as I remember that look after Angie was killed so even though my sister tried to put on a smile, it wasn't what she was feeling within her.

She had just lost her soul mate that now was lying there, dead in a wooden coffin in front of her.

As I left I saw my sister holding Tim's hand and speaking to him. My sister stayed with Tim that night, sleeping in the lounge after the party had finished off the celebration of his life.

The party actually went on all week in that house. My sister stayed with Tim every night so he wasn't alone and so neither was my sister.

She no longer had a boyfriend in her life as Nick and she had broken up.

Nick was more interested in cars since he joined the Rebel Car Club so his club duties took up all of his time and my sister didn't need to be any guys' part time girlfriend so she had the week earlier shown Nick the door though not in a bad way as they still were friends.

It's just a shame Nick wasn't there for my sister that week as she really needed someone to be with her.

On the Thursday was the funeral, the funeral was meant to be the Wednesday but Tim's friends and sister and my sister wasn't letting Tim go anywhere.

They locked the flat and never answered the door to the funeral parlour people as no one wanted to bury Tim as it was too much for them all to say their farewells.

But after many phone calls and visits to the flat including by the police but I think that was due to the loudness of the music and four days of partying.

The neighbours not realizing why that house was rocking n rolling nor did they know that there was a dead body in that house laid to rest.

After the funeral everyone returned to Tim's house and had the final party the wake from the week's long wake, all night long until the music finally finished.

The people, all friends of Tim's and all from different walks of life, all departed from that house and one being my sister who went to her own flat late on the Thursday night and cried herself asleep.

In the night, my sister awoke seeing Tim standing at the end of her bed.

Tim telling my sister, he always will be by her side.

I know in my heart my sister hadn't awoken from no dream and that 100% that was the spirit of Tim visiting my sister as he for one would never leave my sisters side, in life and in death.

There are some people you can always replace in your life, as say when a friend goes and they're never a close friend then you hardly miss them and a new friendship begins with another, who in the end take their place.

Tim, he was one of my sister's friends who for her were never replaceable.

Nor could anyone fill his shoes in the mind of my sister as she had so much love for him.

My sister now with Tim gone, had left a huge void in her life and she had now to go through with the grieving process all over again as she had done when she was only a young child herself with the death of her best friend Angie,

That sorrow over Angie's early death would take a life time to come to terms with and my sister never got over losing her dear friend Angie who she loved so much so how now was my sister going to cope with losing another such dear friend?

We all cope with death differently to each other, some people find death easy to cope with and others it breaks their hearts.

Well with my sister she was already carrying a damaged heart from the loss of Angie and now her heart very much was broken in two by the sudden death of Tim.

As for Tim I am sure he wished to have never died old as he lived his life like many of our friends in the fast lane and they would partied far too much and take risks constantly, be it with drug abuse or drug use.

Really there isn't much different between drug use and drug abuse.

Both can for many people, who are not strong minded and who don't end up with a problem or issues from taking drugs seem to come out the other side all ok but then there are many who sadly lead down the same wrong path, and that in turn is to a very early grave.

Some people call it and know it as rock n roll.

Tim being on top of a roof of that van as it speed down a main road, the only thing that would have put him up there was his drug use.

No straight person, other than a stunt man would have done that and Tim was far from being a stunt man. He was just a kid in his 20s with the rest of his life ahead of him to live but a brain full of drugs and making him do things where he felt he was invincible.

So up he went on that Saturday night, with a belly full of drink and a head full of drugs and being the show man he was.

He never expected it to be the death of him, but sadly it was.

What I thought I wouldn't witness over at his house was everyone who clearly knew it was more than just heading his head that killed him, as if he hadn't been off his head at the time of the crash, his head hadn't been full of drugs, as it were then he wouldn't as I have stated stepped up on top of that van that sadly ended his life so young.

But no one who came to see Tim thought about the dangers of drugs and even though there laid in front of them all was one of their friends bodies laid out cold dead due to the use of drugs.

This for sure should have been a flashing red light for them all and for me.

I stood there looking down at Tim laid in his coffin in his lounge, I saw everyone around me take their lsd trips and pass around the bong to smoke hash and roll up joint after joint for all to get high.

As High as Tim would have been on that fateful night that he passed from the living to the dead.

Leaving behind so many friends who's only way it seemed for them to cope with the grief that I noted was to take lots more drugs and in doing so that took away the pain for them all.

For how long, only as long as they all stayed high as the moment they all came back down to earth and there were their real emotions and feelings that they had to face.

Well for many if not all, it just meant another lsd tap or more dope and coke and booze all mixed together as this was what they all were doing so no one could face the truth nor to truly grief honestly together or either one of them alone.

Was I on the following Friday night doing exactly that as what I had witness all of my sisters friends doing and also some of my peers, whom were also there.

So like normal (my old behaviour pattern) what I always did as seeing them through my eyes growing up, I always copied suite as I didn't have any role models in my life nor did I have a father so these guys were all I had and if they were doing something then I would try my best to copy.

By fitting in and if that meant seeing them cope with death by just getting high, then I was more a fool at that age to do the same so soon came Friday when I would see them again after work and with myself not grieving over the loss of Tim as I had done my very best to put it to the back of my mind but knowing sooner than later it would come to me.

The truth that Tim now was dead and what had happen to him and that what I saw on the Monday pervious was a dead body sitting in his lounge, the dead body of Tim who through my sister I had know over the last 8 years.

How would now I cope with the loss of a friend as he was always a friend to me.

Knowing myself and my many faults that I had back when I was a teenage growing up then the way I copied was just to do as I had stated and that was to follow suite and use the excuse of taking drugs to hold down the emotions of the loss of a friend and also the pain that I saw my sister going through.

Tomorrow was Friday and that day was going to change the rest of my life, the life that up to this point had it seemed finally come good.

Finally for me at last but all good things I was soon to learn always come to an end and usually with a sudden crash.

Life as I knew it was about to even more hit me square in the face.

Chapter 24

THE BEGINING OF THE END

The Friday morning (8th of May 1992) my girlfriend has gone to work with a kiss goodbye. I rolled over and got another hour's short sleep before I had work to go to.

I was told the night before I had a big day ahead, to some it wouldn't have been that big but for me only turning 17years old, a fortnight earlier I it seemed I had been given more trust by some very heavy people in Wellington and these are the people whom I had grown up with in my teenager years since throwing away what would have been a golden education through my contact with drugs at such a early age.

Was it there fault? Their control they had over me? The lack of having a father in my life that leads me down this path?

I had already been let's say burnt by the flames of the world of drugs due to me being expelled a few years back, when I had only reached the age of 13years old.

To me it seemed a world that no other kid was involved in.

My peers were all mid 20s to late 40s.

I had no social circle of my own age group so what my peers were doing, then I was merely learning the trade from constant contact with them over the years, though now I had for once a bright future I could see.

One that meant I no longer had to neither hold their drugs for them nor sell their weed for them.

I had promise Kiren this was going to my last time I would do any more of that for them.

I had an associate come and pick me up from work down on the dockyard and I was driven over down past Wellington airport onto a golf course.

The car was parked in the car park, for another car to meet us shortly after we had arrived.

363

Handed to me in the way of drugs were 30,000 acid trips that had been flown in from the States.

These I had no idea of nor did I know that this was just a small % of what had managed to be flown into New Zealand.

At the time it was the biggest amount of lsd ever to get past the customs and police to land into New Zealand. It had been flown in for what I was to learn was the first time, as normally it had come on ships anyway all this was above my head and here I was now with 30,000 acid trips to get rid of.

In the past the most I ever had was 1,000 and the most I ever stored away and held for them (hidden in my cottage) was 10,000 but that was just to hold for them and never have to sell for them.

This time as so much acid had come through in air freight then they were making me myself sell the 30,000 rather than just hold it for them.

I truly just thought all I would be holding for them is only a few more bags of pot which turned out to be true as instead of the normal two pounds in weight of pot, there were 5 bags there.

That's more than twice the amount but as I had moved the previous bags so quick they thought they would give me more as it seemed I was selling it quicker than ever before.

That was only due to the neighbour selling it for me.

In selling him both the pounds of pot at a knock down price, I had now it seemed shot myself in the foot and even though I said to them there and then no way could I move so much dope, they weren't having none of it.

I was told this wasn't a time and a place to be debating such matters.

The acid alone had street value of $120,000 so this was no child's play.

It was a hell of a lot of acid and what soon flooded the drug market as this in those times before ecstasy had flooded in and what now is big in NZ I have been told the drug P.

Ecstasy though was very much around but over twice the cost of a tab of acid so the market for acid was very much flowing and as for dope well that was always what many folk would want and it went like wild fire.

All on bail as in tick, as of course I didn't have all the funds to cover what had just been thrown at me.

We pulled away from the car park; I had my peers who two were in the car after they were speaking to me telling me how much trust had been put into their decision for me to take all on board.

This for some reason I thought I was the bee knees (ever so grown up) in the eyes of my peers.

I thought I now was in the major league though I really wasn't and only days earlier I didn't even wish to be in this situation, and that was just collecting maybe one more extra bag of weed not now owing them £120,000.

I wasn't thinking of the profile I would be making but just the debit I was now in.

Now it was up to me to move it and move it quick among Wellington and the nightclubs that I had been involved in at a young age - being stabbed and also involved in stabbings and fights and credit card fraud to name a few of the vices that were opened to me.

I was even at a young age known among the door men and clubs and bars through the Wellington area and beyond out of the city as well.

I arrive home and set the sheets of acid up on a clothes line that went the length of my kitchen, sheet after sheet all being five thousand trips on each sheet.

To move them now seemed like a mission and a half but I knew enough people whose game was selling the stuff so first port of call was the Wellington Politick College, the nearest thing to me as in a mini university.

It wasn't too far from my cottage and also full of loads of drug taking students.

I went and had a chat to a few of the students who I knew that just loved the shit and whom I knew on weekends 55% of the students would be taking acid trips as none could afford coke or speed and 70% of the students all would be smoking weed.

I had got to know a few of them really well as they always would buy weed of me and when I didn't have my catering job then at lunch times I would go and have lunch with them and sell them shit loads of weed on campus so whenever I had acid they loved me more as I was the only person their age group who could sort them out without ripping them off.

Many came from wealthy backgrounds so the ones I dealt with always had pure cash on them and they would themselves in turn take weed or acid of me to sell among their own circles, so it suited me fine and they never let me down when it came to money

By late afternoon I had managed to flog them a few of the sheets and was given some cash as one of them popped to a local bank.

He had account his parents had set up for him and he could take large sums of money from across the counter.

He for sure must have had some special gold account as he would always be able to make big withdraws and straight away, not needing to wear a masked anyway the rest of the acid was on tick.

By early evening I was counting the money and cutting trips into smaller sheets of 100 as that evening I would be hitting the acid clubs and also the pubs and then going around certain bike clubs to get rid of more of the acid and weed.

Making calls to find out where certain house parties over that weekend was being held and beach parties.

Any and most parties in New Zealand, people would be smoking weed or doing something more than just having a gin and tonic.

There I was sitting in my lounge cutting away at these acid trips and with gloves as the acid can sweep into the palms of your hands and into your sweat paws and which can cause you to start to trip, which is never a good thing.

My contact who had taken me on that car journey had finished bagging up the weed for me in smaller sizes; I placed them under the cottage. Doing that would end up being a mistake which I would find out to my small loss later.

When I hadn't fought my corner when it came to the extra weed and the surprise of all this acid earlier on in the car (though maybe he hadn't realised that I was actually trying to say no back in the car at golf car park but being told that that wasn't the place to debate it) then next minute my contact laid on some personal coke for me, free of charge.

Now coke was hard to come by in New Zealand, only certain circles ever did have it and it cost so much so to be treated to some was rare but it was his way of praising me.

It meant a after a few lines my job of cutting up the trips was something that I was able to do even quicker.

I called around a few pals who would always join me on the Friday nights in town and tonight was no different, apart from that it was my shout as I didn't have to hand over the payment of the acid till the end of the month so I had a few dollars on me that for now I was safe to spend.

There was no way I was going to be able to move 30,000 acid trips alone, I had given on tick 5 sheets all with 1,000 acid trips on them so I still had 25 sheets to sell.

Yes I knew a hundred people who took acid, but there weren't even 10 in them who would want to take on 1,000 each as many only sold it in a smaller scale as in sheets of hundreds and others, well they only took a few trips here and there.

I started looking at all this acid thinking how the fuck am I going to move every trip.

Standing in front of 25 acid sheets is not like having a few hundred to move.

Before my friends arrive I hid the bulk of the acid as no one ever knew I had drugs in my house apart from my girlfriend and those who would hand it to me to store but even they didn't know ever where I would stored or hide them in my house.

I did trust my three friends but again the words loose lips sinks ships come my mind so I was always ever so careful even with trusted friends.

The paranoia of having so many drugs in the house, I was always worried that someone would attempt to hold me up if people knew I had drugs in my house.

Certain gangs in New Zealand were known to send their younger members to do exactly that and they more than most would turn up in the middle of the night with axes and other weapons.

If you were woken in the pitch of darkness in the middle of the night with your door being kicked in by gang members then you had no chance of protecting yourself that is if you didn't have a shotgun in reach as then no one was going to beat ya and no one was going to nick your gear. Someone would end up being blasted, either them or you.

No one ever knew, outside my girlfriend and it was only this day that these three close friends of mine I asked to help me cut up a few of the sheets.

They like me had never seen so much acid before in their lives.

I gave them all one sheet each which they cut up into sets of 100 and then I asked all three if they would tick a sheet each telling them that it was the very last of the sheets so as it was on tick.

They knew their profits would be high so they agreed to take a sheet each.

I told them I would have it ready for them tomorrow at least now that was 8 sheets that were on tick.

I had 10 sheets in total cut up to 100s so only 12 full sheets left, still so much acid.

The most acid I had ever seen in my whole life and to be honest it wasn't doing much for me as I just knew the hassle of moving the sheets and as for now I couldn't cut up all the acid that I had laid out to cut out by myself so again they sat with me cutting the sheets that I had started on before they arrived.

I would have what now was in the lounge all sorted thanks to their help.

I could trust these three friends as they were like brothers to me and had been a part of my life, all my life.

It was like a no win situation but I wasn't going to let it get to me and after Tim losing his life and then his funeral I had been through a lot this week and I had some good mates around me who was willing to help so I thought after a bad week, I for sure wasn't going to have a bad weekend.

I had a few dollars on me to spend anyway and after a few beers and a few more lines of coke that had been I out on a mirror.

Feeling quite high, sharing the coke around which my mates just loved then we all were very high but serious due to the coke rather than drunk and happy.

We all decided to take a few trips as 50% of the work load had been taken care of and also my girl would be home any minute.

She was used to seeing drugs in the house though nothing compared to this so we started to pack up the acid sheets that I had left out to be cut up.

I parcelled the acid up, hiding it in my bathroom while my friends weren't looking.

I told them to leave the kitchen and go back in the lounge to start the drinking games and to wait for the acid to hit as music had to be sorted for when that moment came so they all rushed in to the lounge fighting over what music to play and to get the shot glasses out of the glass cabinet.

I then removed the acid from the hiding place in my bathroom as didn't feel too safe about where I had hidden it so I took the parcels up to my bedroom to go in my bed base next to my shotgun.

I would hide the acid more carefully the flowing day when I had no guest in the house to deal with.

Soon we started all to feel the acid come on.

Back in those days I can honestly say the trips were all fun and a laugh.

I had never seen anyone have a bad trip nor did I ever.

It was always for me just lots of fun. I am sure it was in the early days of acid such as Woodstock and the late 1960s, be it America or London.

My girl soon came home.

I can remember not being able to take my hands off her so upstairs we went and made love while I dropped some acid in her mouth and we fucked like rabbits while my pals were downstairs tripping among themselves listening to the Grateful Dead on the stereo.

I went to put my supply back after giving her a line of coke and told her that I had some quid for her to go out shopping tomorrow, but when she saw the cash and how much there was she wasn't happy and she asked where it come from as to be honest it was more than I normally would have.

Kiren stayed upstairs and tried to take a look in the bed base to see what was in there which caused a row between us as I told her to mind her own business.

She started a argument with me, demanding me to tell her about the money and what was hidden in the bed base.

She knew I used that as a place to hide my bits and pieces but I wouldn't tell her. Yeah she didn't mind taking drugs and free drugs she knew could only come from me selling them but the scale this time I knew she wouldn't be comfortable with.

I was already high as a skate so I wasn't in a mood to row with her.

Kiren then went mad as she thought that when she had dropped acid it was at the same time as I had, as in that I had waited till she came home.

She couldn't believe that I would drop acid with my friends and not wait for her till she came home if I was getting some acid.

I reminded her how we had had a conversation in the week about these drugs being sold and how they were going to be the very last time as I was going straight after all of this had been sold and with the profiles I would be buying us both tickets to go to London town for a holiday and to see my father as a surprise.

She always wanted to go to London she looked the part already and in many ways was more a London girl than NZ girl.

I tried my best to cheer her up. I couldn't stop smiling and telling her how beautiful she looked.

That was that, she called me a fuckwit and told me that I had to give the acid in the bed base back to my peers. I never told her about the dope that was hidden under the cottage.

I told her that was not going to be the case; there is no way I could hand the shit back.

I would be laughed at and looked upon as some twat but she then put it to me - it would mean her leaving me as she didn't want to date a drug dealer.

I never saw myself as a drug dealer as all I would do is moving some dope and a bit of acid now and there and ok maybe the odd bit of speed as well.

Nearly everyone in NZ either smoked it or could score it so I didn't see myself any different than anyone else and as for the drugs that used to be hidden in the cottage, well they were never my own drugs I was merely being paid to hide and store them so did that make me a drug dealer as she was assuming me of.

I found this strange as all our time together she loved the drug taking.

I could score any drug out there and as for selling it meant we lived in a lovely cottage.

Kerin had anything she wished for and also we could party like kings and drugs were free for us, nightclubs would treat us good so our nightlife was always wicked and we had a massive social circle.

Life was fucking great especially on acid, life seemed great!

How sad it seems looking back, only thinking life was better when on drugs and that my life's decisions seemed to be controlled by my peers.

Any outside contact with them, then I lived by no rules that were set down be in the law of the land or by my mum as I had grown up too fast in my early teenage years.

Was this due not having a father in life in my teenage years?

Was it due to a broken home?

Was it due to spending so much time away from my house when I was so young?

Was it caused from being send to boarding school, there having to step in line or else were you caned and hit with belts?

Was it because once I was back in Wellington, after the all schools in the whole city wouldn't take me after being expelled the second time and my mum not being able to control me with discipline?

Was it the slowly but steady use of drugs ranging from anything out there I was taking?

Was it due to me growing up experimenting with drugs?

Or was it as I had lived a life (that would shock many) being formed into the school of life by career criminals that I had, at times lapped it all up.

It was the only education I was getting once my schooling came to a end, a life of selling drugs up to a recent point when all seemed to finally have good for me, but I had all these last drugs to get rid of before I could even life my new dreams' and achieve my goals that I set myself.

Once the drugs were moved (sold) I could then get out of the life of selling drugs and using them and becoming a chef.

I strongly do believe that if I never started smoking dope when I was young then I wouldn't have gone on to harder drugs, and also of course if I wasn't surrounded by drug users and a social circle that was selling drugs then I would have had a different teenage years when growing up.

But over the years leading up to this point where I just had turned 17 years old, I had gone from a drug user to a drug dealer.

Something here now at the age of 34 years looking back over those years I am not proud to admit and do I have some regrets.

I do think no one should have regrets over their life but as for my early years I have no one to blame apart from myself for the mistakes I made and the way I lead my teenage years.

We are all given chances in life and it's up to what road in life you decided to all walk down when you come to a cross road in one's own life.

The thing is with me I never saw those cross roads as always in front of me was a line of coke or bags of pot to move and they meant dollars.

To me it was a easy way of making a quick buck and having the best things in life.

By now I had come out of youth gangs, and found myself now deeply involved in gangland on the streets of Wellington.

Living a life suited to someone in their mid 20s to 30s rather than a young teenager.

All I can say is if you are young with all your life still ahead of you, and you find yourself in some of the same situations as I did in this book then just don't make the same mistakes as I did nor the same wrong decisions as I did.

Take my advice on that, as sooner or later when you not expecting it, trust me your life as you know it will fall apart. You will lose everything.....oh how I was soon to find out this.

Kieran moaning at me was too much for me to take in as I was buzzing lovingly due to the acid so I left her in the bedroom and I went downstairs to drink a few beers and start on the Jack Daniels.

One of my friends Mr Jack Daniels though it's a bottle of bourbon but hey he came everywhere I went. Drinking was taking place and now Jefferson Airplane was playing loudly on the stereo.

In between songs I heard my girl's voice saying answer the phone as she could hear it ringing from the bedroom though the land phone was in the front room where I was with my mates.

I thought it was just part of the song as more coke was being snorted and speech of another acid tab was on our minds to take. I was in the company of people who just loved the shit and even though one acid trip was so enough, we wouldn't stop by pushing the boat out just a little but firstly I would take the call.

It was my Mum.

There I was out my face on acid, having to speak to my mum down the phone.

I was sitting in my lounge surrounded by my friends so trying to talk tough over the phone but this phone call will stay with me forever as what my mum was saying didn't make sense and it even got me angry by hearing what she was trying to say to me.

That weekend my Mum was going away with her boyfriend Wim as he was taking her away for the weekend as he knew Sunday was a special day for her(Mothers Day) so Wim thought he would make a weekend of it.

Their plan was to go away early Saturday morning then return Sunday late afternoon and meet us for dinner that evening.

We still weren't sure if my sister would be joining us as she was so saddened by Tim's death.

My Mum didn't think it was a good idea to go away for the weekend she felt guilty for some reason that she was going away leaving my sister to cope with the grief by herself and then for us all to be making a huge deal about Mother's Day on the Sunday evening.

My Mum knew how heartbroken my sister was going to be but I still thought it would best for us all still to do the dinner on Sunday night together as a family.

I hadn't seen my sister since Tim's funeral so I wasn't sure what state of mine she was in.

Maybe my Mum was right, we should hold of the dinner but very much hold one before my Mum and Wim were to head to Europe on the following Tuesday.

Before my Mum needed to say whatever she was ringing me for, I told her that Kerin had made up a really special present for her for Mother's Day so at least me and Kerin would on Sunday go over to my Mum's flat when she got back so she got her present.

I said afterwards I would go and visit my sister as I was too busy this evening to do so, and as for Saturday I would still have to move more of the acid, though she didn't know that of course.

Then after I had spoken, my Mum started to talk though what my Mum was saying as I mentioned didn't make any sense at all, and it wasn't the acid that was making me think like.

My Mum was saying if she didn't make it back from her weekend away, that she had already left out her life insurance documents next to her phone in her kitchen at her flat with other such documents.

I asked her what she was taking about and why say things like that to me as it was getting me angry (inside it was upsetting to hear her speak like this).

My Mum tried to explain to me, she had some sort of dream the night before and awoke that morning with a bad feeling about going away this weekend and not returning.

She didn't go into detail about her dream but she made it clear she had a funny feeling that she wouldn't be returning.

When my Mum told me this I swore and told her stop being stupid with what she was saying.

She could hardly hear me when I told her I loved her as the others in the back ground were all dancing around like they were in trances to the song This is the End sang by The Doors.

That song for some reason I didn't like hearing, while at the same time my mum said she loved me and I said the same words back though in a rush and more quieter than she had said them to me.

I didn't want my friends hearing me say those words down the phone in case they had over heard that I had been speaking to my mum as to say those words to your mum in front of friends at the time just didn't seem a cool thing to do.

I am unsure if my mum actually heard that I too had told her that I loved her before the phone line went dead.

The whole phone call caused me to be in a bad mood.

I got snappy and told my friends to turn off that fucking song off.

Seeing everyone's smile just disappears, and then my girlfriend came into the lounge all dressed up and said where we were going tonight?

But as I had all that acid to try and move, I told Kiren she wasn't coming with us.

That caused one of the biggest fights as she started to throw shit at me calling me a wanker, saying I had wreaked her acid trip.

The trip started to come on for her while she was upstairs in the bedroom that's why she had come down in a happy mood as everyone on acid always is when the first waves of the trip hit you.

She asked me who the phone call was from. I told her none of her fucking business. I was such a bastard to her that night to the point she told me she was going to her friends place to enjoy better company that us lot. I told her go then and don't come back.

"Fuck you!" I yelled as she slammed the door.

My mates knew something was up.

They just wanted to get back to the happy state I was in so we all agreed "Women, why can't live with them and you can't live without them." as the record was moved to a new song L.A Woman by The Doors.

That picked up the mood among us all and returned the smiles upon all our faces.

The night was young and another acid tab was spoken about before I had got the phone call, never telling anyone who that was on the phone and not telling anyone about the surreal conversation that I had just had with my Mum.

Putting that at the bad of my mind as I another acid trip was placed in my mouth with a swig of Jack Daniels from the bottle and some up lifting music after we played through The Doors record so the boys put on AC/DC Hells Bells storming out of the stereo.

Our moods were now heightened and we were looking like a right bunch of naughty bastards so yeah my girlfriend did have a point.

We headed out but first I had to quickly see the neighbour two doors down so to hand him a bag of pot.

I placed a smile on his face, and told him that there was more where that came from but for now I was in a hurry as the time now was 630pm so I told him I would see him tomorrow.

He commented that I looked off my nut!

We shook hands and jumped in my mate's car and we were off. Firstly I dropped some acid off to a few dealers I knew in Wellington. None on tick as they all always had cash as they were big time dealers, selling coke and speed and they always took on acid as well.

By 830 pm I had done my rounds and given my pal who had driven a few quid for driving me about, now it was time to treat all three mates to a proper night out.

We all got so pissed and we didn't stop dropping tabs and ended up watching a Madness cover ska band that was puka down at a good little music bar down Cuba St in Wellington.

It was full of skinheads, many of them talking about the F.A Cup Final that was on the following night at around 3am NZ time.

They all were moaning that West Ham Utd weren't in the final, as all the skinheads in NZ all supported the Hammers, and then there was me who was a massive Liverpool FC fan and the good thing for me was that LFC were in the Cup Final that year.

I told my mates that if LFC were to win and due to it being LFC 100 years then I would get another LFC tattoo.

I already had a LFC tattoo but why wait till the end of the match the following night I thought high on acid.

I banged on the door at the local tattoo studio, knowing one of the artists would still be in there as it was Friday night.

He was tattooing a black power member his gang colours, he looked like he was finished.

I asked if he would tattoo me next but he said he was tired and he wanted to finish up so I pulled a sum of cash that was in my jacket pocket (from the acid trips I had sold that evening before hitting town) and gave him an offer he couldn't refused.

The black power member was being finished with his ink so I went to the nearest shop and brought a Shoot magazine and showed him the LFC badge I wanted done including the gates over Anfield and away he went with the ink to my body.

In the end while talking to him, he was a wicked tattoo artist. I ended up selling him some acid as well as paying for the art work.

He done a puka job and quick as well, due to sharing the coke I still had on me.

A few people came in and watched him tattoo away.

Some Chinese tourists took a few photos of him tattooing me. I would have loved to have seen those photos as they would have looked wicked.

Anyway he was done within two hours which is quick but it's not like he rushed the work as it came up good then he crack open two bottles of beer and took his acid so I decided to take another.

By this time I had taken four acid tabs. I left the tattoo studio more flying than any time before.

The band had finished playing and I couldn't find my friends so I wandered up into Manners Mall but there were too many police around.

I still had drugs on me plus I was looking fucked so I headed down to the Diner, where everyone would meet up for late food and drinks.

At the bottom of Courtney Place which is the bottom main road of all the bars and clubs in Wellington at the time was the movie house where I had seen The Doors movie many months earlier with Kiren and the other movies that her and I had seen previously while we both had taken acid and had the movies come alive for us.

This Friday night though there on the outside in big letters were the words The Krays.

Again for some reason those words stuck to me. I wasn't sure if it was due to the acid but it drew me to the movie house. There were people walking in so I just brought a ticket for tonight's screening from a sweet old lady behind the ticket office booth.

In I went being told I could sit anywhere I wished.

(11:59pm Friday 8th of May 1992)

Lights out = movie time.

Chapter 25

THE TRIP

12:00am SATURDAY 9th OF MAY, 1992

I had my hip flask full of Jack Daniels so I had a swig and sat by myself in the movie house.

The big screen light up and so did my mind as now all the acid was doing its magic even more.

I can recall the rushes I was having and the taste of the acid in my mouth for some reason.

What came next was up on the screen was Pink Floyd The Wall and not The Krays.

I hadn't heard of the movie The Wall though my sister had their music and I had the Pink Floyd, Dark Side of the Moon record which is one of the best records ever made.

Of course I knew many of their songs such as the famous song Another Brick In The Wall but as for this movie I hadn't a clue what it was about, and ere where were The Krays.

I tried to walk in the dark, pitch black movie house finally finding the door.

There was no one to help me find my way with a torch and times likes these when u had taken 4 acid tabs, I really needed someone with a torch to guide me through the dark.

What should have taken one minute, must have taken me 15 mins.

One step at a time, I was looking like a robot to the others who were in the movie house.

Down to the desk I headed near where the popcorn was sold and spoke to the old lady behind the screen.

I asked her "Where's The Krays movie?"

She explained that was the evening movie but The Wall is the late showing night movie.

She must have been 60 years old, so I was shocked when she said "Young man by the state of your blue eyes." (That I'm sure were all over the place) "Then The Wall is one movie you're going to love."

When I walked away, I am sure she whispered "How is your Mum, safe I hope?"

I turned back to her and this earlier harmless old lady who was helpful, her face had it seemed turned all very dark and she didn't look friendly at all.

I to be honest was a bit fearful of her as I went back up to the glass and asked what she had said?

She replied "Have a nice evening, safe journey home." But I am sure she said "How's your Mum, returned safe I hope".

I tried to look at her but her face started to move into all funny shapes as if her face was now a jiggle saw puzzle as her eye brows started to meet with her ears.

Her nose was dropping into her open mouth.

Her eyes, they instead of looking friendly (as they had earlier) now looked very black.

A frightening pale of deep darkness came over here facial features.

Either she was a witch, making her face move all around or that by now I had taken too much acid (I think the second).

It was all new to me as I hadn't ever taken this much acid before.

I had only ever only taking max 3 acid trips within a 24 hr period before but never 4 in less than 10 hours.

More acid per mil that was going into my body than ever before, more and more this whole trip stared to come even more a live for me.

I looked down as her face was becoming too hard to keep up with and also as she spoke, her words were coming out of her mouth.

It's as if I could catch them in my hand as like they were like bubbles. Bubbles full of words that once I had touched then popped though none of the words were spelt correctly due to me being dyslexia. They were all miss-spelt as they drifted in the air from her mouth into my hands as I was trying to pop them.

Her final words were telling me to hurry as not to miss any of the movie.

I knew she clearing knew I was on drugs.

I was still convinced at the time, she was some sort of witch.

I was unsure though at the time if she was a friendly white witch or a dark evil witch.

I truly believed she did say something to do with my mum rather than what she retold me that she had first said.

I know I was tripping off my face. As I walked away from the ticket booth where the old lady was sitting in, I couldn't take my eyes of the carpet whenever I looked down.

In my hand I was still holding my movie ticket receipt but I couldn't focus pass that.

The carpet was moving like waves, sloping now up like against a shore of a beach though I couldn't see no beach nor hear any waves as they crashed but it still didn't stop me think I was walking across a beach.

I very much could see all of the carpet acting as if it were waves of an ocean as I turned and went back into the dark of the cinema.

A witch, spoken words being bubbles and her face moving like a rubes cube and carpet acting like the ocean waves – all I wanted to do is take my sit and rub my eyes as by now I was really tripping out.

Yeah it was all down to the acid.....fucking tell me about it!!!!

Fuck though was she right as what a movie and on acid. The movie for sure must have made or even at least thought of while they all were on acid.

It was made for people to watch only on acid, that's for sure!!

It blew my mind and is one of the best movies I ever seen.

SATURDAY May 9th 0:05 am

While I watched this late screening of the film, I didn't know that over at my sisters flat my Mum had after leaving her own flat a few hours earlier rang my sister to see how my sister was.

For whatever reason my mum couldn't sleep, there was something playing on her mind. Something it seemed was worrying her and she couldn't get a good night sleep so she drove her car very late at night and went and saw my sister.

Staying there till 4am in the morning and not driving back to her own flat though she would drive past it but instead she kept on driving and went to Wims house instead after leaving my sisters place.

My sister in latter conversations I have had with her, told me that my mum turned up a few minutes past midnight and that for four hours she spoke to my sister of her childhood.

How she (my Mum) was a twin and that her twin sister had died at birth. It made my Mum feel like half of her was always missing in her whole life.

As my Mum did the week earlier with me, telling my sister about her time in London and also about her marriage and her married life, about the affair that destroyed her marriage.

How much she loved us both and that she couldn't have asked for two better kids and that she was sorry for all the problems that her affair had caused.

Again in a way my Mum was saying to now my sister, her only daughter.

My sister said in later years that her and my Mum had never spoke about the things that did ever before up to that night.

My sister spoke at length about how it affected her when she heard that Angie had been killed and also last week on finding out what happed to Tim.

My sister went on to tell my Mum about being there in the hospital room when Tim's life support machine was turned off, hearing Tim take that last breathe of his.

Though it was a machine that was pumping oxygen into his lungs but my sister saw his chest going up and down and was holding his hand and could feel his pulse and then as the doctors and nurses turned off the machine, she saw his life leave his body.

His chest stop moving as his heart beat stopped for the very last time.

How being a witness to this for my sister, had brought memories back from losing her best friend Angie.

How cruel life was to be losing loved ones, who didn't deserve to die and died too young.

The times spend with my mum really made my sister feel so loved. My sister had felt so alone since Tim's funeral, she wasn't coping too well to come terms with the death of Tim.

I don't and won't ever know how sad it was for my sister that week and with everything that had gone on her life, Angies death, my sisters very near own death with the bike crash and then now with her soul mate leaving her through his own death.

I know that after my Mum had left, my sister finally got a little bit of rest that early morning

For me while my sister and my Mum were still talking over at my sister place unknown to me on the other end of town.

The lights in the movie house came on as the film "Pink Floyd, the Wall" had just come to an end.

Wow! That old lady was right as what a movie and to have watched it on acid, it blew my mind!

I sat there thinking to myself it was one of the best movies I ever seen up to that time of my life, by a mile.

It fucking blew my mind, more so than the "The Doors" movie.

I wished my girl was here to have watched it with me or that my mates had seen it as it was two words......mind blowing.

As for me at just past midnight when my Mum was over at my sisters, I was in the picture house tripping, still trying to work out what the lady behind the box office screen had said to me earlier.

I left, feeling the carpet was moving up and down like I was on a genie rug as I went to leave.

I left the movie thinking I was in the dam movie, hard to describe but I was reliving the movie over and over in my head and just wanted more of it

I thought I would get some nachos and go on home from the Diner but as I got there I saw my mates.

Fucking hell they looked fucked!!

I got us a round of drinks and then another and as The Diner was the only 24 hr joint that ya could drink in after hours(if the manager knew you well enough).

We just stayed on for more drinks while I told them about the movie I had just seen and how unreal was the night.

There I was with a new random tattoo on me as well, though the tattoo wasn't random as in the sense of the meaning of the tattoo, but to get a tattoo just from someone mentioning a football match well yeah that was random I guessed.

If I wasn't on acid, I wouldn't have got the ink done that night.

At least I got what I asked for and that it wasn't of some half devil half girl or some bird on a pillow connected to a phone so I was happy with my new tattoo.

I must have drunk a bottle of Jack Daniels with my friends down at the Diner.

The whole night burnt a hole in my pocket as I had been treating them all night on beers and Jack Daniels etc.

We decided at around 5am to go back to my place to yes drop more acid.

This time though double dip (take two tabs of acid at once).

To take the acid from the bottom of the sheets is where the acid is stronger.

To take one of them is like taking 5 at once, we all had done 3 or 4 already in the night so to top it off with one of these was going to be a step up but we were far too out of it to care.

I always had loads of booze at my mine place so I didn't need to ask for a take out from the manager of the Diner as we left.

I wasn't sure if Kiren would be home, but if she wasn't then I didn't wish to be indoors tripping by myself as for some reason while driving past the street one over from mine in a taxi, (my mate had to leave his car up town as he was just too wasted to be able to drive his own car) I looked at Tim's flat and I am for sure, I saw Tim standing outside knocking on his front door trying to get into his flat.

Whatever it was and I know it was only due to the lsd but it put a shiver up my spin as believed I had seen a ghost. I asked everyone else had they seen what I had seen but no one was looking out the same window as me when we had passed the street.

Soon we were back at mine. I paid the cabbie and in we went into my cottage.

I went up to the bedroom, not turning on the light as not wanting to wake Kiren.

Feeling over the bed and realising that there was no body in the bed so I lifted up the mattress and got in to bed base and unrolled one of the sheets of acid.

Not having anything to cut the bottom row of the sheet so I torn it with my hands making such a mess as I ripped across and upwards of the sheet of acid.

Coming back down with more acid than expected and really by this time not needing anymore as it would mean no sleep from the wicked, and it's not like we had even come down from the last trips.

But us all being young and with mischief of in all our eyes we thought why not, just one more trip and for sure no more after that.

They say you can take one too many and never ever come back from the trip so we would call it a day after the last tab was put down our throats.

Well for sure that trip really hit us all hard and the strength for sure was to be found in it.

Everyone now was expressing (CHANGE WORD) their own trips, rather than earlier the trips of us all coming together.

For some reason the song Ghost Town (sang by the band The Specials) was playing in the lounge. All the music had gone ska while we all were dancing in the cottage to the beautiful sound that is known as Ska music.

Even as a bad dancer, you can always get away to moving ya body to the many different beats of Ska.

The British band The Specials were one of the very best but for some reason this song playing made me think back to the vision I had seen earlier outside Tim's house as it was him that I am sure saw tapping on his door.

Maybe the word ghost in the song made my mind just set on thinking of ghosts as I went to wash my glass up out of old Jack Daniels that I had left before we had gone out many hours earlier.

Knowing the cola I would had added to it, now for sure would be flat so at the kitchen sink I was washing the glass out for a refill when I looked up at the window.

Tim's face was steering back at me.

I nearly shit myself and I screamed like a girl as fuck it gave me a fright.

I told the others, one was chasing a spider up the wall and wasn't too interested and as for the other two who were going through my record collection telling me that I was only tripping out.

And even though I knew I had seen a ghost, it didn't feel like seeing a ghost but what I did see seemed for real.

As I looked again at the window; it seemed someone was standing outside my kitchen window so I went out turning on my security light.

Outside I went around to where I thought someone was standing back of course there was no one there.

I came back in the cottage, looking out again and it seemed that the person had reappeared.

Now my head was playing tricks on me as I went out again but no one was there but every time I came back in, again I would see the outline of someone looking in.

The next time I went out I locked myself out and so I stood at my door knocking to get back in to my cottage.

And then it hit as if what I had seen outside my own house, a vision of Tim knocking on his own front door well here I was knocking on my own front door only an hour later.

What did this mean? I tried to work out. Asking the others who were the person constantly at my window? That only I could see and no one else.

The next song to play was Stairway to Heaven by Led Zep.

I loved that song but I told my friends not now. Not while I was trying to work out who was standing at my window.

My thoughts went past ghosts, now on to death. Was what I saw outside Tim's house just me but a hour later?

Tim had died, was I to die and was that the grim reaper outside my window to come and collect me?

Though the trip hadn't gone bad, I was trying to work out what all this meant when in all honestly the visions I had been seeing were all in my own head, only coming out due to the amount of acid I had taken.

More I went on about it, more my friends apart from spider man (the friend who was connived the spider on the wall was his girl friend who had come to spy on us).

Fuck I was laughing at him even though I was coming out with some mad shit myself.

Still thinking I could see the grim reaper at my window but everything I went out again no one there so I then talked myself into believe he actually was in the glass of the window and that if I were to stand outside my front door to knock or walk on in by the front door then that for some reason was going to bring death closer to me.

I got on the kitchen bench and I opened the window and then jumped out and climbed back in from the window now putting chairs up against the front door, telling my friends they weren't to use the front door as it meant the grim reaper would get to me and maybe them all as well.

Now I was tripping off my face.......and that's putting it lightly.

This did is make them laugh.

Two of them found the Bob Dylan song that had been covered by Guns N Roses Knock Knocking on Heavens Door as a wind up on me.

Now that the window was slightly opened, I still could work out someone outside the window so I knew that it wasn't the plate of glass but it was just from me looking outward of the window that was what was making the imagine appear, a outline of a man standing there.

I tried to stop taking notice of the window as someone had put Kate Bush on. I explained that it was one of my sister's records so I put on the song Waterloo Sunset from the British band The Kinks.

The calming sounds coming from the record player, I loved the song.

As that song was playing I worked out that when I had jumped out the window the first time, while looking back through the window from the outside looking in, I didn't see no figure of a man aka the grim reaper standing on the other side of the window so that was it.

It meant we all had to be outside looking through the window only thus way, all would be ok.

Down came the chairs from the front door that I had barracked up.

I wasn't losing my mind, I merely had taken too much acid and who was madder me or my friend who was asking a daddy long leg spider "Go home and back to bed Sue."

Sue was the name of his girlfriend.

Give me some credit as I wasn't the only one heading off planet Earth.

Anyway with the help of my mates I got the settee outside and we sat outside the cottage.

It was a lovely morning, still dark but soon would be light.

We could hear the music still playing from the opened door and also the opened window but with just the couch outside I felt I needed more so next minute came out the lamp and the coffee table.

Over about the next few minutes, I actually in my front yard had the entire lounge outside in the same way as it had been set up while inside the four walls of the lounge.

Even soon had the TV outside, the stereo too through an extension cord so all the music was still playing.

I looked under the kitchen sink for more extension leads.

For whatever reasons well actually in all honest of course, no reason at all.

Soon I was shuffling the fridge out and other things from the kitchen then taking things out off my bedroom to bring outside.

Luckily we had a walk in wardrobe but as for the night table and the lamp and the phone and the bedside table including the mattress all came out to be arranged next to every other item that was now on display outside my cottage.

The bed base thank God was a wooden base which was stuck to the floor (all you needed to do was just change the mattress) as that would have meant a shotgun and the hidden drugs all would be outside.

I am just glad it was such a bed base that was a under bed cupboard and stooge space as well as a bed base.

Now as it did become light there outside the small cottage of 5a Wright St Wellington, was my house but inside out and me still climbing in and out of my kitchen window apart from when I had been moving things out.

My friend's didn't even stopped me or question why everything was to be laid outside.

They all just agreed it all looked good and once I had completed it all, the feeling of death had seemed to pass from my mind.

I sat out in the sun break and rolling up a smoke sweating from all the heavy work taking a drink of more Jack Daniels.

Me and my pals and a lost spider all got very stoned and spoke random shit that is apart from the spider.

I closed my eyes, feeling my body floating as if I were a cloud and soon with no longer a glass full of Jack Daniel in my hand but the bottle that I had replaced the glass as now even the bourbon tasted so sweet and so was the morning sun against my face.

I just sat there in the back ground with my eyes closed as the time went by soon hearing my friends leave to go home.

Leaving me there alone by 8am, one friend who had also driven up to my house the previous night went to his station wagon motor but couldn't remember how to drive so he just fell asleep on his back seat.

Latter he would tell me when he had got into his car he hadn't got in the front where the steering wheel was but he had got into the back seat.

No wonder he didn't remember how to drive as he didn't have anywhere to put the key nor a steering wheel to fix his eyes on.

His mind already scrambled by acid, was just even more so by facing the back of the driver seats.

As for my two other friends, they had gone to find one of their cars as he had driven us in town the night before.

He had rugby game he wanted to make that Saturday morning.

No way, I doubt he would himself be able to drive home as it was only like 3 hrs ago we took our last trip.

He was doubtful too about making the rugby pitch and if he had, oh I would have loved to see that match. A played on lsd would have been the dog's bullocks!

Can you just picture that now?

I can remember seeing old footage of American G I's who were given lsd by the C I A as experimenter tests, I think in the 1960s before the Vietnam war and these soldiers were only put on drill displays and many of them couldn't march correctly so fuck, imagine someone trying to play a serious game of rugby on that shit.

I soon in the sun fell asleep that morning with now no worries in life.

It seemed after all the stress from yesterday collecting the drugs and being made to take what was given to me (much stress) and from the early part of the week so much sadness over the loss of my sisters friend Tim, now that Saturday my very last thoughts were that this time last week Tim was alive and well.

I pictured Tim waking up probably around this time the week earlier, excited he was going out that evening to some party with his mates to have a great night, never knowing that that night would take his life and only 24 hrs late his body would lay on a life support system, and then his life ending when that machine was turned off.

I then thought in depth again due to the acid as your mind on acid opens up and explores so many inner thoughts as I soon was wondering when someone is brain dead, are the doctors 100% sure that the person though they may seem dead to the world that really he or she can't hear what is going on around him?

It's just isn't it, he or she can't wake from the coma or the brain damaged?

I imagined if Tim or actually anyone while lying there on a hospital bed hearing the decisions that were being made as to his or her life machine being switched off.

I hope not and I know it was the right decision that was made.

I opened my eyes slightly just to reminder myself where I was and that I myself due to the acid had not gone brain dead.

It was all fine, my eyes managed to open and I was lying on my settee looking out at all my furniture that was set out all around me, well at least I was ok for now and that the grin repeater had not come and got me on this very strange night I had, from dropping so much acid.

One thing that I seemed not to have been able to do is (though I thought I had seen Tim knocking on his door trying to get back into his place and then as I thought the grim reaper for some reason was knocking on my own door or standing outside my cottage) not to know some more death was on its way, even after the grim reaper had already taken Tim.

Though yes death seemed to have for a short period been in the air, the trip in whole didn't turn bad.

One thing taking the lsd followed by so much Jack Daniels and also coke from earlier on (and the recent joints that were smoked)it had, meant that the hurt and pain of the loss of someone I were not to feel pain when a friend or a loved one were to die when throwing down my throat loads of drugs or sniffing loads of drugs up my nose.

So to protect myself from any future heart break over losing someone if I were to lose someone close then I would just take a shit load of drugs as I had the night before when grieving over the death of Tim, my sister's soul mate and my mate.

I soon felt like touching the earth again while sitting outside in the morning sunshine.

Though the trip from the night before had pulled me left and right and all over the place I knew I have to become straight for tomorrow when I would be seeing my beautiful Mum to give her, her mother's day present as I wasn't going to disrespectful my mum by being out of it.

That's when I actually thought seriously to myself for the first time in 24 hours.

The thought was that I would after tonight the very last night party it up one more time and move these drugs out, sell them quick so there were never anymore around me which would mean I didn't have the urge to take any more of them.

As for this evening in all to come, it would be the last time I would ever take drugs as come tomorrow when I were to see my Mum I wanted her to hear again the dreams, my goals that I had set and that my future was going to be bright...bright full of sunshine so come tonight Saturday night would be my very last weekend of ever getting high again.

Yes I was looking forward to my very last night of partying but more so to actually never again taking any form of drugs again in my life.

After so many years I knew my mind and my body needed a rest and though due to Tim's death I had again gone a bit wild as in drug taking, I knew I was strong enough to say no in the future.

To give up acid and dope for good and all the other drugs that had come by my way wasn't going to be easy but really in all honesty it wasn't going to be tough either as I wasn't a junkie nor hooked on drugs....I just enjoyed taking them.

If my life wasn't going anywhere or I was in among dark clouds covering my life then it was always easy to fall back on drugs as some sort of soft comfort but if I had things in my life to look forward to then that was a good enough excuse to stop taking any drugs what so ever in the future.

Coping with Tim's passing, to do that would mean for one more night putting it to the back of my mind with the help of drugs and the thought of Liverpool hopefully lifting the F.A Cup.

Tomorrow after I were to visit my Mum, I had planned after wards I would go on and visit my sister, be there for her so she knew I was here for her.

Kieran and I by giving my sister some comfort, that in turn would I am sure make her own grieving process that much better rather than to spend Sunday evening alone by herself if she didn't wish to come out for a family dinner with us all.

Sunday evening would have been exactly a week, seven days to the moment when my sister witnessed Tim`s (her soul mates) life support machine being turned off.

I knew this would be throughout my sisters mind as she would be looking at the clock with her black cat to keep her company though each time her clock went tick it would have remained her of the movement and noises of the life support system that her Tim was connecting to and then when that final hour came, and the final minutes past, those last few seconds of Tim's life.

With that final second that the machine was stopped and Tim`s last breath taken, up on the wall I am sure the time would have been noted to the very second of the minute to the very minute of the hour.

So within her own flat this coming Sunday I was going to make sure that she my beautiful Sister wasn't alone and that her one and only brother would be there for her.

These nice thoughts wandered through my mind and with the heat now from the morning sun and not opening my eyes, I had at this point forgotten that I was still outside of my house.

I knew I was on the couch so just I thought I was in the lounge with the windows opened.

I knew what Wellington radio station was playing on the stereo after the record player had finished and I knew what Rod Stewart song was playing "Sailing Away" but I hadn't remembered I was outside with all my furniture as I was having to many nice dreams and thought of seeing the two most important girls in my whole life, my Mum and my Sister.

I drifted off even more into acid taken dreams, thinking more that I would be visiting them the following day with the other important girl in my life at the time my girlfriend Kieran.

Sleep soon followed and dreams that were acid shaken and acid filled began even more as I was now only finding happiness in these dreams of mine.

Chapter 26

YOURE NEVER WALK ALONE

SATURDAY MAY 9TH 1992

I was awoken by a kick to my shin; a pain went flying up my body as it shooked my body.

Opening my eyes the sun was bright, my face seemed tight due to being out in the NZ sun, and my head seemed all fuzzy from the acid escaping my mind and also from not drinking water.

Having such a thumbing headache, it took me a while to sit up and see who had kicked me or what had run into me.

It was Kerin, I could tell by the outline of her body and also by her blonde hair but soon it didn't take long for me to know, for sure that it was her as she opened her mouth and started to shout at me.

Loudness I didn't need to be hearing and what the hell was I doing outside and with the lamp and coffee table, magazine on top and the house phone that wasn't plugged in of course and with a bottle of very near drunken bottle of Jack Daniels as well on top of the coffee table.

The coffee table and everything else being outside as if they had been set up (as I looked around) in the same fashion as they had been inside the house.

It truly was like if you were looking inside out.

It kind of was quite arty to say the least, but not in Kieran's book did it look in any way an art form what I had done.

My memories soon coming back to me reminding last night, forgetting though about the tattoo till Kieran pointed it out on my arm while still shouting her head off.

That I couldn't be asked for it was far too early in the morning for that though it now had gone past midday so I told her to stop getting her knickers in a twist and that I will bring everything in.

Seeing the neighbour with his two kids coming back from the local shops all with smiles on their faces though they for sure all could have so heard Kerin yelling from streets away.

393

The fact that all our furniture was outside the cottage hadn't it seemed brought too much attention, but once Kiren started with her voice raised then that meant some of the nosey neighbours were steering out of their windows and wondering what all the noise was about.

Unwanted attention I for sure didn't need so I told kiren to shut up for a moment and help me get everything back in the house but she stormed past me and said she had enough as this was just madness and until I put her first before my friends then she wasn't going to be living here any longer.

I asked her what she meant.

Her reply was that due to last night not allowing her to come out with me and that I put my friends first before her and I spend too much time down at the Satan's Slaves' clubhouse, that she now truly had enough being put second.

She felt and her own friends including the friend who she stayed with last night that she was being put second.

This wasn't the truth as I gave Kiren all of my time and anything she ever wanted.

I really couldn't care what her friends had to say as I wasn't dating any them.

I couldn't be asked having a argument with Kerin while I was bringing all the furniture back into the cottage.

I told her to do whatever she wished as truly I wasn't in the mood to be having a row and that last night she only wasn't invited out as I had a few things to do before I even went up town.

It was her who decided to storm out the door when she could have just easier met me up in town once I had finished.

The thing is just to answer her question over her overreacting just meant she would carry it through to the point of carrying on the argument.

That`s exactly what she wanted that morning when she was on her way back to the cottage.........a argument.

The real reason for her rage I can guess was she had thought she had missed out on dam good night and she didn't like me spending my money on my mates as she hardly liked any of them.

She always thought they all were just my friends due to the access they had to drugs through me.

Well many looking back over that time were but the three friends from the night pervious were good solid friends.

I wasn't too fond of a few of her friends but I always kept that to myself as I was never one in a relationship to rock the boat when it was clear to see that there were many others wishing to do that and so being, they would come unstuck.

For now all I wished was to go to bed so as I dragged the mattress up the stairs over my back and threw it on the exposed bed base.

I then with a blanket and a sheet and a few pillows and a very sore head crashed on the bed in one heap but up the stairs, came Kiren still shouting at me.

Trying to tell me I wasn't to go to sleep on her, that she wanted me to sit up and speak to her.

I was just to worn out and exhausted again after bringing everything in to the house.

I needed to catch up on my sleep as I had a big night on this evening so I just placed a pillow over my head to block whatever she was saying out as all of it was negative.

I was already on a come down from the mixture of drugs from the night before. I was now so glad that I only had one more night of being wasted as after that I would never have to go through with a drug come down again.

There would be no drugs going through my body after tomorrow....Fucking great I felt with that thought in my head.

As that nice thought was going through my mind, Kiren lend over me grabbed the pillow and said she was leaving me as she couldn't believe how utterly rude I was being.

The thing is anything I had said was wrong so there was no point getting in to a debate with her as she was on the war path and bulked up with whatever her sado friend had put in her head.

Really there just wasn't any point as clearly I was in the wrong in her mind and all I said; she would just tear it to pieces.

I felt getting lost in sleep rather than in a debate, that would be the way to go for me and bring on a better feeling of bliss.

Still she wouldn't give it up! Now being told she was leaving me so I said with half humour "See ya then." and asleep I went for many hours, though for some reason not enjoying the dreams I were having now while I was tossing and turning, waking up sensing something was wrong.

What I didn't know but I very much could sense, something wasn't right.

I reached over to check the time and it was 6pm so I jumped out of bed and went down stairs plugging the phone back in to the wall and putting on some Bob Marley, listening to his track "No Woman No Cry", that's when I noticed the house looking a little different.

A few things had gone including our suitcases that were always behind the settee.

I went to take a piss in the bathroom and again things were missing in there as well.

Kiren's stuff such as her tooth brush and other items weren't in the places where they had been ever since we moved into the cottage.

I went back upstairs, opening the top set of draws. It was all empty and the other four remaining draws as well were empty.

I knew what I expected to see in the cupboard and I was right as everything had gone. I then checked my draw and a few quid had gone with an I O U note.

That wasn't unusual as she would always borrow a few quid from me when it seemed I had a bit of cash, more than normal and I would borrow a few dollars from her if I was ever short so it's not like she had stolen from me as she wasn't like that, she was very honest in every way.

I didn't need to check the drugs as there would have been no way for her to have moved me and the mattress while I was asleep plus she wasn't a thief.

She never once stole or tamped with the drugs, she may have thought that I was just holding these rolls of lsd as never had I been selling such a huge amount in the past so she would have realise that if this was the case, then it was someone else stock and she knew who my peers were.

Though they were friends, they wouldn't think twice about turning on me as such people whose only interested in that game, is making their own pockets full from the money of drugs.

Thinking of them, I needed to make some calls though I never used the house phone, I always went to phone boxes if the calls were to do with moving gear as again Loose Lips Sinks Ships.

I went out of my cottage, popping around the back of the cottage then crawled under my cottage, taking one of the bags of weed out back with me and then went knocking on my neighbour's door.

I handed him the second bag of weed and asked how he was.

He said he had seen me when he took his kids to the nearby park, and couldn't work out why all my furniture was outside.

He thought that there had been flooding from many a broken water pipe in the cottage or maybe he guessed I was painting the cottage.

He also commented that he had seen Kerin move her stuff out and that she had returned with some gothic girl.

A deep sleep I must have been in when Kieran moved her belongings out.

I didn't hear anything nor did her moving her stuff out wake me.

I thought what I woken to when I sensed something was wrong, was that Kieran had moved out.

Kiren to make some point of her earlier argument had taken it to the extreme by moving out.

I noticed she had the presents we had brought for my Mum which she had put into a basket and arranged so it looked the bee knees.

My neighbour also asked did I know one of my mates was down the path asleep in the back of his car.

After my neighbour handed me some money for some of the weed that he had managed to shift the night before (from the first bag of weed) I wandered down the pathway bagging on my mate's car.

He hadn't even made it home, he had fallen asleep and stayed a sleep so I told him to come inside and get a bite to eat.

He asked if he could have a shower as he was sure he had pissed himself in the back of the car while sleeping.

He went on to tell me he had dreamed he was a fish and he remembers going toilet while being a fish out in a plastic ocean..... Acid ah gets the best of them!!!!

At least he hadn't dreamed of going for a shit as he would have shit himself and slept in it for the day in the back of his car....Yuck!!!!

That would have been bad ah anywhere I told him I had to pop out and make some calls so for him to put his clothes in the washing machine and just to borrow some of mine.

I went out with my black book and made some calls.

I got some good response from my phone calls as some contacts wanted to take on 5 of the acid sheets.

Again tick with some money up front.

I didn't care that most was of the acid so far was out on tick as at this is minor level and it's how things worked.

Not everyone had cash like my peers did and trust wasn't an issue for me among my trusted contacts as I knew them all over years that had gone past so trust was solid as were they.

I was just happy that now I only had 7 sheets left so from 30,000 acid tabs I was down to the last 7,000 and that to me was a great result for the very first weekend.

It was due to the fact the last amount of lsd to get through all had run out many months ago so everyone wanted to get their hands on this new lot and also for themselves to stock up as they were unsure when more would be getting into the country.

All that didn't concern me as I wasn't in my eyes a drug dealer and more so after these last 7 roils of sheets of acid were to be taken then that would be the end of it all for me.

Also I only had three bags of pot to get rid of underneath the house so all was going better than expected and by the way the neighbour was moving each pound of dope was very quick.

In each pound was 16 ounces and most Kiwis who were serious smokers of weed would always buy a ounce to smoke and if not then they would take as much a 9 bar (9 ounces) in one lump.

A 9 bar he could make profile on and I too as well even though I now wasn't even selling it.

I returned back from the phone box and asked if my pal (who by now was rolling a joint) about the madness of last night.

He asked where Kiren was.

I told me to turn off Roxy Music that he had put on, and that I would tell him everything in the car as I needed him to drive down to Island Bay so to get rid of this acid.

I didn't want anyone else first getting to the contact, who asked me for the acid as he said he had called my number that day many times and when he couldn't get through to me, he had called around leaving messages for others who he knew could supply him with what he was looking for.

I knew I had to be the first to get to him before he had brought it from someone else.

I wasn't sure how much lsd had come in off that flight but I knew it was enough to flood the capital of lsd and also within time the entire country.

I was only a peanut in one big jar so I knew there were many peanuts that also had been given sheets of lsd to move among the city and beyond.

I had missed all the calls earlier that day as the phone all day had been outside with me, unplugged.

Also when I finally plugged the phone in, well as I was fast asleep in bed then I didn't hear it ring once as I was out to the world though unlike my friend I wasn't a fish in a plastic ocean pissing myself.

My mate's car didn't smell to bad with every window opened as we spoke about the random night we had just had.

He mentioned tripping out the night earlier so much that he thought the spider on the wall was his girlfriend spying on.

I told him about the grim reaper standing outside the house in my trip.

We laughter when we thought back to the night and what a wicked night we all had together but separately.

I then told him more in-depth of what I could remember about the film I had seen; though I was too wasted to follow the storyline but I went on to tell him about remembering seeing World War Two (The Blitz) in the movie over London.

Which then made the name The Krays pop in to my head and that's when I said it was The Krays that I was meant to have gone and seen?

He asked me who The Krays were?

I told the little I knew what my Mum had told me and how that my father said they had given him lucky break in the 1960s but apart from that I only knew that they maybe were nightclub owners, nothing more I knew.

We both agreed they must have been more than simply nightclub owners for a film to be made about them.

We decided to catch the movie that night.

The F.A Cup wasn't staring on television till 3am in the morning so we decided that once we left the drop off in Island Bay, that we would race home and get on the drink, check to see how much coke we had and even maybe take a trip to start the evening, how we left it off from the night before.

From seeing The Doors Movie, Pink Floyds movie The Wall and the other movies I had seen on acid then why not watch this film also on acid.

We got back to my place like a flash and I called a few more mates, Sasaka came over and though he didn't want to touch the acid, he rolled up some weed and many joints were going around the lounge all at once.

Sasaka was one who didn't enjoy tripping but he very much enjoyed smoking weed so we all got really stoned and went through all the remaining beer.

I gave one of pals some dollars to go down the local bottle store near the cricket ground to get some more beers and booze and also to give Carl the pizza guy (whose father owned the pizza shop) a ounce of dope, in return cash from the till and also some pizzas that would be for our dinner.

I hadn't eaten since I was at the Diner in the middle of the previous night. so I was very hungry plus I never wish to drink more booze on a empty tummy.

We all ate a few of the half dozen pizzas that were given to me. Now we were all full, we could do a line of coke each.....Sorted I thought!!!!

I jumped in the shower while they played some Red Hot Chilli Peppers on the sound system.

After a splash of aftershave and a black shirt was thrown on, two of the three of us dropped a acid tab and went to see the movie. Everyone again feeling high and looking forward to what this movie was going to be about and finally I would get to find out who The Krays were.

I met my best friend Chris Mitchell outside the movie house, he was happy to drop half a tab of acid though not to do a full tab as he wasn't too keen on acid, but he didn't say no to a few lite up joints outside the theatre.

We all went in, not knowing at the time we would have looked like a little firm, though in those day back in NZ I didn't know the word Firm nor what it meant as we only ever called a group of guys who looked a bit tasty as in naughty, a gang rather than the British meaning a Firm.

The movie was (what we all thought) great and I got to see who The Krays actually were. Yes, as my father had said there were naughty indeed but hell even more than that, they were proper naughty British gangsters.

I had never heard of British gangsters, only American gangsters....that were until I saw this movie.

It was such an eye opener. I wasn't to know that the movie wasn't all truth as in the way neither of the twins had great influence over the making of the film, that I wouldn't know for many a years.

For now though the movie blew my mind and the sight of British gangsters (though it was only a movie I had seen but one based on real British Gangsters) and more so these two men... Ronnie Kray and his twin Brother Reggie Kray aka The Krays.

The area of London that had been part of my father's own past, at the age that I now was as my father was only 16 years old when he first went to the East End and he lived there till he was 23 years old (nearly 8 years of his life).

After watching the film I (it would have been again due to the acid trip I was on) wanted to know more as the film finished when they had attended their Mothers funeral in the early 1980s.

I wasn't even sure if they were still alive or had they died in jail or even maybe if they had been released.

Me and even a few of my pals all wanted to know more but it was me who would take it a step further than anyone else and that no one could ever imagine how much I would take it on and also to the extent that I would go to finding more about them The Krays and making contact with them if I could.

But for now was the F.A Cup soon to be watched so we all went and got on the drink throughout Wellington.

I had forgotten my Liverpool Football Club scarf at home so I reached home in a taxi with Sasaka.

I wanted to drop off some of the money that I had been carrying from Island Bay as it wasn't my money and I didn't want to be spending any of it so I put it away and hide it well.

Then I said to Sasaka as I played a Dean Martin record, it remained me of the mob in America.

I called my father; it would have been 11am in the morning in Scotland so I hoped to catch him before he headed to the pub for his first pint.

I again asked him after telling I had seen the movie of The Krays, but he told me to stop asking even more questions about them. He wasn't going to tell me anything to do with the Krays or their whereabouts or if they were still alive and for me not to even think of trying to contact them.

To make contact with them, err that meant they still were alive.

I was quite drunk by now, I said "Well if you not going to help then I will find them myself."

I put down the phone and thought who the hell could I ask if they were still alive? I thought well if the movie portrays them as the most well known gangsters in all of the UK then one place of course would know where they were so I called international dictionary and asked for Scotland Yard.

Now known as New Scotland Yard, I was given a number so I called it and was put through to a man saying "Hello, This is New Scotland yard, how may I help?" so I asked straight up "Where are the Kray twins?"

Now you got to remember I was a teenage kid and one on acid.

One who (that due to my father not willing to answer any of my questions) that with all in my head as in the acid trip made me do what I was doing.

I know for a fact if I had gone to see the same movie straight and not high then it wouldn't have had this effect on me but being high and denied any more knowledge from my Father made me seek out more and more.

What I heard down the phone was for the very first time the word "Bollocks!".

Hand on heart that's what the guy on the other end of the phone said before he hanged up.

I tried Kray surname on international directory for London but there were none listed.

I tried the Blind Beggar pub; I had seen the name of the pub in the film though that number was ex directory.

I don't know why I was trying to call that pub.

I think (I guessed) it must have been run by them though another fact I would be wrong with in time.

I would come to find out that they didn't even drink in that pub; it wasn't theirs or even one of their regular pubs.

Next call was to the Home Office as I didn't know who else would be able to help me.

Back then it's not like these days when you simply at a click of a button such as Google for any information and you're sorted as I don't even think the internet was running then, even so if it was there were no internet cafes, and I didn't even know how to work a computer so the only way I could make movement is by using a telephone and hope for pot luck with whoever was coming into my mind that could possibly help.

It was only the help of the New Zealand telecom women who told me to try the Home Office as New Scotland Yard were of no help though I couldn't blame them as what cheek to call them up in the first place asking where Ronnie and Reggie were.

I was then given my second number that being the Home Office so I called and a lady answered asking me which dept or extension did I wish to be put through to.

I was in luck as when I asked about The Krays she didn't say bollocks nor did she hang up the phone though she said she herself didn't know where either one was though she did know that both hadn't be freed and she couldn't remember if both twins were actually still alive.

She did say she was sure they were still somewhere in the prison system as if one had died it would have been big news and she would have remembered but she couldn't help apart from tell me of a jail directory that was in the public domain and that could be found at libraries (I am sure) she said.

I told her I was all the way in New Zealand, she said she couldn't help anymore. I thanked her for being at least this kind and I took the name down of the directory that she spoke about.

Not knowing that it was the Home Office who held the power to keeping both the twins in jail.

Including Reggie, many years later even after he had served his recommend 30 year jail sentenced.

I just thought the Home Office was like a directories company, themselves that dealt with any subject as in "home meaning the UK" and that as it had the word "Office" on the end of the title meaning it was must just be that, an office.

I hadn't a clue it was part of the British Government.

Well I with Sasaka had come to a dead end but at least I had something which was scribbled down on a piece of paper and as for the phone bill well it was too much to think about for now. I would wait for it when it came in the post to see how much the costs so far would be from my inquiries of whereabouts of The Notorious Kray twins.

As for the internet I didn't have access to that and I never knew how to even turn on a computer so unlike now in these day one has to just Google something but back in the 1990s, I had no idea what the internet was about and there were no internet cafes so I knew my next visit would have to be the library but the time was nearing now midnight.

After all that, for now it all had to be put on hold as in three more hours over in London at Wembley Stadium was going to be the world famous F.A Cup Final.

That was something that I knew a lot about and this evening the best football team in all of the history of the beautiful game, Liverpool was going to be playing against Sunderland.

This to me took my mind off The Krays and very much on to such players such as Ian Rush and Robbie F and John Barns and every player who had a red shirt on with a LFC badge.

LFC were by far the most passionate football team in the world. I had a good feeling that LFC would be lifting that F.A Cup and they would again be the Kings of the F.A Cup.

How great it would be if they could do this, lift the F.A Cup on the year that they had been playing football for 100 years.

I looked down to my tattoo that was still scabbed up, you still could see through the dried blood what it was a symbol of and that was Liverpool Football club "You'll never walk alone".

It made me so proud being a LFC supporter.

Sasaka found two more scarf's, one I had since I we really young and the other one my grandparents in the UK had sent over to me for the recent Christmas, four months earlier.

With these in hands, we jumped in the waiting taxi to meet up with the others as we had three hours of serious drinking to take place. We hurried to reach the others all whom I had convicted them that there was only one team ever to support though I had a feeling a few of them were Manchester Utd closet fans.....There are always a few of them.

We hit the bars and hit them hard and drank (we sure very much did, spending so much money at each bar) and ranking in drinks that I didn't even know what they were as by this time all the bars now had gone trendy in Wellington.

We were doing loads of shots, not just shots off vodka were being served but shots that didn't even taste of booze though all had a massive hit when the cold air had hit us.

One club we went to was playing great live Irish music, that I remember as the music went through my body while I was taking yet another acid trip.

Someone had given me some ecstasy powder that I thought was coke so I snorted it in the toilet of the club for my nose to burn like hell and what turned out to be pure ecstasy.

Fuck did I know it by the time I reached the bar and asked for my normal Jack and coke and a shot of vodka.

I used to drink like a fish when out and about; maybe to be honest I used to drink far too much.

Weekends I would drink so much booze which was due to taking loads of drugs and not being able to get pissed if you were only going to be drinking beers all night.

I wouldn't be a solo drinker of just spirits, but by this time of my life I had already Jack Daniels tattooed on me due to the amount of that type of Bourbon I had already consumed in my teenage years.

Jack would get myself into mischief be in good or bad. If I drank it neat like a litre of it by myself which was a common thing for me to do then I was sure to go to hell and back again after the last drop from the bottle hit my lips and went into my body.

My mates told me the following day that when this club closed and we headed outside, I was all over the show walking along cars bonnets and roof tops of cars on one of the main streets in the city singing for some reason Billy Idol songs...very badly.

They went onto tell me that I was jumping on cars for fun and dancing at a set of traffic lights till they had to pull me down before any police were called.

I wasn't (they said) doing any harm and I wasn't thrashing the cars that I been stepping on, I was just buzzing of my nut and what I thought was my own yellow brick road well if it meant there was a car in the way then over the top I would step.

They got me in to downtown near Courtney Place where the all 24hour Diner was open.

You could get hot food and listen to great music on their juke box; they had a few doormen on as the place would have fights if gang members turned up.

I knew the doormen really well, two Fijian guys, one a very good boxer and both could knock a man out within a second.

True born fighters, they were always sweet with me I had been drinking in this place before they even were on the door here so they knew I was always welcomed and they knew I was part of the Satan's Slaves, so not many doormen would ever turn you away as they knew what would happened.

Normally if they ever turned away a Satan Slave member or prospect, then that doorman/doormen would be confronted within half an hour by men who you wouldn't wish to fuck with or to be followed home by, as no one who upset the Satan's Slaves Motorcycle Club in that city would get away with it.

Most of the members of the Satan's Slaves were mad and very cold hearted, most of them though not all but they wouldn't think of stabbing you or shooting you while smiling and looking into your eyes if you had ever crossed them.

I had my back covered when people knew I was very well connected to the Satan's Slaves and as for the owner of the Diner, he knew that very much so as well.

At this time over seven oceans away in London, United Kingdom on that Saturday afternoon of each year, the most talked about Saturday in the history of England.

Up and down the whole country on every television screen, be it in everyone's homes, every single pub, every single hospital television and even Royal households televisions and every prison, every post office, even customs house, all of their televisions will be turned onto the BBC as this Saturday is the F.A Cup.

Now again Liverpool are the club to have won it many times more than most of the other football clubs and that year was even more heartfelt if they were to lift the cup as it was 100 years of the Liverpool football club that was 1882-1992.

Though this year 2009 while I write this book, its 20 years since 98 of Liverpool fans were killed in a terrible incident as Hillsborough where Liverpool were playing against Nottingham Forest in the semi final of the F.A Cup.

Such horrible scenes happened in the grounds as the police and stewards allowed for some stupid reason thousands upon thousands more fans into the area where Liverpool fans were and it caused people to be crushed to death.

Back in those days there were high fences between the pitch and the crowds, due to crowd troubles back in the 1980s and pitch invasions.

Well it cost young kids and their fathers and many Mothers their lives that evening.

It is something as a child watching on television back in New Zealand with my own father, I will never forget.

It was one horror that will always stay with me as there live on telly, unfolding in front of your own eyes.

That year was one of the hardest finals ever played against their main rival; the only other Liverpool based team Everton.

1989 Liverpool went onto win it, in memory of their fans and all those families that had lost loved ones.

1992 Liverpool were in the final against (a North East team of England)) Sunderland at Wembley and kick off was soon.

Ever since I was a kid I have never missed a F.A Cup final where ever in the world I may have been and whatever age I was.

More so since my Dad died, as this was something that as a young lad I would be woken in the middle of the night so to watch the F.A Cup.

If my Dad was working away at sea in the month of May he took me aboard whatever vessel he was working on so we didn't miss out on the F.A Cup

The early hours of MAY 10TH 1992, after already partying hard all of the evening and not remembering a hour or so that passed (after I had snorted the pure ecstasy by mistake) I was told even more of the remaining night after the game was over though that part I do not have any memory of at all as I hadn't stopped slowing down on drugs or drink as remember this was going to my very last night of ever getting this messy.

I was told I made even Maoris that night became Liverpool Fans and Tongans and a few Cook Islanders as well.

I watched the match from a rugby clubhouse where earlier there had been a wedding reception held in there.

There were loads of people hanging around the entrance of it which I spotted as myself and three of my pals walked pass this rugby club house.

We were on way home to watch the game then I thought of the rugby clubhouse as they always played the matches in the morning hours from major sporting events around the world, such as rugby test matches that were played in the UK.

I thought I would try my luck to see if they were open and showing the F.A Cup as it would have been more fun there than just to watch it on the telly back in the cottage.

I didn't want to miss the kick off that's for sure.

I saw lights on from across the rugby pitch, the time was like 230am in the morning, kick off was 3am New Zealand time.

We headed over, very drunk across the pitch to where the tacky sounding music was being played and the lights were on.

There was many tough looking Pacific Islanders peeing, being sick, fighting and smoking dope in front of us as we walked over to outside the entrance of the rugby clubhouse.

My mates said to me "Christian let's keep on going as it anit a nice bunch of people."

They were right but me being me and slightly drunk, I had just turned 17years old(a few weeks back) so thought I was all grown up now not being 16years old but now 17 years old.

I stepped up and wandered into the clubhouse, up the stairs I went with many wedding guests looking on. Thinking to themselves "Who the hell does he think he is?"

With a yell to my pals who didn't wish to follow me, I shouted at them "Come on lads we need to find a television screen" "We gotti watch the kick off for my Dad over in the UK"

Though my Father and I were many miles apart, we knew each other would be on this single day of our lives be watching the F.A Cup as we had all of my life.

I get to the dance floor to be told by some six foot six heavy that the party was over and who invited me anyway?

As more giants came upon the dance floor, though by the looks of their faces I knew they weren't surrounding me to dance, I knew I was in for a hiding by just the looks on my pal's faces.

My mates all were shitting bricks not for themselves but dear old me being surrounded by Salmons on the dance floor.

The disco lights still flashing different colours of the rainbow and then suddenly the music stopped................

The dj microphone went too loud speaker " There is a taxi for a Mr and Mrs Smith." and with that suddenly the baying mob had turned their attention away from me aka the white kid and started hugging and kissing this couple who were leaving for their awaiting taxi that had just been called out for them.

With all them to one side and only a dj to get pass, I was still in time hopefully to reach the television that was on a brace up at the wall.

This lot, the rugby club couldn't afford a projection screen, or maybe one of the Maoris in the team had nicked it.

I headed towards it but was pulled back by a girl asking if I were someone's cousin?

"Do I look black?" was going to be my reply but no I just said yes, with that I was slapped in the face and told never to sleep with Mary again behind Jenny's back.

Who the hell was Mary?

Why oh why did I say I was someone's cousin?

Well the slap I was given by this angry girl had my mates laughing to themselves.

The first smiles that appeared on their faces since following me up the stairs; also the dj was waging a chuckle to himself so I went over and asked him what was going on, not with the slap but with the party.

He explained it had been a wedding reception and that Mr and Mrs Smith were the newlyweds and that 3am was party time finished so that's why everyone leaving including the bride and groom.

"No I got to watch the kick off at 3am, the F.A Cup!!"

"The what?" he replied

"The F.A Cup, Liverpool against Sunderland" I told him ever so proudly.

"Isn't that where the Beatles are from?" he replied, and with that he put on a Beatles song.

I wasn't there to listen to The Beatles (though I am a Beatles fan, of course) he went on to tell me he was a huge fan of The Beatles.

That's what made him a dj as he was crap at singing, but he loved their music and though he couldn't get much nightclub work as The Beatles weren't really nightclub music so he stuck with weddings where everyone loves The Beatles music being played.

Well I had found a new friend as long as he would switch the telly on so my mates and I could watch the match.

Once the song had played, he informed me that the club caretaker had got so rotten drunk much earlier in the evening that he was sick everywhere so had to go home, and as he (the dj) is a trustee at the rugby club then he the dj was left the keys to lock up after everyone had gone and so he would be more than happy to put the telly on so to see Liverpool play.

It must have been one cheap wedding if even the fucking dj was part of the club.

There still seemed some crates of beer left under a few of the tables but no sign of left over wedding cake.

We took our chairs and sat with the lights dim, the disco light now off.... Thank God.

And with a few drunken Samoans, who couldn't make it down the stairs to the exit point, we were all one happy though drunken wee little family.

75% of them never watched a football game in their lives but all was good.

As the teams lined up in the tunnel of the Wembley stadium, I explained to everyone the history of the F.A Cup.

The pride that Liverpool FC brought to me, and explained that in the UK many miles away was my Dad maybe with my Granddad that would be both watching the same match that we all were about to watch.

I explained to everyone that also this was also on the 100 Years of Liverpool FC 1892-1992 since the club was formed.

Now could there be history written on the walls, could Liverpool F.C win the F.A Cup on this very special year for club, players and supporters and a few drunken Samoans.

LFC did go and win the match and lift the F.A Cup once again.

What a one hell of a party was that afterwards at this little rugby clubhouse in Wellington after the match was played and the F.A Cup had been lifted by Liverpool's team captain and players.

Even the sound of The Beatles music was still being played past 830am in the morning.

It was the kid's Jrn rugby teams and their parents arriving for their kids local rugby games at 9am that stopped the party and the caretaker in hand who thought what the fuck.

"Hey some weddings jus go on and on!"

The dj by now hammered from too much drink, gave us a wink to me and said to the caretaker as we helped him down the stairs with his dj box and disco ball.

I even called my Dad in Scotland at the rugby clubhouse.

I can recall that as the caretaker let me use the phone in the mangers office, he didn't know my father lived in Scotland, until that is when they would have got the phone bill.

I called my Father for him to hear his son's celebrations, "We did it Dad, another F.A Cup!!!!"

"You'll never walk alone!" were my last words as I put down the phone.

I was the happiest young man in the whole world.

My pals and I headed home, how I can't remember as the last thing I recall is taking a kick at the disco ball that was leaning against the dj car and missing the ball completely though making a dent in the side of the dj car.

My pals said we all kept on partying it up back at my place to carry on with the celebrations even getting a few bottles from The Diner over the counter on the way home in the taxis.

Spending a few hundred on that alone and also being told I took one of their ice buckets that I said I was simply borrowing and then when arriving home I told them all that I wanted a party inside and outside the cottage so all the street could hear the celebrations of Liverpool lifting the cup.

They said the Nomad neighbour came over even though it was early hours of the morning.

His dog had had a litter of pups; a few weeks back so I told him drunkenly I would buy one of the puppies for Kiren which I did, giving him £100 for a pit bull pup and then dressing it up with a hat and a sunflower from the back garden.

They said I did the moving of the furniture again for no reason at all but they couldn't stop me as they said I was merely saying I was cleaning the house.....

Again you can only blame the acid.

They all said they left just before midday as they all had to go to their own homes as it was the morning of mother's day 10th of May,1992

Ever since that night the F.A Cup has meant more to me than just football.

The F.A Cup ever since always brings me back to that night when I watched LFC beat Sunderland in that F.A Cup final.

The Liverpool tattoos that I have on me, one that I got on only the Friday evening, the night before of that F.A Cup Final means a lot as it brings me back to this certain weekend in my life.

That certain tattoo is as much of a reminder of that weekend as it has to do with Liverpool FC football club 100 Years.

As for why I got Liverpool football Carlsberg sponsor tattooed on me, I am unsure so again let's blame the acid trip for that one.

As for the crest of the LFC I have well that is now to do with my memories of my Dad as he always was there for me as in my passion for Liverpool FC and throughout my life up to his death so that tattoo again is more than about just football but Family.

As for the Liverpool FC symbol then that's a reminder to a part of my childhood early memoires of happiness as following Liverpool football club has been a huge part of my life and one of the most early childhood memories of mine and dreams of mine that I had wished to have seen LFC play live, be in a F.A Cup final or a home game at Anfield with my Dad but it's one dream, that never was to come true.

Sunday afternoon, my pals had come back to make sure I was ok.

Of course I was and I now had my own family things to do but also I needed to get a little more sleep as I felt dreadful, completely drained.

I said to my mates goodbye and they thanked me for one of their best weekends they had ever had and for me it was as well, more so with LFC lifting the F.A Cup.

Before my friends left I told them that the weekend that just been was a massive blow out as in a binge partying harder than most weekends I had as I was now given up all drug use and also I wouldn't be selling any more dope and I finally was going to take the future by two hands.

Their response wasn't too supportive as I had wished but that didn't bother me as I had made the decision and I didn't care if they still would be carrying on partying without me.

That was fine as at the end of the day they were good mates, it showed that day by them returning to check on me, making sure I was ok.

Friends like that are hard to come by. They weren't users like many other friends who were in my life at the time.

These three friends Chris Mitchell, Sasaka Campbell and Nick Robertson were good people, like brothers in arms.

They left and I went to sleep, shattered I was but with now a puppy running amuck in my cottage.

I fed the pup some nice food from the fridge and then I crashed out.

Nightmares then filled up my sleep.

All very unsettling nightmares they were, not knowing to myself that a real living nightmare soon was to come upon me and one that I wouldn't be able to wake up from.

I would be living it for real within a few hours after I had woken from these nightmares I was suffering from, while I slept on Mother's Day 1992.

Chapter 27

MOTHERS DAY

SUNDAY 10th of MAY 1992

On that Sunday my girlfriend arrived to cottage as she had not heard from me since she moved out the day before.

I hadn't known where she had gone since leaving yesterday. I just guessed one of her friend's houses.

I didn't want to be hassling her yesterday, while she made her point and more so after her yelling at me yesterday morning when she turned up.

I really didn't need the stress and also I had slept all day, then I had to get to Island Bay and then with going to the movies and with the F.A Cup I just didn't find the time to be calling around finding, out where she was.

I knew I would get a frosty reception from some of her friends if I called around asking for Kiren so I didn't bother but I guess I should have.

Kerin pulled into our street, turning the corner to first see what appeared to be our fridge yet again, and then on the outside of our fence was what appeared to be our lounge and coffee table and a empty ice bucket and two glasses.

As she stepped out of her car not knowing what to think as for her it must have felt like did de java as she walked up the pathway to discover on the pathway our washing machine and through the gates to our front entrance of our little two storey cottage was there, our mattress including the bedside table with lamp still sitting on it next to a magazine about motorcycles called Live To Ride.

What the hell must have been going through her mind?

She slowly got out her keys, while calling out my name and placed the key in the door gaining entrance, she noticed that the bathroom window was opened as she looked through the house from the outside looking inwards.

The bathroom window she shut around the back of the cottage, and there she saw me through the window laying outside in the sunshine.

I have been told snoozing away in the morning day light; sleeping like a baby, no cares in the world and a silly smile that was she said years later was on my face.

I may have been in a deep sleep, on acid dreaming the maddest and happiest dreams though I can tell you now that she for sure wasn't smiling as she stepped over me after looking around the house seeing all that was outside that all was meant to be inside.

At the bottom of her feet, she felt the rubbing against her of soft fur. Looking down there was a puppy wearing a homemade tiny torn hat, wagging his or her tail up at my girlfriend.

The hat looked to be made out of a big of straw hat and with a half eaten sunflower sticking out the hat.

The puppy in Kerens eyes, looked like it had just returned from Woodstock.

With that she knew all of this, as in a hippy dog appearing wearing a hat and the content of the house being outside rather than inside where it should be, was all due to acid again.....She wasn't impressed one little bit but did I give a shit, no as she was my ex- she had walked out on me the day before so whatever she thought well I really couldn't give a fuck about.

I and my friends had taken the night before as we saw it and that was to have a wicked night as no way was I going to stay indoors upset that my girl had just left me as one thing I wasn't going to get is all shaken up over her leaving me.

Yes I loved her loads but one thing I never would do and that is walk out on her as she had done on me rather than try and talk things through.

Kiren was thinking here and now she was actually happy that she didn't join us as what the hell had gone on in the time she had stormed out to the time now where she was standing there in her words what seemed like a art house film.

She found herself speechless as she peered out the window now noticing that the out lay of all the belongings outside of the house were in the same position if they had been in the house as in the lounge outside was in the same format when it had been set in our lounge. I am sure in some ways this made her smile and maybe laugh but all in all she just wasn't happy at all.

Things had come too far and this was a trip too far as she called her girlfriend explaining what she had come back to.

Some of her friends loved me; others didn't maybe due to some being free loading girls who loved access to free drugs.

I have known over my life many girls who love ya for that and that alone, many being friends of girlfriends through my life (you all know who you are).

I can spot them a mile away and as they all play the same old game, they truly do think they have always got one up on me but they don't realising they just making themselves to be drug whores, fact !!

Anyway during her conversation from yesterday she decided to move out until I had sorted my shit out as in no more acid to that volume inside the house, our house as she didn't mind a few acid trips to be taken among us, but as for selling the shit on bigger scale than in the past then, she wasn't having any of it.

Until I had give the acid back (was what she demanded) then only then would she move back in as she didn't want to be dating a drug dealer.

Something at the time I didn't really see myself as because I was only ever mainly selling dope.

Dope just made everyone stoned....no harm in that.

It's not like I was hanging around school gates selling the shit to kids and as for acid well there was not one person back in my early days that had a bad trip and to go on acid trips with people was just unbelievable.

It was something else and so many, too many stories to tell of the good times up to this point I had on acid. I loved the shit and so did every kiwi I knew who loved acid back in those days.

As for coke I never sold that, as that were a different game all together different folk and not the type of people I wanted them to know that I was selling any type of drug.

They aren't junkies, they are the type of people who would come knocking at 4am asking for a gram of coke and I didn't need that.

As for ecstasy, it was a expensive drug back in those days the early 1990s in New Zealand.

Ecstasy really had only hit the black market a few years earlier so anyone who had it was selling it only for hard cash and not on tick.

Trust me there were enough people out there who had cash to buy the shit and there were loads of people taking the stuff each and every weekend in every main city throughout New Zealand.

This was before certain people I knew started to make the stuff themselves to sell.

Good people to know until either their house was blown up due to drug making in their kitchens or when the cops would come crashing through their doors busting them for making the stuff.

It was a battle between drug suppliers and the Mr Big vs. the police and it always seemed like Wellington more than any other part of the country was the place where drugs were always in large supply.

Where everyone from every different walk of life wished to spend their weekends in a alter state of mind, be simply just enjoying some weed for the weekend or if they could afford to some coke or if they loved to, then some acid.

I knew city workers who loved the coke, to lawyers and doctors and shop keepers to the girl next door, everyone in many social circles in the 1990s, in Wellington seemed fucking high and that's fact !!

It wasn't just the underclass or the gangs that would be smoking and rolling, it would be every Dick, Tom and Harry that would be spaced out or smiling into the night stars.

My girl as she packed another suitcase upstairs in our bedroom was glad that our wardrobe was a fitted one as that's all that was in bedroom as she loaded up her car once again.

One of her friends and her boyfriend arrived and put all the expensive stuff back into the house as in the telly that sat on our pathway for anyone to nick and the stereo but everything that was of bulk, they left outside.

Kiren went to show her friends me laying there in the middle of the grass in the back small yard but she heard the phone ringing from inside the house so she went inside to answer the phone with a puppy in one hand, she missed the call by seconds.

I always wonder if this call was my Mum before she left on her journey that morning heading back to Wellington after her weekend away.

Had I missed a call that could have changed things?

My Mum was unsure of going on her planned weekend away due to Friday night when she felt something a drift to the point of leaving her insurance documents out for us the kids to find in case something terrible was going to happen.

I and my girl both had brought her something lovely as a gift, in letting my mum know that I loved her dearly.

I had turned 17 only a few weeks earlier so I was no longer 16 years old and now a man in my young eyes.

I didn't have to wait to be 18 years old to be seen as a man as back all those years ago after my father left the house, I was in many ways already a young man.

I just wanted on Mother's Day of this year truly to embrace my Mum for all she herself had been through and how strong of a woman that she was.

With me it all didn't turn out as she had wished for or hoped for in her eyes. I knew she never saw me a failure.

That's because of the kindness that was always throughout my heart and how I never would go out my way to hurt anyone.

How many times I would always put others first and how much of a gentleman I was.

Unlike my Father as in never hitting a women though I did have a flare in me when it came to having blazing rows but that was due to always sticking up for myself and never letting anyone bad mouth me, but in general I had turned out to be a decent kid.

Yes I know the crime involvement I was in, wasn't good nor was the fact that I was selling dope but without the crime related activities that I had found myself being part of over the years, if I hadn't got into drugs on any scale, any level then I myself, the person who I was, was a good kid and with a decent heart.

I was very well liked and a good friend to have. I have to thank my mum for a lot as if it wasn't for her then maybe I would have turned out to be a bastard and I would have gone off the rails at an early age, worse than I did.

Hell with a background I had and my years growing up then of course on my journey in life I would take a few slides and slip here and there.

Fuck up a lot I did but also made up a lot of wasted ground as in of whom I was becoming as a young man up to that age and that was a gentle soul unlike that of my Fathers.

So to have had Mother's Day with my Mum to look forward to, even my own girlfriend knew how important this day was going to be for me so as she left me that day laying there among the grasshoppers and the butterflies flying over me and the bees buzzing around carrying their morning honey.

Kiren promise herself that today after she had calmed down yet again, she would be back so to spend the lovely late afternoon we had planned with my Mum on that Mothers Day 10th of May 1992.

A note written by Kiren (not so much a Dear John note) was left on the front door for me to read as she had locked up all the windows and shut the front door and left.

The only way in this time for me was the proper way in as in using the front door.

Morning soon passed and I still was making more Zzzzzzs laying there.

I wasn't the first to get to read the note, as another friend had rocked up to my place, and only on reading the note that stated my girlfriend had left me sleeping in the backyard was how he discovered me.

He threw some water on me from his bottle of water as I was in a proper deep sleep.

What people didn't know at this time of my life, the sleeping tables that my Mum used to have hidden at her place I used to take some of them, when I first discovered them back when I was young in Miramar?

My Mum used to take them when her and my father used to row and she would be beaten as I am sure this is the only way she found sleep on the nights that she couldn't escape the house.

With such types of drugs such as sleeping tablets, you end up getting addictive to them as times goes by.

Something I would learn for myself over the years, as I used them at such an early age to drown out the noise I would hear coming from my parent's bedroom.

Another reason why I would take them was so I didn't hear the man who I called the monster come tapping on my window during the night.

Now and then I would sneak a few of the tablets as only because I found them next to my mum's bed and the very first time not knowing what they were and maybe guessing they were just adult sweets.

The very first one I took it knocked me out. I do recall the high I got off it first and how the sleep I had was undisturbed which to me was heaven.

All my early years of sleeping were always full of nightmares or waking up not being able to breathe due to asthma.

Some nights awaking up hearing the tapping at my window, be it from that creepy man or other nights from the tree branches that would tap against my window when the winds were howling down the side of my house.

Worse of all that would wake me up was my mum's scream of terror would be heard.

As I got older I would still carry on taking them, not so much when I was send to boarding school but very much when I had been expelled from the second boarding school and I was again living with my mum.

I had no need to take them but on seeing them again in my Mums bedroom I would take a few maybe I guess as like some sort of security blanket or as they did bring me good memoires as in whatever was going on in my life at the time when I first discovered sleeping tablets then to shut all the bad stuff out that was going on in my life.

I would drop a tablet or two and then with a little wait, soon would be followed by a lovely wave of calmness and a gentle close of my eye lids.

I would be in a beautiful place and I can recall my dreams would always be so vita and real like. It was a nice place being asleep and this I kept on returning to as in taking these tablets most of my life.

Addiction to them was so hard to beat. Never knowing how harmful they were to your body and also your mind plus the risks of mixing them with other drug taking.

I always mixed them with booze and other drugs when I got older plus always taking many a times too many, to the point of being so close to dying in my sleep without even knowing.

In my teenage years when I started to take more party drugs and more so acid, well the only way I found to stop a acid trip as I would take a fair few acid tabs (You could trip for days on end) sometimes needing to stop tripping especially in my case when I was selling the shit so I would take a sleeping tablet and that would bring on sleep.

I could function normal the next day, whatever I would be getting up.

Here was my friend throwing that water on me, and waking me up out of a deep sleep because if I had been out in the sun all day, I for sure would have blister.

Without any water either in me and all the drugs going around my system I would have got heat stroke and in sunny countries like New Zealand, though of course more so Australia, you can die from that very quickly.

How weird my main concern was heat strike rather than taking and mixing too many drugs up.

I got to my feet slowly and was taken into the cottage, now I was noticing the fridge and the washing machine outside on the pathway and my bed next to my front door.

It was no longer even funny to me as it meant I would have to yet again bring it all back in again, which I didn't need as I was feeling so dam ruff.

I asked my friend to help me take my bed into the cottage. What was the rush he asked as he said all the furniture outside looked cool but I wasn't in the mood with what looked fucking cool or not.

By this time many of the neighbours had been steering over at us so I really didn't need any more attention to the house.

The bed and the heavy washing machine soon followed by the fridge came in.

Everything that was out there, from the lamp to the Live to Ride magazine then was brought back into my cottage.

We placed most things where they should be and as for the lounge, I just moved the mattress in there as was too exhausted to get it all the way up the stairs.

I moved the lounge against my cottage as that didn't look odd as many places had lounges or chairs and tables outside their front door so you could sit in the sun and drink ya cold beers while chatting to your neighbours across the fence (that is if you got on with ya neighbours).

My mate were putting the washing machine onto the taps again so it would be back in working order and while he was doing this I went upstairs to first feel for my shotgun to make sure it was still there.

I felt the end of the shot gun and down further I reached with my finger tips and could count how many rolled up sheets of acid there was. I knew all was intact and everything was fine as I removed my arm quickly from the bed base and headed back down the stairs, after throwing a blanket over the bed base and some pillows so it formed what looked like a bed for the time being.

My friend had the note that Kiren had left was in his back pocket. He had forgotten he had taken it from the door so passed it up to me. I put it in my pocket for the time being as I went down the remaining stairs to get a much needed glass of water.

He asked me about the night before. I didn't at the time remember much of it though very much did remember the football and really that was it in the latter part of the evening and more so the early hours were blank as in memory.

He said it sounded like a good night to be had by all. He wasn't too far off from that I said to him.

I really had to get more sleep so I asked him could he return tomorrow to discuss in length what he had come to me for.

I thanked him for helping get everything back in for me from outside, and told him I would call him tomorrow "We would do some lunch, go to one of the Chinese restaurants that my Father knew the owners." I said to him as he walked out the door.

The Chinese people behind a certain restaurant always were so good to my Father whenever he dined there.

The restaurant was run by Chinese mafia type people. They all because of my Father respected me whenever I would dine in their restaurants that they run in Wellington.

More so the restaurant I mentioned to my friend for lunch tomorrow.

I was just drained; really needed a few more hours sleep, to get my head right as still felt a bit buzzy. I wanted to give a good appearance when I saw my Mum later.

I fell asleep glad that I wasn't going to be taking anymore drugs again, and how I had given them all up for good so to get my life heading in only one direction, a more positive direction than my life had been for many a years.

Was that, sadly just wishful thinking? Again I wouldn't be able to get to a heighten level of happiness without the use of drugs.

Happiness, I do believed that I did deserve, more so if I was going to give up my old way of life and lifestyle.

I wanted to have a good chat with my Mum before she was to take her trip over to Europe later in the week.

I wanted her returning knowing that I had put in place again my personal goals to achieve, more so positive goals.

Finally my Mum then would be proud of her only son. This I know would very much touch her heart and bring great happiness to her. That's what I very much wanted to achieve, starting with today being Mothers Day when I would be getting to see my Mum with her Mother's Day present.

I finally put all these thoughts to rest as I did just that, rest followed by much more needed sleep though no sweet dreams this time around.

Chapter 28

DEATH COMES KNOCKING AT THE DOOR

I awoke to the sound of the phone not stop ringing, in a semi empty house, as Kieran wasn't there as she always had been and no friends knocking on the door as normal.

I had a feeling of being so alone that seemed to come over me as if something had gone.

Maybe the feeling was due to the comedown of drugs that I taken from over (what was a messy) weekend of mine.

The very last such type of weekend that I wished to take part in.

I was very alone as I had lost my girlfriend, it seemed now very real for me and due to the all the drug use. I didn't really have much to show for it all as all the money I had blown over the weekend since Friday was most of my profit so far, leaving me with not much cash left for myself plus I had blown my wages as well from my catering pay packet.

I came down from the bedroom and sensed there was someone downstairs. I walked into through into the lounge and seen the place had been ripped apart, all the cushions thanks to the puppy.

The wee little man who barked up at me when he saw me thinking that all the mess he had made was something to be proud of.

The lounge was a mess, all the stacks of LPs had been knocked over and then what I stepped in while answering the phone was his little deposit he had kindly left me in the lounge on the carpet...a nice amount of dog shit.

Couldn't he have avoided the carpet and maybe shat in the bathroom on the wipe able floor but no, the wee little man thought he would do one on my carpet that was now being pushed through my toes as I stepped on the present he had left me.

With a phone in my hand and a hangover from hell, I said hello down the phone.

It was my girl; she asked me did I know what the time was? She asked had all my mates fucked off. I said yes and she said "Well I'll come over and pick you up to take you over to your Mums."

Err she still loved me! "Love you babe." I said to her but no reply was given to that as she still was pissed off at me.

At least she rang and had me in mind, more so my Mum and it being Mother's Day.

I was just glad that the dinner had been put off till tomorrow evening with my Mum and Wim and my sister as there was no way I could face sitting in posh busy restaurant feeling this ruff.

I think I was feeling sorry for myself anyway I told her I would call my Mum to tell her that I would be coming over to her flat with Kiren and her Mother's day present, in around a hours time.

Kiren said she would be over in half an hour so I told her to let herself in as I needed to have a shower not telling her about the dog shit that was in my toes and more so on our carpet.

I got off the phone and tide the dog outside to the clothes line so he got fresh air and could have a run about in the back yard on the grass. Hoping he would go for a shit while out there rather than another shit on the carpet..... or anywhere else in the cottage.

I had tied up the dog with a lot of rope to his collar so he could have a lot of the back garden to run about in, without taking off.

Then with some wooden beer crates, I made like a shelter (kennel) for him. It actually looked quite good as I nailed a few together and then with the ripped cushions nailed these inside so to make a soft flooring and then with a sheet of solid plastic made what would have been a water proof roof with a balcony like roof hanging over the entrance so he had a cool little dog house for the wee little man.

I got a huge kitchen pot and filled that up with fresh water and also gave him my steaks out of the fridge so he had those to eat and the bones from some lamb chops to chew on. He was getting the VIP treatment even though only hours earlier he had destroyed the lounge as good as he could and shat in there.

He was only a puppy so he didn't know; he was only doing what puppies do so I couldn't be angry at the wee little man. He was just being a naughty mischief puppy, probably not much difference to what I was like when I was young.... though I never of course shat in my parents lounge on their carpet.

I jumped in the shower making sure the bottom of my feet were as clean as the rest of my body then jumping out of the shower and while in a towel that was wrapped around my waist I knelt down and cleaned up the shit in the lounge and put the LPs back, throwing out the remaining cushions that were un repairable.

I went upstairs to get changed, hearing the door open and Kiren's voice yelling at me thinking I was still in bed so I told her I just getting changed and if she wanted to know, I was naked.

I didn't hear any footsteps coming up those bedroom stairs so I knew she didn't want a quickie before we had to go out.

I popped down stairs after getting changed and went to give her a kiss but was coldly brushed off. That did hurt me but I thought fuck it, if she's still in a mood then I will just let her be.

She asked had I called my Mum and I said no as I needed a shower so she said quite bluntly "Call her then!"

I was already on a bad come down from the drugs so I really didn't need her shit.

I dialled my Mum's number but no answer so I just guessed she was back at Wims place.

I called there but no answer there so I called my Mum's flat again as maybe she herself was in the shower or the toilet but still no answer so I left a voice message and thought maybe they were just late on getting back to where they had spend the day yesterday and last night out of Wellington.

Kiren asked me what did I want to do and so I said to her "Well I guess I will just wait here."

I did call my sister who was over at her flat and asked how she was and she seemed a little better. I asked my sister had she heard from Mum and that's when she told me how our Mum had gone over to her house late Friday night and didn't leave till 5am.

It seemed to have helped my sister a lot. I could tell in her voice after she had spent that time with my Mum.

I told her that I would still be planning to see her later tonight after I seen our Mum to give her, her Mother's Day present. My sister asked me what I had got our Mum so I told her what Kiren and myself had got, and also how Kiren made it look so ever more special.

Before I finished talking to my sister, she said some of her friends were going to be up at her place tonight so I could stay for a drink, that sounded nice so said I thank you and that very much I would like that.

I loved my sister so much though I didn't tell her often that I loved her, actually I don't think I had ever told her.

Kiren then said that she didn't like the thought of me being in the cottage by myself and that she would have stayed with me but she didn't have any clothes here anymore so she needed to go back to her friend's house as all her clothes was now there.

What touched my heart was that she told me to come over with her.

So I left with Kiren, walking out of our cottage overjoyed by her asking me to come with her.

I had forgotten about the wee little man in the back garden while I lead Kiren down the path to her car though he was sorted with all the food I had left me out and the drinking water and more so the shelter I had built him.

We travelled around the bays, ending up in Island Bay Parade above a few shops. We went to a grand flat, it was more of a house above three shops below, and one of my sisters friends lived there Red Head Rachael and also another Rachael whose ex was a ex senior member of the Satan's Slaves Motorcycle Club. There also was one of Kiren friends who lived there so three girls and with Kiren, made four girls, a proper girlie house.

They all were fine towards me, they just nodded their heads in a way of telling me off for being such a little bastard over that weekend as Kiren had informed them of my silliness when my friends and I were high on drugs.

There was a pool table in one of the rooms which was fucking cool to have in a flat so I went in there and played a few games of pool by myself just making, or trying to make shots, non trick shots but still trying my luck.

No I wasn't showing off to anyone. All the girls were in the main lounge watching some girlie video movie flick about boys, and relationships so I knew to keep clear of the main lounge.

Wims oldest daughter Roberta only lived about ten doors down the road on the main route through Island Bay. At one end of Island Bay was at the furthest traffic lights turning into Luxford St past the petrol station on the nearest corner and at the other end of that road was the Satan's Slaves motorcycle club headquarters.

Then at the other end of Island Bay Parade was Island Bay itself, a lively beach that went for miles at both tips and there was the Pacific Ocean.

A lot of surfers would use this line of surf to do just that, surf the waves that came crashing in along the beaches shores.

It soon was like near 730pm. I used Rachel's house phone and again called both my Mum's flat and Wims house but still no answer. Maybe Wim had gone to his daughters' houses first, as he had two daughters Heidi as well as Roberta.

Heidi lived above on of Wims garages on Webb St in town, in a luxury flat that Wim had built. Heidi was living there with a guy by the name of Frank who worked in Wims garage named Speedwell Motors in Wellington. Frank had been very loyal to Wim over the years working hard for him in his garage and being a good trusted mate of Wims as well over the years.

I got on with Frank and he was always a gentleman towards my mum when my mum was at the garage doing the accounts and bookkeeping for Wim. I didn't have Heidi's number but I did call Roberta but Bobby said she hadn't heard from her father.

I didn't let her know where I was as there was no need to so I just asked her to say hello to her boyfriend whose name was Rob, a Samoan guy who was a lovely guy and a very talent softball player. Rob was a proper nice guy, ever since meeting him I always had time for him and he liked me, we got on really well.

I had with Roberta earlier boyfriend Paul, got on well with him as well. Bobby and Paul both came up and took me out for a day out while I was a boarder at Hadlow; he had huge passion for soccer so I used to go down the park with Roberta many a times to watch him play soccer.

Her boyfriend before him was also a good guy, I can't remember his name but he was sound as a pie. He had actually been out to London for a few years working out there and travelling through Europe.

Roberta was gorgeous in looks and so was Heidi, both had been in their time very successful models. There was only two or three years age different between them both and over time they both very much were like sisters to me. I was close to them both and would have many nights out with them getting on the piss and having a proper laugh in their company.

Some nights I would stay over at Roberta's when me and my Mum wasn't seeing eye to eye due to my behaviour. I think Roberta liked having me around as I was the closest thing to her as in a having a brother so we were very close and they both were as well with my sister.

After getting off the phone to Roberta, I guessed maybe Wim and my Mum were just at Heidi flat and that my mum probably had tried to contact me at my cottage, even maybe popping around there, and due to me not being at the cottage and mobile phones neither of us had so she wouldn't have known how to contact me.

Even if she had called my sister, she wouldn't have known I was at Red Head Rachael's flat, where Kiren had moved into but I thought I would at least try my Sister one more time.

On speaking to my sister, she hadn't still heard from my mum. My sister seemed in high spirits when I spoke to her again. Cool Ken was over there and also a few of my sisters friends.

They all were having a drink. The company of good friends was what my sister needed as being alone wasn't doing her any good so with many friends over at her place, she was happier than what she had been through the week that had just past.

Soon it got late evening. Kieran had work the next morning so we both went to bed and made love which brought us for that night closer together and we had a little chat before falling asleep about maybe spending time apart until I had got rid of all the drugs out of the cottage and then she would come back home.

I agreed with her and told her that I myself was no longer going to be partying like I used to and as for personal drug use I had from this day given all my drug use up, with that Kiren fell asleep with a smile on her face.

As for me, my Mum was in my thoughts as I feel a sleep. She was very much alive in my dreams; really strongly I can remember seeing her in my dreams then suddenly being awaked from the dreams with a loud banging on the back door of the house.

I looked at the clock the time was 12 as the cuckoo clock rang out 12 bells. Who could be at the door? Why such a loud banging? Whoever it was, they seemed really wanting to wake the household up.

As it wasn't my house I never went to the back door to check. I tried looking out the window and I could make out it was a male who was knocking but I couldn't tell who it was as there was outside lights on so I could only make just the outline of a male.

Then I heard someone else getting up in the house. What I did do is reach for my knife that I had placed under Kieran's bed as I always slept with a knife near as I was known to have strong connections to the Satan's Slaves Motorcycle then I was a target for other gang members, all whom would always be tooled up so back then you always went out with a knife tucked in your belt or hidden in your jacket. It could mean the difference between life and death if ever you were attacked by a rival gang and you had to defend yourself.

Even with the background in martial arts, that didn't mean I could win every fight and after many years earlier being stabbed in my face and thrown down the set of stairs in the nightclub well I guessed if I had been carrying a knife that night I at least would have been able to protect myself a bit more rather than getting the beating that I took.

As I heard the back door being open by Red Head Rachel (I could hear her sleepy voice), I then heard my name being mentioned and thought who the hell could this be as no one knew I was here so why was my name being mentioned?

The first thing that came to my mind was the police. Was I in trouble with the law? I hide the knife, this time further down the back of the bed and quickly put my jeans on and my t shirt, waking Kiren up who was already half awake as from the earlier knocking of the door.

I told her someone was at the door mentioning my name.

Just as I was putting my Doc Martian Cherry boots on, there was as knock on Kiren's bedroom door.

Rachael's voice calling out my name, I replied to Rachael through the still closed door to give me a second as I did up the shoe laces on my boots and opened the door.

The first thing I noticed was tears in Red Head Rachael eyes.

I asked her what was wrong and who was at the door?

She told me it was Bacon. Bacon was one of the very old school members of the Satan's Slaves Motorcycle Club; he had been part of the club as many years as I had been alive.

Someone who had massive respect from the entire club and many other motorcycles clubs through New Zealand and Australia and around the world among other 1% MC Clubs.

Bacon had one arm, he had been in a bike accident many years ago but he was still able to ride a bike and ride it well.

He had a Triumph motorcycle redone so he was able with one hand, ride the bike.

He was hardcore in his day, once walking into a party of a rival gang who was holding a house party in Wellington but this bike club wasn't allowed to step foot inside Wellington as the Satan's Slaves Motorcycle Club wouldn't ever let any rival bike club to get a foot hold on their manor and there had been talk about this certain house where this house party was being held, becoming a clubhouse for the rival biker gang.

Well Bacon wasn't having any if it so he went to the house, smashed down the front door with an axe and attacked any patched members he saw with the axe. There was no deaths but the biker gang got the message and Bacon fled but not with his tail between his legs as he returned two days later this time with a chain saw and let's say went to town on the house.

The rival bikers who were still inside the house fled while Bacon just saw the house nearly in two as he took the chainsaw to town as in he cut and demotion as much as he could before he was out of breath then he flung the chainsaw on the back of his bike and ride back to the Satan's Slaves clubhouse.

He had destroyed any of the rival bike gang dreams of making that house in to a clubhouse and ever coming back in to Wellington but as they had now been send out of town by one biker, which made them look so soft.

They took up position near the Satan's Slaves headquarters a few days later hiding in a van, watching and waiting till they hoped to see Bacon ride out as they were going to do a hit and run as in what they wanted to do was follow Bacon on his bike in the van then on a straight road at speed come up behind and knock him off the bike while hoping to run him over.

Bacon never came out on his bike but one afternoon, he went to go to the local shop to get some fish and chips and they jumped out of the van and pulled him in, not knowing they had been spotted by another Satan's Slaves who then took chase in a car soon following the rival bike club to their established clubhouse out of Wellington.

The Satan's Slave who had followed in a car then found a phone booth and made certain S.O.S call.

Within a hour there was many members of the Satan's Slaves and also one driving a digger from his work yard smashing into their clubhouse and grabbing Bacon who had been kidnapped but yet had they harmed him though if the backup hadn't come in time then Bacon would have been badly hurt and for sure murdered.

That certain motorcycle never ever entered Wellington and their numbers dropped due to the Satan's Slaves destroying all creditability that motorcycle club had in New Zealand.

As for Bacon he sadly few months later had that bike accident that meant his arm was crushed to the point it had to be cut off though he was still a very much party person.

Bacon calmed down a lot in the years I knew him as he aged with life but as a young man with such stories he was a legend within the history of the Satan's Slaves Motorcycle Club and always a good friend to me.

So on hearing that it was him at the door, I couldn't understand why Rachael was in tears as Bacon was a ladies' man and a kind guy towards girls so I am unsure what he said to Rachael for her to be as upset as she was.

I walked past Rachael who was standing in the hall way crying into her hands, I then entered the kitchen. At the backdoor standing near the microwave oven was Bacon standing there with his patch on which meant he had come on his bike as members never wore their club colours while driving a car.

I said "Hello my friend." and then asked Bacon had I done something wrong? Was I in some sort of trouble?

With that he said "No, of course not Christian."

So I asked again what was wrong.

"Your Mothers dead" "I am so sorry to pass YOU the sad news." "I been riding my bike all over Wellington trying to find you for the last three hours as the police turned up at our headquarters asking for you and gave us the message to pass onto you Christian. "

"I been to your cottage and your mums flat, I wasn't sure where your sister lived and after calling around, someone said that your girlfriend had been seen moving into the two Rachael's house, I was only told this half a hour ago and this was my final place to check if you were here."

All these words that Bacon was telling me, just wasn't going into my brain, they weren't resigning with my brain, as I stood there nodding my head but not speaking.

I just couldn't take it all in but thanked him for all he had done for tracking me down. It was now past midnight; Bacon had been out on his bike since 9pm looking for me. I knew he must have been so tired so I told him to go back to the clubhouse to get rest after he offered to stay with me.

A true friend Bacon was.

Straight away my sister came to my thoughts, my sister who had been through so much only burying her soul mate that week and who I had spoken to only a few hours earlier when she seemed happier in her tone of voice than she had been all week.

I now knew why Rachael was crying as she knew my mum so well. My mum thought a lot of Redhead Rachael as she had been such a close friend to my sister. Redhead Rachael loved my mum loads, all my sisters' friends did, actually anyone who had ever met my Mum had as my Mum was loved by many.

My mum was so beautiful not only in looks but in her spirit. She was such a loving person and with so much good karma and she always gave all her time to her own friends and more so to her family, to her two kids-my sister and I.

My mum was dead.

My mum who I had only a week earlier over at my cottage (with the seafood treats) talking for hours about life, happiness, her proud ness of her son, my dreams and my goals, her own dreams, her goals, her planned trip to Europe, the possible wedding, the marriage that looked on the cards for her and Wim, life and now all this had been taken from her, my mum was dead.

My mum who only 48 hrs earlier had gone to see my sister late at night for them for many hours as she had with me, spending time with my sister opening up and talking about many things , being there for my sister after my sister losing Tim , but now my Mum was dead.

My mum who had called me on Friday while I was high on lsd telling me if anything happen to her then all would-be left by her phone in her flat as in a copy of her life insurance and other documents.

What had she seen in her dreams from the night before? What was it within her, her 6th sense telling her something was wrong?

All this seeming now to come true as now my beautiful Mum was dead.

I went into the other bedroom; Kiren and Redhead Rachael were both in tears.

Kiren asking what was wrong as Rachael hadn't been able to tell Kiren though Kiren for some reason was in tears, and real tears.

I sat on the end of the bed and told her that my Mum was dead.

I needed to reach my sister before anyone else had.

I didn't want the police turning up there telling my sister the news.

The police had been to my flat and to my sisters old flat. It meant they had been to my cottage as well I guessed, but as my sister wasn't register at her new flat then they hadn't been there yet but I guessed if they were looking for me and my sister to tell us the news then they wouldn't be far off from tracking down my sister.

I asked Kiren would she drive me to my sisters and I asked Redhead Rachael if she too would come.

We jumped into Kiren's car and drove through Wellington driving through Kilburnine where my mum's flat was and even passing the main street where I looked up Mahora St and there was my Mum's flat. All the lights were off, apart from the light on the landing just how my Mum had left her flat the last time she was there.

We went up the hill along Prison Road heading up the hill, as if we were driving towards Mt Crawford Prison and before reaching the jail, my sister lived in a set of flats, we parked up and went to the door.

Cool Ken answered the door. I could hear a Janice Joplin song being played and walked on in to the lounge and there was Leigh a good friend of my sisters and there was my sister who was so happy to see me.

My sister stood up and gave me a hug and asked me did we all want a wine. She told me they were celebrating the life of Tim, they all were drunk but in a happy way drunk and I could smell weed had been smoked so they all had big smiles on their faces.

I turned to Redhead Rachael after saying to my sister I didn't wish to have a drink and told Redhead Rachael "I can't tell my sister, please you tell my sister, Rachael."

I could tell Redhead Rachael felt very uncomfortable, my sister picked up on this and asked what was wrong?

As far as my sister could tell we had come over to join them for a drink due to telling her my sister earlier that I would be coming over to have a drink.

My sister then asked again what was wrong?

Before even Rachael could say anything, my Sister looked at me and said "Its Mum isn't it!"

I then had to say as Rachael had burst into tears again, "Mum was dead."

What happened next was my sister, in a state of shock just asking me again and again and again what I had just said and again I said these few words "Mum was dead."

The very last time I said these words, my sister pushed everything that was on the nearest shelve onto her floor and herself as in nearly fainting dropped to the ground.

Leigh jumped of the lounge and held my sister and I reached over and hugged her as she was crying in to my shoulder telling me "This couldn't be true!"

"Why are you telling me such a awful thing!" she kept asking me while crying her eyes out as now tears were falling from my eyes but I didn't want my sister to see my tears as I held her trying to be ever so strong for her.

My sister hitting my chest repeating "It's not true, tell me it's not true."

"Nothing you're saying is true, is it Christian?" She kept on asking me but each time I had to again tell her "Yes it was."

I wanted to burst into tears but still I did my best not to and each time I was telling my sister that mum was dead, even I couldn't believe the words coming out of my mouth.

It all seemed untrue from the moment only 40mins earlier when I had first been told.

Cool Ken didn't know what to do and neither did the girls who all were in sheds of tears and trying to hug both me and my sister.

I got too my feet and looked at Cool Ken who didn't know what to say apart from give me a hug, telling me he was there for both of us.

He was a dam good guy though he had mental health issues, he was still a caring friend and he having this wasn't anything that was his own fault; he was just someone who had this illness.

I got to learn and except the terms of people with mental illnesses through Cool Ken as many a times when he had stopped taking his medication he would been send to a mental hospital, and I would be one friend who would visit him at the mental health hospital out in Porirua.

Kiren would drive me and my sister up to visit him and it was only there at the hospital on speaking to doctors that would give me an insight into this illness, an illness that also Ronald Kray suffered from thought out his own life.

If Ronald Kray had been given the correct care and also drugs that someone like Cool Ken was in, then I wonder if Ronnie Kray would have gone on to commit the cold blood murder/s he had done.

Ronnie had a very violent temper, he was known to switch like a light on anyone including members of his own firm but back in the 1950s / 1960s the illness was so misunderstood than in these day and age.

Finally when Ronald Kray was transferred out of Pankhurst jail on the Isle of Wright to Broadmoor Hospital in Berkshire in the late 1970s to his time throughout the 1980s and up to his death in 1995 (though Ronnie Kray died in an outside hospital in Wrexham). Ronnie Kray, you could say died a free man as he never died behind the bars of a prison or while being held at Broadmoor Maximum Security Hospital.

At least he was on the right meditation in his later years which meant he hadn't those outbursts of violence he had during his reign of power within Gangland Britain during the 1960s.

But many did say due to a change of medication in his final years and the fact he smoked 100 ciggs a day then his health become worse but he wasn't in away a sick man when he died and his sudden fatal heart did bring in many questions as he was only a few years away from his recommend 30 year sentence so was there may have been a more sinister hand at play when it came to his death.

Couldn't he have been saved or was certain hospital staff who were looking after him, being told to let him die or to assist in his death in some way by the British Government?

I am sure other agencies felt Ronnie Kray was still very much a threat to them due his solid links to many members of parliament from the 1960s and to his knowledge and involvement in many British Government scandals.

He was never going to be a threat to the public if he was to be released after 30 years as long as he was taking his medication and the correct care was in place as it was for Cool Ken.

The only similar thing between Cool Ken and Ronnie Kray was they suffered from the same illness.

This Sunday night, Mother's Day will forever stay with me the rest of my life and though I have blanked it for many years until writing this book, I wish not to comment any more on the death of my mother.

My sister and myself and only a very few know how my mum died and the circumstances surrounding my Mother's death.

All out of respect to me and my sister, also for the lasting memory of my Mum then this would never be spoken about again.

In saying this it doesn't meant the subject comes to a end as though my Mum's life was taking away from her, here was both her children - my sister 21 years old and I had just left being 16 years old and now was not even three weeks into being 17 years old.

How a part of me and for sure my sister died that day our Mum was killed.

We both had to face the following day and for me the shock and the reality of my Mum being taken had not reached home as in my thoughts and my head.

I still couldn't believe what I had been told only a few hours earlier.

We all stayed at my sisters flat in what can only be describe as a very surreal dream, a dream that wasn't bringing smiles or laughter. A dream that meant I would never be able to hand my mum her Mother's day present, a dream that was too self destructive all the dreams I had for my life and all the goals I had set myself and worst the promise I had given myself when I woke up that day and the promise I had given Kiren before I fell asleep that night.

What soon was to follow was a complete self destructive of life as I knew it including my own freedom and nearing taking another life.

Chapter 29

KNOCK, KNOCK, KNOCKING ON HEAVENS DOOR

On the Monday after being told 24hrs earlier that my Mum was dead, I hadn't slept and mid way through that night before I cried for so many hours as it had finally hit me that my Mum was dead.

The thought of never seeing her again, this still didn't register in my brain.

All I could think about is how heartbroken my Sister must now truly be as within exactly seven days my sister had lost two of the people in her life who she loved so dearly.

I had keys to my Mum's place.

I left my Sisters in the morning though I wasn't planning going to go by my Mum's place but I asked Kiren to drive by and when we were on her street I asked Kiren to stop the car.

I went to flat 3 / 27 Mahora St Wellington (or 28 I can't remember for now). I climbed the stairs and turned the two keys, one after another into the locks and then I walked in to my mum's apartment.

The first thing I recall was the strong smell of my Mum's perfume (white musk) I could smell it so strong throughout the flat.

My mum's bedroom door was closed but as I turned the door handle, I was for sure going to see her laying there in her bed or getting ready at her dresser even though still after what my sister and I had been told that my Mum was dead.

I was just praying it was wrong news but there as I looked inside my Mums bedroom my Mum wasn't there but what was, was my Mum's nearly made bed and everything in her room was exactly as she had left it when she was last here on Friday.

I still could (as I walked out of her bedroom) smell in the air, her perfume that still stays with me to this day that strong memory.

Though she hadn't been in her flat since Friday why there was such a strong sent in the flat as if she had only been there a few hours before or as if she was there now walking around her flat but I just couldn't see her?

I moved into the kitchen and at the back bay window where the round table in the kitchen was, with my mum's phone on the dining table was also as she said was all these official documents. None made any sense to me and as I looked through them I could only work out that they were her life insurance policy and then at the bottom were her will.

This was too much for me to take in to see that whatever it was in my Mum's dream or whatever made her have a gut feeling that something was going to happen, that she wasn't going to be making it back to Wellington on the Sunday, to the point that she even left out her will.

I couldn't take any more of this so I rushed out of the flat, asking Kiren could she drive me to our cottage as I needed to call my father in Scotland to tell him what had happened.

I just couldn't bare being in my Mum's flat, it was like this was all so not real and I didn't need any more reminders that my beautiful Mum was dead and the fact that she had somehow known something horrible was going to maybe happened, was just too much to take in.

I got to my cottage, telling Kiren if she needed to get to work then do so, but she just wanted to be with me.

I didn't want her getting in trouble at her work and as her work was only down in Newtown which was only a few miles from where we lived on 5a Wright St Mt Cook in Wellington then for her to go to work and if I needed her I would call her.

For now I just needed to call my father.

I shouldn't even have left my sister's house, and I sure shouldn't have gone over to my mum's place as it was too much going there. My sister I know needed me but I just had to sort my thoughts out and work out that my mum was dead and my father lived on the other side of the world and though I had my sister I was feeling very alone.

I actually had been from the moment I woke up on Sunday more so with Kiren having moved out.

I called my Father but he again was out at the pub. He always was at the fucking pub when I called when this time I really needed him the most.

I asked Irene for the number of the pub and I rang it asking to talk to Steve. The land lady yelled out "Stevie the phones for you!"

Next I heard my father's voice and asked him "Why is it every time I fucking call, you are in the pub!!" It was the very first time I ever had sworn at him.

He asked me to check my language and what the hell was wrong......... I said "Mums dead."

I then cried down the phone repeating "Mum is dead!"

I don't think he heard me the first time due to the bad phone line.

He was speechless as though it was hard for me to cope with the fact my Mum was dead, well for my father, my Mum had been the love of his life and though he didn't cry as he was staunch, I could tell how upset he was.

He then asked where my sister was? Was she with me?

I told him no, she was at her flat so he said he would go home straight away and call her.

I got off the phone..... It was silent around me........I was very alone then I heard a noise outside, a barking of a dog.

Fuck I had forgotten about the wee little man (the puppy) so I went outside. The dog was jumping all over me with excitement, still tied up then he went running under the house so I went to pull him back and noticed the remaining bags of weed, all ripped open and the weed was all over the place.

The lead I had made for the dog which I hadn't worked out was so long that he could get access under the cottage and that meant he had torn up all the bags of weed.

The last thing I fucking needed trying to get my body under the cottage and getting what I could of, of some of the weed together.

There was shit loads of it and some which had dogs shit throughout it so there I was, trying to get all the weed together now with dog shit over my hands and the puppy just jumping all over me, licking my face, as he was happy of course to see me but I just couldn't be dealing with all this mess for now.

I went and undone the dog and went over to the neighbours house and banged on the door until he appeared. It was middle of the morning; he looked half asleep when he answered the door. I said to him "You got have this puppy back as I can't look after him."

"My mum had been killed."

He asked how etc but I couldn't be asked talking to him, I told him I would see him later.

He then told me to wait as he went inside his house and gave me a bread bag that was full of money from the two bags of weed I had given him since Friday and he asked did I have more so I told him I was just sorting that out now.

I had dog shit over my hands and grass and dirt on me.

I stupidly told him that I had to recover the dog from the backyard underneath the house and also I told him that I had made up a dog house for the puppy and that the lead was on the washing line if he needed to house the puppy. I then said I would see him that night with the other dope I had.

I needed to have a shower and get changed out of the clothes I was in.

I went back into the cottage and had a shower though hearing the phone ring so I got out of the shower maybe I thought it was going to be my mum and that all was ok as I picked up the phone.

It was my sister telling me that Dad had called her and was I ok as my father told her I was very upset when I had spoken to him.

I told my sister yes I was ok and that I couldn't talk as I was half way through having a shower so I told her I would call her back.

I jumped back in the shower then my phone rang again.

I again thought for some reason it was my Mum so I answered it quickly but it was my Uncle Frank. My uncle, whom I had spend time with him and his wife when I was at boarding school many years earlier.

He was my mum's youngest brother; a very successful businessman who had taken over my Grandfathers saw mills. My Uncle, himself had brought the giant saw mill in Featherstone and renamed it after our families surname on my mum's side of the family.

He was very straight and so strict with his own kids and didn't think much of me after I was expelled from the second boarding schooling for the dope dealing and was even more off with me after I had been expelled for a second time.

He though that I walked all over my Mum and I didn't have any displine in my own life and at one stage he thought it was best if I came and lived with him and my Auntie Beth, to take work up at his saw mill.

I told my Mum back then when I was 15 years old that there was no way I was living away from Wellington, leaving all my mates and my social life to be under his rule and not be able to run amuck.

My Uncle only meant well from it. He just wanted my Mum to have a quieter life but I had already been send away to boarding school and I sure wasn't going to be sent away again to live out of Wellington.

I think that was one of my reasons why I got the cottage and moved in with Kiren so quickly as then no one was going to be able to tell me what to do and if any family member tried to put their two pence in, as in how I should live my life then I could easily just shut the door on them or hang the phone up to them. Once I had a place of my own, then I was king of that castle and no was going to be telling me what to do.

My mum never could, so who gave the right to my Uncle to tell me how to live my life. I did like Uncle Frank a lot but I didn't like when he interfered in my life. Again though he was only trying to help me out and also my Mum, who was his sister who he loved very much.

My uncle told me that he was on his way to Wellington as he had to ID my mum's body and that he was well aware of my Mum being killed and why couldn't he reach me since he was told of the news.

He asked me to be at my Mum's flat that late afternoon so I told him I would meet him there with my Auntie.

For now I had to get back in the shower and get changed into some old clothes and look for a rake so I could get this weed out.

I jumped back in the shower but again my phone rang so out I came yet again and answered the phone.

It was one of my peers who didn't know about the death of my Mum. He was asking (in code) how things were going with the sale of the lsd and the pot and that he wanted me to drop off some of the money.

I explained my Mum had been killed. He said sorry to hear that but coldly he said "When will you be over with my money." so I told him I would count up everything I had and explaining a lot was out on tick as it was the only way I could have moved it.

He didn't care about that, as long as by the end of the month I had every penny for him.

Though the drugs came to a street value of £120,000, that's not the total I had to come up with as I had my own profit plus also what else I was adding on top of my private sales though that was small as I just wanted to get rid of most of it.

Though my profit was a nice amount for a 17 year old kid, I done most of it in bulk so of course I had to drop the price on the acid as I wasn't selling one tab at a time where by I could get $40 for it as I was selling it in sheets of 1,000 and also smaller sheets of 100 so of course the cost of each tab was no way near the $40 mark, anyway I got off the phone to him telling him yes I would be up to his place later.

Back in the shower I got again then the phone went off once again, this time my mood had gone moody as mainly due to how cold the last conversation was towards me(the guy really didn't give a fuck that my Mum was dead).

That hurt me as it showed me how some of my peers were just money bound and they didn't give a fuck about anything apart from their money. Couldn't he just have said "Oh my God, well you take a couple days out and call me at the end of the week." but no he wanted whatever money I made for him and he wanted it by evening that night....wanker!!!!

I picked up the phone this time in now a bad mood as the way I had been spoken to also thinking back to how short my Uncle was over the phone to me as well in his conversation but my Uncle was always like that.

He was always very businesslike in the way he would speak to me and he always thought I was a little shit apart from when I was doing well at the boarding schools or when I was doing well in rugby.

But what I should have thought about, was him rather than myself as my Uncle had just called to tell me he was on the way to Wellington to id the dead body of my Mum, who was his one and only sister so how awful was that going to be for him.

I picked up the phone and asked who it was what the fuck they wanted!

It was Kiren, how I wished I hadn't answered the phone to her like that as all she wanted was to make sure I was ok and that how she felt bad being at work while I was by myself.

I really could have won Kiren back at this time. Something though horrible as in the death of my Mum, really should have brought us closer together but the way I spoke to her just wasn't nice at all.

I now can say the way I spoke to her down the phone was horrible as I was yelling at her for no reason at all.

If she had only been the first of the phones calls and not the last then she wouldn't have got an ear full of abuse.

I put down the phone and finally finished my shower and then went out the back yard as it started to rain down on me, heavily.

I was standing there with a rake and a black bin liner trying to get the rake underneath the house without having to get myself under there again as I had just showered and though I had put on older clothes I really wasn't in the mood to get more dog shit on me nor to be soaking wet.

I couldn't get the rake at the right angel without kneeing on the ground so all I managed to rake out was a half emptied bag with a quarter of the dope that was in it.

I took that inside and bagged it up. It would have been only 5 ounces and in the three bags that I had placed underneath the cottage on the previous Friday in total was 48 ounces in total.

Each bag had 16 ounces in it but as the puppy had got in to it all.

The sight of broken buds of weed that all had been bagged up together were now spread all over the back end underneath the cottage.

To get it all would take me crawling on my hands and chest and getting under there with the rake and a torch.

The way I was doing it wasn't at all getting it all out but I had to get it out as it was money rather weed and more so not my money but my peers money.

Remembering the phone call earlier meant I had to get it all back and ready again for sale so I thought fuck it and out I went in the rain on my hands and knees firstly dragging what was close to the back of the cottage I could reach, and then the heavens just opened up more and it rained down as I was doing it.

I didn't notice the neighbour come up behind me nor hear him call out to me until he tapped me on my shoulder as I was coming back from underneath the cottage.

I got up off my belly with now the dirt turned to mud (due to the rain fall) all over my hands and over my knees of my jeans and the chest of my jumper.

He didn't need to ask me what I was doing as he could see the weed laying around me as I had racked up a fair bit of it and hadn't yet lifted it into the bag next to me as I stood up using the weight of the rake to get me up.

He pretended not to notice the dope and said he had come around to get the dog hut I had made so I pointed over to where it was and as he walked over to the hut I picked up what was on the floor and bagged it all up and then waited till he had the dog hut in his arms and followed him out of the back yard to the front of the cottage.

He walked down into the direction of his house as I went inside and again changed my clothes washing my hands and weighting up what I had in dope.

I then went up stairs and dried the outside of the bag with the towel I had used and placed it underneath the bed base next to the shotgun and also the rolled up sheets of acid.

All of this I really didn't need in my life and wished everything was just one bad dream - my Mum being dead and all these drugs as really I couldn't cope with having the remaining drugs to move as my life had come to a crashing end for the time being and due to still being on the come down of all the drugs that had been in my body over the weekend then to hearing the news that my Mum had been killed, it was just too much.

I went downstairs and put on some music listening to Stevie Wonder and sitting in the lounge it now all was silent again apart from the rain tapping on the windows outside.

I sat there and looked around at my life and though so much had improved as in my job and the cottage, I just didn't like the fact what I had upstairs I started to think about the course of my life so far and I blamed so much on my downfall through my years to my peers but I really only had myself to blame for the situation I was in.

I sat there and listened to the record then put on a Johnny Cash record and reached over and lit up a half smoked joint that was in the ashtray trying my hardest not to think of my Mum being dead.

Though I was earlier thinking about all the drugs in the house and how only yesterday I had promised myself not to ever again do drugs, here I was smoking a joint.

But as I got stoned, all the tension in my chest and my mind full of so many thoughts seemed to all clam down and everything felt numb as I got stoned.

On feeling like this I put on a another record Pink Floyd and closed my eyes and listened to all the songs, they seemed to be taking me away from feeling pain and hurt as I sat back and listened to the whole record of Dark Side Of The Moon.

Half way going upstairs, taking a bud of weed out and rolling a joint that I smoked which hit me so much putting me to sleep.

I hadn't slept since the day before and even then it wasn't a massive sleep.

Looking back now I hadn't had a proper night sleep since Thursday as my weekend was all about lack of sleep.

I awoke to the sound of the phone so off the couch I got and picked it up, noticing the rain wasn't falling as much outside had it earlier.

On the other end of phone was one of my peer asking me if I could come over earlier so I just said "Yes!" and went back up to the bedroom and started to count all the money I had hidden and then I called for a taxi and headed over to his house.

He counted the money in front of me and told me the sum that was outstanding and when did I think I would have the rest?

I informed him that I did have till the end of the month, I didn't have to mention that I had just my lost my Mum as he didn't care less about that.

I asked if he would give me a lift near to my cottage as he was on his way out so he agreed to drop me off in town. There I got another taxi back to mine and on opening the door the phone was ringing. I picked up to make sure I wasn't rude or moody down the phone in case it was Kiren again.

As I wanted to say sorry to her but it wasn't Kiren, it was my Uncle Frank, he was not happy as he had been waiting outside my Mum's flat for me.

My Uncle had been to a phone booth trying to call me without any luck for the last hour while he waited in his car, pouring rain hitting the window screen after Idling my mum's body, which now was back in Wellington at the morgue at Wellington hospital in Newtown.

I told him I am on my way now and that I had just fallen asleep on the couch. I wasn't going to tell him what I had been up that's for sure.

Again I blamed the afternoon on my peer as if he hadn't demanded the money then I would be there for my Uncle rather than at a drug lord house handing him over money.

I called another taxi and off I went to my Mum's flat, getting out of the cab and seeing my Uncle and Auntie waiting for me in their car.

I let them in from the rain and said sorry. My Auntie Beth gave me a hug and I pointed out to my Uncle what my Mum had left out.

He went into the kitchen to read over all the different types of documents that my Mum had left out for some reason on the previous Friday.

I told them both about the very last phone call I took from my mum on the Friday night and what she had said to me.

I spend about an hour with my Uncle and Auntie and then asked them if they could drop me off back to my cottage, which they did.

By the time we got there and open the door, they both could smell weed and wasn't too happy. Neither wishing to come in but that was because they had the long drive back to their house in Greytown as a family friend of theirs was looking after their younger children.

They told me my Mum's body would be in a funeral parlour near my mum's flat, the following day and that they would come back down to see me and my sister at the funeral home as they wanted to see my Nana, who had taken the news very badly.

My Nana I hadn't even thought about which made me feel so bad as I was so close to my Nana she had moved down from New Plymouth when I was young to help my Mum look after me. My Mum had been such a big part of my life and I loved her dearly.

I asked both my Uncle and my Auntie to tell her that I loved her and tomorrow I would see her.

I was hoping Kiren would be at the cottage waiting for me but she wasn't and as it got dark I really didn't want to be in the cottage by myself so I called Redhead Rachael's house, and spoke to the other Rachael who passed the phone to Kiren.

I told kiren sorry for yelling down the phone but would she please come over so she said of course she would and she drove over asking me if I was ok?

What did I want to do so I told her I wanted to go over to my Sister's house to see my sister.

We drove back up in the rain and went to my sister's house. Gladly my sister's friends were there with her. Leigh hadn't left since the day before and nor had Redhead Rachael, who locked so tired.

I really didn't know what to say to my Sister, we all just sat there and I spoke of my day as in that I had seen our Uncle Frank and Auntie Beth, whom my sister told me had called her and informed her of my Mum's body being taken to a funeral parlour the next day.

I stayed at my Sisters for many hours not wanting to leave.

We called our Nana, who was worried about me and my Sister.

Asking if we were ok? I told her yes we were ok?

My Nana had just lost her only daughter after losing my mum's twin when she was born and also another daughter many years ago at birth so all this was so much pain for her. My Nana was such a strong lady; she was being even stronger for me during that phone call.

I left my sisters very late maybe around 2am. I went back to Rachael and Kerens house falling asleep as my head hit the pillow and awaking to Kiren cooking me a breakfast, telling me she wasn't going to be going to work that day but instead taking me to the funeral parlour.

We went there at midday that day. Cool Ken had collected my sister. My Uncle and Auntie had collected my Nana.

We all met there at the funeral parlour. Cool Ken stayed in the car out of respect. The remaining of us went in.

What was behind the closed door was something I really didn't want to see and that was the body of my Mum laying in a coffin. In we went, and there she was.....my Mum.

My Mum just didn't look the same, all her life taken out of her and her eyes closed I really wanted her to stop pretending that she was dead but the fact was she was dead as I reached to touch her hand, never had I touched a dead body before though I had seen a dead body such as Tim only a week earlier.

I put my mum's hand in my hand it was icily cold and I asked her to wake up, then bursting into tears.

My Uncle's words to me were "Toughen up, stop crying Christian."

I could have turned around there and then and hit him as why was he telling me not to cry?

It really hurt me what he said and sorry but there in front of me was my Mum who meant the world to me. Any normal 17 year kids shouldn't be seeing their Mum dead at this age.

My mum was so young she was only 42 years.

My Uncle and Auntie and my Nana (my Nana who was holding onto me) left me in there with my sister as they went to speak to the funeral parlour people. It was only me and my sister; Kiren didn't wish to go in out of respect to us and to the family.

For some reason I wanted to see my Mum's blue eyes, so I lift her eye lit and it was just white, it spooked me out as I couldn't see her eyes and I really wanted to.

I didn't stop crying and nor did my sister as we hugged each other next to my Mum's body then my Uncle called us out so we could speak to the funeral lady but neither of us were ready to be talking about funeral arrangements so we said we would be back tomorrow.

I grabbed hold of Kerens hand, that's when it all came crashing down on me after seeing my Mum's body laying there lifeless.

I still I didn't wish to believe it was all happening and I didn't like feeling the pain ripping through my heart so I asked Kieran if she would drop me off to the Satan's Slaves headquarters as I wanted to thank Bacon.

I told my Sister I would see her tomorrow and that we would collect her from her flat in the morning.

My Sister asked for the keys to my mum's flat so I gave them to her, I then kissed my Nana goodbye and my Auntie and said goodbye to my Uncle (there now seemed tension between my Uncle and me for some reason).

I don't think I was taking in his pain as he still came across all business like and that to me felt cold but everyone was dealing with the pain and loss of my Mum in their own way.

I headed off to towards the Satan's Slaves Motorcycle Club, Kiren didn't want to come in with me so she pulled up outside and dropped me off telling me to ring her when I wanted to be picked up. She was so caring and loving towards me.

I pressed the buzzer though those inside could see me always walking down the drive way on the many security cameras and due to the security beeps that were in place on the driveway, they would know well in advance anyone near the entrance to the clubhouse.

There was a club meeting going on so Bacon wasn't there. There only was a prospect by the name of Craig and another prospect and some close friends of the club drinking in the bar.

They all knew what had happened, all telling me they were sorry to hear about the sad news.

These guys were unlike my peers as though they were dangerous men in their own right they all had hearts.

Soon they got me a beer, one after another after another.

I was still there when Bacon and everyone else returned and all the members stayed up at the bar till I couldn't drink anymore. It was far too late to call Kiren so I stayed the night at the clubhouse, as I wasn't a member or a prospect I wasn't allowed to sleep in the living courters so I fell asleep where the blazing fire was on, using one of the guard dogs as my pillow.

I woke up in the morning to the sounds of bikes leaving the clubhouse. Bacon came over and woke me up saying I could make myself a cooked breakfast in the clubs living quarters (somewhere where only club members were allowed to go).

I then asked if I could use the club telephone. I called Kiren (I was very hung over) as I didn't wish to let my sister down s we had promised her a lift that morning back to the funeral parlour.

Kiren came and collected me, I thanked Bacon again for all he done for and I went and got my sister then we went back to the funeral parlour after collecting my Nana. We spend a hour together with my Mum including Kieran as well this time.

Then my uncle came and done all the business of arranging the funeral though me and my sister picked the coffin and all the little details.

My Nana chose the coffin.

While we were going through all the details of the funeral arrangements, my best friend Chris Mitchell and his brother Daman turned with their parents Kath and John.

Kath was my mum's best friend and her husband was a very close friend to our family, they were like an extended family to me and my sister. They all were so close to me and they had been always there for my Mum when she used to flee the house from my father.

They had been good friends of both my Mum and Father. Kath was my Mums best friend, like a sister my Mum never had.

They offered to drop my Nana back home to her place which was very lovely of them to do so.

Kiren and I dropped my sister off, who said she was exhausted as she hadn't slept the night before.

I offered if she needed me to stay with her but she said she was fine.

I asked Kiren could we go to our cottage and stay the night there but Kiren said she didn't want to stay there. I had to go there as I wanted to pick up some dope to smoke but I didn't want Kiren to know that so I went upstairs and through the black bin liner pulling out a small amount of weed and then running back down to Kieran.

We left the cottage in her car driving over to her new flat.

I needed some rolling papers and so I asked her to stop outside a shop. I went in and as I was asking for rolling papers I hadn't notice Kiren following me into the shop.

She then appeared next to me asking why was I getting rolling papers? I told her because I wanted to have a joint then she said "You promised me you had given up on drugs."

I told her yes I had but I needed to smoke a joint as it helped me the other day. She accused me of being stoned all the time since my Mum had died which that was lies as I had only on Monday smoked one half joint and a full joint and nothing more.

Even at the Satan's Slaves, one of the visitors there offered me to a line of coke and I had said no to that so I didn't need to being accused as a liar so I told her no I haven't but she just went off at me when I got in the car making me feel fucking guilty that I wanted to have a joint.

It got me so wind up as I could have got high the last two days even at my peers house who I drooped the money off to as he had lines of speed he was doing and asked if I wanted a line and I said no to that as well.

I jumped in the car and had a go at Kiren, telling her not to ever call me a liar and she replied "You will never change."

This so got my back up that I just got off the car before she could pull out into the street. I slammed the car door and thought fuck her for turning against me when I needed her the most.

I walked back in the direction of my cottage arriving there and putting on some Iggy Pop and rolled myself a joint then after hearing a few songs of his I put on some Motorhead and smoked the joint.

Turning on the telly for a minute to watch the news as I hadn't watched telly for days now so I didn't know what was going on outside my own little world.

I felt very much again very alone.....stoned and bored and very, very sad.

I went up stairs to lie down but couldn't get off to sleep; it was early for me only 10pm by this time so I got up again and called the Satan's Slaves clubhouse to see who was down there.

I spoke to Zombie and he told me to come down so I went down for a drink seeing Stonney there and always Carl Cumstain and all four of us got really drunk.

I told them about what Kiren said and they all thought she was bang out of order for moaning about me having a joint, which I agreed with them all then but here looking back they had no idea the recent things that had been going on over the weekend and the reason why Kiren had moved out due to finding the cottage inside out.

The boozing second night in a row seemed to kill off the pain but when I went to crash out, this time I was allowed in the bunk room that is inside the clubhouse used for when other bike clubs came down to stay so at least I wasn't on the carpet falling asleep in front of the fire.

I had nightmares that night I can remember of seeing my Mum come alive, reaching out to me in the coffin that I had seen her in the day at the funeral parlour.

The nightmares were very much like night terrors waking me up in the middle of the night, my body sweating a lot. I wasn't able to get back to sleep as I didn't want to revisit the same nightmares.

The following day I had to get back to the funeral parlour. My sister's friend Joana had stayed the night with my sister the night before so at least my sister hadn't spend a night alone as this is something I didn't wish for her to do as out of everyone , it was my sister who needed someone there for her.

Again Cool Ken offered my sister a lift over to the funeral parlour that morning. I went with Zombie on the back of his brand new Harley-Davidson.

Zombie and Cool Ken stayed outside talking while again I went in to see my Mum and spend time with her, my sister and Joanna Smith who with my sister was arranging what my Mum will be dressed in when she is to enter the church. There was talk of my Mum being in an open coffin but then we just wished people to remember my Mum while she was alive.

A very close friend Leonine came over with her husband Carl who was good friends of my Mum. Carl taught me to play cricket when I was a young boy and it was Carl who I got to meet the entire West Indian cricket team when I was kid at boarding school.

Leonine Gill and Carl Gill, I had so much time for them. They had a lovely family I remember her daughter Jackie (from a previous marriage) was also close to my Mum and us.

I still to this day have a photo with them both in which were taken only a week maybe before my mum was killed.

Photos of my Mum I couldn't look at for many years as the photos brought so much hurt so I never had photos ever out also I didn't like everyone asking me how my Mum was killed.

It's something I don't like sharing with anyone, even loved ones here in England.

I spend all afternoon that day with my Mum, right into the early evening as I only had the morning to see her again for my final good bye before the church service where I would never see my Mum again.

It was very hard seeing my Mum in the coffin. I left that afternoon heading over to where I grew up though not going by the old house that I knew as the haunted house but I spend time with my best friend Chris Mitchell and his family.

His mum Kath and father John and also brother Daman as they were so close to us all and I just wanted to be with them as I got comfort from them. I then went and saw my Nana staying with her to very late in to the night hoping that tomorrow never would come, when I had to see my Mum for the very last time.

I got a taxi home; my sister had a few friends stay with her to give her comfort. I went to the cottage which was all dark by the time I had got there. I still hadn't sorted out the weed under the house but I had so many other things to deal with as tomorrow I was saying good bye to my beautiful Mum and that for me was very hard to take in.

While I was home the phone rang, it was Kieran. I didn't want to speak to her as when she drove off the day before, I did think she would have driven back to get me but she didn't and that hurt me so I told her not to turn up to the funeral though by saying that I was only hurting myself more, as the night before my mum's funeral, I really needed her but I wouldn't tell her so.

I just told her again not to turn up tomorrow at the funeral and that I didn't want to see her. I think maybe I was trying to hurt her back, as I just hang up the phone again and didn't answer it when she called back.

I put on some of my mum's music such as The Drifters and then Elvis Presley and some Tom Jones but all this music while drinking alone was too much for me so I went to the only place that I felt more at home with and that was again the Satan's Slaves' Motorcycle Club clubhouse.

I met up with Scotty one of the ex members who was there. He and I got really drunk on vodka. I got so drunk, I don't even remember making it home in a taxi as I drunk probably more booze that night I had ever drunken.

The night before my Mum's funeral, I was in such a state within myself though I wouldn't let any tears fall from my eyes, especially in front of the Satan's Slaves members that I was drinking with.

I tried my best to be staunch but that front could only last so long. Actually, all the grieving that I was doing I was doing in private so everyone was thinking I was handling the death of my Mum better than expected. All that would come apart sooner than later, and everyone didn't need long to witness that happening.

Chapter 30

THE FUNERAL

NOTE : AGED 17 MY MUM WAS KILLED ON MOTHERS DAY 10TH MAY 1992

I awoke the morning of my Mums funeral due to heavy banging on my cottage door. I had been in dead sleep as only leaving the Satan's Slaves clubhouse early hours of that morning. I woke up still feeling drunk and wondering who was banging on my door so loudly also I thought to myself for a very short moment that the week I just had was actually a very bad dream and that my mum **hadn't been killed and I hadn't spend the last few days looking at her body in a coffin.**

I got my trousers on and went down stairs to open the door. Standing there was my Uncle Frank telling me to hurry up. I hadn't answered the phone all morning as I had been crashed down, everyone was worried about me. We had to get over to the church.

So it wasn't a bad dream what I had been dreaming and everything was so very real having my Uncle there at my front door.

I got changed very quickly and next to my bed was a letter I seemed to have written it to my Mum. I could hardly read it so I guessed I must have written it when I had got home after the drinking session as I truly don't remember writing it from any time in the week.

I could hear my stereo system making noise so went in to the lounge to turn everything off and it looked like I had been playing some Neil Young and also there was a Super Tramp LP on the floor, I mustn't have got that far as the LP wasn't out of the cover.

I put on some clothes and shut the door running down the path to get to my uncles car as I really didn't want to be late to my own Mother's funeral.

As I was down the path my neighbour yelled out to me asking when he could collect more weed.

I told him it was my Mum's funeral so I wasn't sure when I could sort it out? I told him I wouldn't be back tonight that's for sure but maybe on Friday, I see what I could do.

I am sure my Uncle heard some of the conversation as his window was down though neither he nor his wife said anything as we drove to the church. On arriving there very much in time, he then told me that I and he with my two remaining Uncles, we would be carrying in the coffin and taking it back out.

I told him though I was happy to lead my Mum into a church but there was no way I was going to carry her out of a church.

He told me not to be a fool but I said no and that was that. He wasn't too happy with me not taking orders from him and couldn't understand what kind of point I was making maybe he thought I was just trying to be awaked but I wasn't. I just didn't wish to carry my Mum's body out of a church.

Also I was meant to say a speech but I was never good at talking publicly since my days when I did debates at the boarding school but as for talking at my Mum's funeral I didn't want to break down in front of everyone so I told him I would simply pass the note I had written and I would give it to the priest to read.

Again my uncle wasn't happy about that but it was as much my Mum's funeral than it was his sisters funeral, and if I didn't want to do what I didn't want to do then no one was going to tell me what to do.

I entered the church carrying my mum's coffin, trying to talk to myself as I took each step and still not wanting to believe all of this, which was happening around me.

I sat down next to my Nana and my Sister. I looked back and the church was packed and also I think I was looking around for Kiren who I really needed.

I couldn't see her though I wondered if I would be angry if I did see her but deep down I wished she had turned up, just as I stopped looking around before the service started, I spotted friends from my earlier years when I went to Worse Bay School.

The Palmerter family had turned up. Campbell was good friend of mine in my earlier years when I was at Worser Bay School, so to see him and his brothers and also both his parents really touched my heart.

I know my mum who by now was in heaven with her two sisters, her brother Peter and her Dad would be looking down so thankful for the Palmerter family to turn up to support me and to say their farewells also Glenis and her three kids including Sasaka was there as well.

Geniis had been so kind in the week to say something in memory of my Mum. They were very good friends and had been through a lot and Sasaka was a good friend of mine and his sister a good friend of my sister and their younger brother was a decent kid with a good heart, who always meant well.

I saw even Bacon standing there from the Satan's Slaves who came for me, and also Grot and Zombie though many of my mum's friends who were straight wondered why bikers had turned up and more so the dangerous Satan's Slaves members.

It was good to know my brothers in arms were there for me as they had been ever since Bacon told me the sad news on the Sunday earlier.

The service I don't remember much as I just tried my best to hold on to my Nanas hand and also my sisters without crying.

Throughout my mind I would tried my hardest to block out everything that was being said and more so what was happening and that was I was sitting at my Mum's funeral.

I do remember Glenis, some of her speech she spoke very much on behalf of everyone there then the priest asked me to stand up but I just handed over the letter that was in my pocket and I let the church read it out.

When the music (some of my mum's favourite songs) started to play this is when tears fell from my eyes as music had always been played in our house growing up and so in my sisters and in my life. Music been came a huge part of all our lives.

Every night or day at my cottage, I would at least listen to two albums a night and so did my sister so I really felt everyone there when Elvis Presley was playing was too in tears, falling from everyone's eyes.

The service was over as quick as it seemed it began though it was an hour service but with me blanking a lot of it out, I didn't listen too much of it.

And when it came to lifting the coffin out, I wouldn't take my position to left the front of the coffin and I just walked outside, that's when as I was walking up through the church I spotted Kiren, she had turned up after all.

One of cousins took my place and the coffin came out and then into the back of a car. Fuck I hated seeing that and as it drive off, a lot of anger came flooding in me and all I wanted to do was get really drunk so to remove the pain that was running throughout this heart of mine.

I didn't know what I had to witness after that as we all went onto another place where they brunt the coffin and body.

When I watched my mum's coffin disappear into what I knew behind the curtains was a fire for her ashes to then be presented to us afterwards in a vase, that's when I was just bending on getting really pissed.

I just wouldn't accept what I had just sat through and witnessed.

I was in Kiren's car on the way to seeing my mum's coffin finally disappear.

I had Chris Mitchell in the car with me as well and my Sister then we went to the Basin Reserve Tavern (just at the start of Newtown), not far from the international cricket ground and near my last college I went to.

I was still in an angry mood though Chris couldn't tell but I think he knew something was up.

We reached the tavern where the wake was being laid on and I was being offered by everyone a drink and each drink I done in one.

I was sinking the drinks very quick that my uncle told me to slow down and then told me I was actually too young to be drinking.

I didn't want to know him and with comments like that but I guess he was just trying to look after his nephew and I should have taken his advice as I got so drunk. I didn't go near the food which I should have as my belly was just so full of booze.

I recall everyone was telling me they would always be there for me and my sister.

You know what I believed them all.

I done more Jack Daniels, when Kiren told me to eat some food as I hadn't eaten all day and at least that would slow down some of the booze I was throwing down my neck but I say no and asked her had she been speaking to my uncle and to get off my back.

Again someone just caring about me but I wasn't there to take any sound advice as all I wished to do is get completely drunk, fall asleep and finally wake up to it all being a dream as I had been hoping all week that it was just really a bad dream but nothing was making this nightmare go away.

Both Wims daughter came over to me with tears in their eyes and gave me a cuddle and then did my Sister but I didn't want all this fuzz made over me.

I stood at the bar with some of the Satan's Slaves who were in the public bar rather than in the salon bar where the wake was taking place also some of my peers had turned up.

I didn't think any of them had hearts but what they did offer me to sober up was some coke so I headed into the toilets with Sasaka as I offered Chris my best friend some and he said no, he wasn't a massive drug taker.

Now and then Chris would smoke some weed but nothing much more than that though hell he could drank as good as anyone for his age so he ordered me another drink for when I came out.

I took a massive line right up my nose and hitting my brain instantly soon as the coke hit my brain I felt so wired up, no longer drunk as I had.

I couldn't handle going back into seeing all my friends and my family especially after taking a line of coke.

Taking the coke and how it made me feel like, was better than the few joints I had smoked in the week, as the coke made me feel strong and not weak, full tears as I had felt all of the earlier part of the day.

For some reason it covered up all the pain in my heart and in my head so I stayed with my peers and also the Satan's Slaves and hit the bar shot after shot.

Chris Mitchell and Sasaka after they both had a shot of whiskey or three went back into the main area that's when Kieran was, asking them where I was?

On finding me, Kiren told me to come back in to all the others and again I told her to stop telling me what to do!

By this time as I was standing with patch members of the Satan's Slaves still so I very much wasn't going to follow her in and when she came out again saying she was just going to go home if I was going to be like this so I told her to go.

I really believe she didn't think I was going to stay and that I was to follow her and when I didn't that's when I think she threw in the towel as I had become too much hard work and all she was doing was trying to be caring but even then I would push her away.

My peers had their hooks in me even more by that line of coke; I think they knew that by offering me another of coke.

With what having that line at this time, when I was very drunk, when my head was all over the place, with losing the person who I loved the most well there and then I truly stopped believing in tomorrow.

I didn't know at the time but this was soon going to be my mind set within a few hours time.

After the afternoon became evening and a lot of people had left the tavern and there were just a few of my friends and many of my sisters friends, Redhead Rachael and the other Rachael said that everyone could go back to theirs.

The Satan's Slaves also said they would bring up some booze so we all went back to the Rachael's house above the sets of shops on the Parade in Island Bay and two of my peers came back as well.

I thought in support but they were asking me had I managed to get rid of any more gear in the week since I saw one of them only a few days earlier so said no.

They both knew I could only move their stuff that I had from Friday onwards due to my job in the evenings and also as I didn't have anyone ever knocking on my door for weed or the acid so they said that was fine as long as I hadn't forgotten that by the end of May, I had to get in the rest of their money.

I couldn't believe I was being hassled even on the wake of my Mother's funeral, they sensed they were being wankers I could tell as the very first thing that they gave me when I got back to Rachael place was another line of coke.

I on that very night, though I had done coke in the past but this very night I was being hooked on it as within an hour I asked them for another line.

One of them said if I wanted another line I would have to buy a gram $300 I didn't have that money on me so they put it as in their words, on my tab.

Next I was snorting huge lines of coke but wasn't getting that buzz again that I had got back at the tavern from earlier on.

I asked them did they have anything else and I was given a matchbox with ten acid trips in.

I did notice as none of my Mum's friends were there, that others had taken acid among my sisters friends and many of my friends were smoking weed so I dropped two acid tabs at once.

I couldn't see Kiren anywhere. I was told she was in her room. I thought if she wanted to act like that and not be part of the wake then that was fine.

I then got impatience with the acid as it hadn't hit me, though I never gave it time to start.

I shouldn't have taken two acid tabs to be truthfully, I shouldn't have even snorted coke and for sure not taken acid but I opened the match box and dropped another three tabs.

I had given five away as I didn't wish to be tripping among all my friends but for me to take five was far too much for anyone to take in one go that much acid, but I was so drunk high on coke and my Mum was dead so I really didn't give a fuck.

As the acid soaked through my body and my mind, whenever I went to the toilet I dared not look in the mirror as due to the acid I kept on thinking I was going to see my Mum in the mirror looking back at me.

I then went in to Kiren's room. She asked to be left alone but I told her she can't just stay in the room and that for her to come out.

When she did come out of her bedroom and was told I had taken acid she called me a prick and told me that we were for sure over and she went crying back into her room.

I went into the other lounge where the pool table was but couldn't play a game as the balls seemed to be moving before I even took a shot.

Everyone was laughing as they all knew I was tripping. I didn't like hearing the laughter and told many people to get fucked.

All my angry I felt earlier now was coming back and more drink I drunk wasn't doing anything.

Also as I now, wouldn't even go in to the bathroom to use the toilet as I was so sure that my mum face would appear in the mirror so I want out to the back door and went for a piss over the stairs.

Kiren's window was open, I could hear her speaking to someone and then I heard a males voice so I went back in to the house and opened her door to see a friend of ours, hugging Kiren as she was crying and him telling her not to worry and that everything would be ok.

I know now and a few days later that he actually was only trying to comfort her as he had seen her go in to her room crying her eyes out, so he was trying to tell her to come back out and that whatever I was saying I didn't mean.

But to me seeing him cuddling the girl I loved and seeing her cry on his shoulder I of course thought more was going on and without even saying anything I attacked me beating him till many others came in dragged him out.

Some turning on him as they all were backing me then Kiren rushed past me to get out of the room so I close the door on everyone including her.

I could hear her telling them it wasn't his fault; I had walked in on him hugging her.

They were knocking on the door; there was no lock on the door but I didn't want to see any one so placed my weight against the door so no one could come in.

I was so angry, still believing that something was going on. I was in such a drunken state I had drunk over a litre of Jack Daniels easily, that's for sure and then all the drugs that were messing up my head.

I got Kiren's bed with all my strength (a big thick wooden bed) that normally of course I wouldn't able to lift up by myself. I placed that up against the door so no one could get in and then I throw down the wardrobe as well against the door, now no one was going to reach me.

Through the open window I could hear the guy who had been holding Kiren speaking to someone on the back stairs slagging me off saying that when all this was finished with, that he would teach me a lesson!

Well wrong thing to say as that just got my blood boiling and now I really wanted to break his jaw after hearing that but I couldn't get out of the room as the bedroom door now had everything in the room up against it.

The only way out for me was through the window so that was that; I clamped out of the window onto a lower roof and jumped off it.

It wasn't a high roof nor was it the roof of the entire house but still thinking back now it was at a height and if it hadn't been for the acid then I wouldn't have jumped off it....actually if it wasn't for the acid I wouldn't be in this state.

As I landed in the back yard, a bush took most of my weight as I flung myself down onto the back yard and landed then rolled over and I was soon up on my feet.

At great speed up the set of stairs before anyone including the guy could say anything as I think they were still in shock from seeing me leap of the roof.

But what I wasn't expecting from him, was he being in a fighting mood as I run up the stairs he caught me with a kick to my chest that flung me back down the stairs.

I do recall some pain but that only got my heart beat up more as I headed back up, this time as he tried to kick me again, I managed to get hold of his foot and with that hold I dragged him down the stairs and laid in to him with all I had.

He was much older than me and very much stronger so he put a good fight up. It was punch for punch, but what I had on my side was everything I had gone through so there was no way I was going to lose this fight and there was no way I was going to let him teach me a lesson as I battered him more and finally he tired out, though he did manage to get away.

He leaped up and took off towards the back gate, undoing the lock before I could reach him.

Chasing him out onto the main road through traffic, till he reached his car that was a flash boy racer type of car, with his keys out he tried to fend me off while he attempted to unlock his driver's door.

I knew if he made it inside his car, he would be off. I knew by the look of his car that this was his pride and joy so I thought I would do as much damage to the car as possible.

I started to kick every panel of the car in, which got his back up as now he found himself chasing me in attempt for me to stop doing damage to his car.

I jumped up on the bonnet of the car, kicking at the front window. Onto the roof I then jumped upon as he was trying to grab at my legs.

I was doing so much damaged to his car, he wasn't able to get a hold of me then with a kick out of my feet as he reached nearer to get hold of me, I struck him right in his face and that made him fly back as he put his hands up to his face, blood came pouring from his nose.

That's when I thought he would be right up for a fight now so I jumped down and managed to get in a beauty of a punch but he didn't fight back, maybe the sight of his own blood have him out of the fighting mood.

What I didn't expect was him running off back to the flat so I just kept on making sure if anyone was taught a lesson it would be him as I smashed off one of the side mirrors.

What I didn't know was that people inside the house were trying to break down Kieran door as they thought I was still inside there.

The other person on the stairs who had seen the fight hadn't told any one of me jumping out the window and no one knew about the street punch up, that was till the guy who I was fighting returned to the house.

Next minute from up at the lounge window people struck their heads out to watch me.

My sister came running down pleading with me to stop and Redhead Rachael as well.

I told them no way as I kept wreaking the car with my hands and feet as I kicked and punched and torn as much of the car as I could with my strength which was more strength than I ever knew I had.

Next a family friend Vince came down telling me the guy was on the phone calling the police then kiren put her head out the window yelling out I was a complete wanker and no way was I to come back inside the house.

She slammed the window shut!

I saw the Satan's Slave member Scotty come down the pathway next to the house above the set of shops.

He for sure was only going to try and clam me down but as he nearly went to take a step onto the road from the pavement, three police cars came flying up the road so Scotty headed back into the house and the police all jumped out of their cars and asked what was going on as they received a call.

I just told them some kids had been seeing kicking in the car and that I had come down to see what was happening.

They told us that they had received three calls so looking around I noted neighbours looking out their windows as what had been going on was very loud.

They asked did we know the owner of the car and we all said no.

I am glad my sister and Redhead Rachael were both backing me up.

As for the guy who owned the car, he was trying to get down to the police but Stonney who now had hold of him with Zombie wouldn't let him out of the house as they had caught him on the phone grassing me.

As he didn't show his face, then the police asked where these so called kids had gone.

I said they run up a nearby alleyway. Next minute there was a dog unit that arrived and heading up the alleyway at that point the police heard a fight inside Rachael's house.

The guy was trying to get free from Stonney, who was holding him so he couldn't get to the police to grass me up.

He was yelling out "Help!" in ear shot of the police, who on hearing his shouts ran up the stairs.

Zombie yelled out "Police!!"

Stonney on hearing this, let go off the guy who then run to the back door and told the police officers what I was wearing and what I looked like and it was me who done the damage to his car.

All this I didn't know was going on and I really thought I was in the clear but I wasn't as two police officers after a radio call grabbed me pushing me head first on the bonnet of the car.

My sister was pleading with them to let me go and Rachael was telling them my Mum had just been buried and to let me go.

They didn't but they allowed me at least to stand up while cuffing me from behind.

Then the owner of the car came down and the grassing prick said yes that was me, next minute with now my sister in tears, I was put into the back of a police car and was placed in the nearest police station in town.

I was so out of it, the flashing lights of the police car when they arrived earlier very much remained me that I was tripping and more so when I was held in a cell.

All the giraffe on the walls were moving around and the blanket I was given was waving up and down as I sat up on the bench in the cell.

A police officer came in and asked me was I ok? Was I handled correctly by the officers?

What was all that about and I thought he was just part of my trip.

I still spoke back and said I was fine.

He told me that the guy who owned the car has since rung up the police station saying it now actually wasn't me who had done it but the police for my own safely (as they said I was far too drunk to be let out) were going to hold me till the morning but I wouldn't be charged with anything.

The police officer said I was not allowed back at the address they had been called to due to someone who lived there requesting that. I knew who that would have been Kiren for sure but by now I didn't give a fuck.

I actually didn't give a fuck even if I had been charge with what they said was criminal damaged and disorder etc as what did I have left in my life, nothing I felt.

I lost my Mum and now my girlfriend, though from the previous weekend that relationship was on the rocks.

It's just a shame how horrible it all ended, more so that on the late evening of my Mum's funeral and that I wasn't there for my sister.

Had the guy changed his story to feel sorry for me as it was my Mums funeral?

No he hadn't due to that, as it was due to Scotty telling him if he didn't then he very much would be a marked man and he would be driven out of Wellington.

He would need to be watching his back as he would be seen as a grass.

This frighten him enough so he called the police in front of Zombie and Stonney and Scotty telling the police he had got it all wrong and it was as first reported, some tearaway kids who had the damage to his pride and joy... his motor.

As the policeman shut the cell door with a loud bang, there I was tripping of my nut in a police cell and with only a moving blanket, it seemed as my company.

Though very drunk I couldn't sleep. I remember for hours I just with my trip changed all the spray paint on the road around from gang symbols to draw pictures of cottages in the country side and animals and other things that seemed to be appearing on the wall without the aid of pens but purely through just tripping off my nut.

All of this actually was very calming and even though I had taken far too much acid, it all still hadn't turned bad on me as in my state of mind though my behaviour was unspeakable and the violence and jumping off a roof then smashing a car up.

My hands and legs didn't hurt at that point.

Hours passed and then sooner than expected, it must have been daylight as a breakfast tray came in the bolt hold but by this time my eyes were closed, though I wasn't a sleep I just could see with my eyes closed, so many different colours of the rainbow.

I didn't want this to fade and I wasn't hungry for breakfast, slowly I fell asleep which only seemed a short time as I was awoke with the cell door open and a lot of noise as everyone else was getting ready for court.

From my cell I was then put into another cell more of a holding cell with gang members who were off to court. I had forgotten about the police officer who came in the night to tell me I wasn't being charged for anything so I just guessed I was going to court with all the others in the cell.

Then a police officer came in and called out my name, a few Maoris said good luck which I thought that was strange as I looked like a skinhead with my tattoo on my head and a skinhead style haircut.

When I was first put into this holding cell I expected a punch up as many looked like brawlers and all looked moody.

I was then giving back my shoe laces and my personal belongs such as my watch and my ring and what cash I had on me at the time plus a piece of paper telling me I wasn't allowed in 100 meters of that house.

It must have been an injunction, I didn't even read it as I threw it in the nearest bin. I just wanted to get out of the police station.

Once I was outside the sunlight hit me and as I walked down the street I felt so hung over again maybe still slightly drunk.

The acid hadn't totally cleared from my system as all the sunlight was more brighten than normal and everything around me seemed faster than normal, be it the traffic or people talking to each other.

It was still very trippy and then on top off this, I felt so ill and also so tired.

All my bones, in my body were so sore especially my hands and feet.

Each step I took, there this was shooting pains in both feet.

Everything from yesterday hadn't yet crossed my mind, not even the funeral of my Mum.

It all was very strange walking down the road, I just wanted to get home as soon as possible so I headed near Manners Mall where I knew there was a cab rank and got in a taxi telling the driver "5a Wright Street, Mt Cook please." winding down the window to get some fresh air as we travelled through Wellington, 24 hours after my Mums funeral.

Arriving at my cottage not to far later.

Up the path I walked holding on the white fence to take my weight off my feet, which were even sorer by now.

I walked on up to find my front door lock busted.

I guessing it might be Kiren, who had come in the night or the morning to get the very last of her things as in some kitchenware and other bits and pieces but then she had her own key still, so she wouldn't kick in the door (not even in a bad mood) and she wouldn't have known that I was released this morning.

I am sure she knew about the guy being forced to call the police last night telling them it wasn't me, so as far as Kiren was concerned I might have been released last night.

I was the last person she wanted to see as by now after all I had done, she didn't want to see me ever again so for sure it wasn't her.

"The drugs, Fuck the fucking drugs!"

I went straight upstairs, slowly making my way up the stairs with all the pain from my body from the night before and seeing my whole bedroom turned upside down even the make shift mattress on the bed base.

I then knew what I was expecting as I put my hand down the gap in the wooden base.

Not only was the acid gone but also the shotgun and the bag of weed that I had got from the back yard and placed into a new black bin bag.

"Fuck!!"

I went downstairs, the cottage hadn't been smashed up, so I knew it wasn't a out of the blue break in, as even my record player was there though my video recorded had been taken and my stereo system but not my television and neither my old record player nor my records though they had been scatted as if someone had been checking in every sleeve as all the records were out of their sleeve covers.

I went in to the bathroom, the washing machine had been undone at the back and also the lid of the toilet was off as I went for a piss looking out through the loafer window. I remembered the dope under neither the cottage.

So I went outside and an extra panel of the cottage had been torn off.

That to me made me now know that whoever it was who had robbed me, knew me personally.

I looked under the cottage and yes all the broken bags of weed had gone though there still was a stoker of weed underneath near the entrance that had been made bigger to get access underneath the cottage.

I went into the house and behind the bathroom door I got the rake and grabbed another bin bag underneath the kitchen sink, all this was a mess and there was only one black bin bag left so I knew that whoever had robbed me, had been using anything laying about in the cottage to help them take out the weed and the acid and the shotgun.

I scrabbled as much as I could of the weed up from underneath the cottage and put it in the last remaining bin bag.

I walked back up to the front door and just then on carrying in the black bin bag of weed, what hadn't come to my mind all of yesterday was my Mum's funeral as I grabbed the yellow pages to call a lock smith.

The very first page, the yellow pages opened to was not on L but on F for funeral services, now my Mums funeral was coming back thick and fast into my head.

I fell back on my lounge. No speakers to listen to any of my music, a lounge that also was upside down but not wreaked, but a life that very much felt wreaked as now I was in debt and in debt to serious people.

I had a gun missing which wasn't sitting well in my thoughts. I had a house that had been broken into, my Mum dead, my girlfriend had left me, a head all mixed up on drugs due to the night before, a body in pain, broken heart, and with only a few hundred dollars to my name as I hadn't worked this week so I had no wage cheque to collect.

As for all the money that was owed out to me, none of that now belonged to me as I no longer had any profit for myself due to being robbed. All the money had to go to the peers now due to being robbed.

The remaining money for sure, my peers (I just knew....fact) would make me cover as it wasn't there problem my house had been robbed and yes I had a pretty good idea who robbed my cottage while I was at my Mum's funeral..... my neighbour, two doors down I guessed, only because he had seen me by the back of the cottage with a bag of weed, so he must have worked out the weed was hidden under there.

Maybe he had broken into the house to get at my cash, I am so lucky that I paid what money was in the house to one of my peers at the start of the week as if I hadn't then I would now be even in more shit.

The little money I had left, I had to use some of it on a lock smith so I went through the yellow pages, I called a locksmith who came over a few house later.

By then I had put the cottage back together.

With the rolling papers I still had on me, I smoked a joint after I had finished.

The lock smith arrived while I was still smoking the joint. I asked if he wanted some of the joint, he said yes so we both got stoned while he put on strengthen deadbolt locks on the cottage door, then he also with his tool kit put on the back of the washing machine as I didn't have any tools in the house.

I was hopeless at DIY so never felt a need to have a tool kit in the cottage.

He thanked me for the smoke, he was a Maori I am sure a ex gang member due to some of this tattoos on his throat but he seemed ok and at that point I just wanted to crash out.

This time waking (fingers crossed) from what I hoped would be all now be the bad dream I was hoping that I had just been through but fuck again it wasn't as everything that had happened over the weekend and up to this moment all wasn't a bad dream........I felt so low and down.

I can't even explain how down I felt there and then in my life at that very moment.

I spend all of that day and afternoon and evening in my cottage, only being woken once by the phone ringing. It was my sister asking where I had been? She was very worried about me and that was uncle Frank was trying to get hold of me as well, she said.

I told her the cottage had been broken into and explained the police let me out that's when she told it was Scotty who had helped me out.

I told her I was exhausted and I wanted more sleep so she let me be and I fell asleep in to a very long dream.

A dream I can't really recall but I know my Mum was throughout the dream.

I didn't wake up again till the Saturday afternoon after such a long sleep.

I so needed it after for all of that week, I must have slept for nearly only 16 hours in total all week.

Friends I was told had knocked on my door and that many people had been calling my phone but I was just in what could have been described as coma like state as the acid was still throughout me and all the lack of sleep from the week earlier and all the boozing then with my body just maybe shutting down to recover and to meant its self.

I was what you could call dead to the world.

I woke up now in lots of pain, my hands were bruised and my feet were so sore, more so than the previous day.

I didn't like that I had slept so long, as knowing the shotgun had been taken, maybe who ever robbed my cottage might think that there was more stuff in the hidden in the cottage and they could come back with me laying there upstairs in my bedroom fast asleep.

I truly didn't feel safe even though I had a proper strong couple of locks put on the door so it would take them a lot to kick in the door but this feeling of being woke to another break in, I didn't like at all.

It reminded me of the man on that New Years Eve night when I was a kid, who had got in to my mum's friends house when I was sleeping over with the other kids while our parents were at a party celebration the New Year.

I don't know why that came to mind and as I made myself a coffee and turned on the telly with lots of thoughts from my past childhood coming through my mind, no thought was on my future, when just prior to my mum dying all my thoughts had been on my future as I had very much put my past in just that....my past.

I had been looking forward to such a bright future but with my mum being alive this time last week to the day then the following day, right out of the blue her life just taken.

As I just slipped on the coffee, how could I ever believe in a tomorrow after what happened to my mum and so any dreams or goals I had of a future were forever gone and no longer could I ever again believe in a future or believe in dreams.

Chapter 31

SHATTERED DREAMS AND A LIFE IN SHATTERS

My life was on free fall starting by the end of the weekend, a week later since I had been told my Mum was dead.

Nothing for me seemed the same, and that was without my Mum being in my life, more so without my Mum having her own life.

Free falling was what, was happening to my life, every aspect of it.

As on the Saturday night I ended up drinking heavily at the Satan's Slaves clubhouse.

By the Sunday I was still there drinking, I didn't want to go back to the cottage.

The cottage that had been broken into, the cottage that was once a loving home for Kiren and me and now she was gone, not just out of the home but also out of my life so life was lonely.

Anytime I went back to the cottage I always had the thought at the back of my mind that someone was watching the place to rob it again and I just didn't want to be in there if that took place also it just didn't feel like a warm loving home, one with good me memoires as it used to have as now it just felt a place that was so sad with too many memories.

Nothing would change that even with new set of speakers I swapped for some of the remaining weed as music hadn't been played in that cottage since the robbery.

It was music that brought good times but even now the sound of music wouldn't lift my mood as I found myself crying alone in the cottage all night on the Sunday...a week since my mum had been killed.

I had work the next morning.

Work just didn't bring anything more for me but I had to work to pay the bills and more so pay the rent that I had to take on myself but a bigger issue that I had to deal with, was the recovery of all the drugs that I put out on bail.

To make sure the money went to my peers but even with all the money out there owed to me, it still was going to be short on what I owed so all my wages had to go towards paying towards the debt as well.

I really wished I knew who had robbed me as I was in the mood to truly do harm to them even if they held the shotgun at me they had stolen as I didn't give a shit about my own life at 17 years old....I really couldn't give a fuck now.

My neighbour, I did have my suspicions but how could I prove it was him?

What was I going to tell the Satan's Slaves that I think he robbed me while he still was my neighbour with no proof at all as that would have brought on gangland war as if they went for him then the Nomads and the Satan's Slaves would have clash and bloodshed would have come either way, though this was the Satan's Slaves city and they weren't scared of anyone but neither did the Nomads fear anyone and their first target would have been me in the middle of a night while I slept in my cottage.

If I had proof then yes I would have been on his doorstep and I would have seek the backing of my brothers in arms the Satan's Slaves but I had no proof and I wasn't silly enough to start a fire that would have spread between one of the country's major gangs and one of the leading motorcycles clubs in the country.

Also I really didn't wish the Satan's Slaves to know about how much drugs I had recently been selling. I am not saying that the Satan's Slaves are a drug free gang or anti drugs but I am just saying they didn't know the extent I had got myself in as in moving drugs for my peers across the city.

I did see my neighbour again on the Tuesday, he asked how I was?

Also he said he had all the remaining money for me, and still did I have some weed left? I gave him the remaining and while standing in his lounge looking around hoping to see my video player or the speakers and my stereo but his lounge was the same it had been, a dinner table, a few chairs and an old telly in the corner, he didn't even have a lounge. Maybe all my stuff had been sold if it was him who robbed me and for him asking I for more weed then that was just a trick, who knows?

As I was stepping out of his house after he had asked how my Mum's funeral was, I told him my house had been robbed and a firearm taken.

Not saying what type but just to see if I could tell in his eyes something that showed me he was guilty but his face nor his eyes changed as his final words were he would keep a look out to make sure my house wasn't hit again.

He went on to say he wished he had heard whoever had broken in, as he said he would have hung them up by their throats.

Well if it wasn't him then I am sure he would have damaged anyone if he caught some one red hand robbing my place but all this talk didn't bring me any closer to who done me and put me now in the shit.

One week soon became another and within in a few days I would have to come up with all the money for my peers.

I was very short then what I thought was a silver lining in the clouds came to me but I wasn't helped out which just got me so mad even more.

My Uncle Frank said he was back in Wellington after going through my mum's will, and speaking to the lawyers of my Mothers Estate.

I was to meet him over at my mum's flat. I hadn't been back to my mum's flat since before my mum's funeral. Walking in the door again, even this time a strong sent of her perfume I still could smell.

Being in there was too much for me as far too many memories of my Mum all around me.

I really couldn't bare it as nothing had changed since the last time my Mum herself was here last.

It felt very airily for me.

I had finished work, the night before I had taken the money from my neighbour to the peers and also I had been collecting more from the students as they had sold on most of the acid they had taken from so at least money was going to the peers each week. I never told them about the break in.

I didn't want to look like I had let them down or been a fool by hiding the drugs just under the bed but for many years when I only used to hold stuff for them well I always had hidden it under the bed as I never felt the threat of being broken in to or railed by the police.

Anyway with the break in of my cottage it showed they hadn't stopped looking and to the lengths they had gone to find the drugs in the cottage as in undoing the washing machine back thinking I had hidden drugs in there, so even if I had hidden the drugs some else, they still I believe would have found them.

The missing gun was playing on my mind more that the drugs and at least maybe I got to be thankful that it wasn't a police raid as I then truly would have been fucked anyway my head just went from thinking it could be any one of my friends.

Even at one stage thinking it was my peers for some reason.

Maybe they thought I wasn't after my Mum's death to be in the right frame of mind to go through with moving the drugs but would they do that to me? I didn't know as I became untrusting of everyone.

As for being in that position in the first place, for once I knew what a fucking fool I was ever to have taken the drugs that day in the car at the golf course. What a fucking idiot to say the least.

All this had built up from starting to smoke dope when I was younger then to selling a little and then to holding drugs for my peers to that point in my life, a few weeks earlier taking what was a very large amount.

Of course to a major drug dealer or drug smuggle, it's really not much but to me a 17 year old, it was. It now was taken over all my thoughts as I had to come up with money and even with wages going towards it I just wasn't going to hit that target.

For now I had to listen to what my Uncle and with what he had to say about whatever he needed to tell me.

Firstly I was told that he had now become my guardian until I turn the age of 18 years old so he was trying to say whatever he said and decided it meant that in his eyes, were law.

He said that there was a sum of $116,000 for me left out of my Mums will. My uncle went onto tell me I could either have the cash or have my mum's flat.

I didn't want my Mum's flat, I never thought of taking it and moving in then in time selling it if I wished, as my mind wasn't thinking straight and all this was above my head so I said I would have the money and my sister to have the house.

She was given all of my Mum's personal belongings and also her car as she had a licence and I didn't have a driving licence.

He also told me that among what my Mum left out that Friday night before she left her flat for the last time, that she had even left her will out.

He asked me about the final conversation I had with him so I told him how she had a bad feeling about going away but he played that down, saying that I must have misheard her, when he said this, we clashed as I heard word for word what my Mum had said to me that night when I last would ever hear her voice again.

He asked about my living arrangements and he said he had been told about the breakdown of my relationship with my girlfriend, though I said that was something in the past and I was getting on with my life.

But in all fact I wasn't as my life (the night Bacon told me my Mum was dead) just stood still.

He offered me to come and live with him and my auntie but I told him I was happy where I was and also I didn't want to be far from my sister.

The conversation was like a business meeting and at the end of it, I asked him when would he be transferring the money into my bank account but he said no I don't get that till I was 20 years old.

What another 3 years! Why not now and if he was the trustee then he could just sign the money off to me now.

But the way he was and only in my latter years I knew he was doing it for the very right reasons as he said he wouldn't be doing anything of the sort and I would just have to wait also he said the best thing for me when I turned 20 was to invest it in some New Zealand forest.

By 28 years time in pine, I would be sitting on a large amount of money. I would been set up for life but again this to me didn't sound any good but it was probably the soundest advise I had been given in my whole life and what a fool I was not to listen. He told me how I could buy one or two houses as well with the remaining money and everything would be good for my future. My mum had left me in a good position but at that time I was just interested in paying off my peers as I had a fair bit outstanding but I couldn't tell him that.

He left me with some lawyer documents and I had to sign some papers as well and then he was off saying he would be checking up on me.

I really didn't need a father figure in my life after all the many years of not having any father but more so no rules to live by.

That night I went with him to see my sister and he had the same nearer enough conversation with my sister and she signed some documents.

I stayed the night at my sisters flat; we didn't speak about my mum or what had happen in the last few weeks. I fell asleep on her couch; walking up in the morning and the very first time not showing up to work then on leaving my sister the next afternoon I just didn't want to go over to my cottage.

I dreaded being in that place by myself so I called a mate who had a car; I collected even more money the final amount that was owed out to me for my peers.

I am just glad no one let me down and I think no one did as everything I had been through as I told all the dealers who I had passed the acid on to that my cottage had been broken in to. Hearing some of their stories when their own houses in the past had taken a knock and everything taken, that's when I though fuck ever living that life.

I was never a drug dealer though what I had been doing was that, but it was something that I never wanted again to get involved in, it just so too much of a head fuck and look where I ended up...in fucking debt.

Debt not to a High St Bank but debt to a nasty outfit of people and they weren't like no bank, so there was no over draft being offered to me.....and I knew that very well indeed.

I took the money and went again for a drink to the Satan's Slaves clubhouse. I now was spending more time down there than even at my own place but they all were fine with me down there.

No one ever told me to fuck off.

I wouldn't break down and nor cry nor would I speak about my Mum as I would just go there to get really hammed drunk. Everything (being that drunk) seemed numb, all the pain that no one knew inside that I was going through.

After getting pissed, I went to my peer's house and gave him more roils of cash and I now had the final week to get the remaining cash but the thing was that the remaining outstanding money I had outstanding, I didn't have no one else now to collect off.

Anyway as I rocked up drunk there, my peer called around a few people and we got on the piss at a night club up town. I was being treated out and so didn't have to put my hand in my pocket but I didn't even have money in my pocket to spend even if I wanted to buy myself a few drinks while out that night.

I was given more coke up my nose, hadn't taken coke since the night of my Mum's wake but here now I was taking it again.

It made me believe that it was again doing me the best of good as it made me just forget about all my problems and issues.

The thing was now with each line of coke I had been given, now was going to become my biggest problem and my biggest personal issue.

The coke in my life throughout my blood vines, all for what, to block out any pain that was in my heart I was holding and not wanting to face up with the truth.

Though thinking I was handling everything ok, having little amounts of coke then wanting more.

By the morning waking up feeling like shit and yet another day of not going to work calling them saying I was ill, well in many ways yes I was ill as I was suffering from the come down that came with cocaine use.

The week was up, a whole week of not going into work and now I had no wage come through and no parent to borrow a few quit of.

I was there now with no money to cover the rent and though through telling the land lord about my mum dying and that I would sort it soon, by another weekend on the piss and partying it up wither Satan's Slaves feeling so safe behind their closed gates, where no problem I had to face and no one hassle me for rent payments, I could just close off from the whole outside world.

But by the Monday morning I was still sat up against the side of the bar, not slept all weekend. Calling work again, this time being told if I didn't show to work tomorrow then that would be my job.

You know what I didn't have my job on my mind as I just wanted to escape again within myself and the way I had found a way to do that as from each line of coke I snorted.

I left the clubhouse and bailed a gram of coke, finding a few pals to have it with and within no time it was gone, all snorted so another gram I got on tick and soon that was gone as when a gram would last all night in the past well now two grams hadn't even last all afternoon. I just wanted more in such a short space of time but wasn't allowed any more as didn't have money for it.

I found myself back at my cottage that's just didn't seem lived in anymore as I had hardly been there.

All these were in the fringe was booze, beers and bottle of half drunken Jack Daniels. My worries were not that there was no food but that there was no mixer to have with the Jack Daniels nor any ice if I wished to have it neat.

It has to be one of my lowest points in my life.

As for dinner, you could say I had that night was 7 cans of beer, glasses quarterly poured of Jack Daniels, and that was it.....my dinner for the evening. The drunkenness putting me to sleep just past midnight, the earliest I had been to bed in many a moon.

I did make it to work the following day but with a hangover and the way I was spoken to well I ended up just telling my boss to fuck himself and I walked.

I wasn't going to be taking no shit, though that was the end of holding a job for the time being, that had done me no wrong but with a head mixed up with the addition of coke then work doesn't even come second , it comes last.

I headed back to my cottage but being at home in the day, I got bored so quick and then took a call which I didn't know whom it be but it was the land lord trying to get hold of me again on the off change I was home, asking for the rent payment or I would be out again on the owed payment.

Lose was easy to, take loss of my Mum, lose of girlfriend and earlier loss of my job. Two things being my fault and now near lose of the roof over my head again my fault, no one else to blame for this mismanaged state of affairs.

I thought I anit going to pay any more money to a place I didn't like living so I packed up all my stuff and got Stonneys to come collect me to take me and my stuff to my Mum's flat.

Dropping it all there and enjoying some weed with him. My mum's place for the first time felt ok for me as long as I closed her bedroom door as that's where the strong sent of perfume was coming from and also that room out of all of the flat was the most reminder of my Mum in so many ways.

With good company and being stoned then I didn't get the feelings I had previously and I was just happy to be finally out of the cottage. I had guessed that the cottage was to blame for a lot of the problems but it was only a tiny bit as most was in my head as in the way I wasn't coping with my Mum's death and for sure not going through the process of dealing with either coming to terms with what had happened.

All I just wanted was to find a comfort zone where everything would be ok, but again for now that sadly was through drug use but no longer could I afford coke.

Yeah I could get weed from friends to share and smoke with them but some strong strains of weed that I started to smoke would bring everything back to the front of my mind when I found myself really high from smoking too much dope.

What I wanted to do was suppress everything and that was not going to happen by just smoking weed so I went to one of the dealers who I had given some sheets of acid to a few weeks earlier before the death of my Mum.

I took off him 300 trips on bail telling him to give me now a few weeks to get the money back to him, he agreed as it was me who in the first place had given him the acid on bail so he couldn't say no to me, even though he had already paid of the acid on tick.

I now stocked up on acid and my very first night now out again up town I took a tab with a pal and tripped out. A trip I remember spending in the end with two hot girls, one my mate pulled and one I did so soon they were on acid with us as well.

We ended getting pissed as I sold a few tabs of acid up town enough to drink all night and party with them, bringing them back to my Mum's flat in the early hours of the morning.

Sleeping with the girl then in the morning not even remembering her name as her and her friend left for work, and me and my pal loving it (the night we had just had) and the success of pulling these two stunners.

But this Friday I had to sort out my shit and fast as I had to see one of my peers that evening, early evening with a bag full of cash that I just didn't have.

I left it at the last minute to call my uncle telling him I really needed some of that money transferee and he said he couldn't just do it there and there as it was in a trust fund with the lawyers Cooke and Co in Greytown.

I demanded to know who the lawyer was dealing with my Mum's will and my money so my uncle said good luck and gave me Juliet Cooke's office number

I called her on the telephone, A very lovely woman and friendly and helpful who informed me that it was my Uncle who had the power and yes he was right if he were to transferee money it would take a lot of paper work and also many days but he could be the only person who could do this and not herself.

I thanked her after she explained a lot and then I called my Uncle again pleading with him but he said though, yes he could, he wouldn't and not to bother him again on this matter.

All I had was a few documents but the documents stated how much money I was due though yes in 2 and half years time, that was about 30 months till I had the money.

Now my peer of course wasn't going to wait 30months but at least I could prove to him that I was trying to recover the remaining money so I went to his house with my documents and told him I had lost the remaining money due to the break in that he already knew about in and also in the time since then I had lost my job and party to hard but that I would have his money in one month's time.

He gave me grace for that but at a cost of a $1000 on top... What a prick, he really had me by the balls so I had to accept it.

Right there in that situation I was being shown my age and how I was far way over my depth when I had got mixed up at this age in that type of drug dealing but at least I was given some more time.

And then as we shook hands after telling him I was hoping and betting on my uncle by the end of the month give me $20,000 off my money he then said after giving me a line of coke knowing that my lights lite up just by the mention of coke.

He then believing I was getting a $20,000 advance on my money from my Mum's estate gave me a bag of coke that was worth around just over $3,500.

Fuck it I thought I will make sure I get at least enough money from my share of my Mum's estate by the end of the month as somehow I would get my uncle to release some money so instead of just turning up to the peers house asking for some extra time on paying him back,

I now ended up leaving his place new in total $4500 more in debt, as $1000 fine you could say and then the coke.

It just shows how I wasn't thinking straight.

I would have been better off hanging myself as that's exactly what, more a less I was doing by accepting even more drugs which just meant more debt and more so....more drug abuse.

The coke, some of it I did sell so by the Saturday night I had a grand in my pocket and a lot of coke left but as the month of June soon faded so did a month of coke taking and also the acid I had and with the money I was getting from selling a bit of coke.

I now had just come back to square one, worse as I was selling coke but with this coke I had it meant I had cash so every night and I mean every night I would be out on the piss, getting drunk and drunken each time the coke wore off.

I would be hit by the volume of booze I had drunken and that would make me agro so slowly I was getting in to a lot of fights, weekend after weekend.

Needing to fight not too cleanly as mainly due to my age having to make sure I won the fights and not to lose face as there I was a teenager in a grown up world.

Even my sister saw the change in me and she didn't like me using my mum's flat for me and my mates to crash over and have girls over, neither did when friends would be sick or break something due to being so drunk in there but I didn't like night time at my mum's place and especially when I was by myself so I would have whoever was up for partying to come on over.

I was sliding fast and so fast I hadn't even noticed the month come to an end.

I had my peer calling me asking what was going on so I said just a few more days then I found myself asking my sister to sell my mum's car as still my uncle wouldn't do anything for me.

My uncle caught on by a friend of mine parent's place, who told him that she believed I was on coke when I had come over to see her son, well my uncle was anti drugs to say the least and he thought the best thing to do was tough love so now for sure 110% he didn't want to help me out at all.

I was honest to him after my sister said no about selling my mum's car, I told him I was in drug debt from self use (not from selling as that was none of his business and again I lived by those early words Loose Lips Sinks Ships.

I told him only that the persons I owed the money to were some heavy people and I had to pay up or they would break my legs.

That they had yet to come for their money, and though they knew me most of my teenage years, when it came to money they wouldn't think twice about doing me harm.

That's just the way it is in those circles and everyone who ever got involved knew what the score was before getting involved so if you let down certain people then you for sure knew what you had coming to you.

I knew that but my uncle Frank didn't believe that and he said "You got yourself in this mess; you get yourself out of it!"

The thing was, out of it 24 / 7 I was but that was "out of it" as in being so high all the time.

I had no job though now any rent to pay and a flat to live in but apart from having a roof over my head I had nothing in my life.....rock n roll, sex and lots of drugs and now even more debt well that doesn't count as all those together were only sending me to what looked very much like a early grave at the young age of only still 17 years old.

Where a few months earlier I had a future to look forward well that for sure was lost in among the mess I had got myself into and nothing it seemed was changing for the good.

I told my peers that I now owed my Mum's car which I didn't and to cover their debt as there was still a delay with my advance on my Mum's money that I would give them their money by selling my Mums car privately.

Again they believed me but again for one more month I was given an extra $1000 hit on top off the now increasing debt.

Now I had to pay back the drug dealer the money for the acid and I didn't have that though at least 200 trips left but I didn't hand them back as in selling a few trips each evening or during the day is what only source of money I was receiving to live on.

I wasn't expecting a knock at my door by him with a few hard nuts all saying they didn't give a fuck I knew the Satan's Slaves.

They were here for their money and their money wasn't here when that knock came so two of them held me with a knife close to my neck.

My television from my cottage that I had at my Mum's was taken out and then my Mum's expensive surround sound stereo system and her huge television that she had only brought near my birthday, was also taken and her bedroom television as well.

I stood watching my Mum's stuff being taken out due to me owing them money, there was no one who I could turn to though it was my Mum's stuff apart from my own telly.

Again who was to blame for this apart from me?

It wasn't a nice thing to witness. The drug dealer even said sorry, the reason for the knife and the two heavies was he knew without them then he could have found himself in a tricky situation as he knew I could easy if he were alone turned the tables on him and it would have been him who could have ended up with a knife to his throat.

It wasn't nice for me but looking back to that moment it wasn't either for him.

The next time I saw him he was too shy or embarrassed to speak to me as he had a lot of shame for what he did but I had the shame now when my sister found out and more so my uncle who forced me out of my mum's flat soon after that.

My sister moved in to take up living there as that's what she had been given in the signed documents.

My sister wasn't going have me homeless but I was just out of control, always on acid and also never listening to her and now I didn't want to know my uncle for him removing me from my mum's flat as really he had just me homeless.

I think within all the family I now had became a black sheep but where was I going to live and this month was also creeping up on me quick.

I stayed at many people's houses, crashing on mates lounges but that wasn't doing me any good and as everyone now saw me as party person....a free spirit.

I had many people wanting to go out drinking with me as I would be some sort of entertainment to them, be it if I get in to a brawl then they all could watch or bait me on also I could get access to decent drugs which many of them couldn't.

When I had my own drugs on me, I would always share as I always wanted others to be tripping with me as its never fun just being on a trip by yourself around others so I would try my best to get everyone on acid and keep the party going.

Though in all truth personally for myself, there wasn't much of a party going on, it was all a front just to stay wasted and escape from facing up to my world falling apart around me.

My sister called me and told me there was a parcel for me from the UK; she thought that maybe it was from my Dad.

I didn't know what it was so I went around there and opened it to find it was the book that whoever from the British Home Office had sent me from that phone call many months earlier when I had called asking about the whereabouts of The Kray twins.

It was huge book, like A to Z of all the prisons, and such places that were in the whole UK.

Seeing it, didn't bring much interest to me.

I was hoping it had been some Liverpool FC shirts from my Father, as in from the recent F.A Cup win but it was just loads of pages and something that I truly couldn't be asked looking through so my sister put it aside for me.

My sister at this time, herself wasn't coping any better than I was with the loss of our Mum.

She found my Mum's place, not nice some evenings to be there alone.

She had good support from a guy call Ian, who was a few years older than her but what was lovely guy.

He remained me very much of a true Bob Dylan, he was a folk singer also and a hippie through and through.

Ian had a beach house up on the Kapati Coast along the west coast of the North Island just outside Wellington (it's known by many as the Gold Coast in New Zealand). My sister started to spend time up there to get away on the weekends but I really needed her in Wellington.

Again I was asking her would she sell my Mum's car as she hardly drove it but still she wouldn't.

One day I popped over to see her while she was at my Mum's place. My best friend Chris Mitchell and his brother Daman were there wanting to see my sister to say hi and make sure she was ok.

Their Mum Kath and John their Father had been over many times to make sure Stacey was ok, and to ask after me. They very much were there for both of us after our Mum was killed.

A few days earlier we had given my Mum's clothes to her best friend Kath.

It was a very hard thing to do, when to empty my mum's bedroom wardrobe of her clothes as it was too much of a remained for my sister. My mum's clothes had the smell of her among them, the perfume hint again but we felt bad given them away but we wanted a good friend of my Mums to have them and that friend of my Mums was her best friend, Kath Mitchell.

Chris and Damien had come over with flowers and a card from Kath and John, letting us know they would always be there for us; it was very much heartfelt by both of us.

When I arrived, it was great seeing the two Mitchell brothers, we all decided to have a drink together.

We would have to get some booze though and as Chris had just passed his driving test then my sister let Chris take the car, telling him that I wasn't allowed to drive it.

I and the Mitchell brothers jumped in the motor, Chris behind the wheel but as soon as we got out of the neighbourhood, and driving through Seaturn Tunnel heading towards the coast line around the bays (the nearby beaches of Seaturn) that's when I asked Chris to pull the car over. Telling him I now was going to be driving the car.

Chris said no, as he didn't want to against my sister wishes but I told him it was my mum's car and I would driving it. I was high on acid when I got into driver's seat, actually so high it only took me the fourth corner to crash the car.

The car with us all in it went flying through a white fence over a cliff, lucky not a major cliff but still one with a steep drop. We flew in the air which seemed like forever but also it did feel like (when you get that awful feeling) a roller coaster like ride. We came crashing down into the beginning of the ocean, the start of the beach.

The car landing on rocks below, all types of smoke came out thankfully none of us were badly hurt though ever so lucky, all of were very shaken up.

We managed to get out of the car and up the side of the beach we clamed up on to the winding road and got out of there as quick as possible managing to wave down a taxi in Seaturn after walking back through the Seaturn tunnel, making it back to my sisters without the car though with the cases of wine that we collected on the taxi ride back near my Mums flat.

My sister didn't believe that I had crashed the car. My sister was in tears as her brother could have been killed and that was too much for her to take in.

Now what made it worse was I had to convince her to call the police telling the police that the car had actually been stolen that she had left the cars keys on the same key ring in her front door when coming home, and that someone must have followed her quietly up the outside stairs and taken the keys while she was inside the house, putting away the food shopping.

The police were told this, none coming to the flat, just telling my sister to come down to the local police station and reporting the crime so get a crime number in print.

As my sister had already been crying then the copper on the front desk made the process very quick but my sister didn't like me making her do this as she had never broken the law nor ever be in trouble with the law like I had.

If I hadn't got her to do this I would have been arrest and as I didn't have a driving licence either then I would have been in serious shit also my sister wouldn't have not got the insurance money for the now wreaked car.

As for me after that, my sister just didn't know what to do with me, by now I was slipping and sliding ever more than I ever had and I was no nearer to paying of the drug debt that still hung over my head.

I couldn't stay in Wellington much longer, I would have killed myself by the way I was carrying on with the massive drug use and all the booze I was sinking every evening with no care for my own life.

Very much living life day by day and due to this, my life was going all downhill and fast.

I had no way paying my peers their money and I didn't want to go out to stay at my uncle Franks house but I had only days to come up with a large sum of money, time was very much against me.

Ian, my sisters friend turned up to my sisters place as he heard how upset my sister was about me crashing the car.

He heard about the situation I was in and also how I wasn't dealing with everything too well and how Wellington it seemed was just taking me apart.

After nearing killing myself by driving my Mums car over a beach cliff with my two dear friends in the car crash, someone in heaven truly must have been looking down on us as for us all to walk away from that crash unharmed, it truly was a miracle.

490

Ian said I could go up and live in his outhouse on the property of his beach house. His daughter whom I knew from my past Mel Berg lived there.

She was my own age; we actually shared the same birth date and year.

Ian had a young talented musician boarding at his house as well, who was in his band, Bryon was his name and he was Ian's drummer.

All this to me sounded like the best get away out of the pits of hell that I could take.

At least he wouldn't be hooting me orders like how I imagined if I lived at my uncle's house so I packed a few things. My sister got into the car with me as well as she was going to come up and stay a few days as well so she wasn't alone in my Mum's flat.

As I went inside to the flat to get a few more things from my mum's flat, I said under my breath "Don't worry Mum, I will be ok."

I went into her bedroom to sit on the bed, looking around still finding it all very surreal and then I saw between her bed and her bedsit table a pack of stillknox, my mum's sleeping pills that my Mum used to take.

I thought maybe they would do me good as when I was young I had taken them when I wanted to block the noise out from my parents fighting or from the constant tapping on my bedroom window from the monster.

With those in my jacket pocket also with still many acid trips that I was in two minds of leaving or taking, I kept hidden in my pocket when in all honesty I should have just thrown them down the loo but I wasn't stronger enough to do that so I kept them in my pocket.

I went to walk out the door, the very last thing I took was the book that had been posted to me from the British Government agency and I then closed the door never knowing when I would be returning.

Off I went through the streets of Wellington and out onto the motorway, on to the beach highway heading up to the Kapati Coast for what was going to be a place that I hoped (and my sister as well) would bring me some peacefulness in my life.

Up there, I would also be out of harm's way and finally I could start to rebuild my life again.

Well that was the plan but was it going to all work out for me and was I going to better myself? The devil inside me it seemed had other plans.

Chapter 32

CAN I SPEAK TO RONNIE KRAY

The first few weeks were easy going, very chilled out and very relaxing. I was living in a beach shake at the back of Ian's massive house, with a forest outside my door and then at the front of the house across the road was the beach and this was just lovely.

It's exactly what you see on a postcard of New Zealand, one of the loveliest parts of NZ, the Kapati Coast. The area is my mum's Maori blood line as we have ownership of Kapati Island through our Maori blood line as this was **Te Rauparaha** stomping ground back in the mid 1880s.

I was really enjoying staying here and I settled in quickly. The first Friday, Ian had lots of musicians over, who all would jam and play music. I was getting on with Mel, Ian's daughter she was my first ever girlfriends many years ago though we didn't get off with each other apart from the odd drunken kiss.

The boarder Bryon was a cool guy, another hippy who loved his weed and for me the first few weeks I hadn't taken any weed nor had I done any of the acid as I was just enjoying chilling out away from the lifestyle and stress that surrounded me back in Wellington, as beach life in NZ is very different than city life.

I would actually use my days up by reading loads of different books from subjects such as the Cuba mission crises and the revolution of Cuba, and many other subjects would take my interest.

Then after reading through all of these books, Bryon told me of a author by the man of Hunter S Thompson so I read a few of his books and being taken in by his style of writing and the stories that he wrote about while having lived them first hand himself.

After reading L&L in Las Vegas, it remained me of the acid I had brought up with me. The following Friday after slowly staring to smoke weed again, I had done so good to last this long but with the weed then followed the normal pattern which many years ago had made me go from weed to harder drugs and that included acid.

This certain weekend and the few following weekends, everyone loved the acid that I would share among them all but then during mid weeks I would find myself reading books that were soaked in drug culture such as the biography of Jim Morrison and then more Hunter S Thompsons books and other drug related books.

I found myself dropping acid just to read a book in the beach shake. The thing was every time I took the acid I either got lost in the book as if the book came alive for me in the photos.

Other times I couldn't read the book as all the words were dancing along the pages also it meant I was just using the books as an excuse to get high.

While Ian and Bryon were just smoking weed during mid week, I would appear on acid trying to convince them all to take acid, even once putting a acid tab in Ian's cup of tea or Bryon's can of beer as I hated tripping alone but that wasn't always smart move.

Though I would tell them soon after what I had done, they just weren't up for tripping. They would just played music louder than normal and a little a drift to say the least, but apart from that where I was sitting all was fine but I could tell neither was too impressed as they hadn't planned to be on an acid trip on a Wednesday afternoon.

Mel wasn't happy I could tell that as it was a week day and these types of days or evenings were only meant for the weekends. Mel's Dad hadn't taken acid before in his whole life until I turned up to live at theirs, but I got to say he loved the shit, he like many though hated the come down. That was with any drug it was ok while you're high but after that then the next few days were always shit.

I was running low on acid maybe only 100 trips left, each one I was selling for $40 so a few sales of that was my food and rent sorted as Ian didn't charge me much, he was a kind soul who would help out any one in trouble.

I started to drink in the local taverns once I got used to the area and many a times I flung people out of one tavern up the road. They didn't have any doorman so I told them I was 20 years old though still only 17 years old and as they noticed me sorting out the trouble more times of course not single handed but the landlady gave me the job as door man on the weekends.

It was ok while it lasted then a bike club who had a clubhouse but didn't wear back patches started to use the place as their drinking hole. I tried my best over the next few weeks to be good to them, getting them on side so they wouldn't start trouble but they were just a pack of wankers and wouldn't give me the time of day when I would tell them to leave at night.

The land lady's husband gave in to them and let them have locks in which I knew they would just take the piss and over time they did just that.

If I had been in contact with the Satan's Slaves, I know they would have come up and help me clear them out but I wasn't in contact with anyone in Wellington due to the money I owed to my peers so if I let the Satan's Slaves know where I was, I know word would have got around where I was hiding out and my peers soon would find out and it would be them who would have given me a visit, and that I didn't need.

I wasn't getting any backing from the land lady now who had first employed me to get shit bags out, well as I had no backing, then more and more the bikers ended up taking over the entire pub.

Once one of their younger guys got a job doing the door with me, that was just a way of the MC Club to wheel their protection racket over the tavern so I thought fuck it, I anit working a long side a scum bag whose only interest was to beat up locals and back up his brothers so I left the job after one final weekend where him and me nearly came to blows, I was dismissed as being a trouble maker.

Trouble maker I wasn't, I was just fearless and wouldn't take no shit from anyone but I was out numbered and so it was a losing battle and one without my own backing, I couldn't win.

This meant back to just partying it up taking acid at least four times a week and then with my come downs which would last longer I started to take my mum sleeping pills, the moment the acid wore off and I was hit with reality that I didn't wish to face even now many months after my mum had died.

I still hadn't given in to grief correctly, using the comfort of drugs covering it all up, all the pain in my heart.

I had read many books and all the drug related ones, no longer where of interest as here I was living the drug fluid life myself. Soon boredom set in and that meant getting bored of having a beach a stone throw away and mixing with all Mel's friends, even the music jams I got bored with as I couldn't play a instrument and neither could I sing

I did miss Wellington, but knew I couldn't go down there even for a night out. I did get to see Cool Ken, he had just come out of a stay in a mental hospital and he was on so many drugs, ones the doctor handed him. He came up once dropping my sister off for the weekend; it was good to see him as I hadn't seen him since my mum's funeral.

He had brought up coke with him which brought back that taste that I had missed the instance high that I had enjoyed. Telling myself it was doing me good plus I was interested in all the downers that Cool Ken had as in his Jack and Jill's.

I asked him to hand me his vs. and a few of the other drugs. I didn't try any of these pills for now but they were in my mind locked away, let say for a rainy day meaning when all the acid had finally run out.

By this stage I truly had taken 100 acid trips from the time of my mum's death as now I was taking an acid trip before I would asleep to see what it was like being on acid while dreaming.

That goes to show how this relaxing hippy style life just bored me as I was a city boy and not a beach sleepy town type of guy. I was just take everything for granted the gorgeous beaches, the safely of being away from Wellington, and being looked after.

Soon I wasn't even being respectful to everything that Ian had done for me when he didn't really have to help me out and what I should have taken with two open arms, I just started to moan how boring everything was, which was disrespectful. I am sorry for how I behaved looking back at that period of my life.

Not even speaking to Ian or Mel for days on end.

After I had finished all the books that I had been reading, I found a local library and on arriving there, I asked out of the blue about British gangster books. I found a Kray Twins book and also one written by Tony Lambrianou, both books I was taken in by though I didn't even finishing reading them as now I started to highlight the book I had been send over from England.

One morning I found his plants growing, so I went to the local bakery, brought a few pies and rolls and drinks, I would just supply myself up while breaking off some buds from his plants and get stoned in the beach shake and for three days, I didn't even appear only entering the house when I wanted to use the down stairs loo so it was really like just a ghost in the night

The following weekend that Ian had gone to spend time in Wellington at my sister place as he had got fed up with my rudeness, I was never rude I just had for some reason stopped speaking to him even though he hadn't done any wrong.

I think it was a mixture of myself taking these downers the pills as I didn't feel talking to anyone and I kind of went inwards. I wouldn't even come up to the main house to eat supper that Ian would put on.

When Ian left that weekend and also Mel went to see her friends, and Bryon had met a girl so he was at her place.

I then had the place to myself so I called my mate Sasaka, who got the next train up from Wellington. We just got in some beers and smoked most of Ian's weed while popping down to a pub and pulling some girls, bringing them back but they weren't up for much more than listening to some music and getting stoned which to me was boring as I wanted to have some fun.

I didn't need them using me for dope and drink so I asked them to leave as I thought they had come back to get up to mischief rather than just drink all the beers and smoke all the weed and listen to The Eagles. It's not my kind of house party at that age being a teenager when there are 6 girls, me and my friend and no one is being naughty.

It was Sasaka who had see The Krays movie with me, and who was with me when I had made those calls all those many months back to England and to my Father trying to find out more about the Krays.

I showed him the book that had been send over from England while I started to ring each jail etc, starting from page one and onwards.

Page one started with A, there was many pages from A onwards, covering from Northern Ireland, Wales, Scotland and England. I didn't have an idea where either twin was.

If I had finished the books about them that I had taken from the library then that would have given me more clues but anyway one after another address in this book from the UK I called asking if Ronnie Kray or Reggie Kray was a inmate or being held there.

Every time I was said no and without any insight or helpfulness as I am sure many of these places that I called thought it was some sort wind up.

I was still calling places at 5am until I got to the letter b and the whole thing had started to become boring in its self but I had made so many phones calls, one after the other using Ian's land line house phone.

Saturday when I woke up, I came in to the main house woke Sasaka up who had fallen asleep on the couch, we done some acid after lunch, my only excuse was that it was a sunny day to do acid.

We went down to the beach fishing, with the sun out and the beach packed full of people. We ended up getting some beers and had wicked day fishing from the shore. Sasaka very nearly catching a sand shark but the line broke and so we went back inside as we too far fucked to change a fishing line while both buzzing of our nut.

Bryon and his girl came over so they dropped some acid and it was great we had the house to ourselves. We started up the bbq, buzzing from just watching the smoke raise then in the evening as Sasaka had a great singing voice, he then jammed with Bryon and it turned into a good night.

Bryon soon after 2am went off to his bedroom to be naughty with his girl, me and Sasaka were left there wide awake nothing to do so due to the time zone we started again on the phone to the UK trying to track down the Kray Twins.

I was getting through the entire Bs in the book and then called a place called Broadmoor which was in the book. Thinking it's just another place which they would who ever answered the phone say no to my questions, more so as it was a hospital rather than a prison.

But what happened next hadn't happened before as the voice down the phone said "Yes we have Ronald Kray, may I ask whose talking?"

I didn't know what to say so I asked could I speak to him, and I was told a flat no.

I had got this far , I had just seven oceans away tracked down one of the Kray Twins, there was no way getting this far was I going to be defeated so I called back and told the person who answered the phone that it was a family related matter.

They put me through to his ward, now I still wasn't sure if it was the correct Ronald Kray and what was he doing in a mental hospital as I didn't know what had taken place while he was serving his time behind bars nor at that stage did I know about his mental illness that he suffered, most of his life.

A nurse male one asked how he could help me, so I asked would he confirm that the Ronald Kray was the twin brother of Reggie Kray, which was confirmed.

I couldn't believe it, I had tracked one of the twins down but now how was I going to get to speak to Ronnie Kray

As I had said it was family related, the reply that was flown back my way by the male nurse was "What was the family related matter that seemed so urgent?"

I said "Its private, I would need to speak to Ronnie to tell him, himself."

I was told that patients weren't allowed to take personal calls and so I would need to leave a message that would be passed on to the patient and that they would not be getting him to speak to me on the phone even when I tried harder, I was again just given the same answer in return from the male nurse.

I then went on to say that I had spoken to Reggie Kray so I unsure why I can't speak to his twin? The male nurse went on to say "Well if the prison allows to u to seek to his twin brother then that's the prison service and not our rules so sorry but all I can do is past on a message to Ronald Kray."

So that didn't help me any closer to speaking to Ronnie Kray.

Though as a 17 year kid from New Zealand what was I going to be saying to him if I had been able to speak to him? I asked one more time if again I could speak to him but still as still no so I said thank and that for now I wouldn't be leaving a message.

I kept on now going through the remaining addresses in the book, calling a few more.

The thing is that both brothers were being held in places that started with B as Reggie Kray was being held in a prison called Blundeston in Suffolk, England which I had called in the Bs of the book but wasn't informed that Reggie was a inmate when I asked maybe they just were allowed to say, and me being short on the phone many times after having a whole book to go through, meant I kept on being given a no.

I had been wondering if maybe Ron was the only twin alive as the 1960s seemed such a long time ago.

I wasn't sure if both twins were alive though I knew Ronnie was and with the male nurse saying that it was the prisons choice in letting me speak to Reggie, then at least I now knew he still was alive and more so serving his sentence that had also been handed down to him, though where he was, I was clueless to.

I did get some of that that question mark answered at while going through the Ls of the book when calling Leicester prison.

A woman who answered said to me only a few years back Reggie Kray was a inmate there so I asked did she know where he was now and she said she wasn't allowed to give that information out, but she never told me how long ago was he a inmate here so this could have been years ago.

I asked was it recent as in the last 5 years and she said yes and even said less than that but that's all she could say and as she was about to say goodbye, I quickly asked one more question was Reggie still alive now?

She quickly said as far as she was aware then yes so I said a big thank you to her.

What I only found out years later was that Leicester prison was actually Reggie last prison and that he had only been transferred onto another jail. She must have thought I was press or a reporter maybe by my quick fire questions.

And now 48 hr later after so many phone calls, I now had tracked down one of the Kray twins Ronnie Kray and as for the other Kray twin I knew he was still in the prison service somewhere but which one I didn't have a clue.

I was only up to L in the book so I kept on going even after Sasaka had fallen asleep and the sun had come up, I kept on calling prison after prison from prison to Long Latrine prison to Nottingham prison, every other prison that also was in the book as not all were marked as jails.

I heard a car pull into the drive way so I got off the phone as Mel was back with two of her friends so didn't need her seeing me on her father's phone and more so calling the UK.

I had been on the phone all night, two nights in a row so I hide all the sheets of paper I had out as I looked like a p I or a journalist with all the notes I had written in trying to track down Reggie and Ronnie Kray.

I didn't think ever to mention what I was doing to anyone, as I didn't even know why I had taken it now this strongly to try and reached and speak to the Kray twins.

It's something that a 17 years old kid wouldn't ever do. Was it because my father wouldn't help, but then again he wouldn't have known where Reggie was and if he did he sure wouldn't have told me.

Thinking back now to the time, who would have guessed in just over two years time I would find myself sitting next to Reggie Kray visiting him in a British prison and then going on to end up working for him in the UK.

Mind blowing when looking back, it all started here and on acid.

I went down to my shake and put my notes away. I just needed another chance to use the phone as I know I was very close though still far in many ways but as least I was on the right route.

I just knew a few more nights I would crack it and I would get to speak to one or both of the Krays twins.

I am guessing it was the acid and also maybe my mind using this; whatever you could call it tracking down The Krays as a way to keep my mind of what I had to deal with as in my mum's death and then the problems with Wellington.

Though it started off with just watching a film, I wanted to finish the journey that I had begun and to get a result.

Nothing was going to stop me from achieving this, in a way as a journalist wants to get a big story that they have been working on, I guess.

Soon Ian was aback as well that night but by this time Sasaka had got the train back to Wellington and I was fast asleep on sleeping tablets (Sleeping all the rest of the weekend through to the Monday afternoon, feeling not too bright when I had awoken).

Another week of nothing to do and all is wanted to do is finish my investigation type work as in finding Reggie Kray but the only time I could call the UK was at night time due to the time zone.

The problem I had was Ian was a night owl and his bedroom was near the lounge so I couldn't use his house phone as night while he finally would slept next door to the lounge , he for sure would hear me if I used his land line.

Worst to come was he himself who hardly used his house phone, I never saw him use the phone much and when he did it was always brief.

I was in his kitchen on the Monday night, making myself a coffee as those sleeping pills really knocked me for ten.

I would feel like punch drunk when waking up after ever taking them and it took ages to get the effects of the sleeping tablets shaken off.

Then I am called over to from Ian who was in his lounge, asking me had I been on the phone and I said yeah I made a few calls to Wellington but nothing more than that. He said the phone line for some reason had a bar put on for outgoing calls.

I guessed the phone bill be what $500. It's the very first time I ever saw Ian get mad as after he called NZ telecom from a local phone box. He nearly hit the roof as all the calls I made and all the questions I would ask each night probably each phone plus all the times I was put on hold and sometimes put on hold for ten mins well it all came to nearer $1000.

He couldn't believe it and he wanted to call my sister to ask her what the fuck was going on with me though to do that would mean he would have to go back to the phone box as he wasn't able to use his own land line, due to me making all those calls to the UK.

He started to yell at me so I warned him not to ever raise his voice at me as no one fucking raiser there voice at me.

I told him I would pay him back and I slammed the kitchen door and though fuck him for yelling at me but he hadn't done anything wrong. He couldn't even make a phone call and had to pay some money over the line to NZ telecom to lift the phone bar around $250 just to get his phone line up and running again for outgoing calls.

He was too angry to call my sister so he got on has Triumph Bonneville motorcycle and went for a ride. Mel came down asking me who had I been calling and how the hell did I get the phone bill that much.

I told her I had been calling the UK but that's all I told her, she wasn't happy and she told me she thinks her father should tell me to go.

I didn't know if she meant it. I was may have now fucked everything up but instead of trying to put things right, I took a acid tab and then regretted for the very first time doing that as I though that's not going to look good when Ian get home.

I didn't really want to hang around so I rolled up a fee joints and also for some reason I took the mixture of pills placing them in my leather jacket and I fucked off to the pub drinking heavily and then wanting to take another acid tab but realised I had left the rest of the acid back at the house.

I really didn't want to go back to face Ian.

I felt so awful after all he had done for me but all I remember was him yelling at me so I just reached into my pocket and dropped about a dozen of these pills.

There were a few blue vs. and white pills I was unsure what they were, and I kept on drinking now at pace I was throwing the booze back.

Sasaka had left me some money so I was using that just to get shit faced and shit faced as quick as possible hoping that by doing this, I wouldn't have to face the music and everything would go away.

While I in the pub, some of Mel's male friends were there, who had grown up in the area with her. They all were my age and maybe a couple years older anyway as I went to pass them to go to the toilet I heard them saying something about me.

When I came out of the bathroom before I opened the bathroom door, I heard them all laughing which stopped when I opened the door and walked again out to near where they were seated, and a few were standing.

As I got just pass them it played on my mind so asked them what the fuck they were laughing at. What the fuck did they think was funny?

They said nothing and told me to sit back down so that started the frightening mood come up in me; I could feel my blood boil. I was very drunk and whatever tablets I had taken turned my mood very violent tempted.

As I told them not to tell to speak shit and more so not to talk behind my back as I would come and get them if I heard one more fucking comment from their mouths about me.

One of them stood his ground and said "Like fuck u will!" "Don't threaten me and my mates and u come near my house later u see what happens!" Then they all just laughed, he laughed in my face thinking he had just stepped me up.

Wrong fucking move in the state I was. It would have just been better they didn't say anything. I walked out the pub knowing where he lived as he lived in the same road as Mel's house so I waited in a nearby bush.

This time the acid had licked differently than ever before or more so with the cocktail of drugs I had taken as in the pills , mixed with the booze I stupidly had taken was making me just shake with angry like I was the hulk as I was build up with so much more angry.

Then about 20 mins later, the guy and his mates walked pass and down across his drive way opening his garage door to where I could see a pool table and other things like a make shift bar.

They passed around bottles of beer as I drunkenly high as a kite came out of the bush, picking up pace on my feet and heading into the garage, going straight up to the one who had laughed in my face back at the pub, taking the bottle of beer he was about to drink out of his hand and just smashed the bottle down on his head.

The bottle didn't break but he fell onto the floor curled up holding his head and then I smashed the bottle against the pool table with it now jarred asking "Who's fucking laughing now!" and "Who wants to fuck with me now?"

All the guys run for their lives leaving their mate who had been the smart ass on the floor. I had all this angry in me, I just dropped the broken bottle out of my hand but punched the shit out of him to the point that I had tired myself out completely from punching him and was throwing up through all the entrance of the garage as I left.

Why did I punch the shit out of him , was because what I could remember was him laughing in my face in a packed pub and one thing I didn't like was any one taking the piss out of me.

I walked away leaving him to clean up his own blood that had dript from his nose all over the garage floor that he laid on.

I was seeing double of everything as I walked down the road, not feeling too good reaching the house and clasping just in time to hit the couch.

I wasn't sure what was happing as I couldn't look straight, the whole room I remember was spinning around and then that was the last thing I remembered.

A light being flashed in my face and the sound of a deep male's voice, that person shaking me, on opening my eyes seeing a pen torch in my eyes, and hearing then Mel's voice.

The man was a medic. Mel had come home and found me what she though not breathing correctly and so called an ambulance.

I sat up and asked what was going on? I was told Mel was concerned for me and she had found a pill that must have dropped out of my pocket.

The medical team on seeing it, knew it as a v tablet so after Mel telling them only recently my world had been turned upside down by my mum's death, the medical team thought I had taken a overdose to try and kill myself which I hadn't, it was just the mixture of so much booze and then the mixture of the pills.

I told them I had been drinking and I had taken a few vs. when I reached home to help me sleep, they informed me that the other types of pills was even more dangerous, more ever so when mixed with booze.

They asked where I got the pills from so, I said none of their business. I was told if I was to go with them to make sure I was ok thought they believed me that I hadn't tried to take my own life and also as I was talking sense with them as in I knew my name and where I was etc. They did think it would be best to go with them and Mel agreed, but then I was told as it was drug related call out that they could inform the police, but in my eyes there was no need for that.

They were just blowing it out of proportion. I said "A pal down at the pub gave me a few Vs to help me sleep, so that's fuck all, and no way that's drug related!" "When all you fuckers have done is woken me from being asleep so fuck off!"

I was fuming now at Mel for even calling them and after they left I asked what was she on?

Why call the ambulance, as the police could easily have been called and turned up as well, I didn't need that as well. Reminding her that her father grew pot so why would she throw all that in the balance as all of us could have ended up being arrested.

You know what she was only caring, being afraid and there I was being nasty when she had only tried what she thought was save my life.

With all the drugs in my body, and being on acid, I wasn't thinking like this though I didn't meant to have a go at her as maybe she had saved my life, who knows if I hadn't been woken up out of that deep sleep.

I could have dropped into more of a deeper coma and then either been sick in my sleep and died or maybe my heart might have just stopped pumping blood through my system.

Mel yell at me that I was a selfish bastard as she ran out of the house and to where, I didn't know, but it was actually to her friend's house, the same friend house who I had been to earlier and beaten up the guy who actually lived there.

I went into my shake at the back of the house when I heard Ian's bike arrive back as I didn't wish to face him, and truly just wanted to fall back to sleep as I was so tired and still feeling the effects of the mixture of drugs that I had taken, though by now the acid had started to wear off a lot.

Mel was in the garage at her friend's house putting an ice bag on his eye as I had battered him quite badly.

She then came back to the house and told her Dad about everything I done as in beating up the guy from down the road and then what she still believed, finding me earlier in a coma due to a suicide attempt.

Ian came down to me asking me what was going on, so I explained to him that the group of boys had been am making a joke of me while I was at the pub and how one had threaten me so I told Ian how I went to the guys house and waited end for him so I could have a go at him.

Ian did not ask what had gone on in his house as he nor his daughter needed to come home to find a dead body in their house as in me.

I told him that it was a bit over the top saying I had tried to kill myself when there was no truth in that at all, as I hadn't tried to kill myself.

All I had dome was take a few pills and maybe yes I shouldn't have taken them, I went onto say I thought they were going to calm me down after he had yelled at me earlier. I didn't know due to booze that it was going to make me good violent.

"What go nuts!" he said.

He left me, he said to collect my thoughts but I didn't need to collect my thoughts as the guy at the pub shouldn't have given me shit as if he hadn't then what happened wouldn't have happened as in him getting a kicking.

As for the pills well yeah I'm as dickhead to have even taken them from Cool Ken not knowing what the hell they were and to drink on them, well I shouldn't have done that's for sure.

I didn't go into the house for a few days but noticed that no one would come over as normal like they had for many, many evenings. I knew I wasn't welcomed anymore also Bryon moved out, and moved in with his girlfriend but that wasn't due to my behaviour as we got on well.

I did feel that Ian wanted his peace and calmness back. The way I had been carrying on, was too much for him as I was such a loose cannon, which being like so then that wasn't bringing any good karma into his beautiful house that was normally surrounded by good karma, music and laughter (all this seemed now to have faded from the house, all because of me and my recent actions).

I knew my time was up staying here so I had to move on though Wellington was still out of the question.

In recent weeks I had been seeing a local girl, and on speaking to her she said she had a spare room at her place so I could move in there though I hadn't ever been back to her place before nor did I know much about her but at least for now it was somewhere to put my head down at night.

Sort out where my life was going as maybe in some way Ian was right as in I needed overall to collect my thoughts.

The girl Emma whose place I was moving to, had just recently broken up with her boyfriend who had been giving her some trouble, so Emma said she would feel more safe with me staying at her place so the flowing morning I packed my stuff up.

I didn't see Ian nor Mel, I just left a note saying how sorry I was for bringing trouble to their home and with that I left for the very last time, never returning to that house ever again in my life time.

It was like that sound of music as finally someone didn't think I was suicidal or nuts, and hey yeah I would go there and of course I would make sure her ex didn't causes her any trouble so I moved out of Ian's while he was over at the beach walking his dog.

By now neither of us was speaking and as for Mel, well I guessed that was the end of our friendship which was a shame as I liked her very much so and actually at one stage of my life, I believe I actually loved her.

As for Ian I still feel so terrible even to this day the way I behaviour at times after all he done and I hope that one day I will get to see him again to share a beer in letting him know how thankful I was for all he done for me back at that period of my life as he is one of the nicest blokes I have ever met in my life.

I have a friend in Bryon though I haven't seen him for over 15 years but he was a good kid.

I moved into Emma's flat, and all was good, she would cook for me though I didn't need her doing all of that so I would cook dinner so she didn't feel the to make sure a fuss over me as she had been doing since I moved in.

One night she added a candle to the dinner table but I didn't wish to be sleeping with her as I had just moved in and I saw her more as a friend.

I just knew it would make the situation living together a bit more than just being friends but within a week after both dropping acid and watching The

Doors movie on video, a movie that I never watched straight always out of it.

One thing leads to another and we were soon making love....high as the sky could go.

Everything seemed fine, everything that is until the ex boyfriend showed up one Friday afternoon.

Emma's front opened, I thought it might have been Emma herself returning from shopping so I didn't take any notice of it and I had my back to the door trying to find batteries for the remote control, turning around when I felt who I thought was Emma walking up behind me.

I was attacked and punched in the back of the head and then to the side of my face.

It put me on the back foot as I wasn't expecting it and I had no idea who this guy was who was laying into me , he threw some good punches into me none I could defend as he was very quick , one after the other.

I worked out through his verbal abuse while he was throwing all these punches that he was Emma's ex boyfriend.

As up to that point I had thought one of my peers somehow found out where I we staying and send someone up to get me.

After taking a few more punches this time on my forearms as I was now protecting myself and the punches really didn't feel that hard, it was just the suddenness of the attack that got me off guard.

It was now my time to fight back and to get through all these many punches as there was no way he could throw many more without tiring himself out and so fight back I did , taking the fight to him , using all my upper body strength to use to push him away.

Once he was off me, within the 20 seconds his nose was broken there was blood everywhere.

Blood wasn't something new to me as all the many fights I had got into over the years I usually presented blood, being it mine but more times being blood from whoever I was fighting as one thing I could do was pack a good punch, and when that punch connected, if ever on someone's bridge of their nose then blood very much would flow.

Emma had come out of her bedroom, she had been in there all of the time and run back inside her room when she saw her ex boyfriend fighting with me.

The ex boyfriend had it in for me. I being a male who had been living in the flat that he had once lived in, and more so sleeping with the girl who he had for many a years. This is why he smashed me as good as he could.

I never knew he had keys to the place, the only thing I am glad is that he came in the daytime, rather during the night while I was sleeping or worse in bed with Emma.

I wouldn't have put it past him to have tried to take my or our lives while we slept as his rage was that much while he still was putting up a fight with me, then a few police officers who were in the area when they got the call came flying as Emma had called the police and let them in.

They held me face down on the floor and I couldn't hardly breathe, and what the fuck were they holding me down for as the other guy was only being held onto while he was on his feet , but I had been taken down to the floor.

I was put into back of a police car and soon told I was being charged with assault, the guy wanted to lay charges against me.

I asked what the fuck was going on.

I had been the one attacked and they said not by the looks of his injures and asked what the fuck did they mean.

I was informed he was the household owner of the property and he didn't know who the hell I was and what I was doing in his house.

Something Emma failed in telling me that it actually it was his flat, more than hers, and when they broke up, he let her stay here.

Though they had broken up, she was still fucking him now and then to keep him happy, and to keep the roof over her head.

I told them I lived there. All my stuff was there in the spare room, but I was told as far as they were concerned I didn't have any right being in his house.

The police officer who was talking to me in the back of the police car was fine but he said I was being charged with assault.

I asked him could he at least get me by belongings that were two bags in the spare room , I had to convince him that they really was my belongings, anyway he agreed and he placed the two bags in the boot of the patrol car.

That was nice of him ah to at least to have done that for me.

As for him with his black and blue face, and for sure broken nose, he was now again king of his castle but a pussy and more so to press charges against me, the wanker!

Emma told me (before the police car drove away) that she would speak to her ex.

He had been on holiday in Australia getting over there recently breaking up. She knew I wasn't happy as I hadn't done anything wrong. Here I was being driven away in the back of a police car.

She said she would ask him to drop the charges and explain to him I had been staying in the spare room and that we hadn't slept with each other.

I doubt he would believe the second part of that but I did believe her that she would convince him to drop the charges against me.

If I had known what I knew then about him, and Emma's set up as in living in his flat and still fucking him now and then, I wouldn't have moved into her spare room as what kind of stupid game was she playing.

She said she liked me a lot, bollocks to that!

I didn't need to have been put in that situation especially with everything that had recently being going on in my life. I was fuming as I was driven away hand cuffed in the back of a police car.

I was driven down the coast to Porirua Police Station in the heart of mongrel mob country, but one thing that was on some my side was my step brothers controlled this city with a iron fist.

I wasn't worried if I were to be sharing a cell with a mobster as maybe just it might be one of my step brothers that I would be sharing the cell with.

Out of four step brothers, three of them were senior members of the mob.

I thought by the way of my appearance didn't fit in at all with the other inmates that were being placed in holding cells as I looked like a skinhead and they all looked like they were true pro mob through and through.

I had that shooting after the AC/DC concert at the back of my mind as well where I had been set upon the mongrel mob members, but here for now I was in my step family (the Manuel's) manor so I knew no harm was to come my way.

What I didn't expect was to be locked up all fucking weekend as I was sure I would get a court appearance on the Saturday but due to Porirua being such a boiling pot of a town, more so any Friday night town as Porirua was one of the country's, if not the toughest town city in all of New Zealand as it we staunch and with some much trouble in the city from the evening before hand then the cells over night just got full up. That meant the Porirua Court House was so busy on the Saturday to more serious matters with others (who by now were also in custody) that not everyone was seen so I was one of the unlucky ones.

It meant it wouldn't be till the Monday morning that I would be seen by a judge and charged with common assault, which meant a whole weekend being locked up in the police station holding cells.

I was asked to appear again in Porirua court after my appearance on the Monday in a month's time.

Like fuck I would!! What for something that I shouldn't be have charged for in the first place.

No way was I going to be travelling back up to that court house again, as on leaving the court house I was nearly attacked as I very much was in the wrong place at the wrong time and more so I was a different colour as in skin tone to all the others that day.

What was I being charged for was, because someone couldn't handled getting his head kick in....the prick!

I hadn't done anything wrong so bollocks to them! I didn't care if it meant no show at court in a month's time, which would lead to warrant out for my arrest.

That for now was the furthest thing from my mind as for now I just needed to get away from the court house and face the music in Wellington. Something for now I didn't wish to be doing but something that I had to do and there wasn't really anywhere else for me to go.

I had been away for over 8months since I last had been in Wellington. I didn't like the feeling as I headed back after hitching a ride with a truck driver who was heading to the capital of New Zealand, that being Wellington.

I really didn't have anywhere to call home. I was 17 years old and you know what, I was homeless.

I had just been on an 8month acid trip as that's how the last 8months up on the coast felt to me.

Hell I wouldn't have made my Mum proud by the way I had lived my life since her death but in all honesty I was in a bad way, and going through a very dark time of my life.

The time on the coast started from the car crash and ended by a punch up and then being locked up in yet a another police cell.

Police cells, by this time in my life I had seen the inside of so many of them. The only thing that ever changed in those police cells was the gang's signs that had been dug into the walls or written over the walls, depending where you were locked up.

I can tell you for sure the only gang logo that was on the walls in that police cell in Porirua was mongrel mob through and through until I managed to add New Order (my old youth gang that was tattooed link on my body back when I was a young teenager).

Right then and there, I was only 5 months time away from turning 18 years.

I had no idea what the next few months were to bring me? I didn't even think as far ahead as to my 18th birthday. In all truth I really didn't even think I would make my 18th birthday. that's how sad things had come ahead as I returned to Wellington, thanking the truck driver for the lift.

My future didn't feel like it was in neither my hands nor what was even to come the following month or even the following day as by now I very much was only living life day by day.

There's no future in that way of living life, and very much so, not for a 17 year old kid.

Chapter 33

RETURNING TO FACE THE MUSIC

XMAS 1992

I arrive back in Wellington 8months after I had left to go to the coast, it felt like I had been away for years.

I didn't want anyone seeing me as I knew I was in serious shit with my peers and I didn't wish to be spotted on just arriving back to Wellington.

The first thing I wanted to do is sort out the mess that I was in, this was on top of my list.

How I was going to do this I was unsure but I wanted to get it sorted straight away before word got around that I was back in Wellington.

My sister was happy to see me, I didn't think she would be but she was after knowing that I hadn't been put on remand for that fight that I had got myself into.

She asked had I tried to take my own life up on the coast but I reassured her of course I hadn't and she then asked me never ever to leave her.

I told her of course I wouldn't, I would always be there for her.

We sat and talked, I told her how serious trouble I was in, more than what she first suspected.

She then went on to tell me people had been to the flat asking for me, and she had seen them in my own social circle before. She had guessed how they were linked within the circle as one thing my sister wasn't, was stupid.

She knew the real friends among my friends and the others who were just my friends for their own causes even if it meant I allowed a few of them to use me as in move their drugs through my circle of friends.

They weren't to be blamed for that as they never came to me, as it was me many years ago who had gone to them.

It was one way of me making quid and being able to keep up with hanging around with an older group but as for my own age group, well I and them

512

were the perfect market when it came to drugs as teenagers are the age group who more than any other take drugs, as if they were sweets.

So in one way I had left myself wide open and it didn't take me long to hang with the rope that they handed me.

For now though I had to get things straighten out and the only way I was going to do that was with hard cash.

A robbery had crossed my mind as many banks throughout NZ would get hit and many a times some folk would get away with such acts but the act of robbing a bank isn't as easy as it seemed in those days by just walking into a bank as a team of robbers and holding the bank up and then doing the disappearing act.

The disappearing act I knew I could pull off as I had just done that for 8months and that was from more meaner guys than the law would ever be but the thing is I wasn't a bank robber and if I ever had been part of a bank team then I always would think myself as being the weakest link on the team.

I wouldn't know where to start in how to pull off such a job.

I didn't wish to let anyone down as that was the last thing I wished to do and if caught then I would just be in the same position as I was now, though many steps backwards rather than forward and forward is where I wanted to be.

I just wanted this great weight lifted off my shoulders and I wanted to have it sorted without going down the same road as many who I guessed had in the past found themselves in this type of a position.

It really did fell like I was looking down the barrel of a shotgun, and that I very much would be, if I didn't get it sorted and sorted fast.

I didn't want this hanging over what was just around the corner, which was Xmas though it would be my very first Xmas with either of my parents.

I was used to not having my father there at xmas time but that wasn't his fault, he just lived too far away to share this day with him, but here not only myself was going to be having a very sad Xmas but also my sister.

In my sisters case she wasn't just without our Mum but she also was without her soul mate Tim so it would be a tuff Xmas for her, more than for me.

We spoke about Xmas and what we would be doing and we decided to not celebrate it at all as really there was no point in either of our minds to celebrate Xmas after the year just been.

What my sister was about to do which in many ways was the true spirit of Xmas and that was giving to another.

She ended up telling me that the cars insurance had come in and it was a higher amount that they paid back as the car she had been told was past repairable so it was ridden off which meant a bigger pay out.

My sister informed me that she was able to take a small loan against the flat which now was in her name as well.

She asked me how much I owed so I wrote down how much I owed but I also wanted to pay more on top so that the debt was repaid in what I classed a fair amount with interest added on top but not the $1000 per month as what was added to start when I was in contact with my peers, as that would work out to be £8000 interest since I last saw them.

I was no fool so I wasn't going to have the piss taken out of me so I wrote on a piece of paper a figure to my sister not telling her that within that amount that some of that amount was what I added as interest as I know she would say no. I knew that if she was going to help me, she for sure wouldn't be giving any more that the amount that was owed to them.

I couldn't thank her enough. Her reason behind giving me the insurance money was the fact that she wasn't even using my Mums car and as I survived the car crash, even if she had got the car back repaired then she wasn't going to want to drive it after what had happened to me.

My sister said this was the very last time she would help me out; she said if Mum was alive and I was in this amount of shit then she knew my Mum would have bailed me out.

I wouldn't be in this shit if my Mum had died and I know that for a fact though that's not saying my cottage wouldn't have been broken in as maybe it still would have as whoever done it, done it looking for my stash of drugs.

I had learned my lesson and never ever again would I ever hold such amount of drugs or any amount of drugs again in my life to sell.

Selling drugs just wasn't my game and it driven me out of my town and could have cost me my life.

My sister the following week while I kept my head low got the money from her account and gave it to me in total.

I never called my peers. I didn't want to pre warn them so what I did was once I had the money, I got a taxi over to one of the peers house just after noon that very same day.

I knocked on his door, not knowing what kind of relation I would be given.

He came to the door; he was very shocked to see me calling.

He lead me in to his lounge and told me to take a seat, asking if I wanted a drink though it was only just midday instead of saying yeah a coffee or a cup of tea, I asked did he have any vodka and so he poured me a vodka over fresh orange juice.

He went onto say "Well, well, well, where have you been?" "People have been worried."

I was thinking yeah I sure they were, not worried about me if I was ok or anything but just worried about their money and that a 17 year kid wasn't going to lose them face.

The thing is I wasn't going to let them down and though they knew about my cottage being broken into, I was still expected to pay back those loses.

I took out all the money and placed it on his table, telling him it all was there plus £3000 on top of what I owed him which was a far bit.

I told him about my cottage being broken into, he told me I should have let them know straight but I knew and he knew even if I had that wouldn't have changed anything, they still would have made me pay every dollar of it back.

I didn't need him trying to act out the nice guy as I knew the form on these guys, hell they had been my peers since I was a young kid so I knew how they operated.

Anyway he thanked me for sorting everything out and told me to have a good Xmas and if I needed someone to have a chat with about anything then he always was there for me.

Now that I believed as though I had disappeared for 8months at least they knew I hadn't run off with their drugs nor their money and that I hadn't changed from the kid that he and the others knew when I was young so I did still respect them for when they were there for me, but define being there for me?

I think back and that was only in educating me how to make a fast buck and educating me on drug dealing, was that truly being there for me?

Well I was young and impressive by them as at the end of the day this tight group of people were my peers.

Before I left he threw me over a small bag, inside it as I unwrapped it was what looked two grams of coke, he said "It's on the house son."

I should have said no thanks but there was that addiction in me, so I left with drugs in my pocket and thanked him.

Was I just going around in circles though now I was debt free?

I went on to spend xmas exactly as me and my sister had planned with no celebrations of a xmas though the Mitchell's had offered to have us over and also the Campbell's but we didn't take up any of the offers.

Other friends of the family did as well and my uncle Frank asked if we wanted to go up to Greytown which was kind of him and his wife (my auntie Beth) but we turned down all offers.

Xmas came and went, no celebrations, it was a very sad Xmas.

I found myself on Xmas day opening not presents but two grams of coke and that was my Xmas in the year that my mum was killed.

I think that was sadder than actually Xmas itself.

Chapter 34

TOOTHLESS

So by this time in my life, all that I seemed to be doing was getting into trouble by the use of my fists and my head being mixed up by constant drug use which after such a long period now leads to drug abuse, rather than simply drug use.

As for the drugs as I no longer was selling any, that meant I had to buy them like everyone else but that was a problem as I no longer had my job or any regular income so I was borrowing money left right and centre of friends, even silly enough I even borrowed some money from my peers.

$1,000 dollars I borrowed and with that I used it on buying drugs from them with a month to pay.

I told them 110% I was getting some advance from my lawyers in Greytown whom were looking after my money from my mum's will.

I was hoping the lawyers would hand me some if I pleaded with them enough and hassled them as well but they were very close with my uncle Frank, who was the trustee so every call I made to my lawyer Juliet Cooke, she would let my uncle know I had tried to get her to go behind his back to hassle them to release me some of the funds.

I soon had my uncle on the phone telling me to back off and leave the lawyer alone. It was the lawyer that he had put in charge so as he was paying her which meant her loyalty very much seemed to be with him.

He did offer me an olive branch as he said I could live at his place and work at his saw mill so I would be away from Wellington and all its negative drawbacks that I seemed to keep on being drawn into.

He didn't know how much addicted to coke I was, he only knew about all the many arrests and the times I had been getting in trouble.

He was my guardian till I turned 18years old.

I knew going to a sleepy town and working for him, the life that I knew would be closed down to me and all I cared about was getting high.

I had court costs to pay and now with money that I borrowed so again I was in debt.

I never paid the court costs and when it came to it, I was issued with a warrant out for my arrest, this time in my real name.

I send the court documents to the lawyers who passed them on to my Uncle and out of his own money after speaking to my Auntie, knowing that me being locked up or being send to a youth detention centre wouldn't do myself or more so my sister any good by being this far away from her so he paid my court costs.

That I was grateful for but I then took the piss and asked would he pay off my personal debt of a $1000, he said no chance!

He left the door open for me to work for him and live at theirs, but I was a teenage who just slammed that door in his face.

Utter rudeness and disrespect on my part towards my Uncle who only was trying to make my life go in the right direction.

I had been staying at my Mums flat, which now was owed by my sister but we couldn't live in the flat together so I looked elsewhere.

I found out that Sasaka was living at the two Rachael's house in Island Bay. I asked Sasaka to have a word with them for me as he said there was a spare room there.

Sasaka called me back and said the two Rachael's had agreed for me to move in, as long as I wasn't going to bring trouble to the house as last time I had been there was the evening of my mum's wake.

I reassured them I wouldn't. They spoke to my sister (Redhead Rachael being a close friend of my sister) and after they had finished speaking then it was agreed that I too move into the place the next day.

I spend the first two weeks there keeping low profile and so not to be a live wire for them and most evenings I would be down at the Satan's Slaves Clubhouse which was about ten mins drive away.

My evenings were spent there so I never saw either of them much.

Sasaka's Mum would come over to the house and make sure that I too was ok while she was checking up on Sasaka.

Sasaka sister would also pop over as well some evenings, and get on the piss with us.

Then nearly at the end of that month, on a weekend everything went Pete Tong for me just when I didn't need it to happen.

I had only one week to pay the debt. I still had a little bit of coke left, not enough to last me the whole weekend and not enough money left to buy more so I brought some speed instead.

I found myself at a party which was held by skinheads and a few mixed up people who didn't know if they were punks or Goths. It was held in a puka house near the Wellington bus tunnel, the house had appeared actually been in one of (New Zealand's famous film director) Peter Jacksons first ever films he made.

Peter Jackson, the famous New Zealand film director of The Lord Of The Rings and the remark of King Kong to name a few of his movies, anyway I made sure I didn't take all my drugs over to the party, but at the party I saw lots of people jacking up. They were doing loads of different drugs. I never dared to do those types of drugs they were doing such as heroin, I always saw Heroin as the dirty drug that it was, and it was a drug that wasn't for me.

I liked getting high and not down so I only took fast drugs anyway I was speaking to one of the skinheads' who I knew quite well and he told me that he had been doing speed balls.

Speed balling in American is the mixture of coke and heroin taken by injection but in New Zealand it's the mixture of coke and speed though still taken by injection.

The skinhead went onto tell me it's the best rush ever, an instant high like no other. I wasn't keen on but the buzz he was explain to me, I very much liked the sound of it and that thought of getting the ultimate rush didn't leave my head all night at the party.

While I was doing another line of coke after another, I kept on thinking back to how he had described this rush like other 100 times better than snorting the shit.

Fuck it what had I got to lose, by now wanting the better high. That's what I was chasing in my life - no more chasing dreams as I had none to chase all my earlier dreams had gone out the window the day my Mum was killed.

I said to the skinhead if I treated him to some of my drugs would he do both of us a speed ball?

He said yes, he would have to go to his place first and get clean needles etc so I told him to meet me over at my place; we both left the party early.

I reached my place hoping everyone was out, but they weren't. Sasaka and his sister were home so was one of the Rachael's.

I waited for my friend to arrive, though very nearly telling him actually I didn't want to go ahead with it, but when he turned up buzzing on the fact that he was going to be doing a speed ball, he went on and on about how much of a hit I will get.

I was already off my face not thinking straight, I agreed that I would go with it so I laid out my drugs and then he went to town and did the business.

He done me first of the bit of coke and speed that he had mixed together, he got out a clean needle and with my belt he jacked up my arm and in it went.

A hit I never ever had experienced but what I hadn't known was that actually he had only ever done this once or twice before so he really was just guessing on what much to mix together of the coke and speed.

He was still a beginner and he just guessed how much of the two to add, not knowing what effect too much would have.

Well as soon as I got up to walk after taking the instant rush through my arm to all over my body, that bit I remember then heading into the lounge, I don't remember anything else apart from a horrible shadow coming over me and the feeling of being pulled down to the earth with great force backwards.

Sasaka and his sister and one of the Rachael's later on to me describe what happened.

They said my body just flung back onto the one of the arm chairs, my eyes rolled up into the back of my head, all they could see was the whites of my eyes as I started to fit out and form at the mouth.

They couldn't stop me from fitting, so they called an ambulance straight away; I was rushed to Newtown into Wellington hospital.

I was injected with something, I am unsure what but some sort of chaser also my stomach was pumped and whatever else the doctors done to me as I was out to it, only coming around seeing my own sister with Sasaka's sister standing there.

Rachael, Sasaka and his sister had saved my life. My mouth felt, sore my jaw was in pain and also my tough as I had bitten it so I had the taste of my own blood in my mouth.

Then I notice two Satan's Slaves members standing there as well, demanding what had happed.

I couldn't say I jacked up on purpose as any use of any use of drugs by needles was a big no, no in the eyes of the motorcycle club.

If they had known at the time what I had done then they would have smashed the fuck of me while I was still in that hospital bed so I had to say it was a suicide attempt. What else could I say; this broke my sister's heart.

As for the guy who actually had nearly killed me, I couldn't bring him into the picture as then they would have known there was needles involved and that I had actually let someone jack me up, so for the time being he got off lightly as I wasn't no grass.

I wasn't going to grass him up, as it was me who gave in and said yes to do a speed ball with him so I didn't dare say a word about his involvement in me being in hospital.

I asked the main doctor please not to tell any of my visitors, he was happy not for anyone to know.

The doctor for now just wanted actually most of the people who had turned up to leave, apart from my sister who I asked to stay.

I told her privately what had happened as I didn't want her to think what I had told her earlier was true as in that it was a suicide attempt as I had only promised her before Xmas that I wouldn't ever leave her.

The only good thing it did was put me off drug use in that fashion ever again.

My sister was terribly upset. I wasn't even 18years old and so far I was living very dangerously.

If I hadn't had other people there when I fitted out, the doctor said for sure I would have died without the quick medical help that I got so I have to again thank my Mum, who I just know was looking down on me that night though probably in so much shame yet again.

I was let out of hospital after having to speak to a head doctor making sure I wasn't going to be trying to kill myself again though I hadn't even tried to but it's what I made out that I had.

Once he knew I was ok, I then went back to the house and got some rest and feel asleep.

Everyone went out the following night to a party and I was told I wasn't allowed to come.

They made me feels even more shit so I thought fuck them apart from Sasaka, who stayed back with me as he was still very concerned about me.

I snorted the very last bit of speed I had left, as there was no coke left and then I took a second trip, listening to the Sex Pistols as loud as I could till noise control turned up threathing to take the stereo if I played the music loud again.

I went from listening to the Sex Pistols to putting on some classical music. Sasaka by this time truly thought I was losing the plot but the thing is I was high on speed and acid and he was just laid back high on grass so our two worlds just weren't meeting in the middle.

I was still in a bad mood with everyone as I wasn't allowed to go partying with them and in the state I was from the drugs I got Rachael's house phone and called through all the places in the UK from the book of the prisons and such places in the U.K still trying to track down Reggie Kray.

Finally going through the entire remaining numbers of the book to call, getting all the way up to W where I called Wayland Prison where yet again I was told no Reggie Kray wasn't a inmate in this HMP Prison.

In years to come this actually was Reggie Krays final jail, he spend time in before his freedom was granted from prison, 8 weeks before he died in 2000.

The Home Office at the time kept Reggie Kray in till the very last minute so he couldn't and wouldn't enjoy any of his freedom that was something I think was terrible but I will come to that at a much later chapter.

After getting so many no's after going through the whole book, I decided fuck it; I am going to call Broadmoor Maximum Security Hospital again.

I told Sasaka what I had in plan; he didn't think it was wise.

Looking back at what I did that night was terrible and not thoughtful.

Not just in my eyes but you got to understand every time I tried to track down Reggie I was always away with the ferries as in so high from the intake of drugs.

High on lsd and other drugs plus booze, I wasn't ever thinking straight and more so as I dial the number to Broadmoor again asking for Ronnie Kray.

Giving my name, being put through to his ward, knowing that they wouldn't put him on the phone if I asked simply just to speak to Ronnie Kray so I simply said I was a lawyer from New Zealand acting on behalf of a relative of The Kray twins.

I made up some name of a great aunt who had I said had died, and that I was in care of the money that was left to Ron and Reg Kray, but if I didn't hear from either of them within 48hrs then it would be placed into a trust fund and over time given to different charities through NZ that I felt fit to give to and they the twins wouldn't be able to claim the money for themselves.

The nurse or whomever I was talking to wrote all this down and asked for a contact number so I gave them the house number telling them it was my office number. He said a member of his staff would pass the message onto Ronnie Kray.

Sasaka was in shock and with what I said and how professional I sounded though he said I was properly off my trolley as I was buzzing so much from the speed, and tripping from the acid trip that I had taken.

Now all I was expecting was a call back expecting it to be Ronnie Kray, whereby I would tell him it wasn't true and I just wanted to speak to him after many months trying my hardest to contact Reggie and himself.

I would add I thought the movie was great and then leave it at that and also of course say sorry.

Well things just didn't turn out to plan....whenever did they in my life, over the last many months.

What I didn't know at the time was that Ronnie took personal lose very deeply and that the hospital gave Ronnie his dose of different medications before telling him the sad news, while being sedated due to the types of drugs the staff given him.

Only while Ron was in this state, then they the hospital staff would pass the message onto his twin brother Reggie Kray where ever he was being held in the U.K serving his 30 year prison sentence.

Reggie Kray who was yes, still in the prison system (I can't recall what prison he was in at this time) on hearing the news from Broadmoor, and being on the ball Reg couldn't work out what great aunt of theirs had passed away and more so one that lived all the way over in NZ.

For Reggie, it all didn't make sense, so he reassured Ron by telephone call that maybe the message had been passed on incorrectly and not to worry.

That cheered Ron up by saying but there had been talk of £250,000 so Ronnie wanted to have it double checked by their lawyers still and that's what Reggie did.

As the weekend went by, we all were in the flat chilling out on the Monday night when the house phone rang. I never answered the house phone, I actually never answer any house phone as I always it expected it to be bad news especially at that late time of night anyway I heard Redhead Rachel get up and answer it and then knock on my door telling me it was a call for me from the UK.

The Krays weren't even on my mind and I never thought it would be either of them, I was actually nearly half a sleep after a quiet Monday evening so I guessed maybe it was my Dad.

I was just hoping that he hadn't heard about my time in the hospital a few nights earlier though I guessed my sister wouldn't have told him as he would have only got more worried.

I said hello and a voice asked "Is this Christian Simpson, the lawyer?"

The penny didn't drop straight away but then it did so I quickly went into Sasaka room, waking him up with the phone glued to my ear.

Placing my hand over the receiver so the caller couldn't hear me, I shook Sasaka till he woke up telling him "It's the fucking Krays!" I then said "May I ask who's calling?" the person on the other end of the phone told me he was a lawyer working on the behalf of The Krays.

He went onto say he wanted to know about the details of this phone message that had been left for his client a Mr Reginald Kray passed on by his twin brother Ronald Kray.

I got to say I was overjoyed as I though sweet all I needed to do is just tell him that I would have to speak to his client over the phone, and only either his client or his clients (The Kray twins) to pass them onto the information but the lawyer said that would not be possible.

He explained as he was their lawyer working on their behalf then it was him who I would be dealing with so all information to be passed on to him and he would relay it to Reggie Kray.

I had got this far only to be defeated at the very last hurled. The earlier sense of victory passed as soon I realised what I had actually said on that previous phone call to Broadmoor when the lawyer said to me that Ronald Kray, his client was very upset on hearing the news.

At the time I didn't know this was a trick as Ronald Kray yes at the time was upset but after speaking to Reggie, he now was fuming and angry.

I had a young kid from NZ just upset the Gangland boss of the biggest crime family in the history of the UK.

The lawyer went on to find me out by asking about non binding interest rates etc of this sum of money and starting to speak all lawyer talk about trust funds etc.

I was being played out into the open when I didn't have the answers at the top of my head to reply back shapely as he was firing of these questions, which in all fact only a lawyer could return in speech with the correct answers.

I had come unstuck in the phone call, and within another six odd minutes the lawyer replied and said

"You clearly lying and worst of all do you really know who you have just upset?"

"Have you no idea who Ronnie Kray and Reggie Kray are?"

I then was now very much thinking what the fuck have I got myself into, and why did I do what I done. What the hell had I been thinking!

I then had to come clean so I told him who I was, my age and that I had merely seen a movie about them, and that my mum mentioned their names to me and I told him my father knew them when he was in the East End back in the 1960s but my father wouldn't answer any of my questions and after my Mum was killed (that wasn't even a year ago to this point in time) that I had tried my best many times to contact Ronnie and they just wouldn't let me speak to him and as for Reggie(I even after over what must have been at least 300 calls in total to the UK) I was just given no's to his whereabouts.

The lawyer just couldn't believe it and though he knew it as the truth what I now was telling him, he just in a semi joking way said "You mad!"

He even finished with a slight laugh but informed me now he would have to tell Reggie Kray the truth.

He went onto say that in my best interests, he wouldn't inform Ronnie first but he would leave that up to Reggie to do as he said Ronnie will go mad as hell over this, so it was Reggie who would be the better one to pass the news onto his twin.

The lawyer ended the call by saying he would call me later after he had spoken to Reggie and that he would tell me what Reggie had said about the matter. He ended the call sounding very serious. He sure put the wind up me that's for sure!

I got off the phone not full of any joy in the slightest.

Sasaka had managed to listen to most of the conversation, and even he was shitting bricks, we both were and when I put the phone down.

Rachael who was going to the toilet asked me who was that, so I said my Dad and went back and sat with Sasaka asking him what had we just gone and done?

Sasaka said "What, you mean what have you gone and done, not us! "This made things even worse.

I just kept on saying "What the fuck have I done then!"

These guys are real gangsters, not to be messed with and I had so wrongly told them in a non direct way that a relative of theirs had died and a lot of money was left for them.

I started to really go off acid as fuck being so wasted on that shit as its the acid which made me pursuit this and look where its ended.

We talked for ages, wondering if they had people in NZ who could find us and kill us for what we had done.

Would they send over hit men do us?

Sasaka said again "What do you mean us?" "You mean you Christian, as I had no part in your mad plan; it's all down to you my mate, and not us!!"

He rolled a joint and stated to laugh to himself which in a way calmed me down and I had laugh to myself then suddenly got such a shock as the phone rang again and now this was many hours later.

I knew it had to be for me as no one else would be calling at the early hours of the morning.

I knew the phone was ringing for me so I went out quickly to the hall way and answered the phone before it woke up anyone else in the house.

It sure was for me as it was the lawyer again who informed me that he had spoken to Reggie who wasn't too happy, and that Reggie that evening would be calling Ronnie to tell him.

The lawyer went on and said "You really are a silly young man, and Reggie wants to speak to you" I said "No way, please just on my behalf tell them both how truly very sorry I am."

The lawyer just said "No you got to say that yourself to Reggie" "Reggie has even arranged with the prison for you or call and say sorry so here's the number and when you call ask for Reggie Kray, explaining who you are as they are expecting your call and they will transfer the call through to his wing"

The lawyer then went on to say "Explain to the prison officer who takes the call who you are as they then will get Reggie so he speaks to you" "You must do it and not to waste any more of Reggie's time as he wants to speak to you before he calls his brother."

Sharply he said "Do u understand?" I said "Yes".

The lawyer replied "I will know if you haven't called or not, and if you don't then you will only be in more serious trouble!"

I was just thinking fucking hell!!

I got off the phone to the lawyer and wished I hadn't smoked more of the joints that by now Sasaka were just constantly rolling as I was so stoned.

Sasaka was now a little more excited than scared but as for me well I wasn't scared but fuck was I worried as I dialled the number that I had written down.

I told the person who answered the call what the lawyer had told me to say and that Reggie Kray was expecting my call.

I was transferred on the phone to a wing and when I told the next prison officer who I was, they told another member of staff to go and get Mr Kray, telling me to wait on the line.

Wait on the line I did.

Next after a few minutes I was informed that the next voice that I would hear would be that of Mr Kray.

Fucking hell, the Reggie Kray who for months I had been trying to track down, now was only minutes away though seeming like a lifetime waiting but then I heard the phone being picked up or handled to someone and a voice said

"Hello this is Reggie Kray, is that Christopher?"

I said "No its Christian, is that really Reggie Kray?"

"Who the fuck do you think it is!" was the reply.

"Yes its Reggie Kray, I don't have much time to talk to you."

I spoke sheepishly saying "I would just like to see how very sorry I am Mr Kray, I really didn't mean any harm by it."

Reggie said to me the lawyer had explained the whole thing. Reg asked who my father was so I said to him Stevie Simpson but the name didn't mean anything to him at the time.

It was only when I showed him a photo, years later on my first visit to see him in Maidstone prison that the he remembered my father from looking at the photo.

I didn't know how my Father knew the Twins, as all I had been told from my mother was that my father knew the twins during his time in the East End but as my father wouldn't say anything more than that, then I was clueless until many years later when I would find out more but for now when Reggie asked me who's Firm was my Father on, I had no idea what he meant by that so I said that to him.

Reg then went on to say "look we not getting anywhere with this!" "Can't you hear me correctly when I ask you a question?"

"I can't really understand you Mr Kray, can you speak up please."

I could hear that my reply didn't go down to well with him, as in asking him to speak up.

He then asked me how old I was.

I didn't want to tell him I was 17 as I saw 17 being the age of a man so I didn't want to look more stupid than I already guessed I was looking so I told him I was 16 years old going on 17 years old.

He asked about my Mum, as the lawyer had told him my Mum had been recently been killed.

I explained that yes my Mum had been killed less than 9 months ago and that she was killed on Mother Day last year.

Reggie said he was very sorry to hear about this, more so as I didn't have my father near as I explained to Reg that my father had returned to the UK to live with his new wife many years ago.

He told me not to worry as my Mother would be in heaven with the other angels.

This comment alone really touched my heart as the angry in his voice had since left and then he said something that would stay for me forever and was the part of the conversation that would stand out for a long time.

Reggie said "As you are only young then I know there is a thin line between youth and stupidly, Christopher" I stop him short by carrying on as I said "No Mr Kray my name is Christian."

"Christian" replied Reg "You have stepped over the line from youth into stupidly, and one thing you must do now is write a letter to my brother Ronnie Kray saying how very deeply sorry you are"

"You are sorry aren't you?"

"You mean that truthfully when you told me earlier, yes?"

"Yes Mr Kray I am sorry." I replied.

"Ok then." he said calmer in his voice and then he added "You sound like a good kid who has been through a lot." "Write the letter to Ron." "Speak to my lawyer again and ask him for his office address and then send the letter to him and he will make sure my brother gets the letter ok!"

"My Brother Ron might reply...he might not."

"Christian make sure you send him some stamps so he can if he wishes post a rely back, do you understand"

"Yes Mr Kray and thank you, sorry, truly sorry."

"Ok then Christian, I got to go now, keep well, God Bless!"

That was that, the phone went down and I had just spoken to Reggie Kray for the first time and it was more than I expected from the phone call as what I expected was him to be threading down the phone to me but instead was a man who yes was angry to start with but that was due to he not being able I guess to catch my accent and I could hardly hear what he was saying when he first spoke.

I didn't understand what he meant by words such as the firm or over the river but when he spoke about heaven and my Mum and then told me to keep well and god bless, I thought what a nice man.

Straight away I got writing a letter to Ronnie Kray, I stayed awake till morning came, thinking back to The Kray movie I had seen and also to the conversation I just had with Reggie Kray.

It was so surreal and what I didn't know of course at the time was something that was to lead onto a very close friendship between myself and The Kray Twins, an unusual friendship, one that started there and then.

After the letter was written and I was given an address from the lawyer, I waited till late morning came and went to the nearest post office and send not only Ronnie a letter but also Reggie a letter as well thanking him for what he had said on the telephone to me. I couldn't add in post stamps as they were New Zealand stamps, not British stamps so I guessed I wouldn't be getting a reply.

I was too worried to give my address so I gave my Mum's address and called my sister to tell her please look out in the post for a very important letter, but my sister told me she was going up to the coast for a few weeks so she wouldn't be at our Mums place so I would have to check the mail, if need be.

I said I would though what was to happen on my very next visit to my Mum's place wasn't nice at all and it made me feel how cold hearted my peers could be.

I took a call from my peers, as now anytime the phone would call I would be the first to answer it thinking it was The Krays lawyer or even maybe Reggie, but it wasn't it was my peers telling me that I had to come up with the £1000 that I borrowed from them and Friday there would be no more excuses.

So I called the lawyers' in Greytown but still they wouldn't hand me any of my money, this made me so angry as at the end of the day, it was my money and my uncle did have the power to hand it to me but he just wouldn't buckle even after I told him I really needed the money.

He just told me to tell who ever I owed the money to that they would have to wait two years before I paid them back.

This made me so angry so there and then I and my uncle fell out.

I thought fuck him as somehow I will work out a way of getting my money before I reached 20. The way I was living my life, well there was no way I would even reach the age of 20 years old as I guessed either I would one night over do the drugs and die that way or in a fight as I was getting into many of fights and maybe I was going to end up dead by a fight going Pete Tong.

Either way I was going to make sure I would go out in blaze of glory. I didn't care if I died or not as long as I spend my remaining days on a high.

I would love to have gone to heaven to be with my Mum as I am sure up there wasn't as painful as living during those times for me. Life for me at the time just seemed like a struggle apart from when I was as high a as kite and loving life through the eyes of an acid trip or from taking loads of coke. I was that drug bound and so loose with no care for myself or my own health...... I was a Lost Youth.

I was just on a self destructive path and going nowhere even if I didn't even make my 18th birthday, I very much was going to make sure I did get at least some of my money somehow.

After all, if I had got so far putting my head into how to contact The Kray Twins, doing so then that wasn't easy going but I kept at it and I got the result so I would just have to work out a way to get my money and get a result on that.

It was going to be a mission, one I was going to make sure of but for now I had to try and get $1,000 together.

Friday soon came and without even a phone call there was a knock on the door. Sasaka's sister opened the door and in came two of my peers.

One asking where his money was and as I tried to ask for a few more days, I was attacked many punches to my face as my head hit the wall and then as I went to fall forward I was then kicked with a steel cap boot straight into my month.

It was the first time I was nearly knocked out. I hadn't been knocked ever in my life but I started to see stars as more blows came my way. I just knew I had to keep on my feet and cover up my face so I put my arms and hands to my face and took more punches.

I knew I couldn't go down as if I had dropped to the floor I for sure would have taken a kicking and it wouldn't take long to have my ribs rebroken so all I could do was take the beating, the worst ever of my life as I was taking it off people who I had known for many years and who for many years I had looked up to and respected over the years.

The blows stopped from the peer who was hitting me the most, he was around 18 stone and I felt all his strength with each punch. He normally would be able to knock any man out, I had seen him do this many times in the past but he just couldn't finish me off.

At least I stood up to everything he was dishing out but I was so near to (as I said being) knocked out.

As I took my hands away from my face I could see blood all over my hands and arms.

Sasaka sister had heard everything going on but she stayed in her brothers' bedroom (Sasaka wasn't at home at the time) as she didn't want to be part of any of this.

I was told I had till Monday to pay the money, now though it wasn't £1000 but £1200 and if I didn't pay up by the Monday then worse was to come.

Dark hair Rachael appeared and called me an ambulance (second fucking ambulance for me that had been called from her place in less than a month). Rachael said my face looked like a balloon but then she went onto say she couldn't handle this anymore in her own home.

I had brought trouble to her own door step now too many times and though it didn't affect her as in she wasn't involved, but at the end of the day it was her house and she had been kind enough to let me move in and all I seemed to do is bring trouble to the house.

This now was just too much for her.

She didn't say anything to me at the time, trying her hardest to look after me till the ambulance arrived.

I went back to Wellington hospital. The ambulance team was asking what had happened and they were keen on getting the police involved which I didn't need so I said I had been attacked by some yobs down at the beach but I didn't want any police involvement.

I just wanted the pain to go way in my face and more so my mouth. I could hardly talk and one of my eyes was closed shut, my nose yes again for sure was broken and my front four teeth, three had been knocked out and one was shattered.

They done all they could, at least I had no broken bones though they had to strap up both my hands due to the back of my hands taken some of the blows.

I was taken to a dentist at the hospital who said I needed urgent work done on my teeth so I was given some dental treatment for now though my mouth was badly swollen up so it was limited what the dentist could do.

I had some injections in my gums as my mouth was in so much pain as it fucking hurts to have three teeth smashed out from their roots in the gums.

By the evening I was released from hospital, my face was a mess, nearly twice the normal size, all over $1000.

How lovely my peers are ah, after everything I done for them though I had taken the piss but I didn't expect such an attack as this.

Well I wasn't going to run nor could I be asked to move out of Wellington all over again, and yeah my main concern was that I wished to get them their money.

I made a few calls to try and borrow $1200, but still without any joy, only getting some broken promises.

By this time the Satan's Slaves had heard about what happened to me. I found out my peers were down at the clubhouse explaining to the Satan's Slaves why they beat me up so they themselves wouldn't fall out with the Satan's Slaves.

Call me mad, but I though bollocks to them I not going to let them drink down there and be proud of what they done to me so like most Fridays nights I would myself go down and drink at the Satan's Slaves clubhouse so that's what I did.

I walked from the hospital in Newtown up to the clubhouse and pressed the buzzer still in my blood stained clothes and looking like I had just been in a car crash.

Zombie answered the door; he took one step back and said "Fucking hell, you got more than just a beating!"

The peers had said they had only given out a few punches, lying bastards as I actually had been serious attacked by them rather than just given a slap.

I couldn't even drink from my mouth as I ordered a beer, my peers couldn't believe the size of my balls by getting a bar stool and sitting up at the bar next to them asking them how was their day, as if nothing had happened.

Being at the Satan's Slaves clubhouse I felt brave to say that as I would love to have seen my peers try and throw just one more punch as though yes I was in the wrong as in owning out money well I knew that if they tried to jump me again while in the clubhouse then the Satan's Slaves members that were in the clubhouse at the time, would have been on them as I had been taught my lesson very much so.

I couldn't see out of my right eye and I couldn't even slip on a can of beer so I was given the vodka jellies that had been previously in the freezer, that's how I got really drunk that night.

As I went to leave hours later, Shane of the senior members of the Satan's Slaves came over to me and said "look Christian, Rachael doesn't want you living at her place anymore so you have to find somewhere else to live."

"Don't worry about your belonging there, as your mate Sasaka also has been asked to leave so he can sort out ya belongs for you as I know he himself was packing up his room, but do me a favour and don't go back there ok."

I respected all the Satan's Slaves very much but more so the senior members such as Greg, Shane, Rob, Scuff, Spoof, Zombie and Red to name only a few so I said "Ok I won't".

I left the clubhouse drunk; the injections in my mouth had all worn off so I was getting the pain from where once my teeth were.

I had nowhere to go and I felt sorry for Sasaka as he hadn't ever done any wrong and it was unfair of him also being kicked out but as for me I was now homeless at the age of 17 years... a month before my 18th birthday.

I knew my sister wasn't at the flat so I caught a bus through Wellington as no taxi driver would pick me up and I reached my mum's flat early hours of the morning.

My mum's flat seemed really airy and I didn't like her bedroom door being opened while I sat in the lounge, my mind was playing tricks on me as I kept on thinking that if I were to go in to her bedroom that my Mum would be laying in her bed, but not asleep but rather in the state of when I last her in her coffin.

That imagine just wouldn't leave my head as you see things on drugs, and reason why I was taking drugs was to block out such imagines and also such memories, emotions and feelings relating to the death of my Mum.

I turned on every light as I didn't want any darkness as again I just believed if I had walked into a room where there was darkness, then that my Mum would come out of the darkness.

It actually felt spookily staying there but I did manage to fall asleep on the settee as I couldn't pull the pull out the bed of the settee as my hands were bandaged up and were to sore.

I awoke in the afternoon the following day and I rang Rachael's house. I spoke to dark hair Rachael, I asked did she tell my peers I was living there as far as I knew they thought I was living at my mum's flat, she told me know it was Sasaka sister who had been seeing one of them, who told him where I was.

That made me so angry as Nat had been such a good friend of mine she was there the week earlier, but now she had only a week later told my peers where I was living so no wonder she had come around that day before to check if I was there so she could call my peers to let them know.

I then spoke to Sasaka, he said "It's all fine my friend."

His Mum had brought a new house and with a flat below, near Courtney Place on a street that actually my Father used to live on, before he went back to the UK.

As for his sister she didn't mean to grass me up he went onto say she wouldn't have, if she knew they were going to do what they did to me as in beat the shit out of me.

He said the flat was two bedrooms so he would be more than happy for me to take the second room if I wanted to.

He knew is Mum wouldn't have minded as she for many years had been so good to me, more so since my Mum was killed.

Sasaka said he would be moving into the flat and that he was happy to leave Rachael's house before the phone bill came in.

He said would he pack up my belongings and brings them over, then by late afternoon he got a people carrier taxi over to my place and had my belongings dropped off to me.

He also couldn't believe how badly beaten up I was. I told him I wasn't happy about his sister grassing me up, though Sasaka didn't wish me to be angry with him as in confronting him over what his sister had done.

Sasaka stayed with me for a few hours, rolling some weed so we got stoned. He then left to go over to his new flat and told me to move in whenever I wished so I said I would some point in the week, and thanked for letting me take the other room. I also told him to say thank you to his mum from me.

I found some wine in my mum's fridge a 2 litre casket so I drunk it dry, glass after glass thinking over my life until I got hammered and then got a taxi over to Sasaka sister flat asking her why the fuck did she grass me up?

Nat had just had her side of body tattooed by Stan, an ex Satan Slaves member (Stan who had done my first tattoos).

Nat was native like many of us were, as she herself started to get deeply involved in drug use, anyone who knew my peers were all hooked on one drug or another drug, that suited the peers very much as it meant more cash for them as that's all they ever cared about.... such is life.

She just thought they were going to visit me to talk to me, I did believe her as she liked me a lot and I knew she wouldn't have wanted such harm to come my way. I just had to clear it up as it was very much playing on my mind, and more so after I had drunk so many glasses of wine.

Drinking on an empty stomach meant it didn't take too long for the wine to hit my head.

I left Nat and headed back to my Mum's flat catching my reflection in the bathroom mirror at my Mum's place as I took a shower as my body was arching from the beating I had taken the day before.

I looked like a homeless man with no front teeth, and the face of the elephant man from all the many punches I taken over the years from fighting, more so from the beating I had recently taken.

The fights I was always getting involved in meant I had a mars bar (scar on my face) and now my nose was broken past repair and my teeth were fucked.

Sunday came and went; I was nowhere closer to getting the money for my peers.

On the Monday they were back, this time to my mum's flat.

Telling them I didn't have their money, they stepped into the flat and took my mum's brand new huge TV which had coasted near $5,000 that my sister had brought out of some of her own savings after my Mums televisions had already been taken from the drug dealer in the past who had given me a visit. They took my sisters stereo system as well which wasn't a cheap one.

I told them this wasn't my stuff but their reply was "Bad luck!" "You were told to have $1200 in cash!" "You failed so we having this to sell to get our money back, that's how the biscuit crumbles." as they walked down my mum's set of outside stairs with the TV and then the stereo in their hands.

Knowing they would with both the items at least get over $3500 so they were the ones now taking the piss, the fucking cunts!!

When they left I would make a point never ever to score drugs from them again, and never have anything else to do with them, actually I wished they rotten in hell as for them to take my sisters stuff was bang out of order.

Things just got worse as the moment they left, my sister arrived back early from her relaxing weekend up on the coast with Ian.

When they walked in they looked so happy, though my sister asked me what the hell had happen to me, I just said I had been mugged.

She didn't believe that as she knew I wouldn't let anyone mug me and get away with it. She noticed the massive television gone and the sterol system, asking now angry "What the fuck was going on where was the television and stereo?"

My sister broke down in tears; Ian just gave me a dirty look, telling me he thought it was best I left so I told him to fuck off.

It wasn't his place to tell me to go; it was my mum's flat so I said to him "Why don't you just fuck off!"

My sister told me to leave, it was actually her flat and she truly couldn't take any more of this.

It was destroying her.

I said don't worry as there still as the TV in mums bedroom and that I would get her a new stereo.

She shouted at me "It's not about the fucking TV Christian, it's all about you, I am sick and tired of worrying about you as very week someone thing else happens to you and I can't sleep at night as I am just so stress out with worry about you."

My sister went onto say "I keep on thinking, I am going to lose you, I even have horrible nightmares that you going to be taken away, and I just can't bear it anymore!"

There and then in front of my own eyes it looked like my sister was having a nervous breakdown, the last thing I wanted to see was my sister this upset so I grabbed my bag and told her "I am sorry I didn't meant to upset you, I will go."

My sister asking where was I going? I just said "Don't worry I will be fine." and then I left.

I felt so embarrassed wherever I went as I looked in such a bad way and I had my mouth broken with no teeth, but more so I felt so terrible for my sister being so upset all due to me and I was fuming at my peers for their daytime robbery of my sisters belongings.

lastly I shouldn't have told Ian to fuck off, that was a bit heavy handed on my behalf.

it was Monday afternoon where the hell was I going as I didn't have Sasaka new address so I went over back to Miramar, over Worser Bay Hill, back to near Shelly Bay, where I had been all those years earlier with the girls from the girls home and the Miramar warriors.

I went along the beach into the bush and to the exact spot where as a youngest I had run away from home with my tent.

I couldn't believe it but there was the tent after all these years, the over grown grass under all the thick bush had grown over it and it had a few tears and also many inserts who had now made it their home.

it wasn't useable, I pulled it up and made what I could out of it as in a small roof between two bushes and a tree so at least I had some shelter as that night I felt a sleep with the stars shinning through the tree tops.

I slept ok which I didn't think I would, as for food there were a few shops darted around the bays so I could go to them and as for showers I would put on a pair of shorts from the bag I had taken from my Mums flat, and I would just go for a swim in the ocean and then use the showers in the bathing rooms along the many beaches.

I would also to save money, eat fresh shellfish I found along the rocks. Some of the shellfish I was taught by the Manuals (my step family) years earlier when I was a young kid what I could eat and what I couldn't.

I used my knife to crack open the shells and eat loads and loads of shellfish. I stayed in the bush for a whole week, not once getting bored as each day I would be down at the beach getting a sun tan and then swimming all day.

It was actually all right and I wasn't getting to cold at night as I had enough clothes in my bag to get by and a little money left that Sasaka had given me, also before I stormed out of my sisters flat, she too handed me some money as though she was very angry at me, she loved me very much.

I was still taking the acid while I lived in the bush; I was down to my very last 11 acid tabs.

I would only take an acid tab in the day time as one night when I took them and I was in the bush I was sure I could see werewolves and other animals and creatures.

I think the werewolves were due to the film I had watched when I was very young called An American Werewolf In London, so that night I actually ended up sleeping on the beach but that wasn't much better as out to sea I could see, well of course I couldn't but to me being on acid, I could see the Loch Ness Monster and that freaked me out big time. I didn't sleep all night and was convinced the Loch Ness Monster was going to come up on the beach and eat me.

Acid ah, makes the mind see some weird shit.

On the following Saturday, I now had been sleeping rough, though rough isn't really the word to use as I was enjoying being free like this, I didn't have to cope with anything in life and though it was lonely as least I wasn't upsetting anyone and nor was I getting into trouble.

Being a beach bum as I called myself was ok but my money was running out.

I was down to my last $10, then on the Saturday afternoon while I was swimming near the shore, I saw a burger van so I walked down to it and as I went to cross over the road I heard the roar not of the sea but of some bikes, and there coming down the road was three Satan's Slaves on their bikes.

They always ride on the white line when they on their bikes, right in the middle of the road,

That's exactly where I was standing while trying to cross the road.

The Satan's Slaves many a time each Saturday would always do a bike ride around all the bays but they weren't expecting to see me, that's for sure.

I had to get out the way as they came flying up, I made it over to the burger van then on being spotted they turned their bikes around and pulled up.

It was Red and his brother Scuff who was the president of the Satan's Slaves as Billy Cluston who had been the president of the Satan's Slaves had been kicked out of the club, I am unsure what for anyway Scuff many months earlier had taken over as no.1 also riding along with them was Zombie.

They told me everyone had been looking for me and there was talk that I had gone and killed myself.

"Why the fuck would I kill myself?"

They thought I had as due to the hospital visit on the Friday three weeks ago.

Zombie said my sister was so worried and he thinks she had called the police saying I was missing.

All the past week I thought everyone would be fine as if I was out of their hair but what had happed was ever more worry and stress on to my sister.

They asked me where I had been staying and so I pointed behind me up to the bush and said there.

They didn't believe me so I took Zombie over and said there look where the tent is.

Zombie said "You can't be sleeping in the fucking bush!"

"This isn't the fucking outback!" "Australian, you fucking are not!"

He then asked Scuff was it fine that I came back with them, and Scuff said "Yes that's fine."

Red was carrying a spare helmet on the back of his brand new Harley-Davidson, he and scuff weren't heading back to the clubhouse so I jumped on the back of Zombies bike and went to the club house leaving the tent for a second time behind me.

My bag on my back that was full of all my belongings that I had to my name as I headed on into the clubhouse.

It was a big weekend as the British's Satan's Slaves were over for the first time since Red and Scuff had returned from their home town of Manchester and met up with the Satan's Slaves chapters in Yorkshire and Shipley and also Manchester and the other chapters while they were in the UK.

The invite was given out for the British lads to come over, and they had as they were arriving in Wellington after doing a club run through the North Island of NZ.

The British Satan's Slaves have more chapters in the UK than any other MC Club, which makes them the biggest 1% MC Club in the UK.

I was allowed to take a shower at the clubhouse and have a shave as I looked like I had been sleeping rough.

Scuff soon returned he had a chat with me as said as I had been such a big part of the club as in my loyalty and friendship, that I could now call this my home but I wasn't to fuck up and I was given my own room within the clubhouse.

The room that Alan who had been too much of a head ach for the Satan's Slaves so they had kicked him out of the club, he had only prospected for a few months. It was good news as the club was back to normal without a live wire trying to beat up everyone.

Scuff said "Take the beer out of your hand, get behind the bar and serve the British brothers what they want."

I couldn't believe that not only had I been given my own room inside the Satan's Slaves MC Clubhouse which was unheard of in the history of the Satan's Slaves, as I was only 17 years old and I wasn't a prospect plus also they bent the club rules by allowing me behind the bar which was only for members and prospects so I felt very honoured.

I served the British members and got on the piss with them, making a call to my sister that all was ok, and that I was fine.

I couldn't be on the phone to her for ages, she was crying down the phone asking where I had been. Why hadn't I been in touch?

I told her not to worry everything would be ok but I had to go and would speak to her in the week.

The Motorcycle club in Upper Hut, Sein Fein MC (no connection to the Northern Ireland Republican Party) was holding their annual Bike and Tattoo Show, the very best Bike show in all of New Zealand that same weekend, just outside of Wellington.

The British brothers were the VIPs so most of the Satan's Slaves ride out there. I myself wasn't allowed to go as I was told to stay at the clubhouse with some ex members and also a few prospects to look after the clubhouse so let's say a little party was held.

A party of mischief and partying, some strippers soon arrived. It was wild to say the least and then they decided it would be funny for me to race a bike from the street down the driveway into the clubhouse over a ramp flying across two pub benches and land safety as the bike touched down after I would have been flying through the air.

The plan sounded sweet so I went into it full on, but on my first run I went flying of the ramp with too much speed and also the bike was too heavy to fly with such a short starting point from start of the run to take off.

I ended up crashing in to the bench and then face first scrapping my face along the ground skinning my face, blood again was what covered in my lower face and jaw.

Fuck it hurt skinning face first along pavement inside the clubhouse without a helmet.

As I got to my feet , there was my 4th broken tooth which was the last one of my front teeth laying there on the floor so that only meant one thing....and that was back to drinking the vodka jellies.

Drink I did do as even more vodka jellies were lined up for me even one I discovered had my tooth added in it a vodka jelly. That vodka jelly was left to drink last. Soon I got through all the other vodka jellies so this one with my broken tooth in it was drunk.

I thought finally bed by 6am but the sounds of at least 30 bikes came roaring in, so the party really had only begun.

It was a party that lasted a few days. I hadn't slept for over 36hrs, I now looked like a very old man due to being toothless.

I didn't flake once and kept up with everyone. The British guys were impressed by my rate of drinking even though it was a diet of vodka and jelly for the Sunday but by mid week I was throwing back the Jack Daniels and also many, many beers.

Life had become so good as I loved living at the clubhouse and getting to meet a few of the British Brothers, who left a few days later for a bike run of the South Island, visiting the 1% bike clubs down there who were friends of the Satan's Slaves.

I needed to get my teeth sorted as I looked like such a fool with no front teeth, the only way I could afford this is if my uncle would release some of my money to get my teeth fixed which was at a cost of over £2500.

I was sent some post to my Mums flat from my lawyer in Greytown. Documents stating all the money that was left for me, also some legal document which requested my signature next to my uncle's signature as that would mean I was getting some of my money at last though it was only for my teeth to be replaced.

Within a week I was at dentist and with the cash, I did spend £300 of the money on a gram of coke and if it wasn't for not liking what I saw in the mirror each time I looked, and seeing a massive gap in my mouth then I would have spend all the money for sure on drugs but at least I had just enough to cover my new teeth and the dentist said I could repay the missing £300.

At least owing a posh dentist didn't mean if I didn't pay him, he was unlikely (like my peers) to come after me and smash my teeth out...my new teeth by now.

After leaving the dentist the first person I wanted to show my new teeth off to was my sister so I went around to her place, she had forgotten to let me know that something else was waiting in the post for me, something all the way from the UK.

Chapter 35

IN TOUCH WITH THE KRAY TWINS

There in the post at my mum's flat was a letter addressed to me. On opening it was send by a Mr Ronald Kray.

I could hardly read the hand writing, it was written in very scruffy writing so it took me a while to be able to read it.

What it did say was "Dear Christian, you took a right fucking liberty, don't ever do it again" then the mood of the letter changed from being angry with fucking liberty unlined, to saying "thank you for your letter, come to England, see you a visit, God bless from Ronnie Kray" and then at the bottom of the page it said "p.s keep out of trouble."

One thing after a while I didn't expect was a letter from Ronnie but the following week he send another two, one asking for me to send photos and tell him about life in New Zealand and the second one asking if I had received the letters and asking when was my birthday was and when was I coming to the UK which gave me a idea as from just receiving a letter then to visit The Krays.

That would have meant I had come full circle from the very moment I had tried to contact the Kray Twins so I wrote back saying yes I got the three letters and that I would let him know when I was able to get to the UK as it would be a honour to visit him as at least I could say sorry to the man's face for the way I went around in making contact with Ronnie in the first place.

I signed off the letter by saying God Bless, then I placed in some photos of myself and send him a book about New Zealand showing how beautiful the country was, as there is no other country like New Zealand on the whole planet, you fucking know that!

The thing is I didn't have the money to get across to the UK though you know I kind of did if my uncle released the money.

I soon spoke to my uncle telling him I wanted to visit my father in Scotland.

My uncle said he didn't think that was a good idea until I had settle down more and stopped being a prick in nearer enough words so again we fell out.

I put it on him saying he had no right in stopping me from reaching the UK to see my father though I also of course would have planned to visit Ronnie and Reggie as well if I could though I hadn't started to write to Reggie, it was just Ronnie.

Soon after I had send the second letter to Ronnie, I got to speak to Reggie again on the phone and he said his brother was pleased that I had written to him such an in-depth letter and he said a moving letter so I had been forgiven by himself and more importantly from his brother Ron.

I can remember years later after this when I first met Charlie Kray he already knew about me and I told him about the very first letter that his younger brother Ronnie had sent me, Charlie said not many if no one ever got away with taking a liberty to Ronnie, he laughed and said his brother must have calmed down in his later years.

I was just had happy that I wasn't swimming with the fishes, if you know what I mean.

I seemed to have a calmed down actually myself for that moment in time, maybe Ronnie Krays advice "keep out of trouble" worked on me but that was short lived.

The following weekend, myself and Sasaka were having a drink at Lord Nelson Tavern near Manners Mall in Wellington and while I was at the bar being served a drink I bumped to another guy by mistake, saying sorry for knocking his beer but he turned around to me and told me to fuck off!

Something that was a bit strong but I let it go, the very first time I had let those words past but I didn't want to wreak the night and also I was having a drink with Sasaka who had been a good friend to me.

I didn't really want to kick off while I was in his company after all he had done for me.

I went to the toilet, took a piss and then went back into the bar and ordered more drinks, spotting one of the politick students who I had sorted acid for in the past and as I was started to feel drunk I asked him was he carrying anything for sale as in drugs.

He asked why I didn't have anything so I explained showing him my new teeth, telling him that I was no longer in that game.

He wondered why he hadn't seen me for so long and then said "Yeah I will treat you to a few lines of Charlie" and he also asked "Do u guys want some acid?"

"I would have to take the money for acid, sorry to ask you Christian, I feel a cheap skate in doing so as you always had been good to me but I need the money as my father has put a limit on my funds" he went onto explain that his younger brother had found coke hidden in his bedroom and told his parents what he had found and now his parents thinks he was some sort of junkie.

Then he goes and says "Parents ah, they so misunderstanding. "

"Well I wouldn't know as my Mum was dead and my Dad was seven oceans away." is what I thought to myself while he spoke about his parents.

It made me even more want to take some acid so I dropped an acid tab. I borrowed the money of Sasaka even though I could have just told the guy to get fuck and actually taken all his drugs off him, but I was never a bastard or a bully so I paid him the money even though this kid had shit loads of money and I had fuck all.

As he had mention his parents, it made me start to think about my Mum, which I didn't wish to be happening as I had only dropped an acid tab so I ended up throwing back drink after drink.

Sasaka even telling me to slow down on the drinks but I was going for it now and then things turned for the worst.

I went around to be served at the bar as there were less people now up there being served, and let's say I was thirsty.

I was standing waiting to be served a drink when I heard someone say "there's that asshole!"

I just knew who ever it was, was taking about me so I looked over , and I was right as there sitting with two others was the guy who had earlier in the night told me to fuck off.

When I made eye contact with them, the guy yelled over at me asking what the fuck was I looking at!

That was it my blooded started to boil and that feeling of rage came over me.

I then asked him what his fucking problem was and he said "You! You asshole"

I then went towards him, Sasaka had seen this go on from where he was sitting and said "No Christian, truly leave it"

"He's not worth it!"

The guy said "What, your names Christian, you're Christian Simpson?"

I said "yes why what's that got to do with you."

He replied "You're ex girlfriend only moved into my flat this week; she heard you lost your teeth a few weeks ago, what you can't take a kicking....pussy?"

"And as for pussy I am sure Kiren has a lovely one!" then he added

"Oi Muppet, I'm going home later tonight to find out if she has as I will make sure I give her a good fucking!"

That was it as I won't have no guy disrespecting her like that as though she was a ex, she was a decent girl and she wasn't no slut, so I told him that I would beat him home first and

I would be waiting to cut this throat when he got there.

By this time I had the doormen asking me to leave and warning me not to start, they even took the glass of Jack Daniels out of my hand and lead me out, Sasaka came out and again told me "Just leave it, it's not worth it."

Fuck that!! I was steaming angry!

I waited in an alleyway up from the front of the pub, and waited and waited, Sasaka knowing by now he couldn't calm me down and also being a good friend waited with me.

Around 45mins later the prick appeared and walked down out to Manners Mall, very near me and Sasaka though he didn't see us as we followed him.

He was now only with one friend so I suggested Sasaka I just do him here and now, but Sasaka pointed out all the police who were in the mall as they always were on a Friday night due to gang tension in the city every weekend more so around this area on a Friday night.

So we kept on following them, keeping our distance, we saw the guy say good bye to his friend and he walked to the taxi rank jumping in one of the Wellington yellow taxis, and we did the same telling the Samoan driver to follow the taxi in front.

It lead all the way through to a hill area of the back of Island Bay, we saw the guy get out of the taxi, putting his keys into a door of a house so we then paid our taxi driver and waited outside the house.

Many stairs leading up to the house, Sasaka asking what we were going to do as we walked quietly up the stairs leading to the front door, all I whispered was "I going to make sure that fucker gets taught not to take right fucking liberties!"

We laughed, as Sasaka knew I had got this saying from the Ronnie Kray letter I had shown him soon after it arrived.

With that laughter in the air I knocked on the door, the prick opened it and that was it, fireworks as I smash him right on the chin and then jumped on top of him while hitting

the floor.

I told Sasaka to find the phone line and to unplug it as I wasn't finished with this bastard as I dragged him up the hall way still fighting.

He was putting up a good fight.

Sasaka showing me the phone I threw it back out the front door and kept on bashing the guy in the lounge, telling him" I told you that I would get you!" He smartly said "Well you didn't beat me home you asshole."

I couldn't believe he still was being abusive so I got Sasaka to hold on to him, while I kicked him right between the legs.

He had fuck all to say about that as he went to the floor in a ball. I picked him up by his hair landing another punch into him and another till now Sasaka was pulling me off him.

What we didn't know was well this was going on, kiren and her new boyfriend was in her bedroom had heard all this and got out the back door running to their neighbour and calling the police.

What didn't seem long we heard the sirens of police cars, though not thinking it was anything to do with us until the front door come crashing in.

I threw the guy to the other side of the room and had what seemed a dozen coppers not only on me and Sasaka but also on the guy, then one police officer asked who Chris love was, and that's when the guy said it was him.

He was let go and again asked his name again. He said his name was Chris love so they sat him in a chair and cuffed both me and Sasaka; I turned to who I now knew as Chris love and warned him, it would be his downfall if he grassed me up. I think he knew how very serious that threat was as for once he didn't call me a asshole and he looked scared.

I was taken with Sasaka to a police station.

I in a patrol car and Sasaka in another one, as I was pulling into the police station I noticed a new nightclub opening across the road, lots of people queuing up, as I went through the gates and around the back to the police station.

Photo taken, prints taken, same old routine, in a cell I was placed, not being told what I was to be charged with but I guess again assault or even worse or whatever else they could think of charging me with.

Three things happen that saved my bacon. One was Chris love explained to the police that he let me into his house, and he told them he knew me and that we were friends, and we had just had a fallen out but he didn't wish to press any charges against me, and he made sure he kept Sasaka right out of the picture nor did he mention the argument back at the Lord Nelson Traven.

Kiren didn't know it was me who had come for Chris, and on hearing what Chris told her about what he said to me, she was furious at him and told him that 100% I would be back for him if he dared grassed on me so he had to not grass me up, that's why he told the police the above.

I was also told that when the police left, Kieran's new boyfriend who was his flatmate gave him a slap so Chris's night didn't end how he wished and I know for a fact he never went around taking right liberties ever again.

As for Sasaka I told the police he had no involvement what so ever. Sasaka was released after a few hours once all the paperwork was done, as for me I thought here another weekend banged up till Monday and another court appearance this time for sure I was not going to get bail and I would be placed in a detention centre but then on the Saturday morning I was woken up and told to piss off after being told that there were no charges being pressed against me as Chris Love didn't want to press charges and as the police didn't witness it and Chris had placed all blame on himself.

I was given a warning to keep out of all licensed venues in Wellington area for no reason at all, apart from being under the age of drinking but they never picked me up from a pub but a private address so I didn't know why I was being told (this though for many a years and more so many times recently before I had gone up to the coast).

I guessed it was due to my details that had been taken down a few times for being in licensed venues drinking piss underage.

I was again explained I was under age to be drinking in any tavern, pub or night club so was given a total ban, by now my name had appeared so many times from so many arrests and I knew this was my last warning that I would be given but then again what could they do if they found me again drinking in one of the many pubs in the city?

Really sweet fuck all! Apart from arresting me for underage drinking (that anit serious) so I really didn't give a fuck what they had to say.

As for Chris love, I would come across him again in the future not till many years had passed.

I was running the door of a live music venue in London, The Mean fiddler in Harlesden North West London, where bands, famous bands and artists and also many at the time unsigned bands would perform anyway one night many years later while checking down the queue of people making sure none were under age, and all who had tickets for the gig were not to wasted or drunk to get into the venue, well there standing in the queue with some other Kiwis and Ausssie was Chris Love.

He hadn't seen me since the night I had kicked the shit out of him, but the first thing he did after getting the shock of his life was extend his hand and ask how I was and he said sorry for that night many years earlier in NZ and introduce me to his friends.

He was staying over in London while backpacking through Europe, and you know one thing he actually was a decent guy as he hadn't any abuse this time to give me and he said how sorry he was. I told him to leave it and it was all in the past, explaining to him how I had left that life behind me back in NZ.

I got him and his guest some V.I.P passes and they ended up having a great night which he thanked me for.

I didn't get to see him again that evening but at least I had done some good karma to wipe out the bad karma I had inflected on him all those years back.

If it wasn't for the police arriving, I really don't know if Sasaka could have stopped me giving the guy more of a beating than I did, anyway it's a event in my life, that I am not proud of but I don't regret it as he deserved a slap for being a smart ass and I am sure he learned his lesson.

I went to the Satan's Slaves clubhouse after being released from the Police Station and slept all day as never got the best of sleeps in a cell especially on acid but my sleep wasn't too last, as I was woken and told to help around the club house.

The clubhouse now had one of my Ronnie Krays letter pin behind the bar as it was the talking point to everyone.

I never told my sister what had happened but did manage to visit her on the Sunday and after again a very close run in with the law, I just knew time wasn't on my side and that I was actually my worst emery through the rages I was getting into and also with the drug abuse that hadn't got any less as in take of drugs such as coke, dope, speed and acid.

It all was just getting too much so I said to my sister how would she like to come overseas with me, I said we do a round the world trip Thailand, L.A, Amsterdam, Paris, London, Scotland and then all the same again on the way back so we get to enjoy each stop over twice and have a few days in each country.

She loved the idea of being able to see our Dad but asked how was I going to be doing that, as I didn't have the money and she wasn't in a position to pay for it as she was still on my behalf paying off the loan against the flat she had taken out to get me out of the shit.

That night on leaving my sisters(my mum's old flat) it was very much something that I wanted to do so I set my mind to make this come true for my sister more than me, but I just knew it would do the best of good for us both.

I spend that evening trying to work out how to get money. I thought of a few people who I knew had plenty of money in business and also in property but then also in drug money though not my peers as I wasn't ever going to do any type of business with them.

On the Monday I set up meeting with Craig the president of the Rebels Car Club as he and his brother had as very successful car business and also they had a few properties throughout Wellington so I put a deal on the table to him and told him to seek advice of his lawyer and

if he wanted to go ahead with it then I would get my now Wellington based lawyer as I wasn't doing any legal business through Juliet Cooke as everything I ever told her, she would just after taking a phone call from me, she would pick up the phone to my uncle and tell him everything so I had called around

Wellington and found my own lawyer, set up my own meetings in private, showing my new lawyer all the legal documents I had to prove I did have over £100,000 in a trust fund with my name on it.

The thing was I was four weeks away from my 18th birthday, not my 20th birthday but that wasn't going to stop me.

I wasn't going to let my sister down, that's how I saw it as I went and sat with the president of the Rebels.

I said to Craig, if he gave me $20,000 then in two years time dead or alive meaning me, he would be paid $40,000.

There was no way a bank would double his money in that time by him just leaving the money sitting in bank account or through any straight investment and this was a 100% return investment.

We spoke for many hours and went for a drink at his clubhouse and then signed the paper work the very next morning at my lawyer's office.

Two days later I had $20,000 cash, I felt on top of the world. I didn't tell a soul and I hide the money in my room at the clubhouse but as I had pulled that off, I now wanted more money , it was like I was addicted to the colour of money as I was to drugs.

Anything I set my mind to I would make sure of it.

I soon had dark hair Rachael calling the clubhouse wanting to talk to me, I couldn't think why and I took the call, she was not happy; her phone bill had come in. I told her please don't panic and don't let anyone know as I didn't wish to get in more shit, and for sure not with the Satan's Slaves as they had been so good to me so I went straight down to her place and handed her over just over a grand and a few hundred more on top, she was a happy bunny.

Then I went to a well known old school Maori drug dealer who had a car breaking yard and he always had plenty of dole.

I knew him from a old friend, though he hated the Satan's Slaves as in the past they had beaten him near to death at a house party.

He was ok with me so again I put it to him about doing a contract this time £30,000 cash for a turnover of £60,000, it took me longer to convince him that it was above board and he was in a win, win situation once he signed on the dotted line.

It was not until a week later unlike how quick it was for Craig to sort the money but this guy was on and off with the deal, and even tried to say no at the last minute but I kept on at him.

Turning up to his breakage yard, finally he agreed.

We meet one night over at his house and counted the cash and then signed over the money, I now had in total just under $50,000.

Fucking hell I was going to have a great birthday that's for sure!

Soon others wanted to do contracts with me though no one knew I had done two contracts as no one knew about the contract I had written up with this guy, they only knew about the Rebel president and me doing business so I signed a $10,000 for $20,000 and also $16,500 for $25,000 to a friend of Cool Kens from Lower Hutt which with that cash on me I ended up staying out in Lower Hutt that night and getting so pissed at some bikers hang out bar in Lower Hutt.

In came members of a certain bike club who were no trouble at all for any one, though the bike club in question isn't really liked by most of the bike clubs up and down the country anyway they weren't doing me no harm, so I kept on partying and then one of their sidekicks started at me.

This wasn't unusual as they would go from pub to pub starting at people, I'm not willing to name what patched bike club it was but I will admitted that I took a hiding with a pool stick that was broken over my back and a bar stool then hit over my back as I wouldn't let go off this wanker but once I had been hit twice I lost my grip on him and then the fight as they came in like a pack of dogs and finished me off.

All I was worried about was the money I had in my jacket and then I thought fuck this as a joke.

I very much was going to take the bastard out of the game and very much so.

That night some of the people from Wellington who I had been drinking with (who got me in a car back to Wellington) had left a few of the others back as these guys were in fear of their lives as they though the bike club would come back with shooters and finish me and them off but the rest of the group of friends stayed out there.

I was told one of the girls who was younger sister of a friend of mine ended up been sexual assaulted, not raped as I always had thought but still some sexual assault that she never told her brother as it would be one fight he wouldn't win alone and she knew it would bring more bloodshed to her family, she didn't want to see her brother being killed over it so she didn't tell a soul apart from me a few days later.

She asked me never ever to tell anyone, it's a promise I have kept to this day and when she told me I gave her a promise back that I would make sure bad karma came to the horrible bastard who done what he done to her.

I wasn't her boyfriend nor her brother but it hurt hearing that she had been touched in such a way against her will as she was a lovely girl.

I hated that and I think men like that are scum and they are no difference to rapists or sick bastards who touch kids as they are the scum of the earth.

Any crime against a woman or a child is a crime that deserves the bastard to be hanged.... full stop, no debate on that! It even makes me angry just thinking about it.

I arrived back to Wellington with the $16,000 as I had spent $500 from the few hours I had been in Lower Hutt.

Black and blue yet again I was though my face wasn't busted up but my back was causing me so much pain.

I didn't want the Satan's Slaves to know about my run in as I shouldn't have been out that far of Wellington and very much not drinking in that certain bar as it was known to be this bike club hang out but I wanted a drink and I was on a high as now I had in near three weeks around $70,000, I was rolling in the money well for a 17 year old kid I very much was.

I booked myself in to a penthouse of a 5 star hotel and counted my money, then took a bath as my back was sore. In the morning I could hardly stand as I was in so much pain but when I opened the safe and saw the money, I thought this was great and thought to get the rest of the money from the clubhouse so I went and got it that afternoon when the clubhouse was quiet as most members were either doing family things and the others were still in bed recovering from their previous night of their own partying.

For me I had my own partying to do but one thing I did do when I collected the money is I went into the kitchen and put $2,000 in cash in the fridge and thought whoever was first to raise from their bed or decide to get a bite to eat would end up being $2,000 up, and they would never know it was me who had left it there for who ever found it first.

I always wondered would whoever found it would they tell the others or share it, or even put half of it towards the club as a whole.

I would never know and whoever did find it, it seemed never let anyone know as there were no conversations that I ever overheard about the money in the fridge.

I returned back to the hotel, boredom sat in so I called my mate Chris Mitchell inviting him over and called a few escorts and we partied it up with $200 an hour girls.

We thought we were rock stars then I called in the drugs to make sure it was more of a rocking roll experience but Chris said no to any of the hard drugs, he had a joint but that was it.

Don't put me wrong he wasn't straight but he didn't take hard drugs like I did, he was much more sensible than me but hell could the guy drink and still very much party it up with the best of them.

I just didn't want to leave I had got the taste to this great room with a view over Wellington harbour, I can't remember what name I had checked in as I made sure it wasn't my own name.

I asked front of house what rate they would give me for a week as my 18th birthday was soon coming, I ended up paying out $10,000 for a week stay then the morning of my birthday I left, getting a taxi across town.

I was sick of having to catch taxis so I thought fuck it I will buy a car but first off all I wanted was to buy myself a decent meaningful birthday present and also a gift for my sister so I booked a 5 star around the world trip for me and my sister that came to over $35,000 business class, and best hotels at each stop over, including spending money.

I then went to my sister place; I had just blown now in total after drugs and escorts and all the booze a hell of a lot of money.............big time and in a very rock n roll manor.

I had turned 18 years old finally but it seemed I hadn't grown up as to blow this sum of money on what I blew on apart from the around the world trip, was stupid to say the least but hell for me I wasn't even going to make my 18th so when I did, I just wanted to celebrate in style, and that's exactly what I did.

My mini bar was being refilled nearly by the hour so that alone had cost me a fair bit and yes I know what a waste of money, what a fool but again I don't have any regrets as though I was left with now only $20,000 and that was 4 weeks later from getting the first bit of cash.

I very much lived the high life and at least I had something to show for it in the end as in the around the world trip and so on my 18th birthday I made my sister shed a tear but one very much of joy and all I needed to do now is wait till June and we would be away, so I rang my father and made his day big time as he hadn't seen me for over 7 years so he was so looking forward to seeing his daughter and his son.

My Father was happy and so were my grandparents in Scotland and so was my Nana in Wellington as she thought she had lost so much of the young grandson who she grew to love as she had seen me just slid down into a very dark hole after my Mum had been killed(her only daughter lost).

I really wish I could make things better between my uncle Frank and I at the time, but I do really think he had given up on me which was sad as he and my auntie too had been there for me and I know for sure if I had taken his advise all the trouble that I was getting myself into would not have happened if I lived at his house and got work at his saw mill as he suggested but I was young and as Reggie had pointed out yes there was a fine line between youth and stupidly.

The very next thing I did when I left my sister's house (leaving our airline tickets with her for safe keeping) I went and saw Stonney who wanted to see me for my birthday as he had somewhere he said he wanted to take me on my 18th birthday.

I was sure it was some parlour to have a few girls though I don't think I could have had any more sex as I so needed the rest after the week I had just had with all the many girls I had come to see me in the hotel room as it was loose to say the least!

They must have through I won the lottery as my door to my suite was like a revolving door as once a few girls had left many more turned up, I didn't catch many of their names but then again they probably didn't mine either as they were in all honesty only there for one thing and that was for the colour of the money rather than my company but that's cool at least I looked after them and all had a good time.

I arrived at Stonneys in another taxi, I was throwing lots of money away on taxis, and there on Stonneys driveway was a car that was an Australian V8 Holden. He had done it up so it was puka, I asked him what he was doing with it as he had been working on it for a while and before he said anything I asked him could I buy it off him.

I didn't even have a driving licence to drive, I hadn't driven such a car before but it beat catching another taxi so the deal was done though I think Stonney thought now I had been given my money as in my trust account money when I turned 18 rather 20 as I paid it of course in cash there and then.

What a powerful car and a lovely one at that as I drove it through Wellington. Stonney said he needed to stop into the Satan's Slaves Motorcycle clubhouse before we were going out so I parked up, in we went and what I didn't know was they laid on a surprise birthday for me, it was Bacons idea as it was coming soon up to exactly a years since I had lost my Mum and they the club just wanted to do something good for me.

I hadn't fucked up while at the clubhouse so they were happy with me, as I had brought no trouble to their front door while living there.

Also I had been helping around a lot, though for the last week when I disappear they all joked and asked had I gone "Walkabout!" as in back to the bush to my tent near the beach.

Oh if they only knew but I couldn't have loads of bikers turning up during my stay at the 5 star hotel as for sure I would have been asked to leave as 100% they would have done the suite more in rock n roll style than me as in a television out of the window and the rest plus I couldn't afford to get them all escorts, I would have been a broke man quicker.

While I was there, there was talk that night that in a few years to come I would be very much more part of the club, they really could see me being their future and that made me feel proud as there guys were like my second family and it felt nice belonging and more so as the drinks flowed and I didn't have to drink vodka jelly shots but more than anything I had made it to my 18th birthday.

I couldn't believe it and I am sure many people had put down personal best among them all thinking I wasn't going to make it either, so I had come along way but I was still very in my drug bubble blocking out everything and still on that slide of a drug hell, my personal battle against drugs wasn't over but still very much in full swing.

I was battling every time I went and took a line of coke that I had scored on the route to Stonney house when I was in the taxi as one thing on the night of my birthday I didn't want to be without was a pocket full of drugs as I wanted to see the night on a high.

The following night my sister was going to be taking me out on a birthday dinner which I was looking forward to so as quick as I could early on this evening I was trying to not drink as much as I could because I didn't want a banging hung over the next day but as for drug taking I just wanted to get as wasted as I could this evening.

I still had rolls of money left on me, so I put up some cash from a bike that the club had taken from a previous prospect of the club.

The bike was never his in the first place, he had been paying it off weekly but had himself fallen out of favour of the club due to not being a 1%er and not being a true Satan's Slaves so he was after also going behind on payments and more, was kicked out of the club, and the bike was taken back so I put money down on it.

This also it seemed was getting me closer to getting to where my life was only heading and that was to prospect for the club and then become a member as my life wasn't going or leading anywhere and very much there wasn't anything positive going on.

I wouldn't have thrown all that money away if I had been a believer in a tomorrow but the pattern of my life, the death of my Mum made very such so that I didn't have a reason to even believe in any tomorrows, let alone in any dreams.

At least one thing I had to look forward to and one thing that could be positive and life changing was in two months time getting on that plane and taking the trip overseas with my sister.

I am sure this could just save my life and I don't mean that lightly, as at that time in my life

I believed it was going to save this life of mine, one thing I needed and that was saving, but this was up to me to do just that.

Again though I couldn't even predict how my life now as an 18 year old was going to take another turn and yet another turn for the worst, this time the very, very worse.

Whose fault was this, I only yet again had me to blame and after the tiny amount of huge celebrations leading up to my 18th birthday and also on my 18th birthday well it was only going to take less than half a day for it all to go Pete tong big time.

Chapter 36

MY LIFES GOING, GONE.......PROPER PETE TONG

Too many people buying me drinks in celebration of my 18th birthday, were they just all being too kind as they felt sorry for me leading up to my Mum's anniversary of her death or were some just being over friendly as they had dollars signs in their eyes.

I am sure I was right to think that among all these people who were celebrating my 18th birthday with me that many would fit into these two catalogues and then there were some who were friends and just liked me for who I was, the young man I had become in the marking of these last 18 years of my life that I have written about through these pages of my book.

Well all I really knew was that I had drunken to much drink, I had taken too many drugs and that was just on this night, not even taking into account all the many other nights I had taken too much of everything, for now I needed to get my head down as I was seeing double, I was that hammered.

I got myself out of the clubhouse as some guests left the clubhouse and I was saying good bye to them, then spotting my new car as I had forgotten about until I saw it in the car park at the front of the clubhouse, the very place where once the skinheads house used to stand before that was burnt down many years earlier.

I got into my car but wasn't in a state to drive so I just lay down and pulled the seat back. I was out quick as a flash. Sleeping like a baby even when Harley Davidson's would be roaring past, not even the sound of the motorcycles woke me up but the sun light soon came through the car windows and that's what woke from my sleep.

I awoke at some time that late morning, waking up in a panic for some reason, thinking I was late to get to my sisters.

I wasn't sure why I had thought the birthday dinner was a lunch being held for me by my sister so I stared the car and drove still clearly half drunk and very much still very high from the amount of drugs in my system from the night before partying (maybe a little too hard as I felt like shit as I drove through Wellington).

I took the ridge along the hills for some reason, I wasn't sure why but I did and this was now the only second time I had driven this powerful motor.

It only took a gentle put down on the petal and that was it, the car would move ever so quick and with the hills bobbing up and down, it's as if I was flying over them.

I am sure I was still drunk and the acid I was for sure half way through the drive hadn't all but worn off as I felt still slightly tripping but I didn't think anything much off it.

Then suddenly from out of nowhere a car Japanese import family type saloon car pulled out in front of me.

I knew if I were to hit the car then whoever was in the car would have probably died so I just grabbed the steering wheel pulling it hard to the left and still through panic my foot was still on the gas as I just headed straight for a bus shelter and a small round about that had earth rocks on it from (it looked) like a oceans bed in the middle.

Some sort of art sight for people at the bus shelter to stand and steer while they waited for their busses.

Well this is what was in my way between the bus shelter and my car with me panicked stricken behind the wheel.

Thank God I had my seat belt on and thank God that on this late morning no one was at the bus stop as I went flying into the arrangement of rocks.

Crashing the car with such forced that the back seats came forward from their bolts and the front of the car, the bonnet was crushed up and smoke and hissing noise came out, as for me yes it hurt....not the about the car but the pain from the impact of the crash.

Let's say I was shaken though not stirred................. I was in shock but more so I had smashed up my new car!

A car I had only brought the day before. I had only owned it for less than 24hrs and now it was not looking like the car that I had first seen in the drive way of Stonneys house.

The car that I avoided hitting hadn't seen the crash but very much I am sure they would have heard it as they continue along the Ridgeway, as for everyone else in nearby houses they very much heard it.

I had a lady come out of her house and over to the car asking if it was ok?

she opened my driver's door and I undone the seat belt, my chest was sore due to the seatbelt I had been wearing but I managed to walk from the crash in one piece.

Again, all I can say is that someone in heaven was looking down on me and that person I knew it could only have been my Mum as for a second time, crashing a car I had come away and unscratched when from certain I was for sure that I would have been injured or could have been killed.

The lovely lady took me over to her house and put me in her kitchen, asking again was I ok?

My neck and my chest was the only pain I could feel but I said I was fine.

I could smell something lovely, I looked over and on top of her stove I noticed a tea towel wrapped over something so I asked her what it was (while she was offering me a glass of water) ?

I didn't get a reply from her but whatever she had baked, the smell from it made me think of my Nana for some reason as she was one who could cook or bake such lovely delights which would always smell like this.

The lady moved into the front of her house where I heard her pick up her phone and ask to speak to what sounded like the police or the medical services.

Fuck, the police! They for sure would have been called by someone who witnessed the crash after receiving a call if not her call, so I had to get the fuck out of there.

I got up on to my feet and unlocked her back door and as I was heading out the back door I took a glance again over at her stove and then stepped over to what was smelling so lovely and lifted up the tea towel and there below was a freshly baked cake...it looked like a carrot cake.

I really wanted a slice, my tummy was emptied and I was feeling sick due to the hangover but the cake hadn't been cut yet into slices. Time wasn't on my side so I just thought I got to have a bite of it so I lifted the whole cake and took a bite out of it.

I was going to of course place it down before she arrived back but as I took a bite, I heard her get off the phone and tell me she would be looking out the front window to let me know when the ambulance and the police were on the way.

Once I heard her say that I leaped out the back door and over her fence down the side of the hill, though in one hand still was the lady's still warm freshly baked carrot cake.

Off I was towards the valley below and not until I reached the bottom did sit down in some bush hidden from the main road below and I ate that cake, not even leaving a crumb for the wild animals that I am sure would have called this part of the wild bush, their home.

I did feel guilty as that lady would have when the medical team arrived, shown them into the kitchen to discovery not only had I done the disappearing act but her freshly cooked carrot cake had also done the disappearing act.

How I wished I could have thanked her for the cake and baked one myself to replace hers but the thing is, even I couldn't have baked such a lovely cake as what she had cooked that morning moments before she would have heard a huge loud crash outside of her house, to peer out of her window after pulling the cake out of the oven to rest on top of the stove, while she went out to help me and make sure I was ok.....so yeah I did feel guilty but for now I had to try and get home and more so let Stonney know asap about the car.

I managed to hitchhike a ride to a friend's house Glyn and I got on his phone telling Stonney what had happened so he knew what to say to the police when they arrived at his house.

He told them (the transport police) when they knocked that his car was parked in his drive way and then when walking out with them, on seeing it not being there well he said he had been sleeping and when he arrived home last night he parked in the drive way.

He went onto say he must have left the keys in the motor which is something not too unusual back in those days in New Zealand if you parked your car on your own land or on your own drive away, anyway they came to the conclusion it had been stolen.

The only thing I had on my side was I had driving gloves on when I crashed the car so my prints weren't on the stirring wheel and as for being on the passager door if my prints had been picked up as that's the side of the car I had gain entry into the car when I fell asleep in it at the clubhouse as it was the nearest door to get into the car from their main entrance, where my car was parked in their car park at the front of the clubhouse.

There would have many other finger prints of other friends of Stonneys who would have been in that car during the week once Stonney had finished working on the car as he had told me in the week that he had taken it out for a spin a few times and more so in my favour was we hadn't signed over paper work as Stonney couldn't find the car documents so I was going to do the register that coming Monday.

For now there was no proof of sale so as far as I was concerned I was in the clear. Lucky I had gone to Glyn house to make that call to Stonney before he had a knock on his door by the old bill.

Of course he wasn't happy with the transport police coming to his door but he now could calm the insurance and he still had my cash in his pocket from the sale of the car the day before.

He was a happy man though he said when the insurance money was to come in then he would give that to me so at least I would get some of my money back but now I was again carless but not homeless so I got a lift with Glyn and went back down to the Satan's Slaves I went.

Once I arrived in the main part of the clubhouse, all the members who were there (still up from partying the night before) had a good laugh at me.

I asked one of the Satan's Slaves could I buy his 1970 Mustang Boss of him again another powerful V8, a car that the member had for many a years so I offered him a deal and said he could hold my bike against the deal as I didn't have full amount in cash to give him as I wanted to save some of my money for my trip with my sister and also to get in at least another week of party in celebrating my 18th birthday so he said that was fine.

He actually said the Triumph bike I had brought from the club, he would get one of the younger members to rebuilt the bike again for me as a birthday present from the club to me and because I had a few weekly payment first to pay back the full amount of the bike first, so he said the remaining car money can come second as they were more concerned I had a bike.

Though I lost out on my car the one I had crashed that late morning, at least with the insurance money I was to get from Stonney, I could hand that to the Satan Slave member who I had brought the car from.

That would be final payment on the British bike, the Triumph Trophy that due to its age they were going to get into shape for me as I didn't have a clue about mechanic work on bikes.

These old Triumphs though solid bikes, had a bad reputation of oil leaks and other problems so they had to get the bike right if I had any chance on going on bike runs with the club trying to keep up with all the Harley-Davidsons.

I now also had another car to replace the crashed one so all was ok, a positive from a negative I seemed to have found and this car though much older than my last car was fucking fast and looked the business though I shouldn't have been driving.

In all fact I should have taken my driving test and correct lessons as I was loose behind the wheel, not as some boy racer but more so as I didn't know the highway road rules so all I really knew was a give way sign, and green, orange and red on traffic lights but apart from that, that was it.

I went over to my sister place in my car, she didn't know about the car crash from the day before and there was no need to tell her so I kept quiet on that.

I handed her some money for us to hide around $5,000 for our spending money on our trip, though my sister said she had her own spending money to take so not to be silly but I said no I really needed her to hold onto that or I would end up spending it before we even left the country.

As for me I had around £3000 left from all the money I had come into over the last few weeks, fuck all to show for it apart from a crashed car, my new car and a Triumph motorcycle and some wild memories of partying it up like a rock n roll star in a classy hotel.

We didn't need to be leaving my sisters till evening to go out for dinner so I said to her I wanted to go around to the Mitchell's to show off my new car to my best friend Chris.

I pulled up with my motor to his house. His mate Brent was there so I said I would take them of a drive but Chris after being in one car crash with me said no way and asked could he drive my car so I threw him the keys and off we went.

Chris was a dam good driver; you could call him a boy racer as he would put foot on the pedal and give it all he had.

His mum and dad asked me when had I passed my driving licence? I told them I had only the week earlier as they wouldn't have been happy that I was driving around without a licence as they cared for me a lot.

Kath and John had heard through Chris's older brother Damien that I had been getting into trouble recently with the police. It was nice that Kath and john cared do much about me, they were such lovely people and true friends of my Mum, and my sister and I.

I went out to one of my favourite Chinese restaurants that my father used to always take me to. My sister treated me to a lovely dinner and the staff who remembered my father, gave me a few bottles of sake on the house, which I was very thankful for.

My father had always known the Chinese community very well in Wellington. I think he had some ongoing business with the Chinese community though unsure whatever it was, and though I knew he knew the main Triads who were operating in New Zealand at the time while my father was in Wellington I don't think it was crime related friendship well anyway whatever it was they did hold respect for my father and so treated me very, very well indeed, though Chinese food wasn't my sisters first choice of food, she still very much enjoyed the dinner.

Then afterwards we went out with her friends and got on the drink. I ended up sleeping with her friend Abby who was a stunner; she was a hippy chick who I always liked.

It was her brother Justin who I had put in hospital at the Diner months earlier by my mistake when he was only trying to stop the fight and for his goodwill he ended up in hospital. I did feel terrible about it but I didn't feel terrible getting into bed with his sister as she was hot.

The rest of the month went by without any worries and the last 9 days of April I was not getting into any trouble and I loved my car.

I was always driving everyone to take them to parties and was going to loads of house parties then on the first week of May, the Satan's Slaves were told of a massive party on a farm in the Happy Valley area of Wellington.

The Satan's Slaves took their bikes, I had a few girls and a prospect jumped in my car and we shot around to the party, everyone being told to go tooled up as it was a big party with many different people attending so there could be gang trouble.

It was the first time I had taken a knife purposely out with me for many years. When you find yourself carrying a knife, it's always close to your mind that you have it on you.

Drugs and drink, I spend maybe $600 before I left for the party so I had a few girls hanging off me so they got a taste of my drugs. They were just drug whores in a honestly but I didn't mind having 4 girls hang off me but some of the older guys there who didn't know me seemed to have a problem with it, more so after many of the Satan's Slaves left around 2am in the morning and I was left just with a few people I knew and many I didn't.

That's when I started to get shoved and asked who the fuck did I think I was? Did I think I was some big man due to having that type of car and with these dolly birds around me?

I was told I was just a boy and then crack I took a punch to the face.

There and then I thought fuck it, I anit even going to dance on my toes and put on a fight so I just stabbed the bastard in the guts. The knife going through his leather jacket then I kicked him backwards and as he lay in the floor I stabbed his mate in the ass who had his back to me leaning over to help his mate up who was on the ground. Both had started at me so both I would teach the bulling pricks, a lesson.

I didn't care one single bit stabbing them and this time I made sure that the girls were safe so I yell at the girls to get in my car and as I had the knife in my hand asking if anyone else wanted to call me a boy then I would stab them up, but everyone else was kind of in shock by what I had just done, though it was random as, I had been baited and I was struck first.

I jumped in my car, a few beer bottles were thrown and I was off back to the clubhouse but told to fuck off from there if I had just stabbed someone.

They didn't need the police coming down here so I left leaving two of the girls there, and dropping one back at her house. She hides the knife for me while I waited in the car as she lived with others, and I had blood on me from my nose bleeding so I held my head back and tried to clot my blood so to stop it from running onto me by the time the girl returned to the car.

She then returned to the car asking me if she could stay on with me for the night so we went around to Stonneys house.

I asked if I could wash the blood off my hands and stay there the night. He said that was fine but I had to pull my car into his garage in case the licence plate had been taken down when I left the party.

I didn't care at the time about stabbing the guy though I do believe knife crime especially these days in London among the youths, is very out of control more than gun crime.

The thing is, when I was only a teenage I really didn't think about the outcome of stabbing someone.

In all fact if you stab someone in the wrong place (and that could be many parts of the body) you even could maybe not wanting to, end that person's life so unlike shooting someone when you know more a less what the outcome is going to be of that when you fire a gun, but as for stabbing someone I stupidly saw it as being harmless to the point of not causing death.

I was foolish to think along those lines but back then I carried a knife for one purpose only, and that was to defend myself if ever under attack.

When you stab someone, you have the problem over blood (serious blood) loss, that can bring on death so the thing is, that with one misuse of a knife in any stabbing, once you stab that person even if it's in self defensive, that single stab wound can easy lead onto that persons lose of live, and your lose of freedom as you know it, taken away from you forever or at least for many, many years so you need to ask yourself seriously is it worth it using a knife? Well if you are asking me it's not.

This didn't go through my mind at the time all those years ago, what did at the time was that the wanker had called me a boy and it was actually him who was trying to act the big man, he reminded of the bullies during my school years.

The thing with them I never let them bully me so I wasn't going to let some dick head wanker try it on me.

I didn't care what pain he was suffering and as for his fool of a mate, while he wouldn't be able to sit for at least two weeks due to being stabbed in the arse so at least he too was taught a lesson, not to be a mouthy bastard anymore.

I stayed out a Stonneys for a few days and nights, not contacting the Satan's Slaves as if anything had happened then they would have got a message up to me.

They knew I was staying at Stonneys house as he had been down to them explaining I was there at his place keeping my head down.

At the time I never thought of the injury that I could have substance to that guy, but within days I got to learn that his heavy leather jacket probably saved his life as it wasn't a bad as I had first thought so I was glad to hear that as I didn't need anything stopping me from going overseas with my sister.

After staying at Stonneys for a few days I took the car over to my sisters place, and there waiting for me was a small parcel from the UK, actually a few.

One was from my Dad, my birthday present that was all Liverpool football Club stuff that I was chuffed with.

The next present was from my Grandmother and Granddad in Scotland, a lovely shirt and warm letter explaining that how happy they were that they would be seeing my sister and me very soon, I loved my grandparents so very much.

The next parcel I opened, it was a card that looked like it was handmade and inside it was a pure gold K pin badge, it was from Ronnie and Reggie, send from Ronnie with a happy birthday inside the card and a God Bless.

I was so cuffed with this, I actually a few years later when I got to meet Reggie Kray, wore it to the prison visit and also I would wear it when ever in my days in London on a suit very proudly at such events as charity parties that Reggie would have me running the security for on his behalf.

I even had the British singer Cliff Richard when I was doing security on his Heathcliff performances at the famous Hammersmith Apollo, ask me what the K stood for and that came how he himself got to know about my friendship that had grown by then with the remaining Kray twin Reggie Kray.

Cliff himself when he started off in show business knew both the twins, he always said good things about them. He even gave me some signed records and a signed programme to take to Reggie Kray on one of my many prison visits to see Reggie.

Reggie was happy with what Cliff had done for him but at the time Reggie wanted more as in he really wanted Cliff Richard himself to come down on the visit. Something (due the negative press that Cliff Richard would have got, and also due to his nightly performances at the theatre) he couldn't get down to see Reggie, though Cliff sent his best wishes onto Reggie at the time.

A few days later I got a signed boxing poster that was dated back to the late 1950s with both the twins and also their elder brother Charlie, when all three Krays were on the boxing card for a boxing show at the world famous Royal Albert Hall and a letter from Reggie wishing me a happy birthday.

Reggie's own handwriting was as hard as Ronnie's to read but after receiving many letters from them over the years I soon got be able to read their letters.

Soon it was May and my birthday was now two weeks behind me, I couldn't use that as a excuse why I was still partying, burning a hole in my pocket but I didn't need a excuse.

I hadn't to give myself a excuse to keep on getting high as my Mum's Anniversary was soon upon me and I didn't want to think about it and nor wake up to the fact that my Mum was dead.

Still by then a year, I believe looking back I still didn't except it and I just didn't want to be anything apart from numb, and to be get numb meant more than just smoking countless joints but to get very, very high.

If I had only more positive things in my life then I would be fine, I know for sure if sport played a huge part of my life at this stage then I could at least channel all my thoughts and also my rage at times which would rear its ugly head more times than I expected.

Anything now, the smallest thing would make me switch and if anyone tried to harm me then I would make sure I got them first or second best, finish them off after they had or said wrong against me.

The weekend before my Mum's anniversary I went out up town, firstly on a Thursday night as there were some punk and heavy metal bands playing at a warehouse in Hopper Street just around the corner from Webb Street in Wellington where Wims main garage was.

The party was held in a warehouse, many parties over the years were held here. You would have to walk up a set of steep stairs to get entry, once inside sometimes you had to pay some money on the door but no one minded as once inside there was always loads of people partying it up to many a times, great kiwi live bands.

Always many different folk in there, and all were cool even the punks and the skinheads would get along; there hardly was never no trouble.

This Thursday night I went out from the Satan's Slaves clubhouse to take a look at the party, as many a times when ever there was a party being held in Wellington, I would be send out to scout it then report back to the clubhouse letting them know who was in attendance at the party i.e. if there was ever any rival gangs.

There were those guys from the AC/DC there but I soon found out they no longer were mob members they had either turned grass against the gang or had fallen out for some reason as none were patched up.

I made sure when I spotted them (being told by someone at the party that these guys had been kicked out of the mob) they didn't see me arrive or go in.

I spoke to some guys outside who said that they were for sure now ex members of the mob and all three had been kicked out of the gang, so they must have done something against the mob and for them to be out of their own social circle meant they were in hiding from the mob as the mob wouldn't never dare come to such a turn out as it was full of skins and other types of social circles who would battle it out with the mob.

I asked these guys outside why weren't any telling these three to leave and I was told they were carrying firearms and that they had already pistol whipped someone and fought a few people.

No one dared called the police as everyone there hated the police but it got a round maybe these three guys were going to try and rob the door takings and the makes shift bars that had been set up but no one dared to stand up to them or tell them to fuck off........neither was I as if they had spotted me, then 100% without doubt they for sure would have shot me there and then.

I had actually been chased after leaving the clubhouse in a private car weeks after the ACDC shooting.

One night when getting out of a taxi near a girls place that I was going around to visit and stay the night as I was kind of seeing the girl on and off anyway I was followed and chased on the footpath as I stepped out of the taxi.

I banged on a random door, actually the nearest house I could reach before I was going to be set upon.

When the front door was opened to me after my heavy knocking on it, I rushed past the poor guy who answered the door and went through his house when I got to the bathroom flung open the window, and then (as they were kicking down the front door that I had slammed behind me) I jumped in the shower and hide behind the curtain rail, so when the door came crashing in hoping they would think I had jumped out the window.

I heard a few tough sounding voices say "He's gone out the fucking window!" and with that they run out the house to the back yard.

I then hide myself under a bed in the very next room to the bathroom as I wasn't going to myself leave the safety of that house for the time being while there were nutcases outside baying for my blood.

I wasn't either going to let the guy (who answered the front door to me) know I was there still in his house in case he informed these fuckers who were out there looking for me.

I just prayed they didn't come back into the house, by this time the house owner had called the police and still no one knew I was hiding under a bed.

I did hear the police ask questions to the home owner and he told them that I had knocked on the door shouting help and as he opened his door I came crashing in slamming the door behind me then running through the house hearing his front door come crashing down.

He then told them how I disappeared into the bathroom and he like the others seeing the opened window had guessed I flung myself out the window before the door came crashing in by these attackers.

I waited for the police to leave. Thought I could sneak out of the house after the police had gone and the nutter's were no longer outside (they had left the area before the police had turned up) as I never heard the police officers speak to the house owner about certain tough guys outside so I knew they must have left before any police were called and had arrived to investigate the 999 call.

I had to wait till after the house owner called every Tom, Dick and Harry about what had happened as he was only in the hallway on a phone outside the bedroom where I was hiding so I couldn't have sneaked out without being seen as for me to reach the front door, I would have had to use the hallway to make my escape.

He then (after speaking to all his mates) called a lock smith so while he was waiting for his lock smith; I had to stay hidden under this oak wooden bed.

Even after the locksmith (when I was hoping then I could get out but still I couldn't) next minute the sound of the door bell went and I heard this time a female voice.

The way they were speaking, I could tell this wasn't his wife who had turned up.

Just my fucking luck, they came into the bedroom I was hiding in under the bed, and they started to make love on the bed.

It seemed to last forever, it was again such a surreal day as I had only been running from who I am sure very much was linked to the shooting outside the AC/DC concert.... running for my life.

I had to keep as quiet as a mouse without trying to laugh then as I heard her having a orgasm, she finished by saying "If only my husband Jimmy could give it to me like you do Bruce." well with that I had to put my hand over my mouth as I was going to crack up.

I had to move weight off one of my legs as I started to get pins and needles, it really hurt as my leg had gone dead.

I tried rotating my foot so to get the blood moving but that caused such cramp in my foot, that I couldn't bear it anymore and crawled out under the bed thinking I just need to reach the bedroom door (that was open) and I will be out of there, but just as I had got my body across the wooden floor, I heard the guy cumin out loud (he sounded like a crap cheesy 1970s porn star).

Next he placed his foot over the bed, which I didn't noticed until his foot stepped on my head and he yelped so loud that I am sure if I was looking up I would have seen him in the air from fright, hitting his head on the ceiling as that is how bad of a shock he got.

I got to my feet and tried my best to run out the door but with pins and needles in my leg I was dragging my left leg as I couldn't move it.

My left leg was like a lead dead weight.

When he got up from the sudden shock, the chase was like a Benny Hill stretch as he chased me around the house.

I just wanted to get the fuck out as now he had a tennis racket in his hand was chasing me around and around a dining table with me saying "I just to get out of your house!" he replying "What the fuck were you doing in my house already."

What could I say to that..........nothing!

Anyway as the blood came back into my leg I was able to get out the front door thought to give him credit he managed to hit me a few times on the back of the head which would have hurt more if he hadn't hit me with the strings of the tennis racket.

The tennis racket each time he struck me, just bounced of my head.

It was very much The Two Ronnie's Television Show and The Benny Hill Show combined together as in the comedy effect and again it had all the Satan's Slaves crackling up falling over with laughter when I managed to get back to the clubhouse telling them off the last few hours what had gone on (after a long walk and more hitch hiking and a lift to their clubhouse).

The Satan's Slaves members said "What are we going to do with ya Christian as every time you leave the clubhouse, you always getting ya self in trouble." anyway back to the story of Hopper st.

I knew that these guys inside had to be stopped whatever they had on their mind and so I went down to the clubhouse and had a quiet chat among a handful of people, who I spoke to is no one business but let's just say they went to the party in two set of cars.

Half an hour later I got on the back of a Harley Davison with Zombie, as we pulled into the street we just saw the windows of the warehouse light up and heard the familiar sound of a gun going off...I heard three shots before we quickly got away from there on the bike.

I am sure I heard some more shots though it could have been just a car in the street at the same time backfiring.

Now back at the clubhouse the two car loads of people who had gone to sort things didn't return that night nor did I actually see them again for a while though no one on our side were hurt and those people who had been kicked out of the mob every one of them very much was thrown out of the party and let's just fireworks went off inside the party and they were on the receiving end of it.

The police sealed off that whole scene and street soon afterwards, well it just shows how they got their bad karma, the three guys who went looking for trouble and ended up getting all shaken up to say the least.

All shaken up was about to come my way, my whole world as I knew it was all going to be all shaken up and it was going to hit home with a boom....a sudden one at that.

Chapter 37

FIGHT OR FRIGHT ....ITS SHOWTIME

It was Friday night, there was talk of going up to the new nightclub which was situated across the road from Taranaki Street Police Station, a police station I had spend in their cells many a times over the last year that has since passed.

Andy Evans a friend of mine (a good friend) who was also a very good Zen Do Kai student and ex prospect of the Satan's Slaves was playing in his band at the nightclub. He played bass in the band. It was a great band, if I can recall correctly was called the buzzards, anyway they were a covers band but they always packed out nightclubs in Wellington whenever they played a live gig.

Wellington nightclubs some nights would turn into live music venues, and live music was massive in Wellington, actually all over NZ.

It sounded very much to be a good night out and it would be good seeing Andy so I rocked up and was enjoying many a drinks, and soon slipping acid tabs down my throat and snorting coke quite heavy as what was some very fine coke which was unusual in New Zealand as all the coke had usually been very badly mixed, but I did enjoy snorting this grade of coke and I went to the bathroom room a few many time shoving line after line of coke up my nose.

I noticed coming back in to the nightclub Craig the president of the Rebels Car Club and his brother Big Mike around the bar so I send them over a few cold beers and then Stephen Rowe who once many years ago had dated my sister was in the bar as well. Stephen had come up with some of the Satan's Slaves though not all of the others who had turned up with Grot hung around very long.

They guessed maybe the police were on the look for them (the police possibly blaming the Satan's Slaves for the shooting in Hooper Street) but that didn't put them off from at least travelling into the city and enjoying a few beers.

Stephen who was also known as Grot who was a patch member of the Satan's Slaves stayed on so did Scotty who now was a ex member (through his own choice) also there was Glyn, Stonney and another friend of mine and his younger sister (the girl who had been assaulted out in Lower Hutt when I had taken a beating out there).

Everyone was having a good night, myself and Glyn got into a earlier fight with some drunken idiots which was straighten out as quick as it started as they didn't put up any sort of a fight. They were all talk but nothing to back it up with.

Soon Glyn's own sister and her friend then turned up as well, they hadn't seen me about for a while so deicide to stay for a drink with me to wish me a belated Happy Birthday.

I was doing straight Jack Daniel's, sinking it like it was water, and high as a dove, loving the Deep Purple music that was being played at that point by Andy's band.

My friends sister (who had joined in conversation with Glyn's younger sister and her friend all having a girlie chat) tucked me on my shirt but I was away with the ferries.

I hadn't even noticed that Grot had left so now there was only Scotty, who had a false leg from a terrible bike accident where he had crash under a timer lorry and nearly lost his life many years earlier.

He had a plastic leg but still was hard as nails and a bit of a nuttier but a dam good guy.... proper friend, old school.

Across the bar among lots of other people were still Craig and his brother Mike.

Stonney was still there, also Glyn was still about, and so I got everyone a drink and send some more beers over to Craig and his brother. They kept on sending over Jack Daniels to the point I had about six lined up on the bar as well as my bottle of elephant beer (Carlsberg strongest beer at the time 9% in volume - it's now called special brew in the UK) and it would send any one nuts if they drunk far too much of it as it was that strong but for now I seemed fine.

I was a bit edgy from the earlier fight that Glyn and I had with two guys but that fight stopped very quick as the doormen knew us all so they just kicked who we told them were the trouble makers.

We kept on partying to the sounds of the British band "The Who" as Andy's band was doing three of their songs back to back which were getting the crowd started.

Lots of people were around dancing, too many in my own personal space so I asked a few long hair heavy metal guys to move away from me.

They just gave me one look and turned their back on me. I had a Zippo lighter on me that Zombie and his girlfriend Tracey at the time had got me for my 18th birthday. I always carried lighter fluid in my back pocket so I just got out the can of the lighter fluid and with that I sprayed them both on the back of their jackets and then pulled out the Zippo lighter and click.

Well one of them must have had so much hair products in his hair as in hair spray as he went up like Michael Jackson on that Pepsi commercial he done (which had gone Peter Tong for him) anyway soon the two long hair guys after patterning themselves down moved away fairy quick, probably they went to the toilets to re do their hair.

I didn't pour loads on them; I wasn't trying to burn them. I just didn't like being crowded around by so many people and did ask them to move away but was only given a blank look so it was one quick way of getting them to fuck off.

The acid was coming on, huge waves of it was rushing through me and I then sit down on a bar stool back going through my lined up Jack Daniels.

Sometimes I can drink too much Jack Daniels but others nights it just seemed so sweet to drink, its only when I was on feet that I noticed how very, very drunk I was and out of it.

My friend's sister was tugging me again for a second time on my sleeves so I asked her what was wrong?

She said to me that the guy who had assaulted her had walked into the nightclub.

Wellington is so small compared to somewhere like London for instance, always a likely chance on a night out, bumping into people you knew or you had fallen out with.

Friends and foes were always easy to bump into every day or every evening, even by just walking down the street you would bump into people you would know or not wish to bump into.

Well she for sure didn't wish to bump into him, but as for me he was the prick who had done wrong to her.

I didn't care if he had beat me in a fight weeks earlier out in Lower Hutt, though he fought dirty by hitting me over the back with a snooker clue and also his coward mate hitting me with a bar stool over my back.

I couldn't believe what balls they had by coming in to central Wellington to a nightclub, their motorcycle club which no one in Wellington were very fond off so all in all in many ways they shouldn't have been in Wellington....they were out of their own manor and now were on Satan's Slaves tuff.

Didn't they think it was going to go off?

He hadn't seen me even while he was in the middle half of the bar ordering a drink. There were around 5 of them. I am unsure if any of the others were from this MC Club but I did recognise his pal who had caught me with the bar stool.

I stood there, my feet starting to move and legs started to shake as my body just knew this wasn't only just from the rushes off the lsd going through my body but this was also from the fight or fright syndrome that any human being gets.

It goes back to when we were cave men millions of years ago, when a man who'd have to go out and fight a wild dangerous animal to kill so to bring back to his cave for his family to feed on. Providing food to eat for any caveman's family was first and foremost back in those days (I guess) as what else was there for caveman to do back in the day......sweet fuck all!!

These animals weren't sheep or deer if you get my drift and nor were they a flock of ducks or a few cows.

We are talking proper dangerous animals that easy could take the man (the caveman/hunters) own life, anyway the human body would trigger of brain activity which meant the cave man would either run or fight, which in turn is now known as the fight or flight syndrome.

Everyone gets these rushes natural throughout their bodies, so much blood circling around the body mainly all near all vital organs and also the brain activity goes a bit wild, as if you had become up against a dangerous animal as well, maybe that's one way of putting it.

But as I was high on lsd and shit loads of coke as well on top through my system, and also taken a E pill I had been given then with all the booze, those double strength beers well I wonder what all this on top of my body natural shaking from the fight and flight syndrome was doing to my body.

I did feel very fucked as if I was going to go into 4th gear of a racing car on a race course or if I was a earthquake going right off the rectal scale.

That's the only way I can think of explaining how high I was on that very night when this guy and his pals walked in to the nightclub and were pointed out to me.

I felt so much for the girl, what this bastard had done to her so I made sure he caught my eye contact but when he did he only laughed and pointed me out to these bikers who gave me evil looks and pushed their chests out like as if they fucking thought, they were Jake the Muse from the New Zealand movie Once Were Warriors.

I'll fucking show them Once Were Warriors, as in my blood line I was a descent on my Mums side from the most feared true Maori Warrior who was ever born and that was the famous **Te Rauparaha** so I will fucking show them some Once Were Warriors.

I now could feel the rage, building up inside of me.

It was like a rage I hadn't ever before and ever since felt to this level, whatever was going on in my head and through my body was for sure making me see more than a red mist.

I wasn't going to be losing this fight that's for sure.

Soon he moved over towards where I was sitting again on my stool so I stood up as he made his way over.

He stopped short of reaching me but he whispered something in the girl's ear, she moved her body away from him as he lend over her.

I could just see sheer terror in her eyes, the poor girl.

He reminded me of the monster knocking on my window and how frighten as a child I felt though in the case of the monster he never got the chance to put his hands on me, but within this situation with the sister of my friend, well her monster (this bastard) had put his hands on her.

I strike him without any warning and what I thought was a great connection as he flew back but it didn't put him on his arse. He came charging towards me, I tried another punch but missed as he ducked under it.

I should have thrown a upper cut as I would have got him very much with that but now he had me flying against a wall, his arms wrapped around me and I kind of knew what was coming next (though I tried to move my head out the way) he slammed his forehead as he brought his head upwards and though not the best of head butts, he still connected to my nose, I had blood pissing out of it instantly. It didn't feel broken; it didn't need to feel broken as it had been so many times in the past.

I grabbed hold of him and tried a judo sweep but he just moved his legs out the way then came in with a knee to my lower ribs and that hurt but it in a way just got me more angry.

I managed to get free of him as I wanted a stand up fight when he was trying to use his strength to wrestle me to the ground. He was much stronger than me, but I knew to keep my distance as I was trying to jab him off but my jabs weren't quicker enough and he kept on coming forward.

If I had my knife that night I would have for sure just pulled it out and stabbed him, this was going through my mind as I just wanted to do the sick bastard.

I wasn't as planned, winning this fight as he would counter punch me, he was getting through so many punches even as I was protecting myself so well but while trying just to land the punch on his jaw that would have dropped him.

I then decided to kick him but that failed and failed big time as he got hold of my leg as it was going towards his knee which was my target as that would have at least stop him short, but with my leg now in his hand, he then before taking me to the ground reached in his back pocket.

I was told by Andy Evans who had been watched this from up on the stage while playing a "Clash" number, that the guy had taken a knife out of the back of his trousers.

Once I saw the blade, I for sure thought on the ground he was going to finish me off.

We hit the ground; Andy just in the nick of time jumped from the stage and grabbed hold of him dragging him away from me, and then Glyn grabbed hold of him, soon I was surrounded by 4 of his mates as I was trying to my feet.

Stonney jumped in and said that's enough and looked over at me telling me to get to my feet and accept the loss.

None of them knew what the monster had done to our pal's younger sister, and as she was there (who had after it had happened to her promised me not to tell a soul).

I couldn't yell that out. I wasn't going to break the promise I had made with her but I wasn't happy that I had beaten in a fight, second time by this guy and second time in front of friends but more so in my own town, I wasn't happy.

He was told to fuck off so he and his mates left that area of the club but instead of fucking off out of the nightclub, once the music stared to play again, he actually just went back around the side of the bar where he had been drinking earlier.

The smart ass bastard was being tapped on his back for winning the fight by his mates, who were buying him drinks as he folder his knife and put it back this time seeing it go inside his jacket pocket.

My pals younger sister thought it was all her fault, I said "No don't be silly, I wanted to do the bastard for what happened out in Lower Hutt so it's not your fault, don't blame yourself for anything babe."

I was handed some tissue paper while Stonney held my head back as my nose was bleeding.

When I finally pulled my head down I saw the guy laughing even more though there was music on I even heard the laughter, well fuck it that was that I was going to kill the cunt now.

Glyn told me to get myself to the toilet to wash the blood from my face and to stop the bleeding from my nose.

I thought yeah actually I should do that so to wipe the blood from my face, and with my nose constantly dripping I probably looked worse for wear.

The constant dripping from my nose, it's all I could think of, was the dripping blood from my nose, the taste of my own blood down the back of my throat. I wanted this bastard to taste his own blood rather than me, here tasting my own after losing the fight to him.

I got off my stool and took in my bottle of Carlsberg elephant beer with me and headed for the bathroom, managing to get into an empty toilet cubical.

There was a knock on the door, a voice I knew among the few friends who were there from inside the club (I won't mention who it was). He told me to put my hand underneath the door of the toilet which I did and he passed me a wrap of coke.

I still had my bit of coke left but with my nose bleeding how the hell was I meant to snort coke then I felt my nose and only right side was bleeding so I sat on the lid of the toilet taking out all the remaining coke that I had, ranking it up in a massive line.

It must have been at least half a gram in one line then I added half of what I had been given as though he told me I could have his wrap I wasn't going to take it but I still rack up a line which must have been over a gram of coke by now.

Blowing my noses clear, one full of blood that trigged down the back of my throat, I then took a big sniff and inhaled through the right side of my nose, the whole line of coke flying up really quick.

I stood up needing to hold onto the back of the toilet door as the coke hit my brain instantly.

I felt the rush of blood through the veins of my heart and I could even hear the rapid beat of my heart.

There and then as I thought earlier before I had left to go the toilet to clear the blood from my face and my bleeding nose, that I was going to go back in there and fucking kill the bastard who had whack me.

I lifted up the toilet seat and on the bowl of the toilet I smashed the head of the bottle of beer so it left a horror looking jagged edge, this was now my choice of weapon and as from the previous fight I had in Happy Valley on the farm at the all night party where I tried to stab the other guy but his leather jacket stopped him getting the knife fully thrushed into him, I wasn't this night going to make the same mistake.

This guy I wanted to cause as much harm as possible to and even it meant killing him as I had gone past the red mist stage and also I knew he had a knife that he had earlier been willing to use so I wouldn't put it pass him using that again on me and killing me so I had to get him first, more so take him out of play as in finish him off good and proper.

I was passed the normal rage that would come over my body in these situations. I was going to make sure that I wasn't going to lose the third fight against this bastard. I was going to do what I thought at the time was right as never again would he ever lay his dirty hands on a girl again or try to rape a girl.

I was going to finish the fucker off, and with so much coke now racing through my body and with the lsd acids trips, all the booze I had drunken then I was now unstoppable.

I undone the lock of the bathroom door and went into the bar area, my eyes were targeted onto him as I saw him in the same space by the area of the bar where he had been drinking earlier.

The nightclub was packed so I had to move my way through everyone and not trying to let anyone notice what was in my hand, even none of my friends including Scotty (the Satan's Slaves motorcycle ex senior member) as if he had known what was about to happen he would have stopped me in my path, to make sure what was about to do didn't unfold.

Who did see me was Craig the president of the Rebels Car Club, I think he knew I was going in for the kill as he could see madness in my eyes as I stepped up to the prick who I wanted to get and I tapped him on his shoulder.

It all seemed to happen in slow motion even the music seemed to have slowed down; I guess this was due to the acid I had taken as the singer on stage was singing a slow Rolling Stones song.

Then next minute came on the song from the Sex Pistols (Sex Pistols is a British punk band) though this was only a New Zealand covers band playing their song, the band very much sounded like the Sex Pistols when they were singing the classic song "Anarchy in the U.K".

The music seemed to fade out as now I could only hear my own breathing that was very raised and then as the prick turned around to see who had tapped him on his shoulder, one of his friends (the guy who had in Lower Hutt put the bar stool over my back) looked around at the same time.

Least I knew where he was as he wasn't getting of lightly either in my mind as he himself was very much on my list to get what had coming to him as well.

"Time to fucking rock n roll you fuckers!" was my last and only words to them both as the bastard turned around, he was near face on to me when I pulled my hand back and then straight direct hit to his left eye and twisted the bottle, pulling it down his face and then that was it multiple stabbing him right between his eyes and right in his face, before he had time to lift his hands to his face.

I had blood pouring from him, his blood sprayed all over me and as I kept on stabbing him soon due to the bridge of his nose and the power of thrusting the broken bottle into his face ,the bottle ended breaking up into my hand.

I was using so much power to smash it time after time in his face.

In the end glass being pushed into my own hand that I felt, but it wasn't going to be as painful as what he was going through as he was screaming like a pig.

Now I became under attack by his friends though one was trying to help him, who I had just done good and proper. I then took to them with my fists, close range and threw what will be forever feel like my best punches I had ever thrown as I done a array of punches, landing them all.

It was like I was in robotic mode as I hit the second guy, constantly again after again, he was being hit with very serious punches that had him soon knocked out.

I was waiting for people to hit back but no one was doing that, everyone just kept away from me, which meant I could finish of the main bastard who now was on the floor in a pool of this time his own blood with his hands up to his face and a face that for sure didn't have no fucking smile beaming from it, and I couldn't hear him laughing now as the prick had just been done good and proper by a kid half his age and he nor his mates could do sweet fuck all about it.

He was on the floor but one of his mates got him to his feet, wrong fucking move as the prick belonged down on the floor like a dog so I done his mate a clear punch to his jaw.

I had now knocked out two of them and there in front of me not being able to see what was going on around him was the sick bastard so I came in with an upper punch that lifted him off the ground and his hands away from his face as he went crashing against the side of the bar.

The same bar where only 10 mins earlier he had been celebrating after beating me up while the fucker was going to stab me back then but now he was the one with holes in him as when I saw his face , I got to say it was a fucking mess like a horror film.

A very huge hole was where his face was once but now mashed up so I threw more punches right between his eyes, he couldn't take much more the bastard and I was tiring out so with one last punch that was it.

I don't think I knocked him out I believe he fainted as he dropped down this time not moving and for all to see.

The doormen behind rushing through the crowd, Glyn grabbed my arm and slung me around towards where he and Stonney were. I looked at Stonney; he was what seemed in shock as he was speechless for the very first time in all the time I had known him.

Craig then came to my aid, if it wasn't for Craig getting me out, away from everyone I am sure even though the doormen knew me I had a feeling when they saw the mess I had done, they might have just thrown me out the front of the club, but that's where I couldn't go as only across the road was the main police station and so I had to get out somewhere else and fast but my head was spinning.

I needed help and that's where Glyn and Craig helped me as Glyn took my hand and said "come on Christian you got to get the fuck out of here now!" as he kicked opened a fire exit and we run down the fire stairs, running through the back alleys and to Glyn's car.

Glyn told me to keep down and out of sight on the back seat so I laid down on the back seat as we drove through Wellington but he didn't want me to take me to his place so he asked me where I wanted to be dropped off to?

He asked could he drop me off at my Mum's old flat, my sisters place and I said "No fucking way, are you joking me, I can't go there!"

Where was I to go he asked, and said "Come on Glyn, to yours!" but he again said "No way, people would have seen me leaving with you and I don't need the police kicking in my door looking for you Christian and then finding you at my place, I really don't need the shit at this of time of my life!"

Where the hell was I going to go? I was bleeding from my hand and my nose had started to bleed again.

I very much needed stitches to my hand but knew not to go to the hospital. Once we were away from town driving through Newtown we started to have a row in the car.

Glyn finally agreed letting me go to his house at least to clean up my hand that was bleeding and work out somewhere for me to go there onwards.

We got to his place, he got a needle, a bottle of Irish whiskey and also what for the stitches was fishing line that he had.

He burnt the needle with my Zippo lighter and then he poured the Irish whiskey over my hand and actually done a good job stitching me up.

I think his mum used to be a nurses or he just had done this previously as he knew exactly what he was doing.

I said to him to get me again across town, I will go the Campbell's house as I know my friend Sasaka will hide me out there and at this time of night then his Mum who lived upstairs (who was a dear friend of my mum's) would be in bed so she wouldn't see me come to the downstairs front door.

Glyn didn't wish to take his car as first he wanted to clean out what blood was on his back seat from where I had been laying down on route to his place earlier from after the attack at the nightclub.

He ended up taking out his sister car from outside on his drive way and then placed his car further up the road, away from his own house.

As quick as he could, Glyn washed down the back seat of his own car and then dried it off with some towels and placed the towels in a bin bag that he took with us telling me as it was my blood then for I to keep the bloody towels to get rid off.

I told him there was no need to use a swear word, and with that he asked what was I on? What did I mean? So I said well no need to say bloody.

He didn't find my joke funny; I was just trying to lighten the mood.

He turned to me and said "You have just half killed a guy , if he isn't dead already and here you are now asking me not to use a fucking swear word........ What the fuck are you on Christian!"

We got to Sasaka flat heading up the winding hills by the international cricket ground Basin Reserve, going past the pub where my Mum's wake was held less than a year ago.

Glyn then said to me "Do you know what shit you going to be in now Christian?" You are fucked if you get caught for this one!"

"You will go to jail for that." And then he went on to say "What the fuck came over you, you were like a mad man." And worse of all he went said "I really don't even know if that guy was breathing when we left so I couldn't even say if you had killed him or not!"

That was something I didn't think about when I left though that was what was going through my mind before I had left the toilet to go out back into the club and do the bastard.

Glyn it seemed didn't wish anything to do with me, well at least he was a gooder enough of a friend to get me out of the club and to fix me up with my hand and drive me to safety so I couldn't say a bad word against him as he for sure showed his true colours that night as a decent proper friend.

We arrive up the road from Sasaka place, I knocked on the lounge window of Sasaka flat, and lucky he had just got home from a snooker club so he said "Yeah come in man."

He thought I had just come over to smoke some weed with him, he lived so close to the city, the city was only 10 minutes walk down the hill from his front door.

I waved off Glyn and went into the flat, without even asking Sasaka rolled up joint and then saw my hand and asked what was wrong with my hand? I told him I had got into a fight with the motorcycle club who had beaten me up a few weeks earlier out in Lower Hutt, but one of them had again beaten up in the newly opened nightclub in town so I ended up stabbing him.

I didn't go into detail but he asked how was the other guy and I just said I think I got him good but was worried that maybe I had over done it.

He asked why where had I stabbed him and so I told him a few times in the face.

Sasaka said "Well at least maybe that's not life threading."

I said "No Sasaka I mean I really done the guy!" and he replied "Well at least you didn't do him in the heart."

I explained to him that someone could be stabbed in the top part of the leg and through blood lose then they could die within 12 minutes so it doesn't matter where you get stabbed.

Sasaka reassured me that if I didn't get him in the throat then I should be ok and it will just been seen as some drunken fight in a nightclub and not to worry about.

I went on telling him what Glyn had told me that I could go to jail for this, but he laughter that off saying "Christian the guy you stabbed doesn't even know your name or who you and the police haven't caught you so sweet as man."

"Here is the joint, man have a smoke and chill out." and smoked I did but chilled out I didn't though I got the munchies so I made myself some pasta and then crashed out in his spare room asking Sasaka before I crashed out if I could stay at his house over the rest of the weekend, and he said of course I could, I could stay at long as I wished.

On Monday I had to get to my Mum's flat to be with my sister as this day was a year when she died so we went to the local church where her service was held then we went and saw my Nana, my Mum's Mum and we spend some time there with my Nana.

My Nana also asking what was wrong with my hand so I said I had caught it on a piece of wire and that is was fine not to worry

My sister knew I had been in fight but didn't know the details of it.

We sat with my Nana telling her about our trip across the world in June(the following month) that we were going to be taken and how we would be seeing our Father for the very first time in many, many years and she was just really happy that we would be seeing our Father.

I tried my best to keep on moving the subject away from my Mums death, I didn't want my Nana to be upset nor did I wish for my Sister to get upset either.

I then went back to my sisters flat and her boyfriend Ian came over so I decided to leave and I went to the Satan's Slaves Motorcycle Club clubhouse.

On arriving there they were joyful as I had done three of the bikers from a certain motorcycle club that the Satan's Slaves and other 1% MC Clubs didn't get on with so they were fairy happy to say the least.

They told me what Scotty had said though they said Scotty was pissed off with me as the police arrived soon after I had gone and that everyone in the nightclub were held inside the nightclub and taken details and that it was a crime scene so no one was allowed to leave straight away after the police turned up.

Scotty said three of the guys were taken to hospital, well at least I had done the fuckers and it was me who now was being tapped on the back.

But by Tuesday morning I was woken up and shown a newspaper and it said that the police were on the hunt (my description was given) and it spoke about the vicious attack that had taken place in a central Wellington nightclub.

Then another news report on a local radio reported it as possible gang warfare after reporting that three of the men injured were members of a notorious bike gang as they used the word gang instead of motorcycle club.

Then they put out a call for any information of who could have done this and any information would be welcomed.

The last report I heard was that the guy who I stabbed up had been in intensive care and that they had to save one of his eye, and he had emergency surgery on his face which due to the attack had ripped out his tear duct which means for ever more he would look like he would be crying constantly as he had no tear duct (which collects the water kept below your eyes to keep them moist) so he would have to always use eye drops plus he was going to be left with a mighty scar and a few at that, over his face.

Maybe I hadn't taken his sight though I couldn't think how they saved his damaged left eye as when I had finished with him, I was for sure he would lose his sight in both of his eyes but maybe that was a good thing in the long run.

At least he was now a ever more uglier basted before and I am sure wouldn't have any more bottle left as in he wouldn't ever start a fight again and more so at least he looked like forever more that he was full of tears but most importantly at least his crime against the girl had caught up with him and that karma had caught up with him as that was what was behind the attack more than just me being beaten by him in the previous two fights.

You know what and yes it may sound nasty and cold hearted, two things that I am not and I wasn't at the time, but he caused many tears to the girl who he had sexual assaulted so what I done to him was nothing compared what he done to my friends younger sister, so now with a tear forever running down his face at least now every time he looks himself in the mirror he sure anit going to forget me and the time he took the biggest kicking off his life.

I can hand on heart say that if this fight had happened only two years earlier to the time it did happen it would never have never turned out to be such a vicious fight and I wouldn't have gone to the extreme I had as all I can say I was so high on drugs that anyone who knows the bad effects of drug use / drug excess will say that you never think straight when taking such drugs and also through all the pain and grief I was carrying from my mum's death then it was, as if I was a time bomb ready to go off, and unlucky for him he was the one who got it when I went off .

He could have avoided it by leaving the nightclub when he was asked by Stonney rather than gloating as he did about giving me a kicking, as if he had left with his mates then that would have been the difference between how he ended up in his own pool of blood on the floor to easy leaving the club with his sight and face intact if only he had left earlier but the smart ass didn't so he ended up getting what happened to him.

More to this when thinking over that very night, I do believe it was karma, and he got his karma back for what he had done to my friend's sister.

Don't think I wasn't expecting bad karma back on me for my own actions as trust me I did believe that something was going to be waiting for me around the corner to dish me up my own slice... let's say of karma.

Well I wasn't wrong to be thinking that and on this Tuesday morning I left the clubhouse and went and saw Stonney to get more details of what had happened after I left the nightclub that evening after I tried my best to killing this scum bag who I had attacked anyway Stonney backed up everything that I had already heard including telling me Scotty was upset with me.

I asked him to drive me over to Scotty's place so I could say sorry and speak to Scotty who just said as I never told them what I was going to carry out after I came out of the bathroom at the nightclub when I should have pre warned them as I didn't know if say Scotty or any of them were carrying anything on them that night, which could have got them arrested and send to prison so I was in the wrong for not telling anyone what I had planned to do.

More so, how didn't I know that these scum bags who I had attacked weren't carrying a gun which would have cost me my own life, as all I knew was that bastard was carrying a knife but I didn't give it any thought what maybe one of his friends could have been carrying.

Scotty was ok with me though he had a tough talk with me saying I had come so far in the eyes of the Satan's Slaves club and he nor the Satan's Slaves club wished to see me come in harm in any way or to throw my life away or worse to lose my life so young.

He like, the club he went onto say remembered me as young kid entering the Satan's slaves clubhouse for the very first time when I was around 8 years of age, playing pool down there without a worry or care in the world and here now only 10 years later I now had my own motorbike and out of the good will of the club they were working on it for me so it would be up and running very shortly.

Scotty also went onto remind me that for the first time in the club history, they had let a non member live there at the clubhouse.

Scotty went onto say how I was being looked after and also noted for the future of mine with the club as long as I didn't get myself in the shit, but after what I have just gone and done, whatever craziness that had come over me then that had damaged me more than the useless prick who I had attacked.

He said that there was other ways, other times and places I could have got the bastard back as he said every dog has his day and I would have in the end caught up with him, but at least that could have been planned and also in private so I could have still got him.

While Scotty was taking to me, Stonney was just agreeing with everything Scotty was saying, like I had let the club down but I didn't see it as such though I knew what Scotty was saying to me but just then he pulled a couple of beers out of his fridge saying "You're a good kid so don't worry too much, you just now got to get your head down as there's a police hunt on though at this stage, at least you are not in the frame for it."

When just then his phone rang and he answered and it's what Scotty told me next, is when everything he had said about me letting the club down in a way, as he got off the phone and said to me "The clubhouse has just been visited by police and they were looking for one person and that person is you Christian and the club is pissed off as they open the gate to the police who had a warrant to search their clubhouse to look for you to see if you were was on the premises as they had been told you was living there."

Someone had fucking grassed me up as there was no camera in the nightclubs back then, it's not like nightclubs today with loads of security cameras.

I couldn't believe it, I had been grassed up, and my name had been given to the police.

I left with Stonney who dropped me off to Sasaka's flat.

I sure didn't tell Sasaka about the police knocking on the Satan's Slaves' clubhouse looking for me as I needed to use his flat as a hide out for the time being.

I thought that the police visiting the clubhouse was a bit over the top as I had only stabbed someone in a fight, it's not like I had killed anyone. There wasn't a dead body so what the fuck was all this about.

Soon my sister got a visit from the police at 6am in the morning to my Mum's place and then at 6am in the morning across town the police also visited Stonneys house, looking there for me as well.

The first thing I did is give Chris Mitchell my car to look after as I wouldn't be using that for a while, he held onto it for a few days before a prospect of the Satan's Slaves came and picked it up from him. I should have just given the car as a present to Chris as he was a good mate and he knew how to drive that motor better than me.

Reason why I sold the car as now I need some cash on me and fast and also I couldn't risk getting caught driving around in the car as that would mean even more charges.

I wasn't even sure what I was going to be charged with over the nightclub attack though there was a rumour, that it was an attempted murder charge.

There I was everyone who was close to me in the circle of the bike club was getting visits' by Wellington C.I.B.

I was being hunted down and the money I had from the quick sale of the car wasn't going to last long.

I was a month way from flying out of the country with my sister, if I dared to go to the airport to catch that flight, of course I would have been grabbed so what the fuck was I going to tell her.

I met away from the clubhouse the president (at the time) of the Satan's Slaves Scuff with Zombie and they gave me some solid advice. Talk to the clubs lawyer Simon who represented for many years all the members of the Satan's Slaves.

Scuff said I would be safe in Simon's hands and to trust him. With that, then they got on their bikes telling me don't risk coming to the clubhouse in case the police have a surveillance team on the clubhouse which wasn't unusual for the Satan's Slaves clubhouse.

The Satan's Slaves were one of the National New Zealand police force main targets in their fight against crime though hey at the end of the day I never saw the Satan's Slaves involved in any type of crime.

They were just bunch of good guys who like riding their bikes and that's all, so could never work out why the police would try and raid their clubhouse and other times always hassle their members as they weren't a gang, they simply were a bike club and there's nothing wrong with that....a bunch of mates riding motorcycles together.

I said to Scuff, I would contact the lawyer Simon asap. They were off on their Harley-Davidsons, leaving me with Simon's business card in my hand so I went to a public phone box and spoke to him.

My future and life was now in other persons hands not even my own but one man and that was my now appointed lawyer who I trusted 110% and who could turn all this round for me and pull it off for me, how I wasn't sure but I knew Simon would do his magic somehow.

I travelled in the back of a taxi after speaking to Simon, heading to his Wellington city office.

Fate which I have huge belief in and faith now had a huge part to play, and also luck I guessed, a hell of a lot of it.

Was I going to come out of as Be Lucky Christian or was the stake of cards come crashing down on me..........it wasn't even 50/50, not even a roll of dice could foreseen how things were going to turn out and if all was going to be good or if as others had said, I would end up behind bars in one of New Zealand's jails.

Who knows as at that point of time, I sure didn't know how things were going to play out for me.

Chapter 38

FUCKED...........FACT

I arrived at Simon's office. I had known Simon over the past years though I never had him representing me as he had more people to look after who were always ever more in the shit than I was....that was up to now anyway.

He asked me to go through everything with him that I did from outlining the very first time I had seen the guy as in the attack on me in Lower Hutt. I never told him about the sexual assault on my pal's younger sister but I did outline that the guy (whoever he was) was a wronging and scum.

I explained about the Friday evening, what happened at the night club how he had beat me in the first of the two fights and that he had actually attempted to stab me as well.

I explained in detail every moment I can remember leading up to stabbing the guy.

Simon also noted the injuries on my right hand.

Then Simon got to town, and he shined in his skills as a lawyer and a fucking good one at that.

We then worked on that my injury was to have been caused by the guy actually stabbing me in the first fight of the night. Saying that suited me fine.

Next the second fight was due to me defending myself after coming back from the toilet, only using the toilet to wash the earlier blood of my face (as of course there would be no mention of taking coke while in there).

Simon said he would let the court know I was very high on drugs at the time and also that I was drinking the very strongest beer mixed with straight Jack Daniels.

He added he would have no mention ever about taking a beer bottle in to the toilet and breaking it down as to shape it in to weapon as then this would be the difference between attempted murder (as that would be a premeditated attack to defending myself in a fight) and he hoped GBH.

Though the other guy took such injuries, at least it would be in self defence on my part.

Simon knew I had x amount of money in a trust account so this was to be mention as in offering the guy money in compensation for his injuries to help with his state of living in the future.

Simon said playing this card would work very much in my favour, and the judge would like that.

I was told to be ever so polite and also to look good natural and sorry during the court case even if I didn't want to be but to make sure I was and to try and grow my hair plus to at least get a suit for the court appearances.

Next my Uncle was called and informed what had taken place and that the police wanted to question me over the attack.

My Uncle said to Simon he would be down tomorrow.

I didn't get to speak to my Uncle as next call was going to be a hard call to make and that was to my sister.

Instead of Simon making the call, I did.

Explaining everything to my sister, she was so upset.

It was actually upsetting listening to my sister being this upset. I tried to tell her that everything could be ok and not yet to panic but what I was thinking about very much, was our planned trip across the world to see our Father.

I really tried to stop thinking about that at the time and I just didn't want to shatter all hope, either of ours.

Next phone call was made by Simon to the Wellington C.I.B to say that his client would come down the following morning but for now he asked them to trust in that, and they were happy with it so no more searching for me would take place, this meant I could then after I had finished with Simon go to my sisters that evening and speak things through with her.

So that night while Simon worked on my case to hold up a good, actually a great defence, I went to my Mum's flat and stayed up with my sister going through everything with her but saying that Simon advised me that more than likely my passport would be asked from me.

If so then I wouldn't be able to travel, that's depending even if I get granted bail as I may end up on remand awaiting the trial.

I woke the next morning after not much sleep, and meet my uncle at my Mum's flat and left with him, kissing my sister goodbye. One thing I had spoken to my sister about was that if I didn't get to travel on the trip then

Simon did say if my passport wasn't asked from me and if I was given bail then I could go overseas but that would mean skipping the country.

If I ever need to return to NZ, I would be returning to be arrested and I would be given a much bigger sentenced as I would have skipped the country on bail so Simon said if I were to do that then he felt it was best that I didn't return after arriving in the UK.

For me that wasn't a option as what happens if something say happened to my sister or a loved one while I was overseas and if I return I would be sent straight to jail on remanded.

Even though I thought of doing a runner, it wasn't worthwhile over all to do a runner.

I really for the very first time in life grew up and grew up fast as what was facing me wasn't child play, I truly was in the shit...let's say up shit creek without a paddle.

My uncle had to now make sure that some funds were ready to cover all the legal costs out of my trust fund. It was going to be expensive but when Simon found out that I actually wasn't working and in all truth I couldn't really have access to my trust fund account till I was 20 years old which was 2 years away, well then he said he would go for legal aid and he believed I would get that legal right.

I drove to the police station with my uncle and my lawyer Simon, on arriving to be arrested facing questions of attempted murder.

I was question in the presence of my lawyer answering no question to each question asked of me then I was told I to be held overnight, so I was lead to a police cell for the night.

My uncle stayed over at a local hotel but he did visit my sister that evening to let her know what was going on.

I feel bad now all these years later for putting my family through all of this - my uncle, my auntie, my sister and also my Nana and my Father after who felt so helpless on the other side of the world.

My father always liked my uncle; he got on with all my uncles during his years in NZ.

While I was in the prison cell, the police came in and took photos of my face and also my hands plus what I and Simon found out not till the next day is when they had taken me down to the cells that had walked me past a two way mirror, and behind the screen was the bar man who had id me (though without the knowledge to my lawyer nor myself).

The bottle that was used in the attack had my fingers prints on it so they would use the broken pieces of that which was taken from the crime scene to use against me when the case would go to trial.

The following morning I was send to the court house in a van and I was charged firstly with the attempted murder, then my lawyer asked of the judge to look through his notes again that he had written up, and the judge looked up and asked what would I be giving as my plead so on advice from Simon who said to me now with witnesses and finger prints then a jury more than likely would find me guilty even if he done his magic so it was best to pled guilty as the judge would take that in a account.

It then was up to the police prosecution changing the charge and also the Judge giving me a low prison sentence or if not a prison sentence at all due to my age and other matters that Simon my lawyer could pull up during further court appearances.

He had offered the police a deal if I were to plead guilty then the police prosecution services would be happy for the change to be dropped to "with intention to use GBH", so I pledged guilty to GBH.

Simon now tried to get the whole case thrown out of court so for me even then that morning I thought I was going to be freed, as Simon said the fact the police came in my cell to take pictures of me that were shown to some witness they had at the police station when I had came in the day before, and also as I wasn't put on a official id parade (slyly was walked past a two-way mirror) without my knowledge nor my lawyers knowledge then this was against the law.

The police came back saying the pictures in the cell were taken as on a previous arrest in my past I had made a complaint against the police for police brutally while in police custody, being beaten up and so the reason of the photos were to show that this time nothing had taken place as I had suggested once before on a previous arrest (beaten up by a police officer in a police cell).

Simon tried his best but the judge wouldn't buck, and now it was for Simon to get me bail which after a lot of debate he managed to do though on the terms my passport was to be given up and also I can't remember how much bail money I was on but I am sure it was either $20,000 or $50,000(my uncle arranged that) and also I would be taken into my uncles care to live at his house away from Wellington.

There were more bail conations' such as each day I would have to attend a police station to sign in and then also the judge put an 8pm to 8am curfew on me as well.

These are what the police requested. I thought it was a bit steep that I wasn't even allowed to live in my own town, hell I was only a teenager and not some criminal.

But due to the serve of the injuries on the other guy and two of his friends then Simon said that it was going to be a hit and miss if was to be placed on remand or get bail so he was happy that I at least got bail, I was as well apart from the fact about the curfew and also having to live over the mountains in Greytown at my uncles and aunties place.

I drove with my uncle after thanking my lawyer for all he pulled off in a short space of time.

Simon said he still had so much more to do but at least we got the first victory.

I felt safe in his hands; Simon very much knew what he was doing.

I went to see my sister again. She was so happy that I wasn't banged up.

I then told her that she was still to go on our holiday and that I would be giving my own ticket away as I would very much like to change it in to Kieran's name for everything Kieran went through (round the time of our break up) and what went on after my Mum's death and how supportive she had been though at the time I was far too high on drugs to notice.

Instead pushing Kiren away further when all she was trying to do is be there for me through such a tough time that I was going through.

My uncle was still there when I called Kiren and told her about letting her have my around the world ticket and everything else that would come with that trip, in saying sorry to her but more so that it meant my sister wouldn't be travelling alone and that my sister still would go on this trip, that my sister had been looking forward to for so long after everything she had been through.

Kiren didn't believe me so I told her to speak to my sister then I left saying my goodbyes again to my sister before my sister called back Kiren in letting her know what I had said to her in the previous conversations was true.

My uncle and I jumped into his car for the long journey out of Wellington.

My sister did say first said no lets cancel it altogether but that was unfair on my sister as she was going on the trip to see our Father, and actually after everything my sister had been through, she really needed this holiday after losing Tim and also my Mum so I cuddle her again before I and my uncle finally drove off.

I went to the Satan's Slaves headquarters with my uncle and collecting my belongings before leaving Wellington.

My uncle wouldn't let me stay for a drink so I said a quick goodbye to all the members feeling a fool I couldn't even have one drink with them.

My uncle was treating me like a kid which I didn't like, anyway the members that were there at the time at the clubhouse (the senior ones) said that if I was sent up to the hill (the name given for the notorious jail that sat up on the hill top looking over the Wellington harbour Mt Crawford) then all the Satan's Slaves members who were in that jail would look after me, making sure no harm would come my way.

They all told me that they were proud of me for sticking up for myself though they joked they thought I was a nuttier but they all knew what I had been going through those last few years and now everything had come on top of me.

Soon though more than likely my own freedom was to be taken away from me.

I left for now with Wellington soon behind me as we headed out of Wellington through Lower Hutt, Upper Hutt, onto the mountains and through the mountain to the other side past my families huge sawmill, Davis Sawmill (that stood in the sleepy township of Featherstone).

On the other side of the beautiful mountains we headed towards Greytown, to my uncles house which would be my home from now on.

A Month went by and soon I settled in at my new surroundings, going everyday to sign on to the police station.

That was really the only thing that went on in my days as my uncle didn't ever let me leave his place which at times it did feel like I was already serving time.

It wasn't his fault, he was just very strict. My uncle had an outhouse so I would sleep in that at night and just help around the place in the day. I did get bored but one thing after about a month I didn't get bored of not having drugs and though the first few weeks of course was hard as I had been used to such a fast life and more so the last few years, getting completely of my face so often.

What I was missing the most was girls.

My uncle and my auntie agreed a girl who I knew from Wellington could come up and visit me, she was a stunner, and her name was Claire.

Claire worked on the share market in Wellington; she was around 23years old and hot. I don't know how I pulled her as she very much was out of my league.

My uncle said it was fine for her to come and visit me and stay over the night which was grand so the following weekend Claire actually came up and stayed over which was like being in heaven.

Two weekends in a row she came but with not much happening in this sleepy little farming town, I knew she herself would soon get bored as well so the next weekend she did come up, we went out to a pub for few drinks.

The time went 8pm (curfew time for me) but we were having such a good time, having a few drinks and also it was Saturday night. I hadn't been out in all the time that I had been in Greytown nor had I even had as much as one drink so though I was meant to be back at my uncles by 8pm as I was under curfew, I just thought fuck it as in all fact I wasn't doing anything wrong or anyone harm.

I was only in a country pub; full of New Zealand farmers and few good hearted Maoris so I stayed on the piss.

It was the very first time I got drunk since being away from Wellington. My uncle and auntie (even though I was 18 years of old) thought I was still too young to be drinking at that age as the legal limit was I think 20 years of or 21 years old, but I had been drinking since I was 10 years old though not heavily when I was young but more so when I reached my early teens.

After having a great time and a few drinks at this country homestead pub, I came back from the pub with Claire in her sports car.

On arriving back my uncle had stayed awake till we returned, saying that by the morning time Claire was to go and she was not allowed to come back.

Claire and I went to the outhouse and laughter our heads off as we truly could believe that my uncle was being so strict as the time was only around 10pm so it's not like I had been out all night and I was 18 years old, not some 12 year kid.

In the morning after my auntie put out breakfast for everyone. Claire and I didn't go into the main house to eat as we were still having sex and also we both were hung over as hell, well it didn't take my uncle long to be knocking on the door and one thing he did was keep to his word as when I jumped out of bed unlocking the door for him, he said after Claire had showered that she was to leave.

He said we had taken the piss the night before from firstly going to a pub and secondly staying out till 10pm.

I felt like a young child being told off and I was so embarrassed. I just thought my uncle was a complete prick, but looking back now he was only trying to keep me out of trouble as if I had been spotted by the local police drinking in the pub then I would have been arrested there and then for breach of my bail conditions.

That would mean I would have been put straight away on remand so he actually was trying to protect me from getting myself into anymore trouble while I was on bail (awaiting my next court appearance).

In any small town in NZ, there was only two coppers, sometimes only even one and in Greytown the two local police officers knew me as every day I had to sign in at their police station so if any of them had spotted me drinking that night in the homestead pub then that's underage drinking so they could arrest me just for that.

My uncle was concerned also if I had got into a fight while I was in the pub and if the fight had turned nasty then either I would have been hurt or I would have ended up being re arrested for again for GBH or even something worse. That for sure, wouldn't have looked good.

The next time I saw Claire was when she came to one of my court appearance while she witnessed the (so-called) victim lash out in court saying my defence was a pack of lies and that myself and my lawyer were liars.

He protested that he had never stabbed me and that he had not attacked me again and I was not using self defence in any way but I had just attacked him viciously.

It was the first time I had see him since the night I had got him, but he was about to get a shook as that's when my lawyer on my behalf offered the sum of $16,500 to the victim and the judge on cue thought this was very good and was happy that though there were some unanswered questions.

The judge felt I had told the truth (all the truth) and that in heat of the moment when the attack happened that the victim couldn't remember the events as clearly as I could as he the victim had suffered shock which could have brought on memory loss.

I found out that the wanker had a record of previous offensives as far as his arm could reach which meant he wasn't such a nice guy (that I already knew).

He was a well known criminal in the court systems so really he didn't have a leg to stand on as he kept on wiping the tears from his face.

He wasn't crying! He just was without a tear duct, the prick!

He still was being abusive towards me in court which wasn't doing him in any favours and by now I had grown my hair and was very well dressed. My uncle had (out of my trust money) brought me a suit so I looked the business when the guy just looked like a scruffy Muppet.

The judge deicide that I would through a scheme (victims support group) would have me come face to face with the victim as in a sit down a private room with him. Of course with a court security officer present and also a councillor and a court person to do with the case would be there.

Though it wouldn't be happening this day as the twat had turned psycho as in the way he was yelling abuse at me from across the court. The judge said it to be taken place another time.

It was in my favour the way the fool was acting, swearing at me even after putting up $16,500 of my own money (actually my mum's own money) in compo for him, something that I didn't like doing but if it meant a lesser sentence, then so be it but in all truth I wished I didn't have to pay the prick fuck all and that he would just roll over and die...the dirty bastard.

On arriving back at my uncle's house with him, I sensed a lot of tension at my uncle's place.

I wasn't happy that he still wouldn't let me have Claire up to see me so I felt like more a less a prisoner as I wasn't allowed to do anything. I didn't even have a penny in my pocket to do anything as that was their way of stopping me going to the pub again.

I got to give my uncle and auntie credit where it as due as in I not being able to go to the pub, only done me the world of good in the long run.

My uncle one day got a call from my other lawyer Juliet Cooke who had said she had received certain signed legal written contracts saying that I had borrowed money against my trust fund money.

My uncle hit the fucking roof!

He went proper mad over hearing this news, I told him how did he think I had been able to pay for the holiday for my sister, that Kiren and my sister were now on.

He said I was sly to do that so I told him to fuck off and get out of my face as it was my money and not his so I could do whatever I wanted to do with it.

I went on to say to him if he only allowed me to have some of my money when I had asked many months ago then I wouldn't have had to go to this length and get these contracts signed up.

He just got so angry and didn't or couldn't calm down so my auntie told me to go into the outhouse as my uncle was under far too much stress.

She suggested they go on a short break away, how fucking cool as then that would mean I would have the whole house to myself but how very wrong was I to be.

They got my cousin from Hawke's Bay to come down to look over their house and more so me while they were away and as he was a builder, they gave me the task to help him paint their hall way and do some work on their lovely house. He was getting a wage from them to do this work for them.

On the very first morning after my uncle and auntie had left for their short break away, my cousin started work on their house. He tried to make me get out of bed to give him a hand so I said yeah that's fine. The first day we worked till late, I helped him out with everything he asked of me.

After we had finished, he said he was off to the pub for a few beers. I got showered quickly and changed into new clothes though when I came out of the outhouse, he was getting in his car.

He said to me "Where do you think you're going?"

I said "Well of course with you to the pub." but he replied "No you anit mate." and then told me that I were to stay at home.

I was a little pissed off so I said well at least give me my days wage so I can at least get something from the local shops and maybe rent out a video movie.

He looked at me with a dazed look saying "What wage?" then telling me that he was the only one being paid, not me so I was to get nothing for all I had done.

With that he drove off to the pub.

I was fucking fuming to say the least, as I always liked Neil (my cousin) but for him to now treat me like this, was just bang out of order! He had been given orders by my uncle so he was sticking to them, but there was no need to be harsh towards me.

Well now I thought fuck him as well so I locked myself in the outhouse for the night.

The following morning he came banging on the door, telling me to get up as we had work today.

"We have work to do!" I shouted out behind the still closed door

"Fuck right off mate!"

"Do it yourself, you wanker!" was my reply through the locked door.

I didn't even unlock the door to speak to him so I stayed in bed all day, every now and then he would be knocking on the door but I just wouldn't even reply.

After he had finished his days work that evening and before he was off to the pub, he then force his way in to the outhouse.

I asked him what the fuck was his game?

He then threaten me. Wrong move as I went for him, which in turn made him lock himself inside my uncles house. Neil was many years older than me and stronger as in strength but he wouldn't have come best off in a punch up with me, that's for sure.

Though how sad it would have been if we had come to blows as we were cousins, we were family and more importantly we were blood family.

Once he locked himself in the house, he told me he was going to call the police. I told him do that and I will make a call to the Satan's Slaves Motorcycle Club.

I yelled out (warning him) "Give them two hours and you will have 30 motorcycles roaring up this road and they will smash their way in and do you good and proper for being a dirty grass, so best thing is you don't call the police."

I couldn't even believe his suggestion of wanting to call the police on me as I hadn't done anything over the top, and he was safe as sound as he was locked in my uncle's house. I was the one standing outside in the rain.

I ended up going back into the outhouse and stayed there for the remaining days while my cousin finished work on the house. We didn't see one another in the remaining time he was there. We didn't even speak to one another and we haven't ever again in all these years now over 16 years on.

My next court appearance I had to go through with the meeting, the one with the victim. I didn't like the term he had been given as in victim as I only saw him as asshole and you got to remember he did in all fact try and use his knife against me until Andy managed to grab him. He had again turned with more heavy people and now I was getting death threats.

What cowards!!!!

Anyway the fool then played the joker card on himself as in front the court official worker after I read out a letter to him saying how very sorry I was for glassing him (in self defensive I may add) and that I forgave him for stabbing me in the hand (giving him a wink as I read out that last piece) which no one saw apart from him with his fucked sight.

This made him go for me. This asshole, whose face was like a railway track due to all the stables and stitches they had to put in his face to hold it together after I done him at the nightclub.

Anyway he attacked me in the private court room. This was him showing his true colours, I let him hit me a few times to now look like I was the victim in front of the security guard and also the court official and the councillor.

They all had to pull him off me while he was stating that my life wasn't worth while living and that his side kicks would do me.

I am sorry but when he threaten me with my life and as no one was holding me back as I hadn't done anything well I just wanted to break his jaw and just before I was about to land one on him, that's when he played the joker card as he came out with a classic.

Which was, he said to me if I was to hand him the sum of $30,000 he would go back on his statement he had given the police against me and say that actually it wasn't me who had stabbed him. The loser had said all of this in front of everyone, what a fucking dickhead to say the least.

The police already had the broken bottle pieces with my finger prints on it, the barman had also given a statement and the victim had himself already pointed me out in court at one of the court appearances in front of everyone (pointing his finger at me) saying "Yes that's him!" ......he grassing me, the scum bag and now he he we asking for a payoff of $50,000.

Well when we walked back into the main courtroom, the report given to the judge by the social worker and the court official (both mention what he had firstly done as in attack me earlier but more so both mentioned what he had said to me in front of them).

It was pure blackmail on his behalf plus trying to lie under oath.

My lawyer tried to get the whole case thrown out due to this as the so-victim just admitted that he was willing to say that he wasn't now to sure it was me who had attacked him in the nightclub (that's if I were to sign over $50,000 to him).

The fucking idol thought I could just write him out a cheque there and then for $50,000.

The judge said as I had already pleaded guilty to the charge, he wasn't throwing the case out of court but as he saw from reading the reports what went on as in a form of blackmail and lowering the court, the judge then took back my original offer at the last court appearance of $16,500 and said he believed due to what he had just read in both reports that now he was only willing that I to hand the guy the victim $4,500 ....fucking result as the wanker had just shot himself in the foot .

Happy fucking days!!!!

I left the court such a happy man and was over the moon with what had gone on as I knew all of the day events , for sure had just swung everything towards me for a better result when it came to me being sentenced.

My next court appearance, the final one which was for sentencing was coming up. My lawyer said I could be looking at maybe 4years though of course I would only do 2 years of that sentence if thing were good.

The max he said I could expect was for 7 years or 6 years but he said no way would I get that term handed down to me, he felt it would be 4 years I would get and do two years of the sentence.

I said what about a youth detention centre and he said on the day, of course he would be asking for this.

The very last week was stressful as my uncle and I just didn't get along.

I thought I wouldn't put him through anymore hassle or worry, so the night before I was due in court to be sentenced I thought come evening once my uncle and auntie went to bed then I would leave while they were sleeping.

As the row that night I had with my uncle (I can't remember what this row was about) I knew it had got to a higher level than our previous rows as I was sure he was about to strike me.

My uncle was a black belt in karate and actually he had three guns in his house so he was either (I guessed) going to try and smashed me or in rage shoot me, though the alter of course he wouldn't think of doing as he wasn't like that at all but as the row got worse and what we were saying to one another which in its own right was very cruel things to say.

I am sure the row was brought on by me feeling nervous about being banged up the following day so maybe I was taking it out on my uncle...all my worries etc.

Well after my uncle and auntie had gone to bed, I walked down to the High St and used a pay phone to call a friend in Wellington; he collected me around 2 and half hours later and drove me back to Wellington.

I wanted to go out for a drink as it was my very last night before I was going to jail but by the time we had reached Wellington, all the pubs were closed and so were many of the nightclubs so we ended driving over to Stonneys house as a surprise.

Stonney got in some girls and we had a party though when my mate pulled out some coke, for the first time in my life (after being away from all types of drugs) I Said no and I felt good in myself from saying no to doing any of the coke and also I felt very proud of myself as this was a huge leap I had made from my old lifestyle as in the past I would never have said no....as the saying goes Never say Never, well that night I said no and I meant it.

I just wanted to shag a girl as I wouldn't be doing that in prison and so when the girls arrived I managed to find myself in one of Stonneys spare rooms with one of the girls.

It's what I really needed.

I really didn't wish to get out of bed I wanted to keep on going like a rabbit rather than go back into the other part of the house where the party was going on as everyone else was talking so much shit from doing coke and as I wasn't high, they all seemed many miles away though the party still was a lot of fun.

Fun I did very much have the night before I was getting sentenced.

Morning of sentencing, I went to court that morning alone.

The night before Stonney did say he would take me in the morning, but when I awoke, I went into his room and he was fast asleep with a girl so I didn't wake him....I let him be.

I did look around in that courthouse when I was standing near my lawyer. I really thought that my uncle would have driven down to be there for me but he wasn't anywhere to be found so I guessed he hadn't forgiven me for the row, we had the previous night.

Right at the end of the sentencing, I did turn around one last time and Angie the Australian stripper was there, blowing me kisses and letting me know she wasn't wearing any knickers... classy lady ah but at least she out of everyone turn up so that was very sweet of her.

The twat was also there. He again had all his gang friends to yell at me that they would make sure I was going to get it in jail.

I turned to them and told them "Give it up as you a lot are standing with a fucking grass!"

I reminded them, that their stupid Muppet of a friend looked like he was crying and then finished saying to them "Oh I forgot.... I had done that to ya wanker friend!"

My lawyer wasn't impressed but as least it meant the victim's friend had been escorted out of the court due to their abusive outburst and that meant my lawyer could carry on doing his very best on my behalf.

Simon went onto explain due to my Mum's death a year ago that single terrible event brining down my down fall in the world of drugs and gambling debts (I don't know where he got this from as I wasn't a gambler but I think due to the contracts of tens of thousands that I had received then he used this as a excuse to where all the money had gone on).

He knew what he was doings so I didn't question him, he then went ahead and explained I had been attacked earlier running up to the fatal night and that this week while drinking heavy leading up to sadly my Mum's anniversary (now there was lot of truth on that though I didn't like my mum's death being brought into it) I was on many drugs to attempt in my own head to ease the pain, so on the night in question when the fight in the nightclub took place, I was not only very intoxicated but also very high on a illegal substances.

Simon then went on to explain how I had again been attacked by the victim and stabbed so I went in to the toilet to wash the blood from the wound in my hand and also of my face.

That then I came back into the area to tell my friends that I was going to leave the nightclub to go due to my hand being stabbed but before I had time to even exit the nightclub again I was attacked a second time and not just by the victim but also by four of his friends (other gang members) so in fearing for my life, I struck one of them on the head (Simon didn't use the sentence "in the face") with a beer bottle out of self defence as I was in fear of my life as I was under attack by grown males who were twice my age and how I was only a teenage.

My lawyer, if he was an actor would have won an Oscar for his performance for this speech. He went on to remind the judge that at the very first court appearance his client(me) pleaded guilty and that I had not caused (unlike the victim) any trouble in court.

Even while Simon was doing his closing speech, throughout the victim was yelling out "fucking liar!!" "You're a fucking liar!" and so he was asked to leave the court house to go and join his wanker mates.

He really never done himself no good, every time he was at court which done me the world of good, every time he had turned up and more so this final day.

I had looked calm and mature in court, when he and his mates had acted like a bunch of silly school kids in a school playground though they thought they were coming across as real tough guys.

It just made me happier as a young kid that I had done them all in the nightclub as that night, let me tell you none were tough in the sightless.

To be grassed up as well just wasn't right and it showed everyone what scum they were as no one ever heard of a Satan Slave ever grassing anyone up, as no one in the Satan's Slaves Motorcycle Club or connected to the Satan's Slaves Motorcycle Club would ever turn grass as we all were old school unlike this prick who had grassed me up from the start.

I left my lawyer to do all the talking as I just kept quiet all the way through. Simon went on to bring again in my age and that a youth dentition centre he felt was best for me.

He finished with reminding the judge finally how I even had offered a huge sum of money for the victim out of the kindness of my own heart and that I was struck after reading the victim a note saying how sorry I was, only then to be attempted blackmailed over a much larger sum of my Mothers money.

That was that, he had done me so proud.

Now it was the judges` turn that went through and agreed on all the points that my lawyer Simon had spoken about and brought up in his closing speech.

There was a" but" actually it turned out to be more than "one but" and they were as follows

One was due to my recent history of being arrested so often and most previous arrests were linked to assaults and violence (drunken or just common misbehave disorders) all which hadn't done me in favours.

But the big "but" was, that the victims injuries that he had received could easy had been life threading if he hadn't had medical attention as quick as he had.

That's what the judge believed and also due to the victim now having near to no vision in one eye and the operation of his tear duck and the facial scaring that he forever will have for the rest of his life then the judge felt that he would have to rule out a youth detention centre sentence for me.

He would be given me (with everything taken in to account) a 2 years jail sentence, on good behaviour I would be out in a year.

That was that, I was off to jail!

I turned and smiled a cheeky smile at Angie, and then I was handcuffed and lead down to the cells beneath the courthouse to wait for what happened next after being given a jail sentence.

I had never been in this situation in my life before (as in heading to prison) and here I was only just turned 18 years old and I was being sent to jail.

Fuck how life can be full of surprises and yeah maybe life is like a box of chocolates, if so then I had tasted all the bad ones in the box.

jail I didn't wish to be going but I just hope it was Mt Crawford that I would be heading to due to remembering the comments that Satan's Slaves members had said to me when I saw them all last down at the clubhouse soon after I had been arrested.

Simon came in to see me in the cell, telling me truly that was even a better result that he had expected and the outcry from the victim could only have worked in my favour.

It showed what a thug the victim was.

I don't even like using the word victim, I didn't see him as one and in all honest I still don't to this day.

We said goodbye to one another, and I thanked Simon for all he had done for me as he truly was a star, and in my case he was more a friend than a lawyer.

Simon over all was a dam good lawyer, if not the best and a dam good friend, a true friend who got me through this all from the moment I called him to the moment he came down to say goodbye while I waited transport out of the courthouse holding cells to serve my jail term that was now upon me.

I don't regret what I did........ I just regret getting caught for it!

The good thing that came out of it was that I had come off drugs and the hold that previously drugs had over me.

While sitting in the court house holding cell, I thought so much about life as I knew it.

There all alone (very alone) which would be seen as one of my darkest hours by others but to me there and then I just had to believe that in every negative, there is a positive so I used that belief system (I didn't want to get down about the situation I was in) and it worked as at least I hadn't killed him so it meant I wasn't sitting in a cell after being sentenced for murder so that was one of my positives I took out of it....he was a lucky man in that sense.

My second positive was that through all of this I was now off drugs, the use of coke was now all a thing of my past and more so that drugs hadn't taken my own life....I was a lucky man in that sense.

I soon was lead out by two prison guards and taken into awaiting prison van with other inmates, some looked slightly hard as nails but you know what I was used to staunch people from the my early years hanging round with the street kinds, to meeting the president of the Black Power gang and members of that gang, to being a part of the Satan's Slave MC Club, to have step brother in the Mongrel Mob.

Yeah I could say I was used to tough people and then there were my two new friends over in England, The Kray Twins well you couldn't get tougher than them two so I didn't care how mean or staunch some of these guys looked, who were travelling with me in the prison van.

My mind that now was so clear that it had ever been before (very much so in these last 12months while I had been out on bail) had to think of my next 12 months that lay ahead of me.

I wonder how Ron and Reg felt when they were in their prison van back in the late 1960s looking at 30 years recommendation.

I couldn't imagine what must have been going through their minds though many years later Freddie Foreman told me that he himself who had been handed a ten year stretch along with Charlie Kray and other members of the firm (who had got steep sentences and of course as well including the twins) were all actually very upbeat and many were singing songs as they were driven through the streets of London after being sentenced.

So many things were going through my mind as the prison van that I was in headed now through Wellington and up the long winding steep road of the hill.

Knowing I wasn't now too far from the jail, feeling quite glad I recall as at least I was heading to Mt Crawford jail.

Soon the prison van reached the jail gates and in we went.

I had arrived, only the age 18 years old the very youngest inmate of Mt Crayford prison history and at the time the youngest ever inmate being held in a high max security jail throughout New Zealand.

What I truly could say this was another chapter for sure of my life.

I just wonder how this chapter of my life was going to unfold and would unfolded in front of me as a year is still year and that to a 18 year kid, well actually too many people even on the outside is a long time so a wonder how long it's going to feel for me being banged up in jail.

Well let's find out, turn that page to read on as I promise you won't find any boredom in the next few many pages, and that's for sure!

Come on in with me and I will show you around Mt Crawford jail, and introduce you to some right characters.

let's just hope reader that its only a year I do on good behaviour unlike the British famous prisoner who went to do 7 and is still in the British prison system now after 32 years Charlie Bronson(hello my friend hope you well and as I enjoyed your many books, I hope you enjoying mine)

God Bless you Charlie from Your Friend Be Lucky Christian

Chapter 39

BANGED UP

MT CRAWFORD JAIL (New Zealand's oldest prison 1927)

I went in with all the other newly arrived prisoners into cell, where there were 5 of us in each cell while we waited to be told where we were going next.

Three of the guys in my cell had been in here before, they all asked what had I done be here as I seemed too young.

I thought them I had been sentenced over a pub fight. One of them commented that it must have been more than a fight, but I didn't want to saying anymore than that.

I didn't want to them to think I was some brawler nor a trouble maker so I just changed the subject.

I didn't ask any of them what they were in for; as far as I was concerned it was none of my business.

They told me that we were in a waiting cell, and that next we would then be seeing the P.O officer and then the Prison Governor.

I was told he would do his same old speech "Keep ya head down and ya time will go quicker." and how he liked a quiet prison.

They went onto say we would be all told to undress and squat over a plastic mirror and if they the screws felt the need, then they would put a glove up your ass, more so if you were on a drug related charge.

Well thank fuck when it came to me as they only asked me to strip and bend over and then squat.

A screw then searched my mouth. I was hoping that the rubber gloves that were placed in my mouth (to search under my tongue to see if I was hiding anything in my mouth) that this screw hadn't earlier done a internet search on any of the prisoners who had gone before me.

All my belongings were taken from me and I was told to get changed into blue jeans, a blue shirt and white trainers.

A blue jumper was also given to me plus blue shorts and a singlet

Guess what colour that was?

Yes, you guessed correctly blue as well.

There were no other colours of choice so I was glad (jokingly) that blue was my colour.

I was then told which wing I was heading off to and was taken with the other prisoners to the wing.

Going through so many locks, gates and grills and doors and then I was there, inside the wing. There weren't many inmates inside the wing as many were out in the two yards. There were some inmates though, who were cleaning the wing and some in their cells with doors opened.

I was taken below a landing, shown a cell that had 2 bunk beds in it.

I was told the empty one at the bottom of one of the bunks would be mine then the door was closed behind me, after being told I would be unlocked when the other inmates were let in from the wing and outside yards.

My cell seemed more spacious than I thought and it had a few things in it a writing desk and a table with four chairs around it plus a toilet which was separated as in it had a moving wooden door which was on tracks though no lock of course.

The windows were high up so I couldn't see out of them apart from if I stood on a chair but then in doing that all I could see was the prison wall and nothing much more apart from the sky and the tops of trees over the wall.

The wing sounded quiet, it felt surreal for me.

I got comfortable on my bunk and then as I did, a lot of noise (general noise) I could hear shortly afterwards (lots of voices).

The cell door soon opened, so I jumped up. In came a biker looking guy, he had a goatee and ginger hair. He was well over 6 foot, his name was Gordon.

I never had seen his face down at the Satan's Slaves Clubhouse so I guessed he was from out of town.

In next was a short Maori bloke, I can't recall his name but he was friendly though he gave me a double look. I could tell (though I had grown my hair) he noticed my tattoo so he probably guessed I was a skinhead.

Next in, was another white guy who was in his 40`s. Stocky but in a fat way, again I can't recall his name maybe Troy. He was the most talkie one, asking me what was I in for?

I knew I would be asked this so many times and I don't know why I said what came out of my mouth next but I think it was due to being fed up with all his questions he was asking me like if he was a copper (though he didn't mean any harm in it) but it was off putting being asked so many questions so I told him I was in for double murder.

Fuck! You could have cut the air with a tooth pick as all their laughing and talking among them just stopped dead.

They all looked like they had shit themselves (very much so the guy who had been asking all the questions) well at least I knew by their reaction that none of them were in for anything worse than that so I said "Of course I am not." "I was just winding you all up."

I have no idea why I said it?

I was thinking "Fuck, I have just met my cell mates, and I come out with that." but they all started to laugh and saw I had a dry sense of humour then the Maori guy said "Yeah but bro, what are you really in for?" so I told them the truth.

I told them the length of my sentence though not going to in detail, apart from just saying I was in a pub fight.

They explained this cell was like only four others in the whole wing.

I was told that next door is also a four man cell, where mainly new comers who come to the jail are placed in these two lower four man cells before they go out on to the landing into two man cells and one man cells.

Gordon pointed up to the roof and said "Up there are two other four man cells." but he said "They are always given to the Satan's Slaves, who run this nick and there is only two single cells on the wing they also are taken up by members of the Satan's Slaves."

They went on to inform me/ warn me "Look kid, one thing while you are doing your time in here, just don't mess with the Satan's Slaves while you are in here as if you do, they will make your life a living hell!"

He carried on saying "Even some of the screws always back up the Satan's Slaves as the Satan's Slaves run this nick that strongly."

He added "even more than the screws at times, but the screws are the next ones don't fuck about with as they too can make your life a living hell but there is one or two who are ok."

I didn't let them know that I knew the Satan's Slaves while we all were chatting away (noting the three other cell mates comfortable through their studying their body langue) knowing that in all honestly I didn't have anything really to worry about as I was sensing that these three were no threat to me and more so all seemed decent guys.

I didn't know there would be 4man cells in the jail but it kind of made sense to new comers who hadn't been in the jail system before. I am glad I was in this cell rather than just thrown in a two man cell though that time would come but for now things were peaceful. Something I couldn't have imagined on my earlier ride up the hill in the prison van.

While two of my cell mates were playing cards, I heard my name being called out.

I recognized the voice; it was Lou, who was a patch member of the Satan's Slaves.

I remember when I was young kid, he was always in the clubhouse then he killed someone in a fight. He cut the guys throat but ended up with man slaughter rather than a murder charge.

His lawyer also was Simon of course, who done his magic for Lou in court anyway Lou had two more years to serve of his sentence.

Now Lou was fucking staunch! He was about 6 foot 6 in height and I could tell he had been working out while he was in jail. He recently had been transferred down from up north as he had been in a few of the jails and finally he had been placed in Mt Crawford to end his sentence, though he wasn't the main guy who run the jail but he was very much the second in charge.

He told me to come up and see P.K

P.K had gone into the jail system as a Satan's Slaves prospect, he had though earned has colours (full colours) while he was serving his sentence.

His brother Greg was a senior member of the Satan's Slaves, never said much but very dangerous man though a kind man. As for P.K, he I found would have more to say than his brother but if you pissed him off, he would then speak with his fists as he was a lethal fighter. P.K was the boss of this jail that's for sure, no one fucked with him.

When I arrived that morning, he was on work leave so he had only just returned back that afternoon as he had done a half day. P.K had been locked up for years but now was very soon getting out of jail maybe in a year's time. I just hoped that he would still be there during my stay as it felt within a few minutes chatting to him, very safe now for me and this was only on my first day.

Both Lou and P.K introduced me to the chaps on the wing. I knew many of them already when in the past I had met them at the clubhouse.

Lou told them all to keep an eye on me. P.K just said "Keep with us and you won't get in trouble." he said "You will be glad to know that this is one jail where male rapes don't take place so don't get any funny ides and decide you want to rape one of the inmates as I won't allow it, Christian." they all crackled up laughing.

P.K pointed out too two cells right down the other end of the wing where the screws box was, he explained in those two cells is Samoan lady boy so the inmates who wish for some ass to fuck then these two cells is where the Lady boy inmate gives other inmates blow jobs and whatever the two lady boy is happy to do.

Well I informed P.K it's not the kind of cell that he would be catching me visiting.

I was told why it's so close to the screws security box, because even the one or two of the screws go in there to get cocks sucked off, if they not getting it at home. A roar of laughter again from all the chaps.

Then Lou explained the real reason is so the lady boys don't get raped and are close to the screws in case some nut case whose anti gay attacks them or in case if some nuttier goes in there and wants ruff sex as in raping either of them, but all in all it means that even with them, rape doesn't go on in as it didn't in general population.

Lou said the Satan's Slaves in here; made sure no male rapes took place and if any one attempted to do so even the screws would let the Satan's Slaves deal with the sick bastard in their own way.

P.K and Lou really did have the run of the jail apart from remand wing on the other side but they didn't give a fuck about the remand prisons apart from if any of their brothers in arms, were in there.

The rapists and sick bastards who had touched kids, and the grasses who were on rule 43 (as it was known in the prison system), Lou told me to look through a open grill across the roofs and said that's there they all held, pointing at another building within the prison grounds.

The scum of the prison all were locked up over there, but he went onto tell me that they do get to them while serving up their food.

Again all the chaps crack with laughter, well at least there was some laughter among them all so all seemed ok.

I left them to it and went back down to my cell. My cell mates who were years older than me asked if I wanted the top bunk and I said no it's fine where I was.

"Why?" I asked them. Gordon went on to say that they just wanted to make sure I was sweet and happy. Followed on by saying to me "you're a Satan's Slave, aren't you?"

I said in my heart I am but I am not a patch member. I explained they were like my extent family and I had been part of the club since I was a young kid, knowing them all with great respect.

Soon we all were banged up and then unlocked an hour or so later to get our dinner.

We had to eat our food in our own cells. Locked up for an hour while eating dinner then at 7pm unlocked and then 830pm back to our cells, all doors locked up at 9pm.

I could hear the sound of a television. My cell mates said "Yeah the Satan's Slaves have a telly in each of the upper cells, we only have a radio."

My cell mate's routine was they listened to music while writing letters home and then switching the lights off at 10pm on the first night and more so on most evenings.

Now and then they would get stoned on pot (that had been brought in to the prison) as one thing that this jail wasn't short of....was drugs.

I couldn't sleep the first night and actually had no thought of writing any letter not on my first night as I thought that would look a bit weak as if I was home sick. Which for me so far wasn't the case as I really didn't feel my first night was too bad in the jail, it was as if I was doing my first night in boarding school all over again, though there were huge differences of course.

There place wasn't some plush posh boarding school as this was one of New Zealand most notorious prisons, housing murderers and rapists and very violent criminals and the odd nutter's, so yeah massive difference between the two.

I don't know why at the time I was thinking it was like my first night at boarding school.

I lay in bed and thought to myself how my sister was going on her trip and wonder if she had called my uncle to find out what I had been given as in my sentence.

Thinking how very close I had come to be going on that trip. I wondered how my life would have turned out if I had not got into the fight that evening that ended up putting me away and more so taking away my freedom.

Where would I be now on my around the world's trip? What was it going to be like if I had actually got to meet The Kray Twins over in England?

I would need to write to Reg and Ron and let them know I now too, was banged up and so I wouldn't be making the visits to see either of them as planned.

My mind went to how my father would be so disappointed.

I mean he would be happy to know I had been standing up for myself and yeah the fight went peter tong but what very much would have been on his own mind was another wait before he could see his son again.

That very much, he had been waiting for the day till he got to see me again. At least though my sister was still on the way over there to see him and family, so his heart hadn't been fully broken and I would one day make sure again in this life of mine to see my father.....When that that time was I was unsure but I would make it happen.

I would also make sure that I would in some part of my future to visit The Krays, that I promised myself as I closed my eyes to fall asleep, hearing the prison officers check the door.

Each hour through the night the screws would check every cell door including ours and outside during that very first night I could hear the prison officers walking around the inside of the fence with their guard dogs.

I couldn't though see them; I could only hear the dogs bark now and then. Even with the barking in the background and some inmates shouting out on the landing for whatever reason, I still managed to get some sleep and fall asleep I did.

Being awoken in the morning told I had to get up. There is no sleep-in, in the jail so up to my feet I got. We had to stand outside our cell door, names were taken and then the screws would look in our cell quickly and comment it had to be kept tidy.

The screws would repeat this along the landing to each cell, though at the Satan's Slave's cells, no screw seemed to look inside. One screw would only pop in their head and never commented to them, that their cell had to be kept clean.

I couldn't believe the power status the Satan's Slaves had over this prison, as yeah I had known for years being at the clubhouse, when members were off to the hill or coming back from serving time, that the Satan's Slaves run the jail but not to this extent as they truly had the place in their control.

I was later told that many of the screws actually lived in the housing units just on the other side of the prison wall and everyone knew that, so they had for many years been a easy target for revenge beatings and other happenings that took place such as firebombing of their houses from ex inmates or friends of inmates.

Many of the screws wouldn't take up that housing so they went onto live among the general population of Wellington.

What I didn't know was one lived on the same road as the Satan's Slaves headquarters and he had become a friend of the club on the outside. He would even unknown of course to the prison board, drink at the clubhouse so he became a very tight connection for the club on the inside.

He would encourage some of the other screws to do little favours and turn the blind eye when I came to the Satan's Slaves in the jail.

That in its self meant straight away the Satan's Slaves had an upper hand on all the other inmates and no one was going to topper them from top position. As far as the Governor was concerned the Satan's Slaves were doing the prison more of a favour if they held them in numbers in the same prison, as it meant the few black power members and the mongrel mob members who were locked up in the jail wouldn't ever be in position to run the prison down and cause much trouble (apart from battle it among themselves).

Battles I would see within my first few days as it was a very violent prison. In New Zealand there are so many gangs and with so many gangs that then means so many gang members in the prison system.

It would go off between all the different gangs as they hated one another, which was a good thing for the Satan's Slaves as it meant all these gangs would never form numbers to go against the Satan's Slaves. This meant their power position was very much intact at all times within Mt Crawford Prison.

It made life very easy for me, and I can't imagine what a different time in jail I would have had if I hadn't the backing from the Satan's Slaves. For my age, I would have been tested so many times and I knew that by just looking in the eyes of some of these gang members who didn't like me from the start.

Fuck them! What could they do? Sweet fuck all as if they ever tried to attack me or do a stand over tactic on me then the likes of Lou and P.K would make their time in Mt Crawford a living hell.

Every day I learned so much, yes about jail life but also all about crime. The professional bank robbers would tell me from their mistakes and how to get it right.

The other criminals would tell me about swindles, and the fraudsters who were so bright would tell me about certain things. It was like being placed in a criminal school.

I do believe jail really is just a breeding ground, more so for the young just to improve themselves in their future lives of crime. What a massive network system prison has, more than such things in this day and age like facebook etc. Inside jail on a criminal level, you would meet so many different connected people so when you were out, you ended up knowing a villain in each town of NZ.

New Zealand really didn't have villains such as Britain or gangsters such as American.... it did though have many high profile gang members.

Not all gangs disliked the Satan's Slaves, there were all the skin head firms inside who would run about for the Satan's Slaves, and then you would have some of the BP members giving equal respect (more so the older guys) and then you had bikers who were friends of the Satan's Slaves on the outside so their friendship bond would grow ever stronger in the jail.

The brotherhood that they had in many prisons, were for all to see especially new comers to the wing who some would try to start shit but soon they would have their life's turned upside down by violent beatings that the Satan's Slaves would dish out.

One good thing was there were no grasses on our wing and no thieving as the last person I was told who stole something out of someone's cell, had his hand crashed in a prison door.

That was a warning to everyone that no one was to steal of each other and while everyone was under the same roof to get the screws off everyone's back then everyone as best as they could, should get along. .

The amount of drugs in the prison system blew my mind, though I had given up drugs but every night you could smell weed down the wing. I think some of the screws though a stoned jail is a quieter jail and that very much was the case as when most of the inmates were stoned then all you could hear were laughter down the wing.

After a week had gone by, I was allowed out of the wing for the first time and placed in the exercise yard surrounded by guard tower blocks. Many inmates would just run around inside the inner wall of the yard to keep fit. Others would be playing poker or card games and the fraudsters would be playing games of chess.

Now and then a rugby ball was thrown in and that meant full contact seven aside touch rugby but it wasn't touch rugby, it was full on and all on cement. That's when the gangs would be able to attack each other and show off their raw strength, it was something to watch the day go by.

I found myself in the yard with none of the Satan's Slaves as P.K was on work leave 5 days a week and Lou run the kitchen so the only protection I had was prospects to watch my back and also a Outlaw MC(unsure if he was a patched member), who was in there.

He was a full on hater of the mob. He was from the Napier area of NZ where the Outlaws MC are based in NZ.

He was staunch and he was the size of a house. His name was Bogga, he could lift two men up with his hands and when it came to the contact sport, even the strongest of the Fijians would go flying and they were tough guys.

Bogga was just full on, he was covered in white power tattoos and he wasn't afraid to let people know his trail of thoughts (which were extreme right wing). Most people kept out of his way in the yard but through boredom he would try and start fights.

The screws didn't like this as he was not so much of a trouble maker to the screws but he would upset the jail population with his outbursts against gang members. One tried to stab him.

The home made knife went into his back but he carried on and removed the home made knife from his back and licked the blood from the blade and then threw the knife over the wall and nearly killed the guy with his bare hands.

He knock him up against a wall in one of the corner of the yard, just in time the screws arrived and made him let the guy go, the other guy was blue in the face, hardly could speak.

Bogga was charged, moved down to the block but due to him throwing the knife away over the wall which the screws saw from the watching tower block, they instead of punishing him for nearly killing the guy, they actually ended up giving Bogga a kitchen job.

He, in their eyes had proved that he was safe around knifes as if he wasn't then he would have stabbed the fellow inmate. The screws felt that by removing him from the yard would do the world of good for the other inmates and with the job in the kitchen then he wouldn't be bored anymore so more of a settled inmate.

Boredom very much was going on in the yard though I enjoyed chess and I loved getting stuck into the touch ruby but not every day as there were wars when the rugby ball would be handed to the gang members in the yard so there were days on end I would just be bored shitless. I couldn't wait till I was locked back up in my cell so I asked for a prison job. Least then, I could spend more time out of the yard.

I was given a wing cleaning job a week later cleaning part of the wing. The Wing was down to me and four other inmates to keep clean. Cleaning the wing meant cleaning everything daily such as the floors, the walls and the shower area and all the security grills, gates, and door handles also had to be cleaned.

Anything that needed cleaning and waxing etc had to be done each day. One thing was the wing its self was spotless.

Each morning after being unlocked, I would get my breakfast then back to the cell to eat then unlocked again and all the work party inmates would go out of the prison but us the cleaners would stay in the wing while general population would go out to the yard.

The Kitchen inmates really would come and go as they wished as they were always prepping food or serving it up and so they would be in their cells resting or reading or for the likes of Lou watching telly, wanking over Australian exercise programme called OZ Style Fitness Show.

That show was on the telly in the mornings so he would kept the whole wing informed what the girls were dressed in, to wind up the other inmates who only got to watch telly in the television lounge and that was only ever in the evenings for a hour and half and then on weekends.

There were other jobs such a laundry, that's where the lady boys would work doing all the inmates clothes and bedding. Down the hill (still in the compound of the jail) up outside the main prison walls, there were some working sheds that other inmates would be doing skilled work.

I was unskilled so I had no chance of getting out of the walls of the main prison but soon things were put in place, for the benefit surely of the Satan's Slaves.

The guy who was doing the bins (he was nearly being released) his prison job was with a trolley he would first collect the tin rubbish bins in the wing and then he would place them on the trolley with wheels.

He would be allowed out of the main gate and just on the far wall (down a bit) was a massive burkes bin and also recycling bins (New Zealand is very green even in the jails) so the rubbish man would have to go throw all the rubbish among the many large bins(arranging all the different rubbish)

He wasn't ever with a prison guard and he done it in his own time, though of course he was on the prison camera system though it never went as far as where the burkes bins were.

He would bring his trolley back up to the short walk to the main gates and with now empty tin bins, he would stack them on each other and maybe the first three at the top would be searched but that was really all as the screws wouldn't want to put their hands throwing dirty smelling bins so the inmate would be let back in.

Then he would go to the remand wing and yard, again do exactly the same as he did in the main wing with the bins and out he would go again.

You can see, this is not a quick job and what was known as the most shittest of jobs as going through all the rubbish, putting them into the correct recycling bins so no one really wished for that job and neither did I.

Once he had done both wings, he would have a wash in the wing and then it would soon be lunch time so he had an hour of free time.

Now free time, you could do weights in the weight room or study a course, say school ceft if you never got it when you were at school or you could use the prison liberty to read books....that was his perk after doing the flirty job.

After lunch he would have to go in to the laundry, followed by collecting all the outside bins within the jail walls (that were scatted around and down the walkways between the wings).

Once he had collected all these bins, out again he would go emptying the bins and then he would finally come in and take all the kitchen waste. There was normally heaps of that so same routine as before but with the food waste he would take further down on the outer wall where there it would be dumped on farm land within the further outside prison fences (low prison fences).

The land on two sides of the hill was farmland and then the rest of the other side of the hill was pure deep forest leading all the way down to the beaches (the same beach at the bottom where I had that tent of mine and the same beach where I had the beach party when I was kid).

The two main roads leading up to the prison were the housing for the screws and then some lovely houses that were owned by people who didn't care living so close to a jail as they just loved the views over Wellington.

These house owners would get magical views that reach past the beautiful Wellington harbour and as far as the naked eye could see.

The prison owed the land as in the farmland and would let it out to city farmers who would collect the food waste for either vegetable patches or feed for the livestock.

Once all the waste was dropped off then the rubbish man/inmate would then be back in the wing, another shower and then locked up in his cell till dinner time and that was his daily routine each day.

So when he was asked by the Satan's Slaves to give his job, telling him to tell the screws he had done his back in. The Satan's Slaves then came to me telling me to put my name down for the job. There were only a few inmates who weren't classed as an escapee risk....I was one of them.

The Satan's Slaves told me to take the job up. What a fucking shit of a job like that.

I thought they were having a fucking laugh but they weren't and told me to go for the job then they told the screw who was their inside man to make sure I was to be given the job.

A few days later I was taken from the wing cleaning job that suited me fine and I was shown the run of the bins. It was the first time I had been out of the prison though it was only to dump rubbish and do the kitchens waste etc.

After a week of doing the job, I was told that by the burke bins would be bottle of vodka and whiskey that had been dropped off and hidden the night before by prospects of the club on the outside. I was told to take the bins, placing the bottles in the bottom of my bins then stacking them high as the screws wouldn't ever go through the first few emptied bins.

I went and done the morning run and got the booze. There was four bottles in total (Gin, rum, and vodka and the whiskey) and a carton of B&H ciggs as well.

I placed them all in the bins then put the bins back in the wing, hiding the booze in my laundry bag. For my hour of free time I asked if I could take my laundry to the laundry room which was housed next to the kitchen.

I took my bag that had these bottles in it and I went to the laundry room where I would then place the booze in the bin underneath the rubbish. The lady boys would make note I had something hidden there for the Satan's Slaves.

I then went back to the wing and would use the weights rooms. I had got a bit stronger from using the weights rooms. I would need to now for my bin job as it was heavy work (than expected) carting around all the heavy metal bins full of rubbish lifting etc them constantly each day etc.

After I had used the weight room, I was given the choice of going to the yard or being locked up in my cell. Fuck the yard so I went back to my cell and was locked up till lunch time. While the Satan's Slaves were serving me my food I wink to let them know I had their booze and where it was (as that's where they had told me for now to put hide the stash).

After lunchtime was over, on my afternoon bin run I collected all the outside bins and the laundry bins. Popping past the kitchen and swapping the laundry tin bins that had the booze hidden under the rubbish and I was given a kitchen bin so my bin count still totalled up the right amount.

Out the gate I went and dumped the rubbish as normal.

I went back inside the prison walls dropping off the bins again to the laundry room and elsewhere they needed to be placed, then I done the kitchen bins. While I was there I went into the walk-in fridge and collected the empty booze bottles as the booze now had been transferred into kitchen containers. I was given a few shots of whiskey that I throw back...I hated whiskey (I was more of a Jack Daniels man) but a drink was a drink.

I placed the empty bottles in my bins, hiding them of course. Out I would go, throwing the booze bottles to the bottom of the burke bin after taking off the labels and trying my best to break up the bottles so they wouldn't be seen from anyone who ever wished to take a interest in the prison burke bins.

I would then cover the broken glass with a lot of rubbish and that was that, all had worked out and most of all I hadn't been caught. I knew the Satan's Slaves would be pleased with the overall result.

After dinner I was called up to Lou's cell, where all the Satan's Slaves were. It was a proper piss up everyone enjoying a decent drink; I must have had at least 12 shots of vodka so I very much was drunk.

I hadn't drunken booze for such a long time so I loved it as this wasn't I thought was going to happen while I was in jail, that's for sure.

I am sure the screws knew what was going on in that cell with the drinking that was taking place.

As long as we didn't let on to the rest of the wing and that we didn't come out of the Satan's Slaves cell drunk as fuck, then all was fine. My cell mates though on lock up could tell I was shit faced and more so in the mornings as I had such a hung over from hell. I wasn't in the best of moods towards them when I was woken up that following morning and my rubbish job was even much slower than normal as I had a banging head ach.

The booze would last ages so it wasn't a weekly thing, doing the booze run. It was around every fortnight I would do it but my routine was changed as one of the lady boys was freed from jail. His job was replaced in the laundry by someone else who the Satan's Slaves didn't trust so no longer could I leave the booze in there.

Instead of collecting the booze in the morning on the first rubbish bin run, I would do it on the kitchen run as then placing it in the kitchen bins which worked better as I would just take the kitchen bins straight into the kitchen and they could take their booze out.

I never then had the hassle of having it in the laundry room or my cell for any period of time as there were random searches of the wings.

More times that most the Satan's Slaves would be told when this going to happen 24hrs in advance due to their contact so they knew when we would be getting turned over so anything they had that they would hide or remove.

The screw who was their friend was in many ways a God send to them as he made sure any changes, they would know well in advance.

A few weeks went by and I was told to do circuit training on my morning hour break in the other exercise yard which one of the screws would teach. He also was the coach of the prison rugby league team. P.K was the team's captain.

The rugby league team would train outside the prison in a nearby army base under prison guard of course.

Once a week they would train for two hours and then play games every Saturday there as well.

I guessed the Satan's Slaves just wanted me to be part of the rugby league team so for me to take part in the circuit training was to get me on the team and get me fit but again there was more to it.

Drugs used to come in for certain people, I won't name who they are as some things don't need to be mention, more so names but some ways how they got the drugs in...I can talk about.

One was for certain people (and only such people) was they would put a fishing wire outside their prison bars where they could open their window (not much) just to allow fresh air in the cells as it could get hot in those cells.

Anyway their inside man whenever he was doing the inner side of the outer main walls, if he was on that duty well some other people would throw over the wall packets of drugs (only when they were informed that this screw was on the wall duty).

He would then find the packs of drugs and hook them up to the fishing lines and tug which was the sign of the inmates in one of the cells to pull up the line and there they now would have the drugs.....be it speed or coke or acid or pot.

These drugs would be sold on the wing for double at times, three times some times more the value and that would bring in a little ongoing business for a few selected inmates.

Another way was some people who were on work parties would now and then bring in a supply of drugs and it was also these certain people who were on outside work duties that would take the money back out of the jail.

Most of the profile would be held elsewhere because any money of a lager sum in the jail that was ever found would mean a crack down on cells.

Also it would mean that person would be placed in the block and transferred as money of any large sum in an inmate's cell meant one thing and that was drug dealing.

I soon found out that the screw didn't mind all the favours he was doing for certain people in the prison but he just didn't like doing this with the drugs as he didn't use drugs himself and if he ever had been caught (doing this) collecting drugs then he himself would be in jail spending time…losing his job.

He would never risk bringing drugs in himself but now he didn't wish to carry on collecting the packets that were thrown over the wall. The inmates who he had been doing this for, said that's fine as they fully understood (they respected his decision) but they still needed drugs to come into the prison for them to make money from.

So the decision was made that I would be the one but not via the rubbish bins as that was safe for drinks but they didn't want to get that fucked up so they had a plan.

That decision, I hadn't even know was made as I was never consulted about it.

And that's how my fitness would play a part in it all. One morning though after doing the rubbish job, getting dressed to do the circuit training.

I had only been given the clearance to possibly make the prison rugby league team the next evening so I was going to be getting a run through at the rugby league practise to see if I matched the grade.

I was very much looking forward to that but then I had two screws at my cell door telling me to get my stuff together as I was being shipped out (as in being transferred to another prison).

"What!"

"Why?"

"What was going on?" I asked.

They said due to my last address being my uncles address (while I was on bail) then the computer prison system stated that I was to be a inmate at the nearest jail to that address which was a fucking bad, bad prison (proper naughty jail) at the back of Upper Hutt.

Out there....there were no Satan's Slaves running that jail.

It was not a easy jail and the rumours I had heard that the prison was in the top five of the most dangerous prisons in NZ.

Though Mt Crawford was no holiday camp and it was a dangerous prison, I was looked after by the Satan's Slaves but this other prison was run by the Mongrel Mob and the bike club (who I had stabbed one of their members). They had many a members in there.

That's all I fucking needed!

I couldn't believe it.

I didn't even get time to say goodbye to anyone. P.K was out at work and Lou was in the kitchen and as for the Satan's Slaves supporters and prospects, they all were in the yard.

Think of your worst nightmare and times it by one hundred as this is the type of place I was heading to.

I was placed in a prison van, driven firstly to Wellington courthouse where some prisoners who had just been given sentences were also to be heading out to this jail in Upper Hutt.

One was a skinhead I knew from Wellington. He had thought he was going to be going up the hill to Mt Crawford, not being taken to Rimutaka Prison (New Zealand's largest prison) but he was wrong as he was heading to the same place as I was.

Going to Rimutaka Prison, just didn't take my fancy in the least.....

I wasn't happy to be heading towards that prison....no fucking way!

Chapter 40

LIGHTS OUT

On arriving at this new jail, it made Mt Crawford look very small in size as this place was huge. It had no wings but units and loads of them, unlike Mt Crawford that only had two wings. In total, Mt Crawford held no more than two hundred prisoners, this jail however held over 1200 inmates.

Red seemed to be the colours of most inmates as every second one of them was the colour of red, and in the New Zealand prison system that means only one thing.....that is the naughty mongrel mob.

Also along the walk to my cell, I noted the security of the place was massive, so many screws.

Unlike at Mt Crawford where we had our own light switch, here after dinner within two hours the call came out "lights out" and that was it the lights were out, though through the big security lights outside and the security light coming through the double strength glass on the door there was natural light still coming into each and every cell so the screws could look in at you whenever they wished.

I was though in a one man cell so at least that was something positive out of the negative.

I knew the only way I would get through my time here was to fight for my life, but also I had firstly to fight for my rights and that would be my biggest fight.

A fight (protest) which was to make sure that I would be taken out of this place.

The very next morning while I was taking my breakfast in a huge hall with hundreds of inmates, I can remember how very nosey and loud it was and just how many inmates there were as I sat down with the skinhead I knew from Wellington and asked him why the fuck did he also end up out of here?

He told me he had only a few months earlier moved out to Upper Hutt (while he was on bail) and so he didn't think that he would be sent here due to his post code as he was a Wellington boy through and through, but had made the mistake to live out of the city while awaiting sentencing, which resulted in ending up him being send to this jail rather than heading up the hill.

I told him I was going to get the fuck out of here once I spoke to my lawyer as no way was I going to stay in here.

He then told me my name had been in the papers some time back about the stabbing, and how word had it that I had a contract on my head of $10,000. "Oh" I said "That's great."

He went on to say how he heard the guy who I stabbed put up $2500 and whoever else I done on that night also matched the money so any one who was willing to shoot me or stab me to death ,his exact words then "They'll be $10,000 better."

"My life was worth more than just $10,000, what a joke" I said "I would have been happy to hear that, if it was with a few extra 0s added on the end."

He said "well that's your fault as you stabbed a guy who was claiming benefits" "The prick couldn't even afford to put all the money up for the contract, how laughable is that, he should have got a loan out from the bank."

We laughed but it stayed with me as these people would easy be capable of getting some drunken drugged up thug to do me for that type of money but it never crossed me this could happen here in the jail.

I was more concerned about the mongrel mob that was giving me dirty looks, especially while we both were sitting together. I had only had my hair shaved off that I grew for my court case a few weeks earlier so we both looked like two skinheads (right wing ones).

Wrong time to get a haircut....I thought to myself.

I asked the screw that I was ready to be escorted back to my cell as the first week in here I was told I would be locked up for 23 hrs a day (apart from when I had one hour of exercise in the yard and also let out to shower once a day and let out for breakfast, lunch and dinner).

All other times for the first week I would be locked up in my cell and they the prison service would work out which unit I would then be sent to while serving the remaining of my time here in this hell hole.

Being locked up for 23 hours a day suited me fine as when after lunch I went back to my cell there under my door a note had been slipped with the words written on it "your card is marked" and with the markings of a motorcycle gang.

I had not seen who had placed it under my cell door but at least I now knew that on my unit there were either members or supporters of the motorcycle gang (they anit no 1% MC) who seeing my name next to my door would have worked out it was me who done three of theirs.

If they knew about the contract on my head then maybe it was in here that I was going to come unstuck.

I didn't feel too brave. I was just glad that for now I wouldn't be mixing with them as I would not know who they were or who the coward was who wrote the note. I guessed that cowards like this would work in numbers and get me only when I wasn't expecting it.

I demanded to speak to my lawyer which took ages to finally be escorted to the screws office to make the call.

I told Simon I have been transferred and also told him about the note. Telling him he has to get me out of here and fast, as for sure I could end up being killed in here.

He told me to keep hold of that note and he would see me tomorrow. He turned up by the following afternoon, by which time I now had three notes that were put under my door.

Well one I had actually had written myself as I thought three notes meant more business than just the two that had been placed under my cell door.

Simon spoke with the prison authorities who said due to my post code they couldn't do anything, so Simon said he would try again but day three still nothing and now I had received even more death threats in notes.

I didn't even have to add anymore as it was like I was receiving fan mail and that everyone wanted to write me a note though the handwriting was the same in each note. I wasn't that stupid nor was I stupid enough to go to the shower rooms.

By day four something changed, as I was still getting at least two notes a day but now in different hand writing. Fucking cowards though as no one said anything to me but simply had just written notes to let me know that I was going to be stabbed up...good and proper.

I had said no to the excise yard for 4 days and no to the shower rooms as well, when the screws came in and said I have to shower.

I said "Bollocks I do!" but they dragged me out and put me under the shower, well that was ok as at least there were more of them than inmates at the time in the shower room so I wasn't going to get stabbed this day that's for sure, but then they said "You going out to the fucking yard!" I said "Make me as I anit going out as I am waiting to hear from my lawyer so fuck off!"

Well that was that as next minute body punches I told from one of the screws. Fuck that hurt. Out I was marched from inside my cell not to a yard but a cage yard, and thrown in.

You could say to the lions as in the corner were four bikers. Well I didn't have to be smart to work out who they were and that at least one of them among them were the writer of some of the letters so I stayed by the gate of the cage.

The cage opened and I was handed not a rugby ball but a football. I loved my soccer so I gave it a mighty good kick.

Just my luck it flew in the air and Whack! Hit one of the bikers right in the side of the head.

It wasn't even meant to go in their direction, I had sliced it of the side of my foot so not like David Beckham and so not like Zico.

It looked like I done it on purpose, a very brave move and one that caught the attention of everyone, including 9 mighty mongrel mob members who were doing Maori carvings with chisels. Can you believe that, they had fucking chisels!! Now in my eyes, shouldn't they not be allowed them outside, let's say yes in a woodwork room but very much so not in a cage around other inmates. Due to them being Maoris, in their culture wooden carvings are a huge part of their culture then they had the right to have those where ever they wished. Well at least none of the bikers were Maoris so for now they weren't tooled up.

I couldn't say sorry to the bikers as that would be seen as a sign of weakness, so it just come out "Don't ever put another fucking note under my door, you bunch of cowards and if you want it...then come and get it on!"

"As I will do you all as good as I done your wanker of a friend!" puffing my chest out as my voice got louder and it looked like I was starting to lose it but I had to show them front or I would have for sure been attacked and I had no one to back me up so I know I would have lost that fight.

What I had just gone and done meant now very much so my card was even marked more.

The football came rolling back to my foot and I kicked it again, this time not in their direction I may add.

I kept on kicking the ball against a side of the cage where no one was near so to make sure I wasn't going to upset anyone else, while keeping an eye on the bikers.

Who all hadn't moved from their part from the cage (maybe they thought I was a compete nuttier) but I knew that wouldn't put them off from going for me so while I kept a steady eye on the path of the football that I was kicking reparative against the cage, I also kept on eye on them at the same time.

After maybe about 30 kicks, suddenly one of the mongrel mob members came over and stood in the path of the ball so the ball didn't reach me. He then picked it up and with one stroke of his chisel stabbed the air out of the ball, telling me to stop making a fucking noise it was putting him off his carving!

Well I couldn't make any noise now with the ball as he had put a mighty hole in it.

There I was without a football to kick about. The popped football the mongrel mob member had, forced it through the cage to one of the screws (who had been keeping watch nearby after my earlier outbursts). I just thought the screw was watching my ball skills but he wasn't, he was ready and waiting for it to go off.

Soon we were unlocked back to our cells and locked up then dinner to the canteen room, where now I could feel I was being watched more than usual.

I sat down and had my lunch with the skinhead who during my burnt-out in the cage didn't come over to me. He seemed to be keeping his distance and then he told me word was going around that by weekend I was going to get it. He had heard it from one of the other skinhead inmates.

The skinheads in there had their own click going on. It wasn't for me, I preferred to stand alone and also I didn't feel the need to mix with others as I was hoping each morning to get out of here back to the safety of Mt Crawford jail.

Even though that sounds weird as in finding safety in any jail but due to the jail I was now in not being controlled by the Satan's Slaves nor actually not even having one of their members in here, well Mt Crawford then was the safest place (while serving my prison sentence) I could be in.

It was Wednesday and now I just had been told, by weekend I would be a dead man as in a dead man walking.

I knew that since the afternoon and I could very much feel this, as I sat there eating my grub.

The next morning I said no again to showers and then I was told I had to go back out to the yard to do an hour to get fresh air as like yesterday. What fun as stood there knowing not to sit down as if I was going to get rushed I would have been better to defend myself had I been rushed while on my feet.

There was more mongrel mob in the cage this day, probably over 25 of them. They were everywhere. I just hoped that things weren't going to go off as I wouldn't have a chance even against a few of them as none would have thought twice about doing me.

I am sure they guessed I was some skinhead. If they knew I was as close to the Satan's Slaves as I was then that would have given them all an excuse to take my head off.

Something I didn't fucking need as I was already watching my back to the death threats from the bikers in there.

The mob were hostile to me but I just ignored them as most of the shit I was getting was only verbal abuse from their prospects and hand on heart honestly on a good day I knew I could have done every one of the prospects, one on one in fight but I couldn't strike out when they had their patch members nearby and in total there were 25 of them...they would have torn me to pieces like a pack of dogs.

After what must have been half an hour, three of them were walking confidently around the inside of the cage, and as they came past me for the 5th time I worded "These fucking screws are treating us like a bunch of monkeys, having all of us in this cage!"

I was meaning that it was like being in a zoo but what I had said was the word "monkeys" and that was the word that the black power had for the mongrels so they stood right in my face and said "What white boy!" "Say that again!"

My reply was "Don't you feel like caged lions?" using the word lion now as realised what I had said that they taken the wrong way, and then they said to me "Don't fucking talk to us you cunt!"

I don't like that word, and I am sure no one reading this book likes that word more so the ladies(I know have used it a few times in this book so forgive me for that).

I like you, reading this book dislike the word and I said politely "Don't call me a cunt, I have step brother in the mob, and they don't call me a cunt and they're family so don't you lot."

I didn't say it in agro way but I did stand up for myself.

They laughter at me, and said "What you?"

"You have step brothers in the mob, fuck off you cunt!"

I really wanted to square up to them but what chance did I ever have to my voice being heard , more so while they would have stamped all over me.

"Really you don't believe me, go and get ya leader!" I said as they were still in my face.

"You're fucking joking, are you mad?" they said with now angrier in their voices.

"Yeah maybe I am mad; don't be calling me a cunt!"

I was pissed of more as they all just laughed louder right in my face asking me what the fuck I was going to do about it.

They were now showing me up in front of everyone, and I hate being called a cunt for the second time.

I asked "Which one over there is the top man?" as their stand over tactics weren't doing fuck all on me and I wanted them out of my face.

"Go fucking find out yourself, you honkey!" which is a racist remark, and one that so deserved a punch being thrown but I wasn't stupid enough to be baited by their stupid games as I walked off thinking to myself "I am going to have you ya racist bastard!"

As I walked across towards where the other mobsters were, the whole mood just changed in all the many inmates who were locked in the cage in with me.

Here I was (someone looking like a skinhead) already in the lion's den and now walking in to an even more very dangerous position as at least 20 of the monsters had tools.

I am sure everyone who was witnessing this, thought for sure a blood bath was about to happen right in front of their eyes.

I had to speak very quickly as being white and being of skinhead appearance and as for some of the mob already taken an interest in me to smash me, I had less than minutes before at least one of the young ones would try their luck to inflict pain upon me.

I asked "Who's the top man?"

One of the mobsters replied "Why do you want to fight him?"

When I heard him say that it reminded me of the great British actor Ray Winstone when he played a role in a certain cult status movie title Scum a classic line was "Who's the Fucking Daddy now!"

Though I had no chance of smashing any of them and getting away with it, to end on a high by repeating those famous words from that movie as I weren't no fucking Daddy in here.

To everyone I was simply a boy as again I was the youngest inmate being held in this jail, and that didn't bring me any favours at all.

Anyway now surrounded by 20 odd mob members, many with facial tattoos and most looked staunch as fuck though they all were just laughing like a pack of African wild dogs as that's what I was to them, a joke in their eyes and they thought they were going to have some fun this afternoon.

Then one of them said "I am the boss!" "What the fuck do you want?"

My reply was "I am the step brother of Patrick Manuel, Billy Manuel and Lenny Manuel, who all who are senior members of the mongrel mob and when I mean senior I mean born leaders and life mobsters."

I didn't even have to keep on going with what I was saying as even half way through, the mob leader tried to speak over me. I wanted to make sure he heard what I had to say, as if not then I wouldn't be walking out of the cage on my feet, that's for sure!

The mobster said "You are Irene Manuel's English husband's boy aren't you?"

I said "Well He's actually Scottish; yeah that's my father Stevie."

He then went on to say to some of the mobsters "Hey remember that wedding years ago in Wellington we all went to, the wedding of Irene Manuel when Patricks mum got remarried."

"This kid isn't telling lies, they're his step brothers!"

With that they all shook my hand and said "You ok kid, your step brothers are legends and we all (every single one of them) have the up most respect for them and their Mother and Family."

I asked "Can you tell those bastards who called me a cunt and also a honkey that if they say it again to my face then I will go for them, and I am totally serious!"

I knew there and then I could now say that plus also I knew if I fought the three who had tried to step me out then I wouldn't have had the back lash of the mob as they wouldn't have wanted to be known for giving Patrick or Billy or Len's little step brother a kicking so at least for now I had won that battle.

They pulled him over (the one who had slagged me off) and in front of everyone he was given a few decent punches which drew blood from his mouth (he must have bitten his lip the poor smart ass bastard).

After that he didn't say sweet fuck all to me as I crossed over the cage and sat again by myself.

At least he was taught a lesson not to use the C word again.

The main boss came over and asked me if I wanted I could sit with them, but I said "I am a Satan Slave supporter through and through but thanks for the offer though it's best I stay to myself."

I had done that, from the moment I came to this prison. He respected my loyalty I had with the Satan's Slaves.

The skin head pal didn't back me once throughout the earlier shit I had been getting from the three mob members. Which in my eyes didn't show a true friendship as if it was the other way around I would have backed him, even if it meant I would end up getting a hiding.

He told me he was shitting himself; he added he didn't want to get involved.

The skinhead asked me what I said to the mob, so I explained about who were my step brothers and also that the big boss in here of the mob would make sure that no threats would be carried out against me as the mob had numbers of at least 200-1 over that certain biker gang, so it was in the best interest of the biker gang not to try anything against me.

I went onto say that no one was going to be now carrying out a coward attack me on me.

Which finally gave me a peace of mind; of course I couldn't be 100% certain as still maybe one of their brave members would have tried their luck and have a go when no one including myself was looking.

For the next two days and all over that weekend, I still watched my own back in case an attack still did came my way? Well it wasn't going to happen in the cage as the mob had my back covered.

One evening while I was eating dinner, a young mobster came over and told me the big boss wanted me to join their table, which was a honour for a inmate to be asked to join that table but I told the young mobster at the end of the day I was Satan's Slaves and so as I had said a few days earlier, it was best I sat alone but thanks anyway.

Mad maybe but loyalty is what it's all about and the mob and the Satan's Slaves were enemies which meant even more so meant no way could I sit with them or have anything to do with the mob while I was in jail.

The big mob boss I knew understood but as for the bike gang, well they couldn't believe it

Here I was their chance of getting me all now out of the window very much so. Their hands were tied behind their back as they couldn't do fuck all but if it wasn't for the mob then that weekend I very much know I would have lost my life or had been viciously attacked. I was by myself without the backing of the Satan's Slaves when I needed them the most.

I ended up having 80% of the jail population protecting me all thanks to my step brothers while I was in this shit hole of a place. At times it seemed the depths of hell but at least it as the mongrel mob hell so for me I couldn't have been in a better position.

My week now was up and I would be going into the whole general population come the Monday morning. I didn't worry as much now as I knew my back was covered by the most unusual set of guys, minders of the mongrel mob protecting a Satan's Slaves supporter (I was not member of the Satan's Slaves).

I am sure up and down the country in all the jails, this hadn't taken place ever before.

I only have my father to thank for that as if he hadn't married Irene Manuel from Porirua then I would be a sitting duck and by now as the weekend was over, I would have been stabbed to ribbons. Maybe worse stabbed to death to die in a pool of my own blood, which was my last thought on that Sunday night when I heard the screws yell out lights out for the very last time.

Chapter 41

AS TIMES GOES BY

Simon my lawyer again came through for me as after spending a week at the Rimutaka prison, I was told I was being transfer back to Mount Crawford jail.

I was a happy man and felt good leaving that prison behind me and not having to spend any more time in there at least I could do my sentence among people who I knew, who I trusted and equally were friends of mine, that being the Satan's Slaves.

I arrived back at Mt Crawford and back into my wing though not in the same cell that I had been in previously, as I was now in a two man cell.

I wasn't sure who I was going to be sharing the cell with also when I asked one of the screws about my rubbish job, he told me that as I had left they had now got one of the other inmates to do it (whom they had trained up as in shown him the rounds) so they were going to leave the job for him.

I was guttered as though a shitty job at least there was a perk in for me as in the booze runs as I would always be invited up for a drink whenever I had got in the booze for the Satan's Slaves .

I saw Lou while he was dishing up dinner(I had been locked up in my cell all afternoon since returning) he invited me up to see the chaps for a drink as there was news they had for me.

So after dinner, being unlocked I went up to see him and P.K and the others. I told them I couldn't get my job back but they said there were more ways of getting booze in than that so I was told to ask all my visitors who came to see me what to bring.

You were allowed gifts such as biscuits, cakes, soft drinks in unopened plastic soft drinks bottles where the seal had not been broken, these three gifts are what I was told to ask of my visitors rather than other things....reason being as all three items could bring on good times.

You wouldn't think with a few biscuits, a slice of cake and a bottle of lemonade that you could have a little party in your cell or the weekends could be more enjoyable.

Lou explained that I was to let one of my visitors tell the others what to do as in with the three items that I would be requesting from all my visitors.

Out of all the people I knew I only would ever allow a few people to visit me as when I first went in and people came and saw me, there were many who were only really interested in what the inside of a prison looked like and who Tom, Dick and Harry were in for and what the food was like.

It got so boring so I decided to only ever invite a few people. My sister came each weekend and so she was the very first visitor who I asked to on her next visit to bring the three items.

The biscuits were to be made out of dope butter so you would get a slight high on them, which everyone enjoyed those types of biscuits.

The cake thought the screws would poke at it so there wasn't anything hidden in the cake, well the cake as well was made from dope butter so again it was another way of getting high for selected inmates.

As for the lemonade bottles of soft drink....well what would happen is the night before a visit, my sister would buy a 2litre of lemonade, boil a pot of water wait for the water to boil then sink the bottle top for the cab of the bottle into the hot water (which would expand due to the heat the plastic seal) then take the cap off with the seal unbroken.

Next pouring out a limit of the lemonade, now pouring in vodka, quickly putting the seal back on and when it had cooled down it would seal the lid of the bottle again.

Thus meaning the following day the screws wouldn't have a clue ever knowing then the bottles would be filled of booze (when being handed to them at the start of the visit by my sister or other visitors).

After the visits, once all gifts were collected and name tagged then I would go and collect what had been left for me and I would alas come away with two litres of booze...........lovely fucking jubbley!!!!

Now the Satan's Slaves (with everyone else who was doing the same stunt) would end up having a proper bar service going on.

We had Black Sambuka, Jack Daniels (both brought in by a cola bottle of course) and every other drink while the black power only had their home brew, and that shit was shit in taste and shit to get drunk on so at least we had some good spirits, and in high spirits we would get.

I had given up drugs, but I would still have the odd biscuit now and then to chill out on a Sunday afternoon after playing cricket in the yard with a few of the inmates who I would sell biscuits to for $2 (which in prison having even a extra $10 on ya could get you a few things like more phone cards etc).

International stamps are what I would spend my money on as when I returned back to Mt Crawford, I would be again in touch with Ronnie and Reggie.

The twins couldn't believe I was now banged up in jail, after Ronnie had written on that first letter "P.S keep out of trouble."

I needed to write to them as I had told them about the trip I had planned to come overseas to visit them so not to expect me now for the time being.

I would promise that I would come over; also at this time Reggie knowing I would be bored in jail put me onto a woman in Chatham in Kent England, whose daughter young daughter was sadly battling Leukaemia.

Reggie was raising money for her, so I wrote to the parents, one being this lady.

My letter saying that I would do my very best once I got out of prison to do a fund raiser in Wellington for their daughter.

I think back to her name I am sure her name was Elaine Crawford, the letters she received from me she said was heartfelt and that Reggie had already raised over £2,000 for her which her and her husband (who was a truck driver) was very touched by and it meant they could provide more health care for their daughter, who had to go to the world famous children's hospital up in London many a times for treatment.

At this same time Reggie put me in contact with a guy from Sittingbourne also in Kent whose name was Danny the knife Henry, he was a young villain from his manor that was trying to change his life around and would visit Reggie in jail.

Reggie tried his best to get the kid on the straight and narrow, and would get him to help Reggie on the outside with charity events, one being Elaine's and her husband fund raising for their poorly daughter.

Danny managed to get some press interest over in the UK, and he sent me over the clippings from his local newspapers.

I found Danny to be a nice kid, he was a few year old than me maybe 24 years old if I am right, and he had been in a lot of trouble through his life, but his own friendship with The Krays had given him some direction in life, he would write to me often while I was in jail.

Now I was back and settled in again at Mt Crawford, I was told to go back to circle training which I did also I ended making the rugby league team.

I shined like a star due to my years of playing rugby. I was by far one of the better players as many of the other players though good, were just thugs on the field though P.K was something else just natural at playing league and a complete all rounder.

There were many benefits being on the team. Every Saturday morning we would go out to play always inside the army base in Seaturn.

Many visitors could come and watch though there was no contact allowed between the inmates and the visitors as the screws weren't silly and knew this was one way drugs in the past had been sneaked back in to the jail through outside contact at the right league games.

Visitors and inmates would still though share the same toilets as the shower block were part of the bathroom faculties so some visitors would hide drugs for certain inmates via a use of a fishing line again.

This time tied around a waterproof packet of drugs, lowered into the toilet and the other end of the fishing line tied around the basin, then the toilet flushed so no one could see the drugs hidden in the pipe line of the toilet.

It meant with the naked eye you wouldn't be able to see it (if inspecting that toilet) then you would want to get the drugs, you would just feel around for the fishing line and pull it slowly till the packet of drugs came to the water and hide it.

Some inmates if the drugs were hidden in a condom then they would sallow it while others would shove the package right up their ass to hide it.

Everyone getting on the bus would be searched, so really most times the second search back at the prison wasn't such an internal search as the guards would already know, and we all had already been searched.

Yeah it didn't feel good but if you carried the drugs for someone you would get a good bit of quid out of it. I did carry a packet back from the league games for some of the chaps who weren't on the team so they didn't get a chance to bring drugs to the prison.

Though at this stage I still wasn't taking drugs though in jail there were lots of drugs going about but I still would say no anytime I had been offered any, but to help out a mate then I would sneak some in for him as I would be handed some cash once the drugs went out through the jail population.

While the rugby league was going good and we were winning most games, P.K the captain said we needed more than just one night practise.

It was agreed if we wanted to win the championship in the grade that we were in, then another night practise had to be given. It was soon granted though it wouldn't take place down at the army base as the army used the rugby pitches for their own use and also rented it out to a local rugby club so we trained on a paddock just down the hill from the prison.

Five guards would walk us down, we would even have some of them practise against us though the Governor wouldn't have been happy to know this, we weren't allowed of course to tackle them so it was more just touch league to get our set plays done. Only two or three screws max would get involved as the others would just stand around and smoke roll ups.

Whoever was on the rugby league team, all were minor risks so no one thought of escaping.

We all were at the end of our sentences and other members of the team were already on day releases and work leave so there never was any risk.

Though among us there were still very dangerous men and some of the players still had a few years to serve so maybe one of them could attempt to do a runner so that's why the guard numbers was high for the 15 of us who would take part in the training sessions.

Being out of the jail walls on rugby league training and then whenever I played the games on the Saturdays down at the army base, Lou told me to apply for outside runs, which I didn't have any idea what he meant by outside runs.

It sounds crazy but the low security risk prisoners out of the rugby league team were allowed each evening out of the prison after dinner to go on a run without a prison guard for a hour around only the hill (at all times on the outside run to stay on prison land) but you were allowed outside the main jail, but not allowed out of the prison grounds.

The paddocks down the hill were ok as that was classed as the prison grounds even though this was past the main fence line so I was told to apply for it.

There was only four members of the rugby league team could apply for it, but none of the others did as they couldn't be asked running around in the evenings when they could just chill watching telly in the TV lounge.

Now to be honest, I couldn't be asked either but I was told if I done it and was granted outside runs then Lou would made sure I got a job into the kitchen (the prison kitchen that he run). Now that was the best job in the whole jail and only the top chaps worked in there so I said ok I would do it.

Outside runs was awarded but as I was already out on Tuesday and Thursdays with the league team so it meant I was allowed outside runs on Monday evenings and Friday evenings as weekends no outside runs were allowed.

The first night I went out, Lou gave me a map of the hill he had got hold of showing the entire hill, all the paths ways and roads and also the forest areas.

Below the forest area was Shelly Bay Navy Base and all the surrounding beaches to the left of the base (which was where I had put my tent up from my early years of running away from home).

Lou showed me a mark on the map and said "If you can get down there in 15min running like hell, meet someone and then run back up and you will still have 30mins to hide something and by the time you get to the gate, you will looked fucked so it will look like you have been running all the time you have been on the outside run and then just before lock up, bring it into my cell and I promise you I will get you a job in the kitchen with me."

So I studied the map and then placed the map in my sock and out the gate I went with a rugby league ball, telling the gate guard that I was going to the paddock down the bottom to do place kicks and I would be also hoping to do some sprint runs. That was it; I was out the main gate.

I run down the paths onto the paddock, setting my stopwatch and checking the time (it had taken me less than 5 minutes to reach here)....I had 55mins left.

I tool out the map to check where I had to get to, at least I could see the roofs down below of the navy base so I knew I would be fine to reach there and then I would run along the tree line until I saw the car that I had to look out for.

I jumped the fence and then placing the ball behind a tree, my plan was if I were coming back up and for whatever reason a screw had come down to check on me then I could just say I kicked the ball too high and it went into the forest so I was regaining the ball, that would save my skin I am sure as it was a good cover to use.

As I went ruining down through all the pine trees (it was really steep) taking me longer than 20mins to reach the bottom. I had 35 mins now to get back up after I had meet Lou's contact (I knew him from my past).

He handed me what was a film canister which was warped in masking tape I didn't ask him what it was as I had already guessed it was.

I left him and headed back up through the forest to the paddock, collecting the ball before I jumped over the fence.

It was fucking hard work, now I had this object to hide and there was no way I was going to put this up my ass....fuck that as a joke.

I put it in between the cheeks of my arse and just prayed I wasn't going to be asked to take my kit off when I got back to the gate.

I had no idea if I would be searched seriously or just lightly anyway by the time I got to the gate; I was over the moon to see the gate guard was the screw that was friends of the chaps so he just patted me down for the cameras and then let me back through.

I went to wing and before I took a shower, I handed whatever it was to Lou.

He was very happy indeed (the biggest smile I seen on his face) in all the time I had been in there.

I just had time to get a shower and then locked up for what I needed was a good nights but as I was locked up, the cell mate who was in with me had different ideas as he decided he needed to go for a shit.

"Like fuck!" I said to him "You anit doing no shit after lock up pal!" I protested "You know the rules!"

"No one shits after locked down!"

That was the general rule and even though I was on the top bunk I didn't need to be smelling his shit, anyway he was just some dickhead from Newlands (just out of Wellington) who got caught selling coke. He thought he was some big drug dealer but so wasn't.

He told me to shut up and that he need to go.

The thing was the window only opened a very tiny amount so any smell wasn't going to leave the cell. I said to him "If it stinks I going to do ya! "

He just laughed that off....the wanker.

My age so went against me in prison, I was the youngest inmate in jail and though big for my age, I wasn't as big as these guys who all were fully grown men anyway I would keep to my word.

As there he was below shitting away and it fucking stunk so I got my empty milk bottle carton and with a lighter I lit it.

While he was on toilet I held it above his head (without him seeing) until it dripped hot plastic onto his head and his back but then as he jumped up screaming, the milk carton set a light even more so I dropped the whole thing on him from a height while he was asking "What the fuck was I doing!"

He had his pants around his knees as the thing dropped on him, he fell forward shaking thinking he was on fire so I jumped off the bed landing my feet on his back and started to kick him, telling him not ever to shut up me.

He could do fuck all, he hadn't his pants up. I flushed the loo and jumped back up to the top bunk warning him not to even think about trying to get me back as one thing for sure I wouldn't be sleeping that night and if I were it would be with one eye opened and one eye closed.

The guy hadn't even had time to wipe his ass.

I ended up by telling him I would tell Lou and P.K who would fuck him up in the gym, if he dared attacked me.

I didn't realise the prick was crying even before I got back up, and what happened next was even more of a shock as he pressed the alarm button in the cell.

Two screws came running down, and the wanker told them I had attacked him so I was put in the block till morning and was then taken out to see the Governor, who asked me was it true I had set him alight?

I could believe the guy had grassed me up.

"It wasn't that I had tried to set him a light, I actually burnt the carton to get rid of the smell." I told the Governor.

"I dropped it as it was on fire, I didn't know he we still on the toilet I thought he had finished so I had though the carton had landed in the bowl of the toilet putting out by the flames"

"I jumped off the bed to flush the loo and he was in my way so there was no fight and more so no attempt to set him alight, that's the truth Gov."

"There weren't any bruisers on him or on his face was there?"

"So of course, I didn't attack him Gov."

I was send back to the block for two days, and wasn't allowed outside runs for two weeks nor rugby league and nor visits in the normal visiting room.

I was told I would have to have my visits behind a glass window to see my visitors (including sister) using a telephone to speak to one another.

I thought back to this time and something that doesn't sit well with me is I never turned up to that visit with my sister as I wasn't going to do a visit this way as I thought this was over the fucking top making me see my visitors like this, more so my sister.

I did leave a message for my sister on her answer machine but she never checked the answer machine so she turned up and was told I wouldn't come out though the screws never told me that Saturday my sister had travelled all the way to see me.

If I had known that then of course I would have gone on the visit as my sister never missed one prison visit to see her brother....me.

I felt so terrible she had travelled the distance to see me and she was left waiting for me. I made sure I never let her down again on visits as it wasn't easy for my sister having to visit me in prison.

She felt for some reason guilty that she had gone on the around the world trip but she had nothing at all to feel guilty about as she out of everyone really needed that holiday after everything she had been through.

As for my cell mate (the grassing fuck) who still I had to share a cell with, never shit in our cell again at night. I didn't speak to him once and I know he now would be the one sleeping with one eye closed and one eye opened.

It wasn't long till he took a proper beating by men his own age for being a grass. One morning after the cell door got unlocked, the Outlaw rushed in and done the guy before he even had a chance to get out of bed and with that beating again he grassed but this time he was placed on rule 43 and as for the Outlaw he had a week in the block and his kitchen job taken off him, that's when Lou got me the job in the kitchen.

I was chuffed and even though it was only for a week until the Outlaw came out of the block, the screws let me stay on in there and as for having to share a cell again with someone else well P.K who had the one man cell decide to move up to the Satan's Slaves four man cell and when the Outlaw got out of the block he had my old cell and I had P.Ks single man cell.

The screws were ok about this change around, Lou was happy as it meant that the Outlaw had a good position now in the middle of the wing so any business that was going on could happen now from there rather than always up on the landing in the Satan's Slaves cell.

P.K didn't want any business going on in the cell he had just moved into. P.K couldn't afford the others being turning over as he shared the same cell which would mean he too would be pulled in if the screws ever found anything which would mean he would (for sure) lose his outside work.

I was well happy with my cell and also with my kitchen job; I did feel sorry for who ever had to share the cell with the Outlaw as he was a proper nuttier at the best of times. It would have been a nightmare for anyone sharing that two man cell with him....big time.

A few weeks later, I was asked again to do the run down to the beach to meet Lou's contact (this time he would be giving me two capsules).

I explained to Lou that I wasn't willing to risk it again but he promised that the screw (inside man) would be again on gate duty so for me not to worry when I came back to the prison gate.

I asked Lou to promise me this as I didn't have long to go now and my birthday was soon as well and after that, I was getting released for a weekend leave though I had to do some anger management course (due to my so called fight with the cell mate and so called setting him alight after he done the stinking shit) before my weekend leave would be grated to me.

"What would I get in return?" I asked Lou as this was big risk more so than any I had done in the past.

Now I know why Lou many months earlier had got me doing the circle training so my fitness level was the peak (that's why I could do the hill so quick).

He explained that the guy would met me half way up the hill as he couldn't afford to get a tug in his car, waiting for me parked up near the prison.

Lou said in return I could have the television in the other Satan's Slaves four man cell. Maybe that to you (the reader) didn't seem much but when you banged up then anything to help the time go by is gold so I agreed.

What I didn't fucking know, was that the prison service was issuing televisions for each of the cells the following month and taken away the TV lounge for the screws office being extended on the wing so the screws didn't need to leave the wing as often to the other buildings (where files and other paperwork were kept) as in the administration building where the prisoners records and reports were kept.

if I had known this then I wouldn't have bloody risked anymore already of my freedom as if it was to go Pete Tong on me then I would have been shipped out of that jail and send to another jail probably half way up the country.

I also would have been charged and given a even much bigger sentence anyway I still done it as the chaps had done me so much for me while I was in prison and I had a lot to thank them for (such as people as Lou).

The following night down the hill I went and found the guy hiding in the forest though it took a while to locate him.

I got the two objects and run up with one now behind my ball sack and the other one push into the checks of my ass. Again no searched was done as I went back in the wing (the television had already been moved in to my cell) and I handed Lou the two film canisters.

I would find out later that each one had a ouches of coke in them (28 grams in each) so Lou for the rest of his time there made a shit load of money and the wing turned from a stoned wing to most everyone high on coke, which brought on more fights and moodiness among many prisoners....I was too get the back lash of one of those moods.

For now though I was never asked to collect any more drugs and my outside runs was just that, outside runs until I got a visit from Angie the Australian stripper (who I had for a few years shagged).

I thought of an idea and told her on the Monday to drive just past Shelly Bay Navy Base (telling her where to meet me in the line of trees at the bottom of the forest).

She did, as there she was when I came running down the hill.

The best outdoor quickie I ever did have, and I kept that one to myself as she would again a few times meet me for shag.

Then I got stupid as I got a mate of mine Nick Robertson who was in the Rebels to meet me in his American V8 monster of a car. He zoomed me over to the Satan's Slaves clubhouse as I thought it would be funny knocking on the clubhouse door even while I was still a inmate, but who was inside there was P.K (who not always let's say turned up to do his outside job as some afternoons he would slip to the clubhouse) who when he saw me speaking to some of the members (I could only stay for 5mins as I had to get back as quick as possible to the prison) well P.K was not happy and told me I was going to get it when he got back and for me to fuck off now before he smashed me.

What I thought was something they all would laugh about, they so didn't and the next morning P.K stop short of giving me a proper kicking....one that I deserved.

While working in the kitchen I had the Outlaw then try to do the same, and said to me "What the fuck were you thinking." and he was confused why P.K hadn't given me a kicking.

But it wasn't the Outlaws place to lay a hand on me!

Yelling at me "You are out of order!"

"Fuck right off!"

"It's none of your business!" I replied but as soon as the words left my mouth, in came a flying punch that threw me across the kitchen as he punched like Mike Tyson.

The hardest punch I had ever had placed on me as I went flying through the kitchen, whacking my back on the sink, blood in my mouth.

I put my hand up to my mouth, the fucker knocked out two of my fake teeth....I couldn't believe it!

It got me mad as hell.

There was no way I was going to win against him as he was a giant so I grabbed a kitchen knife not thinking straight and went for him.

Lou grabbing my arm as I went to put the knife into the Outlaw, as there was no way I was going to take a second kicking from him as I hadn't fucking done him any wrong so I didn't even deserve the earlier punch from him.

Lou told us too stop it! Telling me to see the prison doctor as the screw came out of his kitchen office which was located inside the kitchen. I am just lucky the knife had been taken out of my hand so the screw only saw me standing there with a mouth full of blood.

I was cleaned up by the doctor .The screws asked me what had happen so I said I had slipped on some frying oil on the floor and landed on my face.

They send me back to the wing and as I was walking past the Outlaws cell which was open, I went into his cell undone his bedding and shat a big shit in his bed then placed the blankets back exactly how they were when I first went in.

No one seeing me go in or out of the Outlaws cell.

I went back to my cell and watched telly. I didn't come out when dinner was served as I didn't want to see any of them....I thought they can all go fuck themselves!!

I didn't (as usual) go up to the Satan's Slaves cell for the evening drinks but Lou came down and asked what was wrong?

"Two fucking teeth missing, that's what's fucking wrong due to that ape!"

"What the hell was the doctor meant to do?"

"Hand me out two magic teeth from his draw!"

"Lou, this cost me near $4,000 grand last time and now I got to get done all over again, who the fucks going to pay for that as the ape man sure fucking isn't, is he!"

He left my cell and then went and got the Outlaw who said to me "Sorry mate, I didn't mean to hit you that hard." I replied "Well I was meant to stab you, what a shame."

He thought I was joking and said "look no hard feelings but you did fuck up, but hey we all friends, were brothers in arms remember so let's leave it at that yeah."

The thing is he really did mean sorry, so when I heard all the cells door slammed shut that night and then heard him yell out "You fucking bastard I am going to get you!" well I knew he was talking about me as he would have just got into his shit filled bed.......now that's called karma, you fucking know that!!

The next morning before my cell door opened I knew not to be lying in bed, as in came the Outlaw and though I tried with a punch, which it did land but he just power punched me.

My head was like a boxing bag, back and forth then he left me laying there nearly seeing stars but he was soon back in but this time with a bucket full of piss and shit which he emptied all over me leaving the bucket on my head..........I guess that's what you call good karma.

I knew the bucket well as it's the bucket from the kitchen that we all would shit in, if we could every Thursday night (the night before fish and chips / battled hot dog and chips night) as that's when the bucket full of shit would come back out.

Each evening we would have to serve the sick bastards who were locked up for touching kids (I won't even go into detail of why some of these bastards were locked up as its far to sicken).

We had to serve up them their food in their wing after doing the general population wing of their food then crossing over to the other wing which would hold the rapists, sick minded bastards and also grasses.

First we would fill their tea erne up with all the piss from the bucket that all the kitchen staff including the kitchen screw would piss in each day.

The screws once comment that he was just glad we didn't serve the screws their tea; they the screws had a small mess room for themselves.

Each Wednesday night, all the chaps included myself in the kitchen would eat steak as instead of serving all the other inmates steaks(we would not give out any steak piece as we would eat most) we would make a pie or a sew with the remaining steak pieces.

After eating so much steak ourselves which would make us all want to go for a decent shit, we then (when we needed to take a shit) all would sit over the bucket (one at a time of course) in the back of the kitchen in the bathroom and in the bucket like logs they would go.

We would cover the bucket up and place the bucket sealed up in the walk in freezer then the Friday evenings after we had battered all the pieces of fish and the hot dogs correctly for the general prison population(frying it all off and served it up to the prisoners).

On returning to the kitchen, we would then battered what pieces of shit we had, wearing gloves of course and we would batter pieces of fish and hot dogs mixing them all together so they all looked like pieces of fish and battled hot dogs then deep frying it all though placing the shit pieces in last.

Deep fry them mounting them so they looking exactly like hot battered hot dogs (you really couldn't tell the difference).

We went with the food (the battered shit) serving them up on the sick bastards who had touched kids, and the rapists and the grasses. None of them knew what they were being served and we didn't know always which ones would get the shit.

We knew all would tuck into their food while locked up and if they weren't keeping a eye on their food while eating away then some would have got a mouthful of shit and most probably drinking it down with their cup of tea that was already (due to the tea urn) half filled with piss so either way we were getting the fucking sick bastards.

Whenever they complained to the screws, the screws would do sweet fuck all about it.

It's the only subject that we knew the screws had equal understanding to with us and knew that these terrible bastards deserved everything that got served out, to them.

Hungry got them all every time, as they all would still take the risk the following week of taking battered hotdogs.

We would always think of other ways of getting the dirty bastards, we would even put razor blades in their food or cleaning products in their food. Many of them so got used to the fact that dinner was not worth eating or neither their lunch nor their breakfast as we would be full of surprises.

Anytime they had contact with us, then it wasn't going to be pleasant.

It was only us the kitchen staff who out of the whole prison population that would ever have contact with these scum as that's what they were....scum of the earth.

When I saw all the tellies coming into the wing, I was furious as Lou would know everything through the screws who were pro Satan's Slaves well in advance and he would have known about the whole wing getting television sets for the cells so I asked Lou "Did you know about these TVs before I went and done that last run?"

Lou just smiled and said "Well at least now you get two TV's so TV will never miss a show on the telly again."

With still two missing teeth, I had to contact my uncle. It would be the first time since I had been sentenced that I had any contact with my uncle.

I called him that night before lock up explaining about my teeth and that he would have to release more money for me to get my teeth fixed. He didn't believe me to start so he spoke to the prisons governor the following day, who told him yes I was without two front teeth so arrangements were made that I would be seeing a private dentist in the city.

I had two prisoner guards hand cuff me once we got out of the prison van in the city. I asked why two and they said it's because it meant them looked good in public when they in their uniforms, it's as if they were on the pull.

What sad fuckers, I couldn't believe they really thought that as we walked to the dentist practise, both of them looking like two knob heads as trust me no one was saying "Wow look at those two cool prison officers."

In all fact, people were looking thinking what the fuck has this guy done in the middle to be cuffed to two prison officers.

I said to them "look you frightening people and in all honesty you two look like knob heads."

I think they agreed with my point so one of them uncuffed himself and I was only just cuffed to the other one.

It's not like I was high risk.

Fuck me, I was allowed on outside runs and also was on the league team so why the hell I even had to be cuffed to go to a fucking dentist was a joke.

Arriving at the dentist the first thing we all noticed was how fit and sexy the dentist nurse was as she was hot to say the least so while I waited in the room and she was prepping everything (as the dentist himself was in the adjoining room to us at the time) I asked her for her number.

I didn't have anything to lose and in all truth I wasn't expecting her to give out her number to me, I mean look at me I just walked in a few minutes earlier handcuffed to a prison officer so I doubt that was a good first impression but you know what....she wrote her number down a on a scrap piece of paper and handed it to me.

I was over the moon, making sure I didn't smile so she didn't see the big gap in my mouth where my two front teeth should have been.

I had moulds done and was given a mouth shield and told to come back in two weeks time for my new teeth.

We left the dentist at the top of Manners Mall; I asked the screws could I pop into the post office to ask about a cost of a parcel to England so I would know how much money to give when I wanted something sent in a parcel to The Krays while I was back up the hill.

They said no not really and I said but it's important so they said ok then, still handcuffed I was walked inside the post office at the top end of Manners Mall.

There inside at the end of the queue was my sister. I could believe it but before I could try and give her a hug and explain that I had just been to the dentist, the screws marched me out.

Making out that I had set the whole thing up and that that for sure my sister was trying to pass me something. I was taken straight back to the van and reported to the Governor.

There was nothing at all I had done wrong. The screws didn't seem to think that actually for them to even have taken me into the post office, that they had broken their escort duty so both were giving a telling off and all that happened to me was send back to my cell.

My birthday was next before I got my brand new teeth. I had forgiven the Outlaw for the beating he gave me (the shit and piss bucket) but I didn't forgive him for knocking out my two teeth.

Deep down I was still holding a grudge against him even though he had done me a massive feast in the kitchen for my birthday celebration (which was very kind hearted of him) so I thanked him for the effort he had put into my birthday for me.

My birthday started well, I had the massive feast done by the Outlaw and Lou and then that evening I was given loads of booze and had a puff (first one for age) and a few lines of coke.

I hadn't done coke for so long (hell it was nice) but unlike in the past it didn't make me want to take more and more so I had moved on from my past in that sense.

I was given what looked like lead bits from a pencil, but in fact it was micro dots (very strong doses of acid). I explained I was the king of acid as in how many trips in the past I had taken of acid so two little micro dots were fuck all (though I had never done acid in this form before, only ever taking acid in tabs).

I guessed these two small pencil leads would do shit, but I was warned actually these will really hit me. I thought bullocks so I took five of them; everyone said "Good fucking luck Christian."

Well it was my birthday after all so I could do what I wanted and to try and get the best out of my birthday as at the end of the day I was in prison so I wanted to get something out of it.

I went back to the cell as lock up was being called out. I turned the telly on watching the Paul Holmes Show then next minute Paul Holmes appeared from the TV box into my cell.

What the fuck was going on there I thought to myself?

I asked him what he was doing in my cell jumping out of the TV screen.

Paul Holmes is a very famous TV news and current affairs presenter; he now even has grown his own Oliver oil which is a massive success I have been told in New Zealand.

A year later I would actually find myself as one of the subject of his shows as when Ron Kray died, the news channels and national papers got wind of me knowing The Krays brothers so many wanted to interview me but I would only appear on the Paul Holmes Show.

Paul Holmes got one of his journalists to interview me for his show any way back to the birthday story so there I was taking to Paul Holmes asking him what the hell was he doing in jail? What had he done so wrong?

The conversation must have gone for a hour even at one point the screw (checking each cell door looked in through the guard hole) on checking my cell door asked me who was I talking to so I replied "Paul Holmes of course you fool, now please let us be!" the screw just gave me a funny look and went on his way checking down the wing, all the other cells.

The trip like all past ones was going well, then as I laid down taking in the rushes that were coming more and more over my body, rushing through my mind.

I opened my eyes yet again and noticed that Paul Holmes had gone; also his show was no longer on the telly so I just guessed he had gone back into the television but what had taken his place was a dinosaur bird at my window.... It looked frightening.

I saw it break the glass and try and get past the bars of the window with its long beak trying to get in and bite me. All of a sudden the walls become like forest land, no longer was I in my cell but next minute it seemed I was in a rain forest and the bird was now towelling over me as if I were the birds prey as it started to swoop at me with its giant claws.

I was shouting trying to get out, the bird was going for my eyes so I hide under what I thought was a rotten tree log near one of the fallen trees but the bird was very close on finding me hiding as I could see its huge feet land on the forest floor....close to where I was hiding.

I shouted out for help, hoping someone else was in the forest and that's when I felt the tree log being lifted up. It could only be the giant bird I guessed and that meant only one thing which was it I was doomed to my death.

Then I felt being lifted up and opened my eyes thinking I was about to be eaten but there holding onto my arm was a screw and another screw was holding up my bed.

The forest had gone, my cell had returned. The thing is I was always in my cell, there was no tree log, I had hidden it seemed underneath my bed. 100% there was no giant bird and Paul Holmes for sure hadn't popped out of the telly to join me in my cell.

Let's just say this fucking acid was so strong and I shouldn't ever have taken 5 of them as I was tripping off my nut....big time.

The screws could see how frighten I seemed. The silly thing is one of the screws went into my cell as I was out in the wing and checked then coming back out and how funny is this saying to me "Na, there anit no giant bird in your cell."

I was lead back in to what I still could see was a jungle in there well I just wouldn't go back in there so I was told as I were wasting their time and making a scene then the only place for me was the block.

I was dragged on my feet down to the block as I didn't wish to be heading there either as by this time I was just completely tripping of my face.

Fuck, the acid was so strong (the strongest strength of acid I had ever taken in my life).

The block was just pitch black, no window nor no natural light in there but only a sense of peace and quiet, and thank fuck no giant bird but what did appear next through the wall out of the darkness was my Mum.

My Mum didn't look like her beautiful self as I always knew her as and remembered her, as here her appearance was like how she looked when I saw her laying in the coffin.

It just freaked me out, I was closed my eyes hoping the imagine would go away but every time I opened my eyes there she was reaching out to me. It was just too much to take in, I yelled out but no one came running this time, no screws came to check as I am sure when they heard my outbursts, they probably thought fuck him!

I closed my eyes but only had flashing lights going on while my eyes were closed so now and then I would have to open them.

My Mum stayed there most of the night and also now and then when I would take another quick look, I would see my Uncle Peter (who had passed away when I was younger) and also even Tim would appear and my sister's friend Angie Berg also appeared.

All of this, the whole evening actually had brought on my worst trip ever. I had never experienced a bad trip previously to this and now I knew by morning time fully what people meant by bad trip as it really put me of ever taking acid ever again after so many years enjoying taking acid.

Well after what I went through on this trip then I promised myself never to mess around with acid again as I didn't need that. There was no point where I could just cut it off as the acid trip just grew more and more as that night went on and to suffer my only bad trip while firstly being in prison but more so being banged up in the block was just too much.

It was a living nightmare....a bad fucking trip to say the least.

I was asked what had happened the night before by the Governor, but I couldn't explain it nor was I going to shoot myself in the foot by saying I had taken acid so I told him that maybe I was sleeping walking in some nightmarish dream.

The Governor could see I hadn't meant to cause a scene, he could tell that I had experienced an awful night down in the block so he told the screws to take me back to my cell.

I spelt day to evening till the following morning locked up in my cell. I felt just so drained from the acid trip that I had just been on.

I never have dropped acid again, though I still look back on the years when I did, with fond memories from the very first time I had taken acid but after that evening it really showed me it's not a drug that anyone should take especially young kids as in teenagers as it will fuck your mind up and so no one should take it.

Take my advice on that as when that bad trip comes along its going to be one of your worst experiences that you will ever have and some people never come back down from the trip and end up in metal hospitals or worse causing death or losing their own lives.

I didn't for the rest of my time in jail even go near a neither joint or even bite into any of those magical biscuits or a slice of the special cake.

I had been put off drugs once and for all due to that bad trip. I had done so well for not taking any drugs for such a long time, it was just having to see my birthday in jail which made me take drugs for the first time in such a very long time as all I had while in jail leading up to the lsd and coke on the night of my birthday was the odd biscuit or slice of magic cake.

Even on Christmas Day, when the whole prison was high as a kite I didn't do any drugs. I had Chris Mitchell (my best friend) come and visit me on that day and also my sister and Cool Ken plus the president of the Rebels Craig and his brother, and a dear old friend Campbell Palmerter (from my early years growing up in Miramar).

Craig would bring me in quid when I needed it, he was a dam good friend so often handing me $50 dollar note while on visits. My sister would sneak money to me as well on visits which I would place the money in the crack of my ass as not always did the screws ask you to strip down to nothing after visits.

Other times when the screw who was a friend of the Satan's Slaves members (who were locked up in the jail while I was serving my time) I would simply hide the money rolled up to a small square under my tongue of course never doing a swap from the first hiding place that I mentioned to this one as that would taste like shit....so fuck that for a sunny Saturday after taste.

I had my new teeth waiting for me the following week so again I was taken on a prison escort by two guards. Straight in and straight out once the new two teeth were put into place. Finally after so many weeks I looked normal again with my new teeth though again with a cost of over $2,500....this time it was worth it.

Next was a course I had to do which was an angry management course. I had to take if I were to get out early from my sentence that was handed down to me and also if I was going to be granted my weekend leave that was soon coming up as well.

It was to be taken out of jail, again with a prison escort but only to the venue where it was being held as once we were dropped off then we would be collected again by two prison officers.

We thought they were to stay with us for the day but we were left in the care of the group leaders who took the course (Wellington Quakers).

Nice people, and I do believe I took a lot out of the course and I took it seriously as a good pal a great fighter Brent Vince lived next door to where this course was taken place in Mt Victoria of Wellington and though I saw him and his brother Shane (Shane was a staunch West Hammer Supporter, he would tell me stories of the Inner City Firm who were the hard core supporters of that great fighting British football club from the East End of London - such legends as Cass Pennant come out of that naughty firm) I didn't sneak off to chill with them or get up to any mischief with them as I couldn't fuck things up with this course as it would very much go against me.

It was now the 2 year anniversary of my Mum`s dearth while I was attending the course, so while I and the two other inmates were being transferred in the police van back up to the jail, I asked the screws could I stop off at my Mum's flat so to see my sister very briefly.

It was a big ask, but my Mum's flat was on the route back to the jail and also in my favour was that one of the screws was the screw who was the friend of the Satan's Slaves Motorcycle Club.

If I could get him in agreement then I knew I had a chance he would say yes (which he did).

I thank him for that as it meant a lot to my Sister to see me that evening (even if it was only for all of five mins).

I lit a candle inside my Mum's flat and said a pray then gave my sister a hug. My sister was there with her boyfriend who had just made a dope cake which my sister gave me to me to take back up to the prison with me

Ian by now had forgiven me for my madness (while living at his place on the coast) which was a good feeling knowing this while going away from my Mum's flat that evening back up to the hill to jail.

The screw said I was allowed to take the cake with me, though he of course didn't know it was a dope cake.

I wasn't allowed myself to bring the cake into the prison so he took it from me and said he would leave it in the prison kitchen fridge for me for me to collect it the next day.

I did say he and the other screw was allowed to have a slice each though by the following morning when I started my days work in the kitchen, the cake was still in one piece so at least the two screws hadn't spend the evening feeling slightly stoned, wondering why they had the giggles and munchies as it would have given the game away that the cake was more than simply a chocolate cake.

The next evening after that day, I had let the chaps in the kitchen all have a slice of the cake.

I didn't have a piece myself though I could see all the chaps enjoyed their slice of cake as they all were in good spirits, full of laughter.

When I saw the screw I thanked him for letting me see my Sister and told him his kindness was heartfelt.

Soon I had my weekend leave. I was to have it with many rules set down and also I was only allowed to stay at the Mitchells house. It was nice of them to allow me to gain my weekend leave by signing the prison documents as without them then I wouldn't have been granted the weekend leave.

I wasn't to be allowed to drink booze and nor take drugs (of course). I wasn't allowed to have any contact with the Satan's Slaves which I thought was stupid but it was stated I wasn't allowed to go near the clubhouse address and I wasn't allowed in any licence venues and I had to be at Kath and Johns most of the time that I was to be out on my weekend leave....all very strict rules (too strict I thought).

Kath Mitchell came and collected me. When I arrived at their house, they had put on a huge spread for me with lots of beers.

It made me feel so good that they weren't treating me like a kid, but a grown up.

I got drunk and ate like a king. They were so lovely towards me while I was there and though I wanted to carry on drinking, I went to bed by 9pm like I would do while I was in prison. It was as if I still was on the jail time table as I got up at exactly 7am the following morning.

That day I watched Chris play rugby with his club team and then after him and his brother Damien took me to the rugby clubhouse for a few beers then we headed into Wellington to hit a few bars and have a proper drink.

I thought as long as I didn't get into any trouble then I would be fine and the prison wouldn't know any better but the first pub we walked into, three screws from Mt Crawford were drinking in there.

I couldn't fucking believe it! The first pub I step into and there were the last people I needed to bump into. I am glad that none of them spotted me as we made a sharp exit out of there.

I thought to myself that was a sign that maybe its best we head back home.

I went over to see my sister instead as I wanted to see her and the night was too early to just head home as it was only very early evening.

We all had a few drinks with my sister then by late evening Chris and Damien and I headed back to their place and we all crashed out....all full of beer, beer and more beer.

On the Sunday, Kath took me over to see my Nana and brought her back as John had done a huge roast for us all, so while John caved the meat up and Kath set the table. It was lovely spending time with my Nana as I loved her dearly.

After dinner then my Nana was dropped back home and I was driven back to the prison gates.

When I arrived I was fully stripped searched even to the point of squatting on a sheet of plastic glass and being made to bend over. It was the type of search that I had been given when I first arrived at the jail but I wasn't stupid enough to bring anything back to the jail as I was now very close to being released.

Two day later they done a random drug test on me but I was clear so all was good and soon I was to be freed.

I never told any of the Satan's Slaves or their supporters in the jail when I was being released as I just knew that they would have a little surprise for me and it wouldn't have been a good one as they were sick bastards though I am saying that in the best sense of the term.

I asked the screws the night before I was to be freed, not to tell P.K or Lou (especially) that I was getting out the next day.

The day before I was to be released I had fallen out with an American inmate, who had been arrest for smuggling. He was kind of a Mr Big in the smuggling world, you could say. His sentence was long one handed down to him to do with getting caught for smuggling drugs in to New Zealand.

He had been successful many times, but not getting it right the very last time. He had said something to me I can't remember what but I knew with gate fever at the time I was going through then I was very snappy.

In these last few days anything you do wrong or any trouble you get into then you anit going to reach the gate, you anit going to get released which would bring on a behaviour that wasn't how you normally would act, and this was known as gate fever.

I didn't want to get into a fight with him as I was this close to being released, one day away but I wanted to still get him back for whatever he said to me though it wasn't pleasant at all how I was going to get him back....especially for him, that's for sure!

I had seen this form of sick play at the Satan's Slaves' clubhouse that prospects would do against one another for the enjoyment of the members to watch.

Anyway it's called an enema fight which is two people get a clear tube connecting it to a washing liquid bottle.

Filling the bottle up with warm water (with some of the dish washing liquid still in the bottle) then connect the tube to the bottle, placing the tube up in their ass and squeezing the liquid into their ass.

The other person then would do the same (when both had their fare share of this liquor up their ass) they would turn their backs and take three steps and then each of them would try to spray the contents' of the ass, out onto the other person

It's sick I know but that's what is called an enema fight.

That was years ago but these days you see MTV shows such as Jackass and Dirty Sanchez (the Welsh show) doing the same type of sick acts for as the Irish would say "for the crack!"

Well I done the routine as in with the tube and bottle and walked on down the wing (a tummy full of washing up liquid) into the cell of the American and while he was lying on his bed (watching the night news with a newspaper in his hand) before he could even ask what I was doing in his cell, I dropped my shorts and it was like a fire hose of dirty muddy water that went flying out of my ass at a great speed covering him and his newspaper in all the shit that was in my ass.

It was something like out of a horror film but it felt fucking good getting the wanker back without using violence as this time I didn't do the talking with my fists......hey maybe that angry management course helped more than I even knew.

Coming out of the Americans cell, all the Satan's Slaves were there (laughing their heads off) then I managed to have a quick shower without being pulled by the screws and then it was lock down for the night.

I wasn't sure if he was even allowed to shower though I am sure he was, as he was covered in shit. His cell so very much would have stunk that night big time.......now that's called karma.

I am sure he wasn't a happy bunny.

This was my very last night in jail and though I was happy to be leaving, I very much was going to miss the friends in here and the good times that I had.

Though it was tough and it wasn't an easy ride, I still over all made sure that I very much kept to my own belief and that was always to find positives from any negative.

Thus made me get through my time in prison so much easier plus also without a doubt the fact that I was banged with Satan's Slaves (and they had the overall run of the prison) even to the point I forgot to add that when I had been shipped back a second time from the jail out in Upper Hutt back to Mt Crawford, I was even given my own jeans and my own clothes to wear rather than the prison issued clothes as all the Satan's Slaves were allowed to wear their personal clothes (and so were some of the other inmates).

This was something that I was allowed as well, instead of wearing the prison issued clothes.

It may be something that is small but trust me in jail to be wearing your own clothes was a huge boast to one's self.

The brothers in arms (P.K and Lou) and the others I always more so now, would hold upmost respect for as they were exactly that to me brothers in arms while I was in jail.

I will always be grateful for all the positive things they done for me while I was there.

I proved to them and also myself that I wasn't no boy and though I had come in to jail as a 18 year old kid...I truly would be leaving as a man.

I laid in the bed thinking back to what had put me in here, all the drugs I had taken over my life, the careless and carefree life style I had been living and destroying, the car crashes and all the money I had thrown away, and my mum's death, and the sheer amount of violence that I had been involved in.

Also how as a young man I so had aged many years my age and through that how I had been what I classed as... Lost Youth.

Now though I again was going to be a free man by morning time.

I would be coming out free of drugs, my mind much clearer and though I still hadn't learned how to cope with my Mum's death on personal level, I had come a long way to the person I was before I going to jail.

Jail had yes done the world of good, but I think that was more too how strong minded I was a person and as for my temper then I do believe the angry management course I had done helped me for now to avoid seeing that red mist whenever I lost my temper.

Only the future would tell if I could truly control my temper.

My life for me was soon to change as I had changed so much as a person (I don't believe the jail sentence done that). I still don't believe at such a young age I should have gone to prison.

Reason being as jail out of everything taught me more about crime than I ever did know on the outside so jail for a young teenage can only make them a better criminal(if that's the path in life they wish to choose).

I didn't feel ashamed of being in prison though of course I wished that never ever again would I return to jail and that is one promise I wouldn't break.

Morning time soon came.

The screws as normal unlocked my cell door which usually I would already be on my feet before my cell door was ever opened, as that's when you more than likely to be attacked of guard.

It was my last morning and I hadn't slept too well the night before as I was full of nerves about getting out in the morning so I stayed in bed for a few more minutes......wrong move.

I had also been up most of night writing my final personal letters to my Father, my Grandparents, Danny Henry, Reggie and Ronnie Kray, Elaine Crawford and her family.

There in the morning as I laid in bed I was thinking again over my life(though this time over my whole life from the very first memories I had as a Child living in the haunted house in Miramar, to hearing the domestic violence, to the monster, the street kids, the gangs, the drug use, the many deaths, the drug abuse and then jail) all of it I thought back and you know even then as now a 19 year old kid, I thought I could write a book about my life(truly believed that even back then).

If there was one good message I thought from writing a book then it would be channelled towards the youth of the day to try and steer them away from a life of crime, from gangs and more so from drug use and drug abuse.

I saw it as this, from myself suffering all the bad things that had happened to me in my life at least through good karma, one good thing could come from it all and that would be to steer the youth of the day who had themselves started to get into trouble with the law, drugs or gangs then maybe they would take advise from someone who wasn't many much years older than them and who had lived that life and ended up in prison, due to it all.

As I was thinking all of this (placing one leg out of bed to get up) the American came crashing in to my cell. Punches came down upon me. I couldn't get up as he and also his fuckwit of a cell mate had got me good and proper.

The other reason why I couldn't get up (though they both punched like girls) was because I was still tucked up under my prison issued blankets so I was helpless, but just in the neck of time in came Lou and P.K who with both one punch from each of them had knocked both the American and his cell mate square out..........just like that!

Some water was thrown over them, so they came round and were both kicked up the ass and told to fuck off as they were dragged out of the cell.

Neither knew where the hell they were and what had just happen but then screws came running saying "Christian, you can't afford to get in trouble as you're leaving in 10mins so get your bag together as its time for you to be leaving!"

Lou and P.K looked at each other and said both nearer enough at the exact same time "What you getting out today and you not fucking told anyone.... you fucking devil!"

"Ere officer give us a second with him just to say goodbye." P.K said to the screw.

With that the screw left my cell.

P.K held me while Lou undone my trousers (I was thinking what the fuck is going on here) then Lou got hold of my pot of boot polish and while P.K held me down saying "You little sly fucker, not telling any of the chaps you were going!" while Lou rubbed over my balls, boot polish and then P.K letting me go.

Both of them just laughed their heads off saying "Now you cheeky little bastard try and get that off ya balls when you shower next!"

I think I was still in shock as I pulled up my pants as P.K said "What did you think we were going to do....rape you?" which just had them both laughing even louder.

Finally telling me "Go on mate, get the fuck out of here!" and "Don't ever come back!"

Both gave me hug and helped with my bag as I walked down the wing saying goodbye to the chaps and the good fellas (with boot polish all over my cook and balls).

I didn't care as I now was on my way out of Mt Crawford jail saying goodbye to everyone down the wing and seeing the American and his cell mate who both were on their way to the block............hey ya see, it's all about good karma!

Chapter 42

GOING STRAIGHT

There waiting for me (as I walked out the prison gates for the very last time as she had done when I had been released on my weekend leave a month earlier) was my Mum's best friend Kath Mitchell.

Kath had been such a rock to both my sister and I since my Mum died, though I am not taking anything away from any of my Mums other friends as they all were also there for us all and I am so grateful to all of them but Kath was very much more so.

First of all, being released early from jail I had to give the prison a safe environment of where I would be staying....where I would be calling home.

Being released early from my prison sentence meant that if I did anything while out that was in breaking the law or getting myself arrested then I would be send back to jail to finish my sentence, so I knew I had to keep out of trouble.

I put my stuff in the spare room at Kath and John's house, and had a coffee while waiting for Chris to finish work as by now he had got a job with a bank. My sister popped over to see me which meant a lot.

It was lovely being free and not having to go back there to the jail though I would see them all on Saturday at the rugby league game as I was still asked to continue being part of the team even after I had been released.

I was still an important member of the team which I felt honoured, by them wishing for me still to take part in the games on the Saturdays.

My sister said there was some post for me, whom she had brought along with her to hand me; it was my birthday present from Ronnie and Reggie. They had sent a few books that they both signed, one of the books was the one I hadn't got to finish called Our Story, but here was a book called My Story and also another one called Born Fighter.

I would make sure I thanked them in my next letter as all the time while I was in jail, they would write to me and it as joy to receive their letters and very much so birthday presents sent from them.

Chris soon got home, so I took him down to the Satan's Slaves clubhouse and we got on the piss. I didn't take any nothing else, just drunk beer and celebrated. The Satan's Slaves members had all been told about the attack that morning on me in my cell and how P.K and Lou knocked the two guys out. I showed everyone my balls as I still hadn't been able to get the Kiwi boot polish off them.

It was a good night and I enjoyed seeing every one of them again though one was missing and that was Grot.

He had been kicked out of the club for a very vicious attack on a prospect of another bike club and so he was asked to hand has patch back. He had set a prospect from another club on fire and it nearly cost the prospect his life.

He was in a hospital (out of Wellington) in a burns unit so it wasn't a thing that the club would take on the chin so Grot had to go which I know for a fact (as I knew Grot from when I was only 11 years old) it's something that hurt him deep to lose his club colours.

The Satan's Slaves had been his life for years and to lose his colours was a major blow to him but what he had done was true madness.

The prospect I was told, was in a very bad way in the burns dept (nearly lost his life due to what happened). I found out later that Grot didn't mean to do what he had done, of course he hadn't and also it wasn't so much of an attack or beating the prospect up but more of something going wrong.

Grot had woken the prospect up by pouring petrol on him and then throwing him a light.

I played my game of rugby league and was told that the Outlaw who now was on the team wanted to see me in the toilet. He asked me to on the next game bring him a film capsule full of coke and that he would pay me the following week. I explained to him that I wasn't doing drugs or going anywhere any drugs so I could not help....but he said do it or else.

I thought or else what, as he wasn't even a member of the Outlaws nor was he a prospect so I really didn't need him telling me what to do and he had smashed out two of my teeth a few months earlier while in jail with him.

Something I hadn't got him back for as I wished I had so I said "Yeah ok. I will bring you what you want."

You know what I knew even if I had, he wouldn't have paid me the following week and I wasn't going to be asking my peers for drugs or anyone for that matter as I was going straight.

All drugs had done for me in the past was fuck my life so I decided to buy a huge double A battier and I taped that up with masking tape, so it looked exactly like a film canister wrapped up in masking tape.

The flowing week after the rugby league game, I handed it to him in the toilet watching him stick it right up his ass.

Fuck can you imagine how much that would hurt him (I bet that felt sore). I was sure not to laugh and on the way home all I could think of was the pain the guy must be in though he thinks it's worth the pain as in the end result, only to get to his cell and remove it then unwrap it all only to find that there wasn't film canister full of any coke but just a big double A battery, that he had shoved up his ass after having to sit down on the bumpy bus journey all the way up that hill.

How I wish I had been a fly on the wall in his cell as I would have loved to see his face.........hey that's called karma, I guess.

Well I made sure never to return to rugby league again.

One late afternoon a few weeks later, I saw P.K down at the Satan's Slaves Clubhouse where he could only laugh about what I had done as he told me the guy went off his nut but Lou thought it was classic.

The outlaw soon forgave me as I did send Angie up on a visit to see him, and she handed him something that I know he would have enjoyed so all ended good but at least I had the last laugh and still my two new teeth intact. I felt that little bit better knowing I had got him back, good and proper.

As I had stopped playing rugby league, I went and played for Chris's rugby union team. I out played most of the others on the pitch and so did Chris as he was such a good sportsman in all sports he played; Chris was very naturally gifted on the pitch.

My first game was against a very solid team from the coast. A few of them had worked out that I was a danger to their team so in they came when I had the ball and I was spear tackled. Lifted up in the air and then thrown head first down on the ground.

Their object was to take me right out of the game, and thus they did as I landed with great force hitting the ground.

The St John's ambulance guys (who were the medics for the game) came on the pitch, checking my shoulder that had taken most of my weight and the impact of when I landed as it was giving me pain.

They thought my shoulder had popped out of its socket but that wasn't the case as after they sprayed me with some crap (which didn't do sweet fuck all) I was back out on the pitch but in great pain still.

My left arm wasn't working and so I came off and lifted my rugby jumper and I could see something wasn't right on the top left side of my chest.

After the game Chris and I went to the hospital. I had x rays done and the doctor even knew by just looking at that part of my body what was wrong. I had broken my collar bone.

I was told due to my age and my good health and strength that they didn't feel the need to place a pin it as the bone in time will heal well so I was not operated on but given a frame for my arm and a sling.

I kept that side of my upper body in the same position for it to heal again together over a 8 week period, which meant the end of playing rugby for Chris's team which I was guttered about.

I do believe with Chris and I on the team and also Craig Bell from Miramar (a outstanding player who we had previously when we were young had gone to school with at Worser Bay School) then all three of us (as in how good we were on the pitch) for sure, we would have won the title for the rugby club that year in the grade we were playing in.

I couldn't do anything now for 8 weeks so I spend my days watching television which soon I got bored off so I would find myself again drinking down at the Satan's Slaves clubhouse.

Many nights, sleeping down there (I would be far too drunk to make my way back to Kath and Johns late in the evenings).

I ended becoming a bar fly as I couldn't play pool so I would just sit at the end of the bar and get drunk till I couldn't drink no more.

I wasn't earning any money so I had to ask the club to open me a bar tab at the clubhouse and that meant bad news as soon as it was granted I went from drinking beers back to drinking Jack Daniels like it was out of fashion.

I must have been drinking near to a litre a night which meant my bar tab at the clubhouse was increasing every time I walked in there and sat at the bar ordering myself a Jack Daniels (one after another, after another).

I made sure I got the sling off as quick as possible as I needed to get some work.

Firstly so I could give Kath and John some money towards everything they were doing for me as in roof over my head and feeding me plus I had to pay the tab off down at the Satan's Slaves clubhouse as one set of people I didn't wish to be owning money to, was the Satan's Slaves.

Chris had a job in a bank office but I wasn't that smart nor did I know how to work computers. Chris around this time started to date a Maori girl who became his girlfriend so he would be out most weekends with her.

I couldn't afford any longer to drink down at the Satan's Slaves as my bar tab had gone through the roof so I would spend my evenings in watching television with Kath and John.

I finally got a job that was through a work scheme from prison. It was in a print back door shop. I had no idea how to operate printing machinery but I learned as I went along though it was the most boring job I have ever done in my whole life.

The wages though were actually quite decent which meant every Friday was pay day so after work on a Friday I would have a few dollars in my pocket and sort Kath and John out some board money and then off I would go to get pissed up for the weekend.

I still was staying away from drugs as I never wished for drugs to come back into my life also I had to much respect for Kath and John to ever have thought of having drugs in their home.

One night while out in one of the city bars with a few mates, I seen a girl whom I had seen out in Wellington before but I never spoke to her but due to how drop dead gorgeous she was. I had (and so had most males in any bar that she walked into) noticed her as she was over 6 foot in height and legs that went all the way up plus further more she had a hot body over all and a lovely face with brown eyes, that would melt any man's heart.

She in my eyes was out of my league for sure but that didn't stop me from chatting to her and by the end of the evening we exchange numbers....her name was Alania Hollis.

I took her on lots of dates (for dinner and drinks) also at the time (before meeting Alania) I had taken out the dentist nurse I had meet while getting my teeth fixed plus I took out one of the lawyers who worked for Simon as she was stunning but out of all three of the girls, it was Alania that I like the most.

So then after being a little naughty (before I had dated Alania) with a few girls around Wellington as I needed to when I first come out jail and mores so when I finally had the sling of my arm but after the first few months I had settled down.

I stopped being like a rabbit as I had when first being released from jail (wanting, needing sex big time).

Well I was single and I hadn't had a proper shag for over a year as I had only shagged Angie ever so quick in the bush while I was out on one of my evenings runs (while still banged up) so you couldn't blame me for being a horny little devil

I finally asked Alania out, and she accepted the offer so now we were courting one another and whenever I have been courting in a relationship I have always been loyal.

She was a part time model and also worked an office job. The thing was I was living at Kath and Johns at the time, it wasn't really the place to bring back girls though they were fine with that but I had known Kath and John from the age of five years old so I didn't really want them hearing me shagging.... do you know what I mean!

They were like family to me, also being old fashion I felt it was a bit disrespectful towards them both as their lovely house was a family home and not a half way house.

Then my good mate Sasaka who still living near the city said I could take one of his rooms again in his flat that was owned by his Mum as his flatmate had moved out recently so I did.

Alania and I had looked around at different places to live but we couldn't find anywhere, we liked.

Sasaka place was a great location and more so he was a good friend.

I soon got bored of the printing job even though the money was unbelievable good but I missed actually cooking as I had learned so much while I worked in the prison kitchen with Lou and the others so I took a job back at the coach house style restaurant near Courtney Place.

I enjoyed working there in there. Life in general was doing me fine and though Sasaka would still smoke the weed each night back at the flat, I still didn't even be tempted to have a puff of any of the weed.

Instead I would spend my evenings with Alania or I would be working and then on weekends if I wasn't needed at work I would be down at the Satan's Slaves or with Sasaka hustling money at the snooker clubs. He was fucking good at both snooker and pool when I was only simply a pool shark....a good one at that (at times) not all the time, trust me on that!

I kept clear headed and it just done me the world of good so I was in a good way over all in life.

Unlike the person I had been for many a years on the sliding downward path of drug use and previous years of partying far too hard.

My sister ended up selling my Mum's flat as it brought onto too many sad and upsetting memories for her while living there as it always felt like my Mum's flat still (well for me it always seemed that my Mum still would walk through the door one day as the day she left there for the very last time) it seemed for me that for sure my beautiful Mum would be returning.

Ian had just brought a house bus. My sister and Ian went travelling in that, after my sister had sold the flat. They went down to the South Island, where my sister brought some land in Hokita and they lived of the land and used the house bus as their home. My sister went on and done her art degree while there as she was and still is a great artist.

Their life down in the South Island sounded so cool, and it brought great happiness to my sister's life. They had goats and grew their own vegetables.

Their place in photos that I would see just looked so magical.

I read in one of the newspapers in Wellington a kitchen job that was going in a very trendy restaurant (one of Wellingtons at the time best restaurants called Design Cafe) so I set my sights high as I really wanted to get this job and to get a chance to learn more about cooking as I, like my father had a passion for food....not just eating it but cooking it.

I called up and spoke to one of the owners asking what I would need to get an interview for the job that was advertised in the newspaper. He told me I would need at least three years work experience in a kitchen underneath me and that was just to start at the bottom of the line in their kitchen.

You know what that didn't bother me as all those years ago in the 1960s; my own Father started at the bottom and worked his way up. He was now head chief even in his later years at an Italian restaurant in Scotland.

My Father also had turned around a hotel restaurant in the highlands of Scotland previously to this, so he kept at it and got where he wished to be and that, gave me belief in my own self.

I couldn't say to this guy who owned the Design Cafe in Wellington that I didn't have even three years under my belt as then I wouldn't even have been given a foot in the door for a interview for the job that was advertised in the paper.

I am unsure if the restaurant is still there to this day but in its day it was one of Wellingtons leading trendy upmarket restaurants. I had no chance to get a staff position as I didn't have references and also I had just only recently come out of jail so no way were they going to employ me.

I was only going for a kitchen job though, so it's not like they would do a police check on me so I thought I would still be in with a chance with at least a interview, but I did need refs.

It then came to me; all I needed was a ref from the jail but without it being a jail ref so I spoke to the prison and they put me through to the screw who was a friend of the Satan's Slaves.

I told him I needed a favour. Telling him what the favour was and with the idea I had included.

It wasn't harming anyone and nor was it a massive lie. Ok a white lie but in all honestly I had been working in a kitchen and doing the duties that I spoke off and also I had gained a lot of work experience and learned so much while working in that prison kitchen.

Yes I know prison food is different than a trendy restaurant, but the prepping and the cooking of the types of food are similar.

He then said he was happy to help me out as it meant I was bettering myself and that was a good thing for me and also for him to hear that I was truly going straight, since coming out of jail.

He then got the kitchen screw and also the Outlaw to write a ref for me (one pretending to be head chief and the other one pretending to be manager and Lou as the restaurant owner).

We wanted the restaurant to exist in Wellington but the thing with that is maybe the owners of Design Cafe would ask where this restaurant was.

As this restaurant named in the ref didn't exist apart from a prison kitchen then I would have been found out so it was changed to Crawford Outside Caterers instead of Crawford's Fine Dining Restaurant.

The screw even allowed me to have the direct number of the prison kitchen as for sure Design Cafe would check up on the reference by telephone so for I to have that number was vital.

Everyone knew what to say if any one called asking to speak to someone from Crawford outside Caterers.

Everything was in place; I was sent a reference even with a proper heading on top of the letter.

I was so happy so I booked an interview; I had a feeling that the interview went really well for me so I now just had to wait to see if I got the job.

Someone else was given the job.

I felt guttered but at least I tried.

I then stayed at my job at Fallangans and didn't think much more of it. I continued to look in the newspapers for such a new job as I wanted to be expanding in my knowledge of kitchen work and the art of cooking.

Around about a month later when Design Cafe was all just a thought in my past, I was called to come back for a second interview.

One of the owners told me could I start in the morning as they realized they hired the wrong guy for the job.

I was over the mood so I quit my job at Flanagan's (which wasn't profession to do that without notice but I didn't want anyone else taking this opportunity). The following morning I started work at Design Cafe and loved it.

It just brought the best out of me very much so even while I was under pressure in a fast paced kitchen....I enjoyed that and got a buzz of it.

I then on the side (outside work in my own time) threw a charity fund raising event in Wellington for Elaine Crawford's daughter who was over in Chatham in Kent England, which Reggie Kray was supporting. I raised $1000 (which I sent over to a contact of Reggie Krays out in England to be placed in with the overall money that was being raised) that brought me such a good feeling and a lot of good karma.

The roof over my head that soon changed as though I was busy working hard, I still had a taste for heavy drinking and being in the middle of the city (where the restaurant was based just off Cuba Street) meant I found it far too easy to end up in nearby bars, clubs or pubs with friends and then heading back to the Satan's Slaves clubhouse on the piss.

All the drinking wasn't doing my job any good especially arriving to work some mornings not having no sleep after a big session on the booze from the night before (that sometimes would carry on through till the early hours of the morning).

I was nearly found out one morning as I rocked up to work still pissed as fuck but they sent me home saying I looked green....I blamed another restaurant saying I ate there the night before and I had been sick all through the night after eating from there.

I was very lucky as they could have ended my job and it would have thrown my life back many steps.

All I wished to do was go forward rather than backwards but my lifestyle had to change even that much more.

I had climbed mountains to turn my life around already and been through a hell of a lot and also I had given up all the vices and all the partying but I just was still drawn to the bright lights of Wellington at night.

I had to make a choice or if not, I would end up back drinking far too heavily and partying again even more and end up without my job.

I was 19 years old. I had been a loose cannon all my life (lived a dangerous life) but it was time not to burn the candle at both ends, which meant that Alania and I moved out of Sasaka's flat in the city.

We moved in to Alania parent's house in **Trentham** (a lovely area of Upper Hutt).

Alania's parents were wonderful. They truly both were and they made me feel so at home and they were kind and giving and had a great sense of humour but more so they weren't judgement of me even though I had a tattoo on the side of my head and they knew I had spend some time in jail. They took me in as if I were a son to them. I forever will, always remember them fondly as they both were lovely people and so good to me.

The last time I was in Upper Hutt I was in jail there but now I was living in a family home and living a normal life. Yeah on the weekends, I would still go to the Satan's Slaves as they were like Family to me and I loved the club dearly but no longer would I find myself leaning against the bar at 4am asking for more Jack Daniels or vodka.

As for the bars and clubs of the city well for me to get back home at the end of the night, it meant I couldn't stop in to any of the bars or clubs on the way to the train station as I had to get that last train back (as a taxi fare was near over $100 and I wasn't going to be throwing that type of money away).

Finally I had gone straight in all aspects of my life.

One thing I was missing was sport but I couldn't go back to rugby or rugby league as I was working every week night so I would never make practise.

I did take up Zen Do Kai again with a good friend, who was a master in Zen do kai and was in his time a great boxer (he was a door man at one of the busy bars in Wellington, his name was James).

He would on weekends take me boxing and also intensive Zen Do Kai training.

Bringing both together, he was teaching me free style martial arts so now whenever angry I had these training sessions to channel all my angry through (it done me the world of good).

Chris Mitchell came along a few times as well to do the training. Chris was a decent fighter who could pack a punch, that's for sure.

Soon Christmas was upon me (I was without my sister).

My Nana had Christmas at my uncle's house. I wasn't invited by uncle as we still weren't talking (though my Nana wished I were to be there with her).

I ended up having a lovely Christmas with the Hollis family.

Alania's older brother at the time was living in England in Willesden Green (North West London). He phoned home and wished all his family a happy Christmas which was nice for Alania and her folks.

I was able to call Scotland to speak to my Father and also my Grandparents plus I made a call to Maidstone prison in Kent England and wish Reggie a very Merry Christmas.

He was chuffed that I thought of him and his brother on this very special day which I could hear in Reggie's voice that Christmas meant a lot to him (also I am sure he sounded piss as his words were coming out back to front at times).

Well at least Reg was enjoying Christmas as much as he could as it would have been his and Ron's 27th Christmas behind lock and key (something that I nor you truly could ever imagine).

I was never allowed to speak to Ron, but once a month I was allowed to call Reggie for 5mins.

New Year's Eve, I booked into a lovely hotel along The Parade (the beach near the heart of Wellington Harbour city) for Alania and me to enjoy and to watch the New Year come in.

I party it up with the Satan's Slaves earlier in the evening as they were holding their 25th Year anniversary.

I went along with Craig from the Rebels and his girlfriend and Alania.

It was a loose party to say the lease but a good one of course, and then me and Alania went back to the hotel and ended up staying in the hotel for an extra night.

We had one of the penthouses looking over Wellington Harbour; it had a great view from the balcony where we could actually see over the next bay and up on the hill where Mt Crawford jail stood at the top of the hill.

I thought of everyone who was still up on the hill, a place where the year earlier I had spend my last Xmas and New Years Eve.

The New Year I was hoping to start off how the last part of the previous year ended but I was in for a few shook's and shakes to say the least.

I was invited to a party in Newtown; Alania went back to her family house to look after her dogs as her parents were going away for a few days at the start of the New Year.

I was enjoying myself as normal at the party. Everything seemed fine then as the party died down a little bit; one of the people who lived in the house by the name of Andrew told me and a friend to leave out of all the guests (he pointed me out and my friend).

Neither of us had done anything wrong and to insult us more in front of all the party guests (that were still there) he said " I don't like you bastards!"

"I know you are Satan's Slaves."

"I didn't invite any Satan's Slaves so fuck off out of my back yard!"

Fuck that I thought but I didn't want to stay and have a row as I was past that (that was the old me).

I now had learnt how to simply bite my tongue and walk away (which I did).

I headed up his drive way towards the street to leave when all of a sudden he came marching up behind me and pushed me in the back, telling me to make a move on and to hurry the fuck up.

Well this time fuck that!

I anit biting my tongue that hard for anyone!

(Who is that disrespectful and insulting)

And who laid his hands on me!

I yelled out to Glyn to get a fucking hurry up as I could just feel it within me that it was going to go off (something I didn't wish to happen) but Glyn was too busy still chatting to some tart and really didn't give a fuck that I was taking shit from this fuckwit.

One thing with Glyn, girls (always) always came first when if he believed in the slightest that he was going to get his leg over.

I turned around telling Andrew not to push me and that I was going, but he pushed me in the back again so I just turned to him and whacked him.

He fell against the side of his house and pulled out a knife from the top of one of his cowboy boots (this fool weren't no fucking cowboy, let me tell you that!)

How many times had I had a knife pulled out on me....I really could be asked to get stabbed so I got my vodka bottle and smashed it in the side of his head but not too hard as I just caught him near the ear (the bottle hadn't broken but it done the trick) as he dropped the knife to put his hand up to his ear.

I am sure his ears were ringing and then I lifted him off his feet by a solid upper punch and that was that, he was sparked out.

I took to my feet and went to the Satan's Slaves clubhouse, though after I had left some of the house mates (from the house party I had just been to) found Andrew with Glyn nearby walking up the drive way, dropping his hold of his DB beer he had been drinking out of near where Andrew was laying on the drive way (Andrew coming around from earlier being hit by me) saying one of the Satan's Slaves had hit him with a bottle.

They guessed the broken bottle on the driveway was what Glyn had used to bottle Andrew so they all leaped on Glyn and kicked the shit out of him.

I know as I saw him when he turned up at the clubhouse a hour later covered in blood and that didn't go down to well with the club, who went around and done most of the party guests (as they didn't have Glyn there letting them know who done it).

I know Andrew was knocked out for a second time that evening.

As for me, how stupid was I to use a bottle but this time it really was in self defence but Glyn was fuming at me saying I left him at the party to get attacked which was bollocks!

I had knocked Andrew out then left the party and that was the end of the matter. I wasn't going to hang about and I didn't think in any way Glyn was in any trouble as the last time I looked over at him he was nearer enough getting into some girls` knickers (rather than any trouble).

Glyn should have left with me as then he would have been down the road with me rather than left fighting anyway where was he when Andrew pulled the knife out one me....as its lucky that night I didn't get stabbed.

Glyn and I ended rowing about it down at the clubhouse until both of us was told to shut the fuck up and shake hands as at least we both were fine. Yeah Glyn would have a headache when he woke in the morning (not so a hangover) but by taking a few punches to the head in the attack that was served out to him.

At the end of the day those responsible for it, had all been given a hiding by the Satan's Slaves so the matter was put under the carpet as far as I was concerned.

In March, I went to another party in Wellington. A house party as I tried to avoid the bars and nightclubs on weekends, mainly as I did have a bounty on my head(from the prick who I had stabbed in the nightclub) so I knew I was a marked man by the rival motorcycle club due to the stabbing back in time.

I ended up at this one party with Craig from the Rebels.

Fucking hell as who was there among the people partying but Andrew (who the month earlier I had bottled).

He point over to me telling anyone who was willing to listen that it was me who had done him even though he knew what would happen, if any of his pals decided with him to step up to the mark and fight me.

If I were to lose I would still win in the long run as one phone call to the Satan's Slaves would bring on their worst nightmare, but I wasn't going to hang about to see if I were to win or lose as I would have gone in like a wild fire and if I were to go down I would go down fighting (which wouldn't have turned out nice that's for sure) so as I about to say to Craig "I am out of here!"

I saw Craig leap into the air as he went for Andrew and his mates. Cracking four of them one after another (I have never ever seen any man punch that quickly with such force).

Craig left Andrew for last, doing him with one punch which meant Andrew now had been knocked out three times in the space of four weeks.

I bet he doesn't enjoy house parties due to the very last two he went to and one being his own house party.

Craig just leaps up off his feet like a pit-bull, and just done three others who came towards us.

No one chased us out of that party that's for sure.

Crag just said he didn't want me ending back up on the hill again; he was a good man and true friend.

That was my house parties for me over with, so I would just now keep to the Satan's Slaves club house.

When I was out in Upper Hut I would drink over at the Sinn Fein (not connected to Sinn Fein in Northern Ireland) Motorcycle Club 1% clubhouse, which was only down the road from Alania parents.

I got on with the motorcycle club very well (they had a strong bond with the Satan's Slaves) as all-round they were good group of fellas and they had a puka clubhouse (their president at the time always made me feel welcome).

Then one morning on a Friday while I was at work listening to the radio (it was St Patricks Day) and what I heard being said over the airwaves, I just couldn't believe it.

That night the Satan's Slaves were holding a St Patricks party at their clubhouse so I was looking forward to that until I heard on the radio, news that the British gangster Ronnie Kray had died that day in England. I could believe it as I had only got a letter from him a few days earlier (maybe about a week earlier).

It was a shock so instead of going to the Satan's Slaves party, I went back home and asked Alania's father could I call England, which he said yes of course as he knew it was to try and contact Reggie Kray.

I spoke to Reggie briefly telling him I was so sorry to hear the news and was there anything I could do for him or The Family at the time.

He said no but thanked me for my dearest thoughts during this very unsettling time that he was going through (I could hear in his voice such massive loss).

Reggie Kray was now without his twin brother Ronnie Kray (I couldn't imagine what deep pain he was truly feeling but I can only think it was as if a half of him had now gone...been taken away).

Reggie now had to carry The Family onwards without his twin, who had been there all the way through all these many years (through the good times and more so the bad times).

All I knew was London shall get a huge sending off for their most famous British gangster Ronnie Kray, that his sending off will be something special down to the love of his twin Reggie Kray.

I know that The Krays weren't fucking angels, and what went on back in the 1960s was what many who say was bang out of order but they only hurt their own.

I wasn't there in those times, hell I wasn't even born till 1975 so I am no one to judge them on their past though yes I do know from right and wrong but my friendship with The Kray Twins had been built not on whatever they had done but on how the Twins had been a positive influence in my life.

Not one did I ever wish to go down the same path as them. Why would I look at them both and think they were fucking great......as fucking great wasn't spending your whole life behind bars but fucking great was the honest friendship, the true kindness they had shown me (forgiving me when I had crossed over from youth into stupidity) but more so how they had steered me away from a life of crime.

No one can ever have a debate with me about the Kray Twins, more so no one who never had any contact with them as there were more to the them and the swinging 60s (than just the protection rackets and the odd gangland murder). Many would say they were evil men well in the time up to that point that I had known The Kray Twins, I found both the twins to have good hearts even though yes what they done during their times was in many eyes very unsettling to others (that's putting it lightly) but they neither had ever done me any wrong or harm and I wasn't no one to judge them for their past.

I appeared on the television show The Paul Holmes show as they were asking me for my point of view on The Kray Twins and also asking me about my unusual friendship I had with The Kray Twins (asking to see the very famous first letter that I received from Ronnie Kray many years earlier).

I had a few newspapers and magazines do some articles on me but then I shielded away from all of the press inquires (I seemed to be getting). My only message was that I felt now Reggie Kray who has lost his twin brother should be freed from his jail sentenced for crimes he had committed nearly 30 years previously.

I called Reggie again, a few days after the funeral and told him what I had seen of the funeral and how he very much would have made Ronnie so proud.

There and then (maybe my longest conversation I had with Reggie over the years) Reggie said its time for you to come over and would I like to see him a visit.

This conversation stayed with me over many nights that followed and also the fact that Ron Kray was dead (though I never got to meet him, I was still saddened by his sudden death).

I can say there was only one thing now going through my mind and that was to turn these last few years around from the very moment of making contact with The Krays by meeting the remaining Kray Twin (Reggie Kray).

Less than a month on (the very morning of my 20th birthday) I went to a bank to collect what little money was left for me in my Mum's trust account (I had lost most due to all the contracts I had written up years early when I was living a wild life of partying and excess to say the least).

I called Alania at her work and told her I had enough money left over to buy two air flights to the UK.

I said to Alania that for my 20th birthday I very much would like her and I to go to old London Town to see Reggie Kray.

Of course I would make sure that I would visit my father in Scotland while I was in the U.K

My Father had no idea I was even planning again to come over after losing out on making it over to see him when my sister had gone with my ex.

I just felt England calling and also to now get a personal invite by the gangland boss Reggie Kray then that even had more importance than ever before.

It was a massive decision for Alania to make as she was at the time in her life being treated for kidney disease. Alania managed to get an appointment that early afternoon of my birthday to see her doctor who was her specialist.

Alania was told it was fine for her to travel etc but on best advice to of course take out health insurance (which I would add of course through the travel insurance).

I said to her I would get her an open return ticket as well so whenever she wished to return (or if she had to for any medical reason) then she could get the next flight back.

I think this gave her (and more so her parents) peace of mind.

I would for myself, though get a one way ticket for the time being as I didn't wish to put a date on my return.

I had guessed that we both would try it out for a year and then return to New Zealand as we both were very deeply in love with one another so neither could see us ever being a part.

With that in mind, she agreed so I went and brought the tickets while Alania went home and spoke to her parents.

Alania told her patents, who couldn't believe it but after we all had a good chat together then they that evening drove us to the airport as I had booked us on flights that very same evening (the night of my 20th birthday).

Not having a clue what London would hold for us?

Many others in life, wouldn't have risked such a trip without no forward planning but one thing I had learned through my Mum's death was to live for today as tomorrow may never ever come.

I didn't tell a soul I was flying out. I did though go and visit my Nana that late afternoon as it was very important for me to see my Nana (who I loved dearly).

We spoke for many hours and said our goodbyes.

I never would think that was the very last time I would see my Nana again as she died while I was in the U.K so that very day of my 20th birthday was the last time I saw my Nana.

How very glad I was to have visited her before I caught my flight heading over sevens oceans away leaving New Zealand behind me and also my past and life as I knew it.

I met Alania and her parents over at the airport to say my goodbyes to them both and to thank them for all they had done for me as they had been there for me in those last few months of mine in New Zealand.

I will always hold very good memories of them both and their two pet dogs.

Alania and I got on the flight. It was my 20th birthday, flying out of New Zealand (a place that had been my home for the last 20 years of my life) leaving to visit the remaining Kray twin after over 3 years of writing to one another and speaking to one another, but now I would be meeting him in person....one on one.

You know you could write a book about this as for sure no other had taken up this journey before....more so anyone from the other side of the world (that's for sure).

Many people will think I am mad and of course they could be right but what a hell of a journey was about to take place and then also more than this, I was going to be seeing my Dad for the first time in 10 years.

I had lost out on seeing my Dad a few years earlier when I had been put in jail so this time I very much was looking forward to seeing my Dad again and his wife Irene and my Scottish Grandparents and my Auntie June and Uncle Raymond and my cousins.

Not many 20 years old would have done what I done on the brief of the moment but then again not too many 20 years old would have just lived the life that I had lived and come out of it the other end....in one piece.

I couldn't change my mind as I sat on that plane. I had no idea what was there for me in the U.K and nor how the meeting with the notorious British Gangster Reg Kray was going to be like.

I was full of nerves as the plane took off but also so full of excitement and so was Alania though the Kray Family wasn't a interest for her but she had her blood brother in London so she was very much looking forward to that and to celebrate my 20th birthday as we took off over Wellington....the bright lights of the city below.

All my family including my sister didn't even know neither that I was going nor that I had even left the country.

All my friends had no idea and nor did the Satan's Slaves. I was leaving everyone behind (more so in leaving my whole life behind me which just had come good for me in New Zealand in life and in work) but at least I had my girl with me so I wasn't leaving the love in my heart and in my life behind.

I was taking love with me and to me then life couldn't be any better.

All I can say without adding more is that there is so much more to come in the next many chapters of the story of my life.

If you think this life of mine already was crazy, fun, mad, mischief, sad and at times full of sorrow then what is to come is all of that times one hundred and at even a faster pace that you could ever imagine.

For now I hope you have enjoyed the book that is in your hands and that you are looking forward to what happens next as I promise you all....you won't be let down by laughter, smiles, karma and a hell of a lot of drama with all the above added in as well.

I now am at the end of this part of my book. Ten months in the writing (day after day so many hours and a few tears along the way) as I went somewhere where while writing this part of my book that I hadn't gone or been to for many a years since leaving New Zealand and that place was my past.

In doing so and in sharing it all with you, I do hope it was worth the while and the sadness at times it did return to me but where I sit now I can promise you all that I am very much a happy older man thanks to the love of my beautiful sister and my girlfriend Stacey and her family and my family in Scotland and the few close friends that I have in Old London Town and those back in New Zealand.

I never hoped to have gone and that was back in to my past. A past I left behind me when I leaved my home town on my 20th birthday but here 14 years later through writing this book, I had to relive it all and take memories that I had learned to lock in the back of my head for all those many years that have gone by since I was a kid growing up in New Zealand.

Never wanting to relive many of those dark hours but in doing this book, that's exactly what I have had to do and that is relive them.

All I can say if wasn't for the love of my sister or the love of my girlfriend and the advice of my Godfather Freddie Foreman I wouldn't have been able to do it nor the belief of a very special lady in Australian Bron and her husband Neal, I couldn't have done it or from the encourage of my friend Steve Wraith and the encouragement from Stephen Richards who is a very noted writer, whom when I told him of the idea of putting my life story on paper then he was one who had no doubt that others would very much find great interest in my life story.

One person I want to mention who has (without her even knowing) given me such strength to write this book, is my beautiful daughter Angel-Grace. She is one person who when she grows up I do wish for her to be proud of me as I love her with all my heart and will do forever and ever.

Be it for the life I have lived or to the people who have come in to my life or to the many messages I wish to express throughout my book, hoping to reach out to others who have at times of their own life found themselves in dark places, giving up hope or not being able to believe in dreams of their own.

Well my book very much shows that even in your darkest hour, you still can believe in dreams and over time make those dreams of yours come ever so true against the biggest odds in the world and this will result in you being able to fight your own personal demons and live a good life and a life to be very proud of what ever past you once may have once lived.

I wrote the book alone, but on remembering all who once used to be in my life and the people who are now in my life meant that I never felt alone and for those who have picked up my book to read and you still are here reading the book after so many pages then I thank you for that.

I hope you have enjoyed the journey so far of this life of mine. It's not been a easy one but if success comes from writing this book as in that if I touch some else life then that to me is the karma that I am looking for by writing this book and I do hope I can make a difference even ifs only a little difference on how today's youth lead and live their lives.

I light another ciggie to my mouth, drink from a glass of water and listen to BBC Radio 4.

Oh how things have changed but these three things have been by myself while I write into the late hours of most evenings of mine and some evenings I finds myself still writing away at 7am the following morning, being drained of everything I have put into my heart and soul to attempt to write a book of my life.

Even getting to this point of my book, I look back on all that I have written and I can feel ever so proud, which makes all the late nights at home writing away rather than enjoying a cold beer with friends down at the pub, proves to me how very much my life has changed for the better. When as youngest

I never believed I would even make my 18th birthday let alone being now as old as I am.

If I haven't mention you in my book so far from friends and others who I knew back in my days in New Zealand, you still all are very much in my heart and those of you who have done me good then I only wish forever more good karma upon you all.

And those who have done me wrong well I am now too old to worry about you and I guessing in life you now just found yourself surrounded by bad karma. Well I can only say one thing to you and that is ......such is life - bad karma can creep up on you when you least expecting it.

This is now the end of Volume 1 and now I am about to write Volume 2 of my book. I hope you enjoyed reading this book and are looking forward to now reading my next book.

You shall discover while you find yourself turning the pages to see how this journey of mine is going or where it lead me to.........I am hoping without giving anything away that my life lead onto better things and myself becoming a better person in this life of mine.

I have just spend a whole year, re drafting my book six times over and though I did try my very best to self edit the book, I very much know maybe a lot more work was needed to be done but it has been two years since I wrote Volume 1 of Lost Youth.

I do feel it's time now to tell my story and allow it to be shared around the world for all of you to read.

So here I am now ending the book with a good night and a God Bless from me x

About the Author

Christian Simpson lives in London with his fiancé.

He has a beautiful daughter Angel-Grace from a previous relationship.

He is a successful bodyguard, looking after the rich and famous including foreign royal families.

He recently took two years off work to write two books telling his own story about his incredible life.

He set out on his journey and wrote these books in such places as London, Paris and as far as Australia and Cuba, while it was a struggle from the very beginning, he has never written a book before and suffers from dyslexia, it is something he proudly accomplished.

He has hope that one day he can give up personal security work and become a full time writer so that in the future he can set up a youth club for those kids, who they themselves have had a rocky childhood like his.

At the moment he in talks with the famous British music artist, Tricky in hope that together they will set up a music academy and boxing school for the disadvantaged youth of today, who really just need a second chance in their own lives to give them opportunities of a brighter future for themselves.

Lightning Source UK Ltd.
Milton Keynes UK
26 March 2011

169892UK00002BA/2/P